Minimal Perl

Minimal Perl

For UNIX and Linux People

BY TIM MAHER

MANNING

Greenwich
(74° w. long.)

For online information and ordering of this and other Manning books, please visit
www.manning.com. The publisher offers discounts on this book when ordered in quantity.
For more information, please contact:

Special Sales Department
Manning Publications Co.
Cherokee Station
PO Box 20386   Fax: (609) 877-8256
New York, NY 10021   email: orders@manning.com

Manning Publications Co.   Copyeditor: Tiffany Taylor
209 Bruce Park Avenue   Typesetters: Denis Dalinnik, Dottie Marsico
Greenwich, CT 06830   Cover designer: Leslie Haimes

ISBN 1-932394-50-8
Printed in the United States of America
1 2 3 4 5 6 7 8 9 10 – VHG – 10 09 08 07 06

To Yeshe Dolma Sherpa,
whose fortitude, endurance,
and many sacrifices made this book possible.

To my parents,
Gloria Grady Washington and William N. Maher,
who indulged my early interests in literature.

To my limbic system,
with gratitude for all the good times we've had together.

brief contents

Part 1   Minimal Perl: for UNIX and Linux Users   1

   1   Introducing Minimal Perl   3

   2   Perl essentials   16

   3   Perl as a (better) grep command   53

   4   Perl as a (better) sed command   89

   5   Perl as a (better) awk command   121

   6   Perl as a (better) find command   178

Part 2   Minimal Perl: for UNIX and
          Linux Shell Programmers   203

   7   Built-in functions   205

   8   Scripting techniques   247

   9   List variables   295

  10   Looping facilities   330

  11   Subroutines and variable scoping   362

  12   Modules and the CPAN   388

contents

foreword *xvii*

preface *xix*

acknowledgments *xxii*

about this book *xxiii*

about the cover illustration *xxxiv*

list of tables *xxxv*

Part 1   Minimal Perl: for UNIX and Linux Users   1

1   Introducing Minimal Perl   3

1.1   A visit to Perlistan   3
Sometimes you need a professional guide   5

1.2   Perl can be simple   7

1.3   About Minimal Perl   7
What Minimal Perl isn't   8   ✦   What Minimal Perl is   8

1.4   Laziness is a virtue   9

1.5   A minimal dose of syntax   10
Terminating statements with semicolons   10

1.6   Writing one-line programs   11
Balancing simplicity and readability   12
Implementing simple filters   12

1.7   Summary   14

2   Perl essentials   16

2.1   Perl's invocation options   17
One-line programming: -e   18   ✦   Enabling warnings: -w   18
Processing input: -n   19   ✦   Processing input with automatic
printing: -p   19   ✦   Processing line-endings: -l   20   ✦   Printing
without newlines: `printf`   21   ✦   Changing the input record
separator: `-0digits`   22

2.2 Using variables 23
Using special variables 23 ✦ Using the data variable: $\_$ 24
Using the record-number variable: $. 24 ✦ Employing
user-defined variables 25

2.3 Loading modules -M 27

2.4 Writing simple scripts 29
Quoting techniques 30 ✦ True and False values 32
Handling switches: -s 32 ✦ Using warn and die 35
Using logical and, logical or 37 ✦ Programming with BEGIN
and END blocks 39 ✦ Loading modules with use 41

2.5 Additional special variables 42
Employing I/O variables 42 ✦ Exploiting formatting
variables 43

2.6 Standard option clusters 44
Using aliases for common types of Perl commands 46

2.7 Constructing programs 47
Constructing an output-only one-liner 49 ✦ Constructing
an input/output script 50

2.8 Summary 51
Directions for further study 51

3 *Perl as a (better) grep command* 53

3.1 A brief history of grep 53

3.2 Shortcomings of grep 54
Uncertain support for metacharacters 54 ✦ Lack of string
escapes for control characters 56 ✦ Comparing capabilities
of greppers and Perl 57

3.3 Working with the matching operator 60
The one-line Perl grepper 61

3.4 Understanding Perl's regex notation 63

3.5 Perl as a better fgrep 64

3.6 Displaying the match only, using $& 64

3.7 Displaying unmatched records (like grep -v) 65
Validating data 66 ✦ Minimizing typing with shortcut
metacharacters 67

3.8 Displaying filenames only (like grep -1) 67

3.9 Using matching modifiers 68
Ignoring case (like grep -i) 70

3.10 Perl as a better `egrep`   70
Working with cascading filters   72

3.11 Matching in context   75
Paragraph mode   75 ✦ File mode   77

3.12 Spanning lines with regexes   77
Matching across lines   79 ✦ Using `lwp-request`   80
Filtering `lwp-request` output   80

3.13 Additional examples   81
Log-file analysis   81 ✦ A scripted grepper   84
Fuzzy matching   85 ✦ Web scraping   86

3.14 Summary   86
Directions for further study   88

4 *Perl as a (better) sed command*   89

4.1 A brief history of `sed`   89

4.2 Shortcomings of `sed`   91

4.3 Performing substitutions   93
Performing line-specific substitutions: `sed`   96 ✦ Performing
line-specific substitutions: Perl   96 ✦ Performing record-specific
substitutions: Perl   97 ✦ Using backreferences and numbered
variables in substitutions   99

4.4 Printing lines by number   100
Printing lines by number: `sed`   100 ✦ Printing lines by number:
Perl   100 ✦ Printing records by number: Perl   101

4.5 Modifying templates   101

4.6 Converting special characters   103

4.7 Editing files   105
Editing with commands   105 ✦ Editing with scripts   107
Safeguarding in-place editing   111

4.8 Converting to lowercase or uppercase   113
Quieting spam   113

4.9 Substitutions with computed replacements   114
Converting miles to kilometers   114 ✦ Substitutions using
function results   116

4.10 The `sed` to Perl translator   118

4.11 Summary   118
Directions for further study   120

5   *Perl as a (better) awk command*   *121*

5.1   A brief history of AWK   122

5.2   Comparing basic features of awk and Perl   123
Pattern-matching capabilities   124   ✦   Special variables   126
Perl's variable interpolation   128   ✦   Other advantages of
Perl over AWK   129   ✦   Summary of differences in basic
features   129

5.3   Processing fields   130
Accessing fields   130   ✦   Printing fields   132   ✦   Differences
in syntax for print   134   ✦   Using custom field separators
in Perl   136

5.4   Programming with Patterns and Actions   138
Combining pattern matching with field processing   142
Extracting data from tables   143   ✦   Accessing cell data using
array indexing   145

5.5   Matching ranges of records   151
Operators for single- and multi-record ranges   152   ✦   Matching
a range of dates   153   ✦   Matching multiple ranges   155

5.6   Using relational and arithmetic operators   157
Relational operators   157   ✦   Arithmetic operators   158

5.7   Using built-in functions   159
One-liners that use functions   161   ✦   The legend of nexpr   162
How the nexpr* programs work   164

5.8   Additional examples   165
Computing compound interest: compound_interest   165
Conditionally pluralizing nouns: compound_interest2   166
Analyzing log files: scan4oops   168

5.9   Using the AWK-to-Perl translator: a2p   175
Tips on using a2p   175

5.10 Summary   175
Directions for further study   177

6   *Perl as a (better) find command*   *178*

6.1   Introducing hybrid find/perl programs   180

6.2   File testing capabilities of find vs. Perl   180
Augmenting find with Perl   183

6.3   Finding files   184
Finding files by name matching   184   ✦   Finding files by
pathname matching   187

6.4 Processing filename arguments   188
Defending against `grep`'s messes   189 ✦ Recursive grepping   191
Perl as a generalized argument pre-processor   192

6.5 Using `find | xargs` vs. Perl alternatives   192
Using Perl for reliable timestamp sorting   193
Dealing with multi-word filenames   196

6.6 `find` as an argument pre-processor for Perl   197

6.7 A Unix-like, OS-portable `find` command   198
Making the most of `find2perl`   198 ✦ Helping non-Unix
friends with `find2perl`   199

6.8 Summary   200
Directions for further study   201

Part 2 *Minimal Perl: for UNIX and Linux Shell Programmers 203*

7 *Built-in functions   205*

7.1 Understanding and managing evaluation context   206
Determinants and effects of evaluation context   207
Making use of evaluation context   208

7.2 Programming with functions that generate or
process scalars   210
Using `split`   211 ✦ Using `localtime`   214 ✦ Using
`stat`   215 ✦ Using `chomp`   219 ✦ Using `rand`   221

7.3 Programming with functions that process lists   223
Comparing Unix pipelines and Perl functions   223
Using `sort`   224 ✦ Using `grep`   227 ✦ Using `join`   229
Using `map`   232

7.4 Globbing for filenames   234
Tips on globbing   237

7.5 Managing files with functions   239
Handling multi-valued return codes   240

7.6 Parenthesizing function arguments   242
Controlling argument-gobbling functions   242

7.7 Summary   243
Directions for further study   245

8   *Scripting techniques*   247

8.1   Exploiting script-oriented functions   248
Defining `defined`   249   ✦   Exiting with `exit`   253
Shifting with `shift`   254

8.2   Pre-processing arguments   256
Accommodating non-filename arguments with implicit loops   256
Filtering arguments   257   ✦   Generating arguments   259

8.3   Executing code conditionally with `if`/`else`   259
Employing `if`/`else` vs. `and`/`or`   260   ✦   Mixing branching
techniques: The `cd_report` script   261   ✦   Tips on using
`if`/`else`   264

8.4   Wrangling strings with concatenation and
repetition operators   265
Enhancing the `most_recent_file` script   267   ✦   Using
concatenation and repetition operators together   267   ✦   Tips on
using the concatenation operator   268

8.5   Interpolating command output into source code   269
Using the `tput` command   271   ✦   Grepping recursively: The
`rgrep` script   273   ✦   Tips on using command interpolation   274

8.6   Executing OS commands using `system`   275
Generating reports   277   ✦   Tips on using `system`   280

8.7   Evaluating code using `eval`   283
Using a Perl shell: The `psh` script   284   ✦   Appreciating a
multi-faceted Perl grepper: The `preg` script   286

8.8   Summary   292
Directions for further study   294

9   *List variables*   295

9.1   Using array variables   296
Initializing arrays with piecemeal assignments and `push`   299
Understanding advanced array indexing   300   ✦   Extracting
fields in a friendlier fashion   301   ✦   Telling fortunes:
The `fcookie` script   304   ✦   Tips on using arrays   308

9.2   Using hash variables   308
Initializing hashes   311   ✦   Understanding advanced hash
indexing   312   ✦   Understanding the built-in `%ENV`
hash   313   ✦   Printing hashes   314   ✦   Using `%ENV` in
place of switches   315   ✦   Obtaining uniqueness with
hashes   316   ✦   Employing a hash as a simple database: The
`user_lookup` script   319   ✦   Counting word frequencies
in web pages: The `count_words` script   323

9.3   Comparing list generators in the Shell and Perl   325
Filename generation/globbing   326   ✦   Command substitution/
interpolation   327   ✦   Variable substitution/interpolation   327

9.4   Summary   328
Directions for further study   329

10   *Looping facilities*   *330*

10.1   Looping facilities in the Shell and Perl   331

10.2   Looping with while/until   333
Totaling numeric arguments   333   ✦   Reducing the size of an
image   335   ✦   Printing key/value pairs from a hash using
each   336   ✦   Understanding the implicit loop   337

10.3   Looping with do while/until   338
Prompting for input   339

10.4   Looping with foreach   340
Unlinking files: the rm_files script   341   ✦   Reading a line at a
time   341   ✦   Printing a hash   342   ✦   Demystifying acronyms:
The expand_acronyms script   343   ✦   Reducing image sizes: The
compress_image2 script   344

10.5   Looping with for   345
Exploiting for's support for indexing: the raffle script   347

10.6   Using loop-control directives   349
Nesting loops within loops   350   ✦   Enabling loop-control
directives in bottom-tested loops   351   ✦   Prompting for
input   352   ✦   Enhancing loops with continue blocks: the
confirmation script   353

10.7   The CPAN's select loop for Perl   355
Avoiding the re-invention of the "choose-from-a-menu" wheel   356
Monitoring user activity: the show_user script   357
Browsing man pages: the perlman script   358

10.8   Summary   360
Directions for further study   361

11   *Subroutines and variable scoping*   *362*

11.1   Compartmentalizing code with subroutines   363
Defining and using subroutines   365   ✦   Understanding use
strict   368

11.2   Common problems with variables   370
Clobbering variables: The phone_home script   371   ✦   Masking
variables: The 4letter_word script   372   ✦   Tips on avoiding
problems with variables   373

11.3 Controlling variable scoping 373
Declaring variables with `my` 374 ✦ Declaring variables with
`our` 374 ✦ Declaring variables with `local` 375 ✦ Introducing
the Variable Scoping Guidelines 375

11.4 Variable Scoping Guidelines for complex programs 376
Enable `use strict` 377 ✦ Declare user-defined variables and
define their scopes 377 ✦ Pass data to subroutines using
arguments 383 ✦ Localize temporary changes to built-in variables
with `local` 383 ✦ Employ user-defined loop variables 383
Applying the Guidelines: the `phone_home2` script 384

11.5 Reusing a subroutine 386

11.6 Summary 387
Directions for further study 387

12 Modules and the CPAN 388

12.1 Creating modules 389
Using the Simple Module Template 390 ✦ Creating a
module: `Center.pm` 393 ✦ Testing a new module 395

12.2 Managing modules 398
Identifying the modules that you want 398 ✦ Determining
whether you have a certain module 400 ✦ Installing
modules from the CPAN 401

12.3 Using modules 403
`Business::UPS`—the `ups_shipping_price` script 403
`LWP::Simple`—the `check_links` script 405
`Shell::POSIX::Select`—the `menu_ls` script 408
`File::Find`—the `check_symlinks` script 411
`CGI`—the `survey.cgi` script 414 ✦ Tips on using
Object-Oriented modules 422

12.4 Summary 424
Directions for further study 425

epilogue 426
appendix A: Perl special variables cheatsheet 427
appendix B: Guidelines for parenthesizing code 430
glossary 432
index 443

foreword

Perl is a lamb in wolf's clothing. It has a ferocious reputation for incomprehensibility ("executable line-noise") and excessive power ("the Swiss-Army chainsaw"), but underneath lurks a kinder, gentler programming language than whatever you're using now.

Of course, Perl *can* be complex. After all, very few other popular languages have so many advanced built-in capabilities, which is one reason why Perl rates as one of the most sophisticated programming languages in widespread use today.

Fortunately, unlike many other programming languages, Perl also comes standard with one other vital feature: a gentle learning curve. You don't have to understand a multitude of high-end programming constructs before you can do useful work with it. If you're familiar with the basic tools of Unix/Linux—grep, sed, awk, find, and the shell itself—then many of the features of Perl will seem hauntingly familiar.

Perl's creator, Larry Wall, once described his language as "a cleaned up and summarized version of that wonderful semi-natural language known as 'Unix.'" And that's precisely the direction from which this book leads you into the depths of the language: by showing how Perl has evolved "Unix" into a dialect that is much more powerful but also much easier to use. If you're already fluent in Perl's mother tongue, and you want to discover how expressive and poetic Perl itself can be, you could have chosen no better primer than this book and no better guide than Dr. Tim Maher, a gifted teacher and a decorated veteran of both the Unix world and the Perl community.

So, welcome to Perl! You don't have to come from *nix to work here…but it certainly helps.

DAMIAN CONWAY

preface

In this preface, I'll tell you about the history of Minimal Perl and the origins of this book.

THE HISTORY OF MINIMAL PERL

The seeds of this book were sown many years ago, when I was building up my knowledge of Perl, the greatest programming language I'd ever encountered (before or since). While reading a variety of books on the subject, I was surprised that the authors felt obliged to delve into so many of the different but equivalent *choices* for expressing every basic operation in the language, as well as each of the syntactic *variations* for expressing any one of those choices.

As an example, I've shown here some of the available choices for expressing in Perl the simple idea that B should be executed only if A is True (with those letters representing arbitrary program elements). Both forward and backward variations for expressing the dependency are included:[1]

Forward	Backward
`A and B;`	`B if A;`
`A && B;`	`B if A;`
`A   and  do { B };`	`do { B } if A;`
`A   &&   do { B };`	`do { B } if A;`
`if (A)      { B };`	`B if A;`
`unless (!A) { B };`	`B unless !A;`

Although some are inclined to present symptoms like these of Perl's complexity and redundancy as evidence of its "richness," "versatility," or "expressiveness," many Perl novices would surely have a different reaction—that Perl is needlessly complex and too hard to learn.

Minimal Perl was created to address these obstacles presented by Perl's redundancy and complexity. By emphasizing Perl's `grep`, `sed`, and `awk`-like features, and relying

---

[1] Before you despair, I should point out that Minimal Perl uses only 2 of these variations—which is all anybody needs!

on concepts such as *inputs*, *filters*, and *arguments*, it allows Unix[2] users to directly apply their existing knowledge to the task of learning Perl. So rather than being frustrated with Perl's complexities and disappointed with its steep learning curve, they quickly and painlessly acquire the ability to write useful programs that can solve a wide variety of problems.

My first public presentation on this subject was in a tutorial called *"Minimal Perl for the Impatient"* at the YAPC::Europe 2001 conference[3] in Amsterdam, the Netherlands. The eagerness with which that audience devoured the material confirmed my hunch that many were hungering for an easier way to learn Perl. Since then, I've taught Minimal Perl at other professional conferences, at meetings of Perl Users Groups in the US and Canada, and to many Fortune 500 companies.

THE GENESIS OF THE BOOK

By 2001, the Minimal Perl approach had convincingly proven its ability to help Unix people acquire Perl skills with relative ease. But many who could appreciate its benefits never get to see conference presentations or attend corporate training classes, so I became interested in making this information available to a wider audience.

However, I had some serious reservations about embarking on a book, having heard many sobering stories from colleagues about the travails of authorship. Fortunately, I received some encouragement that was instrumental in helping me decide to go forward with this project, from a good friend—Dr. Damian Conway.

A little help from my friend

Damian and I first met after my presentation on the first "Perl Beautifier" at The Perl Conference in 1998,[4] when he gently informed me that I could have categorized Perl source code into its constituent elements by using a program he had written (in Perl's *module* format), rather than writing my own from scratch to attempt that difficult task.

After examining more of his ingenious modules and reading his excellent book *Object Oriented Perl*,[5] I soon realized that Damian had a deeper understanding of Perl than almost anyone else. To allow others to benefit from his insights, I arranged for him to periodically teach Perl classes through my Seattle-based company (Consultix) and also to present talks to our Seattle Perl Users Group (SPUG, aka Seattle.pm). This worked out wonderfully for Seattleites, who would learn practical Perl incantations

---

[2] In this book, *Unix* is shorthand for "UNIX, Linux, and related operating systems," as detailed in the "Essential terminology" section of "About this book."

[3] See this book's glossary for the definition of YAPC.

[4] For more details, see http://TeachMePerl.com/perl_beautifier.html.

[5] His book is described at http://www.manning.com/conway. It's for a more advanced audience than this one.

from him during the formal daytime sessions and then enjoy his overtly hilarious (yet covertly educational) conference-style presentations by night.

Damian is probably still blushing from my effusive introductions of him as

- The Perl Wonder from Down Under (because he's an Aussie), and
- The Supreme Modulator of Perl.[6]

But I feel vindicated, because by now everybody knows I was correct in my estimation of his uniqueness and importance to the Perl community.

An auspicious weather non-event

During one week while Damian was in Seattle as a visiting instructor for Consultix, we took an extended bike ride along the shore of Lake Washington together—and we didn't even get drenched by rain! As a long-time Seattleite, I knew this to be an *extremely* auspicious sign, so I seized the opportunity to tell him about my interest in writing a Minimal Perl book. Being a fellow fan of the AWK language (which is Perlish, but simpler)—and having a keen interest in making Perl more accessible to novices— he expressed enthusiasm for the project and offered some interesting ideas about how to approach it.

The combination of my ideas with some of Damian's—along with sufficient fermentation and seasoning—ultimately led to the format, content, and approach of the book you now hold. The result is a volume that teaches Perl in ways no book has done before! I hope you enjoy reading it as much as I did writing it.

---

6 This is a reference to his unique ability to crank out amazingly ambitious and advanced Perl modules that mortal hackers dread even to contemplate, let alone code at blazingly high speeds.

acknowledgments

When I founded the Seattle Perl Users Group (SPUG) early in 1998,[7] I half-jokingly told the members that my motivation was to collect as many Perl experts together as possible, so I could learn everything they knew. At the time, I had no idea how *much* I would ultimately learn from them—or how convenient it would be to have ready access to 400+ Perl fanatics when it came time to round up technical reviewers for this book! On both counts, I'm glad to be indebted to so many of the members of SPUG.

I'm happy to acknowledge the assistance of the following individuals for providing insightful comments on early drafts of this book: Kurt deMaagd, Keith Tarbell, Ben Reser, Brian Wisti, Brian Maher (no relation to me), Brian Downs, Randy Kobes, Erik J. Pearson, Michael Wallendahl, Ken Meyer, Gareth Beale, Ashok Misra, Bellam Prakasa, Brian Maddux, Creede Lambard, Chris Whip, Steven Herber, C. J. Collier, Jarod Wilson, Phil Moeck, David Innes, Joel Grow, John Creech, Rob Blomquist, Neil Fryer, Reuven M. Lerner, Paul Campbell, and Stuart Kendrick.

I'm even more deeply indebted to the following intrepid souls, whose generous contributions of time, effort, and sage guidance went far beyond even my most optimistic expectations: Damian Conway, Jon Allen, Christie Robertson, Peter Scott, David Dyck, Joe Knape, Dan Sanderson, and Michael R. Wolf.

I'm also grateful to the helpful folks at Manning for their assistance during all phases of this book's development—especially the publisher, Marjan Bace, for his wisdom, patience, and many indulgences.

Like all JAPHs, I'm grateful to Larry for giving us the gift of Perl, but also for generously answering my questions on Perl's finer details—*even while balancing his laptop on one arm to consult Perl's source code while dashing down the hotel escalator to his next conference talk.* What a guy!

Finally, all my remaining gratitude goes to my wife, Yeshe Dolma Sherpa, who endured seemingly endless periods of husbandly inattention while I was writing this book.

---

[7] Although this group is now also known by its *Perl Mongers* (see http://www.pm.org) moniker of Seattle.pm, that organization didn't yet exist at the time of our formation, so our initial name is still our official one. For more on the history of SPUG, which has been recognized as one of the oldest, largest, and best Perl User Groups, see http://TeachMePerl.com/interviews/tmp_com_interview.html.

about this book

It would have been easy to write a *truly* "minimal" book on Perl by revealing so little of the language that nobody would have been able to do much with it. This isn't that kind of book.

It would also have been easy to write yet *another* "maximal" book on Perl, which would spend so much ink enthusing over its expressiveness, reveling in its redundancies, frolicking through its freakier features, and rampaging through its ribald regions, that there'd be insufficient room left to adequately explain how realistic programs actually work or to give you practical tips on avoiding common problems. This isn't that kind of book either.

This is a new kind of Perl book—one that empowers you to write lots of useful programs, without learning any more about Perl than is necessary.

Why, you may be excused for asking, is this book so *big* for one having *"Minimal"* in its title? There are three reasons. First, it contains dozens of practical programs showing what you can do with this subset of the language, accompanied by detailed explanations of their workings. Second, it shows helpful comparisons between fundamental features of the Shell programming language and their Perl counterparts (in part 2). Third, the essential technical details of all topics are presented in tabular form to maximize the utility of this volume as a reference book.

As a testament to what you can do with Minimal Perl, this book features programming examples drawn from a wide variety of application areas, including system administration, networking, web development, web scraping, HTML processing, CGI programming, databases, log-file analysis, financial calculations, file management, pattern matching, field processing, data validation, report generation, file conversion, and text parsing—among others.

We'll discuss the target audience for this book next.

AUDIENCE AND ORGANIZATION

This book has two parts, aimed at those with different types of prior experience in a Unix environment. The first part is for those with at least a *Unix user's* background, and the second part is for those who additionally have a *Shell programmer's* background.[8]

---

[8] As explained under "Essential terminology," *Shell* refers to a group of related Unix shells.

Part 1: Perl for UNIX and Linux users

Part 1 gives those with at least user-level Unix skills—which includes even the most advanced programmers—a gentle introduction to the core elements of Minimal Perl. After reading it, you'll be able to write custom programs to do the most common types of data-processing tasks.

You're assumed to be familiar with the most basic commands, file-management techniques, and command formats used on Unix systems. For example, you should know how to view the contents of text files, how to change the current directory without getting lost, and how to use the `grep` command to extract matching lines from a file.

Readers with more extensive backgrounds in Shell programming can especially benefit from part 2.

Part 2: Perl for UNIX and Linux Shell programmers

Part 2 helps Shell programmers capitalize on their specialized knowledge to quickly acquire Perl skills that go beyond those learned in part 1. A basic understanding of Shell variables, I/O techniques, flow-control facilities, and other fundamental features of the Bourne, Korn, Bash, or POSIX shells is assumed.

If you lack this more advanced knowledge, you may still benefit from this material after assimilating the lessons of part 1. But you should focus on the Perl syntax descriptions, rather than the Shell-to-Perl translation aids (which aren't designed for your use). The same advice holds for programmers who specialize in the C shell, which is fundamentally different from the Shells emphasized in this book.

We'll discuss the book's other resources next.

Reference materials

Some handy reference materials are provided in the back of the book, including the "Perl special variables cheatsheet" (appendix A) and "Guidelines for parenthesizing code" (appendix B). A glossary is also provided, to explain special terms such as *directive*, *JAPHly*, and *clobberation*.

Some comments on the approach used in writing this book come next.

AUTHOR'S APPROACH

Before diving into this book, it may help you to understand my approach in writing it and the pedagogical tricks and techniques I've used to maximize your benefits from reading it.

First, we'll talk about the features that increase this book's value as a reference work.

Reference value

After your initial reading, you'll want to use this volume as a reference work. To help you bypass the text and rapidly locate the essential technical details, I've packaged them in carefully titled, self-contained tables. I've also included helpful commentary in program listings, so you'll be able to quickly refresh your memory of how the programs work without re-reading the accompanying explanations.

As an avid reader of technical documentation, I value footnotes highly. For this reason, I haven't hesitated to add clarifications in footnotes that may someday be important to you but that shouldn't be allowed to derail your train of thought during your initial reading. So please feel free to postpone the reading of those footnotes until a later time, when you may feel the need to dig deeper into the details of a particular topic.

Many trainers and authors shy away from telling those learning a new language that they'll encounter certain predictable problems. I follow a different approach, which I'll explain next.

Forewarned is forearmed

As you read through this book, I'll periodically warn you about the pitfalls that you're likely to encounter in your early adventures with Perl. I do this because I feel you're better served by being forewarned about the hurdles you'll have to surmount, and by being shown how to handle them, than by being left to grapple with them on your own.

So, pay close attention to the "Tips on using ..." headings, which tell you what might go wrong when you're using certain language features and how you should deal with those situations.

In addition to warning you about potential problems, I'll also try to entertain you.

Entertainment value

I've read many technical books in my career. Many were unbearably *dull*. Others tried too hard to be entertaining, usually by employing the tired formula of silly chapter headings and dumb jokes, and ended up annoying me with their patronizing attitude.

In an effort to avoid these pitfalls and produce a better result, I've drawn on techniques I developed during my multi-decade career as a classroom lecturer and adapted them for use in this book.

For example, I sometimes dramatize Perl solutions for common programming problems by casting famous or fictional characters as workers on similar projects. This approach works well on several levels and has the added benefit of automatically attaching a memorable appellation to each such case study—such as "Rambo's Shopping Cart" or "Britney's Jewelry Database."

As a sampling of what you're in for, here are some of the more memorable characters you'll meet in this book:

- Diggity Dog, a rapper with a reputation to uphold, who *validates his lyrics* with Perl
- Felix and Oscar, Perl programmers who respectively specialize in the *fastidious* and *quick-and-dirty* styles of programming, and who are competing for the same promotion

- Patrick from soggy Seattle, a climatology-data wrangler who consoles himself by proving that Miami and New York are *rainier*
- The wily Bell Labs veteran, who wins a *$200 bar-bet* by writing a one-line Shell script that does complex mathematical calculations
- Ivan, a stamp collector, who needs to compress photos of stamps ranging from *scowling dictators* to *Frank Zappato's tweezer collection* to fit within the storage allotted by his ISP
- Yoko, a bad speller, who compensates by writing a *fuzzy* pattern-matching utility

Any writer of fiction has to choose fitting names for characters and places, and technical writers have to name files and programs as well. To make my life easier and possibly add a hint of intrigue to yours, I've used a few themes in my naming practices, based on my lifelong interests. These include exotic destinations, musical genres, science fiction, television shows, tennis champions, and the fine arts. You'll see what I mean.

I've tried to make this book both informative and entertaining, and I hope it works on both levels for you. But remember, when you're in the mood for getting just the facts, and you don't want to wade through narrative passages looking for them, you should concentrate on the relevant tables and program listings. And by all means, use the index too!

Next, to help you get started, we'll define a few essential terms that are used in the book.

ESSENTIAL TERMINOLOGY

Definitions follow for the most important terms that this book endows with special meanings. You need to understand them before you read the following chapters, so please take a moment to examine them now. If you have any doubts about the meanings of other words later on, please consult the glossary:

- **Camel book**—This is the shorthand name used in Perl circles to refer to the book more properly called *Programming Perl*, which serves as the printed reference manual for the Perl language.
- **Larry**—Larry Wall is the amazing guy who invented the original Perl and who continues to be its major architect and contributor. As an expression of admiration for his creative brilliance and gratitude for his generous gift of Perl to the world, he has been awarded a special honor by members of the Perl community: We refer to him simply as "*Larry*," as you'd refer to *Elvis* and other larger-than-life figures.
- **Newline**—The word *newline* has a special meaning in Perl, as it does in Unix documentation. But instead of representing a particular character (linefeed), as it does in Unix, it stands for the character that's used to split input into separate

records by the operating system (OS) a program is running on.[9] Making new-line a flexible concept allows a Perl program to be run without change on Unix, VMS, Windows, and other OSs, because the Perl interpreter on the target system will automatically choose the appropriate record separator, whether it be *return, return/linefeed, linefeed/return,* or something different. Although we can generally avoid explicit references to newlines in *Minimal Perl*, there are situations where we can't, so you need to know that it's represented in Perl programs as \n within double quotes.

- **Perlistan**—This is an exotic imaginary land, somewhere in Central Asia, populated by refugees from such places as the tyrannical "land of C." Perl is the official language, but many dialects, derived from the mother tongues of the immigrant populations, are spoken. Perlistanis speaking particular dialects identify themselves by marking their foreheads with different geometric shapes, such as circles and squares, so they can recognize each other.

- **Shell**—This term, which is always capitalized, is used to collectively refer to the Bourne shell and its most similar descendants—the Korn shell, the Bash shell, and POSIX-compliant shells. Note that the C shell, which is incompatible with the shells of this group, is not included.

Next, we'll talk about how various typefaces are used to convey different kinds of information.

TYPOGRAPHICAL CONVENTIONS

The following typographical conventions are used in this book.

`Constant width`

This typeface is used within the narrative and its associated tables for terms having special meanings to Unix, the Shell, or Perl—including commands, keywords, operators, built-in functions, subroutines, filenames, and the Shell's command prompt ($). It's also used for code listings, depictions of Shell terminal sessions (see the section on "Displays of commands or code with output"), and output from programs.

For instance, this example shows the syntax of a Unix command:

```
date +%Y
```

And these lines show the contents of the file called `lines`:

```
Line 1
Line 2
```

---

[9] In keeping with established conventions, newline is referred to as a *character* for convenience, despite the fact that it might actually amount to a character *sequence* on some OSs.

Terminal-like sessions, in which commands and their outputs are both shown, are depicted somewhat differently, as detailed in the next section.

Constant width bold

This typeface is used in displays of Shell terminal sessions to differentiate what is typed by the user from the other text that appears on the screen.

Consider the following example. It includes a Shell prompt ($), a command, and the command's output. Only the command is rendered as **bold**, to make it clear that it alone was typed by the user:[10]

```
$ perl -wl -e 'print 22/7;'
3.14285714285714
```

The section on "Displays of commands or code with output" provides additional information about the conventions used in terminal displays.

Italics

Italics are used to:

- Highlight initial uses of special terms in the narrative;
- Identify elements of programming examples as *placeholders* for what belongs there.[11]

For instance, the word *file* in the following example is a placeholder for whichever file the user wishes to display, so it's italicized:

```
$ perl -wnl -e 'print;' file
These are the
contents of the file.
```

Italics are also used to make comments look different from code, as discussed in the section on "Shell and Perl comments".

Markup for highlighting and cross-referencing

To draw your attention to important elements in code listings, commands, or output—called *highlighting*—this book uses several font-style variations. Bold is generally the preferred choice, but if that option is considered too intense for the context or it's already being used for another purpose there, underlining is used instead.

For example, an element within the following pathname would be highlighted in bold:

```
/home/plankton/latest-plan-for-world-domination
```

---

[10] Of course, the <ENTER> key must be pressed to submit the command to the Shell, but that keystroke is shown only when it needs to be emphasized.

[11] Notice that the word *placeholders* is italicized to highlight its initial use in this chapter, in keeping with the rule stated in the first bullet item.

However, if that pathname occurred in the context of a command, it would already be in bold, so underlining would be used instead:

```
$ cat /home/plankton/latest-plan-for-world-domination
```

In addition, there's sometimes a need to *cross-reference* remarks in the narrative to elements in code or program output. This is done by using corresponding style changes to mark the associated elements. For example:

> The following message tells us that a problem was detected on <u>the indicated line</u> of the **specified file**:
>
> ```
> Warning: something's wrong at ./rygel/latest_scheme line 3.
> ```

Underlining is the primary style variation used for cross-referencing, but in cases like this where two variations are needed, bold type is also brought into play.

Special characters

Non-printing characters are referred to by their names in the narrative, such as space and tab, but they're sometimes depicted as <SPACE> and <TAB> to indicate their presence in code listings or to indicate that the user pressing their associated keys in representations of interactive terminal sessions. In the latter case, <SPACE> and <TAB> are shown in a "ghost" font, to emphasize that those symbols represent an invisible character.

In output displays, box characters (□) are used to represent spaces in cases where it's important to know how many are present.

Shell and Perl comments

Shell and Perl comments, which start with a # symbol and end with the next (carriage-) return character, are frequently used to attach commentary to code samples. They are rendered in *italics* to make them look different from the associated Shell commands or Perl code. They're not shown in bold in depictions of interactive commands, because the author types them, not the user (see the section on "Constant width bold" type):

```
$ perl -wl -e 'print "Crikey";'    # This command prints: Crikey
```

Additional details on the depiction of terminal sessions are provided in the next section.

DISPLAYS OF COMMANDS OR CODE WITH OUTPUT

This book includes two types of displays that depict output: one form that shows what appears on the user's screen when a command is typed to the Shell (*command with output*) and another that shows the output that a statement from a Perl program generates (*code with output*).

We'll discuss Shell displays first and then Perl displays.

Shell command-with-output displays

Shell terminal sessions are shown as follows, where the $ at the beginning of the command line is the Shell prompt:

```
$ perl -wnl -e 'print;' one_line_file
Line 1

$ who | sort
shroomy    pts/9     Oct 24 13:42
shroomy    pts/0     Oct 24 14:22
```

As mentioned in the section on "Constant width bold" type, the bold typeface identifies what the user types.

Every effort is made to represent terminal sessions with complete accuracy, which includes backslashing long lines for continuation and showing the Shell's secondary prompt (>) on continuation lines:

```
$ who |
> perl -wnl -e 'print; exit;' # like head -1
contix    pts/0     Oct 24 14:22
$
```

The critical thing to understand about examples like this one is that the Shell itself provides the > symbol at the beginning of the second line—which means a reader trying the command shown will *never* type it. In this case, the trailing pipe symbol (|) automatically triggers a continuation line, leading to the appearance of the secondary prompt, which is the Shell's way of saying *"I can't run the command yet, because you haven't finished typing it."*

In commands like the following, which do *not* naturally end with a command connector like the | symbol, continuation must be explicitly requested by dangling a <u>backslash</u> at the end of each incomplete line:

```
$ meeting_page  -title='Kwiki' -speaker='Brian "Ingy" Ingerson' \
> -date='September Meeting; Tuesday, 9/16/03:' \
> -summary='Ingy talks about "Kwiki"' meeting.tmpl > 0903.html
$            ⬑  Final prompt
```

There's one exception to the policy of always showing sessions exactly as they would appear on the user's screen: to save space, the *final prompt* after the last command is generally omitted, unless its presence adds to your understanding (e.g., by revealing the presence of a blank line at the end of a command's output).

Perl code-with-output displays

This book uses a special method of depicting Perl statements and their output, which is analogous to the way Shell commands are depicted with their output. For instance, the following examples show comparable Shell and Perl ways of printing an array's values:

```
$ echo "${stooges[@]}"   # Shell syntax
arry Moe Curly

print "@stooges";        # Perl syntax; required program omitted
Larry Moe Curly
```

You could type that echo command directly to the Shell as shown to produce the indicated output, as indicated by that command being typed after a Shell prompt.

In contrast, the Perl print statement must be included *within a program* to be processed. But to avoid bogging down examples like this one with extra program material, the book uses this Shell-like code-with-output format to show what a Perl statement *would* produce as output, if run from a suitable program.

The key to differentiating the Shell examples from the Perl examples is to remember that only the former are preceded by the Shell prompt ($).

Ellipsis marks

Ellipsis marks (…) are used to indicate that unnecessary information has been omitted. In addition to being used in the text (e.g., with quotations), they're also used in displays of data files, shell commands, and program output to indicate that something has been omitted:

```
$ chastise file1 file2 ... # can supply many filenames
Chastising on Tuesday, September ...
...
Thank you for running chastise!
```

The three dots of the ellipsis are displayed in the font of the surrounding text, except when they appear in listings of Perl source code, where they're shown in a proportional font (…) rather than the monospaced code font (...). This approach is needed because Perl's range operator looks identical to the ellipsis, as do some regular expressions, and these conflicts could otherwise cause uncertainty about how to interpret ... in Perl source code. So, just remember that "..." in Perl source code *is* Perl code, whereas any occurrence of "…" there signifies omitted material.

CODING CONVENTIONS

The coding conventions used for the Shell and Perl programs are discussed next.

Shell programs

In cases where there's considered to be a relatively conventional way of writing the code for a particular type of command, the examples use that style. On the other hand, in cases where two different styles are in popular use, both are shown, as in these equivalent commands:

```
[ -f "$file" -a -r "$file" -a -s "$file" ]  || exit 42;
[[ -f $file && -r $file && -s $file ]]  || exit 42;
```

Perl programs

Perl allows the programmer to select from a variety of language features when coding program statements,[12] and to exercise wide liberties in how those features are laid out on the pages of the resulting programs.

The features used in this book were included in Minimal Perl for their compatibility with the expectations of UNIX/Linux people, and they're laid out in a manner that is compatible with those expectations. As an additional influence, guidelines from the book *Perl Best Practices*[13] are followed, but only where they don't conflict with our "prime directive" of catering to UNIX and Shell sensibilities.

DOWNLOADING THE SOURCE CODE

You can download the source code for many of the one-line commands and scripts presented in this book from Manning's website. Follow the appropriate links from the http://www.manning.com/maher website to get them.

DEFAULT INVOCATION OPTIONS FOR PERL EXAMPLES

For code snippets shown in tables and interspersed within the narrative, you should generally assume that the w and 1 invocation options are in effect. But for complete scripts that are displayed, you should refer to the *shebang line* (see the glossary) to determine which options are being used.

DEPICTION OF OPTIONAL MATERIAL

In keeping with Unix conventions, optional arguments for commands and functions are shown in square brackets, which are never typed by the user. For example:

```
grep [ -vli ] [ filename ]        # options and filename are optional
print [ items to print go here ]           # items are optional
```

ERRATA

Many conscientious professionals have scrutinized this book to ensure its technical accuracy and grammatical correctness. But proofreading is a difficult job for organisms equipped with automatic error-correction circuitry in their perceptual systems, which hides errors, so it's inevitable that some mistakes have slipped through.

To optimize your experience with this book, please check the *errata* link at the http://www.manning.com/maher website to see the latest list of corrections. In addition, if you find any errors that aren't reported there, we would be grateful if you

---

[12] As illustrated in the preface under the heading "The History of Minimal Perl."

[13] Damian Conway, *Perl Best Practices* (O'Reilly Media Inc., 2005).

would bring them to our attention. The errata page provides the email address for submitting error reports.

AUTHOR ONLINE

Purchase of *Minimal Perl* includes free access to a private web forum run by Manning Publications where you can make comments about the book, ask technical questions, and receive help from the author and from other users. To access the forum and subscribe to it, point your web browser to http://www.manning.com/maher. This page provides information on how to get on the forum once you are registered, what kind of help is available, and the rules of conduct on the forum.

Manning's commitment to our readers is to provide a venue where a meaningful dialogue between individual readers and between readers and the author can take place. It is not a commitment to any specific amount of participation on the part of the author, whose contribution to the book's forum remains voluntary (and unpaid). We suggest you try asking the author some challenging questions, lest his interest stray! The Author Online forum and the archives of previous discussions will be accessible from the publisher's website as long as the book is in print.

ABOUT THE AUTHORS

TIM MAHER, PH D, has many years of experience as a software developer, university professor of computer science, courseware developer, and corporate educator. He has trained thousands of engineers on Unix, Linux, and Perl worldwide. Tim founded Seattle's SPUG, one of the oldest, largest, and most active Perl Users Groups. He serves on the the University of Washington Advisory Board that oversees its Perl Certificate Program. Tim's company, Consultix, offers corporate software training classes to the international community from its base in Seattle, Washington.

DAMIAN CONWAY, PH D, the author of the foreword, is one of the most active members of the Perl community. He is a highly sought after presenter at Perl conferences, a contributor to the *Perl Journal* and a three-time winner of the annual Larry Wall award for Practical Utility. He has written numerous technical and scientific papers as well as three books, including Manning's acclaimed *Object Oriented Perl*. He is also the author of numerous popular Perl modules, and one of the chief designers of Perl itself. He runs an international IT training company, Thoughtstream, which provides programmer education from beginner to masterclass level throughout Europe, North America, and Australia.

about the cover illustration

The figure on the cover of *Minimal Perl* is an "Albanian." The illustration is taken from a collection of costumes of the Ottoman Empire published on January 1, 1802, by William Miller of Old Bond Street, London. The title page is missing from the collection and we have been unable to track it down to date. The book's table of contents identifies the figures in both English and French, and each illustration bears the names of two artists who worked on it, both of whom would no doubt be surprised to find their art gracing the front cover of a computer programming book...two hundred years later.

The collection was purchased by a Manning editor at an antiquarian flea market in the "Garage" on West 26th Street in Manhattan. The seller was an American based in Ankara, Turkey, and the transaction took place just as he was packing up his stand for the day. The Manning editor did not have on his person the substantial amount of cash that was required for the purchase and a credit card and check were both politely turned down. With the seller flying back to Ankara that evening the situation was getting hopeless. What was the solution? It turned out to be nothing more than an old-fashioned verbal agreement sealed with a handshake. The seller simply proposed that the money be transferred to him by wire and the editor walked out with the bank information on a piece of paper and the portfolio of images under his arm. Needless to say, we transferred the funds the next day, and we remain grateful and impressed by this unknown person's trust in one of us. It recalls something that might have happened a long time ago.

The pictures from the Ottoman collection, like the other illustrations that appear on our covers, bring to life the richness and variety of dress customs of two centuries ago. They recall the sense of isolation and distance of that period—and of every other historic period except our own hyperkinetic present.

Dress codes have changed since then and the diversity by region, so rich at the time, has faded away. It is now often hard to tell the inhabitant of one continent from another. Perhaps, trying to view it optimistically, we have traded a cultural and visual diversity for a more varied personal life. Or a more varied and interesting intellectual and technical life.

We at Manning celebrate the inventiveness, the initiative, and, yes, the fun of the computer business with book covers based on the rich diversity of regional life of two centuries ago, brought back to life by the pictures from this collection.

tables

Chapter 1

1.1 Forehead markings for the Perl dialects of Perlistan 6

Chapter 2

2.1 Effects of Perl's most essential invocation options 17
2.2 The data and record-number variables 24
2.3 Employing user-defined scalar variables in the Shell and Perl 26
2.4 Comparison of Shell and Perl scripting techniques 29
2.5 Using switch variables 33
2.6 Shell and Perl techniques for writing messages to STDOUT and STDERR 36
2.7 Special variables for I/O operations 42
2.8 Special variables for formatting output 43
2.9 Standard option clusters for Perl commands and scripts 45

Chapter 3

3.1 String escapes for representing control characters 56
3.2 Fundamental capabilities of greppers and Perl 58
3.3 Matching operator syntax 60
3.4 Essential syntax for regular expression 63
3.5 Compact character-class shortcuts 67
3.6 Matching operator examples 69
3.7 Matching modifiers 69
3.8 Metacharacters for alternation, grouping, match capturing, and match
    referencing in greppers and Perl 71
3.9 Quantifier metacharacters 73
3.10 Examples of matching across lines 78
3.11 Patterns for the shortest and longest sequences of anything or something 78
3.12 Unix and Perl commands for common grepping activities 87

Chapter 4

4.1 Text-modification capabilities of sed and Perl 91
4.2 Substitution modifiers 95
4.3 Substitution operator syntax 95
4.4 Substitution operator examples 96

4.5   String modifiers for case conversion 113
4.6   `sed` and Perl commands for common editing activities 119

Chapter 5

5.1   Differences in pattern-matching capabilities of AWK versions and Perl 125
5.2   Comparison of special variables in AWK and Perl 126
5.3   Loading field data into user-defined variables 131
5.4   Using `undef` in assignments to explicit lists 132
5.5   Syntactic differences for `print` in AWK and Perl 135
5.6   Custom field separator definitions 137
5.7   Patterns and Actions in AWK and Perl 139
5.8   AWK and Perl programs for simple tasks 141
5.9   Illustration of array indexing syntax using the field array, `@F` 145
5.10 Using pattern ranges 153
5.11 Relational operators of AWK and Perl 157
5.12 Arithmetic operators of AWK and Perl 159
5.13 Popular built-in functions of AWK and Perl 160
5.14 Perl counterparts to popular AWK functions 161

Chapter 6

6.1   Syntax for file attribute tests 181
6.2   Comparison of supported file attributes in versions of the
      `find` command and Perl 182

Chapter 7

7.1   Tools for data-type conversion 209
7.2   Useful Perl functions for scalars, and their nearest relatives in Unix 210
7.3   The `split` function 211
7.4   The `localtime` function 214
7.5   The `stat` function 216
7.6   The `chomp` function 220
7.7   The `rand` function 222
7.8   Useful Perl functions for lists, and their nearest relatives in Unix 223
7.9   Data flow in Unix pipelines vs. Perl functions 224
7.10 The `sort` function 224
7.11 The `grep` function 228
7.12 The `join` function 229
7.13 The `map` function 233
7.14 The globbing operator 235
7.15 The globbing operator's FNG metacharacters 236
7.16 Corresponding expressions for the FNG and regex notations 238
7.17 Functions for managing directories 239
7.18 Functions for managing files 240

Chapter 8

8.1   The `exit` function 253

8.2   Using `shift` and `unshift` in the Shell and Perl .255

8.3   The `if/else` construct 260

8.4   Nested `if/else` vs. `elsif` 261

8.5   String operators for concatenation and repetition 265

8.6   Command substitution/interpolation in the Shell and Perl 270

8.7   Controlling and interrogating screen displays using `tput` options 271

8.8   The `system` function 276

8.9   The `eval` function in the Shell and Perl 283

Chapter 9

9.1   Indices and values for the `@stooges` array 297

9.2   Syntax for using arrays in the Shell and Perl 298

9.3   Syntax for advanced array indexing 300

9.4   Array of phone-owners' names 309

9.5   Array of phone numbers for phone owners 309

9.6   Storing phone numbers in a hash 309

9.7   Syntax for using hashes in Perl 310

9.8   Syntax for basic and advanced hash indexing 312

9.9   Common list generators in the Shell and their Perl counterparts 326

Chapter 10

10.1   Looping-related differences between the Shell and Perl 332

10.2   The `while/until` loop 333

10.3   Pre- and post-processing in implicit and explicit loops 338

10.4   Perl's `do while` loop and its Shell equivalent 338

10.5   The Shell's `for` loop and Perl's `foreach` loop 340

10.6   Perl's `for` loop 345

10.7   Corresponding loop-control directives for the Shell and Perl 349

10.8   Enhanced `while/until` loops for the Shell and Perl 353

10.9   The Shell's `select` loop 356

10.10 The `select` loop for Perl 356

Chapter 11

11.1   Syntax for defining and using subroutines 364

11.2   The `my`, `our`, and `local` variable declarations 374

Chapter 12

12.1   Essential functions of the `CGI` module 422

12.2   Form-related functions of the `CGI` module 423

Minimal Perl: for UNIX and Linux Users

Part 1 gives those with at least user-level Unix skills—which includes even the most advanced Unix programmers—a gentle introduction to the use of Minimal Perl's most essential features.

We'll start with a humorous allegory about a Traveler from the world of Unix who's visiting Perlistan, which leads to a discussion of the "less is more" philosophy underlying Minimal Perl. Then in chapter 2 we'll cover the most essential features of the Minimal Perl dialect, which is a strategically crafted subset of standard Perl designed for easy assimilation by Unix people. In the following chapters, we'll use those features to develop tiny Perl programs that surpass the limitations of some of the most important Unix commands—grep, sed, awk, and find.

Because they are relevant to a wide range of problem areas, we'll concentrate on programs that do data validation, file conversion, report generation, and number crunching. For example, we'll discuss programs that:

- *Calculate* the growth of an investment over various time periods
- *Web-scrape* a newspaper's electronic edition for travel deals
- *Scan Unix logfiles* for error messages
- Help bad spellers do successful grepping through use of *fuzzy matching*

Along the way, you'll acquire an impressive set of new tools to use in your data processing activities. In addition, you'll learn how to think like a Perl programmer, and how to effectively use some of the most simple—yet powerful—features of the language.

C H A P T E R   1

Introducing Minimal Perl

1.1 A visit to Perlistan 3
1.2 Perl can be simple 7
1.3 About Minimal Perl 7

1.4 Laziness is a virtue 9
1.5 A minimal dose of syntax 10
1.6 Writing one-line programs 11
1.7 Summary 14

Perl is a great language, with an ingenious mentality underlying it, and a terrific user community gathered around it. Given these properties, it's no wonder it has become so popular.

But Perl is also a large and complex language that offers the programmer many different ways to accomplish the same goal. This can make it hard for beginners to learn the language and for one programmer to understand a program written by another.

In this chapter, we'll discuss the motivation behind the development of Minimal Perl and the philosophy underlying the special subset of the standard Perl language that it employs. But before delving into those matters, we'll begin our journey with a tale of travel that provides a helpful orientation to Perl culture.

1.1   A VISIT TO PERLISTAN

A Unix user visiting the world of Perl may feel like he's in a foreign land, where people use words that sound familiar but that have different meanings than they do back home. Let's observe the adventures of such a *Traveler*, as he tries to understand the way people communicate in Perlistan.

Scene: The main market of Perlistan, a hub of the famous Silk Road, in a high desert region of central Asia. Nomads in tribal dress are haggling enthusiastically for discounts on goods, as camel carts and yak carts compete for space in the narrow lanes of the old city.

As the Traveler pauses to snap a photo of an ornately decorated camel, he overhears a merchant saying to his assistant

> *"Foreach gingko nut in basket, if it passes freshness test, push it in bag."*

The assistant complies, and hands the waiting customer a bag of fresh nuts from the Gingko Biloba tree.

The Traveler can't help but notice the distinctive **triangle** drawn on the merchant's forehead. He's heard that these markings hold a special significance in Perlistani communications, so he makes a mental note of this transaction for later reference.

Across the way, he observes another merchant, also wearing a triangle, getting the same result by telling her identically marked assistant something a bit different:

> *"Test it for freshness and push it in bag, foreach gingko nut in basket."*

It disturbs the Traveler that this instruction was expressed *backwards* relative to that of the first merchant and that and is now playing the conditional role previously played by if. He wonders if it's significant that this merchant's triangle points to the left (from the customer's viewpoint), whereas that of the first merchant points to the right.

Next, he overhears a merchant bearing a large **circle** on his forehead saying to his identically marked assistant

> *"Bag—grep ripe—basket of kiwis."*

The Traveler knows that grep is used back home for selecting items on the basis of *matches*, so he suddenly fells hopeful that he may be able to crack this linguistic code after all. But now he's wondering why the two "triangled" merchants expressed a related request in a completely different way—without any reference to grep!

Then he hears a fourth merchant, also distinguished by a forehead circle, call out:

> *"Bag—grep rand—basket of jerkies."*

An apparently *random selection* of assorted jerkies (dried meats) is put into the bag by his circle-wearing assistant.

Now the Traveler is perplexed. His theory about grep being for matching—which fit the *grep ripe* case perfectly—is discredited by this new evidence. That's because *rand*, unlike *ripe*, wasn't a property of any of the selected jerkies and therefore shouldn't have been usable as a basis for matching. At least, the grep back home doesn't work like that!

Seeking consolation, he buys a few assorted jerkies and commences to gnaw contentedly. A runny-nosed boy interrupts his reverie, offering to change money for him at attractive black-market rates. The Traveler declines, but not before learning that the jerky with the rigid texture and overbearing flavor is made from dried python meat.

Then he notices a merchant sporting a **square** on his forehead, who is accumulating a long queue of impatient customers. Shortly after the merchant finishes intoning the following long-winded set of instructions to his (equally square) assistant, a disgruntled customer finally receives a bag of ripe figs:

> *"Set variable candidate to 0;*
> *set variable selection to 0;*
> *test variable candidate is less than number of figs in basket or finish;*
> *select fig from basket;*
> *if fig passes test for ripeness, mark it with value of variable selection,*
> *   increment variable selection by 1, and put fig into bag;*
> *increment variable candidate by 1;*
> *repeat from 'test variable candidate' step."*

Now the Traveler is mystified. Given the ample evidence that there are more concise ways to express this kind of transaction, why would anyone go to all the trouble to do it this way? Could there be some advantage to this excessively verbose manner of speaking—like, do they get paid by the syllable? Or maybe these squared guys are just meticulous to a fault.

At this point, the Traveler wonders how any visitor could pick up the language of Perlistan, given its many different—and largely unrelated—ways of expressing the same idea. His chances of mastering its nuances seem as remote as those of him being invited to a high tea, catered by Oxford-educated snow leopards, at the den of the Alpha Yeti.[1]

In frustration, he rushes to catch the quickest flight home, and he resolves that his next vacation will be free of linguistic puzzles—and python jerky!

But the Traveler is left wondering if he could have had a better experience in Perlistan, if only he had tried a different approach.

1.1.1 Sometimes you need a professional guide

It's too bad linguistic turmoil ruined the Traveler's vacation. He should have hired a certified guide before venturing into Perlistan's market district—as the brochure had advised. Had he done so, he would have learned that the *JAPH*s (which is what the people of Perlistan call themselves) do indeed share a common language called Perl, which was invented with the founding of the country in 1987.

Rather than being a new creation of whole cloth, Perl was created like a patchwork quilt, incorporating the best features of the languages that were the mother tongues of the JAPHly tribes. But it's not an ugly quilt with a jumble of patterns and shapes

---

[1] Yeti is the Perlistani name for what other cultures call *bigfoot* or the *abominable snowman*.

all forced together, as you might expect. Instead, thanks to the ingenuity of Perl creator Larry Wall ("Larry"), it's a work of art that cleverly coordinates its disparate elements into an aesthetically pleasing result.[2]

Naturally, JAPHs tend to feel most comfortable using the elements of Perl that are derived from their own mother tongues. It shouldn't be surprising therefore that some of these makeshift dialects are so dissimilar as to appear to be different languages because, in fact, they started out that way!

Now you know why the Perlistanis wear dialect-identifying markings—it's so they can easily identify others from their linguistic group.

Table 1.1 summarizes the meanings of the different forehead markings and indicates the subculture associated with each dialect.

Table 1.1 Forehead markings for the Perl dialects of Perlistan

Forehead marking	Perl dialect	Marketplace quote
Right-pointing triangle	UNIX Shell	Foreach gingko nut in basket, if it passes freshness test, push it in bag.
Left-pointing triangle	UNIX Shell (but backward)	Test it for freshness and push it in bag, foreach gingko nut in basket.
Circle	Idiomatic Perl	Bag—grep ripe—basket of kiwis. Bag—grep rand—basket of jerkies.
Square	C language	set variable candidate to 0; ...

With the benefit of this table, we're now equipped to understand the Traveler's observations.

The **triangles** identify those whose mother tongue is Shell and who find Perl's flow-control structures to be refreshingly familiar. These JAPHs come in two varieties, so it's important to notice the direction in which the triangle is pointing. If it points to your right, the individual follows the time-honored tradition of putting control keywords such as `if` and `foreach` at the beginning of the sentence. However, Perl also allows such instructions to be expressed in *backward* order, which those wearing left-pointing triangles consider to be more natural.

Those wearing **circles** have lots of spare time left over after communicating their needs to each other, but they have fewer friends to enjoy it with. That's because they either learned Perl as their mother tongue or have lived in Perlistan long enough to lose their native accents, and they now speak *idiomatic* Perl—which doesn't have much in common with its UNIX-based predecessors.

Those wearing the mark of the **square** need great patience, because it takes them a long time to communicate. Their dialect emphasizes features derived from the

---

[2] Others have commented on the eclectic mix of linguistic ingredients that constitute Perl, such as Yoz Grahame, who wrote an interesting article called "Perl is Internet Yiddish" (available on the Internet).

notoriously hazardous C language, which breeds a mistrust among its users that causes them to compulsively over-specify all aspects of every operation.

But Perl doesn't have to be this complicated.

1.2 PERL CAN BE SIMPLE

As illustrated in the Traveler's tale, Perl provides you with many different ways of obtaining the same result. This is partly due to its extensive appropriation of overlapping features from the UNIX shell languages, the AWK and C languages, and various core UNIX utilities (especially grep and sed), which has endowed it with more redundancies than other languages. The rest is due to Larry's predilection for giving Perl users as much freedom of expression as possible, as celebrated in the Perl motto *"There's More Than One Way To Do It!"*

What's a would-be Perl programmer to do? Given the sorry state of our current time-travel technology, we can't go back to modify the fundamental design decisions that led to the unusual richness and complexity of the modern Perl language. Nor would we necessarily want to; those features have their uses. But there's nothing stopping us from making these factors work *for* us, rather than *against* us.

With the Minimal Perl approach, you learn a Perl subset that's based on familiar features derived from its UNIX-based predecessors. This allows you to continue programming in the AWK style, for instance, while using Perl and benefiting from its many enhancements.

Part 1 of this book, which capitalizes on your existing knowledge of important Unix utilities, is devoted to showing you how to program in this fashion. Part 2 takes this approach a step further, by teaching those with Shell programming experience additional features of Perl—again by capitalizing on existing knowledge.

In addition to UNIX-derived features, Perl also provides others that are unique to Perl, for those who choose to learn them. But you should wait until you've fully mastered Minimal Perl before aspiring to learn the advanced dialect of the circled JAPHs, which is replete with extremely enigmatic expressions!

Next, we'll consider what Minimal Perl is—and isn't—in more detail.

1.3 ABOUT MINIMAL PERL

Many Perl books and training programs try to teach more of Perl than is necessary or can be readily assimilated. By doing so, they impose an unnecessary and counterproductive burden on Perl novices who have modest immediate needs—especially those who know a related language.

From this perspective, setting out to teach a Unix person[3] everything about Perl is like telling a Dutchman who wants to relocate to Zurich that he must learn *every one*

---

[3] A Unix person is a user of Unix command-line utilities, such as grep. This group includes both beginning users and advanced Shell programmers.

of Switzerland's official languages—German, French, Italian, and Romansch—instead of the single language closest to Dutch that's widely understood there: *German*.

That's why this book teaches you Perl from the perspective that's most easily assimilated by those with a Unix background. You'll be able to pick up Minimal Perl quickly and easily, by capitalizing on your existing knowledge of Shell programming and/or basic Unix commands, rather than having to learn everything from scratch. As a result, you'll be able to transfer your existing skills to a more powerful and more portable language, which will enhance your productivity as well as your career prospects.

1.3.1 What Minimal Perl isn't

Before we discuss what Minimal Perl is, we'll discuss what it isn't, to dispel some possible misconceptions.

Is Minimal Perl a dumbed-down version of Perl?

No. It isn't a *version* of Perl at all, in the sense that distinguishes the old Perl 4 from the current Perl 5. Instead, it's a carefully crafted subset of standard Perl 5, designed for easy assimilation by Unix people.

Is Minimal Perl a less capable Perl?

Not really. As a general rule, you can write the same kinds of programs using the techniques of Minimal Perl that you can using the facilities of the full language. The primary exception is that Minimal Perl doesn't include any features for Object-Oriented programming. But there's nothing to stop you from learning additional features, if and when you feel the need, and using them alongside your Minimal Perl skills.

Will learning Minimal Perl restrict my future options?

Not at all. Although Minimal Perl leads you down a narrow path away from the chaotic linguistic conditions of Perlistan's central market area, it's not a one-way path or a dead-end. Nothing will prevent you from learning more Perl later on.

1.3.2 What Minimal Perl is

I created Minimal Perl because I believe it's a good idea to simplify things that are overly complex. This practice is embodied in a principle that is a cornerstone of science, variously called *parsimony*, *Occam's Razor*, and, in more everyday use, *KISS* (Keep it Simple, Stupid).

It has even been expressed by the great blues artist B. B. King, in words to the following effect:

> *Some players use as many notes as they can to make sure they don't leave any good ones out. Great players leave out as many notes as possible, so they can concentrate on the ones they really need.*

We'll talk next about how Minimal Perl fits into its associated cultures.

How does Minimal Perl relate to Unix and standard Perl?

Minimal Perl emphasizes the features of Perl that are most closely related to Unix tools, most applicable to a wide variety of application areas, and most easily learned and used by the corporate engineers who take our training classes. It's "minimal" in the sense that it distills Perl down to its most essential features, by excluding those that are redundant, highly advanced, or overly esoteric.

Like a dialect of a natural language, Minimal Perl consists of more than just a specialized vocabulary and grammar—it also has helpful idioms and powerful techniques that hold it together and make it work. It reduces redundancies, by showing a single good way to accomplish a particular kind of task rather than all the possibilities. It minimizes the amount of grammar you have to learn, by omitting the reversed variants of all the control structures—so you won't also have to learn to *talk backwards* like the **left-triangle** merchant in the Traveler's tale.

Above all, the Minimal Perl approach is practical, eclectic, and willing to take what it needs from beyond the borders of Perlistan. This approach benefits those who already know some Unix utilities, because it's often easier to get the results you want by adding a Perl command to a pipeline of Unix commands than it is to implement all the needed functionality with Perl alone. For this reason, in many of the programming examples in part 1, other Unix commands are exploited to full advantage, to allow the Perl portion to focus on what it can uniquely contribute.

Truly, sometimes less *is* more! That's the philosophy behind Minimal Perl. But before you begin to learn Minimal Perl, you need to embrace your *Laziness*.

1.4 LAZINESS IS A VIRTUE

Some of your envious colleagues may seek to lay a guilt trip on you, once they see the impressive progress you'll be making with the Minimal Perl approach. For lack of a better explanation, they may think you're *cheating* in some way, or at least cutting corners for short-term gains that will come back to haunt you later.

It comes down to the fact that some will think you're lazy for typing a 12-character Perl command to get a particular job done while others are writing and debugging 12-line Perl scripts or 120-line C programs to accomplish the same task.

Your acquisition of Perl skills will go more smoothly if you accept the following simple truth: A willingness to take advantage of the Perl features that simplify your programs doesn't mean you're *lazy*—at least, not in the derogatory sense of the word. It does, however, mean you're *Lazy*, with a capital *L*, as the term is used by Larry in the Camel book.[4]

---

[4] As discussed in the glossary, the "Camel book" is the nickname for the Perl reference manual, more formally known as *Programming Perl*, 3rd Edition, by Larry Wall, Tom Christiansen, and Jon Orwant (O'Reilly and Associates, Inc., 2000).

The highly desirable trait of Laziness refers to a tendency to judiciously exploit available resources to accomplish your programming goals with minimal effort. And that's good, because it enhances productivity. Therefore, as the term is used in the Perl community, Laziness has more to do with using your energy efficiently than indulging in slothfulness or lethargy.

But Perl provides so much scope for the expression of Laziness that it's easy to go overboard. If taken to an extreme, Perl's shortcuts can easily push your programs past simplification into *obfuscation*. And writing programs that nobody else can understand—or even worse, that you can't understand next year yourself—is *not* a recommended practice.

With this perspective in mind, we'll review some of Perl's essential technical features, which allow you to write tiny but powerful programs—*Lazily*! To illustrate this important point, we'll compare the easy way of writing a particular kind of simple program in Perl with the much more complicated approach that's favored by squared JAPHs.

But before we look at our first programming examples, we must first discuss a few important aspects of Perl syntax.

1.5 A MINIMAL DOSE OF SYNTAX

In many languages, new programmers have to learn lots of syntax rules before they can start writing useful programs. Such rules typically decree where spaces are required, where double quotes must be used instead of single quotes, and how to continue a statement onto the next line.

Fortunately, Perl is relatively flexible in its syntax requirements, and is often compliant with Unix conventions. So, Unix-derived habits, such as putting a space after a command name and quotes around its *arguments* (the words that follow the command name), will serve you well in the world of Perl.

1.5.1 Terminating statements with semicolons

As an illustration of the similarity of the languages, consider these Shell and Perl ways of printing a word to the screen:

Shell
```
echo "Greetings"
```

or

```
print "Greetings"
```

Perl
(using l option)[5]
```
print "Greetings";
```

---

[5] Perl's l *invocation option* causes `print` statements to be automatically supplied with terminating *newline* characters, just as the Shell's `echo` is by default. Chapter 2 discusses invocation options in detail.

Notice that the Perl example has a semicolon at the end the argument list for `print`, although the Shell examples don't use that character. This difference is based on the way each language identifies the end of a *statement*—a completed instruction that's ready for processing. In the Shell case, pressing <ENTER> at the end of a line marks a statement as complete, whereas in Perl, typing a semicolon there does that job.

That's all you need to know about Perl syntax for now, although some additional details will be illustrated later as we review other kinds of programs.

Now let's learn how to write one-line programs.

1.6   *WRITING ONE-LINE PROGRAMS*

There are two ways to write Perl programs. With the *script* approach, the program is placed in a file that starts with a `perl` *shebang* line, such as `#! /usr/bin/perl`. With the *command* approach, a `perl` command is typed interactively to the Shell, consisting of a short program preceded by the e invocation option (see the following example).[6]

That e option (for execution of programs) is the foundation on which Perl *one-liners* (one-line commands) are built, because it provides a convenient way for highly compact programs to be conveyed to `perl` without the overhead of creating a script file.

Here's an example of a simple yet useful program that can be written as a one-line command:

```
$ perl -wl -e 'print 22/7;'   # Gimme pi!
3.14285714285714
$
```

The `print` function is the general facility for sending results to the current output destination, which is the user's terminal by default. It's followed, in this case, by an expression describing the division of two numbers, positioned in the argument list of `print`. Accordingly, the result of that calculation gets `printed`.

Just as the pattern argument to a `grep` command would be single-quoted to prevent the Shell from tampering with its contents (e.g., `grep '* On Sale! *' adverts`), the Perl program is also enclosed in single quotes.

The w option enables *warnings*, which are especially helpful for new programmers. The l option (the lowercase *L*) requests automatic line-end processing, which in this case ensures that a Unix-appropriate record separator is printed after the numerical result. That allows the next Shell prompt to appear on a fresh line, as expected. These two options are so beneficial that they're used with almost every program in this book, and they deserve to be used routinely by you as well.

Now you know how to type a simple Perl program directly to the Shell and have its output delivered to the screen. But many programs must collect and process *input*

---

6   Further details on creating Perl commands and scripts are provided in sections 2.1 and 2.4.

in addition to generating output, and doing so requires the use of additional Perl invocation options. We'll cover them in chapter 2.

Next, we'll consider the benefits of striving for simplicity in Perl programming, and an important philosophical principle underlying Minimal Perl.

1.6.1 Balancing simplicity and readability

You'll soon see how the essential behavior of the Unix cat command can be replicated in Perl using various techniques. Along the way you'll learn how to write an elementary *filter program*, which will serve as the foundation for dozens of more interesting ones that are covered later in this book. During this discussion, the Minimal Perl philosophy of employing the simplest practical solution from the rich collection of alternatives will be demonstrated.

Filter programs—such as the grep, sed, and sort commands of Unix—take input, process it in some way, and then emit the results. The single Perl feature that's most valuable for writing filters is the *implicit loop* of the n invocation option, which makes it easy to process lines one at a time. It's much Lazier (and wiser) to use this option than to continually reinvent the wheels of its infrastructure on your own (as squared JAPHs are inclined to do).

One of the more important lessons conveyed in the following sections is that although *"There's More Than One Way To Do It"* in Perl, those ways aren't all equal—some are preferable to others, based on their optimal balance of simplicity and readability.

You'll see some well-crafted programs in the following section, as well as alternatives that are either too large and complex, or too succinct and cryptic. Keep in mind that you won't need to absorb the Perl techniques that are demonstrated in passing at this time, because they'll be covered in detail later. And please note that the complex programs are presented primarily for their *shock value*—they won't be on the test!

> **TIP** Using Perl's n option makes it easy to write tiny but powerful filter programs.

1.6.2 Implementing simple filters

Our exploration of filtering with Perl begins with a consideration of the Unix cat command and a replication of its basic functionality in Perl. Behold the syntax of the humble cat, which is typical of Unix filter programs:

```
cat file file2
```

This invocation causes cat to open *file*, read a line, write that line to the screen, and repeat those steps until all lines have been processed. Then it does the same for *file2*.

For example:

```
$ cat exotic_fruits exotic_jerkies
fig
kiwi
camel
python
```

Now we'll examine some Perl programs that act as cat-like filters. Why? Because the simplicity of cat—called a *null filter*, since it doesn't change its input—makes it an ideal starting point for our explorations of Perl's data-processing facilities.

Here's an example of the *hard way* to emulate cat with Perl, using a script that takes an unnecessarily complex approach:

```
#! /usr/bin/perl -wl

@ARGV  or  @ARGV = '-';
foreach my $file (@ARGV) {
    open IN, "< $file"  or
        die "$0: Open of $file failed, code $!\n";
    while ( defined ($_=<IN>) ) {
        print $_;
    }
    close IN  or
        die "$0: Close of $file failed, code $!\n";
}
```

Only masochists, paranoiacs, or programmers abused in their early years by the C language (e.g., squared JAPHs) would write a Perl program this way.[7] That's because Perl provides facilities to automatically create the filtering infrastructure for you—all you have to do is ask for it!

An equivalent yet considerably simpler approach is shown next. In this case, Perl's *input operator* (<>) is used to automatically acquire data from filename arguments or STDIN (as detailed in chapter 10). Unlike the previous solution, this cat-like program is small enough to implement as a one-liner:

```
perl -wl -e 'while (<>) { print; }' file file2
```

But even this is too much coding! You're busy, and typing is tiresome, error-prone, and likely to give you carpal tunnel syndrome, so you should try to minimize it (within reason). Accordingly, the ideal solution to writing a basic filter program in Perl is the following, which uses the n option:

```
perl -wnl -e 'print;' file file2      # OPTIMALLY simple!
```

The beauty of this version is that it lets you focus on the filtering being implemented in the program, which in this case is no filtering at all—the program just prints every

---

7 There are cases where it makes sense to write your own loops in Perl, as shown in chapter 10, but this isn't one of them.

line it reads. That's easy to see when you aren't distracted by a dozen lines of boilerplate input-reading code, as you were with the scripted equivalent shown earlier.

Where did the `while` loop go? It's still there, but it's invisible, because the n option tells Perl, "Insert the usual input-reading loop for this Lazy programmer, with *n*o automatic printing of the input lines."

A fuller explanation of how the n option works is given in chapter 10. For the time being, just remember that it lets you forget about the mundane details of input processing so you can concentrate on the task at hand.

Believe it or not, there's a way to write a `cat`-like program in Perl that involves even less typing:

```
perl -wpl -e ''  file file2          # OVERLY simple!
```

By now, you're probably thinking that Perl's reputation in some circles as a *write-only* language (i.e., one nobody can *read*) may be well deserved. That's understandable, and we'll return to this matter in a moment. But first, let's discuss how this program works—which certainly isn't obvious.

The p option requests the usual input-reading loop, but with *automatic printing* of each input line after it has been processed. In this case, no processing is specified, because there's no program between those quotes. Yet it still works, because the p option provides the essential `cat`-like behavior of printing each input line.

This bizarrely cryptic solution is, frankly, a case of taking a good thing too far. It's the kind of coding that may lead IT managers to wonder whether Larry has a screw loose somewhere—and to hope their competitors will hire as many Perl programmers as they can find.

Of course, it's unwise to drive your colleagues crazy, and tarnish your reputation, by writing programs that appear to be grossly defective—even if they work! For this reason, the optimally simple form shown previously with the n option and the explicit `print` statement is the approach used for most filter programs in Minimal Perl.

1.7   SUMMARY

As illustrated by the Traveler's tale at the beginning of this chapter, and the `cat`-like filter programs we examined later, the Perl programmer often has the choice of writing a complex or a simple program to handle a particular task. You can use this flexibility to create programs that range from minor masterpieces of inscrutability—because they're so tiny and mysterious—to major masterpieces of verbosity—because they're so voluminous and long-winded. The Perl subset I call Minimal Perl avoids programs at both ends of that spectrum, because they can't be readily understood or maintained, and there are always concise yet readable alternatives that are more prudent choices.

To make Perl easier for Unix people to learn, Minimal Perl favors simple and compact approaches based on familiar features of Unix, including the use of *invocation options* to duplicate the input-processing behavior of Unix filter programs.

Minimal Perl exploits the power of Perl to indulge the programmer's Laziness, which allows energy to be redirected from the mundane aspects of programming toward more productive uses of its capabilities. For instance, the n and p invocation options allow *Lazy* Perl programmers—those who strive to work *efficiently*—to avoid retyping the generic input-reading loop in every filter program they write for the rest of their Perl programming careers. As an additional benefit, using these options also lets them write many useful programs as one-line commands rather than as larger scripts.

In the next chapter, we'll discuss several of Perl's other invocation options. Learning about them will give you a better understanding of the inner workings of the simple programs you've seen thus far and will prepare you for the many useful and interesting programs coming up in subsequent chapters.

C H A P T E R   2

Perl essentials

2.1 Perl's invocation options 17

2.2 Using variables 23

2.3 Loading modules: -M 27

2.4 Writing simple scripts 29

2.5 Additional special variables 42

2.6 Standard option clusters 44

2.7 Constructing programs 47

2.8 Summary 51

This chapter introduces the most essential features of Perl, to pave your way for the programming examples you'll see in the following chapters. Among the topics we'll cover here are the use of Perl's *special variables*, how to write Perl *one-line commands* and *scripts*, and the fundamentals of using Perl *modules*.

But we don't discuss everything you need to know about Perl in this chapter. Further details on this chapter's topics—and more specialized ones not discussed here—are presented in later chapters, in the context of illustrative programming examples.

Some of the language features discussed here won't be used until part 2 of the book, so it's not necessary for you to read this chapter in its entirety right now. If you haven't learned a computer programming language before—or if you have, but you're eager to get started with Perl—you should read the most important sections[1] now (2.1, 2.4.5, 2.5.1, and 2.6, including subsections) and then proceed to the next chapter.

This chapter will serve you well as a reference document, so you should revisit it when you need to brush up on any of its topics. To make this easy for you, when "essential" features are used in programs in the following chapters, cross-references will refer you back to the relevant sections in this chapter. Forward references are also

---

[1] To help you spot them, the headings for these sections are marked with the *θ* symbol.

provided, to help you easily find more detailed coverage in later chapters on topics introduced here.

We'll begin our coverage of Perl with a discussion of its *invocation options*, because you've got to invoke Perl before you can do anything else with it.[2]

2.1 PERL'S INVOCATION OPTIONS

An *invocation option* is a character (usually a letter) that's preceded by a hyphen and presented as one of the initial arguments to a `perl` command. Its purpose is to enable special features for the execution of a program.

Table 2.1 lists the most important invocation options.

Table 2.1   Effects of Perl's most essential invocation options

Option	Provides	Explanation
`-e 'code'`	Execution of *code*	Causes Perl to execute *code* as a program. Used to avoid the overhead of a script's file with tiny programs.
`-w`	Warnings	Enables warning messages, which is generally advisable.
`-n`	Reading but no printing	Requests an implicit input-reading loop that stores records in `$_`.
`-p`	Reading and printing	Requests an implicit input-reading loop that stores records in `$_` and automatically prints that variable after optional processing of its contents.
`-l`	Line-end processing	Automatically inserts an output record separator at the end of `print`'s output. When used with `-n` or `-p`, additionally does automatic *chomping*—removal of the input record separator from input records.
`-0digits`	Setting of input record separator	Defines the character that marks the end of an input record, using octal digits. The special case of `-00` enables paragraph mode, in which empty lines mark ends of input records; `-0777` enables file mode, in which each file constitutes a single record.

Although each of the invocation options shown in table 2.1 is described under its own heading in the sections that follow, it's not necessary to memorize what each one does, because they're commonly used in only a handful of combinations. These combinations, which we call *option clusters*, consist of a hyphen followed by one or more options (e.g., `-wnl`).

Toward the end of this chapter, you'll learn now to select the appropriate options for your programs using a procedure for selecting *standard option clusters* that takes the guesswork out of this important task.

First, we'll describe what the individual options do.

---

[2] A few of these options were discussed in chapter 1's comparisons of easy and hard ways to write `cat`-like commands. To enhance the reference value of this chapter, these options are also included here.

2.1.1　One-line programming: -e

The purpose of Perl's e invocation option is to identify the next argument as the program to be executed. This allows a simple program to be conveyed to `perl` as an interactively typed command rather than as a specially prepared file called a *script*.

As an example, here's a one-line command that calculates and prints the result of dividing 42 by 3:

```
$ perl -wl -e 'print 42/3;'
14
```

The division of 42 by 3 is processed first, and then the `print` function receives 14 as its argument, which it writes to the output.

We'll discuss the w option used in that command's invocation next and the l option shortly thereafter.

2.1.2　Enabling warnings: -w

Wouldn't it be great if you could have Larry and his colleagues discreetly critique your Perl programs for you? That would give you an opportunity to learn from the masters with every execution of every program. That's effectively what happens when you use the w option to enable Perl's extensive *warning* system. In fact, Perl's warnings are generally so insightful, helpful, and educational that most programmers use the w option all the time.

As a practical example, consider which of the following runs of this program provides the more useful output:

```
$ perl  -l -e 'print $HOME;'  # Is Shell variable known to Perl?
(no output)
$ perl -wl -e 'print $HOME;'  # Apparently not!
Name "main::HOME" used only once: possible typo at -e line 1.
Use of uninitialized value in print at -e line 1.
```

The messages indicate that Perl was unable to print the value of the variable $HOME (because it was neither inherited from the Shell nor set in the program). Because there's usually one appearance of a variable when its value is assigned and another when the value is retrieved, it's unusual for a variable name to appear only once in a program. As a convenience to the programmer, Perl detects this condition and warns that the variable's name may have been mistyped ("possible typo").[3]

You'd be wise to follow the example of professional Perl programmers. They use the w option routinely, so they hear about their coding problems in the privacy of their own cubicles—rather than having them flare up during high-pressure customer demos instead!

The option we'll cover next is also extremely valuable.

---

[3] You could say the variable's name was grossly mistyped, because in Perl this Shell variable is accessed as a member of an associative array (a.k.a. a *hash*) using $ENV{HOME}, as detailed in chapter 9.

2.1.3   Processing input: `-n`

Many Unix utilities (`grep`, `sed`, `sort`, and so on) are typically used as *filter* programs—they read input and then write some variation on it to the output.

Here's an example of the Unix `sed` command inserting spaces at the beginning of each input line using its substitution facility, which typically appears in the form `s/search-string/replacement-string/g`:[4]

```
$ cat seattleites
Torbin Ulrich  98107
Yeshe Dolma    98117
$ sed 's/^/    /g' seattleites
    Torbin Ulrich  98107
    Yeshe Dolma    98117
```

The `^` symbol in the *search-string* field represents the beginning of the line, causing the spaces in the *replacement-string* to be inserted there before the modified line is sent to the output.

Here's the Perl counterpart to that `sed` command, which uses a `sed`-like *substitution operator* (described in chapter 4). Notice the need for an explicit request to `print` the resulting line, which isn't needed with `sed`:

```
$ perl -wnl -e 's/^/    /g; print;' seattleites
    Torbin Ulrich  98107
    Yeshe Dolma    98117
```

This command works like the `sed` command does—by processing one line at a time, taken from files named as arguments or from STDIN, using an implicit loop (provided by the n option). (For a more detailed explanation, see section 10.2.4.)

This example also provides an opportunity to review an important component of Perl syntax. The semicolons at the ends of the `sed`-like substitution operator and the `print` function identify each of them as constituting a complete statement—and that's important! If the semicolon preceding `print` were missing, for example, that word would be associated with the substitution operator rather than being recognized as an invocation of the `print` function, and a fatal syntax error would result.

Because `sed`-like processing is so commonly needed in Perl, there's a provision for obtaining it more easily, as shown next.

2.1.4   Processing input with automatic printing: `-p`

You request input processing with automatic printing after (optional) processing by using the p option in place of n:

---

[4] Are you wondering about the use of the "global" replacement modifier (`/g`)? Because it's needed much more often than not, it's used routinely in Minimal Perl and removed only in the rare cases where it spoils the results. It's shown here for both the `sed` and `perl` commands for uniformity.

```
$ perl -wpl -e 's/^/      /g;' seattleites   # "p" does the printing
    Torbin Ulrich    98107
    Yeshe Dolma      98117
```

This coding style makes it easier to concentrate on the primary activity of the command—the editing operation—and it's no coincidence that it makes the command look more like the equivalent sed command shown earlier. That's because Larry modeled the substitution operator on the syntax of sed (and vi) to make Perl easier for UNIX users to learn.

Like the Shell's echo command, Perl's print can automatically generate newlines, as you'll see next.

2.1.5   **Processing line-endings: -1**

Before discussing how automatic processing of record separators works in Perl, we first need to define some terms.

A *record* is a collection of characters that's read or written as a unit, and a *file* is a collection of records. When you're dealing with text files, each individual line is considered to be a separate record by default. The particular character, or sequence of characters, that marks the end of the record being read is called the *input record separator*. On Unix systems, that's the linefeed character by default; but for portability and convenience, Perl lets you refer to the OS-specific default input record separator (whatever it may be) as \n, which is called *newline*.

Perl normally retains the input record separator as part of each record that's read, so it's still there if that record is printed later. However, with certain kinds of programs, it's a great convenience to have the separators automatically stripped off as input is read, and then to have them automatically replaced when output is written by print. This effect is enabled by adding the l option to n or p with perl's invocation.

To see what difference that option makes, we'll compare the outputs of the following two commands, which print the number of each input line (but not the input lines themselves). The numbers are provided by the special variable "$." (covered in table 2.2), which automatically counts records as they're processed.

First, here's a command that omits the l option and features a special Shell prompt (go$) for added clarity:

```
go$ perl -wn -e 'print $.;' three_line_file   # file has three lines
123go$
```

The output lines are scrunched together, because the "$." variable doesn't contain a newline—and nothing else in the program causes one to be issued after each print. Notice also that the Shell's prompt for the next command isn't where it should be—at the beginning of a fresh line. That's about as unnerving as a minor earthquake to the average Unix user!

In contrast, when the l option is used, a newline is automatically added at the end of print's output:

```
go$ perl -wnl -e 'print $.;' three_line_file
1
2
3
go$
```

For comparison, here's how you'd achieve the same result without using 1:

```
$ perl -wn -e 'print $. , "\n";' three_line_file
...
```

This approach requires an explicit request to print the newline, which you make by adding the "\n" argument to print. Doing that doesn't require a substantial amount of extra typing in this tiny program, but the extra work would be considerable in programs having many print statements. To avoid the effort that would be wasted in routinely typing "\n" arguments for print statements, Minimal Perl normally uses the 1 option.

Of course, in some situations it's desirable to omit the newline from the end of an output line, as we'll discuss next.

2.1.6 Printing without newlines: printf

In most programs that read input, using the 1 option offers a significant benefit, and in the others, it usually doesn't hurt. However, there is a situation where the processing provided by this option is undesirable. Specifically, any program that outputs a string using print that should *not* be terminated with a newline will be affected adversely, because the 1 option will dutifully ensure that it gets one.

This situation occurs most commonly in programs that prompt for input. Here's an example, based on the (unshown) script called order, which writes its output using print but doesn't use the 1 option:

```
$ order
How many robotic tooth flossers? [1-200]: 42
We'll ship 42 tomorrow.
```

Here's another version of that script, which uses the 1 option:

```
$ order2      # using -l option
How many robotic tooth flossers? [1-200]:
42
We'll ship 42 tomorrow.
```

As computer users know, it's conventional for input to be accepted at the end of a prompt—not on the line below it, as in the case of order2. This can be accomplished by using the printf function rather than print, because printf is immune to the effects of the 1 option.[5]

---

[5] The name printf refers to this function's ability to do formatted printing when multiple arguments are provided (as opposed to the single-argument case we're using for prompting).

Accordingly, the order2 script can be adjusted to suppress the prompt's newline by adding one letter to its output statement, as shown in the second line that follows:

```
print  "How many robotic flossers? [1-200]:";  # -l INcompatible
printf "How many robotic flossers? [1-200]:";  # -l compatible
```

In summary, the l option is routinely used in Minimal Perl, and printf is used in place of print when an automatic newline isn't desired at the output's end (as in the case of prompts).

Tip on using printf for prompting

In its typical (non-prompting) usage, printf's first argument contains % symbols that are interpreted in a special way. For this reason, if your prompt string contains any % symbols, you must double each one (%%) to get them to print correctly.

2.1.7 Changing the input record separator: -0digits

When the n or p option is used, Perl reads one line at a time by default, using an OS-appropriate definition of the input record separator to find each line's end. But it's not always desirable to use an individual line as the definition of a record, so Perl (unlike most of its UNIX predecessors) has provisions for changing that behavior.

The most common alternate record definitions are for units of paragraphs and files, with a *paragraph* being defined as a chunk of text separated by one or more empty lines from the next chunk. The input record separator of choice is specified using special sequences of digits with the -0digits option, shown earlier in table 2.1.

Look how the behavior of the indenting program you saw earlier is altered as the record definition is changed from a line, to a paragraph, to a file (□ represents the space character):

```
$ perl       -wpl -e 's/^/□□□□/g;' memo    # default is line mode
□□□□This is the file "memo", which has these
□□□□lines spread out like so.

□□□□And then it continues to a
□□□□second paragraph.
$ perl -00   -wpl -e 's/^/□□□□/g;' memo    # paragraph mode
□□□□This is the file "memo", which has these
lines spread out like so.

□□□□And then it continues to a
second paragraph.
$ perl -0777 -wpl -e 's/^/□□□□/g;' memo    # file mode
□□□□This is the file "memo", which has these
lines spread out like so.

And then it continues to a
second paragraph.
```

In all cases, indentation is inserted at the beginning of each record (signified by ^ in the search-string field), although it may not look that way at first glance.

The first command uses the default definition of a line as a record, so every line is indented at its beginning. The second defines each paragraph as a record, so each of the two paragraphs is indented at its beginning. The last command defines the entire file as one record, so the single file is indented at its beginning.

Apart from these commonly used alternate record definitions, it's also possible to change the input record separator to an arbitrary character string by assigning that string to the special variable "$/". That technique is documented in table 2.7 for reference purposes and demonstrated in later chapters (e.g., listings 9.3 and 9.4).

Now we'll turn our attention to Perl's fastest and easiest-to-use mechanism for storing and retrieving data: the *variable*.

2.2 USING VARIABLES

In part 1 of this book, most of the variables you'll see are the simplest kind: *scalar variables*, which can store only one value. All Perl variables have identifying marks, and for scalars, it's a leading dollar sign. That's different from AWK variables, which lack identifying marks, and from Shell variables, whose names must be typed either with or without a leading dollar sign—depending on the context.

Consider a scalar variable called $ring. It could store the text "size 10", or a JPEG image of a gold wedding ring, or even an MPEG movie clip of the climactic meltdown of the "ring to rule them all" from the movie *The Return of the King*.

As these examples illustrate, the scalar variable's restriction about storing only one value doesn't affect the *amount* or *type* of data it can store. But whatever is stored in a scalar variable is treated as one indivisible unit.

In contrast, *list variables* provide for the storage (and retrieval) of multiple individually identifiable values, allowing you to make requests like "give me the MPEG for the Lord of the Rings movie number *N*," where *N* can be 1, 2, or 3, or even "one", "two", or "three". We'll discuss this class of variables in chapter 9.

Both types of Perl variables come in two varieties: special variables that are provided automatically by the language, such as "$.", and user-defined variables that are created by programmers as needed, such as $ring.

We'll look first at the special variables.

2.2.1 Using special variables

For the convenience of the programmer, Perl provides a number of special variables that are built into the language. Table 2.2 describes those that are most useful in the widest variety of small programs. These variables are derived from predecessors in the AWK language, so their AWKish names are shown as well—for the benefit of readers who are AWKiologists.[6]

---

[6] As part of the AWK-like environment provided in Perl, programmers are even allowed to use the original AWK names for the special variables. Type man English for more information.

Table 2.2 The data and record-number variables

Variable	Name	Nickname	Usage notes
$_	Dollar underscore	Data variable	When the n or p option is used, $_ contains the most recently read input record. It's also the default data source for many built-in functions, such as print. AWK: $0
$.	Dollar dot	Record number variable	When the n or p option is used, or the input operator, "$." contains the number of the current input record. AWK: NR

Next, we'll turn our attention to Perl's hardest-working yet most inconspicuous variable.

2.2.2 Using the data variable: $_

The $_ variable has the honor of being Perl's default custodian of data. For this reason, the n and p options store each input record they read in $_, and that variable acts as the default data donor for argument-free print statements.

Consider this example of a cat-like program that shows each line of its input:

```
$ perl -wnl -e 'print;' marx_bros
Groucho
Harpo
Chico
```

The implicit input-reading loop provided by the n option reads one line at a time and stores it in the $_ variable before executing the supplied program. Because print lacks any explicit arguments, it turns to the default data source, $_, to get the data it needs. In this way, each input line is printed in turn, without the need for any explicit reference to the location of the data.

Here's a more explicit way to write this program, which requires more typing to achieve the same effect:

```
$ perl -wnl -e 'print $_;' marx_bros        # $_ can be omitted
Groucho
...
```

The next section shows a case where there's a good reason to refer explicitly to $_.

2.2.3 Using the record-number variable: $.

When you use the n or p option, the record-number variable, "$.", holds the number of the current input record (as opposed to that record's *contents*, which reside in $_). This variable is used in a variety of ways, such as to number lines, to select lines by number for processing, and to report the total number of lines that were processed.

Here's a program that prints each line's number, a colon, and a space, followed by the line's contents:

```
$ perl -wnl -e 'printf "$.: "; print;' marx_bros
1: Groucho
...
```

Notice that double quotes are used to allow the variable substitution request for "$." to be recognized (as in the Shell) while simultaneously causing other enclosed characters, such as ":", to be stripped of any special meanings. (More details on quoting techniques are presented in section 2.4.1.)

The printf function is used to output the line-number prefix, to avoid shifting Groucho to the line below "1:", which would happen if print with its automatic newline were used instead (as discussed earlier). Then "print;" writes out the current input line using its implicit $_ argument, on the same output line used by printf.

There's another way to write this program using only one print, which is preferred for its greater simplicity. It's done by incorporating an explicit reference to the data variable within the double quotes:

```
perl -wnl -e 'print "$.: $_";' marx_bros
```

This second solution is better for two reasons. First, it makes the program simpler by using one print rather than one printf and one print; and second, the double-quoted string serves as a visual template for the desired layout, allowing the reader to visualize the format of the output more easily.

As useful as special variables are, Perl can't offer predefined variables to meet all possible needs, so it also lets you create your own on the fly.

2.2.4   Employing user-defined variables

Perl permits the programmer (a.k.a. *user*) to create new *user-defined variables* that make handy containers for storing and retrieving data. As with the special variables discussed earlier, all references to user-defined scalar variables begin with a $ symbol. But unlike the case with special variables, the next character must be a letter or underscore, optionally followed by any combination of additional digits, letters, or underscores.

As in the Shell and AWK, variables don't have to be declared before they're used, because using them automatically triggers their creation. But in contrast to its context-dependent usage in the Shell, the initial $ symbol is *always* used with a scalar variable in Perl. Like AWK, Perl has the convenient feature of automatically using the empty string or the number 0 as the value of an uninitialized variable, depending on how it's used.

Table 2.3 compares the use of scalar variables in the Shell and Perl.

Table 2.3 Employing user-defined scalar variables in the Shell and Perl

	Shell	Perl	Usage notes
Assignment	name=*value* name="*value*"	$name=*value*; $name="*value*";	In both languages, quoting a *value* being assigned to a variable is generally a good practice but isn't always required.
		$num2=$num1=42;	In Perl, assignments can flow through one variable to another, providing a simple way to initialize multiple variables to the same value.
Access	echo $star	print $star;	With Perl, the result of $*varname* is always the variable's actual contents, but the Shell may replace special characters in the variable by something else on access. For example, if "*" was assigned to the variable, the Shell example would echo filenames.
Access without further processing	echo "$star"	print $star; or print "$star";	If a variable contains a special character such as "*", double quotes must be used in the Shell to prevent further processing (e.g., filename generation). Although they're not needed in Perl, using double quotes doesn't hurt and keeps your Shell habits intact.
Assignment using access	name2=$name name2="$name"	$name2=$name; $name2="$name";	As in the Shell, variables can be assigned values extracted from other variables.

Here are some simple commands that employ user-defined scalar variables:

```
$ perl -wl -e '$message="Hello!"; print $message;'
Hello!
$ perl -wl -e '$fname="Larry"; $sname="Wall";
>       print "$fname $sname is also known as $sname, $fname.";'
Larry Wall is also known as Wall, Larry.
```

As indicated in table 2.3, because one-line commands are already encased in single quotes, double quotes are used to quote the values assigned to their variables. However, in Perl scripts, you're free to choose either type of quote (as discussed in section 2.4.1).

Again, it's important for the Shell-shocked to remember that the $ symbol *always* accompanies the name of a scalar variable in Perl.

Tips on employing user-defined variables

As shown in table 2.3, Perl allows you to put whitespace characters around the = symbol in assignment statements. Although generations of Shell programmers before you have been seduced into exercising that liberty with Perl, you'd be wise to stick with the no-whitespace format, because doing so reduces the interference between your new Perl habits and your ongoing ability to program with the Shell.

For instance, consider these examples of Shell and Perl assignment statements:

Shell
```
performer='Chris Bliss';      # no $, no whitespace around =
```

Perl
```
$performer='Chris Bliss';     # maximally Shell compatible
$performer = 'Chris Bliss';   # minimally Shell compatible
```

My students have taught me that they have enough trouble remembering to drop the Perlish leading $ symbol when assigning values to Shell variables without also remembering to omit the whitespace around = that Perl allows. For this reason, I recommend the maximally Shell compatible approach shown here for beginning Perl programmers.

You'll see user-defined variables used to good effect in several upcoming scripts, and you'll learn about a special subcategory called *switch variables* as well.

Nothing can boost programmer productivity more than avoiding the "reinvention of the wheel". Next, you'll learn how Lazy JAPHs accomplish that goal.

2.3 LOADING MODULES: -M

One of Perl's great strengths is its vast collection of freely reusable modules, which are similar to what other languages call *libraries*. A *module* is a collection of Perl code that's packaged in a special format, which facilitates the reuse of its *functions* or *subroutines* in new programs. Some modules are included with the Perl language, and many others are available from the *Comprehensive Perl Archive Network* (CPAN).[7]

You've already encountered two important functions that are built into Perl: print and printf. The module mechanism allows your program to use other functions with the same convenience, after the relevant modules have been loaded into your program. That's where the M invocation option comes into play—its job is to load the indicated module.

Consider this situation. You need to convert a raggedy-looking text file into one that has evenly filled lines, and numbered paragraphs. The following command handles the paragraph-numbering requirement using techniques covered earlier in this chapter:

---

[7] See chapter 12 for detailed coverage.

```
$ perl -00 -wnl -e 'print "$.: $_";' memo        # -00: paragraph mode
1: This is the file "memo", which has these
lines spread out like so.

2: And then it continues to a
second paragraph.
```

To reformat the text by <u>filling in</u> short lines up to a 60-column boundary, you could filter the output with the standard Unix utility called fmt:

```
$ perl -00 -wnl -e 'print "$.: $_";' memo | fmt -60
1: This is the file "memo", which has these lines spread
out like so.

2: And then it continues to a second paragraph.
```

There's nothing wrong with this approach, except that the paragraph numbers don't stand out as much as they could, and all the work could have been done by Perl. A better solution is to use the CPAN module Text::Autoformat,[8] which will recognize the leading numbers as worthy of out-denting, and make the paragraph numbers stand out more:

```
$ perl -M'Text::Autoformat' \
>     -00 -wn -e 'print autoformat "$.: $_", { right => 60 };' memo
1: This is the file "memo", which has these lines spread
   out like so.

2: And then it continues to a second paragraph.
```

For each input record (a paragraph), the double-quoted string containing the record-number variable and data variable is first filled in with their values. Then that string is presented to the module's autoformat function as its first argument, followed by the format argument that sets the right margin. Next, the output of autoformat (a reformatted paragraph) is provided as the argument to print.

This pure-Perl solution is superior to the earlier one because not only does it produce a better result, but it also does so without depending on an external command (fmt). Moreover, the module it uses is cool in so many ways that it won an award![9]

As powerful and useful as Perl commands like the ones we've been examining may be, there comes a point when you should convert them to a more convenient format, which we'll describe next.

---

[8] The doubled colons in Text::Autoformat tell Perl's module-loading system to look for Autoformat.pm in the installation area under a directory called Text. Because of the way this module works, the l invocation option isn't needed with the command shown.

[9] The "Larry Wall" Award for the best practical utility program of the year 2000 was presented to the module's author, my scarily amazing friend, Dr. Damian Conway.

CHAPTER 2   PERL ESSENTIALS

2.4 WRITING SIMPLE SCRIPTS

Packaging a program as a script lets you execute it by typing the script's name:

```
$ weed_my_email
1,075 SPAM messages weeded out.
   13 valid messages retained.
Valid content: 2.2% -- much higher than yesterday!
```

This style of invocation offers many advantages over retyping the program from scratch on the command line every time you need its services, especially for programs that are large or difficult to remember.

In this section, we'll cover the fundamentals of Perl scripting, as well as some important language features that appear principally in scripts (as opposed to one-line commands).[10]

On a Unix system, a Perl script is one or more Perl statements stored in a file that's marked as executable and readable, and that has an appropriate Perl shebang line at the top. In some ways, it's constructed much like a Shell script, but there are some differences, as detailed in table 2.4.

To illustrate the differences between commands and scripts, here once again is the one-line Perl command that prints each line of its input, along with its scripted counterpart, called `perl_cat`.

Table 2.4   Comparison of Shell and Perl scripting techniques

Shell*	Perl	Comments
`#! /bin/sh options`	`#! /usr/bin/perl options`	As with Shell scripts, Perl scripts need to specify a valid path to the script's desired interpreter on the shebang line, such as the typical `/usr/bin/perl`. Invocation `options` may follow that path.
`$*` `"$@"`	Arguments are handled automatically via the n, p, or s option, or <>.	In Shell scripts, command-line arguments are accessed collectively using "$*" or "$@". In Perl scripts that use the n or p option or the empty input operator, handling of filename arguments is automatic. In those that use the s option, handling of −name and −name=value switch arguments is also automatic.

---

[10] Chapter 8 provides additional information about scripting, with an emphasis on more advanced techniques.

```
$ perl -wnl -e 'print;' marx_bros   # one-liner version
Groucho
...
$ vi perl_cat                       # create the script
```
(editing session not shown)
```
$ cat perl_cat          # examine the script; note that -e is omitted
#! /usr/bin/perl -wnl
print;
```

While creating the scripted version, I copied the command's invocation options to the script's shebang line—*except* -e and its argument (because the program code for a script appears in the script file, not as an argument to -e). Then I placed the contents of the e option's quoted string in the file.

The next steps are to add execute permission to the file and to conduct a test run:

```
$ chmod +x perl_cat                     #  enable execute permission
$ ls -l perl_cat                        # confirm execute permission
-rwxr--r--   10 tim    staff    29 2003-09-30 11:58 perl_cat
$ perl_cat marx_bros            # script gives same results as command
Groucho
...
```

There's a big difference between this script and a comparable one written for the Shell: You don't have to refer to the command-line argument marx_bros in order to access its data—the n option handles that for you automatically.

Now it's time to delve into a subject that strikes terror into the hearts of Shell programmers—until they migrate to Perl, where it's less fraught with danger.

2.4.1   Quoting techniques

With the Perl commands we'll emphasize in part 1, Shell-level quoting is used to allow the program code that follows -e to be safely conveyed as an argument to Perl:

```
$ perl -wnl -e 'program code' filename
```

Single quotes must be used, because they prevent the Shell from making any alterations to the program code. However, because the Shell doesn't allow a single quote to appear within a single-quoted string (i.e., to be *nested*), you're restricted with such commands to using double quotes within the program code.

Perl scripts, on the other hand, aren't first interpreted by the Shell, so you can use both types of quotes within them.

In most cases, single and double quotes behave similarly in the Shell and Perl.[11] In both languages, single quotes cause the enclosed characters to be taken literally (e.g., '-' is interpreted as a hyphen, not a request for subtraction), whereas double quotes allow variable substitutions to occur (e.g., $_ in "Input: $_" gets replaced

---

[11] For a detailed discussion of the cases in which double quotes work differently in these languages, see http://TeachMePerl.com/DQs_in_shell_vs_perl.html.

by the contents of the current input line). However, although the backslash in the Shell can generally be used to quote the character that follows it, in Perl the backslash only acts as a quoting character within quotes (e.g., `print "\$_"` prints $_).

We'll review the most typical uses of the different quoting characters next.

Typical uses of quotes

For reference purposes, common uses of single quotes, double quotes, and the backslash in Perl commands and scripts are summarized below.

Single quotes

- in Unix one-liners
    - convey program code as the argument to the e option:
      ```
      perl -wl -e 'print 84/2;'        # Output: 42
      ```
- in scripts
    - cause enclosed characters to lose any special meanings:
      ```
      print 'The price is $1/@noon';   # The price is $1/@noon
      ```

Double quotes

- represent empty (null) strings more clearly than single quotes:
  ```
  print ''; # is that one double-quote, or two single quotes?
  print ""; # with l option, prints a blank line (as does above)
  ```
- enclose strings in which *string modifiers* (e.g., `\U`; see table 4.5), *string escapes* (e.g., `\t`; see table 3.1), and *variable interpolations* (e.g., `$price`; see table 2.3) can be processed:
  ```
  print "It's \Uonly\E:\t$price lire!";   # It's ONLY:    42 lire!
  ```

Backslashes

- within single quotes within scripts
    - allow nested single quotes to be treated as literal characters (which isn't true of the Shell):
      ```
      print 'Spendy\'s restaurant saves you $$$';
      ```
- within double quotes
    - introduce string escapes that insert special characters:
      ```
      print "\n";  # prints "newline", OS-specific record separator
      ```
    - introduce string modifiers that perform case conversions:
      ```
      print "Upper case signifies \Ushouting\E"   # ... SHOUTING
      ```
    - allow the following special character to be taken literally, if it's not one that signifies a string escape or a string modifier (e.g., $):
      ```
      $price=42; print "Sale price: \$$price"; # Sale price: $42
      ```

Shell programmers may be inclined to call Perl a *liar* when it actually speaks the truth, for reasons we'll cover next.

2.4.2 True and False values

We'll frequently need to distinguish between True and False outcomes of logical tests, and True and False values for variables. The Perl definitions of these important concepts are as follows, stated separately for values treated as numbers or strings:

- For numbers, only values equating to 0 (including 0.0, and so on) are False.
- For strings, only the null string (e.g., " ", ' ') and strings containing exactly zero ("0", '0') are False.
- Any expression that has no value, such as a variable that has not yet been set, is considered False.

In comparison, the Shell has no general way of distinguishing between an unset variable and one containing a null string, and it considers the numeric values of 0 and non-0 as respectively True and False—the *opposite* of Perl's definitions (more on this issue in chapter 8).

NOTE   In the Shell, 0 is considered True, and other numbers are False. In Perl, it's the other way around.

Having discussed how the Shell and Perl have switched their definitions of Truthiness and Falsity, let's examine another kind of switching next.

2.4.3 Handling switches: -s

To let a script work on different data items on different invocations—such as Homer's email address on the first run and Marge's on the second—words with a special significance, called *arguments*, can be presented after the script's name.

As a case in point, the following invocation of a custom script shows how one fictitious IT manager displays her appreciation for her most outstanding software developers (who have quirky login names). Last year, the script was invoked with squidward, gandalf, and peewee as arguments, but this time, different developers have been chosen for special recognition:

```
$ award_cruises 'slurm' 'gollum' 'kryten' # argument order critical
'gollum' awarded Alaska cruise
'slurm' awarded Panama Canal cruise
'kryten' awarded Perlistan Riviera cruise
```

The programmer named in the first argument gets the Panama Canal cruise, the second the Alaska Inside Passage cruise, and the third the Perlistan Riviera cruise (around the desiccated Lake Perlistan; that's a punishment!). This design requires the programmer to know how to access command-line arguments manually, and the user to present them in exactly the right order—or the wrong developer gets the booby prize.

Fortunately, Perl provides an easier alternative, based on the s option for automatic processing of *switch arguments* (a.k.a. *switches*). By supporting the use of switches such as -perlistan, this enhanced version of the earlier script becomes easier to use:

```
$ award_cruises2 -perlistan='kryten' -panama='slurm' \
>     -alaska='gollum'              # argument order is now unimportant
'gollum' awarded Alaska cruise
'slurm' awarded Panama Canal cruise
'kryten' awarded Perlistan Riviera cruise
```

The effect of each switch argument is to assign a value to a like-named switch variable in the program. Here's the part of the `award_cruises2` script that prints the values of its switch variables:

```
print "'$alaska' awarded Alaska cruise";
print "'$panama' awarded Panama Canal cruise";
print "'$perlistan' awarded Perlistan Riviera cruise";
```

The major benefit of this improved version is that it allows cruises to be associated with developers through use of the *-cruise-name=User-ID* switch syntax, which frees the user (and the programmer) from worrying about the argument order.

The upper portion of table 2.5 shows the two formats for switches and explains their differences. The lower portion describes the use of the `our` declaration to mark switches as optional.

Table 2.5 Using switch variables

Syntax on command line[a]	Effect	Comments
-name	Sets $name to True value.	The -name format is used for switches of the on/off type, where all that matters is detecting the switch's presence via a True value or absence via False. For example, script -debug sets $debug to a True value within script.
-name='*stuff*'	Sets $name to *stuff*.	This format is used for switches that need to have particular values associated with their variables. For example, script -email='a@b.ca' sets $email to that address.

Syntax in script	Effect	Comments
our ($color);	Makes the -color switch optional.	Switches that are optional should have their variables listed in our statements at the top of the script, to prevent Perl from issuing warnings when they aren't used.
our ($shape, $size);	Makes the -shape and -size switches optional.	To list more than one switch variable in a single our statement, insert commas between them and parentheses around them.

a. Switches are implemented as scalar variables, so any combination of letters, digits, and underscores can be used in forming a switch name—but the first character should be a letter. When the -name=*stuff* format is used, proper Shell-level quoting must be used on *stuff*—single quotes are appropriate for literal values.

Now you can understand how award_cruises2 works. It employs the s option, and, as you saw earlier, it was invoked with the variable-assignment style of switch syntax (e.g., -panama='slurm'). The = symbol makes it clear that the effect of this switch is to request the assignment of the indicated value to the associated switch variable within the program. In this way, $panama got set to "slurm" with the earlier invocation, $alaska to "gollum", and $perlistan to "kryten", allowing the programmer to access those variables to see who will be cruising where.

Being able to handle command-line switches in such a convenient manner is one of the features that makes Perl so easy to use. You'll see a complete example of a simple switch-using script next.

A switch-driven line-numbering script: show_files

The cat-like show_files script recognizes a -line_numbers ("show line numbers") switch, which causes the script to insert each line's number before its contents. Because there's no need to set the associated variable ($line_numbers) to any particular value, the -name syntax is used instead of -name='stuff' (see table 2.5), causing the variable to be set to a True value.

Here are some sample runs of show_files:

```
$ show_files gilliam_movies          # "-line_numbers" switch not used
Time Bandits
12 Monkeys
The Fisher King
$ show_files -line_numbers gilliam_movies      # switch used
1: Time Bandits
2: 12 Monkeys
3: The Fisher King
```

Note that switches must come before filenames on the command line; otherwise, perl interprets them as filenames:

```
$ show_files gilliam_movies -line_numbers      # switch misplaced
Time Bandits
12 Monkeys
The Fisher King
Can't open -line_numbers: No such file or directory ...
```

Here's the script—notice the -s argument on its shebang line:

```
$ cat show_files
#! /usr/bin/perl -s -wnl
# Usage: show_files filename
#        show_files -line_numbers filename   (for line numbers)
our ($line_numbers);                  # makes -line_numbers optional
$line_numbers and printf "$.: ";  # if switch provided, print line
                                  #    number, without newline
print;                            # print current line with newline
```

This script can print a line-number prefix before each line, but it does so only when the $line_numbers variable is True (reflecting the presence of the -line_numbers switch on the command line). The conditionality of the printf statement on the value of the switch variable is expressed by the logical and operator (discussed in section 2.4.5), which has an "if/then" meaning here (like the Shell's &&).

Notice that the switch variable is named in an our statement, which has the effect of making that switch optional.[12]

A different approach is required for programs that have mandatory switches. An example is award_cruises2, shown earlier, which requires all of -panama, -perlistan, and -alaska to be set on each run (perhaps because the company gets a discount for triple bookings). In such cases, no our declarations should be made for the variables associated with required switches. This allows a warning to be generated for any switch that is omitted, calling the user's attention to the mistake.

For example, here's what happens when the award_cruises2 script is run without the -alaska=*User-ID* switch:

```
$ award_cruises2 -perlistan='kryten' -panama='slurm'   # -alaska?
Name "main::alaska" used only once: possible typo ...
```

The "used only once" message is triggered because the script is being asked to retrieve the value of the variable $alaska, without the value first being set by a corresponding switch argument on the command line. In this way, the user is alerted to her incorrect usage and given a (somewhat vague) indication of what was missing.

You'll see techniques for presenting custom diagnostic messages that are even more helpful next.

2.4.4   Using warn and die

Perl's built-in print function is an important one, but it's not always enough. As with Shell programming, sometimes you need to send a message to the *error channel* (STDERR) rather than to STDOUT, and sometimes a script needs to terminate prematurely upon detection of fatal errors. Table 2.6 compares the Perl and Shell methods for handling these conditions.[13]

---

[12] This kind of our declaration is beneficial when a variable, corresponding to a switch the programmer considers optional, would otherwise appear only once in the program. Using our makes the switch optional, in the sense that no "used only once" warning is generated if the user doesn't supply the corresponding switch argument.

[13] Because we concentrate on Perl *commands* in part 1—whose programs are enclosed in single quotes— we show double quotes being used around function arguments in the table. But in *scripts*, function arguments are generally single-quoted.

Table 2.6 Shell and Perl techniques for writing messages to STDOUT and STDERR

Shell	Perl	Comments
echo "msg"	print "msg";	The examples send msg to STDOUT.
echo "msg" >&2	warn "msg\n"; print STDERR "a", "b";	The examples send their messages to STDERR. The \n tells Perl that warn's message is complete, which prevents the associated line number and filename from automatically being added at its end; the \n should be omitted if that additional information is desired. The advantage of print STDERR over warn is that the former automatically uses the "$," variable to separate its printed arguments (see table 2.8).
echo "msg" >&2 exit 255	Outside a BEGIN block: die "msg\n"; Inside a BEGIN block, using logical operators for conditional execution: $success or warn "msg\n" and exit 255;	The examples send msg to STDERR and then terminate the program, sending an error code to the parent process. die sends code 255 by default; but with the exit function that's used in a BEGIN block (see section 2.4.6), that value can be supplied as an argument. The \n following msg tells Perl not to automatically add the line number and filename to the message's end.

You'll see examples of warn and die in the next four sections. We'll discuss the helpful role a special variable with a self-deprecating name can play in diagnostic messages next.

Using $0 with warn and die

As in the Shell, the $0 variable in Perl contains the name by which the script was invoked. It's routinely used in warn and die messages.

For example, this code snippet can be used to issue a warning if a script has detected that the user has provided more arguments than it needs:

```
warn "$0: Ignoring extra arguments\n";   # sendit: Ignoring extra ...
```

Why is it wise to label such messages with a script's name? Because when a user runs a script along with several others in a pipeline, or runs a script that invokes other scripts, she may have trouble identifying the one that's issuing a particular warn or die message without the help of that label.

As detailed in table 2.6, you can use newline characters, represented by the \n sequence, at the end of warn and die messages to suppress additional information (regarding the line number from which the message was issued and the script's name). The difference is easy to see:

```
$ validate_file -quickly              # uses die "msg\n" format
validate_file: Sorry, no switches allowed
$ validate_file2 -quickly             # uses die "msg" format
validate_file2: Sorry, no switches allowed at validate_file2 line 6
```

The second form is principally used while debugging large scripts, where it's an advantage to the programmer to be told where in the program the early termination occurred.

The most interesting uses of warn and die occur with conditional tests based on Perl's if/else facility, covered in part 2. Here in part 1, we'll focus on their use with the simpler logical and and or operators, which are covered next.

2.4.5   Using logical and, logical or

Logical operators are used to test the True or False status of an expression, and also to express the conditionality of one program element on another. As an example, the show_files script presented earlier uses and to conditionally print the number of the current line before it prints its contents:

```
$line_numbers  and  printf "$.: ";   # print line-number prefix?
print;                               # now print the line
```

First, the True/False value of $line_numbers is checked. If it's True—because the -line_numbers switch was supplied on invocation—then the printf function is executed, because the logical and executes the expression on its right if the one on its left is True. The logical and therefore provides a concise way of expressing a simple if/then condition.

Here's an example taken from another file-printing script, which uses an optional -double_space switch:

```
print;                               # print the current input line
$double_space  and  print "";        # print a blank line on request
```

Depending on the True/False value of $double_space, this script optionally prints a blank line, formed from the empty quoted string and the automatic newline donated by the l option, after each input line.

The logical or is the opposite of the logical and; instead of expressing an if/then condition, it expresses an if/else. This means the right-hand element is executed only if the value on its left is False.

For instance, this example shows how a script can be designed to produce lots of messages by default, but to run more quietly when requested by a -quiet switch:

```
$quiet  or  warn "Processed record #$.\n";   # be quiet if requested
```

Because the optional output is of a different type than the normal output of the program, it's sent to the STDERR channel using warn rather than to STDOUT using print. This allows the script's user to selectively redirect the normal output to a printer, for example, while allowing the warning to remain on the screen.

Shell programmers use the || and && symbols for logical or and logical and, respectively, yielding the following as a Shell equivalent of the previous command:

```
[ -n "$quiet" ] ||    # test for non-emptiness
    echo "Processed record #$counter" >&2
```

Notice that the `>&2` request is required to redirect output to STDERR in the Shell version, whereas Perl's `warn` does that automatically.

Using Perl's logical `or` permits a more polite variation on the `award_cruises2` program, which issues a fairly inscrutable "used only once, possible typo" warning for required switches that are missing. Its successor, `award_cruises3`, identifies missing switches by sensing False values attached to their associated variables, and it issues explanatory messages as needed:

```
$ award_cruises3 -perlistan='kryten' -panama='slurm'   # -alaska?
Designate recipient for Alaska cruise
```

Here's the line that was added to the earlier version to provide that message:

```
$alaska  or  warn "Designate recipient for Alaska cruise\n";
```

If more than one thing needs to be done on the basis of the True/False value of a variable, you can use `and` operators to chain together additional program elements, including calls to functions such as `warn` and `print` that return True:

```
$verbose  and  $error_detected  and  warn "An error was detected\n";
$confirmed_order  and
    $in_stock  and
        print "Your order will ship today";
```

The last statement prints the shipping confirmation message on the joint condition that the user has confirmed he is submitting the order and that the item is in stock. You can think of it as expressing the conditionality of `print` on a combined True value of all the prior conditions, as in "if conditions *A* and *B* are both True, then print".

Tips on using logical *and*, logical *or*

Because the logical `and` is "stronger" than the logical `or` (in terms of *operator precedence*), explicit parentheses are sometimes required in order to clarify your intent and to get the correct result.

For instance, consider this statement:

```
$verbose  or  $debug  and  warn "Entering output section\n";
```

It's interpreted as if parentheses were already placed as shown, due to the higher precedence of `and` over `or`:

```
$verbose  or  ( $debug  and  warn "Entering output section\n" );
```

This statement means: "If $verbose is False, then if $debug is True, then issue the warning." If your intent is to issue the warning if either $verbose *or* $debug is True, then you should write the following instead, with actual parentheses typed as shown:

```
( $verbose  or  $debug )  and  warn "Entering output section\n";
```

Such explicit parentheses are needed wherever a mixture of logical or and and operators would produce the wrong result without them.

Here is an example of a common case (discussed in the next section) that doesn't require the use of parentheses. Its intent is to make both warn and exit conditional on a False value of a variable, which is the meaning that Perl attaches to this statement automatically:

```
$info_provided  or  warn "Provide info\n"  and  exit 255;
```

The negation operator, "!", converts a True result to a False one, and vice versa. It sometimes comes in handy when you're constructing statements involving multiple conditions. For example, if the variable being tested is $no_info_provided rather than $info_provided, the second statement that follows can be constructed using the same logic as the first through use of the "!" operator:

```
  $info_provided     or  warn "Provide info\n"  and  exit 255;
! $no_info_provided  or  warn "Provide info\n"  and  exit 255;
```

That second statement is read: "If it's *not* true that no information was provided (i.e., if information was provided), don't issue the warning."

Another use for Perl's logical and and or is to construct compound conditional tests for use with the if/else facility, as you'll see in part 2.

Next, we'll talk about Perl's special provisions for executing specific code blocks before and after processing input.

2.4.6   Programming with BEGIN and END blocks

Like AWK, Perl provides a special way of indicating that certain statements should be executed before or after input processing occurs. The basic syntax of the so-called BEGIN and END *blocks* is as follows:

```
BEGIN { statement(s); }
END { statement(s); }
```

As usual, you're free to insert additional whitespace characters around the elements (i.e., the keywords and curly braces) as desired.

BEGIN blocks are typically used in such tasks as initializing scalar variables with numbers other than the default of zero, and printing headings for the program output that will follow. END blocks are customarily used to compute summary statistics after all input has been processed (such as averages), and to print final results. Perl allows you to use BEGIN and END together, separately, or not at all in your programs.

In the following example, additional output is produced by statements within BEGIN and END blocks when the -verbose switch is provided on the script's invocation. The END block's statement exploits the fact that after all input has been processed, the record-number variable ($.) holds the number of the last record, which indicates the total number of records that were read:

```
$ cat double_space
#! /usr/bin/perl -s -wnl
# Usage: double_space [ -verbose ] [ file1 ... ]
our ($verbose);   # makes switch optional
BEGIN {
    $verbose  and  print "Running in verbose mode\n";
}
print;              # print the current input record
print "";           # print a blank line
END {
    $verbose  and  print "Processed $. lines\n";
}
$ double_space -verbose marx_bros
Running in verbose mode

Groucho

Harpo

Chico

Processed 3 lines
```

Notice that it's critical that the messages controlled by the $verbose variable occur in BEGIN and END blocks rather than in the body of the program (i.e., within the implicit loop provided by the n option). This allows those messages to be printed before and after the full set of output lines, respectively—rather than before and after the output of *each individual line*, which would be the result if the capital keywords and their associated curly braces were erased from double_space. (Chapter 10 has more on this subject.)

A BEGIN block is often the best place to determine whether a program has everything it needs to do its job, as you'll see next.

Testing and setting variables in the BEGIN block

In scripts that require the user to provide command-line switches, your first task is to determine whether the user has indeed supplied them—and, if she hasn't, to issue a "Usage" message, and exit.

In other scripts, it may be necessary to set special variables to define the manner in which input should be read or output should be written, which must be accomplished before input/output processing begins.

Programs that use the n or p option to request an implicit input-reading loop need to handle these preliminary tasks in a BEGIN block. Here's an example taken from chapter 3, from a script called greperl. It needs to ensure that the user has provided the required pattern before it starts to search for matches with it, which it does using this code:

```
BEGIN {
    # -pattern='regex' switch is required
    $pattern  or
        warn "Usage: greperl -pattern='regex' [ file1 ... ]\n"  and
            exit 255;
}
```

Those statements allow the script to tell the difference between this incorrect invocation

```
greperl somefile
```

and this correct one

```
greperl -pattern='stuff' somefile
```

and to respond properly when the switch variable $pattern has a False value.[14]

A preliminary step in the execution of some programs is the importing of required modules, using techniques covered next.

2.4.7   Loading modules with use

Another important difference between Perl commands and scripts is that the -M'*Module_name*' invocation option isn't used to request the loading of Perl modules in scripts. Instead, you place a "use *Module_name*;" statement below the shebang line. The following comparison between the text-formatting one-liner shown earlier and its script counterpart contrasts the two techniques:

Command version:
```
$ perl -M'Text::Autoformat' -00 -wnl \
        -e 'print autoformat "$.: $_";' file
...
```

Script version:
```
$ cat autoformat
#! /usr/bin/perl -00 -wnl
use Text::Autoformat;
print autoformat "$.: $_";
$ autoformat file
...
```

Notice that the one-liner's argument to the M option was repackaged in a use statement in the script; that the code following the e option became the body of the script, and that the remaining invocation options were included on the script's shebang line.

---

[14] Some False values may be considered acceptable, such as 0 (zero). In section 8.1.1, you'll see an alternative method for validating the contents of the $pattern variable (based on the defined function) which can accept False values.

```
```

2.5 ADDITIONAL SPECIAL VARIABLES

Perl has a few other special variables that are used in part 1, which we'll document here for reference purposes, and discuss in later chapters.

2.5.1 Employing I/O variables

Table 2.7 shows Perl's most important Input/Output (I/O) variables, which include those that determine what constitutes an input record ($/) and how output records should be terminated by print ($\). Although these variables are updated automatically when you uses the -0*digits* invocation option (see table 2.1), that option only allows the setting of single-character record separators. When a multicharacter separator is desired, you must set the relevant variable(s) directly. The table shows the proper technique for doing that, along with the names of these variables in the AWK language.

The $ARGV variable contains the name of the current input file and is typically used to label messages regarding that file's contents. Its relative ARGV, which lacks the leading $ symbol, is a *filehandle;* it's used to exert control over the currently open file.

Table 2.7 Special variables for I/O operations

Variable	Name and *Nickname*	Usage notes
$/	Dollar-slash *Input record separator*	By default, "$/" is set to the OS-specific input record separator character (or sequence) represented as "\n". You can change it to an arbitrary character through use of the -0*digits* option or to an arbitrary multicharacter sequence by assigning a string to "$/". AWK: RS Example: `BEGIN { $/='**'; } # ** becomes input separator`
$\	Dollar-backslash *Output record separator*	When "$/" is set to an arbitrary string, it's generally desirable to set $\ to the same string so that -1 automatically appends to print's output the same string it removed on input. AWK: ORS Example: `BEGIN { $\=$/='**'; } # set both separators`
$ARGV	Dollar-ARGV ("dollar arg-vee") *The filename variable*	When the n or p option or empty input operator is used, this variable identifies the current input source, either by the file's name or by a "-" to represent STDIN. AWK: FILENAME
ARGV	ARGV ("arg-vee") *The file handle*	ARGV is used to exert control over the current input source, especially to close it. (Note: This is not a variable, as indicated by its lack of a $ symbol.) AWK: *No counterpart*
@ARGV	At-ARGV *The argument array*	Program arguments must be accessed manually from this array variable when neither the n or p option nor the input operator is used. AWK: ARGV

It most commonly appears in the form `close ARGV`, which tells Perl to stop reading input from the associated file.

More details on using the features listed in table 2.7, including sample programs, are presented in later chapters.[15]

Next, we'll discuss some special variables that make it easy to format output nicely.

2.5.2   Exploiting formatting variables

The special variables covered in table 2.8 provide for custom formatting of printed output. Their AWK counterparts are indicated also in the table.

Table 2.8   Special variables for formatting output

Variable	Name	Usage notes
`$"`	Dollar double quote	`'$"'` contains the characters that are automatically inserted between elements of arrays whose names appear in double quotes. It's set to the space character by default. AWK: *No counterpart*
`$,`	Dollar comma	`"$,"` is involved in two kinds of special formatting for arguments in `print` statements. Its contents are used on output in place of commas that appear between `print`'s arguments, and also between the elements of unquoted array or hash arguments. It's empty by default. AWK: `OFS`

We'll look at examples of using these variables in printing the contents of the special variable `@ARGV`, the *argument array*, which in this case contains three values: A, B, and C.

As this first case shows, the elements of an array are squashed together when they're printed without any special treatment, because the relevant formatting variable (`$,`) is empty by default:

```
print  @ARGV;    # Unquoted
ABC
```

But if the variable is set to a slash, that character appears between each pair of elements, which looks nicer:

```
$,='/';
print  @ARGV;    # Unquoted, custom $,
A/B/C
```

Alternatively, when an array variable is double-quoted (the most common case), the space character that's the default setting for the associated formatting variable (`$"`) is automatically inserted between each pair of elements:

---

[15] For example, "`$/`" is used in listing 9.4, `$ARGV` in section 5.4.3, `ARGV` in listing 8.7, and `@ARGV` in section 10.4.1.

```
print "@ARGV";    # Double quoted
A B C
```

In this final example, '$"' is assigned a custom comma-space separator to use within the double quotes, which—compared to the earlier SPACEd-out version—looks even groovier:

```
$"=', ';          # Double quoted, custom $"
print "@ARGV";
A, B, C
```

Tip on using formatting variables

Someday, you'll find yourself wondering why the `print` statement you added to a program is displaying funny characters in its output, only to find that those values were assigned to "$," or '$"' earlier in the program. The best defense against this problem is to set such variables using the `local` declaration, as discussed later, in section 11.3.3.

Congratulations!

By this point, you've learned the most essential features of the Minimal Perl dialect, and you're probably eager to start writing tiny yet powerful programs that enhance your productivity and dazzle your co-workers and managers—and make you an even more valuable asset to your firm.

But you won't get far without a better understanding of how to select and assemble the appropriate invocation options for your upcoming creations in the Perl language. We'll cover that vital topic next.

2.6   STANDARD OPTION CLUSTERS

As you know by now, you can use many invocation options with the `perl` command, including w, l, n, and e. What's more, you could conceivably arrange them in many different orders, such as –wnle and –ewnl.

However, it's critical that certain options appear in the correct order relative to others. The e option, for instance, must come directly before the quoted program, and clustering it incorrectly with others (as in –ewnl) is a common error that can be hard to identify. Accordingly, it's prudent to develop good habits for assembling option sequences.

For your convenience, we provide a collection of standard option clusters that are appropriate for different types of programs. If you use them as indicated, you'll find it easy to convey invocation options properly to `perl`.

Table 2.9 lists the most commonly used option clusters. Each is suited to a different type of program, as indicated in the *Application Type* column.

Table 2.9 Standard option clusters for Perl commands and scripts

Primary option cluster	Application type	Example[a]
`-wl`	Output generation	`perl -wl -e 'print "TEXT";'`
`-wnl`	Input or Input/ Output processing	`perl -wnl -e 'print;' /etc/passwd` `who	perl -wnl -e 'print;'`
`-wnla`	Field processing; whitespace separators	`$F[0]` accesses the input record's first field: `perl -wnla -e 'print $F[0];' F`
`-wnlaF'sep'`	Field processing; custom separators	`$F[2]` accesses the input record's third colon-separated field: `perl -wnlaF':' -e 'print $F[2];' F`

Record definition cluster	Effect	Example
`-00`	Enables paragraph mode	Print paragraphs with numbers: `perl -00 -wnl -e 'print "$.: $_";' F`
`-0777`	Enables file mode	Print files with numbers: `perl -0777 -wnl -e 'print "$.: $_";' F F2`

Switch cluster	Effect	Example

`-s`	Enables switch processing	Print lines with optional numbers, using switch -n:
		`$ `**`print_lines -n F F2`**`   # -n sets $n True`
		`...`
		`$ `**`cat print_lines`**
		`#! /usr/bin/perl -s -wnl`
		`$n  and  printf "$.: ";`
		`print;`

In-place editing cluster	Effect	Example
`-i.extension`	Enables in-place editing	Make changes in original file after backing it up as `F.bak`: `perl -i.bak -wnl -e 's/A/B/g; print' F`

Module cluster	Effect	Example

`-M'mod_name'`	Loads the indicated module	Convert tabs in `$_` to spaces before printing (expand is provided by `Text::Tabs`):
		`perl -M'Text::Tabs' \`
		`  -wnl -e 'print expand $_;' F`
		In scripts, employ "use `mod_name`;" instead.

Program cluster	Program type	Usage
`-e 'code'`	Perl command	Include this cluster if the program will be provided by a `code` argument rather than a script file.

a. See section 2.7 for directions on how to use this table in constructing programs.

TIP Using the standard option clusters from table 2.9 will help you avoid problems that afflict many new Perl programmers.

We've already discussed most of the option clusters shown in the table, and you've seen them used in sample programs. The exceptions are the i option for *in-place editing*, which is covered in section 4.7, and the a and F options for *field processing*, which are discussed in section 5.3.

Before we look at a technique that helps you select the options to use in various kinds of programs, we'll discuss an even simpler approach that works with Perl one-liners.

2.6.1 Using aliases for common types of Perl commands

There's no time to waste in our half-day tutorials on Minimal Perl, so we need to make option selection as easy as possible for the students. Toward this end, we provide easily remembered Shell aliases that supply the appropriate invocation options for common types of commands. You may find these aliases useful during your initial adventures with Perl, so we'll discuss them next.

Aliases for Perl commands: Line mode

The first alias is for Perl commands that only generate output:

```
alias perl_o='  perl -wl   '  # Output Generation
```

This next group is for commands that read input:

```
alias perl_io='  perl -wnl '  # Input/Output Processing
alias perl_iop=' perl -wpl '  # I/O Processing, with printing
alias perl_f='   perl -wnla '  # Field Processing
alias perl_fp='  perl -wpla '  # Field Processing, with printing
```

Next, we'll examine paragraph-oriented variations on these aliases.

Aliases for Perl commands: Paragraph mode

The names of these aliases are the same as those of the previous group, except they start with a capital *P* to signify that they process input a paragraph at a time:

```
alias Perl_o='  perl -00 -wl   '  # Output Generation
alias Perl_io='  perl -00 -wnl '  # Input/Output Processing
alias Perl_iop=' perl -00 -wpl '  # I/O Processing, with printing
alias Perl_f='   perl -00 -wnla '  # Field Processing
alias Perl_fp='  perl -00 -wpla '  # Field Processing, with printing
```

If you put these alias definitions in your Shell startup file,[16] log out, and log in again, you'll be able to type typical Perl one-liners without worrying about option selection.

---

[16] Usually .kshrc for the Korn shell or .bashrc for the Bash shell.

All you need to do is type the alias and the -e option before your quoted program, along with any other arguments that are needed.

For example, a program that restricts its activities to "Output Generation" can be written as follows:

```
$ perl_o -e 'print 22/7;' # perl_o provides the perl invocation
3.14285714285714
```

Just keep this in mind: As handy as these aliases may be initially, you'll ultimately have to learn the underlying clusters anyway for use in your scripts, because aliases don't work on shebang lines.

We'll talk next about a procedure that simplifies the selection of appropriate invocation options for your Perl programs and guides you through the construction of both commands and scripts.

2.7 CONSTRUCTING PROGRAMS

You can easily construct Perl programs of various kinds by using the information provided in table 2.9. Here's a detailed list of the steps involved:

1 Select the appropriate *Primary Option Cluster* according to the program's *Application Type* (from column 2), and write it <u>after</u> perl on your scratch pad. If more than one Application Type applies, choose the Primary Option Cluster that has the most keyletters.

   Sample scratch pad:
   ```
   perl -wnl    # for I/O Processing
   ```

2 If you want to use switches, write the *Switch Cluster* on your scratch pad immediately <u>to the right of</u> perl.

   Sample scratch pad:
   ```
   perl -s -wnl
   ```

3 Determine which additional option clusters you need from table 2.9, apart from the *Program Cluster*. For example, if your Primary Option Cluster contains an n, and you don't want the default of reading a line at a time, pick an appropriate *Record Definition Cluster*. Type your chosen clusters <u>to the left</u> of the Primary Option Cluster.[17]

   Sample scratch pad:
   ```
   perl -s -00 -wnl
   ```

---

[17] The techniques described here help Perl novices by taking the guesswork out of proper option selection and ordering—by avoiding certain legitimate option orderings that don't work as they should, and by ensuring that options that may need following arguments (e.g., l and F) are always at the right end of a cluster.

4 Choose an execution method.

  a To use the *one-line command* format, type what's on your scratch pad followed by the -e of the Program Cluster to your Shell, but don't press <ENTER> yet.
  Sample command line:
  ```
  $ perl -s -00 -wnl -e
  ```

  b Alternatively, to use the *script format*, type the contents of your scratch pad on the first line of an appropriately named file (*scriptname*). Then, begin the shebang line by inserting #! and a space followed by your system's correct Perl-path <u>before</u> perl.[18]
  Sample shebang line, in *scriptname*:
  ```
  #! /usr/bin/perl -s -00 -wnl
  ```

  Just as you would do when creating a Shell script, save the file and then run chmod +x *scriptname* to make it executable.

5 Type your program in the appropriate manner.

  a If you're using the one-line command format, type your program in single quotes after -e on the partially constructed command line:
  ```
  $ perl -s -00 -wnl -e 'insert code here;'
  ```

  b Alternatively, if you're using the script format, type your program into *scriptname*, below the shebang line:
  ```
  #! /usr/bin/perl -s -00 -wnl
  insert code starting here;
  ```

6 Now you're ready to test the program. For a command, type any additional arguments (such as names of input files) after the -e 'code' cluster, and press <ENTER>. For a script, type *scriptname* followed by any additional arguments, and press <ENTER>. Then, make corrections to your program until it works correctly.

7 If the program uses the n invocation option and its last line (outside of the END block) is the argument-free "print;" statement, consider deleting that line and changing the n invocation option to p. To enhance readability, you may choose to skip this adjustment; but if you make it, be sure to test the program again as described in step 6 to make sure it still works (as it should!).

Learning to construct a program following these seven steps will make life with Perl a lot easier for you. The next thing we'll do is walk through a couple of examples to show you how to apply these steps in representative cases.

---

[18] You can determine the pathname for perl by issuing the type perl command to your Shell.

TIP
The only option cluster that should be placed to the right of a Primary Option Cluster (e.g., -wnl) is the *Program Cluster* (-e 'code'), and that's only in commands—not scripts.

2.7.1 Constructing an output-only one-liner

Now we'll write a comical variation on the classic program that prints "Hello, world!" Because it's very small, we'll implement it as a one-liner.

In step 1 of section 2.7, we're told to choose the appropriate Primary Option Cluster and place it after perl. Because this program will do nothing but output a message, it fits the Application Type called Output Generation. Table 2.9 prescribes -wl, so we write the following on our scratch-pad:

```
perl -wl
```

Step 2 applies only when the Primary Option Cluster contains an n; because -wl lacks one, this step doesn't apply to the current case.

In step 3, we consider including additional option clusters. But this program won't need to use a nonstandard record definition to handle switches, to do in-place editing, or to use any modules, so we have all the clusters we need.

In step 4a, we decide to make this program a one-liner, so we add the Program Cluster:

```
perl -wl -e 'code'
```

In step 5a, we replace the "code" placeholder with the actual program of interest, yielding the following:[19]

```
perl -wl -e 'print "Good day, world! What a little beauty!";'
```

Step 6 tells us to run the program to see what happens:

```
$ perl -wl -e 'print "Good day, world! What a little beauty!";'
Good day, world! What a little beauty!
```

Because the program works correctly, its output conjures up an image of a wacky Aussie park ranger gushing with admiration over the drooling man-eating beast that's eyeing him with malice. Then the imagined scene suddenly shifts to a commercial, just as the animal's hideously unkempt fangs (no, I'm not talking about Austin Powers) are about to penetrate the Crocodile Hunter's already battle-scarred leg.

---

[19] As fans of the Crocodile Hunter know, the proper representation of his speech pattern is
print "G'day, world! Crikey, isn't she a little beauty!";
(See http://crocodilehunter.com.) But if this line were wrapped in single quotes and presented as an argument to the e option, its apostrophes would interfere with the outer single quotes. Accordingly, his mantra has been changed slightly for this example, so we can avoid getting mired in the intricacies of Shell quoting techniques (detailed in http://TeachMeUnix.com/quoting.html).

But he can't blame that on Perl. Hooray! The program works. *Isn't she a little ripper!* What's more, we're finished, because step 7 is skipped for programs that don't use the n option.

Now let's try a script.

2.7.2 Constructing an input/output script

What about programs that involve *multiple* Application Types? As indicated in step 1 of section 2.7, such cases require the *largest* option cluster (i.e., the one with the most keyletters) from any of the relevant areas.

For example, consider the line-numbering command shown earlier:

```
perl -wnl -e 'printf "$.: "; print;' marx_bros
```

The printing of the record-number variable ($.) via `printf` qualifies as Output Generation, as does the implicit printing of the $_ variable via `print`. Thus far, the -wl Primary Option Cluster seems to be indicated.

But what about the `marx_bros` argument at the end of the command? Its presence reminds us that the program reads input, which specifies the Application Type of Input Processing and the -wnl Primary Option Cluster. That one is larger than -wl, so it wins, and we use it.

At this point in the construction of the program, we have the following:

```
perl -wnl
```

Step 2 doesn't require any adjustments, because we want to use the default of reading a line at a time with the n option.

Step 3 doesn't apply, because no additional option clusters are needed.

We're writing a script rather than a one-liner, so step 4b gives us this:

```
$ cat num_lines
#! /usr/bin/perl -wnl
```

Next we make the script executable:

```
$ chmod +x num_lines
```

In step 5b, we add the code for the program itself, which yields

```
#! /usr/bin/perl -wnl
printf "$.: ";
print;
```

Step 6 reminds us to supply a filename argument for our test run:

```
$ num_lines marx_bros
1: Groucho
...
```

Step 7 tells us that the final `print` can be deleted if we replace the shebang line's n option with p, which would reduce the program to:

```
#! /usr/bin/perl -wpl
printf "$.: ";
```

But that adjustment makes it too easy for a casual reader to mistakenly conclude that the program just prints line numbers, so we'll keep the final print statement in this case. However, when we discuss sed-like Perl programs in chapter 4, you'll see several examples where replacing n with p is recommended.

2.8   SUMMARY

Perl was created as an amalgamation of the best features of various UNIX languages and utilities. But Larry also added some imaginative new features, which represent a departure from UNIX traditions. The result is that Perl is a large and complex language—and a potentially confusing one—because it provides so many distinctly different ways to accomplish the same task.

By focusing on a carefully selected subset of the language, you can easily learn to write small programs that provide the essential infrastructure for many types of data processing tasks. In this chapter, you became familiar with the most essential features of Perl, including the most important *invocation options*, *special variables*, and *functions*.

Let's review some key details. The w invocation option enables warnings, which provide you with valuable feedback about potential problems in a program. The n option enables automatic input processing, which loads the "data variable" $_ with the contents of each input line in turn. The most widely used function in Perl programs is print, which sends its arguments to the output destination. It's often used *without* any arguments, to exploit the fact that it prints the contents of $_ by default.

In addition to learning key elements of the language, you saw how Minimal Perl's guidelines for program construction take the guesswork out of selecting appropriate invocation options for programs and putting together the scripts or one-liners that can do the job.

In the following chapters, you'll learn other features of Perl that provide additional benefits for programs having particular needs. However, we'll retain our focus on doing as much as possible with a small subset of the language. I think you'll be impressed with how much you'll be able to do with the little you'll need to learn!

Directions for further study

Appendix B provides guidelines for using parentheses in code and expands on the discussion provided at the end of section 2.4.5.

To learn more about other topics covered here, you can consult online documentation by issuing the commands listed at the chapter's end, such as man perlintro. Some of those commands use Perl's perldoc utility for accessing online documentation, which is similar to the Unix man command. However, perldoc has additional features, such as the ability to extract and display small excerpts from large documents. Even better, because it's distributed with Perl, it's available on every system that a Perl programmer would use—which cannot be said of man, which is Unix-based.

In cases where both perldoc and man can do the job of delivering the desired documentation on a Unix system, we show the use of man, because it's faster.

For example, you can learn more about CPAN by using this command:

- perldoc **-q** CPAN   # *answers questions about CPAN*

The q option instructs perldoc to search Perl's online Frequently Asked Questions (FAQ) files for matching keywords.

In the interest of keeping things simple in your early days with Perl, you may want to put off exploring the following resources until you feel comfortable with all the material in part 1:

- man perlrun   # *describes invocation options*
- perldoc **-f** print   # *describes the "print" function*
- man perlintro   # *provides beginner orientation*
- man Text::Autoformat   # *describes the indicated module*
- man perlop   # *describes operator precedence*

C H A P T E R   3

Perl as a (better) grep command

3.1 A brief history of grep 53
3.2 Shortcomings of grep 54
3.3 Working with the matching operator 60
3.4 Understanding Perl's regex notation 63
3.5 Perl as a better fgrep 64
3.6 Displaying the match only, using $& 64

3.7 Displaying unmatched records (like grep -v) 65
3.8 Displaying filenames only (like grep -l) 67
3.9 Using matching modifiers 68
3.10 Perl as a better egrep 70
3.11 Matching in context 75
3.12 Spanning lines with regexes 77
3.13 Additional examples 81
3.14 Summary 86

This chapter shows you how to write one-line Perl commands and small Perl scripts that surpass the limitations of the UNIX grep command. We'll start by reviewing grep's history, strengths, and weaknesses, and Perl's superior features, and then we'll show how Perl programs can exceed the limitations of grep.

3.1   A BRIEF HISTORY OF grep

Out of hundreds of command-line utilities provided on early UNIX systems, the grep command rapidly emerged as one of the most important and influential. This became most obvious in the mid 1980s, when implementations started appearing for non-UNIX systems—including versions of the humble DOS.

Although modern versions of grep have additional features, the basic function of grep continues to be the identification and extraction of lines that match a *pattern*. This is a simple service, but it has become one that Shell users can't live without.

NOTE   You could say that grep is the Post-It® note of software utilities, in the sense that it immediately became an integral part of computing culture, and users had trouble imagining how they had ever managed without it.

But grep was not always there. Early Bell System scientists did their *grepping* by interactively typing a command to the venerable ed editor. This command, which was described as "globally search for a *regular expression* and print," was written in documentation as g/*RE*/p.[1]

Later, to avoid the risks of running an interactive editor on a file just to search for matches within it, the UNIX developers extracted the relevant code from ed and created a separate, non-destructive utility dedicated to providing a matching service. Because it only implemented ed's g/*RE*/p command, they christened it grep.

But can grep help the System Administrator extract lines matching certain patterns from system log files, while simultaneously rejecting those that also match another pattern? Can it help a writer find lines that contain a particular set of words, irrespective of their order? Can it help bad spellers, by allowing "libary" to match "library" and "Linux" to match "Lunix"?

As useful as grep is, it's not well equipped for the full range of tasks that a pattern-matching utility is expected to handle nowadays. Nevertheless, you'll see solutions to all of these problems and more in this chapter, using simple Perl programs that employ techniques such as *paragraph mode*, *matching in context*, *cascading filters*, and *fuzzy matching*.

We'll begin by considering a few of the technical shortcomings of grep in greater detail.

3.2   SHORTCOMINGS OF grep

The UNIX ed editor was the first UNIX utility to feature *regular expressions* (regexes). Because the classic grep was adapted from ed, it used the same rudimentary regex dialect and shared the same strengths and weaknesses. We'll illustrate a few of grep's shortcomings first, and then we'll compare the pattern-matching capabilities of different *greppers* (grep-like utilities) and Perl.

3.2.1   Uncertain support for metacharacters

Suppose you want to match the word *urgent* followed immediately by a word beginning with the letters *c-a-l-l*, and that combination can appear anywhere within a

---

[1]   As documented in the glossary, *RE* (always in italics) is a placeholder indicating where a regular expression could be used in source code.

line. A first attempt might look like this (with the matched elements underlined for easy identification):

```
$ grep 'urgent call' priorities
Make urgent call to W.
Handle urgent calling card issues
Quell resurgent calls for separation
```

Unfortunately, *substring matches*, such as matching the substring "urgent" within the word resurgent, are difficult to avoid when using greppers that lack a built-in facility for disallowing them.

In contrast, here's an easy Perl solution to this problem, using a script called `perlgrep` (which you'll see later, in section 8.2.1):

```
$ perlgrep '\burgent call' priorities
Make urgent call to W.
Handle urgent calling card issues
```

Note the use of the invaluable *word-boundary metacharacter*,[2] \b, in the example. It ensures that *urgent* only matches at the beginning of a word, as desired, rather than within words like *resurgent*, as it did when `grep` was used.

How does \b accomplish this feat? By ensuring that whatever falls to the left of the \b in the match under consideration (such as the *s* in "resurgent") isn't a character of the same class as the one that follows the \b in the pattern (the *u* in \burgent). Because the letter "u" is a member of Perl's *word character* class,[3] "!urgent" would be an acceptable match, as would "urgent" at the beginning of a line, but not "resurgent".

Many newer versions of `grep` (and some versions of its enhanced cousin `egrep`) have been upgraded to support the \< \> word-boundary metacharacters introduced in the `vi` editor, and that's a good thing. But the non-universality of these upgrades has led to widespread confusion among users, as we'll discuss next.

RIDDLE   What's the only thing worse than not having a particular metacharacter (\t, \<, and so on) in a pattern-matching utility? *Thinking you do, when you don't!* Unfortunately, that's a common problem when using Unix utilities for pattern matching.

Dealing with conflicting regex dialects

A serious problem with Unix utilities is the formidable challenge of remembering which slightly different vendor- or OS- or command-*specific* dialect of the regex notation you may encounter when using a particular command.

For example, the `grep` commands on systems influenced by Berkeley UNIX recognize \< as a metacharacter standing for the left edge of a word. But if you use that sequence with some modern versions of `egrep`, it matches a literal < instead. On the

---

[2] A metacharacter is a character (or sequence of characters) that stands for something other than itself.

[3] The word characters are defined later, in table 3.5.

other hand, when used with grep on certain AT&T-derived UNIX systems, the \< pattern can be interpreted *either way*—it depends on the OS version and the vendor.

Consider Solaris version 10. Its /usr/bin/grep has the \< \> metacharacters, whereas its /usr/bin/egrep lacks them. For this reason, a user who's been working with egrep and who suddenly develops the need for word-boundary metacharacters will need to switch to grep to get them. But because of the different metacharacter dialects used by these utilities, this change can cause certain formerly literal characters in a regex to become *metacharacters*, and certain former metacharacters to become *literal* characters. As you can imagine, this can cause lots of trouble.

From this perspective, it's easy to appreciate the fact that Perl provides you with a single, comprehensive, OS-portable set of regex metacharacters, which obviates the need to keep track of the differences in the regex dialects used by various Unix utilities. What's more, as mentioned earlier, Perl's metacharacter collection is not only as good as that of any Unix utility—it's better.

Next, we'll talk about the benefits of being able to represent control characters in a convenient manner—which is a capability that grep lacks.

3.2.2 Lack of string escapes for control characters

Perl has advantages over grep in situations involving control characters, such as a tab. Because greppers have no special provision for representing such characters, you have to embed an actual tab within the quoted regex argument. This can make it difficult for others to know what's there when reading your program, because a tab looks like a sequence of spaces.

In contrast, Perl provides several convenient ways of representing control characters, using the *string escapes* shown in table 3.1.

Table 3.1 String escapes for representing control characters

String escape[a]	Name	Generates...
\n	Newline	the native record terminator sequence for the OS.
\r	Return	the carriage return character.
\t	Tab	the tab character.
\f	Formfeed	the formfeed character.
\e	Escape	the escape character.
\NNN	Octal value	the character whose octal value is NNN. E.g., \040 generates a space.
\xNN	Hex value	the character whose hexadecimal value is NN. E.g., \x20 generates a space.
\cX	Control character	the character (represented by X) whose control-character counterpart is desired. E.g., \cC means Ctrl-C.

a. These string escapes work both in regexes and in double-quoted strings.

To illustrate the benefits of string escapes, here are comparable grep and perlgrep commands for extracting and displaying lines that match a tab character:

```
grep            '       '      somefile      # Same for fgrep, egrep

perlgrep        '       '      somefile      # Actual tab, as above

perlgrep        '\011'         somefile      # Octal value for tab

perlgrep        '\t'           somefile      # Escape sequence for tab
```

You may have been able to guess what \t in the last example signifies, on the basis of your experience with Unix utilities. But it's difficult to be certain about what lies between the quotes in the first two commands.

Next, we'll present a detailed comparison of the respective capabilities of various greppers and Perl.

3.2.3 Comparing capabilities of greppers and Perl

Table 3.2 summarizes the most notable differences in the fundamental pattern-matching capabilities of classic and modern versions of fgrep, grep, egrep, and Perl.

The comparisons in the top panel of table 3.2 reflect the capabilities of the individual regex dialects, those in the middle reflect differences in the way matching is performed, and those in the lower panel describe special enhancements to the fundamental service of extracting and displaying matching records.

We'll discuss these three types of capabilities in the separate sections that follow.

Comparing regex dialects

The *word-boundary metacharacter* lets you stipulate where the edge of a word must occur, relative to the material to be matched. It's commonly used to avoid substring matches, as illustrated earlier in the example featuring the \b metacharacter.

Compact character-class shortcuts are abbreviations for certain commonly used character classes; they minimize typing and make regexes more readable. Although the modern greppers provide many shortcuts, they're generally less compact than Perl's, such as [[:digit:]] versus Perl's \d to represent a digit. This difference accounts for the "?" in the POSIX and GNU columns and the "Y" in Perl's. (Perl's shortcut metacharacters are shown later, in table 3.5.)

Control character representation means that non-printing characters can be clearly represented in regexes. For example, Perl (alone) can be told to match a tab via \011 or \t, as shown earlier (see table 3.1).

Repetition ranges allow you to make specifications such as "from 3 to 7 occurrences of *X*", "12 or more occurrences of *X*", and "up to 8 occurrences of *X*". Many greppers have this useful feature, although non-GNU egreps generally don't.

Backreferences, provided in both egrep and Perl, provide a way of referring back to material matched previously in the same regex using a combination of *capturing parentheses* (see table 3.8) and backslashed numerals. Perl rates a "Y+" in table 3.2 because it lets you use the captured data throughout the code block the regex falls within.

Table 3.2   Fundamental capabilities of greppers and Perl

Capability	Classic greppers [a]	POSIX greppers	GNU greppers	Perl
Word-boundary metacharacter	–	Y	Y	Y
Compact character-class shortcuts	–	?	?	Y
Control character representation	–	–	–	Y
Repetition ranges	Y	Y	Y	Y
Capturing parentheses and backreferences	Y	Y	Y	Y+
Metacharacter quoting	Y	Y	Y	Y+
Embedded commentary	–	–	–	Y
Advanced regex features	–	–	–	Y
Case insensitivity	–	Y	Y	Y
Arbitrary record definitions	–	–	–	Y
Line-spanning matches	–	–	–	Y
Binary-file processing	?	?	Y	Y+
Directory-file skipping	–	–	Y	Y
Access to match components	–	–	–	Y
Match highlighting	–	–	Y	?
Custom output formatting	–	–	–	Y

a. Y: Perl, or at least one utility represented in a greppers column (`fgrep`, `grep`, or `egrep`) has this capability; Y+: has this capability with enhancements; ?: partially has this capability; –: doesn't have this capability. See the glossary for definitions of *classic*, *POSIX*, and *GNU*.

Metacharacter quoting is a facility for causing metacharacters to be temporarily treated as literal. This allows, for example, a "*" to represent an actual asterisk in a regex. The `fgrep` utility automatically treats all characters as literal, whereas `grep` and `egrep` require the individual backslashing of each such metacharacter, which makes regexes harder to read. Perl provides the best of both worlds: You can intermix metacharacters with their literalized variations through selective use of `\Q` and `\E` to indicate the start and end of each metacharacter quoting sequence (see table 3.4). For this reason, Perl rates a "Y+" in the table.

Embedded commentary allows comments and whitespace characters to be inserted within the regex to improve its readability. This valuable facility is unique to Perl, and it can make the difference between an easily maintainable regex and one that nobody dares to modify.[4]

---

4 Believe me, there are plenty of those around. I have a few of my own, from the earlier, more carefree phases of my IT career. D'oh!

The category of *advanced regex features* encompasses what Larry calls *Fancy Patterns* in the Camel book, which include *Lookaround Assertions*, *Non-backtracking Subpatterns*, *Programmatic Patterns*, and other esoterica. These features aren't used nearly as often as \b and its kin, but it's good to know that if you someday need to do more sophisticated pattern matching, Perl is ready and able to assist you.

Next, we'll discuss the capabilities listed in table 3.2's middle panel.

Contrasting match-related capabilities

Case insensitivity lets you specify that matching should be done without regard to case differences, allowing "CRIKEY" to match "Crikey" and also "crikey". All modern greppers provide this option.

Arbitrary record definitions allow something other than a physical line to be defined as an input record. The benefit is that you can match in units of paragraphs, pages, or other units as needed. This valuable capability is only provided by Perl.

Line-spanning matches allow a match to start on one line and end on another. This is an extremely valuable feature, absent from greppers, but provided in Perl.

Binary-file processing allows matching to be performed in files containing contents other than text, such as image and sound files. Although the classic and POSIX greppers provide this capability, it's more of a bug than a feature, inasmuch as the matching binary records are delivered to the output—usually resulting in a very unattractive display on the user's screen! The GNU greppers have a better design, requiring you to specify whether it's acceptable to send the matched records to the output. Perl duplicates that behavior, and it even provides a binary mode of operation (*binmode*) that's tailored for handling binary files. That's why Perl rates a "Y+" in the table.

Directory-file skipping guards the screen against corruption caused by matches from (binary) directory files being inadvertently extracted and displayed. Some modern greppers let you select various ways of handling directory arguments, but only GNU greppers and Perl skip them by default (see further discussion in section 3.3.1).

Now we'll turn our attention to the lower panel of table 3.2, which discusses other features that are desirable in pattern-matching utilities.

Appreciating additional enhancements

Access to match components means components of the match are made available for later use. Perl alone provides access to the contents of the entire match, as well as the portions of it associated with capturing parentheses, outside the regex. You access this information by using a set of special variables, including $& and $1 (see tables 3.4 and 3.8).

Match highlighting refers to the capability of showing matches within records in a visually distinctive manner, such as reverse video, which can be an invaluable aid in helping you understand how complex regexes are being interpreted. Perl rates only a "?" in this category, because it doesn't offer the highlighting effect provided by the modern greppers. However, because Perl provides the variable $&, which retains the contents of the last match, the highlighting effect is easily achieved with simple coding (as demonstrated in the `preg` script of section 8.7.2).

Custom output formatting gives you control over how matched records are displayed—for example, by separating them with formfeeds or dashed lines instead of newlines. Only Perl provides this capability, through manipulation of its *output record separator* variable (`$\`; see table 2.7).

Now you know that Perl's resources for matching applications generally equal or exceed those provided by other Unix utilities, and they're OS-portable to boot. Next, you'll learn how to use Perl to do pattern matching.

3.3   WORKING WITH THE MATCHING OPERATOR

Table 3.3 shows the major syntax variations for the matching operator, which provides the foundation for Perl's pattern-matching capabilities.

Table 3.3   Matching operator syntax

Form [a]	Meaning	Explanation
`/RE/`	Match against `$_`	Uses default "`/`" delimiters and the default target of `$_`
`m:RE:`	Match against `$_`	Uses custom "`:`" delimiters and the default target of `$_`
`string =~ /RE/`	Match against `string`	Uses default "`/`" delimiters and the target of `string`
`string =~ m:RE:`	Match against `string`	Uses custom "`:`" delimiters and the target of `string`

a. *RE* is a placeholder for the regex of interest, and the implicit `$_` or explicit `string` is the target for the match, which provides the data for the matching operation.

One especially useful feature is that the matching operator's regex field can be delimited by any visible character other than the default "`/`", as long as the first delimiter is preceded by an `m`. This freedom makes it easier to search for patterns that contain slashes. For example, you can match pathnames starting with `/usr/bin/` by typing `m|^/usr/bin/|`, rather than backslashing each nested slash-character using `/^\/usr\/bin\//`. For obvious reasons, regexes that look like this are said to exhibit *Leaning Toothpick Syndrome*, which is worth avoiding.

Although the data variable (`$_`) is the default target for matching operations, you can request a match against another string by placing it on the left side of the `=~` sequence, with the matching operator on its right. As you'll see later, in most cases the *string* placeholder shown in the table is replaced by a variable, yielding expressions such as `$shopping_cart =~ /RE/`.

That's enough background for now. Let's get *grepping*!

3.3.1   The one-line Perl grepper

The simplest `grep`-like Perl command is written as follows, using invocation options covered in section 2.1:

```
perl -wnl -e '/RE/ and print;' file
```

It says: "Until all lines have been processed, read a line at a time from *file* (courtesy of the n option), determine whether *RE* matches it, and `print` the line if so."

RE is a placeholder for the regex of interest, and the slashes around it represent Perl's matching operator. The w and l options, respectively, enable warning messages and automatic line-end processing, and the logical and expresses a conditional dependency of the `print` operation on a successful result from the matching operator. (These fundamental elements of Perl are covered in chapter 2.)

The following examples contrast the syntax of a `grep`-like command written in Perl and its `grep` counterpart:

```
$ grep           'Linux'              /etc/motd
Welcome to your Linux system!

$ perl -wnl -e '/Linux/ and print;' /etc/motd
Welcome to your Linux system!
```

In keeping with Unix traditions, the n option implements the same data-source identification strategy as a typical Unix filter command. Specifically, data will be obtained from files named as arguments, if provided, or else from the standard input. This allows pipelines to work as expected, as shown by this variation on the previous command:

```
$ cat /etc/motd | perl -wnl -e '/Linux/ and print;'
Welcome to your Linux system!
```

We'll illustrate another valuable feature of this minimal grepper next.

Automatic skipping of directory files

Perl's n and p options have a nice feature that comes into play if you include any directory names in the argument list—those arguments are ignored, as unsuitable sources for pattern matching. This is important, because it's easy to accidently include directories when using the wildcard "*" to generate filenames, as shown here:

```
perl -wnl -e '/Linux/ and print;' /etc/*
```

Are you wondering how valuable this feature is? If so, see the discussion in section 6.4 on how most greppers will corrupt your screen display—by spewing binary data all over it—when given directory names as arguments.

Although this one-line Perl command performs the most essential duty of `grep` well enough, it doesn't provide the services associated with any of `grep`'s options, such as ignoring case when matching (`grep -i`), showing filenames only rather than their matching lines (grep -l), or showing only non-matching lines (grep -v). But these features are easy to implement in Perl, as you'll see in examples later in this chapter.

On the other hand, endowing our grep-like Perl command with certain other features of dedicated greppers, such as generating an error message for a missing pattern argument, requires additional techniques. For this reason, we'll postpone those enhancements until part 2.

We'll turn our attention to a quoting issue next.

Nesting single quotes

As experienced Shell programmers will understand, the single-quoting of perl's program argument can't be expected to interact favorably with a single quote occurring within the regex itself. Consider this command, which attempts to match lines containing a D'A sequence:

```
$ perl -wnl -e '/D'A/ and print;' priorities
>
```

Instead of running the command after the user presses <ENTER>, the Shell issues its secondary prompt (>) to signify that it's awaiting further input (in this case, the fourth quote, to complete the second matched pair).

A good solution is to represent the single quote by its numeric value, using a string escape from table 3.1:[5]

```
$ perl -wnl -e '/D\047A/ and print;' guitar_string_vendors
J. D'Addario & Company Inc.
```

The use of a string escape is wise because the Shell doesn't allow a single quote to be directly embedded within a single quoted string, and switching the surrounding quotes to double quotes would often create other difficulties.

Perl doesn't suffer from this problem, because it allows a backslashed quote to reside within a pair of surrounding ones, as in

```
print ' This is a single quote: \' ';    # This is a single quote: '
```

But remember, it's the Shell that first interprets the Perl commands submitted to it, not Perl itself, so the Shell's limitations must be respected.

Now that you've learned how to write basic grep-like commands in Perl, we'll take a closer look at Perl's regex notation.

---

[5] You can use the tables shown in man ascii (or possibly man ASCII) to determine the octal value for any character.

3.4 UNDERSTANDING PERL'S REGEX NOTATION

Table 3.4 lists the most essential metacharacters and variables of Perl's regex notation.

Table 3.4   Essential syntax for regular expression

Metacharacter[a]	Name	Meaning
^	Beginning anchor	Restricts a match with X to occur only at the beginning; e.g. ^X.
$	End anchor	Restricts a match with X to occur only at the end; e.g., $X$$.
\b	Word boundary	Requires the juxtaposition of a word character with a non-word character or the beginning or end of the record. For example, \b$X$, X\b, and \b$X$\b, respectively, match X only at the beginning of a word, the end of a word, or as the entire word.
.	Dot	Matches any character except newline.
[chars]	Character class	Matches any one of the characters listed in chars. Metacharacters that aren't backslashed letters or backslashed digits (e.g., ! and .) are automatically treated as literal. For example, [!.] matches an exclamation mark or a period.
[^chars]	Complemented character class	Matches any one of the characters not listed in chars. Metacharacters that aren't backslashed letters or backslashed digits (e.g., ! and .) are automatically treated as literal. For example, [^!.] matches any character that's not an exclamation mark or a period.
[char1-char2]	Range in character class	Matches any character that falls between char1 and char2 (inclusive) in the character set. For example, [A-Z] matches any capital letter.
$&	Match variable	Contains the contents of the most recent match. For example, after running 'Demo' =~ /^[A-Z]/, $& contains "D".
\	Backslash	The backslash affects the interpretation of what follows it. If the combination \X has a special meaning, that meaning is used; e.g., \b signifies the word boundary metacharacter. Otherwise, X is treated as literal in the regex, and the backslash is discarded; e.g., \. signifies a period.
\Q...\E	Quoting metacharacters	Causes the enclosed characters (represented by ...) to be treated as literal, to obtain fgrep-style matching for all or part of a regex.

a. chars is a placeholder for a set of characters, and char1 is any character that comes before char2 in sorting order.

Most of those metacharacters will already be familiar to grep users, with the exceptions of \b (covered earlier), the handy $& variable that contains the contents of the last match, and the \Q...\E metacharacters that "quote" enclosed metacharacters to render them temporarily literal.

Nevertheless, it won't hurt to indulge in a little remedial grepology, so let's consider some simple examples. The regex ^[m-y] matches lines that start with a character in the range *m* through *y* (inclusive), such as "make money fast" and "yet another Perl conference". The pattern \bWin\d\d\b matches "Win95" and "Win98", but neither "WinCE" (because of the need for two digits after "Win"), nor "Win2000" (which lacks the required word boundary after the "Win20" part).

We'll refer to table 3.4 as needed in connection with upcoming examples that illustrate its other features.

Next, we'll demonstrate how to replicate the functionality of grep's cousin fgrep, using Perl.

3.5 PERL AS A BETTER *fgrep*

Perl uses the \Q...\E metacharacters to obtain the functionality of the fgrep command, which searches for matches with the literal string presented in its pattern argument. For example, the following grep, fgrep, and Perl commands all search for the string "** $9.99 Sale! **" as a literal character sequence, despite the fact that the string contains several characters normally treated as metacharacters by grep and perl:

```
grep          '\*\* $9\.99 Sale! \*\*'              sale
fgrep            '** $9.99 Sale! **'                sale
perl -wnl -e '/\Q** $9.99 Sale! **\E/ and print;'  sale
```

The benefit of fgrep, the "fixed string" cousin of grep, is that it automatically treats all characters as literal. That relieves you from the burden of backslashing each metacharacter in a grep command to achieve the same effect, as shown in the first example.

Perl's approach—of *delimiting* the metacharacters to be literalized—is even better than fgrep's, because it allows metacharacters that are within the regex but outside the \Q...\E sequence to function normally. For example, the following command uses the ^ metacharacter to anchor the match of the literal string between \Q and \E to the beginning of the line:[6]

```
perl -wnl -e '/^\Q** $9.99 Sale! **\E/' and print' sale
```

In addition to providing a rich collection of metacharacters that you can use in writing matching applications, Perl also offers some special variables. One that's especially valuable in matching applications is covered next.

3.6 DISPLAYING THE MATCH ONLY, USING $&

Sometimes you need to refer to what the last regex matched, so, like sed and awk, Perl provides easy access to that information. But instead of using the control charac-

---

[6] You can save a bit of typing by leaving out the \E when it appears at the regex's end, as in this example, because metacharacter quoting will stop there anyway.

ter & to get at it, as in those utilities, in Perl you use the special variable `$&` (introduced in table 3.4). This variable is commonly used to print the match itself, rather than the entire record in which it was found—which most greppers can't do.

For example, the following command extracts and prints the five-digit U.S. Zip Codes from a file containing the names and postal codes for the members of an international organization:

```
$ cat members
Bruce Cockburn M5T 1A1
Imrat Khan 400076
Matthew Stull 98115
Torbin Ulrich 98107
$ perl -wnl -e '/\b\d\d\d\d\d\b/ and print $&;' members   # 5-digits
98115
98107
```

The command uses "`print $&;`" to print only the match, rather than "`print;`", which would print the entire line (as greppers do).

The regex describes a sequence of five consecutive digits (`\d`)[7] that isn't embedded within a longer "word" (due to the `\b` metacharacters). That's why Imrat's Indian and Bruce's Canadian postal codes aren't accepted as matches.

We'll look next at the Perlish way to emulate another feature of `grep`—the printing of lines that do *not* match the given pattern.

3.7 DISPLAYING UNMATCHED RECORDS (LIKE `grep -v`)

Another variation on matching is provided by `grep`'s v option, which inverts its logic so that records that *don't match* are displayed. In Perl, this effect is achieved through conditional printing—by replacing the `and print` you've already seen with `or print`—so that printing only occurs for the *failed* match attempts.

The main benefit of this approach is seen in cases where it's more difficult to write the regex to match the lines you want to print than the ones you don't. One elementary example is that of printing lines that aren't empty, by composing a regex that describes empty lines and printing the lines that don't match:

```
perl -wnl -e '/^$/ or print;' file
```

This regex uses both anchoring metacharacters (see table 3.4). The `^` represents the line's beginning, the `$` represents its end, and the absence of anything else between those symbols effectively prevents the line from having any contents. Because that's the correct technical description of a line with nothing on it, the command says, "Check the current line to see if it's empty—and if it's not, print it."

---

[7] Although the command works as intended, all those backslashes make it hard on the eyes. You'll see a more attractive way to express the idea of five consecutive digits using repetition ranges in table 3.9.

Another situation where you'll routinely need to print non-matching lines occurs with programs that do data validation, which we'll discuss next.

3.7.1 Validating data

Ravi has just spent the last hour entering a few hundred postal addresses into a file. The records look like this:

```
Halchal Punter:1234 Disk Drive:Milpitas:ca:95035
Mooshi Pomalus:4242 Wafer Lane:San Jose:CA:95134
Thor Iverson:4789 Coffee Circle:Seattle:WA:98107
```

The fields are separated by colons, and the U.S. Zip Code field is the last one on each line. At least, that's the intended format.

But maybe Ravi bungled the job. The quality of his typing always goes into a downward spiral just before tea-time, so he wants to make sure. Using wisdom acquired through attending a Perl seminar at a recent conference, he composes a quick command to ensure that each line has a colon followed by exactly five digits just before its end.

In writing the regex, Ravi uses the \d shortcut metacharacter, which can match any digit (see table 3.5). In words, the resulting command says, "Look on each line for a colon followed by five digits followed by the end of the line, and if you *don't* find that sequence, print the line":

```
$ perl -wnl -e '/:\d\d\d\d\d$/ or print;' addresses.dat
Thor Iverson:4789 Coffee Circle:Seattle:WA:98107
```

It thinks that line is incorrect? Perl must have a bug.

But after spending further time staring at the output, Ravi realizes that he accidentally entered the letter O in Thor's Zip Code instead of its look-alike, the number 0. He knows this is a classic mistake made the world over, but that does little to reduce his disappointment. After all, if his forefathers *invented* the zero, shouldn't he have a genetic defense against making this mistake? Aw, curry. Perhaps a sickly sweet jalebi[8] will help improve his mood.

As his spirits soar along with his blood-sugar level, Ravi feels better about finding this error, and he becomes encouraged by the success of his first foray into Perl programming. With a surge of confidence, he enhances the regex to additionally validate the penultimate field as having two capital letters only.

Much to his dismay, this upgraded command finds another error, in the use of lowercase instead of uppercase:

```
$ perl -wnl -e '/:[A-Z][A-Z]:\d\d\d\d\d$/ or print;' addresses.dat
Halchal Punter:1234 Disk Drive:Milpitas:ca:95035
Thor Iverson:4789 Coffee Circle:Seattle:WA:98107
```

What an inauspicious development. More trouble—and he's fresh out of jalebis!

While Ravi is pondering his next move, let's learn more about *shortcut metacharacters*.

---

[8] For those unfamiliar with this noble confection of the Indian subcontinent, it is essentially a deep-fried golden pretzel, drowned in a sugary syrup. Yum!

3.7.2 Minimizing typing with shortcut metacharacters

Table 3.5 lists Perl's most useful shortcut metacharacters, including the \d (for _digit_) that appeared in the last example. These are handy for specifying word, digit, and whitespace characters in regexes, as well as their opposites (e.g., \D matches a _non-digit_). As you can appreciate by examining their character-class equivalents in the table, the use of these shortcuts can save you a lot of typing.

Table 3.5   Compact character-class shortcuts

Shortcut metacharacter	Name	Equivalent character class [a]
\w	Word character	[a-zA-Z0-9_]
\W	Non-word character	[^a-zA-Z0-9_]
\s	Whitespace character	[\040\t\r\n\cJ\cL]
\S	Non-whitespace character	[^\040\t\r\n\cJ\cL]
\d	Digit character	[0-9]
\D	Non-digit character	[^0-9]

a. The backslashed sequences in the (square-bracketed) character classes are described in table 3.1.

As a case in point, the regex \bTwo\sWords\b matches words with any whitespace character between them. That's a lot easier than specifying on your own that a newline, space, tab, carriage return, linefeed, or formfeed is a permissible separator, by typing

```
\bTwo[\n\040\t\r\cJ\cL]Words\b
```

Another important feature of the standard greppers is their option for reporting just the names of the files that have matches, rather than displaying the matches themselves. The implementation of this feature in a Perl command is covered next.

3.8 DISPLAYING FILENAMES ONLY (LIKE `grep -l`)

In some cases, you don't want to see the lines that match a regex; instead, you just want the names of the files that contain matches. With `grep`, you obtain this effect by using the `l` option, but with Perl, you do so by explicitly printing the name of the match's file rather than the contents of its line.

For example, this command prints the lines that match, but with no indication of which file they're coming from:

```
perl -wnl -e '/RE/ and print;' file file2 ...
```

In contrast, the following alternative prints the name of each file that has a match, using the special _filename variable_ $ARGV[9] that holds the name of the most recent input file (introduced in table 2.7):

```
perl -wnl -e '/RE/ and print $ARGV and close ARGV;' file file2 ...
```

We'll look at some sample applications of this technique before examining its workings.

The following command looks for matches with the name "Matthew" in the addresses.dat and members files seen earlier, and correctly reports that only the members file has a match:

```
$ perl -wnl -e '/\bMatthew\b/ and print $ARGV and close ARGV;' \
>     addresses.dat members
members
```

However, if you search for matches with the number 1, both filenames appear:

```
$ perl -wnl -e '/1/ and print $ARGV and close ARGV;' \
>     addresses.dat members
addresses.dat
members
```

Note that the command reports each filename only once, just as grep -1 would do, despite the fact that there are multiple matching lines in each file.

How do these commands work? The contents of the filename variable ($ARGV) are printed on the condition (expressed by and) that a match is found, and then the close function is executed on the condition (again expressed by and) that the print succeeds.

Why do you need to close the input file? Because once a match has been found and its associated filename has been shown to the user, there's no need to look for additional matches in that file. The goal is to print the names of the files that contain matches, so one printing of each name is enough.

The close function stops the collection of input from the current file and allows processing to continue with the next file (if any). It is called with the *filehandle* for the currently open file (ARGV), which you'll recognize as the filename variable $ARGV stripped of its leading $ symbol.

The chaining of the print and the close operations with and makes them both contingent on the success of the matching attempt.[10]

Next, we'll discuss how to request optional behaviors from the matching operator.

3.9   USING MATCHING MODIFIERS

Table 3.6 shows *matching modifiers* that are used to change the way matching is performed. As an example, the i modifier allows matching to be conducted with insensitivity to differences in character case (UPPER versus lower).

The g option will be familiar to sed and vi users. However, its effects are substantially more interesting in Perl, because of its ability to "do the right thing" in *list context* (more on this in part 2).

---

[9] Although the name $ARGV may seem an odd choice, it was selected for the warm, fuzzy feeling it gives C programmers, who are familiar with a similarly named variable in that language.

[10] Other more generally applicable techniques for conditionally executing a group of operations on the basis of the logical outcome of another, including ones using if/else, are shown in part 2.

Table 3.6 Matching modifiers

Modifier(s)	Syntax examples	Meaning	Explanation
i	/RE/i m:RE:i	Ignore case	Ignores case variations while matching.
x	/RE/x m:RE:x	Expanded mode	Permits whitespace and comments in the RE field.
s	/RE/s m:RE:s	Single-line mode	Allows the "."metacharacter to match newline, along with everything else.
m	/RE/m m:RE:m	Multi-line mode	Changes ^ and $ to match at the beginnings or ends of lines within the target string, rather than at the absolute beginning or end of that string.
g	/RE/g m:RE:g	Global	Returns all matches, successively or collectively, according to scalar/list context (covered in part 2).
i, g, s, m, x	/RE/igsmx m:RE:igsmx	Multiple modifiers	Allows all combinations; order doesn't matter.

Are you wondering about the s and m options? They sound kinky, and in a sense they are, because they let you bind your matches at either or both ends when record sizes longer than a single line are used.

To help you visualize how the modifiers and syntax variations of the matching operator fit together, table 3.7 shows examples that use different delimiters, target strings, and modifiers. Notice in particular that the examples in each of the panels of

Table 3.7 Matching operator examples

Example	Meaning	Explanation
/perl/	Looks for a match with perl in $_	Matches "perl" in $_.
m:perl:	Same, except uses different delimiters	Matches "perl" in $_.
$data =~ /perl/i	Looks for a match with perl in $data, ignoring case differences	Matches "perl", "PERL", "Perl", and so on in $data.
$data =~ / perl /xi	Same, except x requests extended syntax	Matches "perl", "PERL", "Perl", and so on in $data. Because the x modifier allows arbitrary whitespace and #-comments in the regex field, those characters are ignored there unless preceded by a backslash.
$data =~ m% perl # PeRl too! %xi	Same, except adds a #-comment and uses % as a delimiter	Matches "perl", "PERL", "Perl", and so on in $data. Whitespace characters and #-comments within the regex are ignored unless preceded by a backslash.

that table, despite their different appearances, are functionally identical. That's due to the typographical freedom provided by the x modifier and the ability to choose arbitrary delimiters for the regex field.

Next, you'll see additional examples of using the i modifier to perform case-insensitive matching.

3.9.1   Ignoring case (like `grep -i`)

A common problem in matching operations is disabling case sensitivity, so that a generic pattern like *mike* can be allowed to match *Mike*, *MIKE*, and all other possible variations (*mikE*, and so on).

With modern versions of grep, case sensitivity is disabled using the i option. In Perl, you do this using the i (ignore-case) matching modifier, as in this example:

```
perl -wnl -e '/RE/i and print;' file file2 ...
```

Because it uses case-insensitive matching, the output from the following command shows a line from the file that you haven't seen yet, containing the capitalized version of the word of interest. In addition, the "resurgent calls" line that accidentally appeared in earlier output is missing, because the use of \b on both sides of urgent prevents substring matches:

```
$ perl -wnl -e '/\burgent\b/i and print;' priorities
Make urgent call to W.
Handle urgent calling card issues
URGENT: Buy detergent!
```

Even before Perl arrived on the scene, grep had competition. Let's see how Perl compares to grep's best known rival.

3.10   PERL AS A BETTER *egrep*

The grep command has an enhanced relative called egrep, which provides metacharacters for *alternation, grouping,* and *repetition* (see tables 3.8 and 3.9) that grep lacks. These enhancements allow egrep to provide services such as the following:

- Simultaneously searching for matches with more than one pattern, through use of the alternation metacharacter (|):
  ```
  egrep 'Bob|Robert|Bobby'        # matches Bob, Robert, or Bobby
  ```

- Applying anchoring or other contextual constraints to alternate patterns, through use of grouping parentheses:
  ```
  egrep '^(Bob|Robert|Bobby)'      # matches each at start of line
  egrep '\b(Bob|Robert|Bobby) Dobbs\b'   # matches each variation
  ```

- Applying quantifiers such as "+" (meaning one or more) to multi-character patterns, through use of grouping parentheses:
  ```
  egrep 'He said (Yadda)+ again'   # "Yadda", "YaddaYadda", etc.
  ```

Traditionally, we've had to pay a high price for access to `egrep`'s enhancements by sacrificing `grep`'s capturing parentheses and backreferences to gain the added metacharacters (see table 3.9). But nowadays, we can use GNU `egrep`, which (like Perl) simultaneously provides *all* these features, making it the gold standard of greppers.

However, GNU `egrep` has some differences in syntax and functionality from `grep`, as shown in table 3.8. In particular, the parentheses it uses to capture a match aren't backslashed, and they simultaneously provide the service of grouping regex components. By no coincidence, Perl's parentheses work the same way.[11]

As you'll see throughout the rest of this chapter, Perl provides many valuable enhancements over what GNU `egrep` has to offer, including the numbered variables described in the bottom panel of table 3.8. That feature will be demonstrated in examples shown in section 4.3.4 and in the `preg` script in section 8.7.2.

Table 3.8 Metacharacters for alternation, grouping, match capturing, and match referencing in greppers and Perl

Syntax[a]	Name	Explanation
$X \| Y \| Z$	Alternation	This metacharacter allows a match with any of the patterns separated by a vertical bar. The example looks for matches with any of the patterns represented by X, Y, or Z.
`\(`X`\)`	Capturing parentheses (grep)	Capturing parentheses store what's matched within them for later access. `grep` requires those parentheses to be backslashed, unlike GNU `egrep` and Perl.
`(`X`)`	Grouping parentheses (egrep, Perl)	Grouping parentheses cause the effects of associated metacharacters to be applied to the group. They're used with alternations, as in a $(X \| Y)$ b; repetitions of alternations, as in $(X \| Y)$ +; and repetitions of multi-character sequences, as in (XY) +.
`(`X`)`	Capturing and grouping parentheses (GNU egrep, Perl)	With these utilities, parentheses provide both capturing and grouping services.
`\1, \2, ...`	Backreferences (grep, GNU egrep, Perl)	These are used within a regex to access a stored copy of what was most recently matched by the pattern in the first, second, and so on set of capturing parentheses.
Perl enhancement		
`$1, $2, ...`	Numbered variables	These are like backreferences, except they're used outside a regex, such as in the replacement field of a substitution operator or in code that follows a matching or substitution operator.

a. X, Y and Z are placeholders, standing for any collection of literal characters and/or metacharacters.

---

[11] Those clever GNU folks have borrowed liberally from Perl while implementing their upgrades to the classic UNIX utilities.

Next, we'll review the use of the alternation metacharacter in `egrep` and explain how you can use Perl to obtain order-independent matching of alternate patterns even more efficiently.

3.10.1 Working with cascading filters

That TV receiver built into Guido's new monitor sure comes in handy. But all too soon, his virtual chortling over SpongeBob's latest escapade in Bikini Bottom is interrupted by that annoying phone ringing again. *"Hello, may I help you? Sure boss, no problem. I'll get right on it!"*

He has just been given the task of extracting some important information from the `projects` file, which contains the initials of the programmers who worked on various projects. Here's how it looks:

```
area51: ET,CYA,NOYB,UFO,NSA
glorp:  FYI,INGY,ESR
slurm:  URI,INGY,TFM,ESR,SRV
yabl:   URL,SRV,INGY,ESR
```

The boss wants to know which projects, if any, ESR and SRV have both worked on.[12] Being well rested from his cartoon interlude, Guido realizes that the tricky part is avoiding the trap of order-specificity, meaning he can't assume that "ESR" necessarily appears to the left of "SRV", or vice versa.

He decides to start with a `grep` command that matches the word "ESR" followed by the word "SRV", and to worry about the reverse ordering later on. To indicate that he doesn't care what comes between those sets of initials, he opts for `grep`'s "longest anything" sequence: ".*" (see table 3.10). This works because the "*" allows for zero or more occurrences of the preceding character (see table 3.9), and the "." can match any character on the line. Time for a test run:

```
$ grep '\<ESR\>.*\<SRV\>' projects
slurm:  URI,INGY,TFM,ESR,SRV
```

That's a promising start. But Guido soon concludes that's as far as he can go with `grep`, because he'll need `egrep`'s alternation metacharacter to allow for the other ordering of the developers.[13]

Guido whips up a fresh cup of cappuccino, along with a shiny new `egrep` variation on his original command. It uses the alternation metacharacter to signify that a match with the pattern on either its left or its right is acceptable (see table 3.8):

```
$ egrep '\<ESR\>.*\<SRV\>|\<SRV\>.*\<ESR\>' projects
slurm:  URI,INGY,TFM,ESR,SRV
yabl:   URL,SRV,INGY,ESR
```

---

[12] Guido isn't sure, but he thinks those initials stand for Eric S. Raymond and Stevie Ray Vaughan.

[13] He's overlooking the alternative approach based on *cascading filters*, which we'll cover in short order.

It worked the first time! He wisely savors the ecstasy of the moment, having learned from experience that early programming successes are often rapidly followed by outbreaks of latent bugs.

Guido's mentor, Angelo, is passing by his cubicle and pauses momentarily to glance at Guido's screen. He suggests that Guido change the "*" metacharacters into "+" ones. Guido says *Yes, you're right, of course!*—and then he makes a mental note to find out what the difference is.

Table 3.9 lists Perl's quantifier metacharacters (some of which are also found in grep or egrep), including the "+" metacharacter in which Guido has become interested.

The executive summary of the top panel of table 3.9 is that the "?" metacharacter makes the preceding element optional, "*" makes it optional but allows it to be repeated, and "+" makes it mandatory but allows it to be repeated.

By now, Guido has determined that changing the instances of ".*" to ".+" in his command makes no difference in his results, because the back-to-back word-boundary metacharacters already ensure that all matches have some (non-word) character between the sets of initials (at least a comma). But Angelo convinces him that the use of ".*" where ".+" is more proper could confuse somebody later—like

Table 3.9 Quantifier metacharacters

Syntax[a]	Description	Utilities[b]	Explanation
X*	Optional, with repetition	grep, egrep, perl	Matches a sequence of zero or more consecutive Xs.
X+	Mandatory, with repetition	egrep, perl	Matches a sequence of one or more consecutive Xs.
X?	Optional	egrep, perl	Matches zero or one occurrence of X.
X\{min,max\} X\{min,\} X\{count\}	Number of repetitions	grep	For the first form of the repetition range, there can be from min to max occurrences of X. For the forms having one number and a comma, no upper limit on repetitions of X is imposed if max is omitted, and as many as max repetitions are allowed if min is omitted. For the other form, exactly count repetitions of X are required.
X{min,max} X{min,} X{count}	Number of repetitions	GNU egrep, perl	
X{,max}	Number of repetitions	perl	Note that the curly braces must be backslashed in grep.
REP?	Stingy matching	perl	When "?" immediately follows one of the above quantifiers (represented by REP), Perl seeks out the shortest possible match rather than the longest (which is the default). A common example is ".*?"; see table 3.10 for additional information.

a. X is a placeholder for any character, metacharacter, or parenthesized group. For example, the notation X+ includes cases such as 3+, [2468]+, and (Yadda)+.

b. Some of these metacharacters are also provided by other Unix utilities, such as sed and awk.

Guido himself, next year when he needs this command once again—so he opts for the ".+" version.[14]

Guido is happy with his solution, but his boss has a surprise in store for him.

Switching from alternation metacharacters to pipes

Now, Guido's boss wants to know which projects a group of *four* particular developers worked on together. That's trouble, because the approach he has used thus far doesn't scale well to larger numbers of programmers, due to the rapidly increasing number of alternate orderings that must be accommodated.[15]

Angelo suggests an approach based on a *cascading filter* model[16] as a better choice; it will do the matching incrementally rather than all at once. Like Guido's `egrep` solution, the following pipeline also matches lines that contain both "ESR" and "SRV"—regardless of order—but as you'll see in a moment, it's more amenable to subsequent enhancements:

```
$ egrep '\<ESR\>' projects | egrep '\<SRV\>'
slurm:   URI,INGY,TFM,ESR,SRV
yabl:    URL,SRV,INGY,ESR
```

This command works by first selecting the lines that have "ESR" on them and then passing them through the pipe to the second `egrep`, which shows the lines that (also) have "SRV" on them. Thus, he's avoided the order-specificity problem completely by searching for the required components separately.

To handle the boss's latest request, Guido constructs this pipeline:

```
egrep '\<ESR\>' projects |
          egrep '\<SRV\>' |
               egrep '\<CYA\>' |
                    egrep '\<FYI\>'
```

NOTE It's not necessary to format the individual filtering components in this stairstep fashion for either the Shell or Perl—the code just looks nicer this way.

He could also implement a pipeline of this type using Perl instead of `egrep`, but he sees little incentive to do so. Either way he writes it, a cascading-filter solution is an attractive alternative to the difficult chore of composing a single regex that would in itself handle all the different permutations of the initials. But as you'll see next, Perl makes an even better approach possible.

---

[14] After all, what good is having an angel looking over your shoulder if you don't heed his advice?

[15] For example, adding 1 additional programmer for a total of 3 requires 6 variations to be considered; for a group of 5, there are 120 variations to handle!

[16] By analogy to the way water works its way down a staircase-like cliff one level at a time, a set of filters in which each feeds its output to the next is also said to "cascade."

Switching from *egrep* to Perl to gain efficiency

All engineering decisions involve tradeoffs of one resource for another. In this case, Guido's cascading-filter solution simplifies the programming task by using additional system resources—one additional process per programmer, and nearly as many pipes to transfer the data.[17] There's nothing wrong with that tradeoff—unless you don't have to make it.

What's the alternative? To use Perl's logical `and` to chain together the individual matching operators, which only requires a *single* `perl` process and *zero* pipes, no matter how many individual matches there are:

```
perl -wnl -e '/\bESR\b/ and
                /\bSRV\b/ and
                  /\bCYA\b/ and
                    /\bFYI\b/ and
                        print;' projects
```

Note that you can't make any comparable modification to the stack of `egrep` commands shown earlier, because `egrep`'s specialization for matching prevents it from supporting more general programming techniques, such as this chaining one.

There's much to recommend this Perl solution over its more resource-intensive `egrep` alternative: It requires less typing, it's portable to other OSs, and it can access all of Perl's other benefits if needed later.

Next, we'll turn our attention to a consideration of *context* (you know, what public figures are always complaining about being quoted out of).

3.11 MATCHING IN CONTEXT

In grepping operations, *showing context* typically means displaying a few lines above and/or below each matching line, which is a service some greppers provide. Perl offers more flexibility, such as showing the entire (arbitrarily defined) record in which the match was found, which can range in size from a single word to an entire file.

We'll begin our exploration of this topic by discussing the use of the two most popular alternative record definitions: paragraphs and files.

3.11.1 Paragraph mode

Although there are many possible ways to define the context to be displayed along with a match, the simple option of enabling *paragraph mode* often yields satisfactory results, and it's easy to implement. All you do is include the special -00 option with `perl`'s invocation (see chapter 2), which causes Perl to accumulate lines until it encounters one or more blank lines, and to treat each such accumulated "paragraph" as a single record.

---

[17] How inefficient is it? Well, on my system, the previous solution takes about seven times longer to run than its upcoming Perl alternative (in both elapsed and CPU time).

The one-line command for displaying the paragraphs that contain matches is therefore

```
perl -00 -wnl -e '/RE/ and print;' file
```

To appreciate the benefit of having a match's context on display, consider the frustration that the output of the following line-oriented command generates, versus that of its paragraph-oriented alternative:

```
$ cat companies
Consultix is a division of
Pacific Software Gurus, Inc.

Insultix is a division of Ricklesosity.com.
$ grep 'Consultix' companies
Consultix is a division of
```

A division of what? Please tell me!

```
$ perl -00 -wnl -e '/Consultix/ and print;'   # paragraph mode
Consultix is a division of
Pacific Software Gurus, Inc.
```

That's better! But a scandal is erupting on live TV; let's check it out.

Senator Quimby needs a Perl expert

There's trouble over at Senator Quimby's ethics hearing, where the Justice Department's IT operatives just ran the following command on live TV against the written transcript of his testimony:

```
$ perl -wnl -e '/\bBRIBE\b/ and print;' SenQ.testimony # line mode
I ACCEPTED THE BRIBE!
```

His handlers voice an objection, and they're granted the right to make modifications to that command. It's rerun with paragraph-mode enabled, to show the matches in context, and with case differences ignored, to ensure that all bribe-related remarks are displayed:

```
$ perl -00 -wnl -e '/\bBRIBE\b/i and print;' SenQ.testimony
I knew I'd be in trouble if
I ACCEPTED THE BRIBE!
So I did not.

My minimum bribe is $100k, and she only offered me $50k,
so to preserve my pricing power, I refused it.
```

Although the senator seemed to be exonerated by the first paragraph, the second one cast an even more unfavorable light on his story!

He would have been happier if his people had limited the output to the first paragraph by using and close ARGV to terminate input processing after the first match's record was displayed:[18]

---

[18] See section 3.8 for another application of this technique.

```
$ perl -00 -wnl -e '/\bBRIBE\b/i and close ARGV;' SenQ.testimony
I knew I would be in trouble if
I ACCEPTED THE BRIBE!
So I did not.
```

grep lacks the capability of showing the first match only, which may be why you never see it used in televised legal proceedings.

Sometimes you need even more context for your matches, so we'll look next at how to match in *file mode*.

3.11.2   File mode

In the following command, which uses the special option -0777 (see table 2.9), each record consists of an *entire file's* worth of input:

```
perl -0777 -wnl -e '/RE/ and print;' file file2 ...
```

With this command, the matching operator is applied once *per file*, with output ranging from nothing (if there's no match) to every file being printed in its entirety (if every file has a match).

This matching mode is more commonly used with *substitutions* than with *matches*. For this reason, we'll return to it in chapter 4, when we cover the *substitution operator*.

Next, you'll learn how to write regexes that match strings which span lines.

3.12 SPANNING LINES WITH REGEXES

Unlike its UNIX forebears, Perl's regex facility allows for matches that *span lines*, which means the match can start on one line and end on another. To use this feature, you need to know how to use the matching operator's s modifier (shown in table 3.6) to enable single-line mode, which allows the "." metacharacter to match a newline. In addition, you'll typically need to construct a regex that can match across a line boundary, using quantifier metacharacters (see tables 3.9 and 3.11).

When you write a regex to span lines, you'll often need a way to express indifference about what's found between two required character sequences. For example, when you're looking for a match that starts with a line having "ON" at its beginning and that ends with the next line having "OFF" at its end, you must make accommodations for a lot of unknown material between these two endpoints in your regex.

Four types of such "don't care" regexes are shown in table 3.10. They differ as to whether "nothing" or "something" is required as the minimally acceptable filler between the endpoints, and whether the longest or shortest available match is desired.

The regexes in table 3.10's bottom panel use a special meaning of the "?" metacharacter, which is valuable and unique to Perl. Specifically, when "?" appears after one of the quantifier metacharacters, it signifies a request for *stingy* rather than *greedy* matching; this means it seeks out the shortest possible sequence that allows a match, rather than the longest one (which is the default).

Table 3.10 Patterns for the shortest and longest sequences of anything or something

Metacharacter sequence [a]	Meaning	Explanation
.*	Longest anything	Matches nothing, or the longest possible sequence of characters.
.+	Longest something	Matches the longest possible sequence of one or more characters.
.*?	Shortest anything	Matches nothing, or the shortest possible sequence of characters.
.+?	Shortest something	Matches the shortest possible sequence of one or more characters.

a. The metacharacter "." normally matches any character except newline. If single-line-mode is enabled via the s match-modifier, "." matches newline too, and the indicated metacharacter sequences can match across line boundaries.

Representative techniques for matching across lines are shown in table 3.11, and detailed instructions for constructing regexes like those are presented in the next section.

Table 3.11 Examples of matching across lines

Matching operator [a]	Match type	Explanation
/\bMinimal\b.+\bPerl\b/s	Ordered words	Because of the s modifier, "." is allowed to match newline (along with anything else). This lets the pattern match the words in the specified order with anything between them, such as "<u>Minimal</u> training on <u>Perl</u>."
/\bMinimal\b\s+\bPerl\b/	Consecutive words	This pattern matches consecutive words. It can match across a line boundary, with no need for an s modifier, because \s matches the newline character (along with other whitespace characters). For example, the pattern shown would match "Minimal" at the end of line 1 followed by "Perl" at the beginning of line 2.
/\bMinimal\b[\s:,-]+\bPerl\b/	Consecutive words, allowing intervening punctuation	This pattern matches consecutive words and enhances the previous example by allowing any combination of whitespace, colon, comma, and hyphen characters to occur between them. For example, it would match "Minimal:" at the end of line 1 followed by "Perl" at the beginning of line 2.

a. To match the shortest sequence between the given endpoints, add the stingy matching metacharacter (?) after the quantifier metacharacter (usually +). To retrieve all matches at once, add the g modifier after the closing delimiter, and use *list context* (covered in part 2).

As shown in table 3.11, regexes of different types are needed to match a sequence of two words in the same record, depending on what's permitted to appear between them. The table's examples illustrate typical situations that provide for anything, only whitespace, or whitespace and selected punctuation symbols to appear between the words.

Next, you'll see how to combine line-spanning regexes with appropriate uses of the matching operator to obtain line-spanning matches.

3.12.1 Matching across lines

To take advantage of Perl's ability to match across lines, you need to do the following:

1 Change the input record separator to one that allows for multi-line records (using, for example, -00 or -0777).

2 Use a regex that allows for matching across newlines, such as:

- The "longest anything" sequence (. *; see table 3.10) in conjunction with the s match modifier, which allows "." to match any character, including the newline (this is called *single-line mode*).

- A regex that describes a sequence of characters that includes the newline, either explicitly as in [\t\n]+ and [_\s]+, or by exclusion as in [^aeiou]+. (Those character classes respectively represent a sequence consisting of one or more tabs or newlines, a sequence of one or more underscores or whitespace characters, or a sequence of one or more non-vowels.)

For example, let's say you want to match and print the longest sequence starting with the word "MUDDY" and ending with the word "WATERS", ignoring case. The sequence is allowed to span lines within a paragraph, and anything is allowed to appear between the words. To solve this problem, you adapt your matching operator from the sample shown in table 3.11 for the Match Type of Ordered Words.

Here's the appropriate command:[19]

```
perl -00 -wnl -e '/\bMUDDY\b.*\bWATERS\b/si and print $&;' file
```

A common mistake is to omit the s modifier on the matching operator; that prevents the "." metacharacter (in . *) from matching a newline, and thus limits the matches to those occurring on the same physical line.

Several interesting examples of line-spanning regexes will be shown in upcoming programs. To prepare you for them, we'll take a quick look at a command that's used to retrieve data from the Internet.

---

[19] Methods for printing multiple matches at once are shown later in this chapter, and methods for handling successive matches through looping techniques are shown in, e.g., listing 10.7.

3.12.2 Using `lwp-request`

Although interactive search engines are getting more powerful all the time, in some cases you may prefer to obtain information from the Internet using programs of your own. Fortunately, it's easy to do such *Web-scraping* using Perl commands in conjunction with Perl's `lwp-request` script,[20] which provides easy access to the *Library for Web Programming* (LWP, covered in chapter 12).

The simplest thing you can do with `lwp-request` is to download the contents of a web page to your computer, in preparation for further processing. By default, you get the page in its native format, but you can also specify conversions to PostScript, text, or (readability-enhanced) HTML.

For example, to fetch the front page for www.yahoo.com to your system and store its text in a file, you would use a command that requests output in text format:[21]

```
lwp-request -o text www.yahoo.com > yahoo.txt
```

After running this command, you could search within `yahoo.txt` using `grep`-like Perl commands to find material of interest.

Or, to store the web page in PostScript form, for nicer printing, you would use this variation:

```
lwp-request -o ps   www.yahoo.com > yahoo.ps
```

The next section shows you how to use `lwp-request` to "scrape" a web page for travel-related information, such as discounted flights to exotic destinations.

3.12.3 Filtering `lwp-request` output

Suppose you know that the *USA TOMORROW* newspaper always has travel tips on its "Money" page, and you'd like an easy way to display the latest ones on your surfing-enabled Perl-equipped PDA. After figuring out the appropriate URL, you can use the following command to isolate and display the paragraph that contains the latest travel tips:

```
$ lwp-request -o text usatomorrow.com/money/front.htm |
> perl -00 -wnl -e '/\bTravel tips\b/ and print;' # paragraph mode
TRAVEL TIPS AND DEALS
Want to know how you can fly at freight rates?
Simple--just pack yourself in a shipping crate!
Details in Tuesday's edition.
```

But perhaps your only destination of interest is the exotic Indonesian island of Bali. How do you refine this command to better suit your needs? By modifying the regex to

---

[20] If it isn't already on your system, you can download the LWP module from CPAN and install it using the techniques shown in chapter 12.

[21] The o option makes use of the additional modules HTML::Parse and HTML::FormatText; see chapter 12 for installation instructions.

require that the word *Bali* appears in the same paragraph as *Travel tips*, using the Ordered Words pattern from table 3.11: [22]

```
$ lwp-request -o text usatomorrow.com/money/front.htm |
>    perl -00 -wnl -e '/\bTravel tips\b.+\bBali\b/is and print;'
$
```

Note the use of the s modifier to allow ".+" to match across a newline, and the i modifier to ignore case differences (for all you know, those excitable travel writers may be SHOUTING about Bali!).

As you can see, there was no match for Bali in today's paper, but you can try again tomorrow. If you're especially keen on travel, you can store the command in your Shell startup file, so you'll see the latest travel tips every time you log in.

3.13 ADDITIONAL EXAMPLES

Now that we have covered Perl's most important features for matching patterns, we'll discuss some more exotic examples of what you can do with one-line grep-like commands, and we'll illustrate correct and incorrect approaches to composing regexes. We'll start by doing some log-file analysis, which is a common activity of System Administrators (SAs).

3.13.1 Log-file analysis

Many of us play the role of the SA these days, including some who have that official job title and others who maintain their own systems or those of friends and family. As professional SAs will tell you, the only task more important than doing regular disk backups is that of monitoring system log files for error messages.

One day, I developed an interest in identifying hits on my web site that come from sources outside the USA. I started by examining a few records from my Apache web server's access_log file to see how they were formatted. Here are some samples shown with carriage returns inserted after "- -" to let the lines fit on the page:

```
robot.szukacz.pl - - ↲
  [17/Aug/2006:21:05:21 -0700] "GET /bsh.html HTTP/1.1" 200 9519
proxy3.cc.swin.edu.au - - ↲
  [19/Aug/2006:00:44:24 -0700] "GET /Pa1055.jpg HTTP/1.0" 200 7741
crawler14.googlebot.com - - ↲
  [17/Aug/2006:00:46:12 -0700] "GET /robots.txt HTTP/1.0" 200 328
```

The domain name of the visiting surfer is in the first field, which you can see is made up of letters, digits, and dots. Domains ending in two-letter country codes other than .us are "foreign" (to Americans, at least); for instance, the .pl domain stands for Poland, and .au stands for Australia.

---

[22] Although this example works at the time of this writing, there could be a future change in the format of this page that would require modifications to the regex shown. *Caveat scraper!*

Given this information, you could use the following regex to match the lines that start with domains ending in country codes:

```
/^[\w\.]+\.[a-z][a-z] /i
```

The leading caret (^) ensures that each match starts at the beginning of the line. The following character-class ([...]) lists the characters that are acceptable in the subdomain field, based on the evidence that they consist of letters and digits (both handled by the \w metacharacter, covered in table 3.5) and literal period (\ .) characters.[23] The "+" after the character class requests a sequence of one or more of the indicated characters. Following that, a literal period is needed before the country code (a letter followed by a letter), and then a space character. Just in case capital letters appear in some records, the matching operator's i modifier is used to ignore case variations.

That's how you *could* build up a regex to extract lines having domains ending in country codes. *But I wouldn't recommend it!*

There are two problems with this approach: The solution isn't properly aligned with the objective, and it isn't accurate enough to ensure the correct results. Remember, all we're trying to accomplish in this exercise is to match lines whose first field ends in two letters. Complicating the issue by trying to guess which characters might legitimately appear in that field, and getting it *wrong*, costs extra time and effort and is likely to give incorrect results.

What's wrong? *Hyphens* should be permitted in the domain names, but not the *underscores* permitted by \w (in addition to the desired letters and digits). Although this will prevent us from matching hyphenated domain names, allowing underscores probably won't cause any trouble, because such (illegal) domain names shouldn't appear in the file anyway.

> **TIP** Confused about whether a particular *symbol* will have a special or literal meaning in a Perl regex? To ensure the literal meaning, put a backslash before it. For example, "\ ." means a *literal* period.

Sometimes, if you're not sure what something is, it's helpful to consider the other side of the coin and think about what it is *not*.

This problem is more easily solved from that vantage point. Think about this: Have you ever seen whitespace characters, such as a space or tab, in a domain name? Certainly not, because they're expressly disallowed.

Accordingly, let's define the subdomain-portion of the first field, which leads up to the period followed by the two-letter top-level domain-name portion, as consisting of one or more *non-whitespace* characters. (Again, this could theoretically allow some illegal characters to match, but they shouldn't be present in the log file anyway, so this simplification shouldn't hurt.)

---

[23] In the context of a character class ([ ]), the period is taken literally even without the benefit of the preceding backslash. But backslashing it makes the programmer's intention more clear and does no harm.

This approach makes sense because our goal isn't to *validate* the contents of the first field, but instead to scan forward to its end, which is marked by a space, and ensure the top-level domain name has only two letters in it.

The appropriate metacharacter for matching non-whitespace is \S (from table 3.5), and to request one or more, you add "+" yielding this command:[24]

```
$ perl -wnl -e '/^\S+\.[a-z][a-z] /i and print;' access_log
m021182.ppp.asahi-net.or.jp ...
p0915.nas4-asd3.dial.wanadoo.nl ...
robot.szukacz.pl ...
server.stmarys.unimelb.edu.au ...
spider2.cpe.ku.ac.th ...
willynilly.us ...
```

Note the literal period in the regex after the non-whitespace sequence and before the two-letter top-level domain name, because without it, three-letter domains would also match (given that the first letter of each will be non-whitespace).

But what about that willynilly.us domain? Because it's not foreign (from the U.S. viewpoint), its lines should be excluded from a report of foreign visitors to the web site. You'll see how to deal with that case in the next section.

Disqualifying undesirable matches

Earlier in this chapter, you saw how matching operators can be chained together with the logical and to print records that match each of several regexes, using a technique called *cascading filters*. With a slight twist, chains of matching operators can be used to ensure that certain regexes are matched while others are *not* matched. You do this by preceding the matching operators that are required to fail with the negation operator, "!".

To handle the problem of excluding the .us domain, you need to enhance the original command by adding a second "must not match" component:

```
perl -wnl -e ' /^\S+\.[a-z][a-z] / and
               ! /^\S+\.us / and print; ' access_log
```

In words, it says: "Any line that has a two-letter domain name that isn't .us should be printed." With this adjustment, the command successfully excludes U.S. domains such as willynilly.us and prints only the "foreign" ones.

A worthwhile enhancement might be to modify the command's output so that it shows the country codes for the foreign surfers, like so:

```
au jp nl pl sg th
```

Even better, it could print the country names that correspond to those codes, rather than the (somewhat inscrutable) codes themselves:

---

[24] Because the lines in this log file are very long, they have been truncated after the domain name, as indicated by the sequences of three dots.

```
Australia Japan Netherlands Poland Singapore Thailand
```

You'll learn additional techniques that could be used to effect these enhancements in later chapters.

Next, you'll learn how to simplify the use of `grep`-like Perl commands by using a Perl script.

3.13.2   A scripted grepper

As shown earlier, the basic Perl command for finding matches and displaying their associated records is compact and simple to type. But it would be even easier and more foolproof to do your matching using a script. Consider the following session, which shows the use of a script called `greperl`:

```
$ greperl -pattern='\bCA\b' addresses.dat    # find CA customers
Mooshi Pomalus:4242 Wafer Lane:San Jose:CA:95134
```

Note that you specify the desired regex using a switch called `-pattern`, which Perl handles automatically through the s option on the shebang line (introduced in table 2.4).

Here's the `greperl` script:

```
#! /usr/bin/perl -s -wnl

BEGIN {
    # -pattern='RE' switch is required
    $pattern  or
        warn "Usage: $0 -pattern='RE' [ file1 ... ]\n"  and
            exit 255;
}

/$pattern/  and  print;
```

As discussed in chapter 2, the required `-pattern='RE'` switch is tested for a True value[25] in a `BEGIN` block, and a `warn` and `exit` combination is executed in the event of a False result.

As you can imagine, it would be useful to have variations on this script that employed different definitions of the input record separator, different match modifiers, and so forth. But rather than having a multitude of such scripts, a better solution would be to have a single script that lets you select those options through use of command-line switches (as with `grep`). Because it takes additional knowledge to write such programs, we'll defer their discussion until part 2.

Many people have benefited from the use of dictionaries designed for bad spellers. In like fashion, a grepper designed for those who don't quite know how to spell their search patterns can be useful, as you'll see next.

---

[25] One legitimate value, 0, that could be assigned to this switch variable will inadvertently produce a False result and terminate the program. For this reason, a different approach, based on the `defined` function covered in chapter 8, is more proper in such cases.

3.13.3　Fuzzy matching

Unlike computers, the people who use them tend to be fuzzy. Some are certainly fuzzier than others, but as a general rule, humans express themselves with considerably less precision than machines are inclined to require.

A good example is the task of looking for occurrences of a name you're not sure how to spell. This is illustrated by the following session in which Yoko, a fan of the Farscape TV series, is having trouble extracting the records for her favorite characters using the greperl script shown earlier:

```
$ greperl -pattern=Rigel farscape_characters     # No matches!
$ greperl -pattern=Scorpeus farscape_characters  # No matches!
```

Yoko needs a matching program that's as fuzzy as her spelling! So, she writes one called fuzzy_match, which finds the desired matches despite her slightly misspelled patterns:

```
$ fuzzy_match -string=Rigel farscape_characters
Rygel XVI:Imperious Froggy
$ fuzzy_match -string=Scorpeus farscape_characters
Scorpius:Ghoulish Villain
```

The script was easy for Yoko to write, once she found out about the module called String::Approx and downloaded and installed it from CPAN. It provides an *approximate match* function called amatch, which accepts matches if the mismatch with the target string is within an allowed percentage.

Here's the fuzzy_match script:

```
#! /usr/bin/perl -s -wnl

use String::Approx 'amatch';    # must specifically request "amatch"

BEGIN {
    $string  or
        warn "Usage: $0 -string='something' [ file1 ... ]\n"  and
            exit 255;
}
amatch $string, [ "i", "20%" ] and  print; # Ignore case; 20% fuzzy
```

Unlike some modules, this one doesn't automatically export all its functions, so Yoko has to specify amatch explicitly after the module name (see section 12.1.3). She designed the script to use -string for the switch rather than -pattern to emphasize the fact that amatch doesn't support any metacharacters. On the script's last line, the conditional printing of the current line via the logical and is controlled by the success or failure of amatch, just as it's controlled in greperl by the result of the matching operator.

Because of the design of the amatch function, the request to ignore case while matching is presented as an "i" within square brackets. The fuzziness of the matching operation can be increased or decreased by changing the double-quoted percentage value that follows.

Yoko settled on 20 percent fuzziness after some experimentation to determine the smallest value that would let her misspellings obtain their intended matches. If you're happy with the defaults, which provide matching with case sensitivity and 10 percent fuzziness, you can leave out the square-bracketed argument and supply only the $string argument to amatch.

Next, we'll look at a web-oriented application of pattern matching.

3.13.4 Web scraping

One way to use web scraping to good advantage is to obtain a listing of the subjects covered on a particular web page. As a case in point, once I figured out that the bullet symbol used on slashdot.org was character #267, I found that I could easily obtain an outline of the site's front page by extracting lines containing that character. I did so by using the character-generating metacharacter \267 (see table 3.1) in the regex:[26]

```
$ lwp-request -o text slashdot.org |
>     perl -wnl -e '/\267/ and print;'
    · Microsoft Tracking Behavior of Newsgroup Posters
    · SCO Prepares To Sue Linux End Users
    · Talk About A Security Hole, Go To Jail?
```

Another useful command would be one that lets you quickly determine the latest release of a particular CPAN module by looking for it under the dist subdirectory of the CPAN search URL, using a variation on its name in which any doubled colons are replaced by a dash:

```
$ lwp-request -o text \
>     'search.cpan.org/dist/Shell-POSIX-Select'
Shell::POSIX::Select
The POSIX Shell's "select" loop for Perl
Shell-POSIX-Select-0.05 - 11 May 2003 - Tim Maher
...
```

You'll see lwp-request used in additional examples in later chapters (e.g., sections 9.2.8, 12.3.2).

3.14 SUMMARY

From a Perl perspective, the grep command and its relatives impose numerous limitations on applications that need to match patterns against records and display selected aspects of the results. These limitations stem from the fact that some or all Unix greppers lack the following:

---

[26] By the time this book had entered its production phase, Slashdot had changed its web pages to use the "·" entity request as a bullet symbol rather than character #267, but there should be other web pages for which this command will work.

CHAPTER 3   PERL AS A (BETTER) grep COMMAND

- Word-boundary metacharacters (\<, \>)
- Compact character-class shortcuts (such as \d for a digit)
- Control character representations (such as \t for the tab character)
- Provisions for embedding commentary and arbitrary whitespace in regex fields
- Access to match components (e.g., as provided by Perl's $& variable)
- The ability to define custom input records (such as Perl's paragraph mode)
- The ability to match across lines (e.g., as provided for by Perl's single-line mode)
- Automatic skipping of directory files that are inadvertently named as program arguments
- The ability to customize the format used for printing matches within records (as provided for by Perl's '$,' and '$"' variables)
- The ability to do "fuzzy" matching

Another more general problem with the use of Unix commands for pattern matching is that there are variations between different OSs, vendors, and versions with respect to the regex dialects that particular commands employ. This creates uncertainty about the meaning a particular character (e.g., | or {) will have with a specific command on a specific system, and valid concerns about transporting scripts employing such commands to other systems.

The use of Perl programs in place of those unpredictable Unix commands eliminates these problems and provides access to Perl's superior capabilities. For example, you can add the -00 invocation option to display each match in the context of its containing *paragraph* rather than its line, and you can use print $& to display the match *without* the context of its containing record.

Table 3.12 lists the Unix commands for performing the most common types of grepping tasks, their Perl counterparts, and pointers to the sections in this chapter in which those commands were discussed.

Table 3.12   Unix and Perl commands for common grepping activities

Unix command	Perl counterpart	Type of task	Section
grep 'RE' F	perl -wnl -e '/RE/ and print;' F	Show matching lines	3.3.1
grep -v 'RE' F	perl -wnl -e '/RE/ or print;' F	Show non-matching lines	3.7
grep -i 'RE' F	perl -wnl -e '/RE/i and print;' F	Ignore case	3.9.1
grep -l 'RE' F	perl -wnl -e '/RE/ and print $ARGV and close ARGV;' F	Show only filenames	3.8
fgrep 'STRING' F	perl -wnl -e '/\QSTRING\E/ and print;' F	Match literal characters	3.5

In subsequent chapters, you'll learn how to write more sophisticated types of `grep`-like applications and how to emulate the familiar command-line interface of `grep` more closely, while still retaining access to Perl's more powerful capabilities.

Such enhancements will include the following:

- Accepting the regex as an argument to a script rather than via an assignment to a switch variable (as `greperl` does)
- Checking for improper usage and issuing warnings as needed
- Skipping over inappropriate arguments
- Embedding comments within regexes
- Highlighting matches in context (e.g., in *reverse video*)

Directions for further study

To learn more about the topics discussed in this chapter, you can run the following commands to obtain further documentation:

- `man lwp-request`
- `man String::Approx`

After you finish reading part 1, if you feel bold enough to venture out of the UNIX quarter of Perlistan and hang out with the *circled* JAPHs, you'll want to learn more about Perl's regexes and matching operator by issuing the following commands:

- `man perlrequick` *# An introduction to Perl's regexes*
- `man perlretut`   *# A tutorial on using Perl's regexes*
- `man perlre`   *# Coverage of more complex regex issues*
- `man perlreref`   *# Regular expressions reference*
- `man perlfaq6`   *# Regular expressions FAQ*

CHAPTER 4

Perl as a (better) sed command

4.1 A brief history of sed 89
4.2 Shortcomings of sed 91
4.3 Performing substitutions 93
4.4 Printing lines by number 100
4.5 Modifying templates 101
4.6 Converting special characters 103

4.7 Editing files 105
4.8 Converting to lowercase or uppercase 113
4.9 Substitutions with computed replacements 114
4.10 The sed to Perl translator 118
4.11 Summary 118

In this chapter, you'll learn how to write Perl programs that surpass the limitations of the UNIX sed command. We'll start by discussing the historical uses of sed, and then we'll consider its modern-day applications—which are quite different.[1]

Then, we'll explore a variety of commands and scripts that show how Perl can beat sed at its own game.

4.1   A BRIEF HISTORY OF sed

Although it isn't as famous as its brother grep, the sed command is another offshoot of the original UNIX editor, ed. But unlike ed, which needs an interactive user to feed it instructions, sed is a *stream <u>editor</u>* that applies a predetermined set of editing commands to the stream of data flowing through it. The primary contribution of sed to

---

[1] Why? Because sed was relieved of many of its duties by the ascendancy of AWK in the late 1970s.

the UNIX toolkit is therefore that it provides a non-interactive (or *batch*-oriented) interface to ed's capabilities.

sed also has some features that go well beyond ed's, including conditional branching, looping, and character transliteration. For this reason, sed reigned as the primary text-processing utility of early UNIX. But when the ingenious and highly influential AWK language emerged from the Bell Labs in 1977, it quickly supplanted sed for most text-editing applications.

To see why, consider the following solution to the problem of reordering name fields into the "Surname, Firstname" format:

```
$ cat farscapers
Ka D'Argo
John Crichton
. . .

$ sed 's/^\([^ ][^ ]*\) \([^ ][^ ]*\).*$/\2, \1/' farscapers
D'Argo, Ka
Crichton, John
. . .
```

Hello? HELLO? *Are you still there?*

That sed command is certainly a shocker, so I'll give you a moment to regain your equilibrium. But please believe me, despite appearances, that command isn't a cruel hoax—we really used to do field processing like that! In consideration of your traumatized state, I won't try to explain what that command's scary-looking regex is all about. You don't need to know anyway, because in Perl you'd never have to write one like that.

Now, consider the AWK way of doing the same job:

```
$ awk '{ print $2 ", " $1 }' farscapers      # isn't this better?
D'Argo, Ka
Crichton, John
. . .
```

This contrast accurately conveys the message that just about anything sed can do, AWK can do better. UNIX programmers noticed this long ago and started using AWK in preference to sed wherever possible. The result is that nowadays, sed is most commonly used in just two kinds of applications: simple text substitutions (that don't involve fields!), and extractions of lines by number. sed is preferred to AWK for these uses principally because it requires less typing—which, other things being equal, is considered a valid reason in Perlistani culture, where Laziness is highly valued.

In this chapter, you'll first learn how to use Perl to emulate the most popular types of sed applications.[2] Then, we'll examine programs that demonstrate Perl's superiority over sed.

---

[2] You'll learn Perl techniques for printing reordered fields in chapter 5; but as a sneak preview, here's the Perl counterpart to the awk command that reorders the farscapers file:
```
perl -wnla -e 'print "$F[1], $F[0]";' farscapers
```

For example, you'll learn how to do text substitutions while generating replacement strings on the fly, using the full power of Perl to create them. This capability, called *computed replacements*, allows for such feats as converting a dollar amount within a string into one that's 10 percent larger or 20 percent smaller.

Before we examine the impressive capabilities of Perl as a text-processing utility, we'll begin by comparing the basic capabilities of sed and Perl for tasks of this kind, with an emphasis on sed's shortcomings.

4.2   SHORTCOMINGS OF sed

As in the corresponding table for the grep command (see table 3.2), the topmost panel of table 4.1 shows the differences in basic matching facilities provided by sed commands and Perl. Many of the shortcomings of the classic sed are the same as those listed earlier for the classic grep, due to their mutual dependence on the classic regex dialect.

Table 4.1   Text-modification capabilities of sed and Perl

Capability [a]	Classic sed	POSIX sed	GNU sed	Perl
Word-boundary metacharacter	–	Y	Y	Y
Compact character-class shortcuts	–	?	–	Y
Control character representation	–	–	–	Y
Repetition ranges	Y	Y	Y	Y
Capturing parentheses and backreferences	Y	Y	Y	Y+
Metacharacter quoting	Y	Y	Y	Y+
Embedded commentary	–	–	–	Y
Advanced regex features	–	–	–	Y
Case insensitivity	–	–	Y	Y
Arbitrary record definitions	–	–	–	Y
Line-spanning matches	–	–	–	Y
Binary-file processing	–	–	–	Y
Directory-file skipping	–	–	Y	Y
Arbitrary delimiters	Y	Y	Y	Y+
Access to match components	–	–	–	Y
Customized replacements	–	–	–	Y+
File modifications	–	–	Y	Y+

a. Y: has the capability; Y+: has the capability with enhancements; ?: partially has the capability; –: doesn't have the capability

The middle panel of the table compares the kinds of matching the individual commands support, and the lower panel compares the enhanced matching services they provide.

You'll understand what most of the listed capabilities mean, either because they're self-explanatory or because they were discussed earlier in chapter 3. We'll focus on the other capabilities here.

Arbitrary delimiters give you the ability to use an arbitrary character to separate the *search* and *replacement* fields in the substitution syntax, which can greatly enhance readability. For example, the following commands all strip the leading /etc/ from each input line by substituting an empty replacement string (indicated by the adjacent second and third delimiters) for what was matched:

```
sed          's/^\/etc\///g' file            # default delimiters
sed          's|^/etc/||g'    file            # custom delimiters
perl -wpl -e 's|^/etc/||g;'   file            # Perl
```

Isn't the first sed solution hard to read, with those slanty lines falling against each other? This effect, called *Leaning Toothpick Syndrome*, detracts from readability, and can be easily avoided. Like sed, Perl allows the first visible character occurring immediately after the s to be used as an alternative delimiter; it's used here to avoid the need for backslashing literal occurrences of the delimiter character within the regex field.

As the following example shows, Perl even allows the use of *reflected* symbol pairs such as () and {}—whose components are mirror images of each other—to delimit the separate components of the <u>search</u> and **replacement** fields:

```
perl -wpl -e 's{^/etc/ }{ }g;' # reflected symbols for delimiters
```

In recognition of this advanced feature, Perl is accorded a "Y+" (has the capability with enhancements) in the "Arbitrary delimiters" category of table 4.1.[3]

Customized replacements refers to the ability to adapt the replacement string to the specific characteristics of the string that was matched. An example would be substituting "FREDERICK" for "FRED", but "Frederick" for "Fred". The computed replacements mentioned earlier, which are covered later in this chapter, fall into this category, along with the *mapped replacements* discussed in section 10.4.4.

Perl provides automatic *directory file skipping* to ensure that (nonsensical) requests for directory files to be edited aren't honored. In contrast, POSIX sed is happy to dump the edited binary data to the user's (soon to be unreadable) screen. Like Perl, the GNU sed refuses to perform substitutions on data taken from directories, but it does so less gracefully, by issuing an error message that suggests a faulty permission setting:

---

[3] Remember, Perl's matching operator also supports arbitrary delimiters, as shown in table 3.3.

```
sed: read error on /etc: Is a directory
```

File modification means the utility can store changes in the file where the data originated, rather than having to send those changes to the output. Although POSIX versions of `sed` can't directly modify a file, GNU `sed` and Perl can both do that and even
make a backup copy of the original file for you before modifying it. But Perl wins over
GNU `sed` in this category because it allows an automatically updated file extension to
be used on the backed-up file, for greater reliability (see section 4.7.3).

In summary, table 4.1 shows that Perl has the richest collection of text-editing
capabilities, with the GNU version of `sed` coming in second, the POSIX version third,
and the classic `sed` last.

But before you can begin to realize Perl's benefits as a premier text-processing utility, you must first learn to use it for performing simple text substitutions, which we'll
discuss next.

4.3 PERFORMING SUBSTITUTIONS

Several Unix utilities can be used to replace one string of text with another. Text substitutions are performed in `sed` using a <u>*substitution command*</u>:

```
sed            's/RE/replacement/g'  file1 file2 ...
```

The Perl equivalent uses the <u>*substitution operator*</u>, in a command of this form:

```
perl -wpl -e   's/RE/replacement/g;' file1 file2 ...
```

And the `vi` editor's <u>substitution command</u> for modifying the current line is

```
            :s/RE/replacement/g
```

Notice the similarity? It's no accident that Perl's syntax is nearly identical to that of
`sed` and `vi`. Larry, in his wisdom, designed it that way, to facilitate your migration
to Perl.

In each of these three commands, the `s` before the initial slash indicates that a
substitution is being requested, *RE* is a placeholder for the regex of interest, and the
slashes delimit the *search string* and the *replacement string*. The trailing `g` after the
third slash means *global*; it requests that all possible substitutions be performed,
rather than just the leftmost one on each line. (You almost always want that behavior, so in Minimal Perl we use the `g` there by default and omit it only where it
would spoil the command.)

As with all `sed`-like Perl commands, the one shown here uses the Primary Option
Cluster that's appropriate for "Input processing," enhanced in this case for automatic
printing with the addition of the `p` option (see table 2.9).

Now let's consider a simple and practical example of the use of `sed` and Perl
for performing text substitution. The purpose of the following commands is to edit

the output of `date` to expand the day-name abbreviation, which makes its output more understandable:

```
$ date
Sun Dec 25 16:53:03 PDT 2005
$ date | sed            's/Sun/Sunday/g'          # sed version
Sunday Dec 25 16:53:04 PDT 2005
$ date | perl -wpl -e 's/Sun/Sunday/g;'          # Perl version
Sunday Dec 25 16:53:05 PDT 2005
```

As you can see, the `-wpl` option-cluster causes Perl to function like a `sed` substitution command.

That's all well and good, until you realize that these solutions work properly for only one day of the week! It takes seven separate editing operations to do this job properly, which would be most easily handled in `sed` using the "get commands from a file" option, `-f`, along with a file full of appropriate substitution commands:

```
$ cat expand_daynames.sed
s/Sun/Sunday/g
s/Mon/Monday/g
...  you get the idea

$ date | sed -f expand_daynames.sed  # takes commands from file
Sunday Dec 25 16:53:10 PDT 2005
```

Perl has its own ways of handling a file full of editing commands, but the most elementary and `sed`-like approach is to use multiple substitution operators:

```
$ date |
> perl -wpl -e '
>     s/\bSun\b/Sunday/g;
>     s/\bMon\b/Monday/g;
...  you get the idea
> '
Sunday Dec 25 16:53:14 PDT 2005
```

You can do as many substitutions as you want, by stacking them as shown, for execution in top-to-bottom order. But it would be more convenient to package these statements in a script:

```
$ cat expand_daynames
#! /usr/bin/perl -wpl

s/\bSun\b/Sunday/g;
s/\bMon\b/Monday/g;
...  you get the idea
```

This approach works well enough, but you'll see simpler ways to write programs that do multiple substitutions in part 2 (e.g., section 10.4.4).

In addition to allowing you to specify a delimiter of choice, Perl's substitution operator also permits you to specify a data source other than the default (`$_`). Table 4.2 shows examples of these syntax variations.

Table 4.2 Substitution operator syntax

Form [a]	Explanation
`s/RE/new/g`	Using default "/" delimiters, substitutes for all matches of the regular expression *RE* found in the `$_` variable the value *new*
`s:RE:new:g`	Same, but uses custom ":" delimiters
`$somevar =~ s/RE/new/g`	Using default "/" delimiters, substitutes for all matches of the regular expression *RE* found in the `$somevar` variable the value *new*
`$somevar =~ s:RE:new:g`	Same, but uses custom ":" delimiters

a. *RE* stands for a regular expression, and *new* stands for the string that replaces what *RE* matches. The substitution operator returns the number of substitutions it performed—*not* the modified string, as `sed` does.

As with the matching operator discussed in chapter 3, the substitution operator recognizes several modifiers that change the way it works. These modifiers, which are typed after the closing delimiter, are listed in table 4.3. Most of them also work with the matching operator, but the e modifier shown in the bottom panel is a notable exception. Its job is to evaluate the Perl code in the replacement field to generate a replacement string (as demonstrated in section 4.9.1).

Table 4.3 Substitution modifiers

Modifier	Meaning	Explanation [a]
`i`	Ignore case	Ignores case variations while matching.
`x`	Expanded mode	Permits whitespace and comments in the *RE* field.
`s`	Single-line mode	Allows the "." metacharacter to match newline.
`m`	Multi-line mode	Changes ^ and $ to match the ends of the lines within a record rather than the ends of the record.
`g`	Global	Allows multiple substitutions per record, and returns different values for scalar and list contexts (details in part 2).
`e`	Eval(uate)	Evaluates *new* as Perl code, and substitutes its result for what *RE* matches.

a. *RE* stands for a regular expression, and *new* stands for the string that replaces what *RE* matches in `s/RE/new/g`.

Table 4.4 provides examples of using the substitution operator, to help you see how the various syntax variations and modifiers are used together in actual applications. As shown in the table's last row, you can even use the `$&` variable (introduced in table 3.4) in the replacement field, to substitute for what was matched, a variation on that string.

You'll see examples of the features presented in these tables throughout the remainder of this chapter, and also in part 2.

Table 4.4   Substitution operator examples

Example	Meaning
`s/perl/Perl/;`	Substitutes "Perl" for the leftmost occurrence of "perl" in $_. Global (`/g`) substitutions are usually preferable.
`s/perl/Perl/g;`	Globally substitutes "Perl" for each occurrence of "perl" in $_.
`$oyster =~ s/perl/Perl/g;`	Globally substitutes "Perl" for each occurrence of "perl" in `$oyster`.
`$oyster =~ s/\bperl\b/'$&'/ig;`	Globally searches for the word "perl" in `$oyster`, ignoring case, and substitutes for each match that same word (via `$&`; see table 3.4) wrapped in single quotes (i.e., "'perl'" for "perl", "'PERL'" for "PERL", etc.).

We'll look next at how you can exercise more control over where substitutions are allowed to occur.

4.3.1   Performing line-specific substitutions: `sed`

The `sed` command can restrict its attentions to particular lines, specified either by a single line number or by a range of two (inclusive) line numbers separated by a comma, placed before the `s`. For example, the `sed` command in this example restricts its editing to Line 1 of a file, by using **1**`s///g` instead of the unrestricted `s///g`:

```
$ cat beatles          # notice contents of first line
# Beatles playlist, for Sun Jun  4 11:01:10 PDT 2006
...

$ sed '1s/Sun/Sunday/g' beatles
# Beatles playlist, for Sunday Jun  4 11:01:10 PDT 2006
Here Comes the Sun
...
```

The restriction of the editing operation to Line 1 allows the abbreviated month name to be processed on the heading line, while preventing "Here Comes the Sun" from getting changed into "Here Comes the Sunday" on Line 2 (a data line).

With `sed`, you can even specify a range of lines using *context addresses*, which look like two Perl matching operators separated by a comma, as in `/^Start/,/^Stop/`. But that capability is more closely associated with AWK, so we'll cover it in section 5.5.

Next, you'll see the Perl counterpart to the `sed` command that edits the first line of the `beatles` file.

4.3.2   Performing line-specific substitutions: Perl

Because Perl is more versatile than `sed`, some operations that are easily expressed in `sed` require more work to specify precisely in Perl. That may sound strange, or even backward, so let's consider an everyday analogy.

When you want to boil a cup of water, you can tell your microwave oven to cook for two minutes by punching the Minute button twice and the Start button once. That's easily specified, because it's implicit that the operation of interest is *cooking*—that's all an oven knows how to do.

However, if you want to tell your computer to do something for two minutes, instead of saying "*do your thing* for two minutes"—which works splendidly with the microwave—you have to tell the computer exactly *what* you want it do during that period, because it has numerous options.

In the case at hand, sed is like the microwave oven, and Perl is like the computer. Sometimes you have to type a bit more to get Perl to do the same thing as sed—but it's usually worth it. With that in mind, let's see how to perform substitutions on specific lines in Perl.

Although Perl doesn't support the 10,19s/*old*/*new*/g syntax of sed, it does keep track of the number of the current record (a line by default) in the special variable "$." (see table 2.2), if the n or p invocation option is used. This being the case, processing specific lines is accomplished by composing an expression that's true when the line number is in the desired range, and then using the logical and to make the operation of interest conditional on that result.

For example, the following commands perform substitutions only on specified lines, and they unconditionally print (courtesy of the p option) all lines. The result is that a selectively edited version of the file is sent to the output destination:

- Edit line 1:
  ```
  perl -wpl -e '$. == 1              and s/old/new/g;' file
  ```

- Edit lines 3–11:
  ```
  perl -wpl -e '3 <= $. and $. <= 11  and s/old/new/g;' file
  ```

- Edit lines 10–last:
  ```
  perl -wpl -e '$. > 9              and s/old/new/g;' file
  ```

The relational operators (<=, etc.) might look familiar, because they're identical to those used with certain Shell commands. They're covered in more detail in section 5.6.1.

You can see from the first example that the Perl counterpart to the earlier sed command, which edits only the heading line of the beatles file, is

```
perl -wpl -e '$. == 1 and s/Sun/Sunday/g;' beatles
```

But Perl can also perform substitutions on records bigger than a single line, as we'll discuss next.

4.3.3 Performing record-specific substitutions: Perl

Unlike sed, Perl lets you perform substitutions on arbitrarily defined *records*. Consider the following data file, called data_east:

```
Data for Eastern Region

updated: Sun Sep 18 18:40:51
checked: Mon Sep 19 00:00:01
updated: Sun Sep 25 18:40:52
checked: Mon Sep 26 00:00:00

42 56 778 001: Sun Myung
918 42 178 13: Mon Soon
86 574 09 108: Tue Hawt
```

Upper management has been making a lot of noise recently about "bold new innovations" to be announced soon, so Ashanti isn't surprised when she hears their decree that abbreviations for day names are no longer acceptable for presentations in departmental meetings. So before her next weekly meeting, she needs to expand those suddenly taboo day-name abbreviations in the data_east file.

One apparent complication is that there could be any number of "updated/checked" lines in the file, which are the lines with the day-name abbreviations. On the other hand, they're all guaranteed to be in the same chunk of text that's separated by one or more blank lines from the others—and that coincides perfectly with Perl's definition of a paragraph.

Sun, Mon, and Tue in paragraph 3 are people's names—*not* day-name abbreviations—so only paragraph 2 needs to be modified. Accordingly, Ashanti composes the following command to <u>expand</u> its abbreviations:

```
$ perl -00 -wpl -e '$. == 2 and s/\bSun\b/Sunday/g;
>                   $. == 2 and s/\bMon\b/Monday/g;' data_east
Data for Eastern Region

updated: Sunday Sep 18 18:40:51
checked: Monday Sep 19 00:00:01
updated: Sunday Sep 25 18:40:52
checked: Monday Sep 26 00:00:00

42 56 778 001: Sun Myung
918 42 178 13: Mon Soon
86 574 09 108: Tue Hawt
```

The use of -00 enables paragraph mode (see table 2.1), and the equality tests (==) on the values of the "$." variable select the record of interest. Note that the occurrences of Sun and Mon in paragraph 2 were modified as desired, while those in paragraph 3 were correctly exempted from editing.

Now all Ashanti needs to do is run the command again with output redirected to the printer, and she'll be ready for the meeting.

Line and record numbers are also commonly used in connection with selective printing, which we'll discuss next.

4.3.4 Using backreferences and numbered variables in substitutions

Like `grep` (see table 3.8), `sed` recognizes parentheses as literal characters unless they're backslashed, which turns them into parentheses that capture what's matched by the regex between them. In contrast, Perl's parentheses are of the capturing type *unless* they're backslashed, which converts them to literal characters.[4]

The regex notation common to `grep` and `sed` allows you to use numbered backreferences such as \1 and \2 to refer to the captured matches. Although you can use these backreferences in both the search and replacement fields of `sed`'s substitution command, with Perl's substitution operator they work only in the search field; however, you can use their dollar-prefixed relatives ($1, $2, etc.) in the replacement field—and elsewhere in the program too!

Backreferences and numbered variables are useful in substitutions where you need to interject new text between words that match patterns. For example, consider these `sed` and Perl solutions to the problem of inserting an individual's personal name between his (occasionally dotted) title and (variously spelled) surname:

```
$ cat invite                  # Note Mr. vs Mr, and Bean vs. Been
Mr. Bean hereby requests the company of his noble
companion, Teddy, for high tea today with Mr Been.
$ sed        's/\(Mr\.\) \(Be[ea]n\)/\1 Jelly \2/g;' invite
Mr. Jelly Bean hereby requests the company of his noble
companion, Teddy, for high tea today with Mr Been.
$ perl -wpl -e        's/(Mr\.) (Be[ea]n)/$1 Jelly $2/g;' invite
... (same output)
```

Note the backslashing of parentheses and numbered backreferences with `sed` versus the use of plain parentheses and dollar variables with `perl`.

In addition, it's noteworthy that only one substitution was performed by each command, due to the lack of a period after the second occurrence of "Mr". But Perl can treat that period as optional and perform the second substitution, because—unlike `sed`—it supports the "?" metacharacter (see table 3.9):

```
$ perl -wpl -e    's/(Mr\.?) (Be[ea]n)/$1 Jelly $2/g;'  invite
Mr. Jelly Bean hereby requests the company of his noble
companion, Teddy, for high tea today with Mr Jelly Been.
```

Now, we'll turn our attention to another popular use of `sed`, which doesn't involve substitutions.

---

[4] To keep your mind from boggling, Perl's policy is simply this—*any* backslashed symbol is *always* treated as a literal character.

4.4 PRINTING LINES BY NUMBER

Besides performing substitutions, sed is also used to print (i.e., *display*) lines by number. After we review how that's done, we'll discuss alternative Perl techniques that go beyond sed's capabilities.

4.4.1 Printing lines by number: sed

The second most common use of sed in contemporary computing is to extract and print an arbitrary range of lines from a file (or from STDIN).[5] This requires the use of sed's n option, which means "no automatic printing" (as in Perl), along with the p modifier, which selectively prints the lines specified by the range expression. You can use the special character $ to represent the last line (as in ed and vi).

For example, here's how to skip over the heading line from the beatles file ("Beatles playlist") and print the song titles only, using sed:

```
$ sed -n '2,$p' beatles          # omit line #1
Here Comes the Sun
Norwegian Wood
Something
Let it Be
```

Next, you'll see how this is accomplished in Perl.

4.4.2 Printing lines by number: Perl

Printing lines by number is accomplished in the same general way as the line-specific editing discussed earlier. The only differences are that automatic-printing is disabled (i.e., the n option is used rather than p) and a print function is made conditional on the test of the line number, rather than a substitution operator.

As an illustration, the following commands print specific lines from a file:

```
perl -wnl -e '$. == 1              and print;'  F   # line 1
perl -wnl -e '3 <= $. and $. <= 11 and print;'  F   # lines 3-11
perl -wnl -e '$. > 9               and print;'  F   # lines 10-last
```

Given this background, here's the Perl counterpart for the earlier sed example that omits the heading line from the beatles file:

```
$ perl -wnl -e '$. >= 2 and print;' beatles       # omit line #1
Here Comes the Sun
...
```

Next, you'll learn how Perl can be used to print records larger than a single line.

---

[5] Although the head and tail commands are also of some use in this regard, they're specialized to respectively extract the first or last *N* lines. In contrast, you can tell sed to extract, e.g., lines 3–17.

4.4.3　Printing records by number: Perl

As discussed in table 2.1 and demonstrated in section 4.3.3, to operate on records larger than the default of a single line, you can change Perl's record definition using the -0*digits* option.

Consider these variations on the commands shown earlier, which also work by changing the record definition and testing the "$." variable to select the records of interest. Because of the -0777 option, the first example prints a specified *file* rather than a *line*, and the second one prints a specified range of paragraphs rather than a range of lines.

- File mode:
  ```
  perl -0777 -wnl -e '$. == 2              and print;' f1 f2
  ```

- Paragraph mode:
  ```
  perl -00   -wnl -e '3 <= $. and $. <= 11 and print;' f1 f2
  ```

Now that you know how to duplicate sed's most common uses in Perl, we'll use this knowledge in the rest of this chapter to handle typical text processing tasks.

First, we'll discuss how you can write programs that modify *templates*. This technique can be used in many ways, including the personalization of form letters, the generation of web pages, and even the customization of Perl programs.

4.5　MODIFYING TEMPLATES

In this section, you'll see how Perl's substitution operator can be used to convert *templates* containing placeholders into customized documents. This kind of text processing can also be done with sed, but Perl has certain advantages. I'll present this topic by telling you how I came to need a simple template processor at one time, and then we'll discuss the code that implemented it.

For the first six years since its formation in early 1998, I had the privilege of running the Seattle Perl Users Group (SPUG), one of the first, biggest, and most active PUGs on the planet.[6]

How active were we during this period? Well, we always had one technical meeting per month, and for an extended period, we even had *two* meetings per month. That's a lot of meetings!

Why am I telling you this? Because I am a busy guy, and I need all the help I can get to minimize my workload. That included having an easy way to automate the generation of the HTML pages needed to announce each of these hundreds of meetings. And, as you have probably guessed, my salvation was a custom Perl script.

Before I show it to you, consider its user interface, which is designed to make its invocation as foolproof as possible (although there's still quite a bit of typing). Here's

---

[6]　To learn more about SPUG, see http://TeachMePerl.com/interviews/tmp_com_interview.html and http://seattleperl.org.

the command I issued to prepare the announcement for one especially significant meeting that featured long-time SPUG member Brian "Ingy" Ingerson, a prolific contributor of highly creative modules to the CPAN archive:

```
$ make_meeting_page -title='Kwiki' -speaker='Brian Ingerson' \
> -contact='ingy@ttul.org' \
> -date='September Meeting; Tuesday, 9/16/03:' \
> -summary='Ingy will talk about "Kwiki".' meeting.tmpl > 0903.html
```

As discussed in chapter 2, an argument of the form -title='Kwiki' causes the variable $title to take on the value of Kwiki inside the script, when the s invocation option is included on the shebang line (see table 2.5).

The script modifies a copy of meeting.tmpl (a *template*) to replace occurrences of special *placeholders* with the contents of their associated variables. In particular, %%TITLE%% is replaced with the contents of $title (which is Kwiki), %%CONTACT%% is replaced with the contents of $contact (ingy@ttul.org), and so forth. Then, via a redirection request to the Shell, the modified template is stored in a file (0903.html).

Here's the template file used in the previous command, which is a simplified version of the one used by SPUG:

```
$ cat meeting.tmpl
<H2> <I> %%DATE%% </I> </H2>
<CENTER>
<H1><B> "%%TITLE%%" </B></H1><P>
    <B> %%SPEAKER%% </B><BR>
        %%CONTACT%% <P>
    <P> %%SUMMARY%% <P>
</CENTER>
```

And here's the output generated by the invocation of the script shown earlier:

```
$ cat 0903.html
<H2> <I> September Meeting; Tuesday, 9/16/03: </I> </H2>
<CENTER>
<H1><B> "Kwiki" </B></H1><P>
    <B> Brian "Ingy" Ingerson </B><BR>
        ingy@ttul.org <P>
    <P> Ingy will talk about "Kwiki". <P>
</CENTER>
```

Figure 4.1 shows how that file looks when viewed with a GUI browser.

The make_meeting_page script that modified the template to create that announcement is shown below the figure. Note that it uses the x modifier with its substitution operators, which provides for enhanced readability by allowing extra whitespace in the regex field (see table 3.6).

Figure 4.1
A SPUG meeting announcement generated by the `make_meeting_page` script from a template

September Meeting; Tuesday, 9/16/03:

"Kwiki"

Brian "Ingy" Ingerson
ingy@ttul.org

Ingy will talk about "Kwiki".

```
#! /usr/bin/perl -s -wpl
# Template processor for SPUG meeting announcement

s/ %%DATE%%      /$date/gx;
s/ %%SPEAKER%%   /$speaker/gx;
s/ %%TITLE%%     /$title/gx;
s/ %%CONTACT%%   /$contact/gx;
s/ %%SUMMARY%%   /$summary/gx;
```

As mentioned previously, the lack of an our declaration for any of the switch variables ensures that a warning is issued for any missing switch (see table 2.5). This is appropriate because all switches are mandatory for this program.

In contrast, a sed solution wouldn't be able to use automatic switch processing, let alone benefit from automatic warnings about required switches that are missing. Moreover, sed's lack of the x modifier would prevent the columnar alignment of the search and replacement fields, which enhances readability. Furthermore, Perl's more powerful regex dialect and OS portability might provide advantages, in some cases.

Has a use for a templating system already occurred to you? If not, keep this technique in mind, because sooner or later, most programmers find a way to use templating as a productivity enhancer.[7]

Next, you'll see how Perl can help people attain a better appreciation for certain odd characters in the financial world.

4.6   CONVERTING SPECIAL CHARACTERS

A *character set* is a particular mapping of numbers to characters.[8] For example, with the ASCII character set popularized by UNIX systems, 65 means A, 13 means carriage return, and 32 means space. Or, if you want to use octal (base 8) numbers instead of

---

[7]   If your needs go beyond the rudimentary capabilities of the example shown, consider using Perl's freely available Template Toolkit. See http://search.cpan.org/dist/Template-Toolkit for documentation, and type install Template to the CPAN shell to install the software.

[8]   See man ascii (or perhaps man ASCII, on your system) for a complete listing of the ASCII characters and their numeric values.

decimal (base 10) ones, those characters are represented as 101, 015, and 040, respectively. A special group of characters—called *control characters*—are variations on other characters that affect the way devices work. For example, Ctrl-I makes your screen's cursor jump to the next tab stop, and Ctrl-L causes a printer to eject the current page.

As mentioned in table 4.1, Perl, unlike sed, can represent control characters through special codes, such as their numeric values in the character set. This is useful because special characters cause trouble when they reside within a script, due to their propensity to alter the display attributes of the terminal during editing, or to affect printer operations during printing.

I subscribe to a financial newsletter that is delivered to me via email, in plain text. More precisely, although the text *should* be plain, it's not quite plain enough. For some reason, certain characters within the newsletter are always encoded improperly for my viewing purposes. These include apostrophes, and left and right variations on double quotes, which are meant to look like "this". Instead of looking as they should, those characters are represented by my favorite mail reader (mutt) as the strings \223 and \224, and within my standard editor (vim) as ˜ S and ˜ T (representing Ctrl-S and Ctrl-T).

With a little effort, I could figure out how to get mutt to use the appropriate character set when displaying these emails; but I've never bothered to try, because it's easy to fix this with a tiny Perl script. I can tell by the context which characters those funny sequences are meant to represent, so all I have to do is set up the appropriate substitutions to convert them accordingly:

```
$ cat fix_newsletter⁹
#! /usr/bin/perl -wpl

s/\222/'/g;        # apostrophe
s/\223/"/g;        # replacement for LHS of "smart-quote" DQ pair
s/\224/"/g;        # same replacement for RHS of "smart-quote" DQ pair
```

In the first substitution operator, the *string escape* \222 (see table 3.1) tells Perl to look for characters in the current line that have that octal value and to convert them all (via the g modifier) to apostrophes. The other two substitutions replace the left and right double quotes (" and ") with their common ASCII equivalent, which is a straight double quote (").

Armed with this script, I can read a newsletter using this kind of command:

```
fix_newsletter september.txt | more
```

Perl also allows a control character to be represented as \c followed by its associated visible character, allowing, for instance, Ctrl-D to be represented by \cD. This allowed me to come up with a more readable way to write the script's substitutions, after consulting man ascii:

---

⁹ LHS and RHS, respectively, stand for left- and right-hand-side, and DQ stands for double quotes.

```
s/\cR/'/g;          # apostrophe
s/\cS/"/g;          # LHS of "smart-quote" DQ pair
s/\cT/"/g;          # RHS of "smart-quote" DQ pair
```

These techniques for representing characters also work on the replacement side of the substitution operator, as indicated in the following program, which converts each instance of a tab character (\t) at the beginning of a line to a series of four spaces:[10]

```
perl -wpl -e 's/^\t/\040\040\040\040/g;' file
```

This representation is helpful, because once you memorize the association between \040 and the space character, a command like that one is easier to comprehend than one with the corresponding whitespace characters embedded directly in it:

```
perl -wpl -e 's/^    /    /g;' file     # What's going on?
```

Because the programmer issuing that command pressed the actual keys to generate the inscrutable whitespace characters, you can't tell if the command is meant to replace initial space characters by one or two tabs, an initial tab by a bunch of spaces, or something else. In contrast, using \040 or \t would have made the programmer's intentions clear.

Another common type of character conversion is *changing case* from upper to lower, or the reverse. Although that isn't a chore traditionally performed by sed, it's easily done with Perl's substitution operator; we'll cover that topic later in this chapter (section 4.8).

Keep in mind that the results of all the editing operations in the preceding examples appear only on the *screen*—not in the original file. Although sed has historically lacked the capability of storing its output in the original file, that's easy to accomplish in Perl, as you'll see next.

4.7   EDITING FILES

In the examples thus far, you've seen how to read data from a file, make modifications, and send the results to the output. But it's often desirable to have the modifications appear in the original file itself, rather than in an output stream flowing to the screen or to a different file. Accordingly, you'll learn how to do *in-place editing* with Perl next.

4.7.1   Editing with commands

Sometimes, companies behave strangely. And when they do, they usually say, "The lawyers made us do it!" Imagine, if you will, that one day at work while you're minding your own business, the following message appears in your email:

---

[10] It's a good practice to left-pad small octal numbers with leading zeroes to form three digits, to eliminate potential ambiguities that could otherwise cause problems.

```
****************************************************************************
                                 ! URGENT !
                   NEW CORPORATE DECREE ON TERMINOLOGY (CDT)
****************************************************************************
```

Headquarters (HQ) has just informed us that, as of today, all company documents must henceforth use the word "trousers" instead of the (newly politically incorrect) "pants." All IT employees should immediately make this Document Conversion Operation (DCO) their top priority (TP).

The Office of Corporate Decree Enforcement (OCDE) will be scanning all computer files for compliance starting tomorrow, and for each document that's found to be in violation, the responsible parties will be forced to forfeit their Free Cookie Privileges (FCPs) for one day.

So please comply with HQ's CDT on the TP DCO, ASAP, before the OCDE snarfs your FCPs.

```
****************************************************************************
```

What's that thundering sound?

Oh, it's just the `sed` users stampeding toward the snack room to load up on free cookies while they still can. It's prudent of them to do so, because most versions of `sed` have historically lacked a provision for saving its output in the original file! In consequence, some extra I/O wrangling is required, which should generally be scripted—which means fumbling with an editor, removing the inevitable bugs from the script, accidentally introducing new bugs, and so forth.

Meanwhile, back at your workstation, you, as a Perl aficionado, can Lazily compose a test-case using the file in which you have wisely been accumulating pant-related phrases, in preparation for this day:

```
$ cat pantaloony
WORLDWIDE PANTS
SPONGEBOB SQUAREPANTS
```

Now for the semi-magical Perl incantation that's made to order for this pants-to-trousers upgrade:

```
$ perl -i.bak -wpl -e 's/\bPANTS\b/TROUSERS/ig;' pantaloony
$ cat pantaloony
WORLDWIDE TROUSERS
SPONGEBOB SQUAREPANTS
```

It worked. Your Free Cookie Privileges might be safe after all!

Why did the changes appear in the file, rather than only on the screen? Because the `i` invocation option, which enables *in-place editing*, causes each input file (in this case, `pantaloony`) to become the destination for its own filtered output. That means it's critical when you use the `n` option not to forget to `print`, or else the input file will end up empty! So I recommend the use of the `p` option in this kind of program, to make absolutely sure the vital `print` gets executed automatically for each record.

CHAPTER 4   *PERL AS A (BETTER)* sed *COMMAND*

But what's that `.bak` after the `i` option all about? That's the (arbitrary) filename extension that will be applied to the backup copy of each input file. Believe me, that safeguard comes in handy when you accidentally use the n option (rather than p) and forget to `print`.

Note also the use of the `i` match modifier on the substitution (introduced in table 3.6), which allows PANTS in the regex to match "pants" in the input (which is another thing most `sed`s can't do[11]).

Now that you have a test case that works, all it takes is a slight alteration to the original command to handle lots of files rather than a single one:

```
$ perl -i.bak -wpl -e 's/\bPANTS\b/TROUSERS/ig;' *
$                # all done!
```

Do you see the difference? It's the use of "*", the filename-generation metacharacter, instead of the specific filename `pantaloony`. This change causes all (non-hidden) files in the current directory to be presented as arguments to the command.

Mission accomplished! Too bad the snack room is out of cookies right now, but don't despair, you'll be enjoying cookies for the rest of the week—at least, the ones you don't sell to the newly snack-deprived `sed` users at exorbitant prices.[12]

Before we leave this topic, I should point out that there aren't many IT shops whose primary business activities center around the PC-ification of corporate text files. At least, not yet. Here's a more representative example of the kind of mass editing activity that's happening all over the world on a regular basis:

```
$ cd HTML      # 1,362 files here!
$ perl -i.bak -wpl -e 's/pomalus\.com/potamus.com/g;' *.html
$                # all done!
```

It's certainly a lot easier to let Perl search through all the web server's `*.html` files to change the old domain name to the new one, than it is to figure out which files need changing and edit each of them by hand.

Even so, this command isn't as easy as it could be, so you'll learn next how to write a generic file-editing script in Perl.

4.7.2   Editing with scripts

It's tedious to remember and retype commands frequently—even if they're one-liners—so soon you'll see a *scriptified* version of a generic file-changing program.

But first, let's look at some sample runs so you can appreciate the program's user interface, which lets you specify the search string and its replacement with a convenient `-old='old'` and `-new='new'` syntax:

---

[11] The exception is, of course, GNU `sed`, which has appropriated several useful features from Perl in recent years.

[12] This rosy scenario assumes you remembered to delete the `*.bak` files after confirming that they were no longer needed and before the OCDE could spot any "pants" within them!

```
$ change_file -old='\bALE\b'  -new='LONDON-STYLE ALE' items
$ change_file -old='\bHEMP\b' -new='TUFF FIBER'        items
```

You can't see the results, because they went back into the items file. Note the use of the \b metacharacters in the *old* strings to require word boundaries at the appropriate points in the input. This prevents undesirable results, such as changing "WHITER SHADE OF P<u>ALE</u>" into "WHITER SHADE OF P<u>LONDON-STYLE ALE</u>".

The change_file script is very simple:

```
#! /usr/bin/perl -s -i.bak -wpl
# Usage: change_file -old='old' -new='new' [f1 f2 ...]

s/$old/$new/g;
```

The s option on the shebang line requests the automatic *switch processing* that handles the command-line specifications of the *old* and *new* strings and loads the associated $old and $new variables with their contents. The omission of the our declarations for those variables (as detailed in table 2.5) marks both switches as mandatory.

In part 2 you'll see more elaborate scripts of this type, which provide the additional benefits of allowing case insensitivity, paragraph mode, and in-place editing to be controlled through command line switches.

Next, we'll examine a script that would make a handy addition to any programmer's toolkit.

The insert_contact_info script

Scripts written on the job that serve a useful purpose tend to become popular, which means somewhere down the line somebody will have an idea for a useful extension, or find a bug. Accordingly, to facilitate contact between users and authors, it's considered a good practice for each script to provide its author's contact information.

Willy has written a program that inserts this information into scripts that don't already have it, so let's watch as he demonstrates its usage:

```
$ cd ~/bin              # go to personal bin directory
$ insert_contact_info -author='Willy Nilly, willy@acme.com' change_file

$ cat change_file       # 2nd line just added by above command
#! /usr/bin/perl -s -i.bak -wpl
# Author: Willy Nilly, willy@acme.com
# Usage: change_file -old='old' -new='new' [f1 f2...]

s/$old/$new/g;
```

For added user friendliness, Willy has arranged for the script to generate a helpful "Usage" message when it's invoked without the required -author switch:

```
$ insert_contact_info some_script
Usage: insert_contact_info -author='Author info' f1 [f2...]
```

The script tests the `$author` variable for emptiness in a `BEGIN` block, rather than in the body of the program, so that improper invocation can be detected before input processing (via the implicit loop) begins:

```
#! /usr/bin/perl -s -i.bak -wpl
# Inserts contact info for script author after shebang line

BEGIN {
    $author  or
        warn "Usage: $0 -author='Author info' f1 [f2 ...]\n"  and
            exit 255;
}
# Append contact-info line to shebang line
$. == 1  and
    s|^#!.*/bin/.+$|$&\n# Author: $author|g;
```

Willy made the substitution conditional on the current line being the first and having a shebang sequence, because he doesn't want to modify files that aren't scripts. If that test yields a True result, a substitution operator is attempted on the line. Because the pathname he's searching for (`/bin/`) contains slashes, using the customary slash also as the field-delimiter would require those interior slashes to be backslashed. So, Willy wisely chose to avoid that complication by using the vertical bar as the delimiter instead.

The regex looks for the shebang sequence (`#!`) at the beginning of the line, followed by the longest sequence of anything (`.*`; see table 3.10) leading up to `/bin/`. Willy wrote it that way because on most systems, whitespace is optional after the "`!`" character, and all command interpreters reside in a `bin` directory. This regex will match a variety of paths—including the commonplace `/bin/`, `/local/bin/`, and `/usr/local/bin/`—as desired.

After matching `/bin/` (and whatever's before it), the regex grabs the longest sequence of something (`.+`; see table 3.10) leading up to the line's end (`$`). The "`+`" quantifier is used here rather than the earlier "`*`" because there must be at least one additional character after `/bin/` to represent the filename of the interpreter.

If the entire first line of the script has been successfully matched by the regex, it's replaced by itself (through use of `$&`; see table 3.4) followed by a newline and then a comment incorporating the contents of the `$author` switch variable. The result is that the author's information is inserted on a new line after the script's shebang line.

Apart from performing the substitution properly, it's also important that all the lines of the original file are sent out to the new version, whether modified or not. Willy handles this chore by using the `p` option to automate that process. He also uses the `-i.bak` option cluster to ensure that the original version is saved in a file having a `.bak` extension, as a precautionary measure.

We'll look next at a way to make regexes more readable.

Adding commentary to a regex

The `insert_contact_info` script is a valuable tool, and it shows one way to make practical use of Perl's editing capabilities. But I wouldn't blame you for thinking that the regex we just scrutinized was a bit hard on the eyes! Fortunately, Perl programmers can alleviate this condition through judicious use of the `x` modifier (see table 4.3), which allows arbitrary whitespace and comments to be included in the search field to make the regex more understandable.

As a case in point, `insert_contact_info2` rephrases the substitution operator of the original version, illustrating the benefits of embedding commentary within the regex field. Because the substitution operator is spread over several lines in this new version, the delimiters are shown in bold, to help you spot them:

```
# Rewrite shebang line to append contact info
$. == 1 and
# The expanded version of this substitution operator follows below:
#      s|^#!.*/bin/.+$|$&\n# Author: $author|g;
 s|
    ^           # start match at beginning of line
    \#!         # shebang characters
    .*          # optionally followed by anything; including nothing
    /bin/       # followed by a component of the interpreter path
    .+          # followed by the rest of the interpreter path
    $           # up to the end of line
 |$&\n\# Author: $author|gx; # replace by match, \n, author stuff
```

Note that the "#" in the "#!" shebang sequence needs to be backslashed to remove its x-modifier-endowed meaning as a comment character, as does the "#" symbol before the word "Author" in the replacement field.

It's important to understand that the `x` modifier relaxes the syntax rules for the search field *only* of the substitution operator—the one where the regex resides. That means you must take care to avoid the mistake of inserting whitespace or comments in the *replacement* field in an effort to enhance its readability, because they'll be taken as literal characters there.[13]

Before we leave the `insert_contact_info` script, we should consider whether `sed` could do its job. The answer is *yes*, but `sed` would need help from the Shell, and the result wouldn't be as straightforward as the Perl solution. Why? Because you'd have to work around `sed`'s lack of the following features: the "+" metacharacter, automatic switch processing, in-place editing, and the enhanced regex format.

As useful as the `-i.bak` option is, there's a human foible that can undermine the integrity of its backup files. You'll learn how to compensate for it next.

---

[13] An exception is discussed in section 4.9—when the `e` modifier is used, the replacement field contains Perl statements, whose readability can be enhanced through arbitrary use of whitespace.

4.7.3 Safeguarding in-place editing

The origins of the problem we'll discuss next are mysterious. It may be due to the unflagging optimism of the human spirit. Or maybe it's because certain types of behavior, as psychologists tell us, are especially susceptible to being promoted by "intermittent reinforcement schedules." Or it may even be traceable to primal notions of luck having the power to influence events, passed down from our forebears.

In any case, for one reason or another, many otherwise rational programmers are inclined to run a misbehaving program a second time, *without changing anything*, in the hope of a more favorable outcome. I know this because I've seen students do it countless times during my training career. I even do this myself on occasion—not on purpose, but through inadvertent finger-fumbling that extracts and reruns the wrong command from the Shell's history list.

This human foible makes it unwise to *routinely* use .bak as the file extension for your in-place-editing backup files. Why is that a problem? Because if your program neglects to print anything back to its input file, and then you run it a second time, you'll end up trashing the first (and probably only) backup file you've got!

Here's a sample session that illustrates the point, using the nl command to number the lines of the files:

```
$ echo UNIX > os      # create a file
$ nl os
     1  UNIX

$ perl -i.bak -wnl -e 's/UNIX/Linux/g;' os   # original os -> os.bak

$ nl os        # original file now empty; printing was omitted!
$ nl os.bak    # but backup is intact
     1  UNIX

# Now for the misguided 2nd run—in the spirit of a
# "Hail Mary pass"—in a vain attempt to fix the "os" file:
$ perl -i.bak -wnl -e 's/UNIX/Linux/g;' os    # empty os -> os.bak!

$ nl os        # original file still empty
$ nl os.bak    # backup of original now empty too!
$              # Engage PANIC MODE!
```

The mistake is in the use of the error-prone n option in this sed-like command rather than the generally more appropriate p. That latter option automatically prints each (potentially modified) input record back to the original file when the i option is used, thereby preventing the programmer from neglecting that operation and accidentally making the file empty.

Next, you'll see how to avoid damage to backup files when running Perl commands.

Clobber-proofing backup files in commands: *$SECONDS*

For commands typed interactively to a Shell, I recommend using -i.$SECONDS instead of -i.bak to enable in-place editing. This arranges for the age in seconds of your current Korn or Bash shell, which is constantly ticking higher, to become the extension on the backup file.

For comparison, here's a (corrected) command like the earlier one, along with its enhanced counterpart that uses $SECONDS:

```
perl -i.bak      -wpl -e 's/RE/something/g;' file
perl -i.$SECONDS -wpl -e 's/RE/something/g;' file
```

The benefit is that a different file extension will be used for each run,[14] thereby preventing the clobbering of earlier backups when a dysfunctional program is run a second time.

With this technique, you're free to make a common mistake without jeopardizing the integrity of your backup file—or your job security. (Just make sure your Shell provides $SECONDS first, by typing echo $SECONDS a few times and confirming that the number increases each second.)

This technique works nicely for commands, but you should use a different one for scripts, as we'll discuss next.

Clobber-proofing backup files in scripts: *$$*

For scripts that do in-place editing, I recommend an even more robust technique for avoiding the reuse of backup-filename extensions and protecting against backup-file *clobberation*. Instead of providing a file extension after the i option, as in -i.bak, you should use the option alone and set the special variable $^I to the desired file extension in a BEGIN block.[15]

Why specify the extension in the variable? Because this technique lets you obtain a unique extension during execution that isn't available for inclusion with -i at the time you type the shebang line. The value that's best to use is the script's Process-ID number (PID), which is uniquely associated with it and available from the $$ variable (in both the Shell and Perl).

Here's a corrected and scriptified version of the command shown earlier, which illustrates the technique:

```
#! /usr/bin/perl -i -wpl

BEGIN { $^I=$$; }        # Use script's PID as file extension

s/UNIX/Linux/g;
```

---

[14] More specifically, this technique protects the earlier backup as long as you wait until the *next second* before rerunning the command. So if you do feel like running a command a second time in the hope of a better result, don't be too quick to launch it!

[15] Incidentally, the .bak argument in -i.bak winds up in that variable anyway.

Note, however, that the use of $$ isn't appropriate for *commands*:

```
$ perl -wpl -i.$$ -e 's/UNIX/Linux/g;' os
```

In cases like this, $$ is a Shell variable that accesses the PID of the Shell itself; because that PID will be the same if the command is run a second time, backup-file clobberation will still occur. In contrast, a new process with a new PID is started for each script, making Perl's automatically updated $$ variable the most appropriate backup-file extension for use within in-place editing scripts.

4.8   CONVERTING TO LOWERCASE OR UPPERCASE

Perl provides a set of *string modifiers* that can be used in double quoted strings or the replacement field of a substitution operator to effect uppercase or lowercase conversions. They're described in table 4.5.

Table 4.5   String modifiers for case conversion

Modifier	Meaning	Effect [a]
\U	Uppercase all	Converts the string on the right to uppercase, stopping at \E or the string's end.
\u	Uppercase next	Converts the character on the right to uppercase.
\L	Lowercase all	Converts the string on the right to lowercase, stopping at \E or the string's end.
\l	Lowercase next	Converts the character on the right to lowercase.
\E	End case conversion	Terminates the case conversion started with \U or \L (optional).

a. String modifiers work only in certain contexts, including double-quoted strings, and matching and substitution operators. Modifiers occurring in sequence (e.g., "\u\L$name") are processed from right to left.

You'll now learn how to perform a character-case conversion, which will be demonstrated using a chunk of text that may look familiar.

4.8.1   Quieting spam

Email can be frustrating! It's bad enough that your in-box is jam-packed with messages promising to enlarge your undersized body parts, transfer fortunes from Nigerian bank accounts to yours, and give you great deals on previously-owned industrial shipping containers.

But to add insult to injury, these messages are typically rendered ENTIRELY IN UPPERCASE, which is the typographical equivalent of *shouting!* So, in addition to being deceitful, these messages are rude—and they need to be taught some manners.

Unfortunately, the sed command isn't well suited to this task.[16] For one thing, it doesn't allow case conversion to be expressed on a mass basis—only in terms of

---

[16] The Unix tr command can be used to convert text to lowercase, as can the built-in Perl function by the same name. However, because this chapter focuses on Perl equivalents to sed, we'll discuss an easy Perl solution based on the use of the substitution operator instead.

specific character substitutions, such as `s/A/a/g` and `s/B/b/g`. That means you'd have to run 26 separate global substitution commands against each line of text in order to convert all of its letters.

Perl provides a much easier approach, based on its ability to match an entire line and do a mass conversion of all its characters. The following example, which converts a fragment of a typical spam message to lowercase, illustrates the technique:

```
$ cat make_money_fast
LEARN TO MAKE MONEY FAST!

JUST REPLY WITH YOUR CREDIT CARD INFORMATION,
AND WE WILL TAKE CARE OF THE REST!

$ perl -wpl -e 's/^.*$/\L$&/g;' make_money_fast
learn to make money fast!

just reply with your credit card information,
and we will take care of the rest!
```

How does it work? The substitution operator is told to match anything (`.*`) found between the line's beginning (`^`) and its end (`$`)—in other words, the whole current line (see table 3.10). Then, it replaces what was just matched with that same string, obtained from the special match variable `$&` (see table 3.4), after converting it to lowercase (`\L`). In this way, each line is replaced by its lowercased counterpart.

`\L` is one of Perl's string modifiers (see table 4.5). The uppercase metacharacters (`\L` and `\U`) modify the rest of the string, or up until a `\E` (end) marker, if there is one. The lowercase modifiers, on the other hand, affect only the immediately following character.

Are you starting to see why Perl is considered the best language for text processing? Good! But we've barely scratched the surface of Perl's capabilities, so stay tuned—there's much more to come.

4.9   SUBSTITUTIONS WITH COMPUTED REPLACEMENTS

This section shows programs that employ more advanced features, such as the use of calculations and functions to derive the replacement string for the substitution operator. How special is that? So special that no version of `sed` can even *dream* about doing what you'll see next!

We'll explain first how to convert miles to kilometers and then how to replace each tab in text with the appropriate number of spaces, using Perl substitution operators. Along the way, you'll learn a powerful technique that lets you replace matched text by a string that's generated with the help of any of the resources in Perl's arsenal.

4.9.1   Converting miles to kilometers

Like the Unix shells, Perl has a built-in `eval` function that you can use to execute a chunk of code that's built during execution. A convenient way to invoke `eval` is through use of the e modifier to the substitution operator (introduced in table 4.3), like so:

```
s/RE/code/e;
```

This tells Perl to replace whatever *RE* matches with the *computed result* of code. This allows for replacement strings to be generated on the fly during execution, which is a tremendously useful feature.

Consider the following data file that shows the driving distances in miles between three Canadian cities:

```
$ cat drive_dist
           Van         Win         Tor
Vancouver  0           1380        2790
Winnipeg   1380        0           1300
Toronto    2790        1300        0
```

Those figures may be fine for American tourists, but they won't be convenient for most Europeans, who are more comfortable thinking in kilometers. To help them, Heidi has written a script called m2k, which extracts each mileage figure, calculates its corresponding value in kilometers, and then replaces the mileage figure with the kilometer one. Here's the output from a sample run:

```
$ m2k drive_dist
Driving Distance in Kilometers
           Van         Win         Tor
Vancouver  0           2208        4464
Winnipeg   2208        0           2080
Toronto    4464        2080        0
```

Note that Heidi labeled the output figures as kilometers, so readers will know how to interpret them.

Here's the m2k script—which, like much in the world of Perl, is tiny but powerful:

```
#! /usr/bin/perl -wpl

BEGIN { print "Driving Distance in Kilometers"; }
s/\d+/ $& * 1.6 /ge;
```

The print statement that generates the heading is enclosed within a BEGIN block to ensure that it's only executed once at the beginning—rather than for each input line, like the substitution operator that follows it.

The \d+ sequence matches any sequence of one or more (+) digits (\d), such as 3 and 42. (To handle numbers with decimal places as well, such as 3.14, the sequence [\d\.]+ could be used instead.)

The special match-variable $& contains the characters that were matched; by using it in the replacement field, the figure in miles gets multiplied by 1.6, with the resulting kilometer figure becoming the replacement string. The g (for global) modifier ensures that all the numbers on each line get replaced, instead of just the leftmost ones (i.e., those in the "Van" column). As usual, the p option ensures that the current line gets printed, regardless of whether any modifications have been performed—which is why the column headings, which lack numbers, are also present in the output.

Note that you're always free to insert readability-enhancing spaces in the replacement field when the e modifier is used, because it contains Perl code, not literal text.

In addition to performing arbitrary calculations to generate a replacement string, you can also make use of Perl functions, as we'll discuss next.

4.9.2   Substitutions using function results

Another way to use eval in a substitution is to replace the matched text with a transformation of that text that's provided by a function.

For example, Ramon needs to identify lines that are longer than 55 characters, because they can't be successfully printed on the cheap (but narrow) paper rolls that he gets from the Army Surplus store.

He knows about Perl's length function, which can be used to determine the length of a line. But despite his abhorrence of euphemisms, Ramon must admit there's an "issue" with using length: It counts each tab as one character, whereas the printer will treat a tab as from one to eight spaces, depending on where the tab occurs in the line. So before checking each line's length, Ramon needs to use the expand function of the standard Perl module called Text::Tabs to convert all tabs to spaces.

He finds a sample document and runs it through his new script to see what happens:

```
$ check_length ponie
** WARNING: Line 1 is too long:
        So it came to pass that The Larry blessed a Ponie, and
appointed brave Porters, armed with the Sticks of the
Riddle, to train her in the ways of Perl V and prepare
the Engine of the Parrot for Perlitus Sixtus.
```

It works! This file has been properly identified as one that needs to be reformatted to fit on the paper, due to its first line being overly long. That adjustment can be easily accomplished using the autoformat function of Text::Autoformat (introduced in chapter 2).

The check_length script is compact, but powerful—like Ramon himself:

```
#! /usr/bin/perl -wnl

use Text::Tabs;          # provides "expand" function

s/^.*$/expand $&/ge;     # replace tabs by spaces in line

length > 55  and
    print "** WARNING:  Line $. is too long:";

print;                   # Now print the line
```

Ramon's script begins by loading the Text::Tabs module with the use directive. Then, in the substitution operator, the ".*" (longest anything) sequence in the search field matches everything between the line's beginning (^) and its end ($). That line is then replaced by the result of running expand on it (via $&), which converts its tabs to spaces. Once that's done, the length function can accurately assess the number of characters on the line, and a warning can be interjected immediately before the printing of each line that's too long.

Ramon is planning to switch to the cheaper Navy Surplus 53-column paper next week; to pave the way for that transition, he decides to replace the hard-wired 55-character specification in his script with one provided by a new -maxlength command-line switch. Being a cautious shopper, he takes care to test the new version first, before ordering a truckload of the new paper:

```
$ check_length2 -maxlength=53 ponie
** WARNING:  Line 1 is too long:
        So it came to pass that The Larry blessed a Ponie, and
appointed brave Porters, armed with the Sticks of the
** WARNING:  Line 3 is too long:
Riddle, to train her in the ways of Perl V and prepare
the Engine of the Parrot for Perlitus Sixtus.
```

Bull's-eye! This version works, too, on the first try. While Ramon is imagining how he would look wearing the "Purple Camel Award for Outstanding Achievements in Perl Programming" on his flak vest, let's take a moment to look at his new script, check_length2 (the new parts are in bold):

```
#! /usr/bin/perl -s -wnl

use Text::Tabs;          # provides "expand" function

BEGIN {
    $maxlength  or
        warn "Usage: $0 -maxlength=character_count [files]\n"  and
            exit 255;
}

s/^.*$/expand $&/ge;     # replace tabs by spaces in line

length > $maxlength  and
        print "** WARNING:  Line $. is too long:";

print;                   # Now print the line
```

Note the addition of the s option to the shebang line, and the replacement of the number 55 in the original script by the variable $maxlength. Because it's imperative that the user supply the -maxlength switch, Ramon dutifully follows orders and omits the our ($maxlength); declaration that would make it optional (in compliance with the regulations of table 2.5).

Note also that he included a $var or warn and exit condition, which ensures that the program terminates after showing a "Usage" message if the user neglects to supply the -maxlength=N option:

```
$ check_length2 ponie
Usage: check_length2 -maxlength=character_count [files]
```

In part 2, you'll see how the contents of switch variables can be tested more extensively—allowing you to ensure, for example, that a reasonable, positive, integer number is provided as the argument for the -maxlength switch.

Now that you're convinced you should do your future text processing with Perl, what should you do with all your old sed scripts? Why, convert them to Perl automatically, of course, so you can continue to develop them using a more powerful language, and gain OS portability to boot.

4.10   THE sed TO PERL TRANSLATOR

Larry has been considerate enough to provide a sed-to-perl translator with every release of Perl, which makes it easy to convert existing sed scripts into equivalent perl programs. It's valued by those having sed programs that they'd like to use on Perl-equipped but sed-less systems (such as Windows) and by others who have inherited sed scripts that they'd prefer to extend by writing the enhancements in Perl.

The translator is called s2p, for sed-to-Perl, and you may want to check it out. But don't look at the code it generates, or you'll turn into a pillar of salt, and spend the rest of your days being licked by camels!

The reason for this warning is that s2p speaks the ancient dialect of the *ancestors* of the founders of Perlistan, Perl Version 4, which has some keywords, grammatical constructs, and syntactic elements that have fallen into disuse. The code it generates can still be run by modern perl interpreters, but parts of it might look rather strange to you.

4.11   SUMMARY

Nowadays, the Unix sed command is principally used to apply predefined editing commands to text and to print lines by number. But—as you learned in this chapter—with its more powerful regex dialect, its greater flexibility in defining records, its wider variety of options for generating replacement strings, and other advantages, Perl can not only replace sed for these tasks, but also do a better job at them.

For example, you saw in the fix_newsletter script how control characters that need to be replaced by more legible ones can be conveniently specified using *NNN* string escapes with the substitution operator.

Perl's support for embedded commentary within regexes, which is enabled by adding the x modifier to the matching or substitution operator, was used to make the make_meeting_page and insert_contact_info2 scripts more readable and maintainable.

Although sed has historically lacked the ability to modify the files whose contents it edits, this is easily accomplished with Perl by using the -i.bak invocation option, as demonstrated in the change_file script and various commands (see section 4.7).

The Perl programmer's freedom to arbitrarily define what constitutes an input record allows programs to work on arbitrary units of input, such as the paragraphs that were processed by a single substitution operator in the commands of section 4.3.3, or the files processed by a single `print` statement in those of section 4.4.3.

Perl's substitution operator even allows its replacement string to be computed on the fly when the e modifier is used, as the miles-to-kilometers converter `m2k` and Ramon's `check_length` scripts demonstrated. Although the Shell has a code-evaluation facility (`eval`) like the one Perl's e modifier invokes, no mechanism is provided for using it in conjunction with the Shell's counterpart to the substitution operator—the `sed` command. Making its own code-evaluation facility so easy and convenient to use is surely one of Perl's greatest contributions.[17]

Because `sed` lacks the fundamental features that make these tasks so easy to handle in Perl, many of the Perl programs we examined in this chapter couldn't be duplicated using `sed` alone. In fact, advanced skills with the Shell and/or other utility programs would be needed to get the job done. For example, the essential service of the `make_meeting_page` script is to substitute the desired strings for placeholders of the form %%NAME%%. This is something that `sed` could do on its own, but it would need a lot of help from other quarters to duplicate the friendly switch-oriented interface that was so easily incorporated into the Perl script.

For reference purposes, table 4.6 provides a handy summary of the corresponding `sed` and `perl` commands that perform basic editing tasks, along with the locations where they're discussed in this chapter.

Table 4.6   sed and Perl commands for common editing activities

sed command	Perl counterpart [a]	Meaning	Section reference
`sed 's/RE/new/g' F`	`perl -wpl` `-e 's/RE/new/g;' F`	Attempt substitutions on all lines of F, and print all lines	4.3

`sed '3,9s/RE/new/g' F`	`perl -wpl -e '3 <= $.`
	`and $. <= 9`
	`and s/RE/new/g;' F`
		Attempt substitutions on lines 3–9 of F, and print all lines	4.3.1, 4.3.2

`sed -n '9,$p' F`	`perl -wnl -e '$. >= 9` `and print;' F`	Print the contents of F from line 9 through the last line	4.4.1, 4.4.2

`cp F F.bak`
`sed 's/RE/new/g' F > F+`
`mv F+ F`
	`perl -i.bak -wpl`
	`-e 's/RE/new/g;' F`
		Perform substitutions in the file F, after making a backup copy	4.7.1

a. If typed directly to the Shell in the format shown, each of the multi-line Perl commands would require a space-backslash sequence at the end of its non-final lines.

---

[17] What's more, Perl's Shell-inspired `eval` function can be used for much more than substitutions, as you'll see in section 8.7.

Directions for further study

To further explore the features covered in this chapter, you can issue the following commands and read the documentation they generate:

- `perldoc -f length`   *# documentation for function called length*
- `perldoc Text::Tabs`   *# documentation for "expand" function*
- `man ascii`   *# info on character sets*[18]

The following command brings up the documentation for s2p, which, unlike the scary Perl Version 4 code that s2p generates, can be viewed with impunity:

- `man s2p`   *# documentation on sed to Perl translator*

---

[18] If man ascii doesn't work on your system, try man ASCII.

CHAPTER 5

Perl as a (better) awk command

5.1 A brief history of AWK 122
5.2 Comparing basic features of awk and Perl 123
5.3 Processing fields 130
5.4 Programming with Patterns and Actions 138
5.5 Matching ranges of records 151

5.6 Using relational and arithmetic operators 157
5.7 Using built-in functions 159
5.8 Additional examples 165
5.9 Using the AWK-to-Perl translator: a2p 175
5.10 Summary 175

The awk command is surely one of the most useful in the Unix toolkit. It's even more important than grep and sed, because it can do everything they can do and more. That's to be expected, because unlike those commands, awk implements a general-purpose programming *language* (called AWK), which can handle many types of data-processing tasks.

This is why a Unix "power user" who's asked to take the time and effort to learn a new language—such as Perl—can be expected to ask, "What can it do that AWK can't?"[1]

The answer is "Plenty!", because Perl offers many enhancements over its AWKish ancestor. But before discussing those enhancements and showing you a multitude of

---

[1] For the story of the author's initial reluctance to trade in his trusty (and rusty) tools of AWK and the Korn shell for a shiny new Perl, see http://www.perlfoundation.org/pr/newsletter/2002_10-en.html and http://www.TeachMePerl.com/interviews/tmp_com_interview.html.

useful one-liners and scripts, we'll begin with a brief history of the AWK language. This will help you understand why AWK has had such a substantial influence on Perl and why it's a good idea to honor AWK by continuing to use its Pattern/Action model of programming—in Perl!

5.1   *A BRIEF HISTORY OF AWK*

AWK, like its offshoot Perl, has a diverse group of fans, including linguists, artists, scientists, actuaries, academics,[2] hackers, nerds, dorks, and dweebs, and even a few award-winning programming language designers.

I call these people AWKiologists, or, for those who are especially fervent about the language (like me), I sometimes affectionately use the term *AWKoholics*. In addition to its proponents having funny designations, AWK itself has lots of flattering and well-deserved nicknames, including "Queen of UNIX Utilities" and "Jewel in the Crown of UNIX." But it's no ivory-tower sissy, as reflected by its most macho moniker, "Swiss Army Knife of UNIX."

But what is AWK? Like Perl, it was created as an amalgamation of the capabilities of the UNIX Shell, `egrep`, and `sed`, with a little syntax from the C language thrown in for good measure. Although it has many valuable features, it's appreciated most widely for its *field-processing* capabilities, which are superior to those of its traditional competitor, the UNIX `cut` command.

The AWK language has a brilliant design that makes it remarkably easy and pleasant to use and that allows programs to be concise without being cryptic. Indeed, many AWK programs that do substantial data-processing tasks can be expressed in only a *handful* of characters. That's because the language makes certain clever assumptions about what your program will need to do, which allows you to omit much of the boilerplate code that has to be repeated over and over again in other languages.

AWK debuted with the UNIX version of 1977. But due to the governmental regulations of that era, UNIX was distributed only to the Bell System companies and a few universities and colleges. AWK went on to attract an enthusiastic population of users, but they were mostly within the Bell System itself, owing to the fact that detailed lecture/lab courses on AWK's use were provided only in that community (by my colleagues and me).

AWK was especially popular with the clerical and administrative workers of the Bell System, who were already doing a little `grep`-ing and `sed`-ing, but needed a tool for writing simple programs to do data validation, report generation, file conversion, and number crunching—without going back to college first! AWK fit that bill to a tee.

---

[2] E.g., while working in the late 1980s as a senior systems analyst at U.C. Berkeley, I was approached by a researcher about automatically grouping samples of medieval Portuguese poetry into different rhyme-scheme categories. I solved her problem with an AWK program that looked for different patterns in word endings.

Unfortunately, due to the lack of comprehensive documentation on AWK before 1984,[3] even those few outside the Bell System who *did* notice its arrival couldn't fully fathom its abilities or importance. So, despite its greatness and the reverence with which it's viewed by language experts, AWK hasn't had the degree of influence it deserved.

If that first book on AWK had come out a few years earlier, and made it possible for those outside the Bell System to fully appreciate this uniquely valuable tool, I wonder if current languages might proudly reflect ancestry from it, with names like Turbo-AWK, AWK++, Visual AWK, and perhaps even AWK#. AWK is just that good—if it had been more widely known and used early on, it might have changed programming forever.

Nowadays, many programmers still use AWK for certain kinds of programs, but they're more likely to use the *new* AWK (nawk), which came out of the Bell Labs in 1985, or GNU AWK (gawk), which first appeared in 1986, rather than the *classic* AWK of 1977.

Now that you know AWK's history, let's consider its present status. Despite all the developments that have taken place in the world of computing since AWK's emergence in 1977, there's still only one general-purpose scripting language that's better. Guess what—it's called Perl!

This is so because Larry, knowing a good thing when he saw one, incorporated almost all of AWK's features into Perl. Then he added many more, of his own devising, to make Perl even better.

We'll look at some specific comparisons of the capabilities of AWK and Perl next.

NOTE   AWK is totally AWKsome, but Perl is even better; it's Perlicious!

5.2   COMPARING BASIC FEATURES OF awk AND PERL

This section provides an overview of how AWK and Perl compare in terms of their most fundamental capabilities. Later, we'll discuss more specific differences (in built-in functions, operators, etc.) in the context of illustrative programming examples.

Due to the fact that a nearly complete[4] re-creation of an AWK-like programming environment is provided in Perl (albeit with a different syntax), there aren't many

---

[3] AWK's earliest comprehensive documentation was in *The UNIX Programming Environment* by Brian Kernighan and Rob Pike (Prentice-Hall, 1984). The first book devoted to AWK was *The Awk Programming Language* (Addison-Wesley, 1988), by AWK's creators—Al Aho, Peter Weinberger, and Brian Kernighan (hence the name).

[4] AWK does have some features Perl lacks; e.g., all AWK versions allow the field separator to be changed during execution (via the FS variable)—although I've never heard of anyone exploiting this possibility. When I asked Larry why he didn't include an FS-like variable in Perl, his typically enigmatic response was, "AWK has to be better at *something!*"

ways in which Perl can be said to beat AWK at its own game. However, Perl provides features that go well beyond those of its influential predecessor, allowing the use of AWKish programming techniques with a much wider variety of applications (e.g., networked, database-oriented, and object-oriented).

Perl also provides a richer infrastructure that makes its programmers more productive, through its module-inclusion mechanism and the availability of thousands of high-quality pre-written modules from the *Comprehensive Perl Archive Network* (CPAN; see chapter 12).

In consideration of the fact that these languages are both rightly famous for their pattern-matching capabilities, let's see how they stack up in this respect.

5.2.1 Pattern-matching capabilities

Table 5.1 lists the most important differences between noteworthy AWK versions and Perl, which pertain to their fundamental capabilities for pattern matching and related operations.[5]

The comparisons in the upper panel of table 5.1 refer to the capabilities of the different regex dialects, those in the middle to the way in which matching is performed, and those in the lower panel to other special features. By observing the increasing number of Ys as you move from Classic AWK's column to Perl's, you can see that GAWK's capabilities are a superset of AWK's, whereas Perl's capabilities are generally a superset of GAWK's.

Perl's additional capabilities are most clearly indicated in the top and bottom panels, which reflect its richer collection of regular expression metacharacters and other special features we'll cover later in this chapter.

Because AWK has inherited many characteristics from grep and sed, it's no surprise that the AWK versus Perl comparisons largely echo the findings of the grep versus Perl and sed versus Perl comparisons in earlier chapters. Most of the listed capabilities have already been discussed in chapter 3 or 4, so here we'll concentrate on the new ones: stingy matching and record-separator matching.

Stingy matching

Stingy matching is an option provided by Perl to match as little as possible—rather than as much as possible, which is the *greedy* behavior used by Unix utilities (and Perl by default). You enable it by appending a "?" to a quantifier (see table 3.9), most commonly "+", which means "one or more of the preceding."

The stingy (as in *miserly*) matching option is valued because it makes certain patterns much easier to write. For example, stingy matching lets you use ^.+?: to capture the first field of a line in the /etc/passwd file—by matching the shortest sequence starting at the beginning that ends in a colon (the field separator for that

---

[5] There's no separate column for POSIX AWK because its capabilities are duplicated in GNU AWK.

Table 5.1   Differences in pattern-matching capabilities of AWK versions and Perl

Capability [a]	Classic AWK	GAWK [b]	Perl
Word boundary metacharacter	–	Y	Y
Compact character-class shortcuts	–	?	Y
Control character representation	Y	Y	Y
Repetition ranges	–	Y	Y
Capturing parentheses and backreferences	–	? [c]	Y
Metacharacter quoting	?	?	Y
Embedded commentary	–	–	Y
Advanced RE features	–	–	Y
Stingy matching	–	–	**Y**
Record-separator matching	–	–	**Y**
Case insensitivity	–	Y	Y
Arbitrary record definitions	Y	Y+ [d]	Y
Line-spanning matches	Y	Y	Y
Binary-file processing	Y	Y	Y
Directory-file skipping	–	Y	Y+
Match highlighting	–	–	?
Custom output formatting	Y	Y	Y
Arbitrary delimiters	–	–	Y+
Access to match components	–	–	Y
Customized replacements	–	–	Y+
File modifications	–	–	Y

a. Y: has this capability; Y+: has this capability with enhancements; ?: partially has this capability; –: doesn't have this capability
b. Using POSIX-compliant features and GNU extensions
c. Works only with certain functions
d. Allows the specification of a record separator via regex

file). In contrast, many beginners would make the mistake of using the greedy pattern `^.+:` in an attempt to get the same result. This pattern matches across as many characters as needed—*including* colons—along its way to matching the required colon at the end, resulting in fields *one through six* being matched rather than only field one. Perl's ability to do stingy matching gives it an edge over AWK.

Record-separator matching

Perl's capability of *record separator matching* allows you to match a *newline* (or a custom record separator), which is not allowed by *any* of the regex-oriented Unix utilities (`grep`, `sed`, `awk`, `vi`, etc.). You could use this option, for example, to find a "Z" occurring at the end of one line that is immediately followed by an "A" at the beginning of the next line, using Z\nA as your regex. It's difficult to work around the absence of this capability when you really need it, which gives Perl an advantage over AWK (and every other Unix utility) for having it.

Now that we've compared the pattern-matching capabilities of AWK and Perl, we'll next compare the sets of *special variables* provided by the languages.

5.2.2 Special variables

Both AWK and Perl provide the programmer with a rich collection of *special variables* whose values are set automatically in response to various program activities (see table 5.2). A syntactic difference is that almost all AWK variables are named by sequences of uppercase letters, whereas most Perl variables have $-prefixed symbols for names.

The fact that Perl provides variables that correspond to AWK's $0, NR, RS, ORS, OFS, ARGV, and FILENAME attests to the substantial overlap between the languages and tells you that the AWKish programming mindset is well accommodated in Perl. For instance, after an input record has been automatically read, both languages update a special variable to reflect the total number of records that have been read thus far.

Some bad news in table 5.2 for AWKiologists is that the Perl names for variables that provide the same information are different (e.g., the record-counting variables "$." vs. NR), and the only name that is the same ($0) means something different in the languages.[6]

Table 5.2   Comparison of special variables in AWK and Perl

Modern AWKs[a]	Perl	Comments
$0	$_	AWK's $0 holds the contents of the current input record. In Perl, $0 holds the script's name, and $_ holds the current input record.
$1	$F[0]	These variables hold the first field[b] of the current input record; $2 and $F[1] would hold the second field, and so forth.
NR	$.	The "record number" variable holds the ordinal number of the most recent input record.[c] After reading a two-line file followed by a three-line file, its value is 5.

continued on next page

a. Some of the listed variables were not present in classic AWK.
b. Requires use of the n or p, and a invocation option in Perl.
c. Requires use of the n or p invocation option in Perl.

---

6 As discussed in section 2.4.4, $0 knows the name used in the Perl script's invocation and is routinely used in warn and die messages. Perl will actually let you use AWK variable names in your Perl programs (see man English), but in the long run, you're better off using the Perl variables.

Table 5.2 Comparison of special variables in AWK and Perl *(continued)*

Modern AWKs [a]	Perl	Comments
FNR	N/A	The *file-specific* "record number" variable holds the ordinal number of the most recent input record from the most recently read file. After reading a two-line file followed by a three-line file, its value is 3. In Perl programs that use eof and close ARGV,[d] "$." acts like FNR.[c]
RS	$/	The "input record separator" variable defines what constitutes the end of an input record. In AWK, it's a linefeed by default, whereas in Perl, it's an OS-appropriate default. Note that AWK allows this variable to be set to a regex, whereas in Perl it can only be set to a literal string.
ORS	$\	The "output record separator" variable specifies the character or sequence for print to append to the end of each output record. In AWK, it's a linefeed by default, whereas in Perl, it's an OS-appropriate default.
FS	N/A	AWK allows its "input field separator" to be defined via an assignment to FS or by using the -F'sep' invocation option; the former approach allows it to be set and/or changed during execution. Perl also allows the run-time setting (using the -F'sep' option) but lacks an associated variable and therefore the capability to change the input record separator during execution.
OFS	$,	The "output field separator" variable specifies the string to be used on output in place of the commas between print's arguments. In Perl, this string is also used to separate elements of arrays whose names appear unquoted in print's argument list.
NF	@F	The "number of fields" variable indicates the number of fields in the current record. Perl's @F variable is used to access the same information (see section 7.1.1).
ARGV	@ARGV	The "argument vector" variable holds the script's arguments.
ARGC	N/A	The "argument count" variable reports the script's number of arguments. In Perl, you can use $ARGC=@ARGV; to load that value into a similar variable name.
FILENAME	$ARGV	These variables contain the name of the file that has most recently provided input to the program.[c]
N/A	$&	This variable contains the last match.[e]
N/A	$`	This variable contains the portion of the matched record that comes before the beginning of the most recent match.[e]
N/A	$'	This variable contains the portion of the matched record that comes after the end of the most recent match.[e]
RSTART	N/A	This variable provides the location of the beginning of the last match. Perl uses pos()-length($&) to obtain this information.
RLENGTH	N/A	This variable provides the length in bytes of the last match. Perl uses length($&) to obtain this information.

a. Some of the listed variables were not present in classic AWK.
c. Requires use of the n or p invocation option in Perl.
d. For example, see the extract_cell script in section 5.4.3.
e. You can obtain the same information in AWK by applying the subst function to the matched record with suitable arguments (generally involving RSTART and/or RLENGTH).

Another difference is that in some cases one language makes certain types of information much easier to obtain than the other (e.g., see the entries for Perl's "$`" and AWK's RSTART in table 5.2).

Once these variations and the fundamental syntax differences between the languages are properly taken into account, it's not difficult to write Perl programs that are equivalent to common AWK programs. For example, here are AWK and Perl programs that display the contents of *file* with prepended line numbers, using equivalent special variables:

```
awk          '{ print NR  ": "  $0 }' file
perl -wnl -e 'print $., ": ", $_; ' file
```

The languages differ in another respect that allows `print` statements to be written more concisely in Perl than in AWK. We'll discuss it next.

5.2.3   Perl's variable interpolation

Like the Shell, but unlike AWK, Perl allows variables to be *interpolated* within double-quoted strings, which means the variable names are replaced by their contents.[7] This lets you view the double-quoted string as a *template* describing the format of the desired result and include variables, string escapes (such as \t), and literal text within it. As a result, many `print` statements become much easier to write—as well as to read.

For example, you can write a more succinct and more readable Perl counterpart to the earlier AWK line-numbering program by using variable interpolation:

```
perl -wnl -e 'print $., ": ", $_;' file      # literal translation
perl -wnl -e 'print "$.: $_";' file          # better translation
```

It's a lot easier to see that the second version is printing the record-number variable, a colon, a space, and the current record than it is to surmise what the first version is doing, which requires mentally filtering out a lot of commas.

What's more, Perl's variable interpolation also occurs in regex fields, which allows variable names to be included along with other pattern elements.

For instance, to match and print an input record that consists entirely of a Zip Code, a Perl programmer can write a matching operator in this manner:

```
/^$zip_code$/  and  print;
```

Note the use of the variable to insert the metacharacters that match the digits of the Zip Code between the anchor metacharacters.

In contrast, an AWK programmer, lacking variable interpolation, has to concatenate (by juxtaposition) quoted and unquoted elements to compose the same regex:[8]

```
$0 ~ "^"  zip_code "$"
```

---

[7] In Shell-speak, this process is called *variable substitution* rather than *variable interpolation*.

[8] When constructing regexes in this way, AWK needs to be instructed to match against the current input line with the $0 ~ *regex* notation.

These statements do the same job (thanks to AWK's automatic and print, but because Perl has variable interpolation, its solution is more straightforward.

We'll consider some of Perl's other advantages next.

5.2.4 Other advantages of Perl over AWK

As discussed in section 4.7, Perl provides in-place editing of input files, through the -i.*ext* option. This makes it easy for the programmer to save the results of editing operations back in the original file(s). AWK lacks this capability.

Another potential advantage is that in Perl, automatic field processing is disabled by default, so JAPHs only pay its performance penalty in the programs that benefit from it. In contrast, all AWK programs split input records into fields and assign them to variables, whether fields are used in the program or not.[9]

Next, we'll summarize the results of the language comparison.

5.2.5 Summary of differences in basic features

Here are the most noteworthy differences between AWK and Perl that were touched on in the preceding discussion and in the comparisons of tables 5.1 and 5.2.

Ways in which Perl is superior to AWK

Perl alone (see tables 5.1 and 5.2) provides these useful pattern-matching capabilities:

- Metacharacter quoting, embedded commentary in regexes, stingy matching, record separator matching, and freely usable backreferences
- Arbitrary regex delimiters, access to match components, customized replacements in substitutions, and file modifications
- Easy access to the contents of the last match, and the portion of the matched record that comes before or after the match

Only Perl provides variable interpolation, which

- allows the contents of variables to be inserted into quoted strings and regex fields. This feature makes complex programs much easier to write, read, and maintain, and can be used to good advantage in most programs.

Perl alone has in-place editing.

Only Perl has a module-inclusion mechanism, which lets programmers

- package bundles of code for easy reuse;
- download many thousands of freely available modules from the CPAN.

---

[9] Depending on the number of records being processed and the number of fields per record, it seems that AWK could waste a substantial amount of computer time in needless field processing.

Ways in which AWK is superior to Perl

Many simple AWK programs are shorter than their Perl counterparts, in part because and print must always be explicitly stated in grep-like Perl programs, whereas it's implicit in AWK.

It's easier in AWK than in Perl (see table 5.2) to

- determine a script's number of arguments;
- obtain a file-specific record number;
- determine the position within a record where the latest match began.

However, to put these differences into proper perspective, Perl's listed advantages are of much greater significance that AWK's, because there's almost nothing that AWK can do that can't also be done with Perl—although the reverse isn't true.

Now that you've had a general orientation to the most notable differences between AWK and Perl, it's time to learn how to use Perl to write AWKish programs.

5.3   PROCESSING FIELDS

The single feature of AWK that's most widely known and used is its elegant facility for field processing. For example, here's an AWK program that displays the first two fields of each input line in reverse order, using birthday data for 1960s guitar heroes:

```
$ cat birthdays
03/30/45      Eric Clapton
11/27/42      Jimi Hendrix
06/24/44      Jeff Beck      │ Field
    1           2     3   ◁──┘ numbers

$ awk '{ print $2, $1 }' birthdays
Eric 03/30/45
...
```

In AWK, $1 means the first field of the current record, $2 the second field, and so forth. By default, any sequence of one or more spaces or tabs is taken as a single field separator, and each line constitutes one record. For this reason, "3/30/45" was treated as the first field of Eric's line and "Eric" as the second.

After discussing a Perl technique for accessing fields, we'll revisit this example and translate it into Perl.

5.3.1   Accessing fields

Before you can use fields, you have to gain access to them. In AWK, you do this by referring to special variables named $1, $2, and so on. Minimal Perl's main technique for field processing[10] is shown in table 5.3. It involves copying the fields of the current

---

[10] We'll discuss an alternative technique for accessing fields called *array indexing* in section 5.4.3, which uses variables like the $F[0] shown in table 5.2.

Table 5.3 Loading field data into user-defined variables

Syntax[a]	Effect	Comments
`($A, $B)=@F;`	Loads the first field of the current record into $A and the second into $B.	Variables must be provided for each field up to the rightmost one that will be used in the program.
`($A, undef, $C)=@F;`	Loads the first field into $A and the third into $C.	undef in the second position indicates that no variable has been designated to receive the value of the second field.
`$numfields=@F;`	Loads the field count for the current record into $numfields.	For an assignment to a non-parenthesized scalar variable, @F provides the field count.

a. These examples depend on the use of Perl's n and a invocation options to load the fields of the current input record into @F.

record from the field container @F into a parenthesized list of user-defined variables. For instance, the first example in the table assigns the first field of @F to $A and its second field to $B.

In some programs, certain fields won't ever be used, and that requires a different kind of entry in the parenthesized list. Specifically, for unused fields that occur before the rightmost field of interest, the keyword undef (for *undefined*) takes the place of a variable in the parenthesized list (as illustrated by the table's second example).

On the other hand, there's no need to provide variable names or undef keywords for any fields beyond the rightmost one that will be used in the program. This means the assignment statement ($A, $B)=@F can be used with input records having from two to any larger number of fields, as long as only the first two fields are of interest.

As shown in table 5.3, generic variable names such as $A and $B are generally used in programs that don't know what's in the fields they're manipulating. But in cases where the programmer has that information, it's a better practice to use more descriptive names for the field variables, such as $size and $shape.

The table's last row shows how to determine the number of fields in the current input record. You do this by making an assignment to a variable that's *not* enclosed in parentheses (for reasons discussed in section 7.1.1).

Table 5.4 illustrates the assignments of field values to variables and undef keywords in parenthesized lists. The arrows indicate that when a variable name—such as $first—is provided as the target for a particular field, the associated field value (such as "A") is copied into it. In contrast, no copying is performed for an undef target, whose function is just to displace the next variable (or undef) into alignment with the next field value.

Note in particular that there's no effective difference between the last two assignment formats shown in table 5.4, which illustrates the earlier point that you don't need to supply undef entries for fields beyond the rightmost one of interest.

Table 5.4 Using `undef` in assignments to explicit lists

Format of assignment statement (@F contains A, B, and C)	Resulting assignment of values to variables		
`($first, $second, $third)=@F;`	A ↓ `$first`	B ↓ `$second`	C ↓ `$third`
`( undef, $second, $third)=@F;`	A ↓ **undef**	B ↓ `$second`	C ↓ `$third`
`($first,   undef, $third)=@F;`	A ↓ `$first`	B ↓ **undef**	C ↓ `$third`
`($first, $second,  undef)=@F;`	A ↓ `$first`	B ↓ `$second`	C ↓ **undef**
`($first, $second      )=@F;`	A ↓ `$first`	B ↓ `$second`	C ↓

NOTE Minimal Perl's approach of copying field values into descriptively named variables produces more readable programs than conventional AWK solutions.

Now that you know how to access fields in Perl, we'll put that knowledge to use by writing some simple programs that print fields.

5.3.2 Printing fields

Let's construct a Perl counterpart to the AWK command shown earlier, which prints selected fields from the `birthdays` file. To refresh your memory, here's the AWK version:

```
$ awk '{ print $2, $1 }' birthdays
Eric 03/30/45
. . .
```

Our first task is to choose an appropriate Primary Option Cluster from table 2.9, which prescribes `-wnla` for field-processing applications where the default whitespace delimiters are desired. Perl's n option requests the inclusion of an implicit input-reading loop, as we've discussed, and the a option additionally requests the automatic splitting of each input record into fields, which are stored in the @F array.

After consulting the first example of table 5.3 for the appropriate syntax, it's easy to construct a Perl one-liner that displays the first two whitespace-separated fields of each input line in reverse order on the screen:

```
$ perl -wnla -e '($date, $name)=@F; print "$name $date";' birthdays
Eric 03/30/45
...
```

This solution takes more typing than its AWK counterpart, but its descriptive variable names (compared to AWK's cryptic $1 and $2) make it easier to understand.

Next, we'll turn our attention to a program that demonstrates the use of undef, along with named variables, in assignments to explicit lists.

A rock-star biodata system (AWK)

Perhaps because of his name, paranormal researcher Fox Boulder is vitally interested in rock lore. He's currently investigating the rash of rock-star deaths by alleged "accidents" and "drug overdoses" that occurred from 1969 to 1971.

Fox has been a fan of AWK since the last millennium, so he's using it to view selected bits of biodata pertaining to the rock-star deaths. His data file, called X, is shown in listing 5.1.

Listing 5.1 Birth and death dates of rock stars, from the X file

```
Birth           Death           Name
02/28/42        07/03/69        Brian Jones
11/27/42        09/18/70        Jimi Hendrix
11/19/43        10/04/70        Janis Joplin
12/08/43        07/03/71        Jim Morrison
11/20/46        10/29/71        Duane Allman
```

This file may not look suspicious to you, but Fox is a trained observer, so he immediately notices that the order in which the individuals were born is *exactly* the same as the order in which they died. He has several theories about what that means, but all he knows for sure about this case is this—AWK has really come in handy in helping him reformat the data!

For example, here's the command he uses to display each first name and birth date, which requires printing the third field followed by the first field from each line of the X file:

```
$ awk '{ print $3 "\t" $1 }' X
Name    Birth
Brian   02/28/42
...
```

Satisfied with this command, Fox retires to his pyramid-covered hyperbaric bed chamber for some well-deserved rest—but he's soon awakened by a nightmare. As usual, it featured a handsome, dark-haired, bespectacled man sporting a Hawaiian shirt and droopy mustache (i.e., Larry), exhorting him to *Retool from AWK to Perl, exploit the CPAN, and embrace TMTOWTDI!* Hoping it will help exorcise this demon, Fox sets out to convert his AWK birthday-printing command to Perl.

A rock-star biodata system (Perl)

After rummaging through some handouts from a YAPC tutorial on Minimal Perl that the CIA probably won't notice are missing, Fox comes up with the following Perl counterpart to his earlier AWK command:[11]

```
$ perl -wnla -e '($b_date, undef, $fname)=@F;
>         print "$fname\t$b_date";' X
Name    Birth
Brian   02/28/42
...
```

As illustrated in table 5.4, he only had to account for the fields up to the rightmost one of interest (first name) while populating the parenthesized list with variables. Notice also that Fox gave the field variables descriptive names, because he knows that proper labeling of evidence can be critical to the success of a case.

Unlike the corresponding AWK solution, this Perl command can format its output by using variable interpolation (see section 5.2.3) to insert the fields into `print`'s double-quoted argument string. Perl even has in-place editing, so Fox could rewrite the original file in the new format just by adding the i option (see section 4.7):

```
$ perl -i.bak -wnla -e '($b_date, undef, $fname)=@F;
>         print "$fname\t$b_date";' X      # X-file gets transmogrified
$ # Output went back into X
```

We'll explore some additional differences in the use of `print` in AWK and Perl next.

5.3.3   Differences in syntax for `print`

Table 5.5 summarizes the major AWK versus Perl syntax differences for `print` statements involving variables, string escapes, and literal text.

A fundamental difference is that Perl, like many other computer languages, requires commas to appear between arguments. In contrast, AWK *allows* commas to be present in `print` statements—to indicate that arguments should be separated in the output by the value of the OFS variable (see table 5.2)—or commas to be absent, to indicate that the arguments should be concatenated together on output.

---

[11] The Perl solution requires considerably more typing than the AWK one, but for an apples-to-apples comparison, here's an AWK solution that also uses descriptive variable names, which is nearly as large as its Perl counterpart: awk '{ birth=$1; fname=$3; print fname "\t" birth }' X

Therefore, in the AWK example of table 5.5's first row, the juxtaposition of the three arguments causes them to be concatenated, whereas the first corresponding Perl solution needs a comma between each pair of arguments to do the same (and to avoid a fatal syntax error). The second Perl solution in that row, which uses variable interpolation, is the recommended approach.

In the table's second row, the AWK program uses a comma to obtain a space between the printed items, which is explicitly included in the double-quoted string of the Perl version.

Table 5.5   Syntactic differences for `print` in AWK and Perl

AWK	Perl[a]	Explanation

`print name "\t" age`
 	
Output:
`Suzy--->29`
	`print $name, "\t", $age;`
	Or
	`print "$name\t$age";`
	
	Output:
	`Suzy--->29`
		In Perl, arguments can't be placed next to one another without an intervening comma. But because Perl provides Shell-like variable interpolation, items to be printed are generally included in double quotes. The arrow symbol represents the effect of printing the tab character requested by `\t`.

`print name, age`
 	
Output:
`Suzy□29`
	`print "$name□$age";`
	
	Output:
	`Suzy□29`
		In AWK, a comma in a `print` statement requests the insertion of the `OFS` variable's contents (a space, by default, indicated here by a box). In Perl, the space is either included within a quoted argument to `print` or loaded into "`$,`" (see table 2.8).

`print "NR is:", NR`
 	
Output:
`NR is:□13`
	`print "\$. is: $."`
	
	Output:
	`$. is: 13`
		In AWK, the name of a variable is treated as a literal string when it appears within double quotes. In Perl, a backslash is needed before a $ in double quotes to suppress variable interpolation (as in the Shell).

`print name`
 	
Output:
`Suzy`
	`print "$name"`
	Or
	`print  $name`
	
	Output:
	`Suzy`
		When there's nothing in Perl's double quoted string but a single variable name, the quotes have no effect and can be omitted.

a. These examples assume the use of Perl's `l` invocation option.

Similarly, the Perl example in the third row includes a space after "is:" that was provided by a comma in its AWK counterpart.

The examples in the last row make the point that it's optional in Perl to use double quotes around the name of a lone scalar variable, because doing so has no effect on the result. On the other hand, prudent Shell programmers acquire the habit of generally using double quotes in similar cases, to disallow additional processing of the results of substitutions.[12] For this reason, Perl newbies who plan to continue programming in the Shell may wish to keep their Shell-friendly habits intact by using double quotes around scalar variable names in Perl.

With the data files you've seen thus far, the default field separators have been appropriate for extracting the fields of each line. However, sometimes you need to specify *custom separators*, which you'll learn to do next.

5.3.4   Using custom field separators in Perl

By default, Perl's a option splits input records into fields using whitespace characters as field separators. That's fine when you're working with files whose records look like this:

```
01/08/35        08/16/77        Elvis
```

But in other cases, whitespace characters occur *within* fields, so a different character must be used as a field separator, such as the colon in this example:

```
Stimey:Matthew Beard
```

To change Perl's idea of what constitutes a field separator, you specify with the F invocation option (see table 2.9) the desired character(s) or regular expression—as in AWK. Accordingly, this command prints "Stimey":

```
echo 'Stimey:Matthew Beard' |  # Character:Actor
  perl -wnlaF':' -e '($character)=@F; print $character;'
```

Table 5.6 shows examples of custom field separators, which define fields consisting of whatever is found between them in the input.

The field separator definitions are shown in the table with single quotes around their contents, to allow them to work properly when submitted to a Shell.[13]

Yikes! The little hairs on the back of my neck just started tingling—that means it's time to check on Fox.

---

[12] For a discussion of quoting techniques in Shell programming and guidelines for proper quoting, see http://TeachMeUnix.com/quoting.html.

[13] What happens if you omit the quotes? In the case -F'\t', the Shell would convert the unquoted -F\t to -Ft by gobbling up unquoted backslashes—which would make each "t" a field separator, rather than each tab. That wouldn't keep the program from running—just from producing the right results!

Table 5.6 Custom field separator definitions

Separator option and argument [a]	Meaning
`F'///'`	Each sequence of three slashes is a single field separator.
`F'\t'`	Each tab is a single field separator.
`F'\t+'`	Each sequence of one or more tabs is a single field separator.
`F'\s+'`	Each sequence of one or more whitespace characters is a single field separator. Although this is the default definition, it can produce different results when stated explicitly (see text).
`F'[,;!?]+'`	Each sequence of one or more of the characters listed in the square brackets is a single field separator.
`F'[^\w]+'`	Because the list-complementing character (^) is at the beginning of the character class, each sequence of one or more non-"word" characters is a single field separator.

a. Tables 3.4 and 3.5 define the metacharacters used in these examples. The F option works only in the presence of options n/p and a, so it generally appears in the form `-wnlaF'sep'`

Enhancing the rock-star biodata system

Fox is experimenting with his new Perl command that displays rock-star birthdays, when the phone rings. To his surprise, it's an excited guy from TVM—the *television music* network—who has heard about his new rock-star biodata system and wants to make him an offer for it.[14]

But there's a catch—they need him to modify the program so that *both* name components can be manipulated as one unit, so, for example, the last output line prints as "Duane <u>Allman</u>   11/20/46", rather than the current "Duane   11/20/46".

After negotiating an appropriate "license in perpetuity" arrangement for a seven-figure amount, Fox accepts the assignment of modifying his program. He begins by scrutinizing the last line of the X file:

```
11/20/46        10/29/71        Duane Allman
```

The evidence shows a big gap after each date field and a small one between each name component. His intuition tells him that his assistant probably used tabs to separate the three obvious fields while typing the file. He tests this hunch by using a special invocation of the sed command:[15]

---

[14] But Fox had just typed it in on his laptop! How could anybody have learned of its existence? Hmm … his television and ISP services both ride on the same cable; could his ISP be monitoring his keystrokes and sharing them with the TV networks? Naw; it must be an *alien conspiracy*!

[15] The -n option tells sed not to do automatic printing of automatically-read input lines (as with Perl). The l command tells it to list non-printing characters (other than space) in a visible manner, and to mark the end of each line with a $ symbol.

```
$ sed -n l X
Birth\t\tDeath\t\tName$
...
11/20/46\t10/29/71\tDuane Allman$
   1         2           3          ⤆┐  Field numbers
                                        using tabs
   1         2        3       4      ⤆┐  Field numbers
                                        using whitespace
```

The \t sequences reveal tabs between the date and name fields, confirming Fox's hunch. Now he can see that each data line will have four fields when the default separators are used but three fields with tabs as separators.

Armed with the new evidence produced by the arcane sed incantation, he is now ready to solve the case:

```
$ perl -wnlaF'<TAB>+' -e \
>   '($b_date, undef, $name)=@F; print "$name<TAB>$b_date";' X
...
Duane Allman      11/20/46
```

Fox selected the second field-oriented Primary Option Cluster from table 2.9, -wnlaF 'sep', so he could define "one or more tabs" as the field separator. He specified this choice pressing the tab key (<TAB>) in quotes after the F option,[16] and he inserted a tab in the same way within print's quoted argument string.

Shazaam—the program works! Now all Fox has to do is reports its readiness and seal the deal. But suddenly the TVM guy calls, saying they found another source for a rock-star biodata system and won't be needing his after all.

His last remark is still reverberating in Fox's head:

> By the way, my people tell me you could have used \t to represent the tab in the arguments to the F option and print to enhance the program's readability. Whatever. Rock on, dude!

The TVM guy was right! But how did they already know what his new version looked like? Fox vowed he would find out, because *The Truth Is Out There*—somewhere.

Fox is good at identifying patterns in data and taking appropriate actions. That's why he likes AWK so much—it's good at associating Patterns with Actions. You'll see how to make such associations with Perl next.

5.4 PROGRAMMING WITH PATTERNS AND ACTIONS

After field processing, AWK's next most highly prized feature is its ability to combine pattern matching with conditional execution. Why is that so good?

---

[16] Because Fox uses the Bash shell with vi-editing mode enabled, he has to press <Ctrl><V> before the tab character to have it taken literally.

Think for a moment about the most fundamental service provided by `grep`, which is to look for lines that match a pattern and display them. Although this is a useful service, many other things could be done with the match itself, or its associated record, which may at times be more desirable. AWK's creators recognized this fact and engineered it so that *any* of its activities could be dependent on the result of a match. Perl shares this property.

Here's an example of a simple AWKish Perl command that demonstrates the power of the Pattern/Action programming model, in which a conditional element (called the *Pattern*) is paired with an executable element (called the *Action*):

```
$ perl -wnl -e '/^@/  and  print $.;' data
3
17
```

If the Pattern (the matching operator) yields a True result, the Action (`print`) is executed. In consequence, this command reports the numbers of the lines in the `data` file that are marked by an initial @ symbol, which by convention in this IT department identifies those lines as incomplete.

Notice that `grep` isn't up to this task. Its specialty is to print matching lines, and there's no way to persuade it to track their numbers and print them instead. The `sed` command isn't well suited to this job either, because the task involves the reporting of new data (line numbers) rather than the modification of existing data (by substitution).

On the other hand, the Shell can handle this task—if the programmer is willing to write an input-processing loop, manage a line counter, and do some conditional

Table 5.7 Patterns and Actions in AWK and Perl

AWK program type	AWK format & sample programs	Perl format & sample programs [a]	Explanation

Pattern and Action	`Pattern {`
	`    Action`
	`}`
	Example:
	`/RE/ {`
	`    print NR`
	`}`
		`Pattern and Action;`
		
		Example:
		`/RE/ and print $.;`
			Prints record numbers of records matching *RE*. In AWK, regex Patterns are enclosed in slashes, and Actions are enclosed in curly braces.

Pattern only	`Pattern`
	Examples:
	`/RE/`
	`NR > 1`
		`Pattern and print;`
		Examples:
		`/RE/     and print;`
		`$. > 1 and print;`
			The upper examples print records matching *RE*, and the lower ones print all records except the first.

Action only	`{ Action }`
	Example:
	`{ print }`
		`Action;`
		Example:
		`print;`
			Prints every record.

a. The Perl examples assume use of the (AWKish) n option.

branching based on the result of a pattern match. But following this approach would constitute a flagrant violation of the First Virtue of Perl programming: *Laziness*!

Fortunately, Patterns in AWK and Perl needn't be matching oriented; you can use any True/False expression as a conditional element, such as "$. > 42".

Another convenience is that in AWK, a Pattern without an associated Action is automatically provided the default Action of printing the record, and an Action without a Pattern is treated as having a Pattern that selects all records. You can arrange for this behavior in Perl too, by using an appropriate syntax.

Table 5.7 shows Perl counterparts to the three types of AWK programs that can be constructed using a Pattern/Action pair, a lone Action, or a lone Pattern. The examples in the first row of the table associate a Pattern with an Action, to print a line's number if its contents match a pattern. The second row's examples show how to obtain AWK's default `print` Action in Perl, and those in the last row show how to apply a particular Action to all input lines.

To give you a better idea of how the languages compare in practice, table 5.8 shows the implementations in AWK and Perl of some simple programs that perform elementary types of data-processing tasks.

The AWK programs in the upper panel of table 5.8 are of the Pattern-only type, employing the default Action of printing the selected records. Their Perl counterparts need an explicit `and print` clause to obtain the same functionality. Notice also that AWK's `&&` (logical and) used in the compound test of the first example becomes `and` in the Perl version. The examples of the first two rows demonstrate that Patterns don't necessarily involve matching—conditions based on relational operators ("<=", "!=", etc.; see table 5.11) are among the others you can use.

The programs in the table's middle panel are of the Action-only type, in which all records are selected for processing by the Action (with the help of the n option in the Perl versions).

The programs in the bottom panel each use at least one Pattern/Action pair, although that may not be readily apparent. That's because BEGIN and END are pseudo-Patterns that respectively become True *before* any input has been read or *after* all input has been read. Accordingly, the statements in a BEGIN block are the first to be executed in a program, and those in the END block are the last.

As shown in table 5.8's last row, a BEGIN block is used for preliminary operations, such as printing a heading to describe the upcoming output of those programs. The programs then employ an Action-only statement to accumulate a total, and after all the input has been processed, they calculate and print the average of the numbers in and END block.

---

[17] The Perl (or AWK) solution could alternatively use the += compound assignment operator (see table 5.12) in incrementing the variable $total, as in $total += $_.

Table 5.8   AWK and Perl programs for simple tasks

AWK [a]	Perl [b]	Explanation
`1 <= NR && NR <= 3`	`1 <= $. and $. <= 3` `    and print;`	Prints records 1 through 3 of the input.
`NF != 2`	`@F != 2 and print;`	Prints records that don't have exactly two fields. Perl's `@F` corresponds to AWK's `NF` when its context calls for a single value (see chapter 7).
`$2 =~ /^9/`	`$F[1] =~ /^9/ and` `    print;`	Prints records that have "9" at the beginning of the second field.
`{ print $NF }`	`print $F[-1];`	Prints the last field of each line, using negative indexing in Perl's case (see table 5.9).
`{ print NR ": " $0 }`	`print "$.: $_";`	Prepends record numbers to records and prints them.
`END { print NR }`	`END { print $.; }`	Reports the total number of records read.

`BEGIN {`
`    print "AVERAGE:"`
`}`
`{ total=total + $0 }`
`END {`
`    print total / NR`
`}`
	`BEGIN {`
	`    print 'AVERAGE:';`
	`}`
	`$total=$total + $_;`
	`END {`
	`    print $total / $.;`
	`}`
		For input lines consisting of individual numbers, reports the average of those numbers.[18]

a. AWK's special variables are discussed in table 5.2.
b. These Perl programs use the n invocation option, and those employing @F or $F[] additionally use the a option.

The following script, called incomplete, is an enhanced version of the program you saw at the beginning of this section. The original version reported the numbers of the lines that begin with a @ character (which marks them as incomplete). The new one adds value by reporting the *proportion* of incomplete lines at the end of its run. The script uses both the BEGIN and the END block:[18]

```
$ cat incomplete
#! /usr/bin/perl -wnl
BEGIN {
    $count=0;        # to suppress warnings
}

/^@/  and            # this symbol identifies incomplete lines
    print "Line #$. is incomplete"  and
        $count=$count + 1;
```

---

[18] Additional details on BEGIN and END blocks, and how they fit into the use of implicit loops, are provided in section 10.2.4.

```
END {
    print "\n$count lines out of $. are incomplete";
}

$ incomplete datafile
Line #3 is incomplete
Line #17 is incomplete

2 lines out of 38 are incomplete
```

Notice that the variable $count is initialized to zero in the BEGIN block. Although this step is rarely needed in Perl, it's included here for two reasons. One is that an "uninitialized variable" warning would otherwise be issued the first time the variable-incrementing statement is executed, because the underlined instance of the variable would not yet have been given a value. This wouldn't interfere with the addition, because Perl (like AWK) would automatically default to using the desired value of zero for the variable anyway. As in other cases where you know that an "uninitialized variable" warning would otherwise be "crying wolf," you can suppress it through the expedient of explicitly initializing the variable.

A more compelling reason for initializing $count is that if the input lacked any incomplete lines, the variable-incrementing statement would never get executed, and the variable's value would remain undefined. This would cause the print within END to generate an "uninitialized variable" warning for $count, and for Perl to substitute a null string[19] for the variable interpolation request.

Explicit initialization of $count to zero avoids both of these undesirable situations, and is conveniently done in a BEGIN block to ensure that the desired starting value will be in effect from the program's outset.

Next, we'll briefly revisit the topic of field processing to see how it can be used with Pattern/Action programming.

5.4.1 Combining pattern matching with field processing

AWK's Pattern/Action model allows you to combine a record selection step with the conditional printing of selective fields from a record, as in this simple example:

```
/RE/ { print $1, $3 } # if record matches, print 1st and 3rd fields
```

Perl shares this capability but wields it with greater power, due in part to its superior pattern-matching capabilities (summarized in table 5.1). You'll see many programs that demonstrate these benefits later, but first we'll look at an elementary example.

The following command reports the login names and UIDs for Unix accounts having three-digit UIDs that start with 7, which on this system are accounts for students taking a particular class. Printing the report requires matching against the third

---

[19] Why not a zero, as before? Because the double-quoted string provides a string context for the variable, in contrast to the numeric context provided by the variable-incrementing statement discussed earlier.

colon-separated field of the `passwd` file (the UID), coupled with conditional printing of the first and third fields:

```
$ perl -wnlaF':' -e '($name, undef, $uid)=@F;
>    $uid =~ /^7\d\d$/  and  print "$name:\t$uid";' /etc/passwd
raga:    710
theka:   711
tala:    712
...
```

The Pattern is of the matching type and is constructed using the match-binding operator ("`=~`"; see table 3.3) to specify `$uid` as the regex's target. The Pattern's associated Action prints the `$name` and `$uid` fields of the current line in the event of a match.

Next, you'll see how to use Perl's AWK-like capabilities to extract a single chunk of information from a particular location within a file.

5.4.2 Extracting data from tables

As a long-time resident of Seattle, Patrick knows that identifying other cities that have *even more rain* is a popular pastime there during the soggy days of winter. Now that most coffee shops provide WiFi Internet access, the availability of online data should help to quickly settle the inevitable disputes over rainfall patterns.

With a bit of surfing, Patrick finds a U.S. government web site that reports detailed weather data for all major cities in the U.S. and Canada. In preparation for the next "your city is rainier than mine" dispute, he downloads the associated text files to his laptop computer.

Waving from the next table, Patrick's friend Vitas introduces his new friend Guillermo, who has just moved to Seattle from Miami, Florida.

Guillermo mumbles the following, while barely glancing at Patrick: "Hi, Patrick. Please excuse my depressed mood—I'm having trouble adjusting to this dreary Seattle weather—which is so much rainier than Miami!"

Vitas chimes in with: "Yeah, when I like first arrived here from New York, I couldn't believe that human beings would have, like, ever settled in a city so, like, soggy as this one—if you know what I'm sayin'—so I'm down with that!"

Being an IT guy, and freshly armed with the relevant data, Patrick can't resist the opportunity to put these allegations to a test. He pushes aside his coffee, fires up his notebook computer, and begins working on a script to compare the raininess statistics for Seattle, New York, and Miami.

Comparing cities for "mean annual precipitation"

Patrick's first step is to study the data files, so he'll be able to extract the relevant information from the appropriate spots. Looking over his shoulder, you can see in listing 5.2 the first screen of the file for Seattle, with line numbers added for reference purposes.

Listing 5.2   Weather data for Seattle

```
 1                           OPERATIONAL CLIMATIC DATA SUMMARY

 2

 3    STATION: SEATTLE-TACOMA INTL WASHINGTON   STATION #: 727930         ICAO: KSEA

 4    LOCATION: 4727N  12218W                   ELEVATION (FEET):   449   LST = GMT -8

 5    PREPARED BY: AFCCC/DOO, NOV 1998          PERIOD: 7301-9712

 6

 7    ------------------------------------------------------------------------------

 8

 9            SOURCE NO.  JAN  FEB  MAR  APR  MAY  JUN  JUL  AUG  SEP  OCT  NOV  DEC  ANN

10

11    1.   TEMPERATURE ( F)

12    EXTREME MAX      3   64   70   75   85   93   96  100   99   98   89   74   64  100

13    MEAN DAILY MAX   1   46   50   54   59   65   71   76   77   72   61   51   46   61

14    MEAN             1   41   43   46   50   55   60   65   65   61   53   45   41   52

15    MEAN DAILY MIN   1   37   38   40   43   48   53   56   56   53   47   41   37   46

16    EXTREME MIN      3    0    1   11   29   28   38   43   44   35   28    6    6    0

17    # DAYS GE 90     3    0    0    0    0    #    #    1    1    #    0    0    0    3

18    # DAYS LE 32     3   11    7    4    1    #    0    0    0    0    #    4    9   36

19    # DAYS LE 0      1    #    0    0    0    0    0    0    0    0    0    0    0    #

20

21    2.   PRECIPITATION (INCHES)

22    MAXIMUM        3/4 12.9  9.1 12.1  6.5  4.8  3.8  2.4  4.6  6.0  7.8 11.6 15.9 57.6

23    MEAN             3  5.7  4.1  3.8  2.6  1.7  1.4  0.8  1.1  1.8  3.5  5.9  5.9 38.3

24    MINIMUM        3/4  0.6  0.4  0.4  0.2  0.1    #    0    0    0    #  0.5  1.0 20.0

25    MAX 24 HR        3  3.0  3.1  2.7  2.6  1.8  1.8  0.9  1.6  1.7  2.7  3.4  2.1  3.4

26    # DAYS GE .01    3   19   16   17   14   11    9    5    6    9   13   18   19  156

27    # DAYS GE .5     3    4    2    2    1    1    1    0    1    1    2    4    4   22

28
```

Patrick adopts a tentative definition of the city with the "most rain" as the one with the largest number under the ANN ("annual") column on Line 23 of its file, which reports the total of the mean inches of precipitation for all the months of the year. With a few well-practiced mouse maneuvers, he highlights that cell and its row/column endpoints to help him maintain his focus on the pertinent locations in the file (and, coincidentally, to help you spot them too).

But a quick check of the files for the other cities reveals a snag—the statistic of interest doesn't appear on the same line in every file, because some files have more blank lines between the data paragraphs than others (e.g., between Lines 19 and 21). That means Patrick can't access the desired statistic by just grabbing the last field on Line 23. His next idea is to search for "MEAN" to find the line of interest within the precipitation data block, but as it happens, that word occurs within other kinds of data paragraphs too (e.g.,. TEMPERATURE); thus that strategy is equally unacceptable.

Patrick finally settles on the approach of finding the PRECIPITATION data paragraph, locating the intersection of its MEAN line and ANN column, and extracting the number found in that cell.

Such *table*-oriented data wrangling is way beyond the capabilities of grep and its kin, but it's well within the scope of AWK or AWKish Perl. So Patrick solves the problem by writing a script that uses paragraph mode to grab the whole block of PRECIPITATION data, and then uses indexing to extract the value of the appropriate field from the field array.

Before we examine Patrick's script, we'll take a moment to lay the conceptual foundation for the array-indexing technique used in his program.

5.4.3 Accessing cell data using array indexing

As you know, one convenient way to access elements of arrays is to copy them from the array into a list of named variables and then extract the values from those variables. But in cases where you've got dozens or even thousands of values to choose from, this approach isn't practical—typing the ($A,$B, etc.)=@F assignment statement is too burdensome.

The alternative is to use *array indexing* to extract specific values directly from the array. You do this by changing the @ symbol in the array name to a $ sign and appending a pair of square brackets with an integer number (or an expression that evaluates to one) between them.

As shown in table 5.9, Perl is unusual in providing both positive and negative indexing. The benefit is that the last element of the array, for example, can either be retrieved using the index of -1 or the index of *N*-1, where *N* is the total number of elements. (The maximum index is one less than the number of elements, because the indices start from 0, rather than 1.)

Table 5.9 Illustration of array indexing syntax using the field array, @F

	Storage position			
	1st	2nd	3rd	4th (and last)
Positive indexing	$F[0]	$F[1]	$F[2]	$F[3]
Negative indexing	$F[-4]	$F[-3]	$F[-2]	$F[-1]

Now let's examine Patrick's script, called mean_annual_precip, which is compact, sweet, and powerful—like his espresso:

```
#! /usr/bin/perl -00 -wnla
# Parses "Operational Climatic Data Summary" reports to extract
#  and print "mean annual precipitation" statistic for each file.
#
# Find precipitation record, and print its field #33 (index 32)
#
/^ 2\. PRECIPITATION /  and  print "\u$ARGV: $F[32]";
```

The script is designed to read multiple files in sequence (via option n) using paragraph mode (-00) and to automatically load the fields of each record into @F (using a). To home in on the correct portion of each city's data file, the matching operator is used to find the paragraph with the PRECIPITATION heading by looking at the beginning of a paragraph for a space, a 2, a literal dot, and then two spaces before that word.

Next, the logical and is used to print the file's name (via $ARGV; see table 2.7) followed by a colon, a space, and the value of the appropriate field within the record. Notice the use of \u before $ARGV (see table 4.5), which conveniently capitalizes the first letter of each city's name. To help you visualize the implicit lines-to-record mapping that determines the index numbers for the fields in @F, consider the following data file:

```
A B
C D
```

When read in line mode, each line would have two fields, and the maximum index for each record's @F would be 1.

However, if you read the same file in paragraph mode, each field would be considered part of the same record and treated for field-numbering purposes as if the input had looked like this:

```
A B C D
```

Therefore, field "D" would be stored under the index of 3, rather than under 1, as it would be with input records defined as lines.

Using this logic, Patrick determines that the number of the field he's interested in is 33, which means it can be retrieved with the index 32.

Okay, now it's time to run the script, and determine which city is the rainiest:[20]

```
$ mean_annual_precip miami new_york seattle
Miami: 57.9

New_york: 41.2

Seattle: 38.3
```

Patrick gently breaks the news to Guillermo about Miami being rainier than Seattle. After a brief period of shock-induced choking on his carob-iced hemp biscotti, Guillermo congratulates himself on being wise enough to relocate to (relatively) rain-free Seattle.

But Patrick is left wondering why Seattle has such an oversaturated reputation, given that even New York has more rain. In an attempt to reconcile his observations with reality, he speculates that Seattle's distinction might be its *number of days* with significant rainfall, as opposed to its *annual amount* of rainfall.

---

[20] When perl is invoked with the -00 -wnla options, the l option strips *blank lines* from the end of each record, not *newlines*. Field 33 occurs at the end of a line, so it still has the line-ending newline attached at its end. But the l option automatically adds a newline at the end of print's argument list, making the output double-spaced. To avoid this effect, a chomp $F[32]; statement could be added above the print statement to remove any trailing newline present in the field variable. You'll learn more about chomp in section 7.2.4.

Comparing cities for "days of significant rain"

Patrick begins work on a new script to compare the "number of rainy days" statistic from the weather files of the three cities. But instead of writing a script specific to this particular task, he decides to make it a very general one that's configurable by switches, to liberate him from the chore of writing another new script as each new dispute arises in the future.

With the weather-data files, the script could use a matching operator to select the desired record, as mean_annual_precip did. But that technique can't be expected to work with every file, because it requires the record of interest to have a unique marker within it, such as the precipitation record's PRECIPITATION. Accordingly, Patrick opts for the more general approach of selecting records by number.

To give the script the flexibility it needs, he lets the user specify the number of the record and the field of interest within it using command-line switches. Prior to testing his new script against mean_annual_precip, he identifies the number of the PRECIPITATION record in the weather files using this one-liner:

```
$ perl -00 -wnl -e 'print "Paragraph #$.:\n$_";' seattle
Paragraph #1:
                    OPERATIONAL CLIMATIC DATA SUMMARY
...
Paragraph #4:
            SOURCE NO.   JAN  FEB  MAR  APR  MAY  JUN  JUL  AUG  SEP  OCT  NOV  DEC  ANN
...
Paragraph #6:
2.   PRECIPITATION (INCHES)
MAXIMUM        3/4 12.9  9.1 12.1  6.5  4.8  3.8  2.4  4.6  6.0  7.8 11.6 15.9  57.6
MEAN             3  5.7  4.1  3.8  2.6  1.7  1.4  0.8  1.1  1.8  3.5  5.9  5.9  38.3
MINIMUM        3/4  0.6  0.4  0.4  0.2  0.1    #    0    0    0    #  0.5  1.0  20.0
MAX 24 HR        3  3.0  3.1  2.7  2.6  1.8  1.8  0.9  1.6  1.7  2.7  3.4  2.1   3.4
# DAYS GE .01    3   19   16   17   14   11    9    5    6    9   13   18   19   156
# DAYS GE .5     3    4    2    2    1    1    1    0    1    1    2    4    4    22

...
```

Now that Patrick knows that the paragraph number for precipitation data is 6, he can test his new script by specifying that record number[21] along with the number of the desired field within it. The location described by those attributes is like a *cell* in a two-dimensional table, inasmuch as it occurs at the intersection of a horizontal element (in this case, a paragraph) and a vertical one (a column); so, he dubs the new script extract_cell. Patrick then tries it with an invocation that should produce the same results as mean_annual_precip:

```
$ extract_cell  -recnum=6 -fnum=33 miami new_york seattle
Miami: 57.9
...
```

As he hoped, the new more flexible script produced the same output as the earlier one.

---

[21] It will be 6 no matter how many extra blank lines occur between the paragraphs, which is critical, because the weather files for different locations differ in that respect (as mentioned earlier).

But did you notice that the argument for the -fnum switch is 33 with extract_cell, whereas mean_annual_precip used 32 to access the same field? That's because the new script provides the useful service of automatically decrementing the given field number by one to convert it into an array index, so the user won't have to remember to do that.

Here's the extract_cell script:

```
#! /usr/bin/perl -s -00 -wnla
# Prints field indicated by the $recnum/$fnum combination,
#   preceded by filename

BEGIN {
    $fnum  and  $recnum or
        warn "Usage: $0 -recnum=M -fnum=N\n"  and
            exit 255;
    # Decrement field number, so user can say 1, and get index of 0
    $index=$fnum - 1;
}
$. == $recnum  and  print "\u$ARGV: $F[$index]";

# Reset record counter $. after end of each file
eof  and  close ARGV;
```

The script begins by checking that both of the obligatory switches have been supplied and by issuing a "Usage:" message and exiting if they weren't. The last statement of the script senses whether input from the current file has been exhausted by calling the built-in eof function; if that's true, the script closes the current file by referencing its filehandle, ARGV.[22] The effect is to reset the "$." variable back to 1 for the next file, so the program can continue to correctly identify the record number desired by the value of "$.".

It's time to test Guillermo's theory about Seattle being remarkable for its number of days with significant rainfall rather than its mean amount of rainfall. As it happens, section 2 of the precipitation report contains a statistic that seems well suited to this comparison—it reports the number of days per year on which at least half an inch of rain has fallen:

```
          SOURCE NO.  JAN  FEB  MAR  APR  MAY  JUN  JUL  AUG  SEP  OCT  NOV  DEC  ANN

2.  PRECIPITATION (INCHES)
  MAXIMUM       3/4 12.9  9.1 12.1  6.5  4.8  3.8  2.4  4.6  6.0  7.8 11.6 15.9  57.6
  MEAN            3  5.7  4.1  3.8  2.6  1.7  1.4  0.8  1.1  1.8  3.5  5.9  5.9  38.3
  MINIMUM       3/4  0.6  0.4  0.4  0.2  0.1   #    0    0    0    #   0.5  1.0  20.0
  MAX 24 HR       3  3.0  3.1  2.7  2.6  1.8  1.8  0.9  1.6  1.7  2.7  3.4  2.1   3.4
  # DAYS GE .01    3   19   16   17   14   11    9    5    6    9   13   18   19   156
  # DAYS GE .5     3    4    2    2    1    1    1    0    1    1    2    4    4    22
```

---

[22] This is how Perl programmers get "$." to behave like AWK's FNR rather than AWK's NR (see table 5.2).

Oops, there's a snag—Patrick's eyes keep glazing over[23] as he tries to determine the number of the last field within that data paragraph, which is the one on the last line and under the ANN (for "annual") column.

However, once he realizes that there are 12 JAN-DEC columns on each line, plus an extra column at the beginning and end of that group for a total of 14 per line, plus the 3 fields for the paragraph heading and a few more for the row labels, he's able to calculate the field number as 101.

Which of the three cities has the largest number of days per annum with at least half an inch of rain? *May I have the envelope, please:*

```
$ extract_cell -recnum=6 -fnum=101 miami new_york seattle
Miami: 24

New_york: 27

Seattle: 22
```

It's New York! Vitas still can't accept the idea that New York could be rainier than Seattle, so he asks to review the script. Although he is unable to find any fault with it, he does come up with an idea for alleviating the need for those grueling field calculations in the future.

Specifically, he points out that counting 101 fields to identify the last one in the record isn't necessary, because Perl recognizes the index of -1 as referring to that element. Vitas goes on to say, like, in like fashion, -2 could be used to refer to the second element from the end, -20 to the twentieth from the end, and so forth (see table 5.9).

Patrick is excited to learn this, but he realizes that he must modify the script to avoid decrementing arguments to -fnum= that are *already* suitable index values, like -1, while still allowing conventional field-count values, such as 33, to receive the decrementing treatment they require. For additional flexibility, he modifies the script to default to line-mode but to allow paragraph mode to be enabled by a command-line switch when desired. This requires removing the -00 invocation option from the shebang line and selectively enabling paragraph mode by conditionally assigning a null string to $/ (see table 2.7).

Here's the new version, called extract_cell2:

```
#! /usr/bin/perl -s -wnla

# Prints field indicated by $recnum/$fnum, preceded by filename.
# -fnum switch handles field numbers as well as negative indices.

our ($p);        # -p switch for paragraph mode is optional

BEGIN {
  $fnum  and  $recnum or
      warn "Usage: $0 -recnum=M -fnum=N\n"  and
          exit 255;
```

---

[23] He can't help but wonder—could that genetically engineered low-carb zest be to blame?

```
    # Decrement positive fnum, so user can say 1, and get index of 0
    # But don't decrement negative values; they're indices already!
    $index=$fnum;                    # initially assume $fnum is an index
    $index >= 1 and $index--;        # make it an index if it wasn't
    $p  and  $/="";                  # set paragraph mode if requested
}
$. == $recnum  and  print "\u$ARGV: $F[$index]";

# Reset record counter $. after end of each file
eof  and  close ARGV;
```

A quick test shows that the new script successfully extracts the same figures as its predecessor:

```
$ extract_cell2 -p -recnum=6 -fnum=-1 miami new_york seattle
Miami: 24
. . .
```

Notice the use of the -p switch to enable paragraph mode, which isn't hard-coded within the script as it was in the earlier version, and the use of the convenient -1 index rather than the field number of 101, to specify the last field of the record.

Although the script seems to work properly for the data on the first page of the weather file, Patrick wants to be sure the script will work on the subsequent pages too; so, he examines them in greater detail. While doing so, he's excited to find that they all contain a data paragraph called FREQ RAIN AND/OR DRIZZLE, which sounds like a measure on which Seattle might really shine.

Comparing cities for "sogginess"

In preparation for comparing cities for frequency of rain and/or drizzle—which we'll call *sogginess* for short—Patrick improvises a paragraph-numbering one-liner to identify the record number for the relevant data paragraph:

```
$ perl -00 -wnl -e '/12\..*DRIZZLE /  and
>      print "Paragraph #$.:\n$_";' seattle
. . .
```

```
Paragraph #23:
  12.  % FREQ RAIN AND/OR DRIZZLE:
             JAN  FEB  MAR  APR  MAY  JUN  JUL  AUG  SEP  OCT  NOV  DEC  ANN
  00-02 LST   22   19   18   16   11    8    4    4    8   12   23   21   14
  03-05 LST   24   22   21   18   14   11    7    6    9   14   23   22   16
  06-08 LST   24   22   20   19   14   11    7    8    9   14   23   23   16
  09-11 LST   21   20   20   16   11    9    6    6    7   13   21   20   14
  12-14 LST   21   21   19   14   11    8    4    5    7   13   21   22   14
  15-17 LST   21   23   20   15   11    9    5    5    8   14   23   23   15
  18-20 LST   20   22   19   16   12    8    5    4    7   13   24   22   14
  21-23 LST   20   21   19   15   11    7    4    4    6   12   23   21   14
  ALL HOURS   22   21   19   16   12    9    5    5    8   13   22   22   15
```

The appropriate field for comparison is the one in the bottom-right corner of the paragraph, at the intersection of ALL HOURS and ANN. The 15 there indicates that over periods of an entire year, rain or drizzle has occurred 15 percent of the time. Seattle's track record seems like a pretty formidable one to beat, but let's see if Miami or New York is up to the challenge:

```
$ extract_cell2 -p -recnum=23 -fnum=-1 miami new_york seattle
Miami: 5
New_york: 9
Seattle: 15
```

Hooray! Finally, Seattle comes up a winner! Now you can understand why it has such a soggy reputation, despite its relatively unimpressive amounts of annual rainfall and days with significant rain. As any resident can tell you, it's the frequent drizzling that makes Seattle so refreshingly moist and inviting!

Let's sum up what we've learned about Perl from Patrick and his friends. The grep command couldn't have done the job of mean_annual_precip or the extract_cell* scripts, because it's specialized for extracting and displaying entire records. The sed command, on the other hand, could at least have whittled down the appropriate record to the correct field for us—if only it knew how to handle multiline records.

But by using Perl's AWK-like features, it was easy to arrange for the conditional printing of a specified field from a particular record, prefixed by the name of the file from which it came. Along the way, we added a useful tool to our collection—a script that extracts and prints a cell from a table.

Now it's time to discuss a powerful yet easy-to-use feature of AWK and Perl that's not widely known: the ability to apply processing to a *range* of input records.

5.5   MATCHING RANGES OF RECORDS

Consider Martina's problem. She needs help wading through her company's voluminous log files so she can more rapidly identify and correct the problems reported within them. She's particularly concerned about "File doesn't exist" errors in her Apache v2 server's error_log file, such as these examples:[24]

```
[Fri Aug 18 13:35:41 2006]
 [error] [client 127.0.0.1] File doesn't exist: /shruti.htm
[Thu Oct 19 03:03:07 2006]
 [error] [client 127.0.0.1] File doesn't exist: /html/nsiislog.dll
```

One explanation for the first error is that the indicated file used to exist, but now it's gone. Messages like the second one reflect the activities of *bad guys* who are trying to execute vulnerable programs on Martina's system.

---

[24] To save room, we always omit the initial "httpd: " string of these error messages, along with other characters (indicated by ...) when necessary. The nsiislog.dll entry references a file that could be exploited on Windows boxes by hackers.

Her first step is to extract all the lines that report errors of this type, so she constructs the following command. Notice that the apostrophe in "doesn't" is represented by its numeric code, to avoid a clash with the surrounding Shell-level single quotes:

```
$ perl -wnl -e '/File doesn\047t exist:/ and print;' error_log
...
```

The command works, but it produces hundreds of lines of output, so Martina decides to initially limit the analysis to reports within a specific time period. To accomplish this, she uses a *pattern range*.

A pattern range is a facility for selecting a series of records occurring between a pair of pattern matches. In a typical AWK usage, the programmer separates two slash-delimited regexes by a comma, and AWK's default Action is used to print the matching lines along with those that fall between them.

As an example, consider the following command:

```
$ awk '/Monday/ , /Wednesday/' days
Monday
Tuesday
Wednesday
```

It displays the first three weekday names from the days file, using a pattern range to select the lines between Monday and Wednesday:

```
$ cat days
Sunday
Monday
Tuesday
Wednesday
Thursday
...
```

The equivalent Perl program uses the *range operator* (..) between two matching operators:

```
perl -wnl '/Monday/ .. /Wednesday/ and print;' days
```

We'll discuss the two slightly different versions of Perl's range operator next.

5.5.1 Operators for single- and multi-record ranges

Perl provides two variations on the range operator—one that gives AWK-like results using two dots, and one that gives sed-like results using three dots. The difference is that the two-dot version performs the test for the second match on the same line that matched the first one (as AWK does), allowing the same line to satisfy both matches. In contrast, the three-dot version requires the second match to occur with a following record (as with sed).[25]

---

[25] Yes, it's true, sed can also match ranges of records; but that's such a well-kept secret that we discuss this feature in this chapter on AWK, where readers will be more likely to look for it.

TIP
You can keep the range operators straight by remembering that the one with more dots is the one that must match a larger number of records—at least two, rather than just one.

The behavior of Perl's range operators in matching applications is summarized in table 5.10.[26]

Table 5.10   Using pattern ranges

Operator	Sample syntax[a]	Example	Explanation
..	expr1 .. expr2 and something	/START/ .. /STOP/ and print;	Prints all records between the first containing "START" and the first containing "STOP" (which could be the same record), and then repeats that process, looking for the next record containing "START", etc. The operator returns a string ending in "E0" when "STOP" is found (see the scan4oops script).
...	expr1 ... expr2 and something	/START/ ... /STOP/ and print;	Same as the two-dot form, except the first evaluation of expr2 doesn't occur until after the record that yielded True for expr1 has already been processed, thereby preventing both patterns from matching the same record.

a. *something* is a placeholder for the expression that is to be executed for each record matched by the range operator. Although matching operators are often used for *expr1* and *expr2*, any scalar expression can be used. If *expr1* produces a True result, but *expr2* doesn't, all the remaining records are selected.

Remember Martina? She was interested in extracting "File doesn't exist" errors for a particular span of dates—let's see what she's up to.

5.5.2   Matching a range of dates

In an attempt to isolate errors for October 19 and 20, Martina tries using a pattern range. Notice that she's first using a pattern range to select lines within the desired time-period, and then checking each of those lines for the error message of interest:

```
$ perl -wnl -e '/Oct 19/ ... /Oct 20/ and
>   /File doesn\047t exist:/ and print;' error_log    # Output edited
[Thu Oct 19 ...] File doesn't exist: /html/_vti_bin/owssvr.dll
[Thu Oct 19 ...] File doesn't exist: /html/MSOffice/cltreq.asp
[Fri Oct 20 ...] File doesn't exist: /html/nsiislog.dll
```

She notices that the output isn't quite right, because it shows only the first error for "Oct 20", rather than all of them. After some thought, she decides to change the

---

[26] See *ellipsis* in the glossary to learn how to tell the difference between the three-dot version of the range operator and the three-dot ellipsis that indicates omitted material.

range's endpoint to the day beyond the last in which she's interested, so she won't miss any data for the 20th:

```
$ perl -wnl -e '/Oct 19/ ... /Oct 21/ and
>    /File doesn\047t exist:/ and
>    print;' error_log       # Output edited
[Thu Oct 19 ...] File doesn't exist: /html/_vti_bin/owssvr.dll
[Thu Oct 19 ...] File doesn't exist: /html/MSOffice/cltreq.asp
[Fri Oct 20 ...] File doesn't exist: /html/nsiislog.dll
[Fri Oct 20 ...] File doesn't exist: /html/cgi-bin/formmail.pl
[Thu Oct 21 ...] File doesn't exist: /html/nsiislog.dll
```

The output now includes all the errors for the 19th and 20th, as desired—but it also includes one for the 21st, which isn't desired. Using her burgeoning knowledge of Perl, Martina avoids printing the undesirable line by using the negation operator[27] before an additional matching operator, to introduce a "not-match" condition in the chain of logical ands:

```
$ perl -wnl -e '/Oct 19/ ... /Oct 21/ and
>        ! /Oct 21/ and /File doesn\047t exist:/ and
>            print;' error_log       # Output is edited
[Thu Oct 19 ...] File doesn't exist: /html/_vti_bin/owssvr.dll
[Thu Oct 19 ...] File doesn't exist: /html/MSOffice/cltreq.asp
[Fri Oct 20 ...] File doesn't exist: /html/nsiislog.dll
[Fri Oct 20 ...] File doesn't exist: /html/cgi-bin/formmail.pl
```

Now she has the desired result. In words, her command says:

> *Select lines starting with the first that contains Oct 19 up to the next that contains Oct 21, and for the lines that don't contain Oct 21, if the error message is present, print the line.*

It may seem odd to you that to match all the lines for October 20, Martina had to match the first for the 21st and then refrain from printing it; that's the case because the range operator stops yielding a True result when it finds the *first* match with the second pattern ("Oct 21"), rather than the *last* one.

Now that you know how to match "one record too far" with the range operator without printing that record, you'll find it easy to get the results you want while using it in applications like this one.

In contrast to the situation with Martina's error_log file—which holds less than a year's worth of data and will therefore have only one span of dates per file—there are cases where a pattern range can be expected to extract *multiple* spans of records. We'll consider a case of that type next.

---

[27] Covered near the end of section 2.4.5.

5.5.3 Matching multiple ranges

An expression that selects records using a range operator, such as a pattern range, isn't restricted to matching a single span of records—on the contrary, it will match all the qualifying spans it can find.

We'll use the show_fields2_1 script (see listing 5.3), whose purpose is to print the second field of the input before the first, to illustrate the technique. It's a legitimate script, but it's a kind we haven't discussed yet—one that incorporates its own documentation in *POD* format,[28] mixed in with the Perl code.

Listing 5.3   Script with embedded POD documentation: show_fields2_1

```
1    #! /usr/bin/perl -wnla
2
3    =pod
4
5    =head1 Name
6
7    show_fields2_1 - Show field #2 followed by field #1
8
9    =head1 Synopsis
10
11   show_fields2_1 [file1 file2 ...]
12
13   =head1 Description
14
15   For each input line, prints field #2 followed by field #1.
16
17   =cut
18
19   ($A, $B)=@F;      # Copy first field to $A, second to $B
20   print "$B $A";    # Print in reverse order
21
22   =pod
23
24   =head1 Author
25
26   Halchal Punter, IIT Rishikesh 27
27
28   =cut
```

Of course, the embedded documentation must be identified in a special way so it can be distinguished from the program code. You do this by marking the beginning of a

---

[28] This is Perl's native documentation format, whose full name is Plain Old Documentation (see man perlpod). By the way, I wrote the early drafts of this book using home-grown enhancements to POD, UNIX's venerable troff typesetting software, and additional Perl programs I wrote to help them cooperate.

chunk of POD documentation with =pod and its end with =cut. In listing 5.3, I highlighted these regions by using bold type for the directives and drawing a box around the documentation they enclose.

Perl's POD tools (such as perldoc) extract and process the documentation between these markers; conversely, the Perl interpreter filters out these parts and treats what's left as program code.

Here's a command that extracts and displays any POD documentation it finds in a file:

```
$ perl -wnl -e '/^=pod$/ ... /^=cut$/ and print;' show_fields2_1
=pod

=head1 Name

show_fields2_1 - Show field #2 followed by field #1

=head1 Synopsis

show_fields2_1 [file1 file2 ...]

=head1 Description

For each input line, prints field #2 followed by field #1.

=cut
=pod

=head1 Author

Halchal Punter, IIT Rishikesh

=cut
```

Two =pod to =cut chunks of documentation were found and printed.

The utility used to view POD documentation, perldoc, first extracts the embedded documentation in like fashion and then converts it to the Unix manual page format. Here's the documentation for show_fields2_1, as extracted and formatted from the script itself by perldoc:

```
$ perldoc show_fields2_1      # edited for fit

SHOW_FIELDS2_1(1) User Contributed Documentation  SHOW_FIELDS2_1(1)

Name
        show_fields2_1 - Show field #2 followed by field #1

Synopsis
        show_fields2_1 [file1 file2 ...]

Description
        For each input line, prints field #2 followed by field #1.

Author
        Halchal Punter, IIT Rishikesh
```

As you'll see in upcoming examples, Perl's ability to match pattern ranges comes in handy in a variety of contexts and often leads to easy solutions to otherwise difficult programming problems.

But first, we'll discuss some other fundamental resources used in Perl programming—*operators*.

5.6 USING RELATIONAL AND ARITHMETIC OPERATORS

Because AWK is a general-purpose programming language, it provides facilities for branching on the basis of logical tests and for performing numeric calculations. This section shows you how AWK's logical and mathematical operators compare to Perl's and explains how to write Perl programs that compare strings, compare numbers, and perform calculations.

5.6.1 Relational operators

Table 5.11 lists the relational operators of AWK—and their counterparts in Perl.

Table 5.11   Relational operators of AWK and Perl

AWK	Perl numeric	string	Name
==	==	eq	Equal to
!=	!=	ne	Not equal to
>	>	gt	Greater than
>=	>=	ge	Greater than or equal to
<	<	lt	Less than
<=	<=	le	Less than or equal to
N/A	<=>	cmp	Comparison

Unlike those programming in other languages, AWK programmers can compare numbers or strings by using a single set of operators and leaving it up to the language to determine which type of comparison to apply. This is a convenience in the majority of cases, where AWK is smart enough to correctly guess your intentions.[29]

In contrast, Perl programmers use different operators for comparing numbers and strings, which eliminates guesswork of the kind that AWK engages in when such comparisons are made. As shown in table 5.11, Perl uses the mathematical-looking operators of AWK for comparing numbers and word-like ones for comparing strings.

---

[29] I can tell you from hard-earned experience that AWK hasn't always guessed correctly, requiring me to engage in more marathon debugging sessions than I care to remember.

Here's an AWK program that prints Lines 24–42 of its input:

```
awk '24 <= NR && NR <= 42' file
```

Its Perl counterpart has to specify the and print Action that is AWK's default, along with a different logical and operator and a different variable name:

```
perl -wnl -e '24 <= $. and $. <= 42 and print;' file
```

The following programs print the lines after the second that are alphanumerically greater than "L". The result is that the first two input lines are filtered out, along with those that begin with a letter in the range "A" through "L":

```
awk          'NR > 2 &&  $0  > "L"' names
perl -wnl -e '$. > 2 and $_ gt "L"  and print;' names
```

Notice the use of the numeric greater-than operator in the first Perl expression and the use of the string greater-than operator in the second one.

Table 5.11 also shows that Perl has one relational operator that AWK lacks, called the *comparison operator*. Like the others, it comes in two forms: one for comparing numbers (<=>) and one for comparing strings (cmp). Its purpose is to return a number that indicates whether the left operand is less than, equal to, or greater than the right operand.[30] It's most commonly used with the sort function, so it's discussed in chapter 7.

5.6.2 Arithmetic operators

Like AWK, Perl has inherited a rich set of operators for doing arithmetic from their common ancestor, the C language. Table 5.12 lists the most important operators of this set.[31]

The compound assignment operators listed in the bottom panel have a special property in Perl. Consider, for example, the following two Perl statements, which ultimately do the same job, despite their different appearances:

```
$sum=$sum + $_;   # increment value in $sum by value of current line
```

Versus

```
$sum += $_;       # means: $sum=$sum + $_;   (same as above)
```

Each adds the current numeric value of $_ to the current numeric value of $sum before storing the result back in $sum. But if $sum hasn't been initialized by the time the statement is first executed, and warnings are enabled (e.g., via –w), the statements will behave a bit differently. Specifically, an "uninitialized variable" warning will be generated for the first format, when Perl automatically initializes the variable to zero

---

[30] Any functional similarity between this operator and the strcmp() library function of the C language was fully intended by Larry.

[31] For a more complete list of Perl operators, run man perlop.

Table 5.12 Arithmetic operators of AWK and Perl

Operator [a]	Name	Operation
++	Plus plus	Incrementing
--	Minus minus	Decrementing
*	Star	Multiplication
/	Slash	Division
%	Modulus	Remainder of integer division
+	Plus	Addition
-	Minus	Subtraction
+= -= *= /=	Compound assignment	`$A += 1` means `$A=($A + 1)`, etc.

a. Operators sharing the same precedence level are listed in the same panel, with operator precedence decreasing across panels from the top of the table to the bottom. Section 2.4.5 explains the concept of operator precedence.

to permit the calculation to proceed. In contrast, Perl doesn't issue a warning if you use the second format, because it figures you're smart enough to know what you're doing if you use that fancy syntax.[32]

Next, we'll compare the sets of built-in functions supplied with AWK and Perl. These are great productivity enhancers, because by using them effectively, you can reduce the amount of custom code you have to write for your programs.

5.7   USING BUILT-IN FUNCTIONS

A major advantage of AWK over its forebears—grep, sed, and the Shell—is that it comes with a useful collection of built-in functions for processing text, numbers, input and output, and more. Perl also has functions like these, but it does AWK one better—it incorporates a module facility for importing additional functions into programs, letting you extend the language on the fly (as discussed in chapters 2 and 12).

As a case in point, the compound_interest2 script presented later (section 5.8.1) uses a function that conditionally pluralizes a noun—despite the fact that Perl doesn't officially have any such function!

You'll see that script shortly. But first, look at table 5.13, which lists some popular built-in functions for two flavors of the *new* AWK as well as Perl.

We've already encountered several of the Perl functions listed in the table (including length, sqrt, die, print, printf, substr, and warn), and you'll see others used in part 2. You'll find many of their names to be familiar if you have prior experience with the Basic, AWK, C, Shell, or Unix programming environments.

---

[32] See the discussion of the incomplete script in section 5.4 for more on the subject of variable initializations and avoiding the "uninitialized variable" warning.

Table 5.13 Popular built-in functions of AWK and Perl

Type[a]	NAWK	GAWK	Perl
String	gsub, index, match, split, sprintf, sub, substr, tolower, toupper	asort, gensub, gsub, index, length, match, split, strtonum, sub, substr, tolower, toupper	chomp, chop, chr, crypt, hex, index, lc, lcfirst, length, oct, ord, pack, q/*STRING*/, qq/*STRING*/, reverse, rindex, sprintf, substr, tr///, uc, ucfirst, y///
Arithmetic	cos, exp, int, log, sin, sqrt, srand	cos, exp, int, log, sin, sqr	abs, atan2, cos, exp, hex, int, log, oct, rand, sin, sqrt, srand
Input/Output	close, getline, print, printf	close, getline, print, printf, fflush	binmode, close, closedir, dbmclose, dbmopen, die, eof, fileno, flock, format, getc, print, printf, warn
Miscellaneous	system	bindtextdomain, compl, dcgettext, dcngettext, extension, lshift, mktime, rshift, strftime, system	defined, dump, eval, formline, gmtime, local, localtime, my, our, pos, reset, scalar, system, time, undef, wantarray

a. The standard Perl installation provides hundreds of additional functions not listed here, including ones that fall into these categories: Unix system calls, array handling, file handling, fixed-length record manipulation, hash handling, list processing, module management, network information retrieval, pattern matching, process control, socket control, user/group information retrieval, and variable scoping.

However, some of the apparent similarities between the languages mask significant differences. For example, some AWK functions have namesakes that take different arguments in Perl, and certain other functions, such as AWK's sub and match, correspond to operators represented by symbols in Perl, rather than to named functions.

To help AWKiologists migrate to Perlistan, table 5.14 shows the Perl counterparts to the most commonly used (non-mathematical) functions found in popular versions of AWK. Some general differences are that Perl functions are normally invoked without any parentheses around their arguments,[33] and all occurrences of the $0 variable in the AWK examples must be converted to $_ for Perl (assuming use of the n or p option).

Notice in particular that the "offset" argument (#2) of AWK's substr ("substring") function needs to be a 1 to grab characters from the very beginning of the string, whereas in Perl, the value 0 has that meaning.

---

[33] But if you've been cruelly rebuked by other languages whenever you've forgotten to use parentheses around your function arguments, and you consequently feel your Perl programs look shockingly defective without them, feel free to put them in! Perl won't mind.

Table 5.14 Perl counterparts to popular AWK functions

AWK (or GAWK)	Perl
sub("*RE*","*replacement*")	s/*RE*/*replacement*/;
gsub("*RE*","*replacement*")	s/*RE*/*replacement*/g;
match(*string_var*,"*RE*")	$string_var =~ /*RE*/;
substr($0, **1**, 3)	substr $_, **0**, 3;
$0=tolower($0)	$_="\L$_"; Or $_=lc;
$0=toupper($0)	$_="\U$_"; Or $_=uc;
getline	$_=<>;
split($0, *array_var*)	@*array_var*=split;
index, length, print, printf, sprintf, system	Same function names, but Perl doesn't require parentheses.

Another difference is that GAWK's case-conversion functions, toupper and tolower, have two corresponding resources in Perl—the functions called uc and lc, and the \U and \L string modifiers (see table 4.5).

Perl's voluminous collection of built-in functions makes it easy to write commands that do various types of data processing, as you'll see next.

5.7.1 One-liners that use functions

The following command prints up to 80 characters from each input line:

```
perl -wnl -e 'print substr $_, 0, 80;' lines
```

It uses the substr function and specifies an offset of zero from the beginning of $_ as the starting point, along with a selection length of 80 characters. Because the call to substr appears in the argument list of print, substr's output is delivered into print's argument list and subsequently printed.

The following command reads lines consisting of numbers, and prints their square roots:

```
perl -wnl -e 'print "The square root of $_ is ", sqrt $_;' numbers
```

The addition of syntactically unnecessary but cosmetically beneficial **parentheses** changes the previous commands into these variations:

```
perl -wnl -e 'print "The square root of $_ is ", sqrt($_);' numbers
perl -wnl -e 'print substr ($_, 0, 80);' lines
```

Perl won't mind the unnecessary parentheses (see section 7.6, and appendix B), but after you become more acculturated to Perlistan, you'll no longer feel the need to type them in such cases.

Commands like those just reviewed are great for applying the same processing regimen to each input record—but what if you only want to perform a single numeric calculation, such as the square root of 42 or the remainder of 365 divided by 12?

You could write a custom program to generate each of those results. But wouldn't it be even better to write a generic script that could calculate and print the result of any basic mathematical problem?

This valuable technique will be demonstrated next, using a command of legendary significance.

5.7.2 The legend of `nexpr`

We'll begin this section with a discussion of the role played by a certain command in UNIX's early years and how AWK improved on it, and then you'll see how Perl's version is even better. Along the way, you'll learn not only some UNIX history, but also how to win barroom bets by writing one-liners on napkins that can compute transcendental numbers![34]

But first, you need to understand that in the early days of UNIX, C was considered the language of choice for all *serious* computing tasks—such as performing mathematical calculations. In contrast, the early shells were viewed as simple tools for packaging command sequences in scripts and processing interactively issued commands.

For this reason, the utility program that was used to perform calculations in shell programming, expr, was only endowed with the most rudimentary mathematical capabilities:

```
$ expr 22 / 7        # Gimme pi!  And I won't take 3 for an answer!
3
```

Moreover, using expr was horrendously inefficient. For instance, reading 100 numbers from a file and totaling them required 100 separate expr processes—compared to a *single process* on modern systems, using AWK or Perl.

Therefore, even though it was the mathematical mainstay of Bourne shell programming during the late 1970s and 1980s, the expr approach to arithmetic still left a lot to be desired.[35] Given this situation, it's no wonder there was so much interest in improving expr.

Without further ado, I'll now relate to you the *Legend of Nexpr* (for *new* expr), which was initially told to me by my Bell System boss, then extensively embellished by yours truly through hundreds of retellings to my students.

---

[34] Well, at least approximations thereof.

[35] We actually had a great alternative for doing arithmetic starting in 1977—AWK! But most programmers didn't understand its capabilities until the 1988 book came out.

Born in a barroom wager: `nexpr`

One day after work in the early 1980s, three Bell System software engineers stop in a popular New Jersey watering hole. The bearded veteran orders his usual—a pint of Guinness—while the rookies each order a can of the local lager.

"Man," the veteran mumbles, apparently to himself, "the UNIX shell is really awesome for math!"

The first rookie says to the other, "Grandpa over there thinks the shell is good at math! That black sludge he's imbibing must have fouled up his logic circuits."

Fixing his beady eyes intensely on the impudent rookie, the veteran says:

> *I'll bet you $100 each I can write a one-line shell script that calculates the **square root of pi**!* [36]

The second rookie exclaims, "Impossible! The `expr` command used in Bourne shell programming can't even do floating-point calculations, let alone mathematical functions—we accept the bet."

While hastily writing the following script on a napkin—using a nacho-chip dipped in salsa—the veteran says, "I call the script **n**`expr`, for new `expr`":

```
#! /bin/sh
awk "BEGIN{ print $*; exit }"
```

"Read it and weep, and hand over $200!"

If laptop computers running UNIX had been available in those days, the Chumps would surely have typed in the script and tested it on the spot, using this command:[37]

```
$ nexpr 'sqrt(22/7)'   # Becomes: awk 'BEGIN {print sqrt(22/7); exit}'
1.77281
```

(The comment attached to that command shows the `awk` command that is composed and run by `nexpr`, as explained in section 5.7.3.)

The rookies are first shocked, then flabbergasted, and finally angry. They cry foul, arguing that `awk` isn't part of the shell, and therefore what he has written isn't a shell script after all.

The veteran mounts a quick defense by pointing to the script's unequivocally shellish shebang line and reminding them that it's normal for a shell script to use external UNIX commands like `sort`, `grep`, and yes, even `awk`—not to mention the `expr` command they assumed he'd use.

The rookies grudgingly relent and remit payment, admitting they've been outfoxed by the wily vet.

---

[36] You know, the transcendental number that expresses the ratio of the circumference of a circle to its diameter that's represented by the sixteenth letter of the Greek alphabet, .

[37] `expr` can do more than arithmetic, so the `nexpr*` scripts aren't full-fledged replacements for it.

Okay, I hear you. You're wondering, *"What does all this have to do with Perl?"* Quite a bit, actually, because Perl can do just about anything AWK can do—including generating revenues from barroom wagers.

The *nexpr_p* script (Perl)

A script like nexpr is a great asset to those employing a command-line interface to Unix. But the Perl version, which I call nexpr_**p** (for **p**erl), is even better than the original nexpr:

```
$ cat nexpr_p
#! /bin/sh
# This script uses the Shell to create and run a custom Perl
# program that evaluates and prints its arguments.
# Sample transformation: nexpr_p '2 * 21' --> perl ... print 2 * 21;

perl -wl -e "print $*;"
```

Perl is smart enough to exit automatically once it runs out of things to do, so there's no need for an explicit exit statement in this script as there was with the classic AWK of nexpr's era. Nor is there any need for a BEGIN block, which the AWK version requires to position its statements outside the (obligatory) implicit input-reading loop. That's because that (unnecessary) loop can be omitted from the Perl version through use of the −w**l** cluster instead of −w**n**l.

Like nexpr, nexpr_p is capable of performing any calculation that is supported by its built-in operators (such as / for division; see table 5.12) or its functions (such as sqrt; see table 5.13). But the Perl version is even more capable than nexpr, because it has access to a richer collection of built-in functions, along with Perl's other advantages over AWK (especially its module mechanism).

Next, we'll discuss how these nexpr* scripts manage to make the requested computations.

5.7.3 How the *nexpr** programs work

The nexpr_p Shell script works the same way nexpr does—by exploiting the Shell's willingness to substitute the script's own arguments (see tables 2.4, 10.1) for the "$*" variable in a double-quoted string, thereby creating a custom print statement to handle the user's request.

So when the user issues this comand:

```
$ nexpr_p 'sqrt(22/7)'
```

nexpr_p's Shell transforms the Perl source code template in the script from

```
perl -wl -e "print $*;"
```

into

```
perl -wl -e "print sqrt(22/7);"
```

and executes that command.

Next, we'll examine some additional programs that employ techniques presented in this chapter.

5.8   ADDITIONAL EXAMPLES

This section features Perl programs that analyze Linux log files, perform compound interest calculations, and inflect nouns in `print` statements to make them singular or plural as needed. I think you'll find these examples interesting, but feel free to proceed to the next chapter at this point if you prefer.

5.8.1   Computing compound interest: `compound_interest`

Consider the following script called `compound_interest`, which reports the growth of an investment over time:

```
$ compound_interest -amount=100  -rate=18
Press <ENTER> to see $100 compound at 18%.<ENTER>
$118 after 1 year(s)<ENTER>
$139.24 after 2 year(s)<ENTER>
$164.3032 after 3 year(s)<ENTER>
$193.877776 after 4 year(s)<^D>
```

Although the script uses the n option, it's meant to be invoked without any file-name arguments, so it will default to reading input from the user's terminal. This allows each press of <ENTER> to be taken as a request to show an additional year's worth of growth.[38] What's more, when given certain command-line switches, the script will calculate the growth of an arbitrary initial investment at an arbitrary annual rate of interest. I'm sure your interest in examining the script is rapidly *compounding*, so have a look at listing 5.4.

Listing 5.4   The `compound_interest` script

```
1   #! /usr/bin/perl -s -wn
2
3   BEGIN {
4       $Usage="Usage: $0 -amount=dollars -rate=percent";
5
6       # Check for proper invocation
7       $amount  and  $rate  or  warn "$Usage\n"  and  exit 255;
8
9       $pct_rate=$rate/100;        # convert interest to decimal
10      $multiplier=1 + $pct_rate;  # .05 becomes 1.05
11      # Instruct user
12      print "Press <ENTER> to see \$$amount compound at $rate%.";
13  }
```

---

[38] The results demonstrate the *Rule of 72*, according to which an investment of X at Y% interest will approximately double in value every $72/Y$ years. In this case, Y is 18, yielding 4 years for each doubling.

```
14
15   $amount=$amount * $multiplier;          # accumulate growth
16
17   # $. counts input lines, which represent years here
18   print "\$$amount after $. year(s)";
19
20   END { print "\n"; } # start shell prompt on fresh line after <^D>
```

The first thing to notice is that all the operations that can be done in advance of input processing are collected together in the BEGIN block. For example, an informational message is loaded into the $Usage variable on Line 4, which will be printed by the warn function if the user neglects to provide the required switches.

The nominal percentage rate is then converted to a decimal number on Line 9, and the multiplier that will be used to add each additional year's worth of interest to the previous balance is prepared on Line 10. Then a message is printed to inform the user how to interact with the program.

Next, the program waits for a line of input (via <ENTER>) before executing the first line after the BEGIN block, Line 15, which calculates the new balance figure. The result is then reported to the user on Line 18.

Fortunately, although we think of "$." as counting records, in cases where records represent the passage of additional years of investment growth—as they do here—that variable conveniently doubles as a *year* counter.

Notice the need to backslash certain $ symbols in the double-quoted strings of Lines 12 and 18 to make them literal dollar signs, and the absence of that treatment for the $ symbols attached to scalar variable names, which allows variable interpolation for $amount and "$." to occur.

Although this is a useful program, it doesn't do anything that AWK couldn't do on its own—at least, not yet. But we'll teach it how to improve its grammar next, using a valuable programmer's aid that AWK lacks.

5.8.2   Conditionally pluralizing nouns: compound_interest2

As useful as it is, there's something that bothers me about the compound_interest program.

Specifically, it's the output statement that hedges its bets on the singular/plural nature of the year-count, using the phrasing "1 year(s)" and "2 year(s)". Like any literate person striving for grammatical correctness,[39] I'd prefer to see the output presented as "1 year" and "2 years" instead.

Although programmers using other languages—including AWK—may have to settle for such compromises, we certainly don't in the world of Perl! The

---

[39] More candidly, as a survivor of a Catholic grade-school education, something deep inside me still fears the *wrath of the hickory ruler* on my *throbbing knuckles* when I contemplate such flagrant examples of grammatical incorrectness.

easy and entirely general solution to this problem is to use a function from the `Lingua::EN::Inflect` module to automatically *inflect* the word as "year" or "years", so it will match the numeric value before it.

To effect this enhancement, you first download and install the required module from the CPAN (as discussed in chapter 12) and then add the following line at the top of the script:

```
use Lingua::EN::Inflect 'PL_N';
```

That statement loads the module and the needed function, which in this case is one that knows how to conditionally pluralize ("PL") a noun ("N"). Then, the statement that prints the investment's growth is modified to call `PL_N` with arguments consisting of the noun and its associated count.

For comparison, here are the original and `PL_N`-enhanced `print` statements:

```
print "\$$amount after $. year(s)";        # 1 year(s), 2 year(s)

print "\$$amount after $. ", PL_N 'year', $.;  # 1 year, 2 years
```

Notice that the quoted string is terminated after the first "$." in the second version, because the function name `PL_N` would be treated as literal text if it appeared within those quotes.

How does the automatic inflection work? The function `PL_N` returns its first argument as "year" or "years", according to the singular/plural nature of the number in "$.", its second argument. Then, the word returned by `PL_N` becomes the final argument to `print`, providing the grammatically correct output that's desired.[40]

Here's a sample run of the enhanced script:

```
$ compound_interest2 -amount=100  -rate=10
Press <ENTER> to see $100 compound at 10%.<ENTER>
$110 after 1 year<ENTER>
$121 after 2 years ...
```

Listing 5.5 shows the enhanced script in its entirety.

An alternative to using a module-based function to conditionally print "year" or "years" would be to employ Perl's `if`/`else` construct (covered in part 2) to print the appropriate word. But it's equally easy to use the `PL_N` function—and more empowering to learn how to do such things using Perl's modules—than it is to roll your own solution. For this reason, we'll discuss functions and modules more fully in part 2.

---

[40] As detailed in section 7.6, adding optional parentheses may make it clearer to the reader that the final "$." is an argument to `PL_N`, not to `print`:
```
print "\$$amount after $. ",  PL_N('year', $.);
```

Listing 5.5   The `compound_interest2` script

```
1   #! /usr/bin/perl -s -wn
2
3   use Lingua::EN::Inflect 'PL_N'; # import noun pluralizer
4
5   BEGIN {
6       $Usage="Usage: $0 -amount=dollars -rate=percent";
7
8       # Check for proper invocation
9       $amount  and  $rate  or  warn "$Usage\n"  and  exit 255;
10
11      $pct_rate=$rate/100;        #   5 becomes .05
12      $multiplier=1 + $pct_rate;  # .05 becomes 1.05
13      # Instruct user
14      print "Press <ENTER> to see \$$amount compound at $rate%.";
15  }
16
17  $amount=$amount * $multiplier;          # accumulate growth
18
19  # $. counts input lines, which represent years
20  print "\$$amount after $. ",  PL_N 'year', $.;
21
22  END { print "\n"; } # start shell prompt on fresh line after <^D>
```

5.8.3   Analyzing log files: `scan4oops`

Felix has been a happy Linux user since his company installed it on all their notebook computers a few years back. But ever since that clumsy security agent dropped Felix's notebook at the airport, while Felix was frantically trying to grab his freshly X-rayed shoes, his notebook has been crashing periodically. Of course, he did load some experimental device drivers into the kernel during that flight, which could also be the source of the problem.

In any case, he needs to diagnose the problem and get his notebook fixed. He already ran its hardware diagnostic tests several times, and it passed them all with flying colors. So, he needs to try another approach.

The nice people at the local Linux users group suggested he should check the /var/log/messages file for "Oops" reports, because they might indicate why his machine is crashing. When his boss, Murray, heard about this, he requested that Felix formalize his solution in the form of a Perl script so that others in the company (and the users group) could benefit from his efforts.

Felix examines that file and indeed finds an "Oops" report within it. To help the report fit on the page, the timestamp at the beginning of every line, "Aug 17 04:15:14 floss kernel: " has been removed:

```
Oops: 0001
CPU:    0
EIP:    0010:[__remove_inode_page+79/144]    Not tainted
EIP:    0010:[<c01284ff>]    Not tainted
EFLAGS: 00210206
eax: 00003200   ebx: c1063334   ecx: c326c9e8   edx: c1065de4
esi: c326c8b4   edi: c02b2a78   ebp: 0000156d   esp: c9f31f28
ds: 0018   es: 0018   ss: 0018
Process kswapd (pid: 4, stackpage=c9f31000)
Stack: c326c800 c1063334 00000000 c1063334 c01302d0 c1063334 000001d0 c9f30000
        00000c1c 000001d0 00000010 0000001f 000001d0 c02b2a78 c02b2a78 c013055d
        c9f31f88 000001d0 0000003c 00000020 c01305e2 c9f31f88 c9f30000 00000000
Call Trace:    [shrink_cache+656/896] [shrink_caches+61/96] . . .
Call Trace:    [<c01302d0>] [<c013055d>] [<c01305e2>] [<c013079c>] [<c0130808>]
  [kswapd+157/192] [rest_init+0/64] [arch_kernel_thread+46/64] [kswapd+0/192]
  [<c013094d>] [<c0105000>] [<c01073fe>] [<c01308b0>]

Code: 89 50 24 89 02 c7 43 24 00 00 00 00 89 1c 24 c7 44 24 04 ff
```

Isn't that a lovely format? 8-(

Scanning onward in the file, he notices many other "Oops" reports, varying slightly in their details. Realizing he'd probably need to examine them all eventually, he resolves to write a script to extract them.

His first step in attaining that goal is to identify what it is about the "Oops" reports that distinguishes them from the many other reports in the same file, including ones like these:

```
Aug ... floss insmod: Using ... usb-storage.o
Aug ... floss sshd[1079]: Received signal 15; terminating.
Aug ... floss cardmgr[807]: executing: './network check eth0'
```

He finds an easy answer—apart from the "Oops" reports all having multiple lines, the first line is always of this form:

```
Aug 17 04:15:14 floss kernel: Oops: 0001
```

And the last line always ends with a sequence of 20 two-digit hex numbers:

```
Apr 17 00:38:52 floss kernel: Code: 89 50 24 89 02 c7 43 24 ...
```

Having found the distinctive markers that encase each "Oops" report, Felix's next step is to construct regexes to match them.

Constructing a regex to match "Oops" reports

On further scrutiny, Felix notices that the timestamps on the individual reports differ, and that the hostname "floss" that appears within them is unique to his system. So he allows for variations in those fields in the regex he designs to match the initial line of an "Oops" report:

```
^[A-Z]\w+ +\d+ \d+:\d+:\d+ \w+ kernel: Oops: \d+          | Position
A         B    C         D                                ↵ | markers
```

This regex says, starting from position A, "Find records that start with a capital letter, followed by one or more 'word' characters" (that's for the Month-abbreviation).

Then, at B, "there must be one or more spaces followed by one or more digits" (that's for the number of the day, allowing for an extra space before a one-digit day number). Then, at C, "we need a space followed by three sets of digits separated by two colons and followed by a space" (for the hours:minutes:seconds of the time), "followed by (at D) a word and a space" (for the hostname), "followed by the literal text 'kernel: Oops: ', and then some digits."

Being a conscientious programmer who prefers an ounce of prevention to a pound of cure, Felix built up that long regex one step at a time, ensuring that it still matched a sample report's initial line as each component was added, so that he'd know where he'd gone wrong if the match suddenly failed.

The specific numbers on the "Code:" line that ends each report are variable, so he composes an appropriate regex to match them. To save some typing, he copies most of the regex for the initial line of "Oops" reports and then adds the new components (in bold):

```
^[A-Z]\w+ +\d+ \d+:\d+:\d+ \w+ kernel: Code:( [a-f0-9][a-f0-9]){20}
```

Felix used the {20} quantifier (see table 3.9) to concisely specify exactly 20 occurrences of the grouped space/hex-digit/hex-digit sequence that follows Code:. He put parentheses around the sequence that needs to be repeated so the following quantifier would be applied to that sequence, rather than to the item immediately before the opening curly brace (the second [a-f0-9]).

Next, he put each regex into a matching operator, joined them with the "..." range operator, dangled a conditional print at one end and a variable assignment at the other, and packaged it all in the scan4oops script shown in listing 5.6.

Listing 5.6   The scan4oops script

```
#! /usr/bin/perl -wnl
# Extracts and displays "Oops" errors reported by Linux kernel
# User should run "ksymoops" command on each report to decode it
BEGIN {
    @ARGV='/var/log/messages';      # set filename argument
}

# Sample first line of "Oops" report, for Linux kernel v2.4.26:
#   Apr 16 19:30:04 floss kernel: Oops: 0001

# Print lines between first and last (inclusive) of the Oops report
$status=/^[A-Z]\w+ +\d+ \d+:\d+:\d+ \w+ kernel: Oops: \d+/
    ...     # <-- range operator
/^[A-Z]\w+ +\d+ \d+:\d+:\d+ \w+ kernel: Code:( [a-f0-9][a-f0-9]){20}/
    and  print;

# If range operator returned E0, we just printed last line of
# report; print empty string to get blank line before next report
```

Although the structure of the key statement in that script may be hard to discern because of the long regexes, it's really quite simple:

```
$variable=/RE1/ ... /RE2/ and print;
```

Owing to the precedence levels of the various operators (see man perlop), the statement is processed as follows. First, the range operator is evaluated, then its returned value is assigned to the variable, and then the True/False status of the variable's value is tested to conditionally print the current record.

As stated in table 5.10, the range operator returns the special string "E0" to indicate when it has matched the last element of the specified range—in this case, the ending line of an "Oops" report. Accordingly, Felix captures the range operator's return value in $status and checks it against the regex "E0" at the bottom of the implicit loop, so that he can print a blank line for separation after the last line of the current "Oops" report has been printed. This makes it much easier for him to see where one report ends and the next begins, when there are multiple reports.

Felix switches to the root account before running his script so he'll be permitted to read the /var/log/messages file. After some testing, he concludes that the script works.

But he still has no idea what's wrong with his notebook or what these "Oops" reports are trying to tell him! So he checks with the Linux users group again and is informed that the ksymoops command must be used to convert the inscrutable codes of those "Oops" reports into a form more fit for human consumption.

After rerunning his script with output redirected to a file, Felix uses the ksymoops command as instructed to process the single "Oops" report in the file:

```
$ ksymoops oops1    # Edited to save space
Oops: 0001
...     (Rest of Oops report appears here, followed by:)
>>EIP; c01284ff <__remove_inode_page+4f/90>    <=====

>>ebx; c1063334 <_end+d29ed0/a4efbfc>
...
>>ecx; c326c9e8 <_end+2f33584/a4efbfc>
>>edx; c1065de4 <_end+d2c980/a4efbfc>
>>esi; c326c8b4 <_end+2f33450/a4efbfc>
>>edi; c02b2a78 <contig_page_data+d8/3ac>
>>esp; c9f31f28 <_end+9bf8ac4/a4efbfc>

Trace; c01302d0 <shrink_cache+290/380>
Trace; c013055d <shrink_caches+3d/60>
Trace; c01305e2 <try_to_free_pages_zone+62/f0>
...
Trace; c013079c <kswapd_balance_pgdat+6c/b0>
Trace; c0130808 <kswapd_balance+28/40>
Trace; c013094d <kswapd+9d/c0>
Trace; c0105000 <_stext+0/0>
Trace; c01073fe <arch_kernel_thread+2e/40>
Trace; c01308b0 <kswapd+0/c0>
```

```
Code;  c01284ff <__remove_inode_page+4f/90>
00000000 <_EIP>:
Code;  c01284ff <__remove_inode_page+4f/90>   <=====
   0:   89 50 24                  mov    %edx,0x24(%eax)   <=====
Code;  c0128502 <__remove_inode_page+52/90>
   3:   89 02                     mov    %eax,(%edx)
Code;  c0128504 <__remove_inode_page+54/90>
   5:   c7 43 24 00 00 00 00      movl   $0x0,0x24(%ebx)
Code;  c012850b <__remove_inode_page+5b/90>
   c:   89 1c 24                  mov    %ebx,(%esp,1)
Code;  c012850e <__remove_inode_page+5e/90>
   f:   c7 44 24 04 ff 00 00      movl   $0xff,0x4(%esp,1)
Code;  c0128515 <__remove_inode_page+65/90>
  16:   00
```

Felix is happy to see that this report, which converts memory addresses into kernel symbols, shows the actual names of the kernel functions that were called just before the problem occurred. He's feeling optimistic because he's been told that the local "kernel nerds" will be able to help him isolate his problem with the benefit of this information.

However, he's having second thoughts about the robustness of his script. For example, what will happen when the upgrade to the next version of the Linux kernel occurs? Newer versions sometimes introduce changes in kernel error messages, and all it would take to make his regexes fail is the tiniest variation from the current format—such as changing any of its spaces into a tab, or reducing the number of "code" items from 20 to 19.

Given that everybody in the company will ultimately have access to this script, and untold numbers of Linux users groups as well, it seems worthwhile to spend some time to clean it up a bit. That effort leads to scan4oops2, which we'll discuss next.

The enhanced scan4oops2 script

To make his script more modular, readable, and maintainable, Felix breaks its regexes into tiny pieces, and stores those pieces in suitably named variables. This should enable anyone who can interpret a variable name to identify which metacharacters would need to be adjusted to handle any change in the format of a future Linux kernel's messages.

Listing 5.7 shows the new, more maintainable version of the script, called scan4oops2.

In this new script, Felix has made good use of Perl's capabilities by storing regular expression metacharacters in variables, using shortcut metacharacters (such as \w and \d) for conciseness, using the {20} quantifier in $codes to represent 20 hex numbers, and assembling the $timestamp, $oops_start, and $oops_end regexes through use of variable interpolation within double-quoted strings.

Listing 5.7   The scan4oops2 script

```perl
1   #! /usr/bin/perl -s -wnl
2
3   our ($debug);    # debugging switch is optional
4
5   BEGIN {
6     $month='[A-Z]\w+';
7     $spaces=' +';   # for space(s) between month and day number
8     $date='\d+';
9     $hhmmss='\d+:\d+:\d+';
10    $hostname='\w+';
11    $oops_num='\d+';
12
13    # Assemble pieces into more usable form
14    $timestamp="$month$spaces$date $hhmmss $hostname kernel";
15
16    # "Codes" occur in a series of 20 hex numbers,
17    #  so allow digits and letters a-f
18    $hex_digit='[a-f0-9]';
19    $num_codes='20';
20    $gap=' ';        # one space currently, in future could change?
21
22    # RE for $num_codes reps of $gap-prefixed $hex_digit pairs
23    $codes="($gap$hex_digit$hex_digit){$num_codes}";
24
25    # Assemble RE to match first line of report
26    # Sample first line: Apr 17 19:30:04 floss kernel: Oops: 0001
27    $oops_start="$timestamp: Oops: $oops_num";
28
29    # Assemble RE to match last line of report
30    # Sample last line; wrapped onto new line after Code:
31    # Apr 17 19:30:04 floss kernel: Code:
32    # 89 50 24 89 02 c7 43 24 00 00 00 00 89 1c 24 c7 44 24 04 ff
33
34    $oops_end="$timestamp: Code:$codes";
35
36    $debug  and  warn "Oops start RE:\n'$oops_start'",
37        "\n\nOops  end  RE:\n'$oops_end'\n\n";
38  }
39
40  # Now extract and print "Oops" reports
41  $status=/^$oops_start/ ... /^$oops_end/  and  print;
42
43  # If range operator returned E0, we just printed last line of
44  # report; printing "" puts blank line before next report.
45
46  $status =~ /E0$/  and  print "";
```

Here's a sample run, with debugging output enabled so you can see the regexes:

```
$ scan4oops2 -debug   # Output edited
Oops start RE:
'[A-Z]\w+ \d+ \d+:\d+:\d+ \w+ kernel: Oops: \d+'

Oops  end  RE:
'[A-Z]\w+ \d+ \d+:\d+:\d+ \w+ kernel: Code:( [a-f0-9][a-f0-9]){20}'

Oops: 0001
...
Code: 89 50 24 89 02 c7 43 24 00 00 00 00 89 1c 24 c7 44 24 04 ff

Oops: 0002
...
Code: 89 50 04 89 02 c7 46 04 00 00 00 00 c7 06 00 00 00 00 d1 64
```

Satisfied with his result, Felix saunters over to Murray's desk to show off his script (after all, he's still in the running for that promotion):

> *Hi, Murray! Remember that script you asked me to write, to automate the extraction of kernel Oops reports? It's all tested and ready to distribute. Here's the code listing— it's only about 50 lines! What's that? Oscar has already submitted a program that does the same job? What are you scribbling on the board—oh, that's his program? Where's the rest! You cannot be serious—it's a one-liner?*

Felix takes a moment to ponder Oscar's command, as you should too:

```
perl -wnla -e '$F[5] =~ /Oops:/ .. $F[ 5 ] =~ /Code/ and print;' messages
```

Yikes! Felix's polar opposite, Oscar, somehow got wind of this project and seized the opportunity to score a few cheap points with Murray. But Felix must admit, good old cigar-chewing Oscar is an immensely valuable player on their team.

When customers are screaming for immediate action and time is running out, nobody else can step up to the mound and pitch those one-liners with half the speed or accuracy that Oscar routinely delivers. In recognition, he's been voted "Programmer of the Month" and "Most Valuable Programmer of the Year" more times than Felix can remember. In contrast, Felix feels faint when required to work under pressure, and he invariably develops a debilitating migraine and has to go home sick.

Oscar's program should do the basic job well enough—at least, until the report format changes. But unlike Felix's version, it doesn't put blank lines between the individual reports, and it uses the two-dot version of the range operator rather than the more appropriate three-dot version. Oscar probably realized that both patterns would never be able to match the same line in the log file anyway, given its format, so he chose to omit the technically correct—but, in this case, arguably ineffective—third dot. How *lazy!*

Felix also finds it irksome that Oscar included the trailing colon in the "Oops" regex but not in the "Code" one, and that he put spaces around one instance of the array index (5) but not the other.

Sloppy work. **Inelegant** programming! Would it have killed him to add just one tiny comment? *Some people...*

Just then, his scathing but silent code review is interrupted by Murray, who looks up from Felix's code listing and beams at him:

> *Felix, this is a work of art—and compassion! Every variable name is so carefully crafted, and every comment so succinctly yet clearly phrased. I'm really lucky to have both you and Oscar on my team—one programmer who can always be counted on, when the going gets rough, to cobble together an immediate solution to keep us in the game. And another who can provide solutions so elegant and robust and clear that any hung-over bench-warmer can maintain them. By the way, although we initially had only one promotion to award, in recognition of the valuable skills each of you brings to the team, we've decided to promote both of you. **Congratulations!***

In real life, you can't always get a fairy-tale ending like this one, but truly, any IT manager would be fortunate to have the combined talents of an Oscar and a Felix on hand.

In your own career, I'd advise you to develop an appreciation and an aptitude for both the *quick-and-dirty* and *elegant-and-formal* styles of programming, and to cultivate the ability to produce either kind on demand, as circumstances warrant.

5.9   *USING THE AWK-TO-PERL TRANSLATOR: a2p*

As discussed in chapter 4, Larry has always strived to make it easy for programmers using other Unix tools to migrate to Perl, which is why Perl comes with a `sed`-to-`perl` translator.

Guess what—Perl comes with an `awk`-to-`perl` translator too, called a2p! It converts inline AWK programs, such as the quoted portion of `awk '{print $1}'`, as well as stand-alone AWK scripts, such as the one in the file `munge` referenced in the command `awk -f munge`, into Perl scripts.

As with s2p, the code emitted by a2p is based on the venerable but now ancient version 4 of Perl, so this book's coverage of the language won't prepare you to fully understand it. Although that factor reduces the educational value of a2p, it presents no obstacle to those using a2p to adapt existing AWK programs for use on Perl-equipped but AWK-less systems, such as Windows machines and mainframes.

5.9.1   Tips on using a2p

If you need to use a2p on a complex AWK program, look at the CONSIDERATIONS section of its man page. It discusses the AWK expressions that may not always get translated into Perl the way you'd like, and it offers tips on dealing with those cases.

5.10   *SUMMARY*

AWK and Perl have a lot in common. Indeed, the family resemblance runs so deep you can even write AWK-like programs in Perl, using the Pattern/Action style of programming, the record-number variable, and BEGIN and END blocks. But there are some significant differences in their capabilities.

Like the Shell—but unlike AWK—Perl provides *variable interpolation*, which makes print statements substantially easier to read and write.

Like AWK, Perl provides *field processing*, the automatic parsing of input records into fields (via the a option). However, Perl's implementation offers several improvements over AWK's. One is that field processing is *disabled* by default, allowing programs that don't need it to avoid its impact on performance. Another advantage is that Perl's fields can easily be loaded into descriptively named variables (e.g., ($size, $shape)=@F) when readability is important, or directly accessed using positive or negative array indexing ($F[2], $F[-3]) when succinctness is the priority.[41]

Perl shares AWK's ability to match ranges of input records, but it improves on AWK's implementation by also supporting sed-style (non-overlapping) ranges and returning a special code (E0) to allow the last record of the range to be detected, thereby facilitating special processing for that record.

Perl's rich collection of built-in functions and operators is much larger than that of any version of AWK. In fact, in addition to providing AWKish functions such as system and printf, Perl even provides access to the internal functions of Unix systems.

As discussed in earlier chapters, Perl's more powerful regex dialect, more flexible matching options, and support of in-place editing give it substantial advantages in pattern-matching applications over other UNIX-based utilities, including AWK. What's more, the ability of the Perl language to be extended through the inclusion of modules gives it another major advantage over AWK.

The many practical examples featured in this chapter show that Perl can match or exceed the benefits of AWK for applications falling into the latter's traditional fields of expertise: data validation (e.g., incomplete), report generation (mean_annual_precip), file conversion (the Perl rock-star biodata system), and number crunching (nexpr_p and compound_interest). Moreover, the compound_interest2 program goes way beyond AWK's capabilities by importing a function from a module that can, as dictated by the data at hand, inflect a noun into its singular or plural form.

AWKiologists migrating to Perlistan should keep in mind that tables 5.6, 5.7, and 5.13 provide a succinct summary of the major differences in syntax between the languages, and that the a2p command is available to help convert legacy AWK programs into Perl scripts.

---

[41] As you'll see in chapter 9, Perl even provides for the aggregate extraction of arbitrary elements from arrays, using *array slices*.

As a final note, don't forget that when you're down on your luck, you may be able to make a few bucks by soliciting wagers on the mathematical capabilities of the Shell, using the techniques illustrated in the nexpr_p script.

Directions for further study

For more information on other topics covered in this chapter, you may wish to consult these resources:

- man perlop   # operators, and operator precedence
- man Lingua::EN::Inflect   # conditional pluralization, and more[42]
- man perlpod   # Perl's Plain Old Documentation system
- man perldoc   # Perl's documentation-retrieval utility
- man a2p   # AWK to Perl source-code converter
- http://perldoc.perl.org/index-functions.html # the function list

> **TIP**   The range operator is documented in excruciating detail on the perlop man page. Unless you *crave excruciation*, you'd be wise to stick with the more informal coverage provided here.

---

[42] The module's documentation won't be found unless it's already on your system; chapter 12 shows module-installation instructions.

CHAPTER 6

Perl as a (better) find command

6.1 Introducing hybrid `find/perl` programs 180

6.2 File testing capabilities of `find` vs. Perl 180

6.3 Finding files 184

6.4 Processing filename arguments 188

6.5 Using `find | xargs` vs. Perl alternatives 192

6.6 `find` as an argument pre-processor for Perl 197

6.7 A Unix-like, OS-portable `find` command 198

6.8 Summary 200

Scene: Church basement, Seattle, USA. Raining—as usual.

A burly, unshaven, heavily tattooed man is tugging at the sleeve of a woman, who is standing at a podium. She responds to the sleeve-tugger with annoyance.

⟆⟆ ⟆⟆

"Yes Lefty, I know you're upset that they're not serving the tea biscuits on those lovely lace doilies anymore, but given our cash-flow situation—sorry, we'll have to discuss this later.

Testing, testing, 1 2 3. Is this thing on?

Attention!

Would you take your seats please, the meeting is about to begin.

Good evening! As you regulars know, we always begin by welcoming the newcomers. Do we have any first-timers here tonight?

Yes, you sir, with the bushy red hair, would you please introduce yourself to the group?"

[Camera zooms in on a bearded, bespectacled, amber teddy-bear of a man, obviously of Irish descent.]

"Hello, my name's Tim.

*And I am a **loser**."*

[Fade to black]

⁕≈ ≈⁕

As much as I hate to admit it, that statement is 100 percent true! I really *am* a **loser**. What's worse, I am a ***chronic* loser**!

I don't mean that I'm a pitiful ne'er do-well who can never get his life in order. I mean that *I lose things*—all the time! Luckily for me, my wife has what psychologists call *eidetic imagery*, which is more commonly known as a *photographic memory*. All I have to do is ask her, "Have you seen my iPod lately?" and she'll consult her database of mental images and tell me exactly where it is.

Even if you're not a chronic loser like me, you've probably misplaced a file or two on a Unix system by now. This may have motivated you to learn about the `find` command, because it's used to locate and identify files that have certain specified attributes. In a sense, `find` is the Unix system's answer to having a partner with a photographic memory.

The `find` command can certainly come in handy. As a case in point, the other day I made some modifications to the standard Perl script that's used to convert documents from Perl's Plain Old Documentation format (POD) to HTML. The new script worked nicely, and it instantly became a valuable addition to my toolkit.

But then I lost it! I couldn't remember its name, or what directory I had stored it in. But I knew what its attributes were: **owned** by *tim*, **file-type** *regular*, **name** containing *html*, **permissions** of *read, write*, and *execute* for the owner, and **modified** in the *last 24 hours*.

So I issued the following `find` command, and it rapidly found the file for me:[1]

```
$ find /home/tim -user tim -type f -name '*html*' \
>         -perm -0700 -mtime -1 -print
/home/tim/book/publishing/bin/my_pod2html
```

---

[1] The `-perm -0700` option specifies the `rwx` permissions for the file's owner; the time of a file's last access, modification, and attribute change (i.e., its *timestamps*) are respectively accessed via the `-atime`, `-mtime`, and `-ctime` options. Run `man find` for additional details.

In addition to being invaluable to Unix users, `find` is even more important to Unix system administrators, who would have a hard time managing their systems without it.

On the other hand, `find` has some annoying limitations, which have been known to motivate programmers to seek alternatives. What's more, you can only count on `find` being available on Unix systems, so once you grow dependent on it, you'll miss it when using other OSs.

Fortunately, you can easily write Perl programs that surpass `find`'s limitations and extend its reach to non-Unix platforms. You'll see examples of many programs of this type shortly, but first we'll discuss why most of them take a different form than the programming examples shown thus far.

6.1   INTRODUCING HYBRID `find/perl` PROGRAMS

In earlier chapters, we discussed Perl programs that served as more powerful replacements for `grep`, `sed`, and `awk` by exploiting the advanced capabilities of Perl's closely related facilities (e.g., the matching and substitution operators).

Although Perl has less intimate connections to most other Unix utilities, in many cases it can still be used to add value to,[2] if not to completely replace, another utility. Accordingly, we'll approach our discussion of `find` differently than we did the discussions of `grep`, `sed`, and AWK. Specifically, we'll generally use Perl commands to perform additional filtering of `find`'s output rather than to eliminate the use of `find` altogether. This approach allows us to take advantage of `find`'s ability to generate filenames by recursively descending into directories, rather than having to duplicate that functionality in Perl.[3]

Our primary focus in this chapter will be on `find | perl` pipelines that serve as functional *enhancements to* `find` rather than *replacements for* `find`. In addition to this primary theme, we'll also consider possible improvements to `grep` and `sed`-like programs (covered in chapters 3 and 4), which can benefit from many of the enhanced file-finding services we'll be discussing.

We'll begin by comparing `find`'s file-testing capabilities with Perl's.

6.2   FILE TESTING CAPABILITIES OF `find` VS. PERL

Table 6.1 shows the syntax for Perl's file-test operators.[4] You have the option of supplying an explicit filename argument when conducting a file test, as in

```
-r '/etc/passwd'  or  warn "/etc/passwd is not readable\n";
```

---

[2] E.g., I've seen Perl commands used to enhance the interfaces to, and/or outputs emanating from, `crontab`, `date`, `df`, `du`, `echo`, `expr`, `find`, `fmt`, `ifconfig`, `ls`, `mozilla`, `mutt`, `newaliases`, `sendmail`, `sort`, `vim`, `who`, and `users`.

[3] Replacing `find` altogether in Perl programs is accomplished using `File::Find` (see chapter 12).

[4] There's no separate column for POSIX `find`, because its capabilities are duplicated in GNU `find`.

Table 6.1 Syntax for file attribute tests

Syntax[a]	Meaning
-X filename	Tests that filename has attribute X
! -X filename	Tests that filename lacks attribute X
-X	Tests that the file named in $_ has attribute X
! -X	Tests that the file named in $_ lacks attribute X

a. X stands for a Perl file-operator's keyletter, such as the r in "-r memo".

Alternatively, you can omit the filename, causing the data variable ($_) to be accessed as the implicit argument:

```
-r or  warn "$_ is not readable\n";   # filename in $_
```

In addition, the result of a test can be complemented by preceding its associated operator with the "!" character, as in the following reverse-logic variation on the previous example:

```
! -r and  warn "$_ is not readable\n"; # filename in $_
```

Table 6.2 lists a variety of attributes for files and shows, for Perl and significant versions of find, which ones are *impossible, possible,* or *easy* to test. The table also shows, in its rightmost column, the Perl operator that's used to perform each file attribute test.

The most basic file attribute tests (shown in the top panel) are rated as easy to perform with both versions of find as well as Perl. On the other hand, the second panel shows that all permission-related tests that are easy with Perl are impossible to perform with find.

The table also shows that the text-file and binary-file tests provided by Perl (-T, -B) are impossible with find, and the three other tests in the third panel are easier with Perl.

For example, Perl's test for a file's "sticky bit" being set is -k filename, whereas find requires the more complicated -perm -01000. All it takes to bungle the latter test is the omission of the second "-" or the misplacement of the 1 relative to all those 0s, which is why Perl rates an E (for easy), but find a P (for possible) on this test.[5]

The bottom panel shows several tests that are easier with find than Perl, because you have to test for these attributes using the stat function (discussed in section 7.2.3) rather than a file-test operator.

All in all, Perl stacks up relatively well against find, especially when you consider that Perl makes certain extremely helpful tests possible, or even easy (viz., those in the second and third panels). For example, Perl's unique offering of six read/write/execute

---

5 For more information about Unix file types and permissions, consult man ls and man chmod.

Table 6.2 Comparison of supported file attributes in versions of the `find` command and Perl

File attribute[a]	Classic `find`[b]	GNU `find`[c]	Perl	Perl operator
Regular/plain	E	E	E	-f
Directory	E	E	E	-d
Symlink	E	E	E	-l
Named pipe	E	E	E	-p
Character	E	E	E	-c
Block	E	E	E	-b
Socket	E	E	E	-S
Empty	E	E	E	-z
Non-empty	E	E	E	-s
Readable by Real UID/GID	–	–	E	-R
Writable by Real UID/GID	–	–	E	-W
Executable by Real UID/GID	–	–	E	-X
Owned by Real UID	–	–	E	-O
Readable by Effective UID/GID	–	–	E	-r
Writable by Effective UID/GID	–	–	E	-w
Executable by Effective UID/GID	–	–	E	-x
Owned by Effective UID	–	–	E	-o
Owned by Specified UID/GID	E	E	P	stat[d]
Set-UID	P	P	E	-u
Set-GID	P	P	E	-g
Sticky	P	P	E	-k
Text	–	–	E	-T
Binary	–	–	E	-B
Newer than another	E	E	P	stat
Accessed more recently than another	–	E	P	stat
Number of links	E	E	P	stat
Inode number	E	E	P	stat

a. Real and Effective IDs are those of the process running `find` or `perl`.
b. E: test is easily done; P: test is possible; –: test isn't possible.
c. Using POSIX-compliant features and GNU extensions.
d. Covered in section 7.2.3.

tests solves a long-standing problem in Unix programming. Why? Because Perl (on Unix) actually interprets the permissions a file grants to its User (a.k.a. owner), Group, and Others in light of the Real/Effective UID and GID of the person running the test—in the same way the Unix kernel does—and yields a True/False code to indicate whether the specified access would be permitted.

In contrast, `find` only gives you the ability to determine if a particular user owns a file (e.g., `-user nigel`) and whether it has particular permission bits set or not (e.g., `-perm -0400`). What's missing is the all-important logic—provided by Perl—that determines whether the current user will be granted a particular type of access to the file, according to the (rather involved) rules of Unix.

In short, Perl's permission tests report the *implications* of the file's ownerships and permissions on the current user's activities, whereas `find` merely provides *isolated bits of information* from which a programmer must draw her own conclusions.

Each tool has its strengths, so with these differences in mind, let's look at some ways to augment `find`'s capabilities with Perl.

6.2.1 Augmenting `find` with Perl

A useful way to exploit their individual strengths is to use `find` to generate an initial set of pathnames and Perl to eliminate those whose files lack some additional attributes. For example, any of the following commands could be used as the first stage of a pipeline[6] to take advantage of `find`'s ability to locate files according to their *size*, *name*, and *timestamp* attributes:

```
find .     -size  +100   -print |
find /src  -name  'core' -print |
find $HOME -mtime -3     -print |   # starts from /home/tim
```

Then Perl commands, having forms such as these, could be added as the filtering stage in the pipeline:

```
perl -wnl -e '-A and print;'                        # Example 1

perl -wnl -e '-A and -B and print;'                 # Example 2

perl -wnl -e '-A and ! -B and print;'               # Example 3

perl -wnl -e '-A and -B and -C and print;'          # Example 4

perl -wnl -e '( -A or -B ) and print;'              # Example 5

perl -wnl -e '( -A or -B or -C ) and print;'        # Example 6

perl -wnl -e '-A and ( -B or -C ) and -D and print;'  # Example 7
```

In these commands, `-A`, `-B`, and `-C` are placeholders for the file-type attributes of interest, and "`!`" has the effect of negating the meaning of the following test (as it does with `find`). Note also that `or`, being weaker in precedence than `and` (see section 2.4.5), needs parentheses around its arguments.[7]

---

[6] You could alternatively use another pathname-generating command, such as `ls` or `locate`, in place of `find` at the head of such pipelines.

[7] Or, to use the more proper term for an operator's arguments, its *operands*.

Therefore, Example 2 reports files from its input that have attributes *A* and *B*, Example 3 reports those having *A* but not (!) *B*, and Example 6 reports those having at least one of *A*, *B*, or *C*.

Here is a pipeline based on Example 1 that lists regular files under the directory /home/ersimpson that contain text. Although find is used for the regular file (-type f) test, Perl must be used for the <u>text-file</u> test that find doesn't provide:

```
find /home/ersimpson -type f -print | perl -wnl -e '-T and print;'
```

Because many programs work best when users feed them files having exactly these properties, you'll find the Perl component of that pipeline to be useful in many future commands. For this reason, it's worth converting to a script:

```
$ cat textfiles
#! /usr/bin/perl -wnl
# If file named on input line contains text, print its name
-T  and  print;
```

We'll use this script later in this chapter, in an example that provides a file-validating service for grep.

As an example of a case using or, the following command lists files that are regular (-type f) and either <u>empty</u>[8] or **nontext**:

```
find . -type f -print | perl -wnl -e '( ! -s or ! -T ) and print;'
```

The parentheses surrounding or's conditions in that command are critical, due to the higher precedence of and. Without them, a True result from the first test—signifying emptiness—wouldn't lead to the filename being printed as desired, due to **implicit parentheses** being placed as follows:

```
find . -type f -print | perl -wnl -e '! -s or ( ! -T and print );'
```

Now that we've discussed how to find filenames by file attributes, we'll turn next to finding filenames according the characteristics of the names themselves.

6.3   FINDING FILES

Perl's facilities for text processing make it a natural choice when you need to select files whose names have particular properties. We'll look at some typical cases next.

6.3.1   Finding files by name matching

One common use of find is to identify pathnames having certain patterns of characters in their final segments, using the -name option. For example, Don is looking for a text file he created with the vi editor a long time ago. After contemplating the many

---

[8] The -s operator returns the actual size of the file in bytes: For non-empty files, the value it returns is True, so for empty files, "! -s" returns True. Think of "! -s" as meaning "not having contents," or perhaps "no stuff."

possibilities, he concludes that the filename might have been "letter", or it might have contained "memo", or it might have started with "epistle".

He composes the appropriate `find` command, and tries it:

```
$ find $HOME -type f \
> \( -name 'letter' -o -name '*memo*' -o -name 'epistle*' \) -print
/home/donovan/hippie_love_songs/epistle2dippy.txt
/home/donovan/bin/memoize
/home/donovan/bin/order_more_commemorative_plates_of_woodstock
```

Note that it's vital to enclose those alternative -name options joined by -o (or) operators within backslashed parentheses. Unfortunately, due to the way `find` works, the result of omitting them is an incorrect outcome, rather than an error message.[9]

Using a Perl command instead to do the filename matching allows a solution that's less error-prone and more powerful. That's largely because Perl's pattern-matching is based on a powerful regular expression (*regex*) notation with an intuitive `egrep`-like syntax, rather than `find`'s more limited filename generation (FNG) notation coupled with a cumbersome syntax.

In addition, Perl uniquely supports the text-file test, which is appropriate to use when you're searching for files created with `vi`, like the one Don misplaced. Using it eliminates undesirable matches against names of compiled programs, such as the matches with "*memo*" shown in the last two lines of the previous command's output.

Here's Don's improvement on the previous `find` command, which handles the trickier parts of the problem with Perl:

```
$ find $HOME -type f -print |
>       perl -wnlaF'/' -e '-T and
>           $F[-1] =~ /^letter$|memo|^epistle/ and print;'
/home/donovan/hippie_love_songs/epistle2dippy.txt
```

Notice that Don used the a and F options to request the automatic splitting of the incoming pathnames into fields, using "/" as the delimiter. This makes it easier to direct the matching to the final segment of each pathname, to mimic what `find`'s option -name does.[10]

The matching operator is used to scan each pathname's final segment (in $F[-1]) for the exact string "letter", or the substring "memo", or a string starting with "epistle"—with the entire pathname being printed (from $_) for each match.

---

[9] Due to the lower precedence of -o versus the implicit -a (and) before -print, such a command would ignore the "letter" and "memo"-based filenames, and produce the same output as the following command: find $HOME -type f -name 'epistle*' -print

[10] The use of the a and F options, and array indexing with $F[-1], are covered in section 5.3 and table 5.9, respectively.

In summary, Don's vague recollections about his text-file's name were accurate enough to let him write two kinds of commands to find it. The command using the POSIX `find` by itself requires a tricky syntax and uses a relatively weak pattern-matching notation, whereas an approach relying primarily on Perl has the benefits of a more powerful matching facility with a familiar `egrep`-like syntax, and the ability to distinguish text files from nontext files.

We'll next use Perl with a matching operator to select pathnames in another way that POSIX `find` just can't match.

Finding multi-word filenames

Let's consider the intriguing case of Steffi, who has a *lingering thumb*. When using her word-processing application, she saves her documents under multi-word filenames, but because of her "thumb issue", those words may be separated by one space or *several*, depending on how long her thumb lingers on the (automatically repeating) <SPACE> key.

Right now, she needs to rapidly locate a file named "Final Report", or maybe it was "Final report", or possibly "final report", or perhaps even "final Report", or blast it, quite possibly "FINAL REPORT". What's more, because of her thumb issue, she needs to make allowances for various numbers of spaces between the words.

She'll be using the POSIX `find` command, so to save a lot of redundant typing, she simplifies the solution by initially looking for filenames having only one or two spaces of separation between the required words. She also arranges for uppercase and lowercase variations to be allowed for every character, through the highly effective but egregiously cumbersome method of using a character-class for each and every letter.[11] Here's the resulting command:

```
$ find $HOME -type f  \(                                          \
    -name '[Ff][Ii][Nn][Aa][Ll] [Rr][Ee][Pp][Oo][Rr][Tt]' -o     \
    -name '[Ff][Ii][Nn][Aa][Ll]   [Rr][Ee][Pp][Oo][Rr][Tt]'      \
                        \)  -print
```

To handle the case of two spaces between the words, Steffi retyped the first -name line with an extra space between the words to create the second -name line. She needed to match names containing additional spaces as well, but she was already sick of typing by this point and highly motivated to look for an easier solution.

After pleading with a Perlish friend for help, she came up with this alternative:

```
$ find $HOME -type f -print |
    perl -wnlaF'/' -e '-B and $F[-1] =~ /^final +report$/i and print;'
/home/Steffi/first drafts/final   report.stw
```

---

[11] The GNU version of `find` has a `-iname` option that ignores case while looking for files by name, but Steffi's approach has the advantage of working with the `-name` option that's provided in all versions of `find`.

The -B operator checks that the current filename is a *binary* file (i.e., non-text; see table 6.2), which is appropriate because Steffi's word-processing program saves files in a format of that type. The find command can't test for this property, so Steffi couldn't have been certain of finding the right file types with her solution based entirely on it.

The i modifier on the matching operator requests a case-insensitive match, thereby dispensing with all the [Cc][Aa][Ss][Ee]-variation complexities of the find solution with one keystroke.

The "+" quantifier following the space allows for one or more spaces between the words, accommodating much more extreme cases of *thumb-down hysteresis* than the more complex but less powerful find version that Steffi initially coded.

In summary, Steffi's problem is more easily solved with help from Perl because the pattern-matching operations can be handled using the more versatile regex notation, case-insensitive matching can be requested, and non-binary files can be excluded from consideration.[12] Moreover, the Perl solution is also more complete—because it handles any number of additional spaces between words—and more compact than its POSIX find counterpart.

Next, you'll see another way in which Perl's file-finding capabilities exceed those of find.

6.3.2 Finding files by pathname matching

You've seen that Perl can mimic the behavior of find's –name option by matching within a pathname's final segment. But Perl can do something the POSIX find can't do—it can match *anywhere* within the pathname.

I use this feature periodically when I need to find one of my scripts by name. Because I know it resides in one of my *bin directories, I can use this knowledge to avoid matches with like-named files that reside in other directories, such as *man and *lib.[13]

For instance, here's how Homer would locate his scripts for converting images in other formats to JPEGs, using the fact that he employs a *2jpg convention in naming them:

```
$ find $HOME -type f -print |
>    perl -wnla -e '-T and  m:bin/\w+2jpg$:  and  print;'
/home/ersimpson/bin/gif2jpg
/home/ersimpson/public_domain_bin/tiff2jpg
/home/ersimpson/SPUG-bin/png2jpg
```

Notice that the m*X* syntax of the matching operator is used to specify the ":" character as the delimiter, overriding the default of the slash. This allows the slash at the end of "bin/" to unambiguously represent the directory separator in the pathname, which

---

[12] GNU's find can provide the first two of these capabilities but not the third.

[13] In keeping with long-standing Unix conventions, I'm using the FNG notation here to specify that the directories of interest all end with the string bin.

creates a context that ensures the `\w+2jpg$` pattern is only matched as a whole file-name under a `*bin` directory.

By using this technique of matching filenames only within directories matching specified patterns, Homer can avoid undesirable matches such as these:

```
/home/ersimpson/man/gif2jpg
/home/ersimpson/src/graphics/tifflib/tiff2jpg
/home/ersimpson/SPUG-man/png2jpg
```

Next, you'll see how to use a special kind of `find | perl` pipeline for filtering out undesirable arguments for Unix utilities, and how to use Unix utilities for validating arguments for Perl programs.

6.4 PROCESSING FILENAME ARGUMENTS

Have you ever run the `grep` command, only to find yourself suddenly staring at a screen full of blinking graphics characters? Most Unix users should witness this phenomenon sooner or later, because it's not only the closest approximation to the Aurora Borealis you'll ever see on a computer terminal, it's also a rite of passage for Unix newbies.

If you don't know what I'm talking about, feast your eyes on figure 6.1, which shows what happened when a hapless user attempted to search all files *under* $HOME for lines containing the letter e, using POSIX `grep`.

Unfortunately for that user, `grep` doesn't treat $HOME as some kind of magical reference to all the files within the directory it names, as many are prone to assume. Instead, it's taken as the name of the *specific* file that's to be opened and examined for matches! As luck would have it, this directory-file did contain some occurrences of the letter e, so `grep` dutifully sent the associated "lines" to the screen.

But the terminal interpreted something in that data stream as a request to switch character sets, which is why it's difficult to decipher the output of the `who` and `ls -l` commands that came next.

By the way, if you're thinking, "I'm too smart too fall into that trap," consider the related commands shown here, which are just as dangerous in cases where "*" finds a subdirectory it can match:[14]

```
grep 'e' $HOME/*
grep 'e' *
```

It's scary to contemplate, but I know from my decades in Unix IT circles that many users issue commands like these *all the time;* they're just lucky to rarely find matches in the binary files they're inadvertently searching.

---

[14] Because this shortcoming has been rectified in the GNU version, those wishing to use the command formats identified here as dangerous may successfully do so with help from its `-r` (*recursive*) option, as in `grep -r 'e' $HOME`.

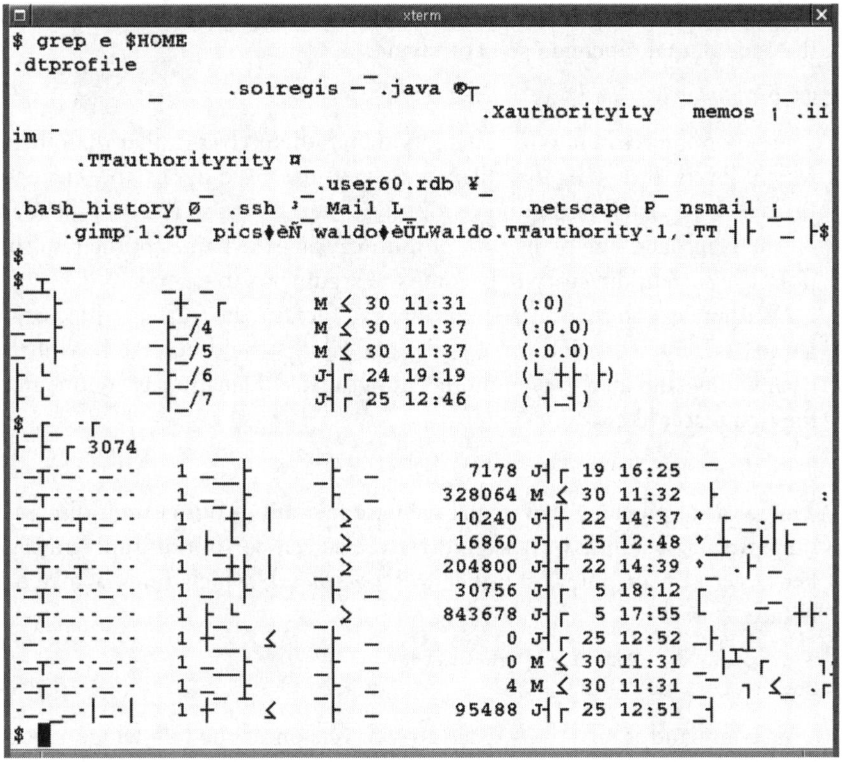

Figure 6.1 Example of screen corruption produced by careless grepping.

Okay, now you understand the problem, and you've seen that it's an easy trap to fall into. So you're probably asking yourself, *"Is there any hope of defending the hordes of accident-prone Unix users from these* grep*ological calamities? And what does this have to do with Perl?"*

Of course there's hope; and, as usual, our salvation is achieved by Perl coming to the rescue.

6.4.1 Defending against grep's messes

A valuable feature provided by the Shell is its ability to replace a command in backward quotes with that command's own output. This facility, called *command substitution*, and its Perl counterpart, called *command interpolation*, are covered in detail in section 8.5. In this section, we'll look briefly at how this powerful feature is used and how you sometimes need to use a command called xargs in its place.

The following command uses the Shell's command substitution facility to execute an ls | perl pipeline and deliver its output to grep as a set of filename arguments:

```
grep 'pattern' `ls -d * | perl -wnl -e '-T  and  print;'`
```

Even better, here's a version using the tiny Perl script presented earlier that embodies the code of that pipeline's Perl command:

```
grep 'pattern' `ls -d * | textfiles`
```

The -d option tells ls to list directory names themselves (rather than their contents), which limits the generated filenames to those residing in the current directory. Because it has backward quotes around it, the ls | textfiles pipeline is replaced on the command line by its own output, causing the names of the resulting text files from the current directory to become the arguments to grep.

With that command, if the only text files in the current directory were ones named Larry, Moe, and Curly, the end result would be exactly as if the user had been willing and able to type those "Stoogeadelic" filenames as arguments to grep in the first place, like so:

```
grep 'pattern' Larry Moe Curly
```

The kinds of pipelines you've just seen are relevant to our current discussion because they provide a simple workaround for the screen-corruption problem discussed earlier. As a case in point, consider this command, which finds a match in the file named Moe:

```
$ grep 'HEAD' `ls -d * | textfiles`
Moe: HEAD STOOGE
```

This command is effectively a screen-safe version of the following, which is suitable only for extreme optimists (and gamblers) when the POSIX or classic grep is used:

```
grep 'HEAD' *
```

Why is the first command of this pair superior? Because it filters the filenames generated by the "*" to remove any troublemakers that don't contain text.

For those restricted to using versions of grep that have the "search in a binary file and corrupt the screen" problem, a scripted version of that pipeline might come in handy.

A screen-safe grepper: text_grep

text_grep implements a case-insensitive grepper for text files:

```
$ text_grep -pattern='Head' Larry Moe Curly bin    # bin is ignored
Moe: HEAD STOOGE
```

Contrary to what you might expect, the textfiles script can't be used directly in implementing text_grep, because the former operates on filenames presented to its input, whereas the latter accepts them as arguments (like a real grep).

But you can easily implement text_grep using the techniques covered in chapter 2. First, test that the current input file has text contents using -T $ARGV. Then, if that test fails, close the filehandle (ARGV) to terminate the processing of the file before any matching is attempted, and to trigger the opening of the next file (if there is one).

Because the script accepts multiple filename arguments, it's important that it identifies each matching line with the name of its associated file, as shown in the earlier run that used $ARGV to prefix "Moe" to the matching line.

Here's the text_grep script:[15]

```
#! /usr/bin/perl -s -wnl

BEGIN {
    @ARGV  and  $pattern or   # must have argument, and pattern
        warn "Usage: text_grep -pattern='RE' f1 [f2 ...]\n"  and
            exit 255;
}

# Close current file, if not text-file, and get next input
-T $ARGV  or  close ARGV  and  next;

# On match, show "filename: matching-line"
/$pattern/i  and  print "$ARGV: $_";
```

This script even has value for those who already have access to improved GNU greppers, because it provides a framework for accessing Perl's superior collection of regex metacharacters and matching options (see table 3.2).

We'll look next at a convenient way to direct a grepper to search within an entire branch of the file-system tree for matches.

6.4.2 Recursive grepping

In the previous section, you saw a filename-filtering technique that prevents non-GNU grep commands from searching within binary files, finding accidental matches, and corrupting the screen. But there are occasions when you really *want* to name a directory as an argument to grep, and have DWIMity[16] prevail—which means grep should search within every file in that directory, and the files of its subdirectories. That's called *recursive grepping*. You'll see how to accomplish this worthy goal next.

Here's the command that formed the initial basis for the text_grep script discussed earlier:

```
$ grep 'HEAD' `ls -d * |
>       perl -wnl -e '-T  and  print;'`
Moe: HEAD STOOGE
```

Only a slight change is needed to allow the user to specify a directory instead of a file and to get the appropriate results from *any* version of grep. You simply replace the ls

---

[15] Placing defined before $pattern would make the script more robust, as you'll learn in section 8.1.1. The next directive is Perl's counterpart to the Shell's continue (see table 10.7).

[16] *DWIMity* is the property allowing a program to *Do What I Mean*—regardless of *What I Say!*

in that pipeline with a `find` command that starts in the specified directory and recursively descends into those below it, finding all regular files.

Here's an example that starts its search in `/home/ersimpson`:

```
$ grep 'HEAD' `find /home/ersimpson -type f -print |
>        perl -wnl -e '-T  and  print;'`
/home/ersimpson/Moe: HEAD STOOGE
/home/ersimpson/stoogetrivia/Shemp: HEAD STOOGE "WANNABE"
```

You'll see a scripted version of this *recursive grep* command in chapter 8, which provides a more `grep`-like interface:

```
rgrep 'pattern' file_or_directory_name(s)
```

Despite its many virtues, it's important to recognize that command substitution, as used in the preceding examples, isn't always the most reliable way to pass arguments to commands. For this reason, we'll examine the `xargs` alternative shortly. But first, we'll wind up this topic with a quick discussion of the widespread applicability of the techniques we've covered thus far.

6.4.3 Perl as a generalized argument pre-processor

Although previous examples focused on the use of Perl commands to preprocess filenames for presentation to the `grep` command, there's no reason to restrict the use of this type of argument-validation service to any particular utility. On the contrary, you can use it to good advantage with *any* command that accepts input from text files named as arguments, including `sed` and `awk`, and dozens of other Unix utilities.

For instance, here are examples of `awk` commands benefiting from argument preprocessing provided by Perl:

```
awk 'program' `ls -d * | textfiles`
awk 'program' `find . -type f -print | textfiles`
```

You'll see additional examples of Perl's usefulness as an argument pre-processor in part 2.

Next, we'll discuss where the much-lauded `xargs` command can provide advantages over command substitution—and where it can't, but Perl can.

6.5 USING *find/xargs* VS. PERL ALTERNATIVES

As shown earlier, `find` can be used to generate filenames that ultimately become arguments to another command. This is such an important service that `find` has its own option for processing such commands, called `-exec`.

How does it work? You insert `{}` symbols anywhere the current filename should be inserted within the `-exec` *command* clause, followed by a "`\;`" sequence to mark the end of *command*'s argument list. The usual command format is therefore

```
find dir(s) attribute(s) -exec command {} \;
```

For simplicity, let's first consider the common task of removing those pesky files named *core*—which can be produced when a program dies—from the branch of the file-system tree rooted at the current directory. The appropriate command is

```
find . -name 'core' -type f -exec rm {} \;
```

If the following three pathnames were found, that `find -exec` command would execute a separate `rm` for each one, just as if you had manually typed these commands:

```
rm ./bin/core
rm ./source/shopping_cart/core
rm ./backups/core
```

Although this approach gets the job done, it's not economical. Why? Because if 100 pathnames were found, it would take 100 processes, one for each `rm` command, to handle them all.

They say that the more processes a task on Unix requires, the more time it takes to run,[17] so to should think about minimizing process utilization—especially if a *single* `rm` command (i.e., one using 1 process with 100 arguments) could do all the work by itself!

Thanks to the efforts of generations before us who have grappled with this problem, modern Unix systems come equipped with a utility program designed to solve it, called `xargs`. Its job is to convert its input lines into arguments for the designated command, allowing the following rewrite of the earlier `find -exec` command:

```
find . -name 'core' -type f -print | xargs rm
```

With this approach, `xargs` bundles together as many filename arguments as possible for submission to each invocation of `rm` that's needed, in compliance with the OS's maximum allowed size for an argument list. This means `xargs` is guaranteed not only to handle all the arguments, but also to use the smallest possible number of processes in doing so. For example, if each command can handle 100 arguments, and there are 110 filenames to process, there will be two invocations of the command, respectively handling 100 and 10 arguments.

As is the case with any powerful tool, you must be careful not to use it improperly. After all, a rocket-propelled grenade is an appropriate device for punching holes in tanks, but it's not recommended for manicuring toenails. Unfortunately, Unix users are in constant danger of shooting themselves in the foot by using `xargs` in places where it doesn't belong. For a thorough briefing on how to use Perl to avoid these types of *friendly fire* situations, report to the next section—pronto!

6.5.1   Using Perl for reliable timestamp sorting

A classic problem is that of identifying the most recently modified (i.e., newest) file within a particular branch of the file system, which might reflect the most recent

---

[17] This guideline is most applicable to single-CPU computers.

order received, the latest blog uploaded, the last Unix configuration file modified, and so forth. To find the newest file, a knowledgeable Unix programmer might compose a command like the following:

```
find . -type f -print |
    xargs ls -lrdt |
        tail -1
```

What does that pipeline do? The `find` command emits the pathnames of the relevant files; the `xargs` command submits them as arguments to `ls`, whose `-lrdt` options sort their listings in ascending order by modification time; and then the `tail -1` command peels off the listing that comes out last—the one for the newest file. At least, you'd *expect* it to be the pathname of the newest file, on the basis of (dodgy) advice from books or colleagues, or your own experiences with similar commands.

As discussed earlier, it's considered fiendishly clever to use `xargs` with `find` instead of an `-exec` clause, because doing so is guaranteed to minimize the number of processes required to handle all the arguments. In fact, the `find | xargs` approach is so efficient, and so highly revered in Unix culture, and so impressive to your colleagues, and so, well, *cool*, that the only bad thing you could possibly say about its use for this task is: ***It's not guaranteed to produce the correct results!***[18]

Why can't it be trusted? Because the `ls` command isn't guaranteed to sort all the filenames in *one batch*. That can lead to an incorrect result, because the most recent file from the final batch is always the last one provided as input to `tail` and therefore the one emitted by the pipeline. Therefore, if so many filenames are presented to `xargs` that it has to divvy them up for processing by two or more `ls` commands, there's no guarantee that the file of interest will be processed in the critical final batch and that the correct pathname will emerge from the pipeline.

Note that this isn't a criticism of `xargs` itself, which does an admirable job of running the separate `ls` commands as efficiently as possible. The problem is that sorting isn't an operation that can be done in *piecemeal fashion*—all the filenames must be sorted in one batch. For this reason, the `find | xargs` approach just isn't suited to solving this problem.

The modified solution shown next uses a custom Perl script called `most_recent_file` instead of `xargs`, which has two distinct advantages:

- It always produces the correct answer.
- It works even on non-Unix systems that have Perl.[19]

---

[18] Unfortunately, that doesn't prevent it from being widely used this way. I hope the results aren't being used to control any nuclear reactors!

[19] Which brings with it the `find2perl` command (see section 6.7), which can play the role of a Unix `find` command for systems that lack one.

Here are the results from using the `xargs`-based technique shown earlier—and its Perl alternative—for finding the most recently modified file under `/etc` on my Linux-equipped laptop:

```
$ cd /etc
$ find . -type f -print |
>      xargs ls -lrdt |
>            tail -1
-rw-r--r-- 1 root    root     28005 2006-07-31 12:53 ./ld.so.cache

$ find . -type f  -print | most_recent_file    # the correct answer!
./mtab
Tue Aug  1 11:41:29 2006
```

As you can see, the commands identify different files as the newest—and they can't *both* be right.

The wrong answer is the one produced by the first pipeline, because `find` generated so many arguments that `xargs` couldn't present them all to `ls` in one batch. In contrast, `most_recent_file` (shown in Listing 6.1) always produces the correct answer.

Listing 6.1   The `most_recent_file` script

```perl
#! /usr/bin/perl -wnl
# From pathname inputs, emits name of one most recently modified
# Gives correct answer where pipelines of this form may not:
#    find . -print | xargs ls -lrdt | tail -1

# NOTE: Use find or locate to provide input, or ls -d dir/*,
# but *not* simply "ls dir" (dir won't be present in pathname)

# Sample invocations:
#      locate '*.c' | most_recent_file
#      ls -d /etc/* | most_recent_file
#      find /local -name 'somescript' | most_recent_file
#      most_recent_file < filelist

BEGIN {
        $newest=0;  # initialize modification-time reference point
}
# Get file's numeric modification time; 10th value from stat
$mtime=(stat $_)[9];     # indexing into output of stat
if ($mtime > $newest) {  # if True, current file is newest yet seen
        # Remember mod-time for comparison to others,
        #  and remember filename for final report
        $newest=$mtime;
        $name=$_;
}

END {
      print $name;
}
```

That script may look intimidating at first, due to its size, but if you look more closely, you'll see that it's mostly comments.

It starts by using the `stat` function to obtain the file's data.[20] The value it returns for the index of 9 is the time of the file's last modification, represented by a large integer number that represents the seconds that elapsed to that time from an ancient reference point.

The rest of the script is devoted to keeping constant track of the most recent modification time seen thus far, along with its associated filename, and then printing the "winning" name after all input has been processed (in the END block). The logic goes like this: If the current file's `$mtime` value is larger than the largest one seen thus far (stored in `$newest`), the current filename replaces the earlier one as our latest idea of the one most recently modified.

That's all it takes to write a Perl script that avoids the predilection of the `xargs`-based solution for identifying the *wrong file* as most recently modified, when many must be examined.

Next, we'll discuss another limitation of `xargs`, and how Perl can once again be of assistance. It involves wrangling pathnames that contain whitespace characters, which has historically been a vexing problem for Unix system administrators.

6.5.2   Dealing with multi-word filenames

As discussed earlier, the `find | xargs` approach to handling filenames has the advantage of using fewer processes than the `find -exec` alternative. However, there's a limitation of the `xargs` approach that's important to understand. Specifically, filenames containing whitespace characters are split into separate pieces at those positions, preventing them from being handled properly.

Let's say we need to count the number of characters (via `wc -c`) in each of the regular files within or below the current directory. The `find -exec` approach isn't bothered by filenames containing whitespace characters (represented by □):

```
$ find . -type f -exec wc -c {} \;
    177 ./multi-word□name
    258 ./regular_name
```

but the `find | xargs` approach certainly is:

```
$ find . -type f -print | xargs wc -c
wc: ./multi-word: No such file or directory
wc: name: No such file or directory
    258 ./regular_name
    258 total
```

---

[20] `stat` is related to the Unix function that `ls -l` and `find . -ls` use to obtain a file's properties. The `(stat $_)[9]` syntax is discussed in section 7.2.3. In section 8.4.1, we'll enhance this script to show *multiple* filenames as "most recent" when there are ties.

As you can see, each part of multi-word name was presented as a separate argument to the wc command.

This problem can easily be rectified by using a Perl command in place of xargs, because Perl can also report file sizes, but it doesn't automatically do word-splitting on input lines:

```
$ find . -type f -print | perl -wnl -e 'print -s , " $_"'
177 ./multi-word□name
258 ./regular_name
```

The -s operator provides the byte-count for the file named in the current input line (see table 6.2), and $_ provides the filename itself, so printing these elements—with a space before the filename—produces a report that resembles wc's output.

The result is a solution that handles whitespace embedded in filenames properly, like find's -exec option, but that's even more economical with processes than xargs—the Perl command uses only *one*, versus one process for xargs and from one to an astronomical number for the required wc commands.

We discussed the benefits of pre-processing arguments for other commands with Perl in section 6.3. But turnabout is fair play, so next we'll discuss the use of other commands, such as find, as argument pre-processors for *Perl*.

6.6 find AS AN ARGUMENT PRE-PROCESSOR FOR PERL

Back in chapter 4, we covered simple Perl commands that offered improvements on sed, including examples that automatically edited large numbers of files with commands like these:

```
perl -i.bak -wpl -e 's/\bpotatos\b/potatoes/g;' *

perl -i.bak -wpl -e 's/\bWireless\b/WiFi/g;' site[12]/*.html
```

The first example edits every file in the current directory,[21] whereas the second one edits all the HTML files in the directories called site1 and site2.

That format works nicely for processing *all files* within directories, but what if you want to select *particular* files on the basis of their attributes—including files that reside in subdirectories? That problem can be solved by using find to feed filenames to a Perl command—which filters out the inappropriate ones and passes the others on to xargs—which in turn feeds arguments to another Perl command.

Here's an example:

```
find $HOME -type f -print |                        # only regular files
   perl -wnl -e '-T and print;' |                  # only text files
      xargs perl -i.bak -wpl -e 's/\bPRE-OWNED\b/USED/g;' # be honest
```

---

[21] More precisely, it edits only non-hidden files—which are also regular files, because Perl automatically skips other types presented as arguments (see table 4.1).

This can be simplified a bit more by using the `textfiles` script from this chapter along with the `change_file` script from chapter 4, yielding the following:

```
find $HOME -type f -print |
  textfiles |
    xargs change_file -old='\bPRE-OWNED\b' -new='USED'
```

As discussed previously, the use of `xargs` ensures that every pathname emitted by `find | textfiles` is eventually presented as an argument to `change_file`, even if the OS won't allow a single instance of the script to handle them all.[22]

Of course, the invocation could be simplified even more by enclosing this pipeline in a script. One user interface might look like this:

```
change_text_files  -dir=$HOME  -old='\bPRE-OWNED\b'  -new='USED'
```

Another interface might dispense with the switch options and assign meanings to arguments by position instead:

```
change_text_files2  '\bPRE-OWNED\b'  'USED' $HOME
```

You'll learn techniques for processing *positional parameters*, such as the three arguments of that last command, in section 8.1.3.

Next, you'll see how Perl lets you enjoy the benefits of the Unix `find` command on Windows.

6.7 A UNIX-LIKE, OS-PORTABLE `find` COMMAND

When the Perl language is installed, some useful ready-made scripts are installed along with it, which can be of considerable value—even to those who think a Perl is something manufactured by irritated mollusks! As a case in point, we'll discuss `find2perl` next, which provides the valuable service of emulating the Unix `find` command for systems that lack it.

6.7.1 Making the most of `find2perl`

Many Unix users are accustomed to having the power of `find` at their disposal. That allows powerful commands like the following to be quickly unleashed to burrow through the file system and process the indicated files:

```
# Show JPEG files last accessed in 24 hours (< 1 day)
 find . -name '*.jpg' -type f -atime -1 -print

# Compress my regular, not recently read, big files
 find $HOME -type f -atime +30 -size +1000 | xargs gzip
```

But what's the hapless Windows user or system administrator to do? Is she doomed to wade forever through the "friendly" GUI interface of *Search>All file and folders,*

---

[22] The fundamental advantage of cmd1 | xargs cmd2 over cmd2 `cmd1` is that the latter fails altogether when cmd1 generates more arguments than the OS can deliver to cmd2.

cutting and pasting its output into delete commands in a `cmd.exe` window? Fortunately, after installing Perl (and therefore `find2perl`), such people can use `find` commands like those shown previously.

The procedure is as follows. The `find2perl` command is run with options appropriate for the real Unix `find` command,[23] with its output redirected to a file. That file then contains a custom-crafted Perl script that implements the functionality of the particular `find` command that the options specified. Then, the script is executed (perhaps after being shipped to a different Perl-equipped system), and its results are obtained.

Here's a sample session, from a DOS-like session on a Windows box:[24]

```
C:\> find2perl . -name "*.jpg" -atime -1 -print > find_script
```

```
C:\> perl find_script
./images/dalailama.jpg
./images/spongebob.jpg
./images/slowhand.jpg
```

That's just about all there is to using `find`-like commands on non-Unix systems, except for taking care to comply with local filename conventions.

For example, the following command on a Unix system creates a script that lists all the filenames of the indicated directories:

```
$ find2perl /tmp /local/tmp -print > find_script
```

But a comparable script destined for a Windows system may have to specify drive key-letters:

```
$ find2perl C:/tmp D:/tmp -print > find_script.4win
```

Fortunately for those with Unix habits, using *slashes* (rather than backslashes) in Windows pathnames will work, because Perl automatically handles such OS-specific conversions for you anywhere filenames are expected (see http://TeachMePerl.com/Perl_on_non-Unix_systems.html for additional details).

By the way, the `find2perl` approach to script-generation works on Unix systems too, and there are cases where it's useful to run `find2perl` rather than the real `find` on Unix. One such situation is described next.

6.7.2   Helping non-Unix friends with `find2perl`

Do you know someone who could benefit from the power of the Unix `find` command but doesn't have it on his system, and wouldn't know how to use it even if he did? If so, and Perl is installed on his computer, you can generate an appropriate script

---

[23] At the time of this writing, `find2perl` translates the popular `-ls` option into code that won't run on most non-Unix OSs, but perhaps this will be fixed by the time you read this.

[24] To eliminate the need to type that leading `perl` command, Windows systems are typically modified so that files with the `.pl` or `.plx` extension are automatically interpreted by Perl.

WinDude:

Hey PerlDude,

On this @&%!-ing Win/XP box, I need to remove all regular files under the current directory that are larger than 1024 blocks and not read within the last week. FYI, I've got Perl, but IMHO, I don't know anything about it, AFAIK. Can you help? TIA!

PerlDude:

Sure! I've emailed you a custom Perl script that will do the job. FYI, I generated it on my Linux box like so:

```
find2perl . -type f -size +1024 -atime +7 -exec rm {} > script
```

On your end, just put it in the desired directory, and run it as:

```
C:\some_dir> perl script
```

HTH, & FYI, YMMV, & IANAL,

--PerlDude (RHCE, HWP, NS, JAPH, POD, EIEIO)

Figure 6.2 PerlDude coming to rescue of WinDude with `find2perl`

on *your system* using `find2perl` and email it to your friend for him to use. And you won't even need to be *on* a Unix system when you do that! All you need is a Perl environment, an understanding of `find`'s syntax, and (for certain `find` commands) an understanding of the pathname conventions on your friend's system.

Figure 6.2 illustrates the concepts with a fictional interchange.[25]

It's as simple as that! By using this technique of composing a custom file-finding script and supplying it to a friend in need (or to yourself on a non-Unix platform), anybody who has a working Perl installation can reap the benefits of the Unix `find` command—without having access to it, or even knowing how to use it.

Are you wondering how well the Unix `rm` command, shown with the `-exec` option in the figure, works on Windows? Perfectly, in fact, because `find2perl` watches for the frequently used `rm` command and translates it into its native Perl equivalent, `unlink` (see table 7.18). But other Unix commands aren't automagically transformed, so as a general rule, commands specified with `-exec` must be restricted to those that will be present on the system that will run the script.

6.8 SUMMARY

The Unix `find` command is a valuable tool for finding files that have particular attributes. But some attributes are more easily specified with Perl than with `find`, such as whether a file is readable by the current process, or whether a file's name

[25] Unix people have the luxury of eschewing `-exec` in favor of the more economical `xargs`, but those using other OSs will happily settle for `find2perl`'s offering of `-exec`.

matches a non-trivial pattern. What's more, Perl uniquely offers tests for some especially useful attributes, such as the -T operator for identifying text files.

You can easily overcome many of these limitations of find with a little help from Perl. A simple yet effective method is to use find | perl pipelines, where find is used to generate an initial set of pathnames, and Perl to provide additional filtering on specified attributes. In some cases, it's sufficient to let the output of such a pipeline flow to the screen; in others, the output is presented as the argument list for another command, using Shell-level command substitution, or the xargs command—the input-to-argument converter of Unix.

You saw how augmenting find's capabilities with Perl can produce enhanced grep-like scripts that can automatically disregard non-text files and process directory arguments as requests for recursion into the file system, as users expect. You also saw these techniques used to handle classic problems in Unix file-wrangling, such as the proper treatment of multi-word filenames.

Savvy Unix users are wise to be fond of find's sidekick—xargs—which is prized for its ability to efficiently allocate arguments to processes. However, they shouldn't let their admiration for it blind them to its intrinsic limitations. As a case in point, the use of xargs in sorting applications can lead to incorrect results, so you should use dependable Perl scripts such as most_recent_file instead.

Finally, although there's generally no Unix-like find command available on other OSs, you can use the find2perl script that's part of the standard Perl distribution to create custom find-like scripts that will run on any Perl-equipped system. With this technique, find-savvy individuals can create find-like scripts that can be used by anyone who has access to Perl.

Directions for further study

You can learn more about the topics covered in this chapter from the following resources:

- man find   # describes the Unix find command
- man xargs   # describes the Unix xargs command
- man perlfunc   # describes -T, -r, etc.
- http://TeachMePerl.com/Perl_on_non-Unix_systems.html

Further details on additional topics introduced here are discussed in part 2:

- Section 7.2.3 describes Perl's stat function.
- Section 8.5 describes command interpolation.
- The use of the module on which find2perl relies—File::Find—is discussed in section 12.3.4.

Minimal Perl: for UNIX and Linux Shell Programmers

Part 1 focused on ways in which simple Perl programs can provide superior alternatives to standard Unix commands. Along the way, you learned the features of Perl that are relevant to emulating or *surpassing* the functionality of grep, sed, awk, and find. Although those features are an essential subset of Minimal Perl, there's more for you to discover.

In part 2, our focus will shift to rounding out your view of Perl. Accordingly, you'll learn to use additional language features that will let your programs solve a wider variety of problems, and to do so with greater efficiency and OS portability.

The topics we'll cover are diverse, including the following:

- Special programming techniques used in *scripts*
- The most essential *built-in functions*
- Storing and retrieving data using *arrays* and *hashes*
- *Compartmentalizing program code* for easier access and reuse
- Preventing *name-clashes* between variables
- Downloading, installing, using and creating *Perl modules*

We'll also discuss how to go beyond the implicit loop by writing *explicit* ones, and how to automate your menu-oriented programming with Perl's new Shell-inspired `select` loop—developed especially for this book!

Unlike part 1, part 2 assumes an understanding of basic Shell programming techniques. If you lack this background you may still benefit from reading part 2, but you should focus on the discussions of the Perl features themselves rather than the Shell-to-Perl translation aids that accompany them.

CHAPTER 7

Built-in functions

7.1 Understanding and managing
     evaluation context 206
7.2 Programming with functions that
     generate or process scalars 210
7.3 Programming with functions that
     process lists 223

7.4 Globbing for filenames 234
7.5 Managing files with functions 239
7.6 Parenthesizing function
     arguments 242
7.7 Summary 243

One of the properties of a programming language that makes it easy and gratifying to use, or the opposite, is the collection of *built-in functions* it provides. Perl has literally hundreds of these, including the relatively mundane ones called print, printf, warn, and die that you encountered in part 1. But Perl has much more advanced functions as well, such as one that provides the basic infrastructure for implementing arbitrary data transformations,[1] which can be a great productivity enhancer.

In contrast, the Unix shells have only a few built-in commands (cd, echo, export, etc.), because they're designed to obtain most of their services from Unix utility programs (such as grep and sort).

Other things being equal, programs written in languages having rich sets of built-in functions, such as Perl, run more quickly and are much more OS-independent than those that rely on external utilities (as does the Shell). But as you learned in part 1,

---

[1] The map function, covered later in this chapter.

other things are generally *unequal* in comparisons between Perl's built-in resources and Unix's utilities—in particular, Perl's facilities tend to be distinctly superior.[2]

This combination of characteristics gives Perl programs a significant advantage over Shell programs—not only are Perl's facilities better, but they're also faster and more OS-independent, due to their built-in status.

This chapter teaches you how to use Perl's most important built-in functions so you can parse text, convert data types, make random decisions, tell time, manage files, and sort, filter, and transform data. With this background, you'll be prepared to write many kinds of useful programs, and to understand the roles these functions play in the more complex scripts featured later in part 2.

Another thing you'll learn—which may come as a shock, albeit a pleasant one—is that some components of Perl programs are able to sense the "context" (*scalar* or *list*) in which they're used, and modify their behavior appropriately.

In keeping with this scalar/list distinction, which is deeply ingrained in Perl, we'll cover functions oriented toward scalar data and list data separately. Later, we'll discuss the use of file-management functions, which come in both scalar and list-oriented varieties.

Before delving into these topics, we first need to discuss Perl's unusual context-sensing feature, which is called *evaluation context*.

7.1 UNDERSTANDING AND MANAGING EVALUATION CONTEXT

Perl was developed by a linguist, who strongly feels that it's the role of computer-language designers to make things easy for programmers—rather than the role of programmers to endure whatever makes things easiest for language designers (the guiding principle behind certain historical languages!).

One way that Perl provides the all important property of DWIMity ("doing what I mean") is through its recognition of evaluation context. This means that the way an expression is used can signify whether it should be evaluated in scalar context or list context, with its results being adjusted accordingly.

Consider this assignment statement, which will be familiar from earlier chapters:

```
$num_fields=@F;        # NOTE: @F contains three fields
```

This is a request for a scalar variable to be loaded with a value derived from an array, which in this case contains three elements of the "field" type (see section 5.3). However, because a scalar can store only a single item, Perl must characterize the contents

---

[2] Some Perl facilities that are superior to their Unix counterparts: the matching operator vs. the `grep` command, the substitution operator vs. the `sed` command, and some file operators vs. options of the `find` command.

of the array as a single value. Its policy is to use the array's number of elements in such cases, resulting in the number 3 being assigned to $num_fields.

But what about this assignment statement,

```
@all_fields=@F;
```

or this one?

```
($f1, $f2)=@F;
```

Although these examples have the same right-hand side (@F) as the earlier one that initialized $num_fields, in these cases Perl represents @F as a list of its component elements rather than the number of its elements. This results in the @all_fields array becoming an exact copy of @F, and $f1 and $f2 being assigned the first two elements of @F.

Have you surmised how Perl knows what the programmer wants in these examples, so it can treat @F appropriately in the different cases?

Unlike you, Perl can't look for clues in the names of the target variables of the assignment, so there must be some other indicator. All it does is check what's on the left-hand side of the assignment! If it's a scalar variable, the scalar representation of @F (its element count) is used. If it's an array variable[3] or a parenthesized list of variables, the list representation is used.

This means that *you* control evaluation context by the way you write your program, as discussed next.

7.1.1   Determinants and effects of evaluation context

Evaluation context is important! And you, the programmer, are responsible for specifying the context you want for a particular expression. For these reasons, it's vital for you to understand what effects various contexts have, and how they can be requested. This information is provided next, along with illustrative examples.

List context can be requested by

- **assigning** to a <u>list variable</u>:
  ```
  @all_fields=@F;
  ```
- **assigning** to <u>variables within a parenthesized list:</u>
  ```
  ($first, @rest)=@F;
  ```
- placing an <u>expression</u> in a **function**'s argument list:
  ```
  print @F;          # prints the array's elements
  ```

Effects of list context:

- Allows a list of values to be treated as a list of values
- Causes some functions to return a list rather than a scalar

---

[3] Or a hash variable, as discussed in section 9.2.

- Has no effect on a scalar value, such as `'Fred'`:

```
@names='Fred';  # assigns Fred,   list context
$names='Fred';  # assigns Fred, scalar context
```

Scalar context can be requested by

- typing **scalar** before an <u>expression</u>:

```
print scalar @F;     # prints the number of elements
```

- **assigning** to a <u>scalar variable</u>:

```
$num_fields=@F;
```

- using an <u>expression</u> with an **operator** that provides a scalar context:

```
@ARGV      or  warn "No arguments!\n";
@ARGV > 1  and warn "Too many arguments\n";
```

- using an <u>expression</u> to **subscript** a variable (i.e., using an index):[4]

```
$F[@F]='New last value';
```

Effects of scalar context:

- Causes a list to be converted to its scalar representation
- Causes some functions to return a scalar rather than a list
- Has no effect on a scalar value

Perl programmers have some special tools for working with evaluation contexts, as you'll see next.

7.1.2 Making use of evaluation context

It's important to understand how to override the list context that otherwise applies in cases like `print @array_name`, which is accomplished by placing `scalar` before the list variable. Doing so imposes a scalar context on the argument, causing it to be converted to its scalar form:[5]

```
print scalar @array_name;     # print the number of arguments
```

Although the *element count* is Perl's standard way of representing a list in scalar context, it's not the only possible representation. For example, the built-in `localtime` function (covered later in this chapter) returns a list of numbers in list context, but a string that looks like the output of the `date` command in scalar context.

Moreover, as you'll see in chapter 11, programmers have the ability to define any type of list-to-scalar conversion (or vice versa) that they please. For example, a user-

---

[4] Assuming the array `@F` initially had two values, stored under the indices of 0 and 1, the subscripting expression would cause the string to be associated with the index of 2 (`@F`'s value), which was initially beyond the end of the array but becomes its new end.

[5] This works because functions in a series are processed from right to left, causing the scalar conversion of `@array_name` to be processed first, leaving its (scalar) result to be (un)affected by the list context provided by `print`.

defined function called `april_precip` might return the precipitation recorded for each day as a list of 30 numbers—when called in list context. But in scalar context, it could return a number indicating the *total precipitation* for the month—or even a PDF file containing a discussion of how this April's rainfall compared with last year's, illustrated with daily precipitation graphs.

We'll look at Perl's most fundamental facilities for converting scalars to lists, and vice versa, next.

Converting data types

Table 7.1 lists two Perl facilities for converting scalars to lists and three for converting lists to scalars.

Table 7.1   Tools for data-type conversion

Scalar to list	List to scalar
The `split` function	The `scalar` function
The `-wnla` and `-wpla` option clusters	Double quotes
	The `join` function

As a counterpart to the `scalar` function, you might expect there to be a function called `list` for converting a scalar to a list. There is such a function, but as the table shows, it's called `split`, because it "splits" an arbitrary string into a list of its constituent elements. We'll cover it in detail in section 7.2.1.

As demonstrated in section 5.3.1, option clusters incorporating the `n` or `p` option—along with the `a` option—provide convenient ways of doing scalar-to-list conversion for records processed by Perl's implicit input-reading loop. For list-to-scalar conversion, double quotes can be used to join array elements with spaces (or whatever else is in '`$"`'; see table 2.8) and form the result into a string, as illustrated by this code fragment:

```
"@ARGV"              # means "arg1 arg2 arg3"
```

In this statement, the left-hand side calls for a scalar value, but because a quoted string is already a scalar, no conversion is needed:

```
$args="@ARGV";       # assign space-separated arguments to $args
```

That's a lot different from the following case, whose right-hand side is of the list type and therefore needs to be converted to a scalar prior to the assignment:

```
$num_args=@ARGV;     # assigns number of elements to variable
```

The following example may look a lot different from the one that assigned to `$args`, but it receives similar treatment:

```
print "@ARGV";       # prints space-separated arguments
```

The double quotes around the argument are processed first, forming a string from the space-separated list elements; then, the list context provided by the function is applied to that result. But a quoted string is a scalar, and list context doesn't affect scalars, so the existing string is left unmodified as print's argument.

The join function listed in table 7.1 provides the same service as the combination of '$"' and double quotes and is provided as a convenience for those who prefer to pass arguments to a function rather than to set a variable and double quote a string. We'll discuss this function later in this chapter.

Now you understand the basic principles of evaluation context and the tools used for converting data types. With this background in mind, we'll examine some important Perl functions that deal with scalar data next, such as split. Then, in section 7.3 we'll discuss functions that deal with list data, such as join.

7.2 PROGRAMMING WITH FUNCTIONS THAT GENERATE OR PROCESS SCALARS

Table 7.2 describes some especially useful built-in functions that generate or process scalar values, which weren't already discussed in part 1.

Table 7.2   Useful Perl functions for scalars, and their nearest relatives in Unix

Perl built-in function	Unix relative(s)	Purpose	Effects
split	The cut command; AWK's split function; the Shell's IFS variable	Converting scalars to lists	Takes a string and optionally a set of delimiters, and extracts and returns the delimited substrings. The default delimiter is any sequence of whitespace characters.
localtime	The date command	Accessing current date and time	Returns a string that resembles the output of the Unix date command.
stat	The ls –lL command	Accessing file information	Provides information about the file referred to by stat's argument, or the symbolic link presented as lstat's argument.
lstat	The ls –l command		
chomp	N/A	Removing newlines in data	Removes trailing input record separators from strings, using newline as the default. (With Unix utilities and Shell built-in commands, newlines are always removed automatically.)
rand	The Shell's RANDOM variable; AWK's rand function	Generating random numbers	Generates random numbers that can be used for decision-making in simulations, games, etc.

CHAPTER 7   BUILT-IN FUNCTIONS

The counterparts to those functions found in Unix or the Shell are also indicated in the table. These provide related services, but in ways that are generally not as convenient or useful as their Perl alternatives.[6]

For example, although split looks at **A**<TAB><TAB>**B** as you do, seeing the fields **A** and **B**, the Unix cut command sees *three fields* there by default—including an imaginary empty one between the tabs! As you might guess, this discrepancy has caused many people to have difficulty using cut properly. As another example, the default behavior of Perl's split is to return a list of whitespace-separated words, but obtaining that result by manipulating the Shell's IFS variable requires advanced skills—and courage.[7]

We'll now turn to detailed consideration of each of the functions listed in table 7.2 and demonstrate how they can be effectively used in typical applications.

7.2.1   Using split

split is typically used to extract a list of fields from a string, using the coding techniques shown in table 7.3.

Table 7.3   The split function

Typical invocation formats[a]	
@fields=**split**; @fields=**split** /RE/; @fields=**split** /RE/, string;	

Example	Explanation
@fields=**split**;	Splits $_ into whitespace-delimited "words," and assigns the resulting list to @fields (as do the examples that follow).
@fields=**split** /,/;	Splits $_ using individual commas as delimiters.
@fields=**split** /\s+/, $line;	Splits $line using whitespace sequences as delimiters.
@fields=**split** /[^\040\t_]+/, $line;	Splits $line using sequences of one or more *non*-"space, tab, or underscore characters" as delimiters.

a. Matching modifiers (e.g., i for case insensitivity) can be appended after the closing delimiter of the matching operator, and a custom regex delimiter can be specified after m (e.g., split **m:/:;**).

split's optional first argument is a matching operator whose regex specifies the delimiter(s) to be used in extracting fields from the string. The optional second argument overrides the default of $_ by specifying a different string to be split.

---

[6] Perl has the advantage of being a modern descendant of the ancient Unix tradition, so Larry was able to address and correct many of its deficiencies while creating Perl.

[7] Why courage? Because if the programmer neglects to reinstate the IFS variable's original contents after modifying it, a mild-mannered Shell script can easily mutate into its evil twin from another dimension and wreak all kinds of havoc.

In the simplest case, shown in the table's first invocation format, split can be invoked without any arguments to split $_ using whitespace delimiters. However, when *input records* need to be split into fields, it's more convenient to use the n and a invocation options to automatically load fields into @F, as discussed in part 1. For this reason, split is primarily used in Minimal Perl for secondary splitting. For instance, input lines could first be split into fields using whitespace delimiters via the -wnla standard option cluster, and then one of those fields could be split further using another delimiter to extract its subfields.

Here's a demonstration of a script that uses this technique to show the time in a custom format:

```
$ mytime       # reformats date-style output
The time is 7:32 PM.

$ cat mytime
#! /bin/sh
# Sample output from date:  Thu Apr  6 16:12:05 PST 2006
#     Index numbers for @F:  0  1  2    3     4   5
date |
  perl -wnla -e '$hms=$F[3];   # copy time field into named variable
                ($hour, $minute)=split /:/, $hms;   # no $seconds
                $am_pm='AM';
                $hour > 12  and  $am_pm='PM'  and  $hour=$hour-12;
                print "The time is $hour:$minute $am_pm.";
                '
```

mytime is implemented as a Shell script, to simplify the delivery of date's output as input to the Perl command.[8] Perl's automatic field splitting option is used (via -wnl**a**) to load date's output into the elements of @F, and then the array element[9] containing the **hour:minutes:seconds** field ($F[3]) is copied into the $hms variable (for readability). $hms is then split on the ":" delimiter, and its hour and minute fields are assigned to variables. What about the seconds? The programmer didn't consider them to be of interest, so despite the fact that split returns a three-element list here, the third subfield's value isn't used in the program. Next, the script adds an AM/PM field, and prints the reworked date output in the custom format.

In addition to splitting-out subfields from time fields, you can use split in many other applications. For example, you could carve up IP addresses into their individual

---

[8] An alternative technique based on *command interpolation* (like the Shell's *command substitution*) is shown in section 8.5.

[9] The expression $F[3] uses array indexing (introduced in table 5.9) to access the fourth field. The named-variable approach could be used instead, with some additional typing:
(undef, undef, undef, $hms)=@F;

numeric components using " . " as the delimiter, but remember that you need to back-slash that character to make it literal:

```
@IPa_parts=split /\./, $IPa;    # 216.239.57.99 --> 216, 239, 57, 99
```

You can also use `split` to extract schemes (such as http) and domains from URLs, using " : / / " as the delimiter:

```
$URL='http://a.b.org';
($scheme, $domain)=split m|://|, $URL;    # 'http', 'a.b.org'
```

Notice the use of the m syntax of the matching operator to specify a non-slash delim-iter, to avoid conflicts with the slashes in the regex field.

Tips on using `split`

One common mistake with `split` is forgetting the proper order of the arguments:

```
@words=split $data, /:/;        # string, RE: WRONG!
@words=split /:/, $data;        # RE, string: Right!
```

Another typical mistake is the incorrect specification of `split`'s field delimiters, usu-ally by accidentally describing a *particular* sequence of delimiters rather than *any* sequence of them.

For example, this invocation of `split` says that each occurrence of the indicated character sequence is a single delimiter:

```
$_='Hoboken::NJ:Exit 14c';
@fields=split /:/,   $data;   # Extracts two fields
```

The result is that "Hoboken::NJ" and "Exit 14c" are assigned to the array.

This alternative says that *any sequence* of one or more of the specified characters counts as a single delimiter, which results in "NJ" being extracted as a separate field:

```
$_='Hoboken::NJ:Exit 14c';
@fields=split /[:]+/, $data;   # Extracts three fields
```

This second type of delimiter specification is more commonly used than the first kind, but of course what's correct in a specific case depends on the format of the data being examined.

Although `split` is a valuable tool, it's not indispensable. That's because its func-tionality can generally be duplicated through use of a matching operator in list con-text, which can also extract substrings from a string. But there's an important difference—with `split`, you define the *data delimiters* in the regex, whereas with a matching operator, you define the *delimited data* there.

How do you decide whether to use `split` or the matching operator when parsing fields? It's simple—`split` is preferred for cases where it's easier to *describe the delim-iters* than to describe the delimited data, whereas a matching operator using capturing parentheses (see table 3.8) is preferred for the cases where it's easier to *describe the data* than the delimiters..

Remember the `mytime` script? Did its design as a Shell script rather than a Perl script, and its use of `date` to deliver the current time to a Perl command, surprise you? If so, you'll be happy to hear that Perl doesn't really need the `date` command to tell it what time it is; Perl's own `localtime` function, which we'll cover next, provides that service.

7.2.2 Using `localtime`

You can use Perl's `localtime` function to obtain time and date information in an OS-independent manner, using invocation formats shown in table 7.4. As indicated, `localtime` provides different types of output according to its context.

Table 7.4   The `localtime` function

Typical invocation formats

`$time_string=localtime;`
`$time_string=localtime timestamp;`
`@time_component_numbers=localtime;`
`$time_component_number=(localtime)[index];`

Example	Explanation

`$time=localtime;`
`print $time;`
Or
`print scalar localtime;`
	In scalar context, `localtime` returns the current date and time in a format similar to that of the `date` command (but without the timezone field).

`print scalar localtime` `  ((stat filename)[9]);`	`localtime` can be used to convert a numeric timestamp, as returned by `stat`, into a string formatted like `date`'s output. The example shows the time when *filename* was last modified.

`($sec, $min, $hour, $dayofmonth,`
`  $month, $year, $dayofweek,`
`  $dayofyear, $isdst)=localtime;`
	In list context, `localtime` returns nine values representing the current time. Most of the date-related values are 0-based, so `$dayofweek`, for example, ranges from 0–6. But `$year` counts from 1900, representing the year 2000 as 100.

`$dayofyear=(localtime)[7] + 1;` `print "Day of year: $dayofyear";`	As with any list-returning function, the call to `localtime` can be parenthesized and then subscripted as if it were an array. Because the `dayofyear` field is 0-based, it needs to be incremented by 1 for human consumption.

Here is a command that's adapted from the first example of the table. It produces a `date`-like time report by forcing a scalar context for `localtime`, which would otherwise be in the list context provided by `print`:

```
$ perl -wl -e 'print scalar localtime;'
Tue Feb 14 19:32:03 2006
```

Another way to use `localtime` is shown in the example in the table's third row, which involves capturing and interpreting a set of time-related numbers. But in simple cases, you can parenthesize the call to localtime and index into it as if it were an array, as in the "day of year" example of the table's last row.

Here's a rewrite of the mytime script shown earlier, which converts it to use localtime instead of date:

```
$ cat mytime2
#! /usr/bin/perl -wl

(undef, $minutes, $hour)=localtime;    # we don't care about seconds
$am_pm='AM';
$hour > 12  and  $am_pm='PM'  and  $hour=$hour-12;
print "The time is $hour:$minutes $am_pm.";

$ mytime2
The time is 7:42 PM.
```

This new version is both more efficient and more OS-portable than the original, which makes it twice as good!

Tips on using localtime

Here's an especially productivity-enhancing tip. When you need to load localtime's output into that set of nine variables shown in table 7.4's third row, don't try to type them in. Instead, run perldoc -f localtime in one window, and cut and paste the following paragraph from that screen into your program's window:

```
#  0    1    2    3    4    5    6    7    8
($sec,$min,$hour,$mday,$mon,$year,$wday,$yday,$isdst) =
                                        localtime(time);
```

Then, edit that assignment as needed by replacing some variables with undef, removing localtime's argument, etc.

You'll see examples featuring stat next, like the one shown in the second row of table 7.4.

7.2.3   Using stat

One of the most frequently used Unix commands is the humble but absolutely indispensable ls -l. It provides access to the wealth of data stored in a file's *inode*, which holds everything Unix knows about a file.[10]

Perl provides access to that per-file data repository using the function called stat (for "file <u>stat</u>us"), which takes its name from a related UNIX resource. Table 7.5 summarizes the syntax of stat and shows some typical uses.

---

[10] Well, almost everything; the file's name resides in its directory.

stat is most commonly used for simple tasks like those shown in the table's examples, such as determining the UID or inode number of a file. You'll see a more interesting example next.

Table 7.5   The stat function

Typical invocation formats	
($dev, $ino, $mode, $nlink, $uid, $gid, $rdev, $size, $atime, $mtime, $ctime, $blksize, $blocks)=**stat** *filename*;	
$extracted_element=(**stat**)[*index*];	

Example	Explanation
(undef, undef, undef, undef, $uid)= **stat** '/etc/passwd'; print "passwd is owned by UID: $uid\n";	The file's numeric user ID is returned as the fifth element of stat's list, so after initializing the named variables as shown, it's available in $uid.
print "File $f's inode is: ", (**stat** $f)[1];	The call to stat can be parenthesized and indexed as if it were an array. The example accesses the second element (labeled $ino in the format shown above), which is the file's inode number.

Emulating the Shell's –nt operator

Let's see how you can use Perl to duplicate the functionality of the Korn and Bash shells' –nt (*newer-than*) operator, which is heavily used—and greatly appreciated—by Unix file-wranglers. Here's a Shell command that tests whether the file on the left of –nt is newer than the file on its right:

```
[[ $file1 -nt $file2 ]] &&
    echo "$file1 was more recently modified than $file2"
```

The Perl equivalent is easily written using stat:

```
(stat $file1)[9] > (stat $file2)[9] and
    print "$file1 was more recently modified than $file2";
```

The numeric comparison (>) is appropriate because the values in the atime (for access), mtime (for modification), and ctime (for change) fields are just big integer numbers, ticking off elapsed seconds from a reference point in the distant past. Accordingly, the difference between two mtime values reveals the difference in their files' modification times, to the second.

Unlike the functions seen thus far, there are many ways stat can fail—for example, the existing file /a/b could be mistyped as the non-existent /a/d, or the program's user could be denied the permissions needed on /a to run stat on its files. For this reason, it's a good idea to call stat in a separate statement for each file, so you can print file-specific OS error messages (from "$!"; see appendix A) if there's a problem.

Following this advice, we can upgrade the code that emulates the Shell's −nt operator to this more robust form:

```
$mtime1=(stat $file1)[9]  or  die "$0: stat of $file1 failed; $!";
$mtime2=(stat $file2)[9]  or  die "$0: stat of $file2 failed; $!";
$mtime1 > $mtime2 and
    print "$file1 was more recently modified than $file2";
```

The benefit of this new version is that it can issue separate, detailed messages for a failed stat on either file, like this one issued by the nt_tester script:[11]

```
nt_tester: stat of /a/d failed; No such file or directory
```

stat can also help in the emulation of certain Unix commands, as you'll see next.

Emulating `ls` with the `listfile` script

We'll now consider a script called listfile, which shows how stat can be used to generate simple reports on files like those produced by ls −1. First, let's compare their results:

```
$ ls -1    rygel
-rwxr-xr-x  1  yumpy   users 415 2006-05-14 19:32 rygel

$ listfile rygel
-rwxr-xr-x  1  yumpy   users 415 Sun May 14 19:32:05 2006 rygel
```

The format of listfile's time string doesn't match that of ls. However, it's an arguably more user-friendly format, and it's much easier to generate this way, so the programmer deemed the difference an *enhancement* rather than a bug.

Listing 7.1 shows the script, with the most significant elements highlighted.

Line 6 loads the CPAN module that provides the format_mode function used on Line 17.

Listing 7.1 The `listfile` script

```
1  #! /usr/bin/perl -wl
2
3  # load CPAN module whose "format_mode" function converts
4  #    octal-mode --> "-rw-r--r--" format
5
6  use Stat::lsMode;
7
```

---

[11] In contrast, the original version would report that $file1 was more recently modified than $file2 even if the latter *didn't exist*, because the "undefined" value (see section 8.1.1) that stat would return is treated as a 0 in numeric context.

```
 8   @ARGV == 1  or  die "Usage: $0 filename\n";
 9   $filename=shift;
10
11   (undef, undef, $mode, $nlink, $uid, $gid,
12     undef, $size, undef, $mtime)=stat $filename;
13
14   $time=localtime $mtime;      # convert seconds to time string
15   $uid_name=getpwuid $uid;     # convert UID-number to string
16   $gid_name=getgrgid $gid;     # convert GID-number to string
17   $rwx=format_mode $mode;      # convert octal mode to rwx format
18
19   printf "%s %4d %3s %9s %12d %s %s\n",
20     $rwx, $nlink, $uid_name, $gid_name, $size, $time, $filename;
```

Line 12 assigns stat's output to a list consisting of variables and undef placeholders that ends with $mtime, the rightmost element of interest from the complete set of 13 elements. This sets up the six variables needed in Lines 14–20.

On Line 14, the $mtime argument to localtime gets converted into a date-like time string (a related example is shown in row two of table 7.4.)

Lines 15 and 16, respectively, convert the UID and GID *numbers* provided by stat into their corresponding user and group *names*, using special Perl built-in functions (see man perlfunc). The functions are called get**pw**uid, and get**gr**gid because they get the user or group name by looking up the record having the supplied numeric UID or GID in the Unix password file ("**pw**") or group file ("**gr**").[12]

Line 17 converts the octal $mode value to an ls-style permissions string, using the imported format_mode function.

The printf function is used to format all the output, because it allows a data type and field width—such as "%9s", which means display a string in nine columns—to be specified for each of its arguments.

As mentioned earlier, the way localtime formats the time-string is different from the format produced by the Linux ls command, so some Unix users might prefer to use the real ls. On the other hand, listfile provides a good starting point for those using other OSs who wish to develop an ls-like command.[13]

Tips on using stat

For over three decades, untold legions of Shell programmers have—according to local custom—*groused*, *whinged*, and/or *kvetched* about the need to repeatedly respecify the filename in statements like these:

---

[12] As usual, it's no coincidence that these Perl functions have the same names as their Unix counterparts, which are C-language library functions.

[13] The first enhancement might be to use the looping techniques demonstrated in chapter 10 to upgrade listfile to listfiles.

```
[ -f "$file"  -a  -r "$file"  -a  -s "$file" ]  ||  exit 42;
[[ -f $file  &&  -r $file  &&  -s $file ]]  ||  exit 42;
```

To give those who've migrated to Perlistan some much-deserved comfort and succor, Perl supports the use of the *underscore character* as a shorthand reference to the last filename used with stat or a file-test operator (within a particular code block).

Accordingly, the Perl counterpart to the previous Shell command—which tests that a file is regular, readable, and has a size greater than 0 bytes—can be written like so:

```
-f $file  and  -r _  and  -s _  or  exit 42;
```

Here's an example of economizing on typing by using the underscore with the stat function:

```
(stat $filename)[5] == (stat _)[7]  and
    warn "File's GID equals its size; could this mean something?";
```

To get the size of a file, it's easier to use -s $file (see table 6.2) than the equivalent stat invocation, which is (stat $file)[7].

As a final tip, when you need to load stat's output into those 13 time variables, don't try to type them in; run perldoc -t stat in one window, cut and paste the following paragraph from that screen into your program's window, and edit as needed:

```
($dev,$ino,$mode,$nlink,$uid,$gid,$rdev,$size,
    $atime,$mtime,$ctime,$blksize,$blocks)
        = stat($filename);
```

Next, we'll look at the chomp function, which is used to strip trailing newlines from input that's read manually, rather than through the auspices of the implicit input-reading loop.

7.2.4 Using chomp

In Minimal Perl, routine use of the l option, along with n or p, frees you from worrying about trailing newlines fouling-up string comparisons involving input lines. That's because the l option provides automatic *chomping*—removal of trailing newlines—on the records read by the implicit loop.[14] For this reason, if you want your program to terminate on encountering a line consisting of "DONE", you can conveniently code the equality test like this:

```
$_ eq 'DONE'  and  exit;     # using option n or p, along with l
```

That's easier to type and less error-prone than what you'd have to write if you weren't using the l option:

```
$_ eq "DONE\n"  and  exit;     # using option n or p, without l
```

---

[14] See table 7.6 for a more precise definition of what chomp does.

As useful as it is, the implicit loop isn't the only input-reading mechanism you'll ever need. An alternative, typically employed for interacting with users, is to read input directly from the standard input channel:

```
$size=<STDIN>;              # let user type in her size
```

The angle brackets represent Perl's *input operator*, and STDIN directs it to read input from the standard input channel (typically connected to the user's keyboard).

However, input read using this manual approach doesn't get chomped by the 1 option, so if you want chomping, it's up to you to make it happen. As you may have guessed, the function called chomp, summarized in table 7.6, manually removes trailing newlines from strings.

Table 7.6   The chomp function

Typical invocation formats[a]	
chomp $var; chomp @var; chomp ($var1, $var2, @var, ...);	

Example	Explanation

`printf 'Enter your size: ';`
`$size=<STDIN>;`
`chomp $size;`
`# now we can use $size without`
`# fear of "newline interference"`
	An input line read as shown has a trailing newline attached, which complicates string comparisons; chomp removes it.

`chomp ($flavor, $freshness, @lines);`	chomp can accept multiple variables as arguments, if they're surrounded by parentheses.

a. The value returned by chomp indicates how many trailing occurrences of the input record separator character(s), defined in $/ as an OS-specific newline by default, were found and removed.

The first example in the table shows the usual prompting, input collecting, and chomping operations involved in preparing to work with a string obtained from a user. After the string has been chomped, the programmer is free to do equality tests on it and print its contents without worrying about a newline fouling things up.

As a case in point, the following statement's output looks pretty nasty if $size hasn't been chomped, due to the inappropriate intrusion of $size's trailing newline within the printed string:

```
print "Please confirm: Your size is $size; right?"
Please confirm: Your size is 42
; right?"
```

The table's second example shows that strings stored in multiple scalar variables and even arrays can all be handled with one chomp. However, it's important to realize that chomp is an exception to the general rule that parentheses around argument lists are optional in Perl. Specifically, although parentheses may be omitted when chomp has a single argument, they must be provided when it has multiple arguments.[15]

Tips on using *chomp*

Watch out for a warning of the following type, which may signify (among other things) that you have violated the rule about parenthesizing multiple arguments to chomp:

```
chomp $one, $two;                                          # WRONG!
Useless use of a variable in void context at -e line 1.
```

In this case, the warning means that Perl understood that $one was intended as chomp's argument, but it didn't know what to do with $two.

Here's another common mistake, which looks reasonable enough but is neverthe-less tragically wrong:

```
$line=chomp $line;    # Store chomped string back in $line?  WRONG!
```

This is also a bad idea:

```
print chomp $line;                                        # WRONG!
```

That last example prints nothing other than a 1 or 0, neither of which is likely to be very satisfying. The problem is that chomp doesn't return the chomped argument string that you might expect , but instead a numerical code (see table 7.6). In conse-quence, chomp's return value wouldn't generally be printed, let alone used to overwrite the storage for the freshly chomped string (as in the example that assigns to $line).

But surprises aren't always undesirable. Having just discussed how to avoid them with chomp, we'll now shift our attention to a mathematical function that's designed especially to *increase* the unpredictability of your programs!

7.2.5   Using *rand*

The rand function, described in table 7.7, is commonly used in code testing, simula-tions, and games to introduce an element of unpredictability into a program's behavior. The table's first example loads a (pseudo-)random, positive, floating-point number, less than 1, into $num. Let's look at a sample result:

```
$ perl -wl -e '$num=rand; print $num;'
0.80377197265625
```

You generally won't need this much precision in your random numbers, and integers are easier to work with than floating-point numbers anyway, so rand allows you to provide a *scaling factor* as an argument. Using this, you can get a bit closer to working with integers:

```
$ perl -wl -e '$num=rand 10; print $num;'  # Range: 0 <= $num < 10
4.93939208984375
```

---

[15] See section 7.6 for more details on parenthesization.

Table 7.7 The rand function

Typical invocation formats

`$random_tiny_number=`**`rand`**`;`
`$random_larger_number=`**`rand`** `N;`
`$random_element=$some_array[` **`rand`** `@some_array ];`

Example	Explanation
`$num=`**`rand`**`;`	Assigns a floating-point number N, in the range $0 <= N < 1$, to $num.
`$num=int (` **`rand`** `10 ) + 1;`	Assigns an integer number N in the range $1 <= N <= 10$ to $num.
`$element=$ARGV[` **`rand`** `@ARGV ];`	Assigns to `$element` a randomly selected element from the indicated array. In this case, it's a random argument from the script's argument list.

If you modified this command to discard the decimal portion of each random number, it would print integers in the range 0 to 9 (inclusive). To shift them into the range 1–10, you'd use the algorithm shown in the table's second example. It works by first truncating the decimal portion of each random number with the int function and then incrementing its value by 1,[16] thereby converting the obtained range from 0.*x*–9.*x* to 1–10.

As an example, the following code snippet has 1 chance in 100 of awarding a prize each time it's run:

```
int (rand  100) + 1 == 42   and          # range is 1-100
    print 'You\'ve won $MILLIONS$!',
        ' But first, we need your bank account number: ';
```

The third example in table 7.7 takes advantage of Perl's 0-based array subscripts, and the facts that @ARGV in scalar context returns the argument count and the int function is automatically applied to subscripting expressions. The result is the random selection of an element from the specified array,[17] with very little coding.

In section 8.3, we'll cover if/else, which can be controlled by rand to make random decisions about what to do next in a program.

In the next section, we'll shift our discussion to list-oriented functions and demonstrate, among other things, how rand can be used with grep to do random filtering.

---

[16] The parentheses around rand 10 prevent it from getting 11 (10 + 1) as its argument. See section 7.6 for more information on the proper use of parentheses.

[17] You'll see this technique used in a practical application in section 9.1.4.

7.3 PROGRAMMING WITH FUNCTIONS THAT PROCESS LISTS

Table 7.8 lists some of Perl's most useful functions for list processing—which provide reordering, joining, filtering, and transforming services, respectively, for lists. The table also shows each function's nearest relative in Unix or the Shell.

Table 7.8 Useful Perl functions for lists, and their nearest relatives in Unix

Built-in Perl function	Unix relative(s)	Purpose	Effects
sort	The Unix sort command	List sorting	Takes a list, and returns a sorted list.
reverse	Linux's tac command	List reversal	Reverses the order of items in a list. Primarily used with sort.
join	The Unix printf command; AWK's sprintf function	List-to-scalar conversion	Returns a scalar containing all the elements of a list, joined by a specified string.
grep	The Unix egrep[a] command	List filtration	Returns selected elements from a list.
map	The Unix sed command	List transformation	Returns modified versions of elements from a list.

a. It's like grep, too, but egrep's regex dialect is more akin to Perl's.

You shouldn't read too much into the family relationships indicated in the table, because the designated Unix relatives all work rather differently than their Perl counterparts. For example, although the Unix egrep command reads files and displays lines that match a pattern, Perl's grep is a general-purpose filtering tool that doesn't necessarily read, match, or display *anything!* As you'll soon see, Perl's grep can indeed be used to obtain egrep-like effects, but it's capable of much more than its Unix relative—as are the other functions listed in table 7.8.

Next, we'll discuss the similarities and differences in how data flows between commands and functions.

7.3.1 Comparing Unix pipelines and Perl functions

Although there are distinct similarities between Unix command pipelines and Perl functions, we need to discuss one glaring difference to avoid confusion. Specifically, data flow in pipelines is from left to right, but it's in the *opposite direction* with Perl functions, as illustrated in table 7.9.

You'll learn how Perl's sort and grep functions work soon, but for now, all you need to know is that the Perl examples in the table do the same kinds of processing as their Unix counterparts. Note in particular that with Perl, a data stream is passed from one function to another just by putting their names in a series (e.g., sort grep

Table 7.9 Data flow in Unix pipelines vs. Perl functions

Unix pipeline	Perl function
Input → *command(s)* → Output	Output ← *function(s)* ← Input
Examples	

```
ls | grep 'X'          > X_files    @X_files=         grep { /X/ } @fnames;
ls | grep 'X' | sort > X_files.s  @X_files_s=sort grep { /X/ } @fnames;
```

in table 7.9); there's no need for an explicit connector of any kind, equivalent to the Shell's "|" symbol.

With that background in mind, we'll now examine the functions of table 7.8 one at a time.

7.3.2 Using sort

The sort function, described in table 7.10, does what its name implies to the elements of a list.

As shown in the table's first set of examples, all it takes is a few characters of coding to convert an array's elements into ascending alphanumeric order. The second exam-

Table 7.10 The sort function

Typical invocation formats [a]
sort *LIST*
reverse **sort** *LIST*
sort { *CODE-BLOCK* } *LIST*
reverse **sort** { *CODE-BLOCK* } *LIST*

Example	Explanation
`@A=`**sort** `@A;        # A-Z order`	The first example rearranges the elements of @A into alphanumeric order. The second shows the explicit way of requesting the same result by stating the default sorting rule, which uses the cmp string-comparison operator. reverse rearranges list elements from ascending order to descending order, and vice versa.
`# Explicit version of above` `@A=`**sort** `{ $a cmp $b } @A;`	
`# Reversal of above; Z-A order` `@A=reverse `**sort** `@A;`	
`@B=`**sort** `{ $a <=> $b } @B;`	Modifies array @B to have elements reordered according to numeric sorting rules using the numeric comparison operator. reverse reorders the list into descending order.
`@B=reverse `**sort** `{ $a <=> $b } @B;`	
`$,="\n";` `print `**sort** `@C;`	Displays elements of @C in alphanumerically sorted order, one per line.

a. In the common case where *CODE-BLOCK* consists of a single statement, it's customary to omit the trailing semicolon.

ple shows explicitly the *CODE-BLOCK* that the first example uses by default, which defines the sorting rule that's used. To understand what that *CODE-BLOCK* does, and how to write your own custom code blocks, you have to know how sorting rules are processed.

Here's how it works. For each pairwise comparison of elements in *LIST*, sort

- loads one element into $a and the other into $b;
- evaluates the *CODE-BLOCK*, and if the result is
  - < 0, it places $a's element *before* $b's;
  - 0, it considers the elements to be tied;
  - > 0, it places $a's element *after* $b's.

Perl's string (cmp) and numeric (<=>) comparison operators[18] return -1, 0, or 1 to indicate that the value on the left (such as $a) is respectively less than, equal to, or greater than the one on the right ($b). Because these are exactly the values that a sort *CODE-BLOCK* must provide, these operators are frequently used in sorting rules.

To convert lists in ascending order to descending order and vice versa, you can use the reverse function after sorting, as shown in the third example of table 7.10.

The table's second set of examples shows comparisons based on the numeric form of the comparison operator, <=>, which is used for sorting numbers. As a practical example of numeric sorting, the intra_line_sort script uses split and sort to reorder and print input lines containing a series of numbers:

```
$ cat integers
111 10 19 88 43 55 81 23 04 40 12 2 1
2 1 10 91 88 43 55 18 23 40 17 21 000

$ intra_line_sort integers
1 2 04 10 12 19 23 40 43 55 81 88 111
000 1 2 10 17 18 21 23 40 43 55 88 91
```

The effect of the sorting is easier to see when the script's -debug switch is used:

```
$ intra_line_sort -debug integers
111 10 19 88 43 55 81 23 04 40 12 2 1 <- Original
1 2 04 10 12 19 23 40 43 55 81 88 111 <- Sorted

2 1 10 91 88 43 55 18 23 40 17 21 000 <- Original
000 1 2 10 17 18 21 23 40 43 55 88 91 <- Sorted
```

Listing 7.2 shows the script.[19]

---

[18] Introduced in table 5.11.

[19] When the execution of two or more statements must depend on a single condition, the if construct, covered in section 8.3, is preferred to repeated independent uses of the logical and (as shown).

Listing 7.2 The `intra_line_sort` script

```
#! /usr/bin/perl -s -wn

our ($debug);            # make switch optional

$debug  and  chomp;      # so "<-" appears on same line as $_
$debug  and  print "$_ <- Original\n";

$,=' ';                  # separate printed words by a space

# split lines of numbers on whitespace, and sort them
print sort { $a <=> $b } split;   # numeric sort

$debug  and  print " <- Sorted\n";
print "\n";              # separate records in output
```

Do you notice anything unusual about the shebang line of this script? It's one of only a handful in this book that doesn't include the l option for automatic line-end processing. That's because it needs to `print` the sorted list of numbers without a newline being appended, so that the "`<- Sorted`" string can appear on the same line.[20]

You have complete control over how Perl sorts your data, allowing special effects, as you'll see next.

Sorting randomly

Just so you don't get the idea that either `cmp` or `<=>` must always be used in sorting rules, here's an example that uses `rand` to reorder the letters of the alphabet:

```
$ perl -wl -e ' $,=" ";        # set list-element separator to space
>     print sort { int((rand 2)+.5)-1 } "a".."z"; '
b g e a c p d f o h i k j l q n s r m t w u y z x v
```

The two dots between "a" and "z" are the range operator we used in chapter 5, for matching pattern ranges. But here we're using its list-context capability of generating intermediate values between two endpoints to avoid the work of typing all 26 letters of the alphabet. It works for integer values too, in expressions such as 1..42 (consult man perlop).

To arrange for the sorting rule to yield the sort-compliant values of -1, 0, and 1, rand's result in the range 0 to <1 is first scaled up by a factor of two, yielding a number in the range 0 to <2. Then that value is incremented by .5, shifting the range to

---

[20] We can't use printf rather than print to avoid the l option's automatic newline, because that only works when there's a single argument to be printed (see section 2.1.6). For this reason, the script omits the l option and does its own newline management.

0.5 to <2.5, in preparation for the truncation of decimal places by int. The resulting value of 0, 1, or 2 is then decremented by 1, to yield -1, 0, or 1 as the result.[21]

Tips on using sort

A commonly needed variation on alphanumeric sorting is *case insensitive* sorting, which you obtain by converting both the $a and $b values to the same case before comparing them with cmp. Here's a sorting rule of this type, which is adapted from the first example of table 7.10 by converting $a to "\L$a" and $b to "\L$b":

```
@A=sort { "\L$a" cmp "\L$b" } @A;   # case-insensitive sorting
```

In cases like these where everything in the double-quoted string is to be case-converted, \L (for lowercase conversion, see table 4.5) can be used without its \E terminator to reduce visual clutter. Note also that the effects of the case conversion are confined to the double-quoted strings used in the comparison; therefore, they don't affect the strings ultimately returned by sort.

Having already learned in chapter 3 about Perl's powerful and versatile matching operator, which can be used to write grep-like programs, you may be surprised to hear that Perl also has a grep function. As you'll see in the next section, Perl's grep certainly does have some properties in common with its Unix namesake, but it's an even more valuable resource.

7.3.3 Using grep

This section discusses Perl's grep function, which, despite what its name suggests, isn't just a built-in version of a Unix grep command. Table 7.11 illustrates some uses of grep. Like its Unix namesake, it can selectively return records that match a pattern. But one difference is that it obtains those records from its *argument list*, not by reading them from a file or STDIN.

Unlike its namesake, Perl's grep is a programmable, general-purpose filtering utility. It works by temporarily assigning the first element of *LIST* to $_, executing the *CODE-BLOCK*, returning $_ if a True result was obtained, and then repeating these actions until all elements of *LIST* have been processed. The *CODE-BLOCK* is therefore essentially a programmable filter, determining which elements of *LIST* will appear in the function's return list.

The first example in the table shows how to use a matching operator to select the desired elements from @A for copying into @B. Unlike the case with the grep *command*, the second example shows that other operators, such as the directory-testing -d, can also be used to implement filters with Perl's grep.

---

[21] As an alternative to using sort for shuffling list elements, most JAPHs would use the shuffle function of the standard List::Util module. Modules are discussed in chapter 12.

Table 7.11 The `grep` function

Typical invocation formats [a]	
`grep { CODE-BLOCK } LIST`	
Example	**Explanation**
`@B=grep { /^[a-z]/i } @A;`	Stores in `@B` elements from `@A` that begin with a letter.
`@B=grep { -d } @A;`	Stores in `@B` elements from `@A` that are names of directory files.
`@B=grep { rand >= .5 } @A;`	Prints elements from `@A` that are randomly selected (`rand` returns a number from 0 to almost 1).
`$,="\n";` `print grep { length > 3 } @A;`	Prints elements from `@A` that are longer than three characters.

a. In the common case where *CODE-BLOCK* consists of a single statement, it's customary to omit the trailing semicolon.

As shown in the table's other examples, filters can also be defined to select elements according to the number of characters they contain, or even to select them at random, among myriad other possibilities.

The last example of the table shows that the "`$,`" variable (introduced in table 2.8) comes in handy for separating list elements that would otherwise be squashed together, when `grep`'s output is passed on to `print`.

Remember the `textfiles` script from chapter 6? It reads filenames from STDIN and filters out the ones that don't contain just text, as determined by Perl's `-T` operator. Here's the script again, to refresh your memory:

```
$ cat textfiles
#! /usr/bin/perl -wnl

# If file named on input line contains text, print its name
-T and print;
```

Because this script is meant to obtain its filenames from a pipe, it doesn't handle filenames presented directly as arguments, as a user might expect:

```
$ textfiles /bin/cat /etc/hosts     # incorrect invocation!
$
```

With this invocation, the script extracts *lines* from each of the named files and treats each one as a *filename* to be tested. The lack of output indicates that no line in any file was recognized as the name of a text file—which is understandable, because the file `/bin/cat` contains binary instructions for the CPU, and `/etc/hosts` contains IP addresses paired with hostnames!

But a script for reporting which filename arguments are *themselves* the names of text files can be easily written using `grep`:

```
$ cat textfile_args
#! /usr/bin/perl -wl
```

```
# If file named as argument contains text, print its name
$,="\n";                          # print one filename per line
print grep { -T } @ARGV;
```

$ **textfile_args /bin/cat /etc/hosts**
/etc/hosts

Notice that the n option is absent from the script's shebang line, because this script needs to do manual processing of its arguments, rather than having the n or p option automatically read input from the files they name.

The programmer saved a few keystrokes by taking advantage of the fact that $_, which contains the list item being currently processed by grep, is also the default argument for -T (as it is for many other operators and functions). The setting of "$," to newline causes print to insert that string between each pair of the arguments it gets from grep, which results in each of the selected filenames appearing on its own line.

You'll see additional examples of how grep can be used for filtering arguments in chapter 8, including scripts that perform sanity-checking on their own arguments.

Next, we'll discuss the function that's the opposite of the split function we discussed in section 7.2.1.

7.3.4   Using join

Table 7.12 shows typical uses of the join function, which you use to combine multiple scalars into a single scalar. The multiple scalars may be specified separately, as shown in the table's first example, or provided by a list variable (e.g., an array), as shown in the other examples. (You'll learn more about arrays in section 9.1.)

Table 7.12   The join function

Typical Invocation Format	
join *STRING, LIST*	
Example[a]	**Explanation**
$properties=**join** '/', $size, $shape, $color;	Joins the values of the scalar variables into a single string, with a slash character between each pair of elements. Sample result in $properties: huge/irregular/clear.

$string_with_NLs=**join** "",
              @strings_with_NLs;
 	
$string_with_NLs=**join** "\n",
              @strings_without_NLs;
	Joins the individual elements of the array into a single string of newline-terminated records, by inserting an empty string between each pair of elements (for strings already terminated with newlines) or by inserting a newline between them (for strings lacking newlines), respectively.

a. NLs stands for *newlines*.

The first example in the table shows individual scalars being joined together with a slash. A classic variation on this technique is to assemble a Unix password-file record by joining its separate components with the colon character, which acts as the field separator in that file:

```
$new_pw_entry=join ':', $name, $passwd, $uid, $gid,
                       $comment, $home, $shell;

print $new_pw_entry;
snort:x:73:68:Snort network monitor:/var/lib/snort:/bin/bash
```

The examples in the table's second row join an array of strings into a single new string. You'll see an example that demonstrates a use for this type of conversion next.

Matching against list variables

Here's a common mistake made by Perl novices, along with the warning message it triggers:

```
@bunch_of_strings =~ s/old/new/g;        # WRONG!
Applying substitution (s///) to @array will act on scalar(@array)
```

The warning informs you that the substitution operator imposes a scalar context on the array expression, which means if there are 42 elements in the array, the code is effectively trying to change *old* to *new* in—*the number 42!*

This result is obtained because the matching and substitution operators only work on scalar values. You therefore have to choose whether you want to process the elements of the list individually,[22] or to combine them into a single scalar and process them collectively. The former approach is appropriate when all the matches of interest can be found within the individual elements, and the latter when matches that *span* consecutive list elements (i.e., start in one and end in another) are of interest.

A typical task that requires the collective-processing approach is that of doing matches or substitutions across the line boundaries in a text file. For example, you might initially read the lines of a file, store them in an array, and strip them of their newlines (using chomp; see section 7.2.4), in preparation for some kind of line-oriented processing. Then, to look for line-spanning matches, you would create a file image by joining each adjacent pair of elements with a newline, and then match against that scalar variable:

```
$file=join "\n", @lines_without_NLs;    # join lines into file form

$file =~ /\bUnix(\s)system\b/  and      # match against file image
    print 'The phrase was found';
```

---

[22] This could be done using the map function discussed in section 7.3.5 or the looping techniques discussed in chapter 10.

Notice that that *any* whitespace character (\s) is allowed—including newline—to appear between the words, to allow for "Unix" at the end of one line, and "system" at the beginning of the next.

You could also perform *substitutions* throughout the text of the file that preserve the whitespace character that was matched within the capturing parentheses around \s, by referencing the associated numbered-variable in the replacement string:[23]

```
$file =~ s/\bUnix(\s)system\b/Linux$1OS/g;  # 1st set of parens-->$1
```

After doing the matches and substitutions, you could once again convert the file-image string into its constituent lines, if desired, using split:

```
@lines_without_NLs=split /\n/, $file;  # split file image into lines
```

> **TIP**   The matching and substitution operators only work with scalars, so when you need to find matches that span the consecutive elements of a list, use join to convert them into a scalar first.

Next, you'll see how join can help in the generation of HTML code.

Developing HTML documents with join: The fields2lists script

The fields2list script converts the tab-separated fields of each input line into the HTML code for a separate unordered (i.e., bullet) list.[24] Here's a sample run:

```
$ cat list_data
Wallace<TAB>Gromit
Wanda Sykes

$ fields2lists list_data > lists.html

$ cat lists.html
<P>
<UL>
<LI>
Wallace
<LI>
Gromit
</UL>

<P>
<UL>
<LI>
Wanda Sykes
</UL>
```

---

[23] Capturing parentheses and numbered variables are discussed in section 3.10.

[24] The CGI module provides prefab functions that create HTML lists—see section 12.3.5.

```
$ w3m lists.html      # check results, using text-mode browser
* Wallace
* Gromit

* Wanda Sykes
```

The script uses the a option for automatic field processing and a BEGIN block to initialize some variables before constructing each line's list from its constituent fields:

```
$ cat fields2lists
#! /usr/bin/perl -wnlaF'\t'

BEGIN {
    $list_start=join "\n", '<P>','<UL>', '<LI>';
    $list_end="</UL>";
}
# Convert the fields of each input line into the elements of a list
$list_elements=join "\n<LI>\n", @F;

# Now send the list to the output
print "$list_start\n$list_elements\n$list_end\n";
```

As anybody who maintains it will be quick to tell you, it's much easier for humans to read HTML code when newlines are placed between the elements. The trick, of course, is to achieve this result without repeatedly typing the newlines. Accordingly, the script uses join to insert a newline between each pair of HTML tags it loads into $list_start, and also to insert "\n<LI>\n" between each pair of the current line's fields while loading $list_elements. After newlines are appended to the variables in print's argument string, the code for the HTML lists is ready for displaying on the screen, or storing in a file.[25]

Next, we'll discuss Perl's general-purpose data-transformation function.

7.3.5   Using map

The map function provides a *list transformation* service. Its syntax is similar to grep's, and both have the property of evaluating the code block for each of the list elements. Where they differ is that grep determines whether to return each element on the basis of that evaluation, whereas map returns the result of that evaluation itself— which effects the transformation.

Table 7.13 shows map's syntax and several transformations that you can perform with it. Although the results of the first two examples appear only in @B, it's possible to have the transformations affect the original list, as shown in the third example. You accomplish this simply by storing the transformed results back in the original array (i.e., @A).

---

[25] We could alternatively have written this script without join by switching the setting of "$," from "\n" to "\n<LI>\n" and back again while printing the various substrings, but that approach yields code that's a bit more difficult to write and harder to read.

Table 7.13 The **map** function

	Typical invocation format [a]
	map { *CODE-BLOCK* } *LIST*

Example	Explanation
@B=**map** { sqrt } @A; @B=**map** { "\L$_" } @A;	Stores the square root or lowercase conversion, respectively, of each element of @A in @B.
@A=**map** { "$_\n" } @A;	Stores the newline-appended conversion of each element of @A back in @A (i.e., converts @A's values to have appended newlines).
$,=' '; print **map** { "'$_'" } @A;	Prints each element of @A enclosed in single quotes and separated by spaces (due to the setting of print's "$," variable).

a. In the common case where *CODE-BLOCK* consists of a single statement, it's customary to omit the trailing semicolon.

The bottommost example displays each element of a list within single quotes. Note the use of double quotes in the code block to remove the special meanings of the inner single quotes.

Next, you'll see how to convert numbers in a file using map.

Converting Celsius to Fahrenheit: The c2f script

The c2f script converts Celsius temperatures to Fahrenheit ones, using map:

```
$ cat celsius          # Celsius temperatures
0 16 32 48

$ c2f celsius          # Fahrenheit temperatures
32 60.8 89.6 118.4
```

Here's the script:

```
$ cat c2f
#! /usr/bin/perl -wnla
# Converts Celsius to Fahrenheit

BEGIN { $,=' '; }   # separate each of print's arguments by a space

print map { $_ * ( 9 / 5 ) + 32 } @F;   # transform each field
```

After each line is read by the implicit loop, its fields are extracted and loaded into @F (courtesy of the a option), and then each field is transformed by map and delivered as an argument to print.[26]

Now that you're familiar with some typical uses of map, we need to discuss a problem you'll surely have with it sometime soon.

---

[26] As demonstrated by the m2k script of section 4.9.1, this type of processing can also be accomplished using a matching-based approach with a substitution operator. Which is best depends on the relative difficulties of extracting the fields of interest with a regex, and specifying what delimits them with a field separator.

Tips on using `map`

Because `map` returns the value of the last expression evaluated within its code block, you sometimes have to make special arrangements to get the result you want. Consider this command, which is meant to convert semicolons in its arguments to colons:

```
$ perl -wl -e '  $,="\n";
>     print map { s/;/:/g } @ARGV; '  '1st; Think' '2nd; Act'
1
1
```

Weird, isn't it? All that came out was a bunch of *1s*!

Get used to seeing that result, because as your adventures in Perlistan continue, one of your own programs *will* eventually manifest this classic *"Column of Ones"* bug. The good new is that the underlying cause is always the same, so the single cure we're going to discuss will fix the bug in all its myriad forms.[27]

The confusion stems from the fact that the output of the `sed 's/;/:/g'` command—which looks a lot like a Perl substitution operator—*is* in fact the modified string, whereas the substitution operator returns something very different—a report of the number of successful substitutions (see table 4.2).

What's the cure? Simply to arrange for `map` to return the (possibly modified) `$_` value, by using `$_` as the final statement in `map`'s code block:[28] It may look strange at first to see `$_` just dangling there before the closing curly brace, but with `map`, that's sometimes required to obtain the desired transformation:

```
$ perl -wl -e '  $,="\n";
>     print map { s/;/:/g; $_  } @ARGV; '  '1st; Think' '2nd; Act'
1st: Think
2nd: Act
```

Transforming data, even with a tool as nifty as `map`, can strain your brain. Accordingly, we'll look next at an operator that generates its own output, which will let us relax as we shift our perspectives from that of data manufacturers to data consumers.

7.4   GLOBBING FOR FILENAMES

The Shell has the valuable capability of generating filenames from "wildcard" characters. This facility is known as *filename generation* (FNG) in traditional AT&T UNIX culture and *file globbing* in Berkeley UNIX.[29]

---

[27] Are you experiencing "*Déjà vu* all over again"? That's appropriate, because this is essentially the same bug we discussed in "Tips on using `chomp`" under section 7.2.4.

[28] As mentioned previously, it's considered good form to use semicolons within a `grep` or `map` *CODE-BLOCK* sparingly, to make it easier to spot the more important one at the end of the surrounding statement. In this case, we can't leave out the one separating the statements, but we *can* omit the one after `$_`.

[29] To me, *globbing* is a more fitting name for what happens to the shoes of a small child on a hot summer day when he holds his ice cream cone at an inappropriate angle for too long. But of course the obvious name *file matching* was too mundane for those wacky Berkeley types (I know; I was one of them!).

In Perl, the language feature that generates filenames is called the *globbing opera-tor*, and the act of generating filenames is referred to as *globbing*. In addition to these terms, we'll use FNG to describe the notation that's used to construct the filename-generating patterns.

TIP The *globbing operator* brings the Unix filename-generation service to all systems that have Perl.

With its globbing operator and FNG notation, Perl duplicates the filename-generation service provided by the UNIX shells. But because Perl does this using built-in functions, Perl programmers can do globbing on any system equipped with Perl.

The globbing operator is invoked by putting (unquoted) angle brackets around a filename specification. Table 7.14 shows the operator's syntax and some usage examples.

Table 7.14   The globbing operator

Typical invocation formats	
`<pattern>` `<pattern1>, <pattern2>, etc.`	
Example	**Explanation**
`@files=<pattern>;`	Stores filenames matching `pattern` in `@files`.
`@files=(<pattern1>, <pattern2>);`	Stores filenames matching `pattern1` or `pattern2` in `@files`. When assigning globbing results directly to a variable, separate multiple globbing operators by commas and parenthesize the group.

`$,="\n";`
`print <pattern1>, <pattern2>;`
 	
`print sort <pattern1>, <pattern2>;`
	Prints filenames matching `pattern1` or `pattern2` with `"\n"` between them. The matches for `pattern1` are printed first in alphanumeric order, followed by `pattern2`'s matches in alphanumeric order. The second example sorts the entire set of matching filenames before printing.

As indicated in the table, the filenames returned by a globbing operator are generally stored in an array for later access, or else sent to the output by `print`.

When you don't want to get your matching filenames from the current directory, you can specify an alternative directory within the globbing operator:

`@html_files=</local/web/*.html>;`

When a single pattern won't suffice to describe all the files of interest, you can use a parenthesized, comma-separated list of globbing operators instead:

`@temporary_files=(</tmp/*>, </var/tmp/*>);`

Variables can also be used in globbing, as can special directory names such as "..", which stands for the parent directory:

```
$html_dir='/local/web';
$html='htm';
$text='txt';
@files=(<$html_dir/*.$html>, <../*.$text>);
```

Table 7.15 describes the meanings of the FNG metacharacters used in globbing, including "*", and shows illustrative examples of the filenames that would be matched by different patterns.

Table 7.15   The globbing operator's FNG metacharacters

Metacharacter[a]	Meaning[b]	Example	Sample matches
?	Any (one) character	<f?.txt>	f2.txt, fX.txt
		<.?>	.., .a, .9
[xyz]	Any character explicitly listed in the square brackets (called a *character class*), implicitly indicated by being in the range *c1-c2* (inclusive), or indicated by being omitted from the characters listed after a leading "!", which complements the list	<[abc].txt>	a.txt, b.txt, c.txt
[c1-c2]		<f[0-9].txt>	f2.txt, f8.txt
		<f[!0-9].txt>	fX.txt, f%.txt
[!xyz]			
[!c1-c2]			
*	Any character(s), or no characters ("anything goes")	<*.txt>	f2.txt, fX.txt, H.txt
		<f*>	f2.txt, fX.txt, fud

a. *c1, c2, x, y,* and *z* are placeholders; *c1* must come before *c2* in sorting order.
b. No metacharacter is allowed to match a leading ".", which on Unix systems is the mark of a hidden file. Within a character class, all standard metacharacters lose their normal meanings, and two take on new special meanings: "–" as a range specifier, and "!" as a list complementer.

Note that the wildcard expressions in the table's Example column look just like they would in Shell programming, apart from being surrounded by angle brackets. For example, within the square brackets of the character class, a hyphen between two other characters can be used to represent a range of consecutive characters. Moreover, the filenames generated by each globbing operator are returned in alphanumerically sorted order, as in the Shell.

As a practical application of globbing, a program that works on the HTML files of its current directory might start like this, to free the user from having to specify the filenames as command-line arguments:[30]

---

[30] Additional techniques for generating arguments in the BEGIN block are shown in section 8.2.3.

```
BEGIN { # get names of HTML files
    @ARGV=<*.html>  or  warn "$0: No html files!\n"  and  exit 255;
}
```

The matching filenames (if any) are first loaded into the argument array (@ARGV), and then that array is evaluated for non-emptiness in the scalar context provided by the or operator. The resulting True/False value controls the execution of warn and exit.

7.4.1 Tips on globbing

Because the angle-bracket symbols play more than one role in Perl, you'll run into a problem if you put your entire FNG pattern into a single variable:

```
$pattern='/local/web/*.html';  print <$pattern>        # WRONG!
readline() on unopened filehandle ...
```

The solution is to surround the variable name with (unquoted) spaces, which won't affect the file specification:

```
print < $pattern >                                      # Right.
```

Because Perl incorporates most of the syntax of the UNIX regular expression (regex) and filename generation (FNG) notations, Perl programmers need to be wary of the same pitfalls that Shell programmers do. In particular, the strong similarities between the two non-identical notations can sometimes create confusion over which symbol to use. As a case in point, beginners often mistakenly attempt to use "*" in regex notation to mean "anything goes".[31] But that's its meaning in the FNG notation—in the regex notation, ".*" is used for that effect.

Programmers who write a lot of FNG patterns may eventually fall into the trap of attempting to use "!" to complement the list of a regex character class:

```
/[!aeiou]$/  and  print "Line ends with non-vowel"; # WRONG!
```

That statement prints the lines that *do* end with vowels—or with a "!" symbol! This is a particularly undesirable kind of error, because the Perl compiler can't help by spotting it for you. The fix is to employ the complementing character that's correct for the regex notation, ^, by writing

```
/[^aeiou]$/  and  print "Line ends with non-vowel"; # Right.
```

To help you keep the notations straight, table 7.16 shows the different yet equivalent expressions that are most commonly confused. The top panel of the table

---

[31] If you make this mistake, you *may* get a "quantifier follows nothing" error from Perl—or not. It depends on the context.

focuses on differences between metacharacters, and the second deals with differences related to anchoring.

The differences shown in the top panel of the table are based on the use of different symbols to perform the same function (e.g., "?" vs. "."), whereas those in the second panel reflect the fact that only FNG expressions have implicit anchoring. For example, A means "starts and ends with A" in FNG, due to its implicit anchoring, but in regex notation, it takes ^A$ to express that idea.

Table 7.16   Corresponding expressions for the FNG and regex notations

FNG	Regex	Meaning
?	.	One character [a]
*	.*	0 or more characters [a]
[a-z]	[a-z]	One lowercase letter
[!a-z]	[^a-z]	One character that's not a lowercase letter [a]
a*	^a	Starting with "a"
*a	a$	Ending with "a"
abc	^abc$	Exactly "abc"
N/A	X?, X*, X+	0 or 1, 0 or more, or 1 or more successive Xs

a. FNG metacharacters aren't allowed to match a leading dot in a filename, to prevent accidental references to hidden files. Regex metacharacters don't have this limitation.

Another concern, signified by "N/A" in the table's bottom panel, is that there are potentially bothersome limits on what you can accomplish with the humble FNG notation, which is considerably less expressive and powerful than its regex cousin. The solution in such cases is to use regex notation to enhance your globbing, as discussed next.

Employing regex notation for filtering filenames

As we discussed earlier in connection with the find command (section 6.3.2), you can arrange to do your globbing with the regex rather than the FNG notation. You begin by performing a rough selection of filename candidates using FNG with the globbing operator, and then you employ the more sophisticated regex notation to do additional filtering, using grep with a matching operator.

For example, we can use this regex with a matching operator to specify more precisely the filenames we want from the globbing operator's rough initial selection:

```
@files=grep { /^80[23]?86$/ } <80*86>;   # files for certain old CPUs
```

As a result, @files is loaded with any filenames from the desired set of 8086, 80286, and 80386 that are present in the current directory—but not with other filenames that would also be matched by the FNG pattern itself, such as 80486 and 80586.[32]

Now that you've seen examples of the globbing operator being used in relative isolation, you'll see some typical ways it's used with functions that supply file management services.

7.5   MANAGING FILES WITH FUNCTIONS

Perl is heavily used for general-purpose file wrangling—by system administrators and others—using built-in Perl functions that provide the functionality of their Unix counterparts. As tables 7.17 and 7.18 show, most of these functions have names similar to their Unix relatives; an exception is unlink, which does the job of rm. Another difference is that there's no chgrp function corresponding to the Unix chgrp command, because Perl's chown can change both the UID and GID for a file.[33]

Table 7.17   Functions for managing directories

Function	Unix relative	Invocation format	Explanation
chdir	cd		Depending on *Function*, changes to (chdir), creates (mkdir), or removes (rmdir) the directory *dirname*—or terminates the program (via die). For rmdir to succeed, the directory must be empty. A True/False value is returned to indicate success or failure.
mkdir	mkdir	*Function dirname* or die "$0: *Function* failed: ", $!;	
rmdir	rmdir		

Table 7.17 shows the invocation format for functions that process directories. It contains an or die clause, because when these functions fail, it's generally undesirable to proceed with the program.

For example, imagine how many files you'd have left in your current directory after executing this code, which is meant to remove files from /tmp/playpen but unfortunately isn't restricted to operating in that directory:

```
$dirname='/temp/playpen';
chdir $dirname;            # I hope this chdir works!
unlink <*>;                # Search and Destroy!
```

---

[32] Actually, the FNG pattern would even match "800 868-6886" and "80 + 6 = 86", but we're assuming that only CPU model numbers appear in the filenames of this directory.

[33] Just like the Berkeley-derived versions of the Unix chown command can do.

Perl's unlink (see table 7.18) removes the specified filenames by ruthlessly—and irreversibly—removing them from their directories (just as Unix's rm does). Unfortunately, after chdir fails to change to the misspelled directory, this program will blithely proceed to unlink the files of the *current directory* instead!

All it takes to prevent such disasters is to add an appropriate or die clause, as shown in table 7.17, whose use is strongly recommended:

```
chdir $dirname  or  die "$0: Couldn't chdir to $dirname: $!";
```

Next, you'll see how to handle functions whose return values aren't simple True/False codes.

7.5.1 Handling multi-valued return codes

Like chdir, mkdir, and rmdir, the functions depicted in the middle panel of table 7.18 also require special handling, but of a different type. That's because they

Table 7.18 Functions for managing files

Function	Unix relative	Format, or sample invocation	Explanation [a]
umask	umask	umask 0022; # +w only for owner printf "Umask is: %04O\n", umask;	Sets (or reports) the octal bit-mask that removes permissions granted by default to newly created files. 0022 denies the group and others write permission.
chmod	chmod	$successes=chmod perm_num, file(s);	Combines octal permission specification perm_num (e.g., 0755) with umask value to set permissions for file(s).
chown	chown, chgrp	$successes=chown UID_num, GID_num, file(s);	Associates file(s) with owner UID_num and group GID_num.
unlink	rm	$successes=unlink file(s);	Removes names of file(s) from their directories. [b]
rename	mv	rename old, new or die "$0: rename failed: $!";	Renames existing file old to new. move is more dependable and OS-portable.
move	mv	use File::Copy; # load module move old, new or die "$0: move failed: $!";	Moves existing file old to new in an efficient and OS-portable manner.
copy	cp	use File::Copy; # load module copy old, new or die "$0: copy failed: $!";	Copies existing file old to new in an efficient and OS-portable manner.

a. umask returns its previous setting if invoked with an argument, otherwise its current setting. The functions in the middle panel return the number of files that were successfully processed, whereas those in the bottom panel return True/False to indicate success or failure.

b. As with the rm command, the file itself will live on until its last hard-linked directory entry is removed.

return the *number of successfully processed files*—rather than a simple binary Success/Failure code—when supplied multiple filename arguments.

This kind of *multi-valued* return code therefore represents a point on a continuum ranging from complete failure (0) to complete success (>0), with the latter result achieved only when the return code equals the number of filename arguments. For this reason, with the functions chmod, chown, and unlink, this approach

```
$successes=function @files  or  die;
```

will only terminate a program when *none* of the files named in @files is successfully processed (i.e., when $successes is 0), because any non-zero number is equally True.

In contrast, the following approach arranges for the program to continue only if *all* files are successfully processed:

```
@files=<*.txt>;
$num_files=@files  or  exit;     # exit if no files to work on

$successes=chmod 0600, @files;  # $successes contains success count
$successes == $num_files or
  die "chmod only succeeded for $successes of $num_files files\n";
# Code for remaining processing goes here
```

The program will terminate with a message of the following form unless it succeeds in setting the permissions of *every* *.txt file in the current directory:

```
chmod only succeeded for 3 of 7 files
```

But how can we report the *names* of the files that were associated with the failed processing attempts? That's a problem, because that information isn't be provided by unlink. To handle this situation, in section 10.4.1 we'll demonstrate a technique based on *looping* that presents each filename as the lone argument to the desired function (e.g., unlink, chmod, etc.). This approach allows a detailed error message—which includes the file's name—to be generated if the operation fails.

Tips on file-management functions

Perl has many additional file-oriented functions that provide useful services, but some (e.g., open, pipe, glob) are of marginal interest to programmers who already know their more convenient alternatives favored in Minimal Perl (viz., the n and p options, command interpolation, and <*FNG*>).

Now that you know how to use built-in functions, you need to know something else—where to use parentheses around their argument lists to prevent Perl from misinterpreting your intentions. That's our next topic for discussion.

7.6   PARENTHESIZING FUNCTION ARGUMENTS

In Perl, you can usually omit parentheses around argument lists, because the language is smart enough to understand what you want and to do the right thing without them. However, there are certain situations where Perl just can't read your mind, so you need to handle them properly to avoid trouble. To help you understand the problems of the JAPHly population at large, we'll look first at a vexing problem that bothers many Perl programmers—but not those following the Minimal Perl approach.

7.6.1   Controlling argument-gobbling functions

Consider this statement:

```
print sort @F, "\n";
```

Because functions are *greedy* in gobbling up their arguments—and those on the right get to eat first—that newline won't be allocated to `print` as its final argument, as intended. Instead, it's treated as the final argument to *sort*. In consequence, the newline won't be printed to the right of the sorted `@F` values, as you might expect, unless alphanumeric sorting puts it in that position.

We'll demonstrate the problem in the following program, which prints markers before and after the output of interest to make the misplaced newline (represented by " ⬇ ") easier to spot (`@F` contains the values A, B, and C):

```
$,=' ';                  # separate values by a space; -l not in effect
print "Start:\n";  print sort @F, "\n";  print "End:\n";
Start
⬇
 A B CEnd
```

The newline argument of the middle `print` came out first in sorted order, giving a double-spacing effect when combined with the newline at the end of the "Start:" string. The "A" gets indented because a space was automatically inserted between it and the newline that `sort` placed before it, as requested by the "`$,`" setting.

As always in such cases, explicitly limiting `sort`'s argument list with parentheses is the solution to allocating arguments to functions in the desired manner:

```
print "Start:\n";  print sort (@F), "\n";  print "End:\n"; # -l off
Start
A B C
End
```

You can tell that Minimal Perl's strategies for insulating you from unnecessary complications are working, because we've successfully avoided this pesky issue of argument parenthesization for hundreds of pages thus far. The 1 option deserves most of the credit, because it eliminates the most common source of this problem—interference between the trailing newline argument on a `print` statement and nearby function arguments. As a case in point, enabling the l option allows us to rewrite the earlier code in a more intuitive manner:

```
$,=' ';
print "Start";  print sort @F;  print "End";  # -l on
Start
A B C
End
```

In addition to its manifestations with print, this argument-gobbling problem can occur anywhere functions are used in series. For instance, this line has three functions:

```
$string=join "\n",  reverse sort  @F,  'another value';
```

This statement is interpreted to mean that "another value" should be sort's last argument. But what if that string was meant to be *reverse*'s last argument instead? In that case, parentheses would be needed around sort's intended arguments to prevent it from claiming "another value":[34]

```
$string=join "\t",  reverse sort (@F), 'another value';
```

On the other hand, if that string were meant to be *join*'s last argument, the following syntax would be needed, to arrange for all the values resulting from the parenthesized segment to be delivered to join before "another value":

```
$string=join "\t", (reverse sort  @F), 'another value';
```

The upshot of this discussion is that if you use the l option as Minimal Perl prescribes, you'll avoid the most common situations involving print that require parenthesization of function arguments. But for expressions involving a series of functions, you may need to add parentheses to help Perl identify a function's intended arguments.

To help you write your programs correctly, helpful guidelines on the use of parentheses, are provided in appendix B.

7.7 SUMMARY

Perl has a rich collection of built-in functions, and many provide enhancements to facilities found in Unix and the Shell. The especially valuable property of being sensitive to *context* allows a function to behave differently in situations that call for a singular result, or a plural one, and effectively lets a single function do the work of two separate but related ones. (When you learn how to write your own functions in chapter 11, you'll appreciate how Perl's sensitivity to context can really boost a programmer's productivity.)

---

[34] Another approach would be to use a more conventional style of parenthesization, in which the argument lists for the various functions are explicitly indicated. It requires more typing, and is arguably harder to read, but it's possibly easier to comprehend:

```
$string=join ( "\t", reverse (sort (@F), 'another value') );
```

Some of Perl's functions, such as localtime, stat, and sort, can serve as built-in alternatives to related Unix commands (date, ls, and sort), leading to programs that are not only more efficient but also OS independent. Other functions, such as map, provide unusual yet valuable services that have no direct counterpart in the Unix toolkit.

The split function separates a string into a list of its constituent fields, using whitespace delimiters by default, or else the delimiters provided in an optional argument. Because the a invocation option in conjunction with n or p automatically provides this service for input records, split is generally used for secondary splitting in Minimal Perl, to extract subfields from input fields using different delimiters.

The localtime function allows programmers to access information describing the current time and date in an OS-independent manner. It can provide a nicely formatted report that resembles the Unix date command's output.

The stat function provides a wealth of administrative information about the specified file, which on Unix consists of all the data residing in the file's inode. It can be used to write programs that mimic the behavior of the Unix ls -l command, as demonstrated in the listfile script.

Trailing newlines on input records can foil string-equality tests and disturb the formatting of output messages. This is why Minimal Perl routinely uses the l invocation option to automatically strip newlines while input is being read by the implicit loop of the n and p options. For input read through other methods, such as from <STDIN>, newlines can be stripped by using chomp.

Unpredictability is usually an undesirable trait in computer programs. Nevertheless, a capability for making pseudo-random decisions is often needed in programs that do source-code quality-control tests, simulations, or games. Perl's random number generator is called rand; you'll see it used to select random "fortunes" in section 9.1.4.

As the counterpart to the Unix sort command, Perl has its own function called sort. But Perl's version is unique in giving the programmer complete control over where each element $a—in a pairwise comparison of list elements—goes relative to element $b. A reverse function is also supplied, to allow convenient conversion of lists in ascending order to descending order, and vice versa.

As the mirror image of split, which does scalar to list conversions for strings, Perl's join function performs list to scalar conversions. It inserts a specified delimiter between each adjacent pair of the strings provided, to create a new composite string.

Perl's grep takes its lead from its Unix namesake, but it goes where no grep has gone before! It's a programmable, general-purpose filtering tool that passes to its output the elements of a list that produce True outcomes for a specified code block. Although it can be used to write grep-like commands, that's more easily accomplished with the /RE/ and print approach shown in section 3.3.1.

The `map` function is a programmable, general-purpose tool for transforming the elements of a list into another form. It can be used, for example, to convert a list of strings to lowercase by using `"\L$_"` in its code block.

Perl's globbing operator and FNG notation are also valuable resources, allowing programmers to use Unix filename-generation techniques in an OS-portable manner.[35]

We ended this chapter with a discussion of the proper use of parentheses in Perl, which are sometimes needed to override default groupings of code elements prescribed by Perl's operator precedence levels. Although JAPHs can generally omit almost all the parentheses that would be required in other languages, there are certain situations in Perl where they must be used to obtain correct results, as described in section 7.6 and appendix B.

Because Perl is a rather unusual language, and we're delving more deeply into "Perlocity" here in part 2, it's likely that some of the concepts and principles revealed in this chapter came as a surprise to you. But like the immigrants to Perlistan who came before you, you'll soon find yourself wondering how you ever put up with languages that were insensitive to contextual cues, or lacked `grep` and `map` and an OS-portable FNG notation, or made you put parentheses in your programs in places where any compiler worth its salt would have already known they belonged!

Directions for further study

To obtain specific documentation on particular functions (`sort`, `grep`, `chmod`, etc.) or *named* operators (e.g., `scalar`, but not "+"), replace *name* in the following command with the name of the desired resource:

- `perldoc -f name`   `# specific coverage of "name"`

You have to use special techniques to retrieve the documentation for certain functions. In particular, documentation for the globbing operator is found under `glob`—which is the name of the function underlying the `<FNG>` syntax, and documentation for `printf` is best obtained from your Unix system, using one of these commands:

- `man  -s3 printf`   `# for some UNIX systems`
- `man -s3c printf`   `# for other UNIX systems`
- `man 3 printf`   `# for Linux systems and their relatives`

We'll discuss some additional functions that are generally used only in scripts in chapter 8 (e.g., `eval`). But Perl provides many other functions (and operators) as well, which provide more specialized services. You can see them listed by category

---

[35] See http://TeachMePerl.com/Perl_on_non-Unix_systems.html for more details on OS-portable programming with Perl.

in table 5.13, and you'll find detailed documentation on them in these man pages, in which they're covered in alphabetical order:[36]

- `man perlfunc`   `# coverage of perl functions`
- `man perlop`   `# coverage of perl operators`

As useful as they are, Perl's built-in functions can't anticipate all your needs, so you'll learn in chapter 12 how to extend Perl's capabilities by importing functions written by other JAPHs from the voluminous CPAN archives, as well as how to write your own custom subroutines to handle your unique requirements in chapter 11.

---

[36] The functions vs. operator distinction is fuzzy in Perl, so some operators are documented in `perlfunc` and some functions in `perlop`, so it's best to try `perldoc -f name` before resorting to looking for *name* in the `perlfunc` or `perlop` man pages.

C H A P T E R   8

Scripting techniques

8.1 Exploiting script-oriented
     functions 248
8.2 Pre-processing arguments 256
8.3 Executing code conditionally
     with if/else 259
8.4 Wrangling strings with concatena-
     tion and repetition operators 265

8.5 Interpolating command output into
     source code 269
8.6 Executing OS commands using
     system 275
8.7 Evaluating code using eval 283
8.8 Summary 292

Those nifty one-line commands you saw in part 1 are easy to type, and they're adequate for an impressively wide variety of common tasks. And gosh darn it, you might even say they're cute, if not downright *elegant.*

But sooner or later, you'll need to write programs that can validate their arguments, handle arguments that aren't filenames, capture and manipulate outputs from Unix commands, process inputs from interactive users, select particular branches of code to execute, or even compose and execute new Perl programs on the fly. This chapter teaches you the language features and programming techniques that are used to perform such tasks.

For instance, you'll learn how to write programs that accept arguments, and the benefits of doing so. As a case in point, the following grep commands can look for different patterns in different places—despite the fact that they're all running the same program—because grep accepts arguments:

```
grep 'SpamMeister@scumbags\.com' inbox
grep 'Mr\. Waldo Goodbar'        WhereCouldHeBe
grep 'Loofabob Circletrousers'   bikini_bottom_of_another_dimension
```

Arguments can also be used in emulating a familiar user interface. For example, we'll discuss a grep-like script called `perlgrep` that accepts the search pattern as its first argument:

```
perlgrep 'RE' filename
```

That's a more natural user interface for a grepper than this switch-oriented one we employed in section 3.13.2:

```
greperl -pattern='RE' filename
```

Another technique you'll learn is how to run Shell commands from within Perl programs, using the `system` function or Perl's version of the Shell's *command-substitution* facility. Although using these techniques reduces a script's OS portability, it's sometimes the best way—or the *only* way—to obtain certain kinds of vital information.

For example, what if you need to know if there is enough disk space in the current directory's partition to accommodate the needs of your program? Executing this Perl statement in a program running on Unix will help you make that determination, using *command interpolation*[1] to capture the output of the back-quoted `df` command:

```
$free_space=`df -k .`;
```

The `system` function also runs OS commands, but it works differently. For this reason, `system 'df -k .'` would *not* be an alternative way to obtain the same information. Accordingly, you'll learn where each technique should be used in preference to the other.

When you combine the scripting techniques you'll learn in this chapter with the built-in functions of the previous one—and the techniques for data storage and retrieval you'll learn in the next one—you'll be able to write scripts that are more robust, versatile, and advanced than those featured in part 1, as well as more OS-portable and efficient than Shell scripts.

We'll begin by discussing some special functions and variables that are primarily used in scripts.

8.1 EXPLOITING SCRIPT-ORIENTED FUNCTIONS

Certain built-in functions are used more commonly in scripts than in one-line commands like those you saw in part 1. These include Perl's `shift` and `exit` functions, which resemble their Shell namesakes, and `defined`, which is unique to Perl. We'll discuss the applications and benefits of these functions next, so you'll understand how they're used in the scripts that appear later in this chapter.

---

[1] Which is Perl's name for what the Shell calls *command substitution*.

8.1.1 Defining `defined`

To help you appreciate the value of `defined`, we'll first illustrate a common problem that it can solve. Consider these lines from `some-script`, which might appear at the top of a script that requires arguments:

```
$ARGV > 0  or  warn "$0: No arguments!\n"  and  exit 255;
$pattern=$ARGV[0];
```

If the program reaches the assignment statement, we know for sure that at least one argument was provided. But to handle the case where that argument is present but *empty*, we might want to add this third statement:

```
$pattern  or  warn "$0: Bad first argument!\n"  and  exit 250;
```

This extra precaution detects potential slip-ups like the following one, which, through a combination of conscientious quoting and bad typing, winds up invoking the script with an empty first argument:

```
$ RE='helium';                          # set the variable
$ some-script "$ER" hynerians           # pass $RE's contents as arg1
some-script: Bad first argument!
```

But what does an expression of the form `$pattern or `*`something`* do? It determines whether *`something`* will be evaluated on the basis of the True/False value of `$pattern` (see section 2.4.2). The `warn` message is triggered in this case because the null string that gets assigned to `$pattern` is one of Perl's False values (the other is 0).

However, there's a complication. Some scripts may *want* to accept a False value—especially 0—as a legitimate argument. After all, with a `grep`-like script, shouldn't the user be allowed to look for records containing zeroes? This one disallows that:

```
$ some-script '0' luxans           # pass 0 as pattern argument
some-script: Bad first argument!
```

Unlike most languages, Perl provides an elegant solution to this problem, by allowing you to conduct separate tests to identify undefined, empty, and False values. This gives you the ability to treat certain Falsely-valued expressions—such as those associated with missing or empty arguments—differently than others, such as an argument of 0.

False values can be sensed using logical operators (`$pattern `<u>`or`</u>` whatever`), and empty values can be identified using the string comparison operator (`$something `<u>`ne`</u>` ""` or warn; see table 5.11). The property of being *defined*, on the other hand, is determined using the `defined` function, which returns a True/False value according to the status of its argument.

What does it mean to be "defined"? Simply that the expression (usually a variable) has been assigned a value. If it hasn't—e.g., because it's accidentally being used before it's been initialized—a warning is triggered:

```
print $name;              # What's in a $name?
$name='Willy Nilly';
Use of uninitialized value in print ...
```

With this background in mind, let's look at a practical example that can benefit from the use of defined:

```
$tip=shift;                              # tip amount is in argument
$tip  or  die "Usage: $0 tip_to_waiter_in_dollars\n";
```

That code must have been commissioned by the Waiters Union! It forces the diner to tip the waiter a non-zero amount, because an argument of 0 is False and therefore causes die to terminate the script.

Instead of asking the question "Does $tip have a True value?" the code should ask these two questions: "Does $tip have a value?" and if so, "Is its value non-empty?"

Here's an improved version that applies these tests and doesn't reject a null tip for a bad waiter (the improvements are in bold):

```
$tip=shift;
defined $tip  and  $tip ne ""  or
    die "Usage: $0 tip_to_waiter_in_dollars (0 or more)\n";
# Now report the tip to the IRS
```

If defined returns False (because no argument was provided), the or-branch is executed, which terminates the program. If defined returns True, the next test is whether $tip contains something other than a null string. If it does—even if it's just the (False) number 0—the program lives on. On the other hand, if a null-string argument is provided (as demonstrated earlier), the program terminates—as it should.[2]

That, in a nutshell, is why we need Perl's defined function—so we can test whether an expression *has* a value, independently of whether that value is True or False. You'll find a more detailed explanation of how Perl treats undefined values in the next section, but feel free to skip it for now if you wish.

Using defined for keyboard input

As shown earlier (in table 7.6), you can read input from the standard input channel by using the angle brackets of the input operator with STDIN. In such cases, a prompt is typically used to solicit the input, leading to a printf/variable-assignment sequence like this one:

```
printf 'Email resignation letter? YES to confirm, <^D> to exit: ';
$answer=<STDIN>;
```

In cases like this where you're dealing with a live user providing input from a keyboard, you have to be ready for these possibilities:

---

[2] The following additional test could be added before the or keyword, to ensure that a positive integer number was provided: and $tip =~ /^\d+$/.

1. The user types some characters, such as "maybe", and then presses <ENTER>. Because $answer contains "maybe\n", which isn't a null string, its string-value is True (see section 2.4.2).

2. The user just presses <ENTER>. Because $answer contains "\n", which isn't a null string either, it's also True.

3. The user presses <^D>, which signifies the "end of file" condition for typed input. In this special case, $answer receives nothing but is marked as "undefined", which makes it a False string.

4. The user kills the program by pressing <^C> (or some other fatal-signal-generating character), which terminates the program immediately—thereby liberating the programmer from concerns about handling user input!

The programmer would identify the case at hand by conducting various tests on $answer and then provide an appropriate response.

One obvious approach would look something like this:

```
#! /usr/bin/perl -wl

printf 'Email resignation letter? YES to confirm, <^D> to exit: ';
$answer=<STDIN>;                      # omitting chomp to simplify

$answer ne "YES\n"  and        # This is line 6
    die "\n$0: Hasty resignation averted\n";

print 'Sending email';         # (emailing code unshown)
```

This technique works nicely for cases A and B, which result in something usable being stored in $answer (a newline or more).

But with case C, this output is produced:

```
Email resignation letter? YES to confirm, <^D> to exit: <^D>
Use of uninitialized value in string ne at line 6.
...
```

The good news is that the user still has time to reconsider her resignation, because the undefined value in $answer didn't equate to "YES\n", thereby causing the program to die.

But what about that warning message? That's Perl's way of telling you that one of the operands for the string inequality operator (ne) did not have a *defined* value—and you know that it can't be complaining about "YES\n", so it must be $answer. The program is allowed to continue, but Perl fudges in a null string as $answer's value to allow the comparison to be performed. That's why it issues a warning—so you'll know it's working with "best- guess" data rather than the real thing.

Here's what's happening behind the scenes. When Perl encounters an end-of-file immediately upon reading input, it returns a special value called "undefined" to signify that no usable value was obtained. Accordingly, when $answer=<STDIN> calls on Perl to assign the value returned by the input operator to $answer, Perl marks

$answer as undefined This signifies that the variable has been brought into existence, but not yet given a usable value.

The solution is to add an additional check using the defined function, like so:

```
(! defined $answer  or  $answer ne "YES\n" )  and
    die "\n$0: Hasty resignation averted\n";
```

This ensures that the program will die if $answer is undefined, and also that $answer won't be compared to "YES\n" unless it has a defined value. That last property circumvents the use of a fabricated value in the inequality comparison, and the "uninitialized value" warning that goes with it.

With this adjustment, if $answer is undefined, the program can terminate without a scary-looking warning disturbing the user.[3]

The rule for avoiding the accidental use of undefined values, and triggering the warnings they generate, is this:

> *Always test a value that might be undefined, for being* defined, *before attempting to use that value.*

But there is an exception—copying a value, as in $got_switch, never triggers a warning—even when $answer is undefined. That's because moving undefined values around, as opposed to using them in significant ways, is considered a harmless activity.

Tips on using defined

The following statement attempts to set $got_switch to a True/False value, according to whether any (or all) of the script's switches was provided on the command line:

```
$got_switch=defined $debug  or  defined $verbose;     # WRONG!
```

Here's the warning it generates:

```
Useless use of defined operator in void context
```

That message arises because the assignment operator (=) has higher precedence than the logical or, causing the statement to be interpreted as if it had been typed like this:[4]

```
( $got_switch=defined $debug )  or  defined $verbose;
```

Perl's warning tells the programmer that it was useless to include the or defined part, because there's no way for its result to be used anywhere (i.e., it's in a *void context*). As with other problems based on operator precedence, the fix is to add explicit parentheses to indicate which expressions need to be evaluated before others:

```
$got_switch=( defined $debug  or  defined $verbose );  # Right.
```

---

[3] Which might result in you being paged at 3 a.m.—prompting you to consider your *own* resignation!

[4] The Minimal Perl approach minimizes precedence problems, but they'll still crop up with logical operators now and then (see "Tips" at the end of section 2.4.5, appendix B, and man perlop).

In many cases, a Perl program ends up terminating by running out of statements to process. But in other cases, the programmer needs to force an earlier *exit*, which you'll learn how to do next.

8.1.2 Exiting with `exit`

As in the Shell, the `exit` command is used to terminate a script—but before doing so, it executes the END block, if there is one (like AWK). Table 8.1 compares the way the Shell and Perl versions of `exit` behave when they're invoked without an argument or with a numeric argument from 0 to 255.

Table 8.1 The `exit` function

Shell	Perl	Explanation
exit	exit;	With no argument, the Shell's `exit` returns the latest value of its "`$?`" variable to its parent process, to indicate the program's success or failure. Perl returns 0 by default, to indicate success.[a]
exit 0	exit 0;	The argument 0 signifies a successful run of the script to the parent.
exit *1-255*	exit *1-255*;	A number in the range 1–255 signifies a failed run of the script to the parent.

a. Because it's justifiably more *optimistic* than the Shell.

As indicated in the table, Perl's `exit` generally works like that of the Shell, except it uses 0 as the default exit value, rather than the exit value of the last command.

Although the languages agree that 0 signifies success, neither has established conventions concerning the meanings of other exit values—apart from them all indicating error conditions. This leaves you free to associate 1, for example, with a "required arguments missing" error, and 2 with an "invalid input format" error, if desired.

As discussed in section 2.4.4, Perl's `die` command provides an alternative to `exit` for terminating a program. It differs by printing an error message before exiting with the value of 255 (by default), as if you had executed `warn "message"` and `exit 255`. (But remember, in Minimal Perl we use the `warn` and `exit` combination rather than `die` in BEGIN blocks, to avoid the unsightly warning messages about aborted compilations that a `die` in BEGIN elicits.)

The following illustrates proper uses of the `exit` and `die` functions in a script that has a BEGIN block, as well as how to specify `die`'s exit value by setting the "`$!`" variable,[5] to load the desired value into the parent shell's "`$?`" variable:

---

[5] Later in this chapter, you'll learn how to use Perl's `if` construct, which is better than the logical `and` for making the setting of "`$!`", and the execution of `die`, *jointly* dependent on the success of the matching operator.

```
$ cat massage_data
#! /usr/bin/perl -wnl

BEGIN {
    @ARGV == 1  or  warn "Usage: $0 filename\n"  and  exit 1;
}
/^#/  and  $!=2  and die  "$0: Comments not allowed in data file\n";
...

$ massage_data
Usage: massage_data filename
$ echo $?
1

$ massage_data file    # correct invocation; 0 is default exit value
$ echo $?
0

$ echo '# comment' | massage_data -      # "-" means read from STDIN
massage_data: Comments not allowed in data file
$ echo $?
2
```

We'll look next at another important function shared by the Shell and Perl.

8.1.3   Shifting with `shift`

Both the Shell and Perl have a function called `shift`, which is used to manage command-line arguments. Its job is to shift argument values leftward relative to the storage locations that hold them, which has the side effect of discarding the original first argument.[6]

Figure 8.1 shows how `shift` affects the allocation of arguments to a Shell script's *positional parameter* variables, or to the indices of Perl's @ARGV array.

Shell			
Variable	$1	$2	$3
Original value	A	B	C	Before shift
New value	B	C		After shift

Perl			
Array index	0	1	2
Original value	A	B	C	Before shift
New value	B	C		After shift

Figure 8.1
Effect of `shift` in the Shell and Perl

---

[6] A common programming technique used with early UNIX shells was to process $1 and then execute `shift`, and repeat that cycle until every argument had taken a turn as $1. It's discussed in section 10.2.1.

As the figure illustrates, after `shift` is executed in the Shell, the value initially stored in $1 (A) gets discarded, the one in $2 (B) gets relocated to $1, and the one in $3 gets relocated to $2. The same migration of values across storage locations occurs in Perl, except the movement is from `$ARGV[1]` to `$ARGV[0]`, and so forth. Naturally, the affected Perl variables (`@ARGV` and `$#ARGV`) are updated automatically after `shift`, just as "$*", "$@", and "$#" are updated in the Shell.

Although Perl's `shift` provides the same basic functionality as the Shell's, it also provides two new features, at the expense of losing one standard Shell feature (see table 8.2). The new feature—shown in the table's second row—is that Perl's `shift` *returns* the value that's removed from the array, so it can be saved for later access.

Table 8.2   Using `shift` and `unshift` in the Shell and Perl

Shell	Perl	Explanation
shift	shift;	`shift` removes the leftmost argument and moves any others one position leftward to fill the void.
N/A	$variable=shift;	In Perl, the removed parameter is returned by `shift`, allowing it to be stored in a variable.
shift 2	shift; shift; OR $arg1=shift; $arg2=shift;	The Shell's `shift` takes an optional numeric argument, indicating the number of values to be shifted away. That effect is achieved in Perl by invoking `shift` multiple times.
N/A	shift @any_array;	Perl's `shift` takes an optional argument of an array name, which specifies the one it should modify instead of the default (normally @ARGV, but @_ if within a subroutine).
N/A	unshift @array1, @array2;	Perl's `unshift` reinitializes @array1 to contain the contents of @array2 before the initial contents of @array1. For example, if @array1 in the example contained (a,b) and @array2 contained (1,2), @array1 would end up with (1,2,a,b).

That allows Perl programmers to write this simple statement:

```
$arg1=shift;     # save first arg's value, then remove it from @ARGV
```

where Shell programmers would have to write

```
arg1="$1"        # save first arg's value before it's lost forever!
shift            # now remove it from argument list
```

Another improvement is that Perl's `shift` takes an optional argument that specifies the array to be shifted, which the Shell doesn't support. However, by attaching this new interpretation to `shift`'s argument, Perl sacrificed the ability to recognize it as a numeric "amount of shifting" specification, which is the meaning `shift`'s argument has in the Shell.

Now that you've learned how to use `defined`, `shift`, and `exit` in Perl, we'll use these tools to improve on certain techniques you saw in part 1 and to demonstrate some of their other useful applications. We'll begin by discussing how they can be used in the pre-processing of script arguments.

8.2   PRE-PROCESSING ARGUMENTS

Many kinds of scripts need to pre-process their arguments before they can get on with their work. We'll cover some typical cases, such as extracting non-filename arguments, filtering out undesirable arguments, and generating arguments automatically.

8.2.1   Accommodating non-filename arguments with implicit loops

The `greperl` script of section 3.13.2 obtains its pattern argument from a command-line <u>switch</u>:

```
greperl -pattern='RE' filename
```

When this invocation format is used with a script having the s option on the she-bang line, Perl automatically assigns *RE* to the script's $pattern variable and then discards the switch argument. This approach certainly makes switch-handling scripts easy to write!

But what if you want to provide a user interface that feels more *natural* to the users, based on the interface of the traditional `grep`?

```
grep 'RE' filename
```

The complication is that filter programs are most conveniently written using the n invocation option, which causes all command-line arguments (except switches) to be treated as filenames—*including* a `grep`-like script's pattern argument:

```
$ perlgrep.bad 'root' /etc/passwd    # Hey! "root" is my RE!
Can't open root: No such file or directory
```

Don't despair, because there's a simple way of fixing this program, based on an understanding of how the implicit loop works.

Specifically, the n option doesn't start treating arguments as filenames until the implicit input-reading loop starts running, and that doesn't occur until after the BEGIN block (if present) has finished executing. This means initial non-filename arguments can happily coexist with filenames in the argument list—on one condition:

> *You must remove non-filename arguments from @ARGV in a BEGIN block, so they'll be gone by the time the input-reading loop starts executing.*

The following example illustrates the coding for this technique, which isn't difficult. In fact, all it takes to harvest the pattern argument is a single line; the rest is all error checking:

```
$ cat perlgrep
#! /usr/bin/perl -wnl

BEGIN {
    $Usage="Usage: $0 'RE' [file ...]";

    @ARGV > 0  or  warn "$Usage\n"  and  exit 31; # 31 means no arg

    $pattern=shift;   # Remove arg1 and load into $pattern
    defined $pattern  and  $pattern ne ""  or
        warn "$Usage\n"  and  exit 27;  # arg1 undefined, or empty
}
# Now -n loop takes input from files named in @ARGV, or from STDIN

/$pattern/  and  print;   # if match, print record
```

Here's a sample run, which shows that this script succeeds where its predecessor
perlgrep.bad failed:

```
$ perlgrep 'root' /etc/passwd
root:x:0:0:root:/root:/bin/bash
```

The programmer even defined some custom exit codes (see section 8.1.2), which may
come in handy sometime:

```
$ perlgrep "$EMPTY" /etc/passwd
Usage: perlgrep 'RE' [file ...]
$ echo $?   # Show exit code
27
```

Once you understand how to code the requisite shift statement(s) in the BEGIN
block, it's easy to write programs that allow initial non-filename arguments to precede
filename arguments, which is necessary to emulate the user interface of many traditional Unix commands.

But don't get the idea that perlgrep is the final installment in our series of
grep-like programs that are both educational and practical. Not by a long shot!
There's an option-rich *preg* script lurking at the end of this chapter, waiting to
impress you with its versatility.

We'll talk next about some other kinds of pre-processing, such as reordering and
removing arguments.

8.2.2 Filtering arguments

The filter programs featured in part 1 employ Perl's AWKish n or p option, to handle
filename arguments automatically. That's nice, but what if you want to exert some
influence over that handling—such as processing files in alphanumeric order?

As indicated previously, you can do anything you want with a filter-script's arguments, so long as you do it in a BEGIN block. For example, this code is all that's
needed to sort a script's arguments:

```
BEGIN {
    @ARGV=sort @ARGV;        # rearrange into sorted order
}
# Normal argument processing starts here
```

It's no secret that users can't always be trusted to provide the correct arguments to commands, so a script may want to remove inappropriate arguments.

Consider the following invocation of change_file, which was presented in chapter 4:

```
change_file -old='problems' -new='issues' *
```

The purpose of this script is to change occurrences of "problems" to "issues" in the text files whose names are presented as arguments. But of course, the "*" metacharacter doesn't know that, so if any *non*-text files reside in the current directory, the script will process them as well. This could lead to trouble, because a binary file might happen to contain the bit sequence that corresponds to the word "problems"—or any other word, for that matter! Imagine the havoc that could ensue if the superuser were to accidentally modify the ls command's file—or, even worse, the Unix kernel's file—through such an error!

To help us sleep better, the following code silently removes non-text-file arguments, on the assumption that the user probably didn't realize they were included in the first place:

```
BEGIN {
  @ARGV=grep { -T } @ARGV;  # retain only text-file arguments
}
# Normal argument processing starts here
```

grep selects the text-file (-T; see table 6.1) arguments from @ARGV, and then they're assigned as the new contents of that array. The resulting effect is as if the unacceptable arguments had never been there.

A more informational approach would be to report the filenames that were deleted. This can be accomplished by selecting them with ! -T (which means "non-text files"), storing them in an array for later access, and then printing their names (if any):

```
BEGIN {
  @non_text=grep { ! -T } @ARGV; # select NON-text-file arguments
  @non_text   and
      warn "$0: Omitting these non-text-files: @non_text\n";
  @ARGV=grep { -T } @ARGV;        # retain text-file arguments
}
# Normal argument processing starts here
```

But an ounce of prevention is still worth at least a pound of cure, so it's best to free the user from typing arguments wherever possible, as we'll discuss next.

8.2.3 Generating arguments

It's senseless to require a user to painstakingly type in lots of filename arguments—which in turn burdens the programmer with screening out the invalid ones—in cases where the program could generate the appropriate arguments on its own.

For example, Uma, a professional icon-designer, needs to copy every regular file in her working directory to a CD before she leaves work. However, the subdirectories of that directory should *not* be archived. Accordingly, she uses the following code to generate the names of all the (non-hidden) regular files in the current directory that are readable by the current user (that permission is required for her to copy them):

```
BEGIN {
    # Simulate user supplying all suitable regular
    # filenames from current directory as arguments
    @ARGV=grep { -f  and  -r } <*>;
}
# Real work of script begins below
```

The <*> expression is a use of the globbing operator (see table 7.14) to generate an initial set of filenames, which are then filtered by grep for the desired attributes.

Other expressions commonly used to generate argument lists in Perl (and the Shell) are shown in section 9.3, which will give you additional ideas of what you could plug into a script's BEGIN block. You can't always automatically generate the desired arguments for every script, but for those cases where you can, you should keep these techniques in mind.

Next, you'll learn about an important control structure that's provided in every programming language. We've managed without it thus far, due to the ease of using Perl's logical operators in its place, but now you'll see how to arrange for conditional execution in a more general way.

8.3 Executing code conditionally with if/else

The logical or and logical and operators were adequate to our needs for controlling execution in part 1, where you saw many statements like this one:

```
$pattern or warn "Usage: $0 -pattern='RE' filename\n" and exit 255;
```

However, this technique of using the True/False value of a variable ($pattern) to conditionally execute two functions (warn and exit) has limitations. Most important, it doesn't deal well with cases where a True result should execute one set of statements and a False result a different set.

So now it's time to learn about more widely applicable techniques for controlling two-way and multi-way branching. Table 8.3 shows the Shell and Perl syntaxes for two-way branching using if/else, with layouts that are representative of current programming practices. The top panel shows the complete syntax, which includes branches for both the True ("then") and False (else) cases of the condition. In

Table 8.3 The `if/else` construct

Shell[a]		Perl
		`if (condition) {`
`if`	`condition`	`    code;`
`then`	`commands`	`}`
`else`	`commands`	`else {`
`fi`		`    code;`
		`}`
`if cond; then cmds; else cmds; fi`		`if (cond) { code; } else { code; }`

a. In the bottom panel, *cond* stands for *condition* and *cmds* stands for *commands*.

both languages, the `else` branch is optional, allowing that keyword and its associated components to be omitted. The table's bottom panel shows condensed forms of these control structures, which save space in cases where they'll fit on one line.

We'll examine a realistic programming example that uses `if/else` next, and compare it to its and/or alternative.

8.3.1   Employing `if/else` vs. and/or

Here's a code snippet that provides a default argument for a script when it's invoked without the required one, and terminates with an error message if too many arguments are supplied:

```
if (@ARGV == 0) {
   warn "$0: Using default argument\n";
   @ARGV=('King Tut');
}
else {
  if (@ARGV > 1) {              # nested if
    warn "Usage: $0 song_name\n";
    exit 255;
  }
}
```

For comparison, here's an equivalent chunk of code written using the logical and/or approach. It employs a style of indentation that emphasizes the dependency of each subsequent expression on the prior one:

```
@ARGV == 0   and
    warn "$0: Using default arguments\n"   and
        @ARGV=('King Tut')   or
            @ARGV > 1   and
                warn "Usage: $0 song_name\n"   and
                    exit 255;
```

This example illustrates the folly of stretching the utility of and/or beyond reasonable limits, which makes the code unnecessarily hard to read and maintain. Moreover, matters would get even worse if you needed to parenthesize some groups of expressions in order to obtain the desired result.

The moral of this comparison is that branching specifications that go beyond the trivial cases are better handled with `if/else` than with `and/or`—which of course is why the language provides `if/else` as an alternative.

Perl permits additional `if/else`s to be included within `if` and `else` branches, which is called *nesting* (as depicted in the left side of table 8.4). However, in cases where tests are performed one after another to select one branch out of several for execution, readability can be enhanced and typing can be minimized by using the `elsif` contraction for "`else { if`" (see the table's right column).

Table 8.4 Nested `if/else` vs. `elsif`

`if/else` within `else`	`elsif` alternative

```if (A) {```
 ```   print 'A case';```
 ```}```
 ```else {   # this brace disappears -->```
 ```   if (B) {```
 ```   print 'B case';```
 ```   }```
 ```   else {```
 ```   print 'other case';```
 ```   }```
 ```}   # this brace disappears -->```
	```if (A) {```
	 ``` print 'A case';```
	 ```}```
	
	 ```elsif (B) {```
	 ``` print 'B case';```
	 ```}```
	 ```else {```
	 ``` print 'other case';```
	 ```}```

Just remember that Perl's keyword is `elsif`, not `elif`, as it is in the Shell.

Next, we'll look at an example of a script that does lots of conditional branching, using both techniques.

8.3.2 Mixing branching techniques: The `cd_report` script

The purpose of `cd_report` is to let the user select and display input records that represent CDs by matching against the various fields within those records. Through use of the following command-line switches, the user can limit his regexes to match within various portions of a record, and request a report of the average rating for the group of selected CDs:

- `-search='RE'`   Search for *RE* anywhere in record
- `-a='RE'`   Search for *RE* in the Artist field
- `-t='RE'`   Search for *RE* in the Title field
- `-r`   Report average rating for selected CDs
- `(default)`   Print all records, under column headings

Let's try some sample runs:

```
$ cd_report rock        # prints whole file, below column-headings
TITLE                    ARTIST            RATING
Dark Horse               George Harrison 3
Electric Ladyland        Jimi Hendrix      5
Dark Side of the Moon    Pink Floyd        4
Tommy                    The Who           4
Weasels Ripped my Flesh Frank Zappa        2

Processed 5 CD records
```

That invocation printed the entire rock file, because by default all records are selected. This next run asks for a report of CDs that have the word "dark" in their Title field:

```
$ cd_report -t='\bdark\b' rock
TITLE                    ARTIST            RATING
Dark Horse               George Harrison 3
Dark Side of the Moon    Pink Floyd        4

Processed 5 CD records
```

As you can tell from what got matched and printed, the script ignores case differences.

The next invocation requests CDs having "hendrix" in the Artist field or "weasel" anywhere within the record, along with an average-rating report:

```
$ cd_report -a='hendrix' -search=weasel -r rock
TITLE                    ARTIST            RATING
Electric Ladyland        Jimi Hendrix      5
Weasels Ripped my Flesh Frank Zappa        2

        Average Rating for 2 CDs: 3.5

Processed 5 CD records
```

Now that I've piqued your interest, take a peek at the script, shown in listing 8.1. Notice its strategic use of the if/else and logical and/or facilities, to exploit the unique advantages of each. For example, if/else is used for selecting blocks of code for execution (e.g., Lines 18–20, 21–33), logical and is used for making matching operations conditional on the defined status of their associated switch variables (Lines 23–25), and logical or is used for terminating a series of tests (Lines 23–25) as soon as the True/False result is known.

Let's examine this script in greater detail. First, the shebang line includes the primary option cluster for "field processing with custom separators" (using tabs), plus the s option for switch processing (see table 2.9).

Then, the initialization on Line 6 tells the program how many tab-separated fields to expect to find in each input record, so it can issue warnings for improperly formatted ones. The next line sets $sel_cds to 0, because if Line 29 isn't executed, it would otherwise still be undefined by Line 38 and trigger a warning there.

Listing 8.1   The cd_report script

```perl
1   #! /usr/bin/perl -s -wnlaF'\t+'
2
3   our ( $search, $a, $t, $r );              # make switches optional
4
5   BEGIN {
6       $num_fields=3;                        # number of fields per line
7       $sel_cds=0;  # so won't be undefined in END, if no selections
8
9       $options=( defined $r  or  defined $a  or        # any options?
10          defined $t  or  defined $search );
11
12      print "TITLE\t\t\tARTIST\t\tRATING";  # print column headings
13  }
14
15    #####  BODY OF PROGRAM, EXECUTED FOR EACH LINE OF INPUT   #####
16  ( $title, $artist, $rating )=@F;    # load fields into variables
17  $fcount=@F;                         # get field-count for line
18  if ( $fcount != $num_fields ) {     # line improperly formatted
19      warn "\n\tBad field count of $fcount on line #$.; skipping!";
20  }
21  else {                              # line properly formatted
22      $selected=(         # T/F to indicate status of current record
23          defined $t  and  $title  =~ /$t/i  or  # match with title?
24          defined $a  and  $artist =~ /$a/i  or  # match with artist?
25          defined $search  and  /$search/i    or  # match with record?
26          ! $options          # without options, all records selected
27      );
28      if ( $selected ) {              # the current CD was selected
29          $sel_cds++;                 # increment #CDs_selected
30          $sum_ratings+=$rating;      # needed for -r option
31          print;                      # print the selected line
32      }
33  }
34  END {
35      $num_cds=$.;                    # maximum line number = #lines read
36      if ( $r  and  $sel_cds > 0 ) {
37          $ave_rating=$sum_ratings / $sel_cds;
38          print "\n\tAverage Rating for $sel_cds CDs: $ave_rating";
39      }
40      print "\nProcessed $num_cds CD records";      # report stats
41  }
```

Line 9 sets the variable $options to a True or False value to indicate whether the user supplied any switches.

The BEGIN block ends with Line 12, which prints column headings to label the upcoming output.

Line 16, the first one that's executed for each input record, loads its fields into suitably named variables. Then, the field count is loaded into $fcount, so it can be easily compared to the expected value in $num_fields and a warning can be issued on Line 19, if the record is improperly formatted.

If the "then" branch containing that warning is executed, the else branch comprising the rest of the program's body is skipped, causing the next line to be read and execution to continue from Line 16. But if the record is determined to have three fields on Line 18, the else branch on Line 21 is taken, and a series of conditional tests is conducted to see whether the current record should be selected for printing—as indicated by $selected being set to True (Line 22).

Let's look more closely at these tests. Line 23 senses whether the "search in the Title field" option was provided; if so, it employs the user-supplied pattern to test for a match with $title. If that fails, matches are next looked for in the $artist and $_ variables—if requested by the user's switches. Because logical ors connect this series of "defined and *match*" clauses, the first True result (if any) circumvents the remaining tests. If no option was provided by the user, execution descends through the "defined and *match*" clauses and evaluates the ! $options test on Line 26, which sets $selected to True to cause the current CD's record to be selected.

If the current record was selected, Line 29 increments the count of selected CDs, and its rating is added to the running total before the record is printed on Line 31.

The cycle of processing then resumes from Line 16 with the next record, until all input has been processed.

Because an average can't be computed until all the individual ratings have been totaled, that calculation must be relegated to the END block. Line 36 checks whether an average rating report was requested (via the -r switch); if that's so, and at least one CD was selected, the average rating is computed and printed.

As a final step, the script reports the number of records read. To enhance readability, the value of "$." is copied into a suitably named variable on Line 35 before its value is printed on Line 40.

8.3.3 Tips on using if/else

The most common mistake with the if/else construct is a syntax error: leaving out the closing right-hand brace that's needed to match the opening left-hand brace, or vice versa. In common parlance, this is called *not balancing* the curly braces (or having an *imbalance* of them). Users of the vi editor can get help with this problem by placing the cursor on a curly brace and pressing the % key, which causes the cursor to momentarily jump to the matching brace (if any).

Another common mistake beginners make is appending a semicolon after the final curly brace of if/else. That's somewhat gratifying to their teacher, because this reveals their awareness that semicolons are required terminators for Perl statements and critical elements of syntax. However, curly-brace delimited code blocks are *constructs* that *encase* statements, rather than statements themselves, so they don't rate the semicolon treatment.

For help in spotting these syntax errors and others, try running your code through a beautifier. You can learn about and download the standard Perl beautifier from http://perltidy.sourceforge.net.[7]

As a final note, Perl, unlike some of its relatives, doesn't permit the omission of the curly braces in cases where only a single statement is associated with a condition:

```
if ( condition )   statement;          # WRONG!

if ( condition ) { statement; }        # {}s are mandatory in Perl
```

So get used to typing those curly braces—*without* terminating semicolons!

Having just discussed an important flow-control structure that's highly conventional—which is an unusual occurrence in a Perl book—we will regain our Perlistic footing by looking next at some valuable yet *un*conventional operators for string manipulation.

8.4 WRANGLING STRINGS WITH CONCATENATION AND REPETITION OPERATORS

Table 8.5 shows some handy operators for strings that we haven't discussed yet. The *concatenation operator* joins together the strings on its left and right. It comes in handy when you need to assemble a longer string from shorter ones, or easily reorder the components of a string (as you'll see shortly).

The *repetition operator* duplicates the specified string the indicated number of times. It can save you a lot of work when, for example, you want to generate a row of dashes across the screen—without typing every one of them.

The concatenation operator doesn't get much use in Minimal Perl, for two reasons. First, our routine use of the 1 option eliminates the most common need for it

Table 8.5 String operators for concatenation and repetition

Name	Symbol	Example	Result	Explanation
Concatenation operator	.	`$ab='A' . 'B';`	AB	The concatenation operator joins together (*concatenates*) the strings on its left and right sides. When used in its compound form with the assignment operator (.=), it causes the string on the right to be appended to the one on the left.
		`$abc=$ab . 'C';`	ABC	
		`$abc='A';`	A	
		`$abc.='B';`	AB	
		`$abc.='C';`	ABC	
Repetition operator	x	`$dashes='-' x 4;`	----	The repetition operator causes the string on its left to be repeated the number of times indicated on its right.
		`$spaces=' ' x 2;`	☐☐	

---

[7] To learn about the *first* Perl beautifier, see http://TeachMePerl.com/perl_beautifier.html.

that others have. Second, in other cases where this operator is commonly used, it's often simpler to use quotes to get the same result.

For example, consider this code sample, in which `random_kind_of_chow` is an imaginary user-defined function that returns a "chow" type ("mein", "fun", "Purina", etc.):

```
$kind=random_kind_of_chow;
$order="large chow $kind";                    # e.g., "large chow mein"
```

That last statement, which uses double quotes to join the words together, is easier to read and type than this equivalent concatenation-based alternative:

```
$order='large ' . 'chow ' . $kind;
```

But you can't call functions from within quotes, so the concatenation approach is used in cases like this one, where the words returned by two functions need to be joined with an intervening space:

```
$order=random_preparation . ' ' . random_food;   # flambéed Vegemite?
```

On the other hand, concatenation using the compound version (. =) of the concatenation operator[8] is preferred over quoting for lines that would otherwise be inconveniently long.

For instance, this long assignment statement

```
$good_fast_things='cars computers action delivery recovery⌐
reimbursement replies';
```

is less manageable than this equivalent pair of shorter ones:

```
$good_fast_things='cars computers action delivery';
$good_fast_things.=' recovery reimbursement replies';
```

The syntax used in that last statement

```
$var.=' new stuff';
```

appends ' new stuff' to the end of the variable's existing contents.

The compound form of the concatenation operator is sometimes also used with short strings, in applications where it may later be necessary to independently change, conditionally select, or reorder them. For instance, here's a case where the tail end of a message needs to be conditionally selected, to optimally tailor the description of a product for different groups of shoppers:

```
$sale_item='ONE HOUR SALE on:';
if ($funky_web_site) {
    $sale_item.=' pre-weathered raw-hemp "gangsta" boxers';
}
else {   # for posh sites
    $sale_item.=' hand-rubbed organic natural-fiber underpants';
}
```

---

[8] See the last panel of table 5.12 for more information.

This use of the concatenation operator is also helpful for aggregating strings that become available at different times during execution, as you'll see next.

8.4.1 Enhancing the `most_recent_file` script

Remember the `most_recent_file` script, which provides a robust replacement for `find | xargs ls -lrdt` when sorting large numbers of filenames?[9] It suffers from the limitation of showing only a single filename as the "most recent," when others are tied with it for that status.

This shortcoming is easily overcome. Specifically, all that's required to enhance `most_recent_file` to handle ties properly is to take its original code

```
if ($mtime > $newest) {       # If current file is newest yet seen,
    $newest=$mtime;           # remember file's modification time, and
    $name=$_;                 # remember file's name
}
```

and add to it the following `elsif` clause, which arranges for each filename having the same modification time to be *appended* to the $name variable (after a newline for separation), using the compound-assignment form of the concatenation operator:

```
elsif ($mtime == $newest) { # If current file ties newest yet seen
    $name.="\n$_"; # append new tied filename after existing one(s)
}
```

Next we'll look at a code snippet that, when used as intended, will annoy law-abiding Netizens with its deceitful claims and awphul shpelink mistakes. Its redeeming qualities are that it illustrates some important points about the relative precedence of the concatenation and repetition operators, and the code-maintenance advantages of using the concatenation operator.

8.4.2 Using concatenation and repetition operators together

Here's a code snippet that uses both the repetition and concatenation operators in their simple forms, as well as the concatenation operator in its compound assignment form:

```
$pitch=($greedy_border='$' x 68 . "\n"); # initializes both variables

$pitch.="\t\t   You con belief me, becauze I am laywers. \n";
$pitch.="\t\tYou can reely MAKE MONEY FA\$T with our cystem!\n";
$pitch.= $greedy_border;

print $pitch;
```

In the first statement, because the string repetition operator (x) has higher precedence than the concatenation operator, the $ symbol gets repeated 68 times before

---

[9] See listing 6.1.

the newline is appended to it. Then that string is assigned to `$greedy_border`, and also to `$pitch`.

Here's the output from `print $pitch`:

```
$$$$$$$$$$$$$$$$$$$$$$$$$$$$$$$$$$$$$$$$$$$$$$$$$$$$$$$$$$$$$$$$$$$$$$$$$$$
              You con belief me, becauze I am laywers.
           You can reely MAKE MONEY FA$T with our cystem!
$$$$$$$$$$$$$$$$$$$$$$$$$$$$$$$$$$$$$$$$$$$$$$$$$$$$$$$$$$$$$$$$$$$$$$$$$$$
```

The `$greedy_border` variable is used to draw a line of $ signs across the screen, using the string repetition operator.[10] Note that newlines must be added to all but the last line appended to the variable `$pitch`, because the l invocation option only supplies a single newline at the end of `print`'s argument list.

So, you ask, what's so great about this piecemeal-concatenation approach to string building that makes it so popular with HTML jockeys? Simply this: If a later report from a focus group indicates that the "MAKE MONEY FA$T" line would work better coming *before* the "laywers" claim, the affected sentences can be reordered by simply exchanging the associated code lines:[11]

Before exchange:
```
$pitch.="\t\t   You con belief me, becauze I am laywers. \n";
$pitch.="\t\tYou can reely MAKE MONEY FA\$T with our cystem!\n";
```

After exchange:
```
$pitch.="\t\tYou can reely MAKE MONEY FA\$T with our cystem!\n";
$pitch.="\t\t   You con belief me, becauze I am laywers. \n";
```

See chapter 12's listing 12.7 for an example of building up a complete HTML document using this piecemeal-concatenation approach.

8.4.3 Tips on using the concatenation operator

The most common mistake when using the concatenation operator to build up a string one piece at a time is this: accidentally using a plain assignment operator when you should use the compound concatenation operator instead. For example, the second statement of this pair correctly appends a second string after the first one in the variable `$Usage` to build up the desired usage message:

```
$Usage="Usage: $0 [-f] [-i] [-l] [-v] [-n] [-d]";
$Usage.=" [-p|-c] [-m] [-s] [-r] 'RE' [file...]\n";        # Right.
```

---

[10] With a slight change, you can determine the current window-size of an emulated terminal (such as an xterm) and supply the appropriate repetition value automatically (see listing 8.4).

[11] In vi, for example, all it takes is three keystrokes (ddp) to switch these lines, after placing the cursor on the upper line.

But this mistaken variation *overwrites* the first string with the second one:

```
$Usage="Usage: $0 [-f] [-i] [-l] [-v] [-n] [-d]";
$Usage=" [-p|-c] [-m] [-s] [-r] 'RE' [file...]\n";        # WRONG!
```

So when you're using this coding technique and you find that the earlier portions of the built-up string have mysteriously disappeared, here's how to fix the problem. Locate the assignment statement that loads what appears at the beginning of the incomplete string (in this case, " [-p|-c] ..."), and change its "=" to the required ".=".

Next, we'll discuss an especially useful programming feature that Perl inherited from the Shell, which allows the output of OS commands to be manipulated within Perl programs.

8.5 INTERPOLATING COMMAND OUTPUT INTO SOURCE CODE

The Shell inherited a wonderful feature from the venerable MULTICS OS that it calls *command substitution*. It allows the output of a command to be captured and inserted into its surrounding command line, as if the programmer had typed that output there in the first place. In a sense, it's a special form of output redirection, with the current command line being the target of the redirection.

Let's say you needed a Shell script to report the current year every time it's run. One way to implement this would be to hard-wire the (currently) current year in an `echo` command, like so:

```
echo 'The year is 2006'     # Output: The year is 2006
```

But to prevent the frenetic refrain of your beeper from rudely awakening you the next time January rolls around, you'd be better off writing that line as follows:

```
echo "The year is `date +%Y`"
```

Here's how it works. The back-quotes (or *grave accents*) and the string they enclose constitute a command-substitution request. It's job is to write `date`'s output over itself, making this the command that's ultimately executed:

```
echo "The year is 2006"     # `date ...` replaced by its own output
```

The benefit is that a script that derives the year through command substitution always knows the current year—allowing its maintainer to sleep through the night.

Perl also provides this valuable service, but under the slightly different name of *command interpolation*. Table 8.6 shows the syntax for typical uses of this facility in the Shell and Perl.[12]

---

[12] As indicated in the left column of the table, the Bash and Korn shells simultaneously support an alternative to the back-quote syntax for command substitution, of the form `$(command)`.

Table 8.6　Command substitution/interpolation in the Shell and Perl

Shell[a]	Perl	Explanation

`var=`cmd``
OR
`var=$(cmd)`
	`$var=`cmd``	The *cmd* is processed for variable substitutions as if it were in double quotes, and then it's executed, with the output being assigned in its entirety to the variable. *cmd*'s exit value is stored in the "$?" variable.

`array=(`cmd`)`
OR
`array=($(cmd))`
	`@array=`cmd``	*cmd*'s output is processed as described above, and then "words" (for the Shell) or $/ separated records (for Perl) are assigned to the array.

`cmd2 `cmd`` OR `cmd2 $(cmd)`	`function `cmd`` OR `function scalar `cmd``	*cmd* is processed, and then, in the Shell case, the individual words of the output are supplied to *cmd2* as arguments. In Perl's list context, each record of the output is submitted to *function* as a separate argument, whereas in scalar context, all output is presented as a single argument.

`"`cmd`"`
OR
`"$(cmd)"`
	``cmd``	In the Shell, double quotes are needed to protect *cmd*'s output from further processing. In Perl, that protection is always provided, and double quotes aren't allowed around command interpolations. The Shell examples yield all of *cmd*'s output as one line, whereas the Perl example yields a list of $/ separated records.

a. *cmd* and *cmd2* represent OS commands, *var*/*$var* and *array*/*@array* Shell/Perl variable names, and *function* a Perl function name.

When a Unix shell processes a command substitution, a shell of the same type (Bash, C-shell, etc.) interprets the command. In contrast, with Perl, an OS-designated command interpreter (/bin/sh on Unix) is used.

As indicated in the third row of the table, when command substitution (or interpolation) is used to provide arguments to another command (or function), the arguments are constructed differently in the two languages. The Shell normally presents each *word* separately, but it will use the entire output string as a single argument if the command substitution is double quoted. Perl, on the other hand, presents each *record* as a separate argument in list context, or all records as a single argument in scalar context.

Another difference is that the Shell automatically strips off the trailing newline from the command's output, and Perl doesn't. To make Perl act like the Shell, you can assign the output to a variable and then chomp it (see section 7.2.4).

Because of these differences, the corresponding Shell and Perl examples shown in table 8.6 don't behave in exactly the same way. However, Perl can generally be trusted to give you what you want by default—and anything else you may need, with a little more coaxing.[13]

The major differences in the results provided by the languages are, as usual, due to the Shell's propensity for doing additional post-processing of the results of substitutions (as discussed earlier). We'll discuss this issue in greater depth as we examine some sample programs in upcoming sections.

The command we'll discuss next is held in high esteem by Shell programmers, because it makes output sent to terminal-type devices look a lot fancier—and, consequently, makes those writing the associated scripts seem a lot cleverer!

8.5.1 Using the `tput` command

The Unix utility called `tput` can play an important role in Shell scripts designed to run on computer terminals or their emulated equivalents (e.g., an `xterm` or `dtterm`). For instance, `tput` can render a script's error messages in reverse video, or make a prompt blink to encourage the user to supply the requested information.

Through use of command interpolation, Perl programmers writing scripts for Unix systems can also use this valuable tool.[14]

The top panel of table 8.7 lists the most commonly used options for the `tput` command. For your convenience, the ones that work on the widest variety of terminals (and emulators) are listed nearest the top of each of the table's panels.

Table 8.7 Controlling and interrogating screen displays using `tput` options

Display mode	Enabling option	Disabling option
standout	smso	rmso
underline	smul	rmul
bold	bold	sgr0
dim	dim	sgr0
blink	blink	sgr0
Terminal information	**Option**	**Explanation**
columns	cols	Reports number of columns.
lines	lines	Reports number of lines.

---

[13] I was put off by these disparities when I first sat down to learn Perl, but now I can't imagine how I ever put up with the Shell, and I'm pleased as punch with Perl.

[14] There's a Perl module (`Term::Cap`) that bypasses the `tput` command to access the Unix terminal information database directly, but it's much easier to run the Unix command via command interpolation than to use the module.

Highlighting trailing whitespaces with `tput`

People who do a lot of grepping in their jobs have two things in common: They're fastidious about properly quoting `grep`'s pattern argument (otherwise they'd wind up unemployed), and they *hate* text files that have stray whitespace characters at their ends. You'll see how `tput` can help them in a moment. But first, why do they view files having dangling whitespaces with contempt? Because such files thwart attempts that would otherwise be successful to match patterns at the ends of their lines:

```
grep 'The end!$' naughty_file # Hope there's no dangling space/tab!
```

Because the `$` metacharacter anchors the match to the end of the line, there's no provision for extra space or tab characters to be present there. For this reason, the lack of any matches could mean either that no line ends with "The end!" or that the lines that do visibly end with that string have invisible whitespace(s) afterwards.

Figure 8.2 shows how `tput` can help with a simple script that makes the presence of dangling whitespace characters excruciatingly clear. It uses "standout" mode to draw the user's attention to the lines that need to be pruned, to make them safe for grepping.

Listing 8.2 presents the script. As with many of the `sed`-like scripts covered in chapter 4, this one uses the p option to automatically print the input lines after the substitution operator processes them.

Listing 8.2   The `highlight_trailing_ws` script

```
1   #! /usr/bin/perl -wpl
2
3   BEGIN {
4       $ON =`tput smso`;     #  start mode "standout"
5       $OFF=`tput rmso`;     #  remove mode "standout"
6   }
7   # Show "<WHITESPACE>" in reverse video, to attract eyeballs
8   s/[<SPACE>\t]+$/$ON<WHITESPACE>$OFF/g;
```

The script works by replacing trailing sequences of spaces and/or tabs with the string "<WHITESPACE>", which is rendered in standout mode (usually *reverse video*) for additional emphasis.[15] Once the presence of dangling whitespace has been revealed by

```
$ highlight_trailing_ws seattleites
Torbin Ulrich    98107
Yeshe Dolma      98117<WHITESPACE>
Michael Wolf     98107<WHITESPACE>
Will Grates      98039
$
```

**Figure 8.2
Output from the
`highlight_trailing_ws` script**

---

[15] You might think it sufficient to highlight the offending whitespace characters themselves, rather than an inserted word, but reverse video mode doesn't affect the display of tabs on most terminals.

this tool, the "data hygiene" team could give some refresher training to the "data entry" team and have them correct the offending lines.

This is a good example of using `tput` to draw the user's attention to important information on the screen, and I'm sure you'll find other places to use it in your own programming.

Command interpolation is used to solve many other pesky problems in the IT workplace. In the next section, you'll see how it can be used to write a `grep`-like script that handles directory arguments sensibly, by searching for matches in the files within them.

8.5.2 Grepping recursively: The `rgrep` script

As mentioned in chapter 6, a *recursive* `grep`, which automatically descends into subdirectories to search the files within them, can be a useful tool. Although the GNU `grep` provides this capability through an invocation option, a Perl-based grepper has several intrinsic advantages, as discussed in section 3.2. What's more, writing a script that provides recursive grepping will allow us to demonstrate some additional features of Perl that are worth knowing.

For starters, let's observe a sample run of the `rgrep` script, whose code we'll examine shortly. In the situation depicted, the Linux superuser was having trouble with a floppy disk, and knew that some file(s) in the `/var/log` directory would contain error reports—but he wasn't sure which ones:

```
$ rgrep '\bfloppy\b' /var/log          # output edited for fit
/var/log/warn:
kernel: floppy0: data CRC error: track 1, head 1, sector 14
/var/log/messages:
kernel: I/O error, dev 02:00 (floppy)
```

These reports, which were extracted from the indicated files under the user-specified directory, indicate that the diskette was not capable of correctly storing data in certain sectors.[16] The script can be examined in listing 8.3.

Listing 8.3 The `rgrep` script

```
1   #! /usr/bin/perl -wnl
2
3   BEGIN {
4       $Usage="Usage: $0 'pattern' dir1 [dir2 ...]";
5       @ARGV >= 2  or  warn "$Usage\n"  and  exit 255;
6
7       $pattern=shift;     # preserve pattern argument
8
9       # `@ARGV` treated like "@ARGV"; elements space-separated
10      @files=grep { chomp; -r  and  -T } # <-- find feeds files
11                      `find @ARGV -follow -type f -print`;
```

---

[16] Which is one reason this venerable but unreliable storage technology has become nearly obsolete.

```
12      @files  or  warn "$0: No files to search\n" and exit 1;
13      @ARGV=@files;   # search for $pattern within these files
14  }
15  # Because it's very likely that we'll search more than one file,
16  # prepend filename to each matching line with printf
17
18  /$pattern/  and  printf "$ARGV: "  and  print;
```

Because this script requires a pattern argument and at least one directory argument, the argument count is checked in Line 5 to determine if a warning and early termination are in order. Then, Line 7 shifts the pattern argument out of the array, leaving only directory names within it.

The find command on Line 11 appears within the back quotes of command interpolation, but these quotes are treated like double quotes as far as variable interpolations are concerned. The result is that @ARGV is turned into a series of space-separated directory names, allowing the Shell to see each as a separate argument to find, as desired. The -follow option of find ensures that arguments that are symbolic links (such as /bin on modern UNIX systems) will be followed to their targets (such as /usr/bin), allowing the actual files to be processed. The result is the conversion of the user-specified directories into a list of the regular files that reside within them (or their sub-directories), and the presentation of that list to grep as its argument list.

In Line 10, grep filters out the filenames emitted by find that are not readable text files.[17] But before applying the -T test to $_, which holds each filename in turn, chomp is employed to remove the newline that find appends to each filename.

Line 12 ensures that there's at least one searchable filename before proceeding, to avoid surprising the user by defaulting to STDIN for input—which would be highly unexpected behavior for a program that takes directory arguments!

Finally, Line 18 attempts the pattern match, and on success, it prints the name of the file—because multiple files will usually be searched—along with the matching line.

Although this script is useful and educational, you won't be seeing it again. That's because it will be assimilated by a grander, more versatile Perl grepper, later in this chapter.

8.5.3   Tips on using command interpolation

Perl's command-interpolation mechanism is different in some fundamental ways from the Shell's command substitution. For one thing, the Shell's version works within double quotes, allowing literal characters and variables to be mixed within the back-quoted command:

```
$ echo "Testing: `tput smul`Shell"
Testing: Shell
```

---

[17] The -T operator has to read the file to characterize its contents, so it doesn't return True unless the file is readable—making -r redundant. Accordingly, we won't show -r with -T from here on.

In contrast, Perl treats back-quotes within double quotes as literal characters, requiring individual components to be separately quoted:

```
print 'Testing: ', `tput smul`, 'Perl';
Testing: Perl
```

Another difference is that what's tested for a back-quoted command in conditional context is the True/False value of its *output* in Perl, but of the command's *exit value* in the Shell:

Shell

```
o=`command`  ||  echo 'message' >&2    # warns if command's $? False
```

Perl

```
$o=`command` or warn "message\n";       # warns if output in $o False
```

You can arrange for Perl to do what the Shell does, but because the languages have opposite definitions of True and False, this involves complementing *command*'s exit value. With this in mind, here's the Perl counterpart for the previous Shell example:

```
$o=`command` ; ! $? or  warn 'message';        # warns if $? False
```

And here's the same thing written as an `if`:

```
if ($o=`command`; ! $? ){ warn 'message'; }    # warns if $? False
```

As mentioned earlier, Perl has a simpler processing model than the Shell for quoted strings, which has the benefit of making the final result easier to predict.[18] One conspicuous side-effect of that tradeoff is Perl's inability to allow command interpolation requests to be nested within double quotes—but that's a compromise worth making.

Next, we'll talk about the `system` function, because no matter how richly endowed with built-in resources your programming language may be, you'll still want to run OS commands from it now and again.

8.6   EXECUTING OS COMMANDS USING `system`

In cases where you want to use an OS command in a way that doesn't involve capturing its output within the Perl program—such as simply displaying its output on the screen—the `system` function is the tool of choice. Table 8.8 shows sample invocations of `system`, which is used to submit a command to the OS-dependent command interpreter (`/bin/sh` on Unix) for execution.

---

[18] See http://TeachMePerl.com/DQs_in_shell_vs_perl.html for further details.

Table 8.8 The system function

Example	Explanation
`system 'command(s)';`	*command(s)* in single quotes are submitted without modification for execution.
`system "command(s)";`	*command(s)* in double quotes are subjected to variable interpolation before being executed. In some cases, single quotes may be required around command arguments to prevent the Shell from modifying them.
`system 'command(s)';` `! $? or warn 'failed';`	Just as "`function or warn`" reports the failure of a Perl function, "`! $? or warn`" reports a failed command run by `system`. The "`!`" converts the Unix True/False value to a Perl-compatible one.

As indicated in the table, it's important to carefully quote the command presented as system's argument, because

- special characters within the command may otherwise cause Perl syntax errors;
- judicious use of single quotes, double quotes, and/or backslashes may be required to have the command reach the Shell in the proper form.

Let's say you want to do a long listing on a filename that resides in a Perl variable. For safety, the filename should appear in single quotes at the Shell level, so if it contains whitespace characters, it won't be interpreted as multiple filenames.

The appropriate invocation of system for this case is

```
system "ls -l '$filename'";  # filename contains: ruby tuesday.mp3
```

which arranges for the Shell to see this:

```
ls -l 'ruby tuesday.mp3'
```

The double quotes around system's argument allow the `$filename` variable to be expanded by Perl, while ensuring that the single quotes surrounding it are treated as literal characters. When the Shell scans the resulting string, the (now unquoted) single quotes disable word-splitting on any embedded whitespace, as desired.[19]

As shown in the last row of table 8.8, when you need to test whether a system-launched command has succeeded or failed, there is a complication—on Unix, the value returned by system (and simultaneously placed in "`$?`") is based on the Shell's definitions of True and False, which are the opposite of Perl's.

The recommended workaround is to *complement* that return value using the "`!`" operator and then write your branching instructions in the normal manner. For example:

```
system "grep 'stuff' 'file'";
! $? or  warn "Sorry, no stuff\n";
```

---

[19] For a more detailed treatment of the art of multi-level quoting, see http://TeachMeUnix.com/quoting.html.

CHAPTER 8 SCRIPTING TECHNIQUES

Next, we'll look at two programs that use system to format "news flashes" on the screen.

8.6.1 Generating reports

Instead of returning a string that adjusts the terminal's display mode, tput's lines and cols options (see table 8.7, bottom panel) return the number of lines and columns on the terminal. The latter option is useful for drawing borders across the screen, among other things. These options also work with many terminal emulators (such as xterms) to report their current dimensions.

Figure 8.3 shows two sample runs of the news_flash script, which uses tput to print a heading across the width of the user's terminal. As you can see, the heading is centered within each of the differently sized windows, and the dashed lines occupy each window's full width.

Listing 8.4 shows the script.

Listing 8.4   The news_flash script

```
1   #! /usr/bin/perl -wl
2
3   $width=(`tput cols`  or  80); # supply a reasonable default
4   $line='-' x $width;           # make a line the width of screen
5
6   $heading='NEWS FLASH:';
7   $heading.=' ' . `date '+%X'`;  # append date's formatted output
8   chomp $heading;                # remove date-added newline
9
10  # Calculate offset from left, to center the string
11  $heading_length=length $heading;
12  $offset=($width - $heading_length) / 2;
13
14  # Offset may have decimal component, but Perl will
15  # convert to integer automatically for use with "x" operator
16  $padding=' ' x $offset; # generate spaces for calculated offset
17
18  print "$line";              # dashed line
19  print "$padding$heading";   # the centered heading
20  print "$line\n";            # dashed line
```

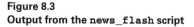

Figure 8.3
Output from the news_flash script

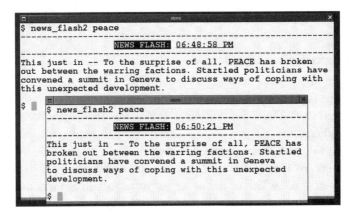

Figure 8.4 Output from the `news_flash2` script

The script uses command interpolation rather than the implicit loop to obtain the information it needs, so it doesn't need the n option or its associated BEGIN block. It works by constructing a dashed line that's the width of the screen (Lines 3–4), building a heading string (Lines 6–8), determining its length (Line 11), calculating the offset needed to center it (Line 12), and then printing the left-padded heading string (Line 19) between dashed lines (Lines 18, 20).

By being more creative in the use of tput, and with a little help from system, we can make the heading look even fancier. Figure 8.4 shows an enhanced version, which uses both reverse video and underlining to decorate the heading, and formats the text of a news article to fit within the screen width.[20]

The script is shown in listing 8.5.

As indicated in the shebang line, the script supports a command-line switch (via -s) called -debug, which is declared on Line 3. It checks for a first argument that's the name of a text file in Line 6, and it issues a "Usage:" message and dies if it doesn't get one.

Listing 8.5 The `news_flash2` script

```
1   #! /usr/bin/perl -s -wl
2
3   our ($debug);                       # make switch optional
4
5   $file=shift;                        # get filename of news article
6   if (! defined $file  or  ! -T $file) {
7       die "Usage: $0 filename\n";
8   }
9
```

---

[20] The Text::Autoformat module could reformat the string, but our emphasis in this section is on demonstrating the use of Shell-based processing options rather than pure-Perl ones.

CHAPTER 8 SCRIPTING TECHNIQUES

```
10   # Get the display control sequences
11   $REV=(    `tput smso`  or   "");     # use null string by default
12   $NO_REV=(`tput rmso`   or   "");
13   $UL=(     `tput smul`  or   "");
14   $NO_UL=( `tput rmul`   or   "");
15
16   # Get the terminal's width
17   $width=( `tput cols`   or   80);     # supply standard default
18   chomp $width;                        # remove tput's newline
19   $line='-' x $width;          # make a line the width of screen
20
21   $heading='NEWS FLASH:';              # store heading string
22   $date=`date '+%X'`;                  # store date string
23   chomp $date;                         # remove date's newline
24
25   # Calculate needed offset from left, to center the string
26   $msg_length=length "$heading $date";
27   $offset=($width - $msg_length) / 2;
28
29   # Offset may have decimal component, but Perl will
30   # convert to integer automatically for use with "x" operator
31   $padding=' ' x $offset; # generate spaces for calculated offset
32
```

Then the script sets some variables for controlling the user's display, taking into account the possibility that tput might not succeed in obtaining the requested display-control string for the user's terminal. Specifically, for each display attribute, tput's return value is tested for being False (to detect the "undefined" value), in which case a null string is assigned to the variable instead.[21] This allows those variables to be used without triggering any warnings about uninitialized values, with null-strings standing-in for any requested (but unavailable) display-control strings.

The parentheses are needed in those assignments (Lines 11–14) because the assignment operator has higher precedence than the logical or. In consequence, tput's output would be assigned to each variable directly without them, leaving the or "" portions just dangling there uselessly.

In the case of the $width variable, we can do better than fudging in a null string for its value if tput cols returns False, so it's set in Line 17 to the standard width of a terminal.

The two parts of the heading line are stored in variables on Lines 21 and 22. They're kept separate so that the different display-control sequences can later be inserted around them (Lines 34–35). After the usual calculations are performed to center the heading string, it's printed between the dashed lines generated on Lines 33 and 36.

---

[21] There's no need in this case to check tput's output for being merely defined as opposed to True, because the number 0 could never be a display-control string anyway. But here's how the defined-based coding would look:

```
$REV=`tput smso`; defined $REV  or  $REV="";
```

```
33   print $line;                               # dashed line
34   print $padding, $REV, $heading, $NO_REV, " ",
35       $UL, $date, $NO_UL;                     # the heading
36   print $line;                               # dashed line
37
38   # Assemble command in string
39   $command="fmt -$width '$file'";  # e.g.,   "fmt -62 Reuters.txt"
40
41   $debug  and  warn "Command is:\n\t$command\n\n" and
42       $command="set -x; $command"; # enable Shell execution trace
43
44   system  $command;                 # format to fit on screen
45
46   # show error if necessary
47   ! $? or  warn "$0: This command failed: $command\n";
```

The next step (Line 39) is to construct the Shell command that reformats the contents of `$file` to fit within the terminal's width, using the Unix `fmt` command. As you'll see in an upcoming example, storing the command in a variable is better for debugging purposes than passing the command as a direct argument to `system`. Note that `$file` is placed between Shell-level single quotes, to guard against the possibility that it may contain characters that are special to the Shell.

The command is executed on Line 44. If it fails, a warning is issued on Line 47.

The `news_flash2` script's use of `system` to run `fmt file` is appropriate, because it lets the command's output flow to the screen. However, if a script needs to repeatedly reenable reverse-video type, it's more economical to run `tput smso` once using command interpolation and save its output for later reuse, than to repeatedly run `system 'tput smso'`.

In the next section, we'll first discuss some general techniques for debugging Shell commands issued by Perl programs, and then you'll learn how to debug an actual problem that once afflicted `news_flash2`.

8.6.2 Tips on using `system`

The first and most important tip on successfully using `system`, as mentioned before, is to make sure you provide the necessary quotes at the Shell level to allow your command to be interpreted correctly. But no matter how hard you try, you may mess that up, so an even more important tip is to write your script with ease of debugging in mind.

In listing 8.5, you may have wondered why the `system` command for `news_flash2` was coded (Lines 39, 44) as

```
$command="fmt -$width '$file'";
...
system $command;
```

rather than more directly as

```
system "fmt -$width '$file'";
```

Using a variable to hold system's command has much to recommend it, because it facilitates

- printing the text of the command for inspection before running it (Line 41);
- showing the text of the command in a diagnostic message (Line 47);
- conditionally enabling the Shell's execution-trace mode for debugging purposes (Lines 41– 42).

As a case in point, when I first tested this program, one of the lines currently visible in listing 8.5 had gone missing (as in all such cases, I blamed vi—*bad* editor!). This caused the script to print the heading, and then just *stall* (or *hang*), as shown in Figure 8.5.

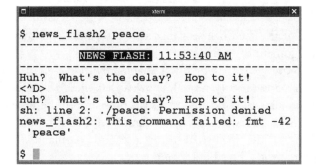

Figure 8.5
Strange behavior of the
news_flash2 script

I've been goofing up commands on Unix systems for decades—so I know that when a program appears to be stalled, it's not taking a siesta, but waiting patiently for the user to type some input. So, I typed the "Huh?" line shown in figure 8.5 and pressed <^D>. That same line was immediately sent back to the screen, followed by a message indicating that the permissions were incorrect for the file peace. So I checked to see if that file was readable by me, and indeed it was!

Examining the output more carefully, I took comfort in seeing that the last line on the screen confirmed that the command, fmt -42 peace, was indeed the one I intended—even though the filename peace had wrapped around at the screen boundary (more on this in a moment).

Because I had written the script with debugging in mind, my next step was to run it again using the -debug switch, as shown in figure 8.6.

The first thing that caught my eye was the strange formatting of the output under "Command is:". Checking the listing (Line 41), I confirmed that there was supposed to be a newline-tab combination before the command appeared, but there definitely shouldn't have been a newline between the -42 option to fmt and that command's

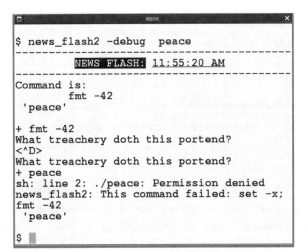

```
$ news_flash2 -debug  peace
-----------------------------------------
            NEWS FLASH: 11:55:20 AM
-----------------------------------------
Command is:
        fmt -42
  'peace'

+ fmt -42
What treachery doth this portend?
<^D>
What treachery doth this portend?
+ peace
sh: line 2: ./peace: Permission denied
news_flash2: This command failed: set -x;
fmt -42
  'peace'

$
```

Figure 8.6
Debugging the
news_flash2 script

intended filename argument. The Shell sees that as two separate commands, rather than one with a final argument of 'peace'.

The Shell's *execution-trace mode*,[22] which was enabled by the –debug-based code prepending set -x; to $command (Line 42), showed that the ("+"-prefixed) command being executed was just fmt -42. And that's the problem: In the absence of the intended filename argument, fmt was waiting for input from STDIN! After I signaled the end of input with <^D>, the Shell tried to run a second command whose name was peace, while reading from "line 2" of its input.

Finally—making the script's defect even more apparent—the "command failed" warning hit the screen-edge differently this time, allowing me to clearly see that the filename argument (peace) had a newline before it within $command.

The reported "permission problem" was now also clear, signifying that peace wasn't *executable*, as any self-respecting command (which it isn't) would be. I felt a momentary urge to set its execute bit (impulsive attempts for quick fixes can be *so* appealing), but I decided it would be wiser to deal with the pesky newline between $width and the filename instead, which was the real culprit.

The remedy is to insert the chomp $width statement shown on Line 18 of listing 8.5, which wasn't there during my initial testing. Doing so removes the trailing newline from the variable if tput's output initializes it, without doing any harm to the newline-free value of 80 if that is used as the initializer instead.

You can find other tips on using system, including techniques for increasing security by preventing /bin/sh from interpreting its arguments, and for recovering

---

[22] Execution-trace mode shows the (potentially modified) text of the original command after it's been subjected to nearly a dozen stages of processing, allowing the programmer to see the actual command that's about to be executed. Perl's processing model is much simpler, obviating the need for any similar mechanism.

the actual Shell exit codes from the values that are encoded in "$?", by running `perldoc -f system`.

One of the most useful and powerful services that a script can provide is to compile and execute programs that it constructs on the fly—or that the user provides—while it is already running. We'll discuss Perl's support for this service next.

8.7 EVALUATING CODE USING `eval`

Like the Shell, Perl has a code-evaluation facility. It's called `eval`, and its job is to compile and execute (i.e., "evaluate") Perl code that becomes available during a program's execution.

That might sound like a description of the `nexpr_p` script we discussed in chapter 5, which evaluates an expression formed from arguments supplied by the user, but there's a big difference.

To jog your memory, here's `nexpr_p`:

```
#! /bin/sh
perl -wl -e "print $*;"    # nexpr_p '2 * 21' --> print 2 * 21
```

It uses the Shell to construct a Perl program, which Perl runs in the usual way. As an alternative, the Perl program could have been designed to accept the specification for the desired program as an argument and to run it on its own. That's where the judicious use of `eval` would be required.

Why is `eval` needed in such cases? Because programs contain special keywords and symbols that are only recognized during the program's compilation phase, which has completed by the time the program starts running. Accordingly, the benefit of `eval` is that it lets your running program handle code that wasn't present during that program's initial compilation.

Examples of tokens that require `eval` for recognition are keywords, operators, function names, matching and substitution operators, backslashes, quotes, commas, and semicolons. Table 8.9 shows the syntax for `eval` in both the Shell and Perl.

Table 8.9   The `eval` function in the Shell and Perl

Shell	Perl

`eval 'command'`
`error=$?`
`(( $error > 0 )) &&`
   `echo "failed: $error" >&2`
	`eval 'stuff'; # sets $@`
	
	`$@ ne ""   and`
	   `warn "failed: $@";`

N/A	`eval;    # evaluates code in $_`

A similarity is that `eval`'s argument is shown in quotes for both languages in table 8.9, because proper quoting—with single quotes, double quotes, and/or backslashes—is often required for success.

Some differences are that the Shell provides an integer exit code for the `eval`'d command, whereas Perl provides a null string or a diagnostic message in the "$@"

variable. Also, there's no need to make a copy of Perl's "$@" to avoid losing access to it, because it's not overwritten in Perl by every subsequently evaluated expression—as "$?" is in the Shell by every subsequently executed command. Another difference is that only Perl allows the invocation of eval without an argument (as shown in the table's bottom panel), in which case it defaults to using $_.

We'll look next at a simple yet surprisingly powerful application of eval that can be used to good advantage by every JAPH. It's based on a script I developed for one of our training courses (like most of the examples in this book).

8.7.1 Using a Perl shell: The `psh` script

The psh script is a dramatic example of how easy it can be to write useful scripts with eval that could never work without its help. psh, a *Perl shell*, prompts the user for a Perl statement, compiles and executes that statement, returns any errors that it generated, and then continues the cycle until <^D> or exit is entered. Its major benefit is that it lets you quickly try some Perl code without writing a script first to do so.

Some of psh's applications are as follows:

- Rapidly developing a prototype of a small program
- Determining the proper syntax for a particular language feature
- Helping teachers demonstrate the error messages associated with certain mistakes

A sample psh session is shown in Figure 8.7.

The student whose psh session is depicted in the figure was learning how to code the printing of a sorted list of numbers. The syntax error that Perl reported was caused by the understandable tendency to place a comma after sort's code-block argument (see table 7.10). She corrected that mistake in the next line, only to find that the numbers were being squished together on output, which reminded her to set the "$," variable to a suitable separator. But this adjustment revealed that sort's arguments were being treated as strings rather than as numbers, leading to the replacement of the string comparison operator by its numeric counterpart, <=> (see table 5.11).

```
$ psh
psh> print sort { $a cmp $b }, 100, 3, 20;
syntax error at (eval 1) line 1, near "},
psh> print sort { $a cmp $b } 100, 3, 20;
100203
psh> $,="\n" ;
psh>
psh> print sort { $a cmp $b } 100, 3, 20;
100
20
3
psh> print sort { $a <=> $b } 100, 3, 20;
3
20
100
psh>
```

Figure 8.7
The Perl shell as a learning tool

CHAPTER 8 SCRIPTING TECHNIQUES

Voilà! The student figured out how to print a sorted list of numbers without engaging in the cycle of repeatedly editing a file, saving it, and submitting it for execution. That makes psh a valuable tool for explorations of this type.[23]

Listing 8.6 shows the psh script. As with many sophisticated and powerful Perl programs, there's almost nothing to it!

Listing 8.6   The psh script

```
1   #! /usr/bin/perl -wnl
2
3   BEGIN {
4       $ON=`tput smso`;
5       $OFF=`tput rmso`;
6       $prompt="${ON}psh>$OFF ";
7       printf $prompt;            # print initial prompt
8   }
9
10  eval;   # uses $_ as argument, loaded by -n loop
11
12  $@ ne ""  and  warn $@;       # if eval produced error, show it
13
14  printf $prompt;               # print prompt for next input
15
16  END {
17      # If user pressed <^D> to the prompt, which leaves $_
18      # undefined, we need to print a newline so the shell's
19      # prompt will start on a fresh line.
20
21      ! defined  and  print "";   # -l appends newline after ""
22  }
```

In Lines 4–5, the back quotes of command interpolation are used around each tput command to capture its output for assignment to a variable. Then those variables are used to render psh's prompt in reverse video (Line 6), to make it stand out (see figure 8.7).

Line 7 issues the first prompt. Then, for each line of input the user provides, eval compiles and executes it (Line 10). If necessary, a diagnostic message is printed on Line 12.

The prompt for the next input is then issued (Line 14), and the cycle of reading and evaluating input continues until <^D>—or an input consisting of exit—requests termination. For the exit case, the user-supplied <ENTER> serves to position the

---

[23] In contrast, the somewhat similar Perl debugger (invoked via -d) has some very non-Perlish properties, which—unlike psh—may require you to stop thinking Perlishly when you use it! For this reason, I prefer to debug most problems using print statements for information gathering (as Larry does)— with an occasional dash of psh.

Shell's upcoming prompt on a fresh line of the terminal, but with <^D>, the program must supply a newline on its own. That's handled on Line 21, where the programmer saved some typing by exploiting the fact that $_ is the default argument for defined.

And now, without further ado, it's time to reveal our much-ballyhooed comprehensive Perl grepper—which sports a name worthy of an *obstetrician's pet ferret*.

8.7.2 Appreciating a multi-faceted Perl grepper: The `preg` script

There's no getting around the fact that grep is one of the most important and popular Unix utilities, despite its limitations. That's why we've discussed so many Perl programs that behave like grep or one of its cousins, fgrep and egrep.

But do we really need to carry all of greperl, text_grep, perlgrep, and rgrep around in our toolkits?[24] That's too much of a good thing. Wouldn't it be better to have a single script that could provide the services of any of those specialized versions through options? It sure would, but there's a reason you haven't seen that script thus far—eval is needed to make it work.

preg, short for "Perlish relative of enhanced grep", is a veritable "Swiss Army knife" of Perl greppers compared to what you've seen thus far. It supports the following options, each of which enables a special kind of grep-like (or grep-*eclipsing*) functionality:

-f:	**f**grep style; disable metacharacters in the pattern.
-i:	**I**gnore case differences.
-l:	**L**ist filenames that have matches (not their matching records).
-v:	Only show records that don't contain matches.
-n:	Prepend record **n**umbers to the records that are shown.
-d:	**D**isplay matches within their records using screen's standout mode.
-p:	**P**aragraph mode; use blank lines as record separators.
-c='*S*':	**C**ustom delimiter mode; use string *S* as a record separator.
-m:	**M**ulti-line mode; ^ and $ match ends of lines, not ends of record (used with –p or –c).
-s:	**S**ingle-line mode; "." matches newline.
-r:	**R**ecursive search; descend into arguments that are directories.

Here are some sample runs, matching against a short version of the UNIX "fortune cookie" file, to give you an idea of preg's versatility:

---

[24] Respectively covered in sections 3.13.2, 6.4.1, 8.2.1, and 8.5.2.

```
$ preg -l        'eve'        fortunes    # just list filename
fortunes

$ preg           'eve'        fortunes    # show matching record
Eagles may soar, but weasels never get sucked into jet engines.

$ preg -d        'eve'        fortunes    # display match in record
Eagles may soar, but weasels never get sucked into jet engines.

$ preg -p -d     'for.*the'   fortunes    # paragraph mode; no match

$ preg -p -d -s  'for.*the'   fortunes    # now . can match newline
The problem's solution is trivial and is left as an exercise for
the reader.

$ preg -p -d -m  '^t\w+'      fortunes    # display initial t-words
The solution of this problem is trivial and left as an exercise for
the reader.

$ preg -r -i '\bWaldo\b|\bGodot\b' testing   # search directories
testing/waiting_place:Mr. Godot ain't here yet!
testing/hiding-place:waldo is virtually invisible.
```

The output of the last command indicates that Waldo and also Godot (no relation to
http://godot.com) were found in the indicated files that reside under the directory
testing.[25]

Now it's time to ogle the code! The script is shown in listing 8.7.

Listing 8.7 The preg script

```
1   #! /usr/bin/perl -s -wnl
2   our ($f, $i, $l, $v, $n, $d, $p, $m, $s, $r); # switch vars
3
4   BEGIN {
5     $Usage="Usage: $0 [-f] [-i] [-l] [-v] [-n] [-d]";
6     $Usage.=" [-p|-c] [-m] [-s] [-r] 'RE' [file...]\n";
7
      # Must at least have pattern argument
9     @ARGV > 0  or  warn "$Usage"  and  exit 255;
10
11    # Can't have mutually-exclusive switches
12    defined $p  and  defined $c  and
13      warn "$Usage\n\tCan't have -p and -c\n"  and  exit 1;
14
15    $X='g';           # set modifier to perform all substitutions
16    $ON=$OFF="";       # by default, don't highlight matches
17
18    if ($d) {          # for match-displaying with -d
19      $ON=(`tput smso`  or  ""); $OFF=(`tput rmso`  or  "");
```

---

[25] See sections 3.2.3 and 3.3.1 for information on what various grep commands do when given directory
arguments.

```
20    };
21
22    $p  and  $/="";      # paragraph mode
23    $c  and  $/=$c;      # custom record separator mode
24    $i  and  $X.='i';    # ignore case; add to modifiers in $X
25    $m  and  $X.='m';    # multi-line mode
26    $s  and  $X.='s';    # single-line mode
27
28    $pattern=shift @ARGV;            # remaining args are filenames
29    $f  and  $pattern='\Q' . $pattern . '\E'; # "quote" metachars
30
31    $r  and  @ARGV=grep { chomp; -T }
32      `find @ARGV -follow -type f -print`;
33    $multifiles=@ARGV > 1;    # controls "filenames:match" format
34
35    $matcher="s/$pattern/$ON\$&$OFF/$X";
36    $v  and  $matcher="! $matcher";     # complement match result
37  }
38  #####  BODY OF PROGRAM, EXECUTED FOR EACH LINE OF INPUT  #####
39  $found_match=eval $matcher;       # run sub-op, to try for match
40  if ( $@ ne "" ) {                 # show eval's error
41    warn "\n$0: Eval failed for pattern: '$matcher'\n\n";
42    die  "Perl says:\n$@\n";
43  }
44  elsif ( $found_match ) {
45    if ($l) { print $ARGV; close ARGV; }        # print filename\n
46    elsif  ($multifiles) { printf "$ARGV:"; } # print filename:
47    if (! $l){                      # don't show match if listing filenames
48      $n  and  printf "$.:";  # prepend line number to record
49      print;                        # show selected record
50      $p  and  print "";      # separate paragraphs by blank line
51    }
52  }
```

The shebang line includes the s option for automatic switch processing, which is used heavily in this script—so it begins by calling our on all the variables corresponding to its optional switches.

In the BEGIN block, the $Usage variable is constructed in two steps to keep the lines short, with the help of the compound-assignment version of the concatenation operator.

Like grep, this script requires at least a "pattern" argument, so it issues a warning and exits on Line 9 if it's missing. In similar fashion, Line 12 checks for an attempt to simultaneously use mutually exclusive switches, and exits the script if appropriate.

Line 15 initializes the variable that holds the match modifiers with the g (for /g) that is the script's default, in preparation for other modifiers being appended to it later.

If the match-displaying switch was chosen, the screen-highlighting variables initialized to null strings in Line 16 are overwritten in Line 19 with the appropriate terminal escape sequences (see section 8.5.1 for details on `tput`).

Lines 22–26 check for switches, and set their associated variables as needed.

Line 28 extracts the pattern argument from `@ARGV`, leaving only filenames as its contents (or nothing at all, to obtain input from STDIN).

If the `-f` (fixed-string, like `fgrep`) switch was chosen, the next line places `$pattern` between `\Q` and `\E` metacharacters, to render any metacharacters within it as literal. The concatenation operator is a good choice here, because the double-quoted alternative is more error prone, requiring doubled-backslashes to get single ones into the variable:

```
$pattern="\\Q$pattern\\E";                 # stores: \Q ... \E
```

If the "recursive" switch was used, Line 32 uses `find`[26] to convert any arguments that are directories into a list of the regular files residing within or below them, while preserving any arguments that are regular files. Then `grep` extracts the text-files from that list (Line 31) and stores the results back in `@ARGV`.

For example, given initial arguments of

```
/home/plankton
```

and

```
/tmp/neptunes_crown.txt
```

the final contents of `@ARGV` might become

```
/home/plankton/todo_list.doc
```

and

```
/home/plankton/world_domination_plan.stw
```

along with the originally specified

```
/tmp/neptunes_crown.txt
```

Line 33 sets a variable to True or False according to the number of filenames to be searched, so that `grep`'s functionality of prepending filenames to matched records can be conditionally provided in Line 46.

Line 35 assembles the text of the expression that will do the matching. A substitution operator is used, because matching-plus-replacement is required to support the "display matches" feature of the `-d` switch, and it can also handle the other cases.

---

[26] The use of command interpolation to provide arguments to a script, as in `script `find ...``, is subject in extreme cases to buffer-overflow problems requiring an `xargs`-style remedy (as discussed in section 6.5). However, in this case, the output of `find` is delivered to the already-running process through other channels, so these concerns don't apply.

For example, with -d, the substitution operator replaces the match by the values of ON&$OFF to highlight the match; without -d, it replaces the match by itself ($&), because $ON and $OFF have null values in that case. Either way, the substitution operator returns a True/False value on Line 39 to indicate the success or failure of the substitution (and, by extension, the match), and that's used to control the reporting of results (on Line 44).

Back in Line 35, the backslashing of the $& variable's dollar symbol delays the variable's expansion until the matching text has been stored within $&, which happens during the eval on Line 39. In contrast, the values of the $pattern, $ON, $OFF, and $X variables are immediately placed into the string on Line 35, because they're already available and won't change during execution. Also notice that the contents of $X are appended after the substitution operator's closing delimiter, which is how the script communicates the user's choices for match modifiers to that operator.

Line 36 prepends the complementing operator (!) to the contents of $matcher, if the (grep-like) -v switch for displaying non-matching lines was supplied.

And that's the end of the BEGIN block! Now all that remains to be done is—the real work of the program.

On Line 39, our old friend eval is used to evaluate the string representing a substitution operator that's stored in $matcher. This is required because it includes tokens that can only be recognized as having special meanings at compile-time. The substitution operator returns the number of substitutions it performed, which equals the number of matches it found, and eval assigns that value to $found_match. This allows the code block following elsif ($found_match) on Line 44 to be executed only if a match is found.

But first, Line 40 checks whether eval had problems with the $matcher code. If it did, the offending code is displayed, along with Perl's diagnostic message. This situation shouldn't arise as long as the user provides a syntactically correct pattern and the script assembles the substitution operator properly, but to make sure the diagnostic message doesn't go unnoticed, die terminates the script after printing the message found in $@.

If a match was found, the conditional statements starting on Line 44 are evaluated next; if not, the next input record is fetched, and the processing cycle continues from Line 39.

On Line 45, if the "filename listings" switch was provided, the filename (only) for the matched record is printed. As with grep's -l option, the filename should only be printed once, no matter how many matches it might contain. This means there's no point in looking for additional matches after finding this first one, so the current filehandle is closed, which triggers the opening of the next file named in @ARGV (if any; see section 3.8).

Line 46 checks whether multiple files are to be searched; if so, it prints the matched record's filename followed by a colon (just as grep does), with no following newline (thanks to printf).

Line 47 ensures that "filename listing" mode isn't in effect, because if it is, all the output for the current match is already on the screen. Then, if the user asked for line numbers, the current record's number is printed using `printf`. The matched record itself is then printed, on the same physical line to which the `printf` on Line 46 may have already made a contribution.

If paragraph mode is in effect, Line 50 prints a blank line to provide separation between this record and the next.

It may all sound rather complicated when scrutinized at this level, but don't lose sight of how straightforward the processing is in the simplest situation, when there are no switches and only one input file. In that case, after finding a True result on Line 44, Line 49 prints the record. Then, the next input record is fetched, and the cycle continues from Line 39.

I use this multi-faceted, Perlishly enhanced grepper all the time, and I trust you'll find it as useful as I do. But you need to be aware of a few gotchas, which are covered next.

Tips on using `preg`

Consider this attempt to run `preg` with an improperly constructed pattern argument, and the associated diagnostic message:

```
$ ps auxw | preg '?'                        # syntax error; ? needs \
preg: Eval failed; sub-op is: 's/?/$&/g'

Perl says:
Quantifier follows nothing in regex; marked by
    <-- HERE in m/? <-- HERE / at (eval 1) line 1, <> line 1.
```

What's happening? Well, when `eval` fails while compiling and/or running the code it was given, `preg` displays the text of the substitution operator (sub-op) it constructed, because that's where the error has got to be. `preg` also shows Perl's diagnostic message, and, as you can see, the `<--HERE` pointer makes it abundantly clear that the quantifier metacharacter "?" caused the trouble. Why? Because when it appears in the substitution operator's regex field, it's supposed to be preceded by the element whose quantity it's specifying—but it wasn't.[27]

To fix the problem, you can either backslash the "?" to remove its special meaning as a quantifier or use the `-f` switch, which enables `fgrep`-like automatic quoting of all metacharacters:

```
$ ps auxw | preg -f '?' # show terminal-less processes; edited
root      1  0.0  0.0    448   64 ? S     Dec08  0:04 init
root    411  0.0  0.0   1356  220 ? S     Dec08  0:09 /sbin/syslogd
bin     586  0.0  0.0   1292    0 ? SW    Dec08  0:00 /sbin/portmap
root    795  0.0  0.0   1416  128 ? S     Dec08  0:00 /usr/sbin/cron
...
```

---

[27] For example, _X_? would allow 0 or 1 occurrences of _X_; see table 3.9 for details.

The command shows reports on processes that are not attached to terminals, as indicated by the "?" character in the seventh field.

One more word of caution on using preg: If your pattern includes a slash character, you'll have to backslash it, even when using the -f switch, because preg uses that character as the delimiter for the substitution operator itself:

```
preg -f 'TCP/IP?'      # WRONG!
preg -f 'TCP\/IP?'     # Right.
```

Now you're ready to use this powerful and OS-portable grepper, in place of: grep, fgrep, egrep, rgrep, text_grep, greperl, and perlgrep[28]!

8.8   SUMMARY

Perl provides a variety of tools that are principally used in the kinds of programs that are sufficiently large to be worth storing in a file, which we call *scripts*.

You saw how defined is used to test for the mere existence of a value, independently of its True/False status. As a general rule, you should always use defined to ensure that a variable that might be unset actually has a value, before you attempt to use that value. We reviewed examples showing how defined is used with other operators in validating arguments (e.g., as readable text files) and in proofreading interactive input from users (e.g., as a confirming "Yes").

We discussed how non-filenames—such as a *pattern*—can coexist with filenames in a script's argument list, as long as the non-filenames are removed from @ARGV by shift in a BEGIN block. An advantage of Perl's shift over the Shell's is that it returns the value being removed from the array, making it easy to preserve that value for later access.

You also learned how to *pre-process* script arguments in various ways, such as using grep to filter out the ones that have the wrong properties, and using sort to reorder them. The *generation* of filename arguments, by using the globbing operator in a BEGIN block, was also illustrated.

Perl's exit does the same basic job as the Shell's, but it differs by returning the "success" code of 0 by default.[29]

Perl's die function, which is like warn *'message'* coupled with exit 255, provides an alternative to exit for terminating a script. In cases where a custom exit code is desired, you can set "$!" to the required number before calling die, to override the default of 255.

---

[28] You can download this script, along with the others featured in this book, at this web site: http://manning.com/maher.

[29] This is appropriate because, IMHO, Perl—as a better-designed, easier-to-use, harder-to-abuse, and more DWIM*errific* language than the Shell—has more reason to be optimistic about its scripts completing successfully than the Shell does!

We showed the limitations of the logical and/or for controlling non-trivial conditional execution requirements, and how to control multi-way branching in such cases by using if/else instead. The cd_report script demonstrated the use of if/else to handle a program's large-scale branching needs, while using and/or to construct compound tests, so that the unique benefits of each facility could be realized.

The string-concatenation operator comes in handy for joining short strings into longer ones, which can make programs easier to read and maintain. It's also used to store newly acquired data after existing data, by appending to the contents of a variable. We demonstrated that technique in an upgrade to most_recent_file, which allows it to properly handle files whose modification times are tied.

You learned about a special benefit of the compound-assignment form of the concatenation operator—it allows the statements that were used to build up the contents of a variable to be easily reordered, if desired, to change the order in which the substrings are loaded. This capability was exploited in the example that promises to help web surfers MAKE MONEY FA$T.

You can easily live without the string-repetition operator, but only if you're willing to do a lot of unnecessary typing to do so. It specializes in replicating strings, and you saw it used to construct a string consisting of a series of dashes, which was displayed across the width of a terminal.

Command interpolation and system are valuable tools that let Perl run commands provided by the host OS. You saw how judicious use of these tools obviates the need to re-invent the functionality of existing OS resources, at the expense of reducing a program's portability to other OSs. Command interpolation is used when a Perl script needs to capture an OS-command's output so it can be manipulated in some way. In contrast, system is used when it's sufficient merely to run the command without any access to its output.

A Unix command that's especially useful for scripts running on terminals is tput, which—by making it easy to control display modes such as reverse video, underline, and bold—can really spruce up an otherwise drab display of characters on the screen. tput can also report the terminal's current height and width, which is valuable information for scripts running in re-sizable windows. This capability was used by news_flash to draw full-width lines across windows having uncertain dimensions.

During our examination of news_flash2, we discussed the Shell's execution-trace mode, which shows exactly what each command looks like before it's executed. You saw how enabling this facility in a Perl script can help debug mysterious problems with commands run by system.

Like its Shell namesake, Perl's eval function is a powerful utility for compiling and executing code that's acquired or manufactured during a script's own execution. Through use of eval, programs can be endowed with advanced capabilities—as illustrated by psh, the Perl shell, and preg, a multi-faceted Perl grepper. Keep psh in mind during your further adventures with Perl, because it will come in handy when you want to quickly try out some Perl code—*without* the bother of first creating a script to do so.

Directions for further study

To obtain information about specific Perl functions covered in this chapter, such as `defined`, `exit`, `shift`, or `system`, you can either browse through the output of `man perlfunc` (not recommended) or use `perldoc` to zero in on the documentation for each specific function:

- `perldoc -f` *function-name* `# coverage of "function-name"`

For additional information on other topics covered here, you may wish to access these online resources:

- `man perlop`   `# operators, and command interpolation`
- `man perlsyn`   `# basic syntax, including if/else`
- `man tput`   `# command that retrieves terminal information`
- `man Term::ANSIColor` `# module for coloring terminal text`

C H A P T E R   9

List variables

9.1   Using array variables 296
9.2   Using hash variables 308
9.3   Comparing list generators in the Shell and Perl 325
9.4   Summary 328

By this point, you've learned how to use Perl's most important built-in functions and the special techniques employed in scripts. So you're nearly ready to start slinging around huge quantities of data and wrangling their values until you get what you're after—like a professional data munger!

But first, you need to learn how to classify, store, and retrieve those copious amounts of data. This brings us to the topic of *list variables*.

The main property that distinguishes list variables from the scalar variables we've already discussed is how many distinct items of data each can hold. The limit for a scalar variable is one, but a list variable can hold many thousands of items, each of which is—guess what?—a scalar value.

> **NOTE**   The essential job of a list variable is to provide each of the elements in a data collection with a private cubbyhole having its own address.

List variables come in two types, distinguished by their characteristic symbols. We've already discussed *array variables*, such as @F and @ARGV, and we'll discuss *hash variables*, such as %ENV, later in this chapter.

List variables are important because they let you easily manage a collection of data elements as a whole, while still allowing you to process them one at a time when you please.[1]

In addition to variables of the array and hash types, lists also appear in other forms in Perl. One important form is what we call an *explicit list*, which consists of one or more items appearing within parentheses:

```
($pizza_size, $crust_type )=@F;
```

Does that look familiar? That's the syntax introduced in chapter 5 for initializing a list of scalar variables with values from the field array (@F), which is automatically loaded with the fields of the current record when the n and a options are used. The statement shown causes the first value in the array to be copied into the scalar variable $pizza_size and the second to be copied into $crust_type.

Another variation puts the explicit list on the other side of the assignment, to initialize the array with the indicated values:

```
@drink_order=( $flavor, $packaging );
```

Literal strings could also be assigned, instead of values taken from variables:

```
@drink_order=( 'ginseng', 'carry-out' );
```

The special property of a hash (known as an *associative array* in AWK) is that it associates a *key* with each stored value, rather than an integer number (0, 1, etc.) as an array does. You can use this property to make programs more readable and manageable, as shown in this hash-based version of the earlier array example:

```
%drink_order=(flavor => 'ginseng', packaging => 'carry-out');
```

Note the use of the special arrow operator (=>), which links each key with its associated value.

Now that you've had a taste of what's in store, we'll look more closely at how arrays and hashes work in Perl and see representative examples of their many uses. For example, you'll see a program that tabulates word frequencies for web pages like popular search engines do, another that generates reports from simple databases, and even a program that retrieves random quotes from the classic *Star Trek* series.

We'll begin by exploring array variables, which you already know something about, in greater detail.

9.1 USING ARRAY VARIABLES

The array is the classic data structure for storing separate but related pieces of information in a single named variable. The distinctive properties of an array are that its

---

[1] With a little help from other language features, such as the *loops* discussed in chapter 10.

values are maintained in a particular order, and they're associated with integer indices ranging from 0 to *N*-1 (where *N* is the number of array elements).

Consider this assignment statement:

```
@stooges=( 'Larry', 'Moe', 'Curly' );
```

It loads the names in order, causing them to be stored under the indices 0 to 2, as indicated in table 9.1.

Table 9.1   Indices and values for the @stooges array

@stooges	
Index	**Value**
0	Larry
1	Moe
2	Curly

Array names can be fashioned from any combination of letters, digits, and underscores, but a digit can't come immediately after the @ symbol. That's why this array is called @stooges rather than the more obvious (but disallowed) @3stooges.

You can retrieve the complete set of an array's values by using its name in a list context or in a double-quoted string. Here's an example of the latter case, which makes use of the fact that the values of an array whose name appears within double quotes are separated by the space character (by default):

print "@stooges";

```
Larry Moe Curly
```

When you need to extract an individual value from an array, indexing into it with a subscript is the most direct approach. Doing so requires the use of the $ symbol in place of @ (because an individual value of an array is a *scalar* data type) and square brackets around the index:

print "Who'd have thunk it? $stooges[1] hit $stooges[0] again!";

```
Who'd have thunk it? Moe hit Larry again!
```

Table 9.2 contrasts the Shell and Perl ways of initializing arrays and retrieving values from them.

The major syntactic differences between the languages in array usage are these:

- In Perl, curly braces aren't used around an array name and its subscript.
- Perl normally requires commas between array initializers, rather than whitespace alone.
- Perl only uses the $ symbol before an array's name when it's being subscripted with a single index—otherwise, @ is used.

Table 9.2   Syntax for using arrays in the Shell and Perl

	Shell	Perl [a]	Remarks
Assigning a value	`n[0]=13`	`$n[0]=13;`	In Perl, the $ symbol is always used with the variable name when referring to a scalar value. With the Shell, it's only used when retrieving a value.
Retrieving and displaying a value	`echo ${n[0]}`	`print $n[0];`	The Shell requires the array name and index to be enclosed in curly braces.
Deleting a value	`unset n[0]`	`delete $n[0];`	The Shell deletes the designated element, but Perl maintains the element's slot after marking its value as undefined.

Assigning multiple values	`n=(13 42)`	`@n=(13, 42);`
		
		`@n=qw/13 42/;`
		`@n=qw!\ | /!;`
			The Shell recognizes whitespace as separators in the parenthesized list of initializers. By default, Perl requires a comma, and allows additional whitespace. With the qw**X** syntax, *only* whitespace separators are recognized between paired occurrences of the **X** delimiter.[b]

Retrieving and displaying all values	`echo "${n[@]}"`	`print "@n";`	See text for explanation.

a. The examples using `print` assume the use of Perl's `l` invocation option.
b. Examples of the qw*X* quoting syntax are shown in chapter 12.

As shown in the table's last row, the Shell uses the special @ index to retrieve all values, preserve any whitespace within them, and separate them from each other by a space. As usual, double quotes are also required if further processing of the extracted values isn't desired.

With Perl, on the other hand, all values are retrieved by using the array name *without* an index. The only effect of the double quotes is to separate the values on output with the contents of the '$ "' variable—they're not needed to suppress further processing of the extracted values, because that doesn't happen anyway.[2]

Next, we'll look at different ways to initialize arrays.

---

[2] See http://TeachMePerl.com/DQs_in_shell_vs_perl.html for details on the comparative use of double quotes in the two languages.

9.1.1 Initializing arrays with piecemeal assignments and `push`

As shown in the top row of table 9.2, you can initialize arrays in *piecemeal* fashion:

```
$stooges[2]='Curly';
$stooges[0]='Moe';
$stooges[1]='Larry';
```

Alternatively, you can use explicit lists on both sides of the assignment operator:

```
($stooges[2], $stooges[0], $stooges[1])=('Curly', 'Moe', 'Larry');
```

When it's acceptable to add new elements to the end of an array, you can avoid managing an array index by using `push @`*arrayname, 'new value'*. This technique is used in the `shell_types` script, which categorizes Unix accounts into those having human-usable shells (such as `/usr/bin/ksh`) or "inhuman" shells (such as `/sbin/shutdown`):

```
$ shell_types | fmt -68     # format to fit on screen
```

THESE ACCOUNTS USE HUMAN SHELLS: root, bin, daemon, lp, games, wwwrun, named, nobody, ftp, man, news, uucp, at, tim, yeshe, info, contix, linux, spug, mailman, snort, stu01

THESE ACCOUNTS USE INHUMAN SHELLS: mail, sshd, postfix, ntp, vscan

Because the listing of "human" account names produces a very long line, the Unix `fmt` command is used to reformat the text to fit within the width of the screen.

The script's shebang line (see listing 9.1) arranges for input lines to be automatically split into fields on the basis of individual colons, because that's the field separator used in the `/etc/passwd` file, which associates shells with user accounts.

The matching operator on Line 8 checks the last field of each line for the pattern characteristic of "human" shells and stores the associated account names in `@human` using `push`. Alternatively, Line 12 arranges for the names of the accounts that fail the test to be stored in `@inhuman`.

Listing 9.1 The `shell_types` script

```
1   #! /usr/bin/perl -wnlaF':'
2
3   BEGIN {
4       @ARGV=( '/etc/passwd' );          # Specify input file
5   }
6
7   # Separate users of "human" oriented shells from others
8   if ( $F[-1] =~ /sh$/ ) {
9       push    @human, $F[0];
10  }
11  else {
12      push    @inhuman, $F[0];
13  }
```

```
14   END {
15       $"=', ';
16       print "\UThese accounts use human shells: \E\n@human\n";
17       print "\UThese accounts use inhuman shells:\E\n@inhuman";
18   }
```

To make the output more presentable, Line 15 sets the '$"' variable to a comma-space sequence, and \U is used to convert the output headings to uppercase.

In programs like this, where you don't care what position a data element is allocated in the array, it's more convenient to push them onto the array's end than to manage an index. In other cases, it may be more appropriate to do piecemeal array-initializations using indexing (see, e.g., section 10.5), to maintain control over where an element is stored.

Next, we'll look at the syntax and rules for using more advanced indexing techniques.

9.1.2   Understanding advanced array indexing

Table 9.3 shows the association between array values and indices of both the positive and *negative* varieties, both of which are usable in Perl. Negative indexing counts backward from the end of the array and is most commonly used to access an array's last element. Another way to do that is by using an array's *maximum index variable*, whose name is $#*arrayname*.

Table 9.3   Syntax for advanced array indexing

Initialization	@X=('A',	'B',	'C',	'D');
Stored value	A	B	C	D
Ordinal Position	1	2	3	4
Positive indexing	$X[0]	$X[1]	$X[2]	$X[3]
Negative indexing	$X[-4]	$X[-3]	$X[-2]	$X[-1]
Indexing with maximum-index variable				$X[$#X]
Result	A	B	C	D
Slice indexing	@X[2,3]		"@X[2,0..1]"	@X[3,0..2]
Result	CD		C A B	DABC

As an alternative to repeatedly indexing into an array to access several values, Perl allows a collection of values—called an *array slice*[3]—to be addressed in one indexing expression (as shown in the table's bottom panel). You do this by arranging the comma-separated indices within square brackets in the order desired for retrieval (or assignment) and putting @*arrayname* before that expression. The @ symbol is used rather than $, because multiple indices extract a list of values, not a single scalar value.

You can also specify a *range* of consecutive indices by placing the range operator (..) between the end points, allowing the use of 3..5, for instance, as a shortcut for 3, 4, 5.

The following Perl command retrieves multiple values from an array using a slice:

```
$ cat newage_contacts   # field number exceeds index by 1
(510)   246-7890   sadhu3@nirvana.org
(225)   424-4242   guru@enlighten.com
(928)   312-5789   shaman@healing.net
 1/0       2/1          3/2          ⏎   Field numbers / indices

$ perl -wnla -e 'print "@F[2,0,1]";' newage_contacts
sadhu3@nirvana.org (510) 246-7890
guru@enlighten.com (225) 424-4242
shaman@healing.net (928) 312-5789
```

We could have written the Perl command without using an array slice, by typing print "$F[2] $F[0] $F[1]" in place of print "@F[2,0,1]". But that involves a lot of extra typing, so it's not Lazy enough!

Because each array slice is itself a list, you can set the '$"' formatting variable to insert a custom separator between the list elements:

```
$  perl -wnla -e '$"=":⌴\t"; print "@F[0,2]";' newage_contacts
(510):⌴sadhu3@nirvana.org
(225):⌴guru@enlighten.com
(928):⌴shaman@healing.net
```

We'll continue with this theme of finding friendlier ways to write array-indexing expressions in the next section, where you'll see how a script that lets the user think like a human makes access to fields a lot easier.

9.1.3   Extracting fields in a friendlier fashion

Sooner or later, every Perl programmer makes the mistake of attempting to use 1 as the index to extract the first value from an array—rather than 0—because humans naturally count from 1. But with a little creative coding, you can indulge this tendency.

---

[3] The indexed elements needn't be adjacent, and subsequent slices needn't run parallel to earlier ones (as with *bread* slices), so a better name for this feature might be an *index group*.

As a case in point, the show_fields2 script allows the user to select fields for display using human-oriented numbers, which start from 1:

```
$ cat zappa_floyd
Weasels Ripped my Flesh Frank Zappa
Dark Side of the Moon    Pink Floyd

$ show_fields2 '1' zappa_floyd        # 1 means first field
Weasels
Dark
```

It works by using unshift (introduced in table 8.2) to prepend a new value to the array, which shifts the existing values rightward. As a result, the value originally stored under the index of *N* gets moved to *N*+1.

As depicted in Figure 9.1, if 0 was the original index for the value A, after unshift prepends one new item, A would then be found under 1.

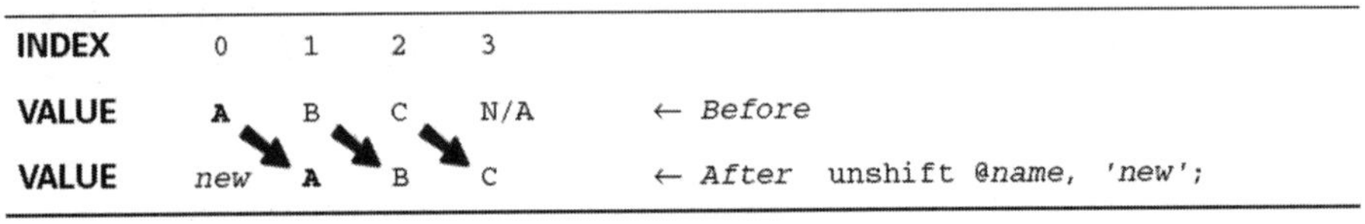

Figure 9.1 Effect of unshift

The show_fields2 script also supports index ranges and array slices:

```
$ cat zappa_floyd    # field numbers added
Weasels Ripped my Flesh Frank Zappa
   1       2    3    4    5     6
Dark Side of the Moon    Pink Floyd
  1   2   3   4    5      6     7

$ cat zappa_floyd | show_fields2 '2..4,1'    # indices 1..3,0
Ripped my Flesh Weasels
Side of the Dark
```

It even issues a warning if the user attempts to access (the illegitimate) field 0:

```
$ show_fields2 '0' zappa_floyd        # WRONG!
Usage: show_fields2 '2,1,4..7, etc.' [ file1 ... ]
       There's no field #0! The first is #1.
```

The show_fields2 script, which uses several advanced array-handling techniques, is shown in listing 9.2.

Line 7 pulls the argument containing the field specifications out of @ARGV and saves it in the $fields variable. Then, a matching operator is used to ask whether

`$fields` contains only the permitted characters: digits, commas, and periods.[4] If the answer is "no," the program terminates on Line 11 after showing the usage message.

```
1    #! /usr/bin/perl -wnla
2
3    BEGIN {
4        $Usage="Usage: $0 '2,1,4..7, etc.' [ file1 ... ]";
5        # Order of field numbers dictates print order;
6        #   the first field is specified as 1
7        $fields=shift;
8
9        # Proofread field specifications
10       defined $fields  and   $fields =~ /^[\d,.]+$/g  or
11           warn "$Usage\n"  and  exit 1;
12
13       # Convert 5,2..4 => 5,2,3,4
14       #   and load those index numbers into @fields
15       @fields=eval " ( $fields ) ";
16   }
17
18   if (@F > 0) {    # only process lines that have fields
19       # Load warning message into 0th slot, to flag errors
20       unshift @F,
21           "$Usage\n\tThere's no field #0! The first is #1.\n";
22       print "@F[ @fields ]";  # DQs yield space-separated values
23   }
```

The next step is to turn the user's field specification into one that Perl can understand, which requires some special processing. The easy part is arranging for the request for field 1 to produce the value for the element having index 0. This is accomplished (on Line 20) by using `unshift` to shift the original values one position rightward within the array. A combined usage and warning message is then placed in the freshly vacated first position so that the program automatically prints a warning if the user requests the (illegitimate) field #0.

Now for the tricky part. In Line 15, the user's field specification—for instance `1,3..5`—needs to be converted into the corresponding list—in this case `(1,3,4,5)`. You may think that placing `$fields` into an explicit list and assigning the result to an array would do the trick, using `@fields=( $fields )`, but it doesn't. The reason is that commas and double-dots arising from variable interpolation are treated as literal characters, rather than being recognized as the comma operator and the range operator.

---

[4] The "." becomes a literal character within square brackets, like most metacharacters (see chapter 3).

Accordingly, after the variable interpolation permitted by the surrounding double quotes in Line 15 yields the contents of $fields, the expression (1,3..5) must be processed by eval—to allow recognition of "`..`" as the range operator and the comma as the list-element separator.[5] The end result is exactly as if @fields=(1,3..5) had appeared on Line 15 in the first place,[6] resulting in the assignment of the desired index numbers to the @fields array.

Line 18 checks the field count, to exempt empty lines from the processing that follows. As mentioned earlier, unshift loads a special message into the now illegitimate 0th position of the array; then, the contents of the @fields array are inserted into the subscripting expression for use as indices, to pull out the desired values for printing.

Having just seen a demonstration of how to carefully control indexing so that the *wrong* number can produce the *right* result, we'll next throw caution to the wind, forsake all control over indexing, and see what fortune has in store for those who *randomly* access arrays.

9.1.4   Telling fortunes: The `fcookie` script

In the early days of UNIX we were easily entertained, which was good because the multi-media capabilities of the computers of that era were quite rudimentary. As a case in point, I remember being called over one December day by a beaming system administrator to gawk in amazement with my colleagues at a long sheet of paper taped to the wall. It was a fan-fold printout of a Christmas tree, with slashes and backslashes representing the needles and pound signs representing ornaments. Shortly after this milestone in the development of ASCII art was achieved, "comedy" arrived on our computers in the form of a command called fortune, which displayed a humorous message like you might find in a verbose fortune cookie.

We'll pay homage to that comedic technological breakthrough by seeing how Perl scripts can be used not only to emulate the behavior of the fortune program, but also to do its job even better.

But before we can use them for our script, we need to understand how fortunes are stored in their data files. Let's examine a file devoted to Star Trek quips:

```
$ head -7 /usr/share/fortune/startrek
A father doesn't destroy his children.
              -- Lt. Carolyn Palamas, "Who Mourns for Adonais?",
                 stardate 3468.1.
%
```

---

[5] eval evaluates code starting with the compilation phase, allowing it to detect special tokens that cannot otherwise be recognized during a program's execution (see section 8.7).

[6] Allowing a user to effectively paste source code into an eval'd statement could lead to abuses, although the argument validation performed on Line 10 of show_fields2 is a good initial safeguard. For more on Perl security, including Perl's remarkable *taint-checking* mode, see man perlsec.

```
A little suffering is good for the soul.
            -- Kirk, "The Corbomite Maneuver", stardate 1514.0
%
...
```

As you can see, each fortune's record is terminated by a line containing only a % symbol. Armed with this knowledge, it's easy to write a script that loads each fortune into an array and then displays a randomly selected one on the screen (see listing 9.3).

Using the implicit loop, the script reads one record ending in % at a time, as instructed by the setting of the $/ variable, and installs it in the @fortunes array. A suitable array index for each record could be derived from the record number variable ($.), as shown in the commented-out Line 8, but it's easier to use push (Line 9) to build up the array. Then, a random array element is selected for printing, using the standard technique of providing rand with the array's number of elements as its argument (see table 7.7), and using its returned value as the index.

Listing 9.3   The fcookie script

```
1   #! /usr/bin/perl -wnl
2
3   BEGIN {
4       @ARGV=( '/usr/share/fortune/startrek' );
5       $/='%';      # set input record separator for "fortune" files
6   }
7
8   # $fortunes[$. -1]=$_;   # store fortune in (record-number -1)
9   push @fortunes, $_;      # easier way
10
11  END {
12      print $fortunes[ rand @fortunes ];    # print random fortune
13  }
```

Here are some test runs:

```
$ fcookie
A man will tell his bartender things he'll never tell his doctor.
            -- Dr. Phillip Boyce, "The Menagerie", stardate unknown
```

```
$ fcookie
It is a human characteristic to love little animals, especially if
they're attractive in some way.
            -- McCoy, "The Trouble with Tribbles", stardate 4525.6
```

Yep, that's space-grade profundity all right. But I crave more! And I don't want to reissue the command every time I want to see another fortune—nor do I want to see any *reruns*.

These problems will be solved in the next episode.

fcookie2: *The sequel*

fcookie2 is an enhancement that responds to the newfound needs of the increasingly demanding user community (consisting of me, at least). It illustrates the use of a *dual input-mode* technique that first reads fortunes from a file and stores them in an array, and then takes each <ENTER> from the keyboard as a request to print another randomly selected fortune.

Here's a test run that uses the Unix yes command to feed the script lots of y<ENTER> inputs, simulating the key presses of an inexhaustible fortune seeker:

```
$ yes | fcookie2
Press <ENTER> for a fortune, or <^D>:
There is a multi-legged creature crawling on your shoulder.
        -- Spock, "A Taste of Armageddon", stardate 3193.9
...
Vulcans never bluff.
        -- Spock, "The Doomsday Machine", stardate 4202.1
...


fcookie2: How unfortunate; out of fortunes!
```

You can do a "full sensor scan" of the script in listing 9.4.

Listing 9.4 The fcookie2 script

```perl
 1  #! /usr/bin/perl -wnl
 2  # Interactive fortune-cookie displayer, with no repeats
 3
 4  BEGIN {
 5      @ARGV  or  # provide default fortune file
 6          @ARGV=( '/usr/share/fortune/startrek' );
 7      push @ARGV, '-';  # Read STDIN next, for interactive mode
 8      $/='%';            # Set input record separator for fortunes
 9      $initializing=1;  # Start in "initializing the array" mode
10  }
11          ############ Load Fortunes into Array ############
12  if ($initializing) {
13      push @fortunes, $_;          # add next fortune to list
14      if (eof) {     # on end-of-file, switch to input from STDIN
15          $initializing=0;     # signify end of initializing mode
16          $/="\n";       # set input record separator for keyboard
17          printf 'Press <ENTER> for a fortune, or <^D>: ';
18      }
19  }
20          ############ Present Fortunes to User ############
21  else {
22    # Use random sampling without replacement. After a fortune is
23    # displayed, mark its array element as "undefined" using
24    # "delete", then prune it from array using "grep"
25
26      $index=rand @fortunes;                # select random index
```

```
27      printf $fortunes[ $index ];        # print random fortune
28      delete $fortunes[ $index ];        # mark fortune undefined
29      @fortunes=grep { defined } @fortunes;   # remove used ones
30      @fortunes  or  # terminate after all used
31          die "\n$0: How unfortunate; out of fortunes!\n";
32   }
```

The BEGIN block starts by assigning the pathname of the startrek file to @ARGV if that array is empty, to establish a default data source. Next, it adds "–" as the final argument, so the program will read from STDIN after reading (and storing) all the fortunes.

Lines 8–9 set the input record separator to % and the $initializing variable to the (True) value of 1, so the script begins by loading fortunes into the array (Lines 12–13).

As with all scripts of this type, it's necessary to detect the end of the initialization phase by sensing "end of file" (using eof, Line 14) and then to reset $initializing to a False value, set the appropriate input record separator for the user-interaction phase, and prompt the user for input.

Line 26 obtains a random index for the array and saves it in a variable, which is used in the next statement to extract and print the selected fortune. printf is used for the printing rather than print, because the fortune already has a trailing newline,[7] and print (in conjunction with the l option) would add another one.

Line 28 then runs delete (see table 9.2) on the array element, which isn't quite as lethal as it sounds—all it does is mark its value as undefined.[8] The actual removal of that element is accomplished by using grep to filter it out of @fortunes and reinitialize the array (see section 7.3.3), using

```
@fortunes=grep { defined } @fortunes;
```

That's all the coding it takes, because defined operates on $_ by default, and grep stores the list element that it's currently processing in that same variable.

If the user has sufficient stamina, he'll eventually see all the fortunes, so Line 30 checks the remaining size of the array and calls die when it's depleted. Alternatively, because the implicit loop is reading the user's input, the program can be terminated by responding to the prompt with <^D>.

One final word of caution, for you to file away under "debugging tips": Any dual input-mode script will behave strangely if you neglect to reset the "$/" variable to

---

[7] Why does it have a trailing newline? The input record separator ($/) was defined as %, so that's what the l option stripped from each input record, leaving the newline that came before it untouched. An alternative approach would be to set "$/" to "\n%" to get them both stripped off and to use print to replace the newline on output.

[8] In contrast, delete removes both the index and its value when used on a hash element, as we'll discuss shortly.

newline before entering the interactive phase. As a case in point, `fcookie2` will keep gobbling up the lines of your response to the first `Press <ENTER>` prompt until you happen to press the `%` key—if ever! So whenever you set "`$/`" to a custom value in a program that later needs to read keyboard input, make sure you reset it to newline before the user-interaction phase begins.

9.1.5 Tips on using arrays

Use `push` to populate arrays whenever possible. Doing so eliminates the need for you to manage an index, without imposing any restrictions on how you may later access the stored values (i.e., you can still use indexing to retrieve them).

You're supposed to change the `@` symbol in an array's name (and the `%` in a hash's) to a `$` when using a single subscript, but that's not a serious error—Perl will do what you wanted it to anyway, after mildly rebuking you with a warning of this form:

```
Scalar value @array_name[0] better written as $array_name[0]
```

> **NOTE**   Arrays aren't used as frequently in Perl as they are in other languages, because we have the option of using a more versatile data type for managing lists instead—the *hash*.

We'll now turn our attention to that other variety of list variable, the hash.

9.2   USING HASH VARIABLES

As useful as arrays are, it's very limiting for a programmer to be restricted to storing and retrieving data using integer subscripts. For example, if you were developing a system to keep track of the repair records for your organization's computers, don't you think it would be more user-friendly to employ the computers' names as identifiers ("ELVIS", "AREA-51", etc.), rather than their 27-digit (integer) serial numbers?

To support this kind of association between data elements, Perl provides a data structure called a *hash*, which maps string-based indices to scalar values.[9] Hashes are somewhat like arrays, but they're superior in certain ways. To realize their potential, you need to adopt different ways of thinking about mechanisms for data storage and retrieval, and learn some specialized techniques.

We'll begin by considering a small hash called `%phone`, which has two key/value pairs, as depicted in table 9.4.

This tabular representation does a good job of conveying the message that non-integer indices are permitted in hashes. However, the table's implication that Joe's

---

[9] The name derives from the use of "hash table" data structures in Perl's hash implementation. AWK calls its related facility an associative array. The 1993 Korn shell introduced limited support for associative arrays, but most Shell programmers haven't used them, so we won't assume that knowledge here.

Table 9.4   Storing phone numbers in a hash

%phone	
Key	**Value**
Joe	789-9834
Jan	897-7164

phone number is stored in the first slot and Jan's in the second slot is misleading, because hash elements aren't stored like that. But "who's on first" is irrelevant, because with hashes, what's important isn't where a value resides in the underlying data structure—instead, it's which key is *associated* with that value.

For instance, it would be of little use to know that "somebody's" phone number is 789-9834, but it might be very useful to know that it's Joe's number. You could determine this using the following coding:[10]

```
print "Joe's number is $phone{Joe}"
Joe's number is 789-9834
```

Note that using an array to manage the information in table 9.4 would require the use of more elaborate strategies than just using the key "Joe" to retrieve the associated value from the hash. For example, one technique would involve the creation of an array of phone-owners' names, as shown in table 9.5.

Table 9.5   Array of phone-owners' names

@phone_owners	
Index	**Value**
0	Joe
1	Jan

To find Joe's phone number, we'd search the values of this array to find "Joe" and then use the corresponding index (0) with a paired second array (see table 9.6) to retrieve his number.

Table 9.6   Array of phone numbers for phone owners

@phone_numbers	
Index	**Value**
0	789-9834
1	897-7164

---

[10] Hashes use curly braces rather than square brackets around their subscripts, as shown in table 9.7.

The processing steps would therefore involve first looking up the <u>entries of interest</u> in the specified arrays and then retrieving the **desired values**:

@phone_owners: <u>Joe</u>   ->   **0**

@phone_numbers: <u>0</u>   ->   **789-9834**

Of course, you'd have to be careful not to disturb the precise synchronization between the arrays when making modifications to them, or else the storage/retrieval system would break down.

Because an array-based approach is so inconvenient, error-prone, and burdensome, hashes are the data structure of choice for associating strings with values. As shown in table 9.7, hashes are used like arrays, except % replaces @, and curly braces are used rather than square brackets as indexing symbols. Their names follow the same rules as those for arrays, which means a digit can't come first after the variable's identifying symbol (%).

Table 9.7   Syntax for using hashes in Perl

	Examples[a]	Remarks
Assigning a value	`$h{A}=1;` `$h{'B C'}=2;`	The $ symbol is used when referring to a single scalar value in a hash. Multi-word keys must be quoted.

Retrieving and displaying values	`print $h{A};` `# prints 1`
	`print $h{'B C'};` `# prints 2`
	`OR`
	`exists $h{A} and print $h{A};`
		If there's any doubt about whether a hash has a particular key, its presence can first be tested with `exists`.

Deleting entries	`delete $h{A};` `delete $h{'B C'};`	The `delete` function causes the indicated key and its value to be deleted from the hash.

Assigning multiple values	`%h=( A      => 1,`
	`      'B C' => 2 );`
	`OR`
	`%h=list_generator;`
		A hash can be initialized with an explicit list of comma-separated *key* `=>` *value* pairs. A variety of other expressions (called *list generators*) can also be used to initialize hashes (see section 9.3).

Retrieving and displaying all elements	`$,="\n";`
	
	`print sort values %h;`
	`print sort keys   %h;`
	
	`print map { "$_=$h{$_}" }`
	`   sort keys %h;`
	`OR`
	`foreach $key (sort keys %h) {`
	`   print "$key=$h{$key}";`
	`}`
		The `values` and `keys` functions are used to extract elements from the hash, with `sort` added to impose order on their results. The `map` operator or `foreach` loop is typically used to print hash elements in the "*key=value*" format.

a. The examples using `print` assume the use of the `l` invocation option.

Unlike the case with arrays (see table 9.2), when `delete` is used on a hash, it actually removes all traces of the specified element. This obviates the need to reinitialize the data structure after removing its deleted values, as `fcookie2` (listing 9.4, Line 29) has to do with its `@fortunes` array.

Next, we'll discuss hash initialization techniques.

9.2.1 Initializing hashes

As with arrays, you can initialize hashes using an aggregate syntax or a piecemeal syntax (see table 9.7). Here's an example of piecemeal initialization for a hash called `%stooges_by_hairstyle`. For each of those wacky morons of the silver screen, his distinctive hairstyle-type is used as the key for storing his name. Note the use of curly braces around the indices, rather than the square brackets used with arrays, and the need to quote the <u>multi-word</u> key:

```
$stooges_by_hairstyle{bald}='Curly';
$stooges_by_hairstyle{'soup bowl'}='Moe';
$stooges_by_hairstyle{fuzzy}='Larry';
```

Here's an equivalent way of creating the same hash using aggregate initialization:

```
%stooges_by_hairstyle=(
    bald         => 'Curly',
    'soup bowl'  => 'Moe',
    fuzzy        => 'Larry',
);
```

The commas after `'Curly'` and `'Moe'` are required, because they come between key/value pairs. In contrast, the one after `'Larry'` isn't required, and would even be a syntax error in most programming languages. But it's good that Perl allows it, because that gives you the freedom to reorder the lines without having to worry about adding or removing trailing commas.

> **NOTE** Hashes have no counterpart to the `push` function of arrays, because there's no "next key" for storing each newly added value.

Tips on initializing hashes

It's a common mistake to replace the parentheses in aggregate hash initializations with curly braces, due to the association of those symbols with hashes:

```
%wrong={ key1 => 'value1', key2 => 'value2' };   # WRONG!


%right=( key1 => 'value1', key2 => 'value2' );   # Right.
```

Unfortunately, rather than triggering a fatal syntax error, this mistake just causes Perl to assign a more exotic interpretation to the statement than you had in mind, which makes your program behave strangely. If you make this mistake with warnings enabled (as they routinely should be, via –w), you'll see a warning of one of the following types:

- Reference found where even-sized list expected
- Odd number of initializers

You'll learn next how to *slice* a hash, and why that's not considered a hostile act.

9.2.2 Understanding advanced hash indexing

Table 9.8 shows the indexing techniques most commonly used with hashes. Note that there's no concept of a range of indices as with arrays, because hash keys aren't restricted to integer values.

Table 9.8 Syntax for basic and advanced hash indexing

Initialization	%X=(A => 1,	B => 2,	C => 3);
Stored value	1	2	3
Indexing	$X{A}	$X{B}	$X{C}
Result	1	2	3
Slice indexing	@X{A,B}	"@X{C,A,B}"	@X{C,B,A}
Result	12	3 1 2	321

You code hash slices by supplying multiple keys within the curly braces of the subscript. The result is a list of values, so the $ symbol that would be used with a single index gets changed to @, just as it does with array slices.

When the keys and values functions are used to extract their namesakes from a hash, those items may emerge in an undesirable order. (The order is a consistent and repeatable one, but it may appear to be random to a casual observer.) However, you can completely control the retrieval order of hash values by using a pre-ordered set of keys with a hash slice.

For example, here's a script that presents the names of the Fab Four in their default hash-retrieval order, and then in the conventional order:

```
$ beatles    # Everybody knows them as John, Paul, George, & Ringo
UNCONTROLLED ordering:
PAUL    JOHN    GEORGE  RINGO
Bass    Guitar  Guitar  Drums

CONTROLLED ordering:
JOHN    PAUL    GEORGE  RINGO
Guitar  Bass    Guitar  Drums
```

Here's the source code:

```
$ cat beatles
#! /usr/bin/perl -wl

%musicians=(   JOHN => 'Guitar',   PAUL => 'Bass',

               GEORGE => 'Guitar', RINGO => 'Drums' );
$,="\t";
print 'UNCONTROLLED ordering:';
print keys   %musicians;                # Disorderly column headings
print values %musicians;

print "\nCONTROLLED ordering:";
@names_in_order=( 'JOHN', 'PAUL', 'GEORGE', 'RINGO' );
print @names_in_order;                   # Orderly column headings
print @musicians{ @names_in_order };
```

At first glance, the script's last line may look like it's referring to two arrays, but the curly braces indicate that it's extracting a slice from the %musicians hash using keys provided by the @names_in_order array.

That's a good example of a situation where you'd want to supply a set of indices to a hash by using an array. But the syntax doesn't look as different as you might expect when you index into an *array* by using another array. Here's the comparison:

```
@array3[ @ordered_array_of_array_indices ]; # indexing an array

@hash42{ @ordered_array_of_hash_indices  }; # indexing a hash
```

Note that it's the indexing symbols—square brackets or curly braces—that tell you whether the variable being indexed is an array or hash. That's because in both cases, the result of slice-indexing is an ordered list of values—requiring the use of the initial @ symbol with the variable's name, whether it's a hash or an array!

In summary, here are the codings for the three basic ways of retrieving data from hashes:

```
%hash               # no indices; yields all key/value pairs
$hash{ key }        # single index; yields scalar
@hash{ key1, key2 } # multiple indices; yields ordered list (slice)
@hash{ @key_list }  # multiple indices via array; same as previous
```

Next, we'll talk about an important built-in hash that's chock full of useful information.

9.2.3 Understanding the built-in %ENV hash

By the time the Shell gives you your first prompt of the day, several *environment variables*—including TERM and PATH—have been initialized on your behalf. These variables convey information to the programs you subsequently run, which may affect the way they behave. For example, the vi editor will send different escape sequences to remove deleted characters from your screen if TERM is set to "xterm" versus "adm3a".

Perl makes these environment variables available through its `%ENV` hash, in which the names of the variables serve as the keys. As a simple usage example, here are the corresponding Shell and Perl ways of printing the value of the LOGNAME variable, and the whole environment:

Shell
```
echo "$LOGNAME, your ENV is: ";  env
joe, your ENV is:
TERM=xterm
PATH=/bin
LOGNAME=joe
...
```

Perl
```
print "$ENV{LOGNAME}, your ENV is:\n", %ENV;
joe, your ENV is:
TERMxtermPATH/binLOGNAMEjoe
...
```

As the Perl output demonstrates, you wouldn't normally want to print a hash using `print %somehash`, because that approach tends to make the output hard to interpret. In fact, if the keys of the hash weren't all capitalized in this case, we'd have a difficult time identifying where each one ends and its associated value begins.

You'll see better ways to print hashes next.

9.2.4 Printing hashes

We can make the output of `print %ENV` look more like that of the Shell's env command by being more clever about how we format the results. One approach is based on map (see section 7.3.5), as shown in the last row of table 9.7:

```
$,="\n";
print map { "$_=$ENV{$_}" } sort keys %ENV;
LOGNAME=joe
PATH=/bin
TERM=xterm
...
```

How does it work? The map function delivers key-sorted "*key=value*" arguments into `print`'s argument list, and the "`$,`" setting inserts newlines between them. Then, a final newline is provided at the end of `print`'s argument list by the shebang line's l option (unshown).

Another option for printing key/value pairs, also shown in table 9.7, is to use the `foreach` loop. It's similar to the Shell's for loop, in that it assigns a value from a list to the designated *loop variable* for each iteration through a block of statements. Here's the way it would be used to produce output identical to that of the map example:

```
foreach $key (sort keys %ENV) {
    print "$_=$ENV{$_}";
}
```

Because this approach runs a separate `print` for each "*key=value*" string, the newline provided for each `print` by the `l` option separates the strings on output. For this reason, there's no need to manipulate the "`$,`" variable, as in the map-based version.[11] We'll cover the `foreach` loop in detail in section 10.4.

Next, we'll explore a valuable use for environment variables in Perl programming.

9.2.5   Using %ENV in place of switches

You can use a command-line switch of the form `-debug` or `-debug=value` to trigger optional diagnostic messages in a script, if you include the `s` option for automatic switch processing on the shebang line (see section 2.4.3). Alternatively, that effect can be obtained by passing an environment variable to the script, which has certain advantages over the switch-based alternative.

There are two ways to do it:

```
$ DEBUG_script27='anything'  script27    # export from script27
```

or

```
$ export DEBUG_script27='anything'       # export from current shell
$ script27
```

The second example sets the variable in the current shell, for delivery to all its subsequently executed commands until it's removed from the environment by `unset`. In contrast, the first one sets the variable in the process running `script27`, for use by that script and its descendants. By restricting the change to a smaller group of processes, the latter method minimizes the possibility that setting the variable will affect unintended programs.[12]

You can employ the usual Perl techniques in `script27` to detect and respond to the environment variable's contents (whether or not the `s` option is enabled), such as

```
defined $ENV{DEBUG_script27}  and  warn "$0: So far so good!\n";

...

defined $ENV{DEBUG_script27}  and
    $ENV{DEBUG_script27} eq 'verbose'  and
        warn "$0: Entering output section at ", scalar localtime;
```

---

[11] On the other hand, this approach has the drawback of requiring one call to `print` for each variable, whereas the map version uses a single `print` to handle all variables. You can use the standard `Benchmark` module to determine which version runs faster, if that's of interest.

[12] Those unintended influences are especially likely if generic names like DEBUG and VERBOSE are used.

A potential benefit of using an environment variable is that it's available to the script's offspring, whereas a switch variable affects only the script itself. Therefore, in Perl scripts that start up other scripts, the environment-variable approach may be preferable to its switch-based alternative.

Next, you'll learn why, thanks to hashes, Perl doesn't need a built-in function similar to Unix's `uniq` command.

9.2.6   Obtaining uniqueness with hashes

Just as arrays store their values under unique indices, hashes store their values under unique keys. For this reason, if you assign a value for the same key (or index) more than once, the prior value is overwritten, leaving only the most recently assigned value available for retrieval. You'll see how this property can be used for "unique-ifying" arguments and inputs in the next sections.

Rendering arguments unique

The fact that hashes have unique keys can be used to good advantage. For example, consider a script that sends a message to each email address provided as an argument. To avoid sending email to any address more than once, such a script might first want to eliminate duplicates from its argument list.

Here's a sample run of a script that performs that service:

```
$ DEBUG_unique_args='yes' \
>     unique_args a b c a b a
unique_args: Initial arguments (sorted):
        a
        a
        a
        b
        b
        c

unique_args: Final arguments:

        a
        b
        c
```

Listing 9.5 shows `unique_args`, which provides the foundation for any script that needs to render its arguments unique before processing them further.[13]

---

[13] The unique-ifying code would go in a BEGIN block in a program using the n or p option (as shown), or before the custom argument-handling loop of a program that doesn't (see table 10.3).

Listing 9.5 The `unique_args` script

```
1   #! /usr/bin/perl -wnl
2
3   BEGIN {
4       $debug=defined $ENV{DEBUG_unique_args};
5
6       if ($debug) {        # use shorter variable name
7           $,="\n\t";       # indent output for better visibility
8           print "$0: Initial arguments (sorted): ", sort @ARGV;
9           print "";        # separate from following output
10      }
11
12      foreach $arg (@ARGV) {
13          # following line supplied automatically
14          # ! defined $unique{$arg}  and  $unique{$arg}=0;
15          $unique{$arg}++;    # count each argument's occurrences
16      }
17      @ARGV=sort keys %unique; # retain unique args
18
19      if ($debug) {
20          print "\n$0: Final arguments: ", @ARGV;
21          exit 0;                   # terminate here during debugging
22      }
23  }
24  # BODY OF PROGRAM GOES HERE
```

The job of the `foreach` loop[14] that starts on Line 12 is to count how many times each argument has occurred. But the first time a particular `$arg` is used as an index for the `%unique` hash (Line 15), it will not yet have an associated value there.[15]

An obvious way to handle this situation would be to write the statement shown in Line 14, which initializes the key's associated value to 0 if it wasn't already defined. However, this situation comes up so frequently in Perl that it's handled *automatically*, so such a statement isn't needed.

In Line 17, the (necessarily unique) keys are extracted from the hash, sorted, and assigned back to `@ARGV`, eliminating any duplicates that may have been present.

If the user requests debugging information by setting the relevant environment variable, the script prints the initial arguments and final arguments (Lines 8, 20), to reveal the effects of the processing.[16]

---

[14] Covered in detail in section 10.4.

[15] Attempting to access a variable that doesn't exist is sure to instill dread in the heart of a squared JAPH, because in C, such a program would crash—but not before spewing blinking graphics characters all over the screen to obscure any error messages.

[16] By default, changing "`$,`" (on Line 7) affects all subsequent uses of `print`, which is generally undesirable; section 11.4.4 shows how to `localize` such changes to a particular program region.

Related but somewhat different techniques are used to render *input records* unique, as discussed next.

Rendering inputs unique

Listing 9.6 shows another script that unique-ifies data, but this one works on input lines, rather than arguments. Unlike its argument-wrangling predecessor, unique_inputs is a complete program, designed to duplicate the functionality of certain Unix commands.

Listing 9.6 The unique_inputs script

```
1   #! /usr/bin/perl -wnl
2
3   $unique{$_}++;                        # increment counter for each input
4
5   END {
6     @inputs=sort keys %unique;          # determine unique inputs
7     if (defined $ENV{DEBUG_unique_inputs}) {
8       foreach $input (@inputs) {
9         $unique{$input} > 1   and
10          print "$0: '$input' appeared $unique{$input} times";
11      }
12      print "";     # for spacing
13    }
14    # Now print the sorted, unique, inputs
15    $,="\n";                           # re-supply newlines stripped by -l
16    print @inputs;
17  }
```

We'll test this script by having it show the unique list of currently logged-in users on a Linux system, with its input provided by who's output:

```
forrest    :0        Dec   6 09:07 (console)
forrest    pts/0     Dec   6 09:08
forrest    tty1      Dec   6 09:37
willy      tty2      Dec   6 09:43
willy      tty3      Dec   6 09:48
gloria     pts/1     Dec   6 17:03
gloria     pts/5     Dec   8 09:36
```

But first, that output will be reduced by an awk command[17] to its first column, to isolate the user names:

---

[17] Although Perl has many advantages over AWK (see chapter 5), this AWK solution is just as good here and considerably more compact than the equivalent perl -wnla -e 'print $F[0]; '.

```
$ who | awk '{ print $1 }' | unique_inputs
forrest
gloria
willy
```

The script produces the same result as the UNIX `sort -u` command, as it should:

```
$ who | awk '{ print $1 }' | sort -u
forrest
gloria
willy
```

But unlike `sort`, `unique_inputs` has a debugging mode that includes in the report the number of times each unique line was seen in the input:

```
$ who | awk '{print $1}' | DEBUG_unique_inputs='yes' unique_inputs
unique_inputs: 'forrest' appeared 3 times
unique_inputs: 'gloria' appeared 2 times
unique_inputs: 'willy' appeared 2 times

forrest
gloria
willy
```

Although the format is different, that's the same information `sort | uniq -c` provides:

```
$ who | awk '{ print $1 }' | sort | uniq -c
      3 forrest
      2 gloria
      2 willy
```

Of course, the value of `unique_inputs` is not that it duplicates the functionality of certain combinations of Unix commands, but rather that it shows a general technique for unique-ifying inputs using Perl's resources alone.

Another place where hashes are commonly used is in the implementation of simple database systems, as you'll see next.

9.2.7 Employing a hash as a simple database: The `user_lookup` script

Due to their innate abilities to associate indices with values, arrays and hashes are often used in simple *database* (i.e., storage/retrieval) applications. The fcookie* scripts of section 9.1.4 are examples, in the sense that each accesses a database of fortunes while providing its services. The script we discuss here is similar—but more likely to impress its users. Why? Because its ability to associate keys with values is more *apparent*.

The `user_lookup` script provides a report of a Unix user's `passwd`-file entry in response to input of a login ID—*or* a numeric user ID:

```
$ user_lookup
```

Enter login-ID or UID: **spug**   ↵   <u>**256**</u> **would work too**

```
        ID:    spug
        UID:   256
        GID:   104
        NAME:  Seattle Perl Users Group account
        HOME:  /home/spug
        SHELL: /bin/bash
```

Enter login-ID or UID: **plankton**

```
No such user: 'plankton'
```

Notice that the script was smart enough to know that it didn't have a record for "plankton". Making this determination requires the use of a special technique that wasn't needed in the fcookie* scripts, which you'll soon see.

The script is shown in listing 9.7. As is appropriate for the /etc/passwd file—which supplies all the information the script reports—the shebang line sets the field separator to a colon.

Like the fcookie2 script discussed earlier, this one has two phases of operation: data storage and data retrieval. The current processing phase is signified by the value of the $initializing variable, which is initialized to a True value in the BEGIN block.

Line 9 sets some variables—whose names refer to the fields of passwd-file records—to the integers from 0 to 6, using a special service provided by the range operator (introduced in table 5.10). These variables are used later as indices for the @F array, to make the indexing operations more understandable.

Line 12 loads the pathname of the passwd file and the "-" symbol into @ARGV, which tells the implicit loop to read from STDIN after passwd so user input can be accepted.

Line 14 loads the prompt string into a variable, because prompts have to be issued from two places, and it would be undesirable to duplicate the message string.

Once the BEGIN block has finished executing, the script reads input lines and either uses them as hash initializers (Lines 17–34) or interprets them as data-retrieval requests (Lines 38–46), depending on the processing phase indicated by $initializing.

While initializing, the program constructs a report for each user by assembling fields pulled out of the @F array (Lines 23–28) into a string, which is then loaded into the %user hash under two keys: the numeric UID (Line 22) and the alphabetic login ID (Line 21).

Why record each value under two keys? Because it's more convenient for the user if either specification can be used to retrieve the record, and it's hardly any additional work for the programmer. The double initialization (Lines 21–22) is accomplished using a hash-based variation on the $b=$a=1 syntax shown earlier (in table 2.3).

Listing 9.7   The user_lookup script

```
 1   #! /usr/bin/perl -wnlaF':'
 2   # Prints report of passwd-file data for users specified
 3   #    interactively, via login-ID or numeric UID
 4
 5   BEGIN {
 6       $initializing=1;                        # start with TRUE value
 7
 8       # Use field-name variables for field-number indices
 9       ($id, undef, $uid, $gid, $name, $home, $shell)=(0..6);
10
11       # Read passwd file first, then STDIN (-) for user input
12       @ARGV=( '/etc/passwd', '-' );
13
14       $prompt="\nEnter login-ID  or  UID: ";   # Prompt string
15   }
16
17   if ($initializing) {
18
19     # Assign formatted string to both ID and UID keys
20     # E.g., for "root", store under both '0' and 'root'
21       $user{ $F[$id] }=
22           $user{ $F[$uid] }="
23                   ID:     $F[$id]
24                   UID:    $F[$uid]
25                   GID:    $F[$gid]
26                   NAME:   $F[$name]
27                   HOME:   $F[$home]
28                   SHELL: $F[$shell]";
29
30       if (eof) {
31           $initializing=0;   # Signifies start of retrieval mode,
32           printf $prompt;    #   so prompt for user's first input
33       }
34   }
35
36   # Finished loading hash from file, now interact with user
37
38   else {
39       if (exists $user{$_}) {    # Avoid attempts to use bad IDs
40           print $user{$_};
41       }
42       else {
43           warn "No such user: '$_'\n";
44       }
45       printf $prompt;                        # Prompt for next input
46   }
47
48   # On entry of <^D>, program comes here before exiting
49   END {
50       print "";        # Ensure newline before Shell's next prompt
51   }
```

Now, let's examine the humble but critical Line 30. Its job is to detect the point at which all the lines from `passwd` have been read, by using `eof` to test for the "end of file" condition (as in section 9.1.4's `fcookie2`). If the result is True, the `$initializing` variable is set to a False value to signal the beginning of the interactive phase, during which the user can retrieve the stored reports for user accounts.

Line 32 supplies the prompt for the user's first input. After the user presses <ENTER>, Line 39 is executed on the next iteration of the implicit loop, which tests whether the user's input is a registered key in the hash by using the `exists` function (see table 9.7).[18] If it is, the associated value is printed, and if it isn't, a warning is issued (Line 43).

Line 45 prints the prompt for the next input, and then the program continues prompting and reporting until the user presses <^D>. As with any interactive program using dangling prompts, this script needs to print a newline before turning control over to the Shell; this is accomplished in Line 50 by printing a null string (which will be followed by an automatic newline, courtesy of the `1` option).

So that's how it works. But I can already hear the user community clamoring for an upgrade! Why? Because hash keys are case sensitive, which means that an attempt to look up "SPUG" (instead of "spug") will fail with this program. However, that problem is easily fixed by coercing all inputs into a standard case before using them as keys. This can be achieved by changing the current Line 21

```
$user{    $F[$id]  }="...";
```

into a form that lowercases the field value before it's used as an index:

```
$user{ "\L$F[$id]" }="...";
```

We also have to coerce the user's input into the same case, by adding the following line before the current Line 39:

```
$_="\L$_";
```

The techniques illustrated in this program are general ones that are relevant to a wide variety of applications. For example, some system administrators might wish to define hostnames and/or IP addresses as keys, to allow users to retrieve reports about those hosts. Or a manager might wish to retrieve project-related information, a car dealer inventory information, or a student lecture notes, using programs based on this model.

Next, you'll learn one way that hashes are used in Internet search engines.

---

[18] The `exists` function is used less frequently with arrays, because uncertainty about indices is more prevalent in hash-based programs. The script under discussion is an excellent example, because its indices are determined by the contents of a file—not by the programmer.

9.2.8 Counting word frequencies in web pages: The count_words script

Ever wonder how Google does such a good job of instantly directing you to relevant web pages on the basis of your search terms? A lot of it has to do with the prior characterization of those pages according to relative word frequencies. That's why when you ask for pages related to "rocky road", you might see results dedicated to off-road driving, ice cream, or even songs by Weird Al Yankovic, depending on which pages have those words occurring in the largest proportions. Guess what? Many Internet search engines use Perl to prepare these statistics, because its hashes make word counting so easy.

As an example, here's a sample run of a script that breaks each input line into words, and shows each word's frequency of occurrence as a proportion of all words on the page:

```
$ echo 'Testing, testing ... is this thing on?' | count_words
       WORD      FREQUENCY
         is      0.166667
         on      0.166667
    testing      0.333333
      thing      0.166667
       this      0.166667
```

Let's try the script on the text of a web page, using lwp-request (see section 3.12.2) to fetch it. We'll sort the output so the words that appear most frequently come out first:

```
$ lwp-request -o text ukuleleworld.com |   # output edited
>    count_words |
>      sort -r -n +1 |  # reverse numeric sort, skip over WORD field
           WORD      FREQUENCY
        ukulele      0.047442
           uke      0.012093
            or      0.010233
         music      0.010233
        paypal      0.009302
            of      0.009302
             a      0.009302
            us      0.008372
       hawaiian      0.004409
```

. . .

You'd be correct to infer that this web page would be of interest to those who want to order a ukulele (uke) or Hawaiian music online, from a merchant that accepts payments by the PayPal service.

The script is shown in listing 9.8, with the lines that do the bulk of the work highlighted.

Listing 9.8   The count_words script

```
1   #! /usr/bin/perl -wnlaF'\W+'
2
3   foreach $word ( @F ) {
4       # Use word as hash index, and increment its count
5       #  but coerce to lowercase, to ignore case-differences
6       $lc_word="\L$word";
7       $count{$lc_word}++;  # count another occurrence of this word
8
9       $total++;                # keep running count of word total
10  }
11
12  END {   # Show frequency for each word, in word-sorted order
13      printf "%20s%14s\n", 'WORD', 'FREQUENCY';
14      foreach $word (sort keys %count) {
15          $frequency=$count{$word} / $total;
16          # Print $word as string in 20-char field,
17          #  $frequency as floating-point number in 14-char field
18          printf "%20s%14f\n", $word, $frequency;
19      }
20  }
```

The script's shebang line specifies that any sequence of one or more *non* word-characters (spaces, commas, periods, etc.) constitutes a delimiter (see table 3.5). This definition is used rather than the default of whitespace characters, because we don't want punctuation symbols to remain attached to the extracted words (i.e., we want "spam", not "*%#&spam!!").

In Line 3, foreach assigns each of the fields of the current line from @F to the $word variable in turn, for one iteration of the loop. Line 6 converts the current word to lowercase, so we can treat "THE" and "the" as instances of the same word. Line 7 counts another occurrence of the current word. To facilitate the later calculation of relative word frequencies, Line 9 keeps track of the total number of words processed thus far.

After all the words have been counted, control transfers to the END block, which prints the column headings. The formatting specifications on Line 13 say, "Print WORD and FREQUENCY right-justified in adjacent fields of 20 and 14 characters, as strings (%20s, %14s), followed by a newline (\n)." That newline is needed because the l option affects only print, not printf also (see section 2.1.6).

Line 18 uses a similar format, but it specifies that the second value ($frequency) should be printed as a floating-point (**f**) number (i.e., one with decimal places) rather than as a string, as the word itself and the column headings are printed.

As this script demonstrates, it's easy to calculate relative word frequencies with Perl—the most involved part is printing the results! Now you understand why Perl is so widely used for this type of activity, in web-crawling robots and the search engines they supply with data.

At this point, we've finished our coverage of the essential features of arrays and hashes and how they're used with special programming techniques in representative applications. We'll conclude this chapter by comparing Shell and Perl techniques for generating lists, so you'll be familiar with the Perl counterparts to the Shell idioms you may already know.

9.3 COMPARING LIST GENERATORS IN THE SHELL AND PERL

Shell programming terrifies me. ... Is it trying to remember what the rules are for all the different quotes? Is it having to look up the multi-phased interaction between filename expansion, shell variables, quotation, backslashes and alias expansion?

—Olin Shivers, author of `scsh`, 1994

As many have noticed, it can be a challenge to understand all the intricacies of the way the Shell processes command lines. Fortunately, Perl's approach is much simpler—without being less powerful—and it's also easier to comprehend.

In this section, which is aimed at intermediate to advanced Shell programmers, we'll review the commonly used Shell idioms for generating lists and show you their closest Perl counterparts. This knowledge will help you transfer your Shell skills into the Perl domain and make you a more proficient Perl programmer.

Lists can be generated through variable, command, or filename substitution (or *interpolation*, in Perltalk) in both languages. The Shell may then perform additional substitutions on the results of variable or command substitutions, before re-parsing the final result in the processing stage called *word-splitting*.[19] As the name implies, the major effect of this processing stage is to convert a string into a list of its constituent "words".

Because the programmer needs to control which substitutions will be subjected to these additional processing steps, the Shell provides a mechanism for selectively disabling them: *quoting*. But you don't need quoting for this purpose in Perl, because it doesn't perform those additional processing steps anyway. Conversely, emulating the Shell's treatment of unquoted substitutions with Perl often requires additional processing steps to be explicitly requested (using, for example, `split`).

For your convenience, table 9.9 presents examples of the most common types of list-generators used in Shell programming, along with their closest Perl equivalents.

---

[19] This is also called *IFS* (for Internal Field Separator) *processing*, after the Shell variable of the same name.

You can use this table to select the Perl counterparts for the Shell expressions you already know, without the burden of working out the Perl equivalents yourself.

Table 9.9   Common list generators in the Shell and their Perl counterparts

Shell name	Perl name	Shell examples	Perl examples[b]
Filename generation	Globbing	`*` `[!a]*.txt`	`<*>` `<[^a]*.txt>`
Command substitution	Command interpolation	`` `cat memo` `` `$(cat memo)`	`split /\s+/, `cat memo``
		`(TRICKY)*` `` `find . -print` ``	`` `cat memo` `` See `File::Find` in chapter 12.
Variable substitution	Variable interpolation	`"$@"` `"${names[@]}"`	`@ARGV` `split /\s+/, "@ARGV"`

		`$*`
		`${names[*]}`
		`$names`
			`@names`
			`split /\s+/, "@names"`
			`split /\s+/, $names`

N/A	Input operator	N/A	`<>` `<STDIN>`
N/A	Matching operator	N/A	`/\w+/g`

a. _TRICKY_ means that it may be possible to arrange a result in the Shell that matches that of the Perl example, but it's not necessarily easy.
b. List context is assumed where required.

We'll discuss the Perl counterparts to the three different types of Shell processing covered in that table—*filename generation*, *command substitution*, and *variable substitution*—in the sections that follow.

9.3.1   Filename generation/globbing

The first row of table 9.9 compares techniques for generating filenames. As discussed in chapter 8, filename generation (FNG) metacharacters, such as "*", must appear within the angled brackets of the globbing operator to be recognized in Perl. Another difference between the languages is that the metacharacter that complements a character class is "!" in the Shell but "^" in Perl (see table 7.16).

Now we'll discuss differences between the languages in the way that command output is imported into programs.

9.3.2 Command substitution/interpolation

Although Perl shares one of the Shell's syntaxes for command substitution/interpolation (`` `command` ``; see the table's second row), the languages may nevertheless treat *command*'s output differently. For example, the result provided by `` `cat memo` `` in the Shell is a list of the file's whitespace-separated "words", but in Perl it's a list of its lines instead. If desired, you can use `split` to convert those lines into words (see section 7.2.1), as shown in row 2 of table 9.9.

However, even after that conversion, the languages might not have the *same* words in their lists! This is possible because if any FNG metacharacters (?, *, etc.) are present within the words, the Shell might replace them with *filenames*.[20]

Another disparity is that the result provided by `` `cat memo` `` in Perl—which by default is the eminently sensible "each line is one list element"—has no direct counterpart in the Shell, which returns a list of individual words for an unquoted command substitution, or a single string containing all the original data for a double-quoted one.[21]

Next, we'll discuss some differences in the way the languages handle requests for the values of variables.

9.3.3 Variable substitution/interpolation

Thanks to the special behaviors exhibited by certain built-in variables and array indices when they're double-quoted in the Shell, the upper examples of table 9.9's third row produce identical results in the two languages. However, the Shell's infamous propensity for doing further processing on the results of most types of substitutions (filename generation is the exception) means that the Perl list generators shown in the bottom examples of the third row can't be trusted to behave identically—in all cases—to their indicated Shell counterparts.

For instance, if any of those unquoted Shell examples of variable substitution were to yield a "*", that character would be replaced by all the (non-hidden) filenames in the current directory. In contrast, the "*" would remain unchanged in the Perl counterparts to those examples.

For what it's worth, I—like many other immigrants to Perlistan—prefer Perl's "no surprises" approach to the uncertainties of the Shell's processing model.

Conclusion

It's fortunate that most files and script arguments don't contain FNG metacharacters, because there's no easy way to defend against their unwanted conversion to filenames

---

[20] E.g., if "Jos?" were in the file, the Shell would convert it to "Jose" and "Josh"—if files with those names were present in the current directory. The same result could be arranged in Perl, but it wouldn't happen *by accident*, as it may in the Shell.

[21] Although with sufficient manipulation of the Shell's IFS variable and intermediate storage of output into temporary variables, the same effect might be achievable.

in the Shell. Why? Because the only tool you've got for disabling substitutions on results of prior substitutions is double quoting—but that also prevents word-splitting, which might be required!

Nevertheless, for the *majority* of cases you'll encounter in common programming practice, the Perl counterparts shown in table 9.9 for Shell list-generating commands will serve as functional equivalents.

9.4 SUMMARY

Perl's arrays allow multiple data values to be stored in—and retrieved from—named variables, using integer indices that refer to individual storage locations within the array. Unlike most languages, Perl lets you use negative indexing to access elements relative to the array's end (as in the shell_types script), and to use groups of indices to store or retrieve multiple values ("slices") in one operation (as in show_ fields2, section 9.1.3).

In cases where it's acceptable for new values to be appended at an array's end, you can use the push function, which lets Perl generate the appropriate indices automatically.

With some applications, a method for retrieving values from arrays that resembles the extraction of lottery numbers from a fishbowl is appropriate, as illustrated by fcookie (section 9.1.4), which extracts random "fortunes" from an array that functions as a simple database.

Perl's hashes (called associative arrays in AWK) expand on the concept of arrays by allowing strings to be used as indices. Because the essential services performed by hashes and arrays are the same—data storage and retrieval—hashes tend to be used more frequently than arrays in Perl, because strings generally make more convenient indices than integers.

Array indices range from 0 to one less than the number of elements in the array, which makes it easy to extract every stored value in a methodical manner. In contrast, the keys of a hash (42, 'AC/DC', 'slurm') aren't necessarily predictable or restricted to a pre-determined range. For this reason, functions called keys and values are provided to facilitate the extraction of their namesake elements from a hash, often with the aid of the foreach loop (see section 10.4), which makes it easy to process each element in turn.

A common application of hashes is the removal of duplicates from a list, as you saw in the unique_args and unique_inputs scripts. This technique could be used, for example, to avoid the mistake of sending a particular email to the same address more than once.

Hashes are well suited to tasks such as word counting, where each word acts as a key and its corresponding value is the number of times it appears in the input. You saw how simple scripts like count_words (section 9.2.8) can generate statistical reports like those used by Internet search engines, for recommending web pages on the basis of search terms.

The user_lookup script (section 9.2.7) uses a hash to retrieve the passwd-file data for the indicated user. Because numbers and strings can both be used as keys in the same hash, the user of that script can specify a Unix user by either his numeric UID or his alphabetic login name, which is a valuable feature that's difficult to implement with arrays.

Arrays and hashes are often used together, such as when an array supplies an ordered list of keys for extracting a slice of values out of a hash in a pre-determined order (as in the beatles script of section 9.2.2).

Although unindexed arrays and hashes have different initial symbols (@stuff vs. %stuff), those are both replaced by the $ character when the variables are singly indexed. But Perl can still tell the data types apart, because arrays and hashes use different symbols around their subscripts (e.g., $stuff[$array_index], $stuff {$hash_index}).

The %ENV hash provides access to a program's environment variables, such as PATH and DISPLAY on Unix systems. You saw how environment variables can be used in place of command-line switches to affect a program's behavior, in scripts such as unique_args (section 9.2.6).

In the Shell, lists of values can be obtained from filename generation, command substitution, or variable substitution requests. We discussed the closest Perl counterpart for each type of Shell list-generator (e.g., <*> vs. *) and the Shell's propensity for doing additional processing on the results of prior substitutions—which can sometimes be more of a liability than an asset. You can program Perl to emulate the Shell's behavior, but unwanted substitutions don't occur by accident in Perl, as they may in the Shell.

Directions for further study

To obtain information about specific Perl functions covered in this chapter, such as keys, values, shift, unshift, delete, exists, or printf, you can use that function's name in a command of this form:

- perldoc -f function-name # coverage of "function-name"

The following document provides additional information on Perl's data types:

- man perldata   # discusses scalar, array, and hash variables

The standard List::Util module provides several useful utility functions for lists of all kinds—explicit lists, arrays, and hashes. For example, it provides functions that shuffle (randomly reorder) a list's values, and that return their minimum and maximum values. Run the following command for additional details:

- man List::Util   # describes utility functions for lists

C H A P T E R   1 0

Looping facilities

10.1 Looping facilities in the Shell
      and Perl 331
10.2 Looping with while/until 333
10.3 Looping with do while/until 338
10.4 Looping with foreach 340

10.5 Looping with for 345
10.6 Using loop-control directives 349
10.7 The CPAN's select loop
      for Perl 355
10.8 Summary 360

Recapitulation. Repetition! Redundancy!! The redundancy of repetition. The repetitive monotony of redundancy. The monotony of endlessly repeating a mundane task—*repetitively!*

Repetition is annoying—and dangerous. It can drive people crazy! Fortunately, civilization has evolved to the point where we have unfeeling mechanical agents who exist just to perform an endless variety of mind-numbingly repetitive tasks for us. The ones we call *computers* can process operations repetitively through a process called *looping*, which refers to the repeated execution of program code.

Before we discuss how looping in Perl relates to looping in the Shell, let's consider a typical kind of activity that looping makes a lot easier.

As you know, most Unix commands can handle multiple arguments. That's why you can get a long listing of every file that ends in .txt for the current directory by using this command:

```
ls -l *.txt
```

There's no need to run the command separately for each of the files, because the command processes the filename arguments supplied by *.txt one after another—using a loop.

But adventurous Shell programmers will eventually encounter standard Unix commands that don't work this way. For example, both `tr` and `col`[1] are designed to read only from STDIN, not from filename arguments, so processing multiple files with them requires different techniques.

The following command shows a common use of `tr`. It converts each character in a file from *upper-* to *lowercase*, using redirection of the command's input from an existing file, and redirection of its output to a new file:

```
tr '[A-Z]' '[a-z]' < memo.txt > lc_memo.txt
```

This approach is fine for a single file, but what if you needed to convert *all* the `*.txt` files in the current directory? That would require execution of the `tr` command with different input and output files each time. This goal could be conveniently accomplished with some help from the Shell's `for` loop:

```
for file in *.txt; do tr '[A-Z]' '[a-z]' < $file > lc_$file; done
```

Each filename that matches the pattern `*.txt`, such as `memo.txt`, has its input converted to lowercase and then written to a related filename, in this case `lc_memo.txt`. The loop variable (`file`) holds each filename in turn, allowing the command's invocation to be customized for each filename through variable substitution for `$file`. Looping makes the job easier by allowing the programmer to specify the operation only once, but to have it applied as many times as necessary to handle the files at hand.

Think of the alternative—if 100 files needed this processing, and you didn't know how to use a loop, you would have to compose and submit 100 `tr` commands (one per filename) to get all the work done. *Monotony!*

This is why every serious programming language provides a facility for looping, and Perl, despite its carefree nature, is no exception. But Perl is exceptional in having such a complete collection of looping facilities. (We have the eclectic flair and good taste of Perl's creator, Larry, to thank for that.)

In this chapter, we'll discuss how Perl's standard looping facilities compare to those of the Shell. In addition, you'll see how the Shell's `select` loop, arguably its friendliest feature, can also be used in Perl programs—despite the fact that it isn't a part of the Perl language!

10.1 LOOPING FACILITIES IN THE SHELL AND PERL

Loops are generally classified according to whether they iterate over a *list* of items, or until a *condition* produces a True (or False) value. For loops of the second type, an additional distinction is whether the condition is tested before or after the code block has been executed (i.e., top- or bottom-tested).

---

[1] The `tr` command can transliterate characters from one listed set to another, or delete specified characters. The `col` command can delete control characters; it's been used to remove over-striking from man pages prior to grepping: `man` *whatever* `| col -bx | grep -i '`*something*`'`.

The Unix shells offer three kinds of loops:

- The functionally similar `foreach` (from the C shell) and `for` (from the other Shells), which are top-tested list-handling loops
- The closely related `while` and `until`, which are condition-evaluating loops that support both top and bottom tests
- The `select` loop, which is a uniquely useful hybrid that provides menu-oriented list-handling in a top-tested, condition-evaluating loop

Perl provides four loops:

- `foreach`, which is like the Shell's `for`
- `while`/`until` and `do while`/`until`, which together cover the same ground as the Shell's `while`/`until` loop
- `for`, inherited from the C language, which is a top-tested, condition-evaluating loop that's especially useful for handling arrays in certain ways

This chapter compares each Shell loop to its Perl counterpart and shows translations of representative Shell examples into Perl. In some cases, both *literal* and *figurative* translations are provided, to respectively show a direct mapping of features as well as a more idiomatic way of expressing the code in Perl.

Both languages allow flexibility in how the elements of loops are laid out. To help you gain familiarity with two representative formats, we show typical *expanded* and *condensed* code layouts for each loop, which differ only in whitespace characters (e.g., see table 10.2).

To help you relate what you already know to Perl, table 10.1 summarizes the fundamental similarities and differences between the languages in looping-related concepts, terms, and syntax.

Table 10.1   Looping-related differences between the Shell and Perl

Feature	Shell	Perl
Code block delimiters	`do` `done`	`{   }`
Contents of code block	Commands	Statements
Individual script arguments	`$1`, `$2`, ...	`$ARGV[0]`, `$ARGV[1]`, ...
Collective script arguments	`$*` `"$@"`	`@ARGV` *(in list context)*
Number of script arguments	`$#`	`@ARGV` *(in scalar context)*
Explicit list of literal values	`'Pat'  'Kim'`	`(  'Pat',  'Kim'  )`

Most of the table's entries are self-explanatory, but Perl's concept that list versus scalar *contexts* provide different meanings to `@ARGV` (see section 7.1) is worth a quick review. Essentially, if you're using an array name in a context that calls for a single value (i.e., a scalar result), such as `@ARGV > 0`, Perl provides the number of elements in the array.

But in a context that calls for a list of values, such as `print @ARGV`, Perl provides the elements themselves. Other differences listed in table 10.1 will be discussed in more detail in connection with upcoming examples.

We'll begin our examination of Perl's loops with `while` and `until`, which iterate until the required True/False result is obtained.

10.2 LOOPING WITH `while`/`until`

These two variations on one loop continue executing the code block until the termination criterion is met, based on the True/False value provided by the command before `do` (called the *controlling condition*, or condition for short). The loops differ only in `while` iterating *while* the condition remains True, and `until` iterating *until* it becomes True.

The `while`/`until` loops of both languages are shown in table 10.2. The expanded forms are shown in the top panel, and the compressed forms, suitable for loops that will fit on one line, are on the bottom.

Table 10.2   The `while`/`until` loop

Shell[a]	Perl

while
    condition
do
    code
done
	while (*condition*) {
	    code;
	}

while *condition*; do *code*; done	while (*condition*) { *code; }

a. *condition* is a placeholder for the True/False expression that controls looping, and *code* for the block of one or more commands/statements processed on each iteration. The `until` variations look the same, apart from the `until` keyword replacing `while`.

You can see that semicolons are required in the Shell's condensed format to provide the punctuation given by the return character in the expanded format, although no such adjustment is required with Perl.[2]

Next, you'll see an example of a Shell `while` loop performing a simple mathematical task, along with its Perl counterpart.

10.2.1   Totaling numeric arguments

In the terminology of Shell programming, *positional parameters* are a special class of variables. They hold copies of the script's arguments—the words the user typed after the script's name on the command line.

---

[2] A semicolon isn't used after the closing curly brace that marks the end of Perl's code block (although many beginners are inclined to place one there).

A common technique for processing all positional parameters is to process the first one ($1) and then execute shift[3] to discard it, which moves the remaining parameters one position leftward. Those steps are then repeated using a while loop until every argument has taken its turn residing in $1.

The following program uses this technique to sum the numbers in its argument list:

Shell
```
while
       [[ $# -gt 0 ]]                 # while an argument remains
do
       (( total=$total + $1 ))   # each parameter takes turn as $1
       shift                           # $2 becomes $1, $3 becomes $2, etc.
done
echo "The sum is $total"
```

The condition tests whether the current number of positional parameters ($#) is greater than 0. If so, the value of the first argument (in $1) is added to the prior total and stored back in the total variable. Next, $1 is discarded, and the remaining arguments are moved leftward one position via shift, with the former $2 becoming the new $1, and so forth. Then the number of positional parameters is tested again, and the next argument is added to the total, until all arguments have been processed.

Perl
The Perl version is similar, apart from the syntactic variations discussed earlier and the usual difference that the variable $total never appears without its $ symbol:

```
#! /usr/bin/perl -wl
while ( @ARGV > 0 ) {              # while an argument remains
       $total=$total + $ARGV[0];  # each argument takes turn as #0
       shift;                       # $2 becomes $1, etc.
}
print "The sum is $total";
```

If the test of the argument count yields a True result, the first argument is obtained from the array using a zero-based index and added to the running total. In contrast, the Shell stores its arguments in individual variables whose names correspond to their ordinal positions on the command line (see table 10.1). This leads to the use of $ARGV[0] in Perl versus $1 in the Shell to access the first argument.

Tips on using while for list processing

Although the looping approach shown in the argument-totaling example will be refreshingly familiar to many Shell programmers, Perl's foreach loop is generally preferred to while for list processing tasks, because it's easier to use (see section 10.4).

---

[3] Covered in section 8.1.3.

We'll look at another application of `while` next, where it's used to manage data compression for image files.

10.2.2 Reducing the size of an image

Consider Ivan's plight. Having finally conceded that email is here to stay, he decides to liquidate his vast collection of exotic postage stamps and start collecting "From:" headers on foreign spam messages instead. But after scanning his stamps and comparing the total disk usage of the resulting files to the amount of storage he'll be allocated on his favorite auction site, he realizes they won't fit.

Ivan knows all about data compression, but he thinks it's best reserved for text. He shudders to think how his lovely stamps would look with JPEG artifacts superimposed on their colorful scenes of soaring birds, magnificent palaces, and scowling dictators. Nevertheless, he has to raise money for the new disk farm to house his From–header collection; so, as a compromise, he resolves to compress each image to the minimum degree possible. After doing some quick math with a Perl one-liner,[4] he determines that each image can use up to 25KB of storage.

Then he writes a program to progressively compress an original image until its size falls below that threshold. Because this is clearly a case of iterating until a criterion is achieved, he chooses a `while` loop to do the job.

Here's what the program looks like in action:

```
$ compress_image -fname=tibet-lhasa.jpg
Size of tibet-lhasa.jpg: 31072 bytes
Size of tibet-lhasa.jpg: 28084 bytes
Size of tibet-lhasa.jpg: 24701 bytes
```

As you can see, the program stopped automatically once the compressed size fell below the 25KB mark, to preserve as much of the image's initial quality as possible. Listing 10.1 shows the script.[5]

The program begins by copying the image file to the `/tmp` directory, which requires complementing the value returned by `system` before testing it in the usual Perlish way for a failed result (Line 9; see section 8.6). Then, if its size (determined via `-s`; see table 6.2) exceeds the target size (Line 14), the image is compressed to "quality" level `$qual` using the <u>convert</u> command of the ImageMagick package (Line 16).[6]

---

[4] Of the following form:
```
perl -wl -e 'print "Max bytes for file: ", space / num_stamps;'
```

[5] For filenames containing special characters, proper Shell-level quoting would be required in the calls to `system`, as demonstrated in section 8.6.

[6] See http://www.imagemagick.org.

Listing 10.1 The `compress_image` script

```
1   #! /usr/bin/perl -s -wl
2
3   $DEBUG=1;      # for extra feedback during testing
4   $qual=80;      # starting quality value
5
6   $fname  or  die "Usage: $0 -fname=imagefile\n";
7
8   # Copy original image to another directory
9   ! system "cp $fname /tmp/$fname" or  die "$0: cp failed\n";
10
11  $DEBUG  and  # show initial size
12    print "Size of $fname: ", -s $fname, ' bytes';
13
14  while ( -s $fname > 25_000 )  {  # 25_000 means 25,000 in Perl
15    # Compress copy using $qual; store under original name
16    ! system "convert -quality $qual /tmp/$fname jpg:$fname"  or
17      die "$0: convert failed\n";
18
19    $DEBUG  and   # show new size
20      print "Size of $fname: ", -s $fname, ' bytes';
21
22    $qual=$qual - 5;    # reduce for next iteration
23  }
```

convert writes its results in the format specified by the prefix on its last argument (jpg) to the filename specified in that argument, which in this case is the original file. Additional iterations are executed as needed until an acceptable size has been reached, by compressing the unaltered data in the copy of the original file (named /tmp/$fname) to a larger degree (Line 22) and storing the result once again in the original file.

After reviewing the results for a few images, Ivan is pleased with the quality produced by his "just sufficient" compression strategy. But now he needs a way to process the hundreds of remaining images that doesn't involve typing hundreds of commands! We'll help him solve that problem a little later, when we discuss foreach.[7]

In the meantime, we'll discuss the use of while, along with its companion each, in the printing of hashes.

10.2.3 Printing key/value pairs from a hash using each

In Perl, the *environment variables* provided by the OS are accessible through the %ENV hash (see section 9.2.3) Here's a simple script based on a while loop that shows the contents of any environment variable whose name contains the string "PATH". In the

---

[7] In the meantime, Ivan should remember that the Shell can help via
```
for image in *.jpg; do compress_image -fname="$image"; done
```

CHAPTER 10 LOOPING FACILITIES

lingo of hash processing,[8] the script searches each key for that string and then prints the matching keys along with their associated values:

```
$ cat show_pvars
#! /usr/bin/perl -wl

while ( ($key, $value)=each %ENV ) {
    $key =~ /PATH/  and  print "$key=$value";
}
```

The each function returns another key/value pair from the hash each time it's called, and after all pairs have been returned, a False condition is detected by while. The returned values are typically assigned to an explicit list of two scalars (as shown), providing easy access to the key and value in the body of the loop. Here's a sample run of the program, with "PATH" strings within keys highlighted:

```
$ show_pvars
PATH=/usr/local/bin:/usr/bin:/usr/X11R6/bin:/bin:/opt/gnome/bin
MANPATH=/usr/local/man:/usr/share/man:/usr/X11R6/man:/opt/gnome/man
INFOPATH=/usr/local/info:/usr/share/info:/usr/info
```

As you can see, the output lines aren't sorted according to either keys or values, which is one of the limitations of this approach. In consequence, each tends to be used when the convenience of directly accessing key/value pairs via simple scalar variables (such as $key and $value) is more important than processing the elements in sorted order.

In section 10.4 on the foreach loop, you'll see examples that illustrate the opposite tradeoff—they benefit from the ability to sort keys at the expense of having to use indexing (e.g., $ENV{$key}) to obtain their corresponding values.

Now that you've seen the while loop used in several representative applications, we'll peek under Perl's hood and see what fuels the handy n and p invocation options.

10.2.4 Understanding the implicit loop

Among the most useful of Perl's invocation options is n (covered in part 1). Now that you understand the while loop, you're in a position to understand what that option really does, which is to wrap the following *implicit loop* around the bulk of your program:

```
while ( <> ) {
    PROGRAMMER'S CODE GOES HERE
}
```

The empty input operator (<>) tells Perl to look for input in the files named as arguments to the script or, in their absence, to read input from STDIN. Most Perl programs that need to process input are happy to comply with these Unix conventions for input acquisition, so it's convenient to get this loop for free by using the n option.

---

[8] See section 9.2.

When you use that option, the entire program is enclosed in the implicit loop by default, although you can use BEGIN and/or END to specify code blocks that should be executed before or after that loop. The same effect can be achieved with an explicit loop simply by positioning the desired code above or below it, as shown in table 10.3.

For completeness, the explicit loop in the table is labeled LINE, just as the implicit loop (invisibly) is, which allows the programmer to employ loop-control directives such as next and last on it via that label (covered later in section 10.6).

Table 10.3 Pre- and post-processing in implicit and explicit loops

Implicit loop (provided by –n)	Explicit loop
BEGIN { *Pre-input code goes here* }	*Pre-input code goes here*

LINE: while (<>) {
    INPUT-HANDLING CODE GOES HERE
}
	LINE: while (<>) {
	    INPUT-HANDLING CODE GOES HERE
	}

END { *Post-input code goes here* }	*Post-input code goes here*

The next looping facility we'll examine is an upside-down variation on the while/until loop, which comes in handy when the information that's meant to control looping isn't available up front.

10.3 LOOPING WITH *do while/until*

The Shell's while loop executes the code block between do and done while the condition returns True. But some situations require commands to be executed *before* each test of the condition, rather than after. That's why Perl has do while and do until, which position the test at the loop's bottom (see table 10.4).

The Shell lacks upside-down variations on while and until, but that hasn't stopped crafty programmers from rolling their own. The unusual format shown for the Shell's while in table 10.4 arranges for its preliminary code to be executed before the condition, repeatedly, until the condition stops returning True. The null

Table 10.4 Perl's do while loop and its Shell equivalent

Shell[a]	Perl

while
    prelim_code
    condition
do
    : # *null command*
done
	do {
	    prelim_code;
	} while (*condition*);

while *commands*; do :; done	do { *prelim_code*; } while(*condition*);

a. *prelim_code* stands for "preliminary code"; *commands* represents the combination of *prelim_code* and *condition*.

command (:) does nothing, as its name implies, apart from providing a syntactically required command between do and done.

Testing a loop at its bottom is achieved in Perl by using do while or do until, as illustrated in the right column of the table.

With both languages, you achieve the do until effect—which causes iteration to continue *until* the condition returns True—by replacing the while keyword with until and adjusting the logic of the condition

> **TIP** A common, fatal error is omitting the semicolon that's required after the parenthesized condition at the end of do while/until.

Next, we'll look at a typical case where you'd use a bottom-tested loop.

10.3.1 Prompting for input

Interacting with a live user is always a challenge, but in some cases it's absolutely necessary—such as when you need to confirm that the user *really* wants an irreversible, destructive action to be performed. Here's a code fragment written for the Shell that seeks confirmation for such a case:

Shell
```
while
        echo 'Remove all files? [y/n]'
        read answer
        [[ $answer != 'y'  &&  $answer != 'n' ]]
do
        :               # null command
done
# Code to handle y/n choice goes here
```

This bottom-tested Shell while loop issues a prompt, loads the answer into a variable, and then repeats those operations while the answer isn't "y" or "n".

Perl

The equivalent Perl loop needs to remove the trailing newline character from $answer before testing the acceptability of the input:[9]

```
do {
    printf 'Remove all files? [y/n] ';
    $answer=<STDIN>;
    chomp $answer;      # remove newline
} while ($answer ne 'y'  and  $answer ne 'n');
# Code to handle y/n choice goes here
```

---

[9] Remember, the l option strips trailing newlines only from input read via the implicit loop of the n or p option, not from input read by the input operator.

The do until variation is very similar, apart from using equality (eq) rather than inequality (ne) tests in its condition, and a logical or rather than and to connect them. Most would probably agree that this variation reads most naturally for this application:

```
do {
       printf 'Remove all files? [y/n] ';
       $answer=<STDIN>;
       chomp $answer;       # remove newline
} until ($answer eq 'y'  or  $answer eq 'n');
# Code to handle y/n choice goes here
```

The three loops you've just seen will all repeatedly prompt the user until they get what they need. But what if you want to let the user leave the loop on input of <^D>, which is a Unix convention for requesting release from an input-reading program?

The conventional Shell solution would be to rewrite the read answer command as read answer || break. Unfortunately, no analogous adjustment will work for Perl's do while or do until—because *neither responds to loop-control directives!* We'll revisit this issue in section 10.6.2, and see how to deal with it.

Next, we'll look at everybody's favorite Perl loop, which is also one of the few features it adapted from the C shell.

10.4 LOOPING WITH *foreach*

QUESTION: *What's the best loop in Perl?*
ANSWER: *As any JAPH worth his camel jerky will tell you, it's* **foreach**.

The while and do while loops discussed thus far continue iterating while the condition's True/False value permits it. In contrast, the distinctive property of the for and foreach loops is that they continue iterating until they run out of list elements to assign to the loop variable.

The syntax for the Shell's for loop is shown in table 10.5 alongside that of its Perl counterpart, foreach.

Table 10.5   The Shell's for loop and Perl's foreach loop

Shell[a]	Perl

for *var* in *LIST*
do
   code
done
	foreach $var (*LIST*) {
	       code;
	}

for *var* in *LIST*; do *code*; done	foreach $var (*LIST*) {code;}

a. *var* and *$var* are placeholders for the name of the loop variable, *LIST* for its associated list of values, and *code* for the code block to be processed on each iteration. The elements shown in the ghost font are optional.

Various commands (in the Shell) or expressions (in Perl) can be used to generate the *LIST*.[10] If in *LIST* is omitted with the Shell, the script's double quoted arguments ("$@") are used by default. Perl requires *LIST* to be present, but it allows the loop variable to be omitted and uses $_ in that case, which is a convenient feature.[11]

We'll look at some practical applications of foreach next, starting with an upgrade to a script from an earlier chapter.

10.4.1   Unlinking files: the `rm_files` script

As discussed in section 7.5.1, when you run unlink with multiple filename arguments, you can't get detailed explanations for why particular files couldn't be removed.[12] But now that you know about foreach, you can easily rectify that problem by unlinking files one at a time:

```
$ rm_files junk shangri-la kumari-devi    # only junk gets trashed
 rm_files: Unlink failed on 'shangri-la'; No such file or directory
 rm_files: Unlink failed on 'kumari-devi'; Permission denied
```

There's not much to the script, because foreach makes it so simple:

```
$ cat rm_files
#! /usr/bin/perl -wl

foreach (@ARGV) {
    unlink $_  or  warn "$0: Unlink failed on: '$_'; $!\n";
}
```

A loop like this one could come in handy in a script that creates temporary files and wants to report any problems later when removing them.

It's much easier to process files a line at a time with Perl's foreach loop than it is with the Shell's for, as you'll see next.

10.4.2   Reading a line at a time

Shell scripts that need to process lines from files typically use command substitution (see section 8.5) on the cat command to provide the *LIST* used by the for loop. The tricky part is that some special manipulations of the IFS variable are required to arrange for cat's output to be parsed into *lines*, rather than the default of *words*:

---

[10] Section 9.3 shows expressions commonly used to generate lists in the Shell and Perl. On the web, http://TeachMePerl.com/DQs_in_shell_vs_perl.html documents the effects of double quotes in the two languages. You may wish to consult these resources while reading this section.

[11] The Perl programmer also has the option of providing a scope-defining *declaration* for the loop variable (see section 11.3).

[12] That's because the OS-error message variable, "$!", can only hold a single error message at a time.

```
 Shell
OIFS="$IFS"                     # save for restoration
IFS='
'               # Internal Field Separator is now "carriage return"
for line in `cat somefile`     # or: `cmd1 | cmd2`, etc.
do
      IFS="$OIFS"              # reinstate original setting ASAP
      echo "Processing $line"
      # Processing code goes here
done
```

A savvy JAPH wouldn't usually write a loop to handle this scenario, because the n option provides a more convenient solution. However, that approach can't always be used—e.g., the filename might not be available from the user until after the script is already running, when it's too late to provide that information as an argument.

Here's a Perl solution that you can use in such cases:

```
 Perl
printf 'Enter filename: ';    # prompt for input
$filename=<STDIN>;            # store the filename
defined $filename  or  exit;  # exit on <^D>
chomp $filename;              # strip trailing newline
-T $filename  or  die;        # test for readable, text contents

foreach $line ( `cat $filename ` ) { # Or: `cmd1 | cmd2`, etc.
      print "Processing $line";
      # processing code goes here
}
```

After the filename has been obtained and validated, the rest of the coding is considerably simpler than the Shell version. That's because Perl processes the output of command interpolation one *line* at a time by default, whereas the Shell's default is to process it one *word* at a time (necessitating the tricky IFS manipulations).[13]

Next, you'll see how to print hashes using a foreach loop, which offers certain advantages.

10.4.3 Printing a hash

Because hashes return their key/value pairs in a seemingly haphazard order,[14] a common application of foreach is to print each pair in *key-sorted* order. The following loop prints the variable-name/value pairs of the environment variables, which are provided by the Shell to its child processes (such as this code's program), in alphanumeric order:

---

[13] See section 9.3 for a detailed comparison of the languages with respect to *list generators*.

[14] The order in which keys and values are returned is a consistent and repeatable one, but it seems haphazard because of its unpredictability (see table 9.7 and section 9.2.2).

```
foreach $variable_name ( sort keys %ENV ) { # show variables/values
    print "$variable_name => $ENV{$variable_name}";
}
```

Here's some sample output from a Linux system; note that the keys are in alphanumeric order:

```
COLUMNS => 80
EDITOR => vim
HOME => /ward/bond
```

To pay for the privilege of sorting the keys, we assume the responsibility of indexing to get their values—which are the opposite tradeoffs to those obtained by using each in a while loop (see section 10.2.3).

Next, you'll see how Perl can—IMHO, help you—AFAIK, to decipher those cryptic acronyms—FWIW, in your email messages. *HTH!*

10.4.4 Demystifying acronyms: The `expand_acronyms` script

Many people save keystrokes and thwart carpal-tunnel syndrome by using cryptic acronyms in email messages. But Gabriella got frustrated trying to decipher the ones she didn't understand, so she wrote an "acronym expander" to explain them. Because it needs to map strings like "FWIW" into their expanded equivalents, she uses a hash to associate each acronym with its expansion, as shown in listing 10.2.

Listing 10.2 The `expand_acronyms` script

```
#! /usr/bin/perl -wpl

BEGIN {
    %expansion=(
        FWIW  => "for what it's worth",
        IMHO  => 'in my humble opinion',
        AFAIK => 'as far as I know',
        YMMV  => 'your mileage may vary',
        JAPH  => 'Just Another Perl Hacker',
    );
}

foreach $acronym ( keys %expansion ) {
    s/\b$acronym\b/$expansion{$acronym}/ig;
}
```

This script reads a line at a time using the p option, and then it uses the foreach loop to attempt a case-insensitive global substitution in the current line for each acronym in turn. Once that's done, the resulting line is printed automatically (courtesy of the p option).

Here's a sample run with a suitable file:

```
$ cat jive_talkin
FWIW, IMHO,
YMMV, AFAIK.

- JAPH

$ expand_acronyms jive_talkin
for what it's worth, in my humble opinion,
your mileage may vary, as far as I know.

- Just Another Perl Hacker
```

Having just learned how to process hash keys in sorted order, you might be surprised to see that keys isn't preceded by sort in the list of the foreach loop. But that wouldn't offer any advantage in this program, because the order in which the substitutions are made is unimportant.

Remember Ivan, the guy who's switching hobbies from stamp collection to email-header collection? He's got a problem, which foreach can help solve.

10.4.5 Reducing image sizes: The compress_image2 script

Ivan is currently typing the twenty-seventh invocation of his image-compressing script, this time for the stamp memorializing Franco Zappato's famous tweezer collection. He needs to work *smarter*! In particular, his compress_image script needs to be enhanced with a foreach loop so it can compress *all* files named as arguments, allowing Ivan to process all his images with one invocation of this form:

```
$ compress_image2  *.jpg     # processes 242 *.jpg files
...
Size of Idi_Amin_medals.jpg: 33272 bytes
Size of Idi_Amin_medals.jpg: 29184 bytes
Size of Idi_Amin_medals.jpg: 24889 bytes
Size of Imelda_flip-flops.jpg: 36782 bytes
...
```

As highlighted in listing 10.3, the significant changes to the original script are the addition of Lines 7 and 25 to provide the enclosing foreach loop, and the removal of the -s option from the shebang line. Although that option made it easy for him to specify the filename using the -fname=*filename* switch with the earlier script, it also limited that script to processing one file per invocation, which has become an undesirable restriction.

The new version still uses the $fname variable, but now it's reset to the next filename from the list at the beginning of each iteration, courtesy of the foreach loop. That makes life a lot easier for Ivan, who's got better things to do than re-issue hundreds of commands by hand.

Now it's time to talk about Perl's for loop, which is valued in cases where the programmer needs to deal directly with array indices.

Listing 10.3 The `compress_image2` script

```
1   #! /usr/bin/perl -wl
2   # Usage: compress_image2 image [image2 ...]
3
4   $DEBUG=1;     # for extra feedback during testing
5   $qual=80;     # starting quality value
6
7   foreach $fname (@ARGV) {
8     # Copy original image to another directory
9     ! system "cp '$fname' '/tmp/$fname'"  or
10        die "$0: cp failed; $!\n";
11    $DEBUG  and  # show initial size
12      print "Size of $fname: ", -s $fname, ' bytes';
13
14    while ( -s $fname > 25_000 )  {  # 25_000 means 25,000
15      # Compress copy using $qual; store under original name
16      ! system "convert -quality $qual " .
17        " '/tmp/$fname' 'jpg:$fname' "  or  # Shell-quote fname
18          die "$0: convert failed\n";
19
20      $DEBUG  and  # show new size
21        print "Size of $fname: ", -s $fname, ' bytes';
22
23      $qual=$qual - 5;    # reduce for next iteration
24    }
25  }
```

NOTE   The Shell's **for** loop is similar to Perl's **foreach** loop, not Perl's for loop.

10.5 LOOPING WITH *for*

Although the Shell's for is like Perl's foreach, Perl does have a for loop of its own, derived from the C language. It conveniently bundles together the initialization, condition-testing, and incrementing steps typically used to process arrays in that language. Table 10.6 shows its syntax.

Table 10.6 Perl's for loop[a]

```
for (init; condition; increment) {
    code;
}
```

```
for (init; condition; increment) { code; }
```

a. *init* is a placeholder for a variable initialization, *condition* for the True/False expression that controls iteration, *increment* for an expression that increments the loop variable, and *code* for the statements processed on each iteration.

The for loop processes its elements as follows:

1 It executes *init* (which typically initializes the loop variable);

2 It executes *condition*, using scalar context;

3 If *condition* is True, the loop executes *code*; if not, the loop is finished;

4 It executes *increment* (which typically increments the loop variable by 1); then, it returns to step 2.

Here's a simple example that prints each of a script's arguments. It uses the handy $index++ notation (see table 5.12) to increment the loop variable by 1 after each iteration:

```
for ( $index=0; $index < @ARGV; $index++ ) {
    print $ARGV[$index];
}
```

The <u>condition</u> checks that the current value of $index is still less than the number of elements in the array, which is appropriate because $index starts from 0.[15]

Now that you understand how the for loop works, you should know something even more important about it: It isn't used very often for list processing in Perl! To understand why, consider the following alternative to the for loop just shown:

```
foreach $arg (@ARGV) {
    print $arg;
}
```

Which would you rather type?

From a C language perspective, the for loop helps the programmer by bundling together the elements required to micro-manage the minutiae of array processing. In contrast, the Perlthink perspective is that in many cases, for represents the *hard way* to iterate over a list of values, as a comparison of the previous code samples demonstrates. For this reason, foreach is generally preferred to for in Perl for list processing.

However, there certainly are programs that can benefit from the use of Perl's for loop. These include programs that need to keep count of the number of iterations they have performed, and programs that need to search for particular elements in arrays and retain their indices for later use.

We'll look next at a list-processing program that benefits from for's support for indices.

---

[15] An alternative way to phrase the test would be $index <= $#ARGV, using the special variable that contains the number of elements in its associated array. But that requires two characters of additional typing (= and #), so I recommend the shorter approach.

10.5.1 Exploiting `for`'s support for indexing: the `raffle` script

During a period when The Perl Foundation (TPF) was funding such amazing guys as Larry Wall, Damian Conway, and Dan Sugalski to work full-time on Perl, we had frequent TPF fund-raising events at the meetings of the Seattle Perl Users Group (SPUG). These included such activities as auctioning Perl books autographed by their *actual* authors (when convenient),[16] and the selling of raffle tickets to those wishing to compete for geekworthy prizes.

We couldn't use the old technology of dropping business cards in a fishbowl in running these raffles, because we wanted the chances of winning to be proportional to the numbers of dollars contributed—and there were precious few SPUGsters packing mass quantities of business cards. So, we decided to simulate the fishbowl electronically, using Perl. The program I wrote ended up having *two* `for` loops, which makes it an excellent example to show you now.

Here's a test run with the `-debug` switch enabled for extra feedback, for a hypothetical raffle in which Andy contributes $3, and Dora $2:

```
$ raffle -debug andy 3  dora 2   # Debugging run
Inserting 3 tickets for ANDY
Inserting 2 tickets for DORA

Fishbowl contains: ANDY ANDY ANDY DORA DORA

Selecting a ticket ...

And the winning ticket is #4, owned by "DORA"
```

Here's a production run, showing what would appear on the auditorium's big screen during an actual raffle:

```
$ raffle andy 39  dora 42  colin 40  ingy 41   # Production run

Selecting a ticket ...
                          ↵ Pregnant pause here
And the winning ticket is #108, owned by "COLIN"
```

Listing 10.4 shows the `raffle` script.

This program requires some explaining, so we'll walk through the interesting parts while referring to the following invocation, which shows argument numbers along with their corresponding indices in the @ARGV array:

```
         1  2   3   4    ↵ Argument number
$ raffle andy 3 dora 2
         0  1   2   3    ↵ Index number
```

---

[16] Having live access to a book's actual author wasn't always possible, so on certain magical evenings, you could bid on a copy of Damian Conway's *Object Oriented Perl* signed by none other than renowned SPUGster Brian Ingerson!

Listing 10.4   The SPUG `raffle` script

```
1   #! /usr/bin/perl -s -wl
2   # Simulates "hand in fishbowl" method of picking raffle winner
3
4   $Usage="Usage: $0 [-debug]  name1  num_tickets1 ...";
5
6   # Process args in pairs; requires incrementing by two
7   for ($index=0; $index < @ARGV; $index+=2) {
8       $name="\U$ARGV[$index]";       # uppercased contestant name
9       $tickets=$ARGV[$index+1];      # arg after name is count
10
11      # Given "andy 3  dora 2", fishbowl gets 3 ANDYs, 2 DORAs
12      $debug   and
13          warn "Inserting $tickets tickets for $name\n";
14
15      for ( $tcount=1; $tcount <= $tickets; $tcount++ ) {
16          push @fishbowl, $name;  # put in another "$name"
17      }
18  }
19  @fishbowl  or  die "$Usage\n";  # empty fishbowl, no drawing
20  $debug  and  print "\nFishbowl contains: @fishbowl";
21
22  print "\nSelecting a ticket ...";
23  $rand_num=int rand @fishbowl;   # range is 0,#elements-1
24
25  $debug  or  sleep 2;     # Engender suspense (unless debugging)
26  print "\nAnd the winning ticket is #$rand_num,",
27       " owned by: \"$fishbowl[$rand_num]\"";
```

The first `for` loop starts on Line 7. Its job is to process one contestant's name and donation on each iteration, so it needs to process two arguments at a time. The initialization expression sets `$index` to 0, to start with the first argument, as you'd expect. However, the incrementing expression is unusual because it has to increase the argument counter by two, which is accomplished using the compound assignment operator (see table 5.12). In this way, the first iteration processes andy via `$ARGV[0]` (and 3 via `$ARGV[1]`), and the second processes dora via `$ARGV[2]` (and 2 via `$ARGV[3]`). As dictated by the condition on Line 7, the loop finishes when `$index` reaches 4, the number of arguments provided.

To enhance readability and avoid repeated indexing, Lines 8 and 9 load variables named `$tickets` and `$name` with the associated values pulled out of the argument array. Note that the `$tickets` value is obtained by using the current `$index` plus 1, to access its following ticket count (3 for andy). For additional dramatic impact on the big screen, the `$name` variable is loaded with the uppercased (via `\U`) name of the contestant on Line 8.

The second, nested `for` loop starts on Line 15. Its job is to load three instances of ANDY and two of DORA into the simulated fishbowl, so that their probabilities of winning will be proportional to the number of tickets they've purchased. The initialization and incrementing expressions for this loop ensure that the number of ticket-granting iterations for the current contestant is equal to the number of tickets purchased, by stopping after $tcount (the ticket counter) equals the number of tickets purchased (because we're counting from 1 this time).

The fishbowl is loaded by using push (Line 16) to add additional elements at the end of the @fishbowl array.[17]

Line 19 does a sanity check and bails out (via die) if there aren't any tickets in the fishbowl. If everything is okay, Line 20 shows the fishbowl's contents, if debugging mode is enabled (via the -debug command-line switch).

Line 23 uses the customary technique for selecting a random index for an array, based on rand @arrayname (see table 7.7).

All that's left is a suspenseful pause of two seconds on Line 25, to get the audience excited, and then the winner is announced.

This program makes good use of the special capabilities of for by manipulating $index to process pairs of arguments in the outer loop, and $count to issue the correct number of tickets to the current contestant in the inner loop.

Now that we've covered all of Perl's standard loops, we'll turn our attention to its special directives for exerting additional kinds of control over loops.

NOTE   Some former C programmers are inclined to habitually use for in place of foreach. But having already escaped from the tyrannical *Land of C* and arrived in Perlistan, they can now let down their guard and exploit such labor saving shortcuts with impunity.

10.6   *USING LOOP-CONTROL DIRECTIVES*

Like the Shell, Perl provides facilities to control iteration in loops, as shown in table 10.7.

Table 10.7   Corresponding loop-control directives for the Shell and Perl

Shell	Perl
continue *loop-number*	next *loop-label*
break *loop-number*	last *loop-label*

The Shell's continue is like Perl's next, forcing the completion of the current iteration, and break is like Perl's last, forcing the loop's termination. But the loop of interest is specified in Perl in a different and more practical way—instead of counting nesting levels to get the *loop-number*, as Shell programmers must do, Perl programmers refer to loops using descriptive *loop-labels*, such as PROCESS_URLS and WRITE_OUTPUT_LINES.

---

[17] We don't care where the contestants end up in the array, and there's no other advantage to working with indices here, so push is the best choice (see section 9.1.1).

As a Perl programmer, you have a valuable option triggered by `next` that's unavailable in the Shell: You can define a `continue` block whose statements are executed before the start of the next iteration (covered in section 10.6.4). This is useful in cases where additional work must be done—such as incrementing a variable, closing a file, or printing user feedback—before each subsequent iteration can begin.

Okay, I've held my tongue as long as I could—now it's time to reveal one of Perl's dirty secrets. `do while/until` isn't a *real* loop, and for that reason it can't respond to loop-control directives! But with a language this powerful, there are always alternative ways of getting things done, so you'll see a general technique for implementing a fully-functional bottom-tested loop in section 10.6.4.

Loops often appear in groups in which some are located within others, like nested Russian dolls. Next, you'll learn some special loop-control directives that let you specify which loop in a nested set you want the CPU to visit—or to leave.

10.6.1 Nesting loops within loops

When you're working with nested loops—loops within other loops—it's important to be able to designate the one that's meant to be the target of a particular loop-control directive. The Shell programmer does this using a number related to the nesting depth, which varies for a given loop according to the location of the reference. For example, the `while` loop in listing 10.5 can be exited via `break 2` on Line 9, or `break 1` on Line 12.

Listing 10.5   Shell syntax for loop-control directives

```
 1 while
 2    COMMAND_RETURNS_TRUE
 3 do
 4    for item in LIST
 5    do                               # MEANING:
 6      TRUE_CONDITION && continue 1   # next iteration: for
 7      TRUE_CONDITION && continue 2   # next iteration: while
 8      TRUE_CONDITION && break 1      # leave: for
 9      TRUE_CONDITION && break 2      # leave: while
10    done
11    # "leave: for" comes here
12    TRUE_CONDITION && break 1        # leave: while
13 done
14 # "leave: while" comes here
```

In contrast, the Perl programmer uses unchanging labels in referring to loops, as shown in listing 10.6, which is the Perl counterpart to the pseudo-code program of listing 10.5. To create a label, you use a Perl identifier followed by a colon; to refer to that label, you use the identifier without the colon along with a loop-control directive. The identifier is subject to the same rules as variable names, meaning it can use letters, digits, and underscores, but it can't start with a digit. Lines 1 and 4 of listing 10.6, respectively, illustrate the setting and using of the `while` loop label called OUTER.

```
 1 OUTER: while ( COMMAND_RETURNS_TRUE ) {
 2   INNER: foreach $item ( LIST ) {    # MEANING:
 3     TRUE_CONDITION   and   next INNER;   # next iteration: foreach
 4     TRUE_CONDITION   and   next OUTER;   # next iteration: while
 5     TRUE_CONDITION   and   last INNER;   # leave: foreach
 6     TRUE_CONDITION   and   last OUTER;   # leave: while
 7   }
 8   # "leave: foreach" comes here
 9   # following exits while; same effect and coding as Line 6
10     TRUE_CONDITION   and   last OUTER;   # leave: while
11 }
12 # "leave: while" comes here
```

For heightened visibility, loop labels consisting of capital letters are recommended, as shown in listing 10.6.

In both languages, you can omit the loop specifier—the Shell's number or Perl's label—if your intent is to affect the innermost enclosing loop.

Don't you like the Perl approach better? I certainly do, because there's no ambiguity about the meaning of a statement like last OUTER. In contrast, the Shell's break 2 and break 1 may mean different things—or the same thing—depending on the position at which each appears in the code! Moreover, it's easier to make the mistake of typing break 1 when you mean break 2 than to type something more meaningful like PROCESS_ROW when you mean PROCESS_COLUMN.

Next, you'll see how to use these loop-control directives in representative Perl programs.

10.6.2 Enabling loop-control directives in bottom-tested loops

As stated previously, Perl's do while/until doesn't respond to loop-control directives, which makes it unsuitable for use in any but the most trivial loops requiring bottom-tested conditions. So no matter how desperately you may need to do so, you can't code a do while loop like this:

```
do {
  preliminary_code;
  condition1  and  next;   # start next iteration
  condition2  and  last;   # leave loop
} while (condition);
```

But here's a workaround that uses an *infinite* while loop—one whose condition is always True—to manage the iterations, along with a bottom-tested condition linked to a loop-control directive to arrange for the loop's termination:[18]

---

[18] The parentheses shown around the controlling condition prevent precedence interactions between the or/and after the condition and other operators within the condition itself. Even better, they make that line look more like an official loop-control statement!

```
while (1) {                     # or, until(0)
    preliminary_code;
    condition1 and next;        # start next iteration
    condition2 and last;        # leaves loop
    # Here's the "controlling condition"
    (condition) or last;        # leaves loop when condition False
}
```

The until variation differs only by starting with until(0) and ending with (condition) and last.

This looping format provides the basic behavior of do while, but with the added benefit of functioning loop-control directives. Next, we'll consider some applications where this kind of loop can be used to good advantage.

10.6.3   Prompting for input

It's impolite to hold a user captive to an interactive session that he might want to escape, so it's conventional to recognize input of <^D> as a request for program termination. In the Shell, you can provide an escape from a prompting loop by executing exit when read returns False, which happens on input of <^D> from the keyboard. Here's an example, with loop-control directives highlighted:[19]

Shell
```
while
        echo 'Remove all files? [y/n] '
        read answer || exit    # terminate on <^D>
        [[ $answer = "" ]] && continue
        [[ "$answer" != 'y' -a "$answer" != 'n' ]]
do
        :
done
# Code to handle y/n choice goes here
```

This loop continues prompting for a y/n answer until it gets one or the user presses <^D>. Note that if $answer is empty, continue starts the next iteration immediately, bypassing the next set of tests.

Perl
Here's the Perl counterpart to the Shell example:

```
while (1) {
    printf 'Remove all files? [y/n] ';
    $answer=<STDIN>;
    defined $answer or exit;    # terminate on <^D>
```

---

[19] For simplicity, we're omitting newline-suppression for the echo command, because the syntax differs between shells. There's little benefit from next, or the comparable continue in its Shell counterpart, because the empty answer will fail the string-equality tests anyway. But in other cases, it might be beneficial to use next as shown to avoid executing the controlling condition.

```
        chomp $answer;                     # remove newline
        $answer eq ""   and next;      # re-prompt if only <ENTER> typed
        ($answer ne 'y' and  $answer ne 'n')  or  last;
}
# Code to handle y/n choice goes here
```

Next, you'll see a way to obtain even greater versatility from this kind of bottom-tested loop.

10.6.4   Enhancing loops with `continue` blocks: the `confirmation` script

An unusual and valuable feature of the Shell's `while`/`until` loop is that it permits an arbitrary number of commands to appear between the opening keyword and `do`, as well as between `do` and `done`. This makes it easy to implement solutions that require preliminary code to be executed before the condition is tested, and then for other code to be conditionally executed afterward.

Table 10.8 shows the full syntax for the Shell's `while`/`until` loop, along with its closest Perl counterpart.

Table 10.8   Enhanced `while`/`until` loops for the Shell and Perl

Shell	Perl

`while               # or until`
`    preliminary_code`
`    condition`
`do`
`    conditional_code`
`done`
	`while (1) {        # or until(0)`
	`    preliminary_code;`
	`    (condition)  or  last;`
	`}`
	`continue {`
	`    continuation_code;`
	`}`

Shell

As a variation on an earlier example (see section 10.3.1), the following loop uses an `echo` command between `do` and `done` where there was previously a null (`:`) command:

```
while
        echo 'Remove all files? [y/n] '
        read answer || exit      # terminate on <^D>
        # [[ $answer = "" ]] && continue
        [[ "$answer" != 'y' -a "$answer" != 'n' ]]
do
        echo "Please respond with 'y' or 'n'"
done
# Code to handle y/n choice goes here
```

The added `echo` command (highlighted) arranges for an instructional message to be provided when the user supplies incorrect input. The command from the original version that checks `$answer` for a null value is now commented-out, because executing `continue` would start the next iteration immediately, bypassing the newly added instructional message.

Perl doesn't provide a looping mechanism that's entirely equivalent to the full syntax of the Shell's while/until. However, it does let you attach a continue block—which contains code to be executed before the loop's next iteration—to any loop. Using this feature lets you match the functionality of the Shell's enhanced while/until loop and achieve additional benefits as well.

The right column of table 10.8 shows the syntax for this "enhanced" Perl while/until loop. It's set up as an infinite loop (see section 10.6.2) with a bottom-tested condition that causes either the continue block to be executed (for the True case) or the loop to be exited via last (for False).

We can use this loop to duplicate the functionality of the earlier Shell example, as shown in the confirmation script. The program components that can trigger the execution of the continue block are highlighted:

```
$ cat confirmation
#! /usr/bin/perl -wl

while (1) {                              # seek confirmation
    printf 'Are you sure? [y/n] ';
    $answer=<STDIN>;
    defined $answer  or  exit;        # exit on <^D>
    chomp $answer;                    # remove newline
    $answer eq ""  and  next;        # execute continue; re-prompt
    ($answer ne 'y'  and  $answer ne 'n')  or  last;
}
continue { # executed before all prompts after first
    print "\nPlease respond with 'y'  or  'n'";
}
# code to handle y/n choice goes here
```

The next directive is conditionally executed for inputs that are empty after chomping, which results from the user pressing only <ENTER>. That causes execution of the continue block, as does a True value for the bottom-tested condition.

Here's what the script looks like in action:

```
$ confirmation
Are you sure? [y/n] Say what?

Please respond with 'y' or 'n'
Are you sure? [y/n] <ENTER>

Please respond with 'y' or 'n'
Are you sure? [y/n] N

Please respond with 'y' or 'n'
Are you sure? [y/n] n
```
⮐ **Program proceeds to next phase**

Note that when the user responds to the prompt with only <ENTER>, the `continue` block is executed via `next` within the preliminary code, without the condition even being evaluated.[20] That's a desirable effect in cases where the continuation code is needed to make the required preparations for the next iteration, no matter how its execution is triggered. Unfortunately, the Shell's `while` doesn't provide this service.

Let's review! Adding a `continue` block to a bottom-tested `while`/`until` loop provides two improvements over Perl's `do while`/`until` loop:

- It allows loop-control directives to work;
- It allows a `continue` code-block to be executed before each subsequent execution of the preliminary code.

In some applications, such as the one that interactively seeks confirmation of a choice, this is exactly the behavior you need.

You've now learned about all of Perl's "native" loops, but the best is yet to come. It's a loop that was implemented especially for this chapter!

10.7   THE CPAN's `select` LOOP FOR PERL

The `select` loop of the Korn and Bash shells is unique in several ways. It's the friendliest control feature in any Unix shell, it's the only Shell loop that's missing from standard Perl, and it's one of the few flow-control features for Perl that's ever been implemented as a module-based enhancement.

But what does a `select` loop do? Given a list of values, it generates a numbered menu of selections, prompts the user to select one by number, and then executes a code block with a variable set to that selection. In other words, it automatically provides the infrastructure needed to write terminal-based menu-oriented programs.

Here's an example that lets a user select a `*.txt` file for more-*ification* using the Shell's `select`:

```
$ select fname in *.txt
> do
>       more $fname
> done
1) awk.txt
2) bash.txt
3) ksh.txt
#? 2
BASH(1)                                                        BASH(1)

NAME
        bash - GNU Bourne-Again SHell
...
#? <^D>
$
```

---

[20] Hence the use of the term *continuation code*, rather than *conditional code*, for this loop in table 10.8.

From a Perlish perspective, you can think of select as a special kind of interactive variation on a foreach loop. But rather than having each list-value assigned automatically to the loop variable for one iteration, select only assigns values as they are selected by the user.

Next, you'll see how you can avoid "re-inventing wheels" by using this loop.

10.7.1 Avoiding the re-invention of the "choose-from-a-menu" wheel

Although Perl has no counterpart to the Shell's handy select loop, its functionality is provided by a CPAN module called Shell::POSIX::Select.[21] It provides its services through *source-code filtering*, which means it extracts the select loops from your program and rewrites them using native Perl features. As a result, you can use a feature that's missing from Perl as if it were there!

The benefit of bringing the select loop to Perl is that it obviates the need for terminal applications to provide their own implementations of the *choose-from-a-menu* code, which indulges the programmer's noble craving for Laziness—and thereby increases productivity.

Table 10.9 shows the syntax variations for the Shell's version of the select loop.

Table 10.9 The Shell's select loop

```
select var            ; do commands; done      # Form 0
select var in LIST; do commands; done          # Form 1
```

If in LIST is omitted (as in Form 0), in "$@" is used by default to provide automatic processing of the script's (or function's) argument list.

Some of the major forms of Perl's select loop are shown in table 10.10. These take their inspiration from the Shell and then add enhancements for greater friendliness and, well, *Perlishness*.

Table 10.10 The select loop for Perl

```
use Shell::POSIX::Select;
select                ()        { }            # Form 0
select                ()        { CODE; }      # Form 1
select                (LIST)    { CODE; }      # Form 2
select        $var    (LIST)    { CODE; }      # Form 3
```

As you can see, Perl's select lets you omit any or even *all* of its components (apart from the punctuation symbols). For example, if the loop variable is omitted, as in Forms 0, 1, and 2, $_ is used by default. If the LIST is omitted, as in Forms 0 and 1, the appropriate arguments are used by default (i.e., those provided to the script or the

---

[21] Written by yours truly, a long-time Shell programmer turned Perl proponent, while writing this chapter—so I wouldn't have to say "the best Shell loop is missing from Perl".

enclosing subroutine), as with its Shell counterpart. And if *CODE* is omitted (as in Form 0), a statement that prints the loop variable is used as the default code block.

Because system administrators have the responsibility for monitoring user activity on their systems, they might find the following application of select to be of particular interest.

10.7.2 Monitoring user activity: the `show_user` script

This program allows the user to obtain a system-activity report for users who are currently logged in:

```
$ cat show_user
#! /usr/bin/perl -wl

use Shell::POSIX::Select;

# Get list of who's logged in
@users=`who | perl -wnla -e ' print \$F[0]; ' | sort -u`;
chomp @users;    # remove newlines

# Let program's user select Unix user to monitor
select ( @users ) { system "w $_"; }
```

This script uses the who command to get the list of current users, and then a separate Perl command to isolate their names from the first column of that report. Note the need to backslash the $ to prevent the Perl script from providing its own (null) value for $F[0] before the who | perl | sort pipeline is launched. sort is used with the "unique lines" option to remove duplicate user names for those logged in more than once. The w command, which reports the selected user's activity, won't appreciate finding newlines attached to the ends of those names, so the @users array is chomp'd to remove them.

Here's a sample run of the script:

```
$ show_user

1) phroot  2) tim

Enter number of choice: 2

 3:51pm  up 4 days, 17:57, 7 users, load average: 0.00, 0.00, 0.00
USER    TTY     FROM        LOGIN@   IDLE   JCPU   PCPU  WHAT
tim     pts/1   lumpy       Mon10am 3days 18.91s  1.19s  -bash
tim     pts/3   stumpy      Mon10am 28:16m  0.48s  0.48s  bash -login
tim     tty5    grumpy      Sun 3pm 28:16m  1.71s  1.04s  slogin lumpy
tim     pts/0   bumpy       Sun 4pm  1.00s  4.03s  0.14s  w tim
<ENTER>

1) phroot  2) tim

Enter number of choice: <^D>
```

Note that the user pressed <ENTER> to redisplay the menu and <^D> to exit the loop, just as she'd do with the Shell's `select`.[22]

Next, you'll see how `select` can facilitate access to Perl's huge collection of online man pages.

10.7.3 Browsing man pages: the `perlman` script

One of the obstacles faced by all Perl programmers is determining which one of Perl's more than 130 cryptically named man pages covers a particular subject. To make this task easier, I wrote a script that provides a menu interface to Perl's online documentation.

Figure 10.1 shows the use of `perlman`, which lets the user choose a man page from its description. For simplicity's sake, only a few of Perl's man pages are listed in the figure, and only the initial lines of the selected page are displayed.[23]

```
$ perlman

1) Perl built-in functions
2) Perl cheat sheet
3) Perl data structures
4) Perl data structures intro
5) Perl operators and precedence
6) Perl regular expressions quick start
7) Perl source filters
8) Perl syntax


Enter number of choice: 7
PERLFILTER(1)      Perl Programmers Reference Guide      PERLFILTER(1)


NAME
        perlfilter-Source Filters

DESCRIPTION
        This article is about a little-known feature of Perl
        called source filters. Source filters alter the program
        text of a module before Perl sees it, much as a C prepro-
...

1) Perl built-in functions
2) Perl cheat sheet
3) Perl data structures
4) Perl data structures intro
5) Perl operators and precedence
6) Perl regular expressions quick start
7) Perl source filters
8) Perl syntax


Enter number of choice:
```

Figure 10.1   Demonstration of the `perlman` script

---

[22] For those who don't like that behavior (including me), there's an option that causes the menu to be *automatically* redisplayed before each prompt. I wish the Shell's `select` also had that feature!

[23] The `select` loop is a good example of the benefits of Perl's source-code filtering facility, which is described in the selected man page, `perlfilter`.

Before we delve into the script's coding, let's discuss what it does on a conceptual level.

The first thing to understand is that man perl doesn't produce "the" definitive man page on all things Perlish. On the contrary, its main purpose is to act as a table of contents for Perl's *other* man pages, which deal with specific topics.

Toward this end, man perl provides a listing in which each man page's name is paired with a short description of its subject, in this format:

perlsyn   Perl syntax

As illustrated in the figure, the role of perlman is to let the user select a man-page name for viewing from its short description.

Listing 10.7 shows the script. Because it's important to understand which of its elements refer to the man-page names versus their corresponding descriptions, distinctive highlighting with bold type (for man-page names) and underlined type (for descriptions) is used.

Listing 10.7   The perlman script

```
1   #! /usr/bin/perl -w
2
3   use Shell::POSIX::Select;
4
5   $perlpage=`man perl`;    # put name/description records into var
6
7   # Man-page name & description have this format in $perlpage:
8   #     perlsyn              Perl syntax
9
10  # Loop creates hash that maps man-page descriptions to names
11  while ( $perlpage =~ /^\s+(perl\w+)\s+(.+)$/mg ) { # get match
12
13      # Load ()-parts of regex, from $1 and $2, into hash
14      $desc2page{$2}=$1;       # e.g., $hash{'Perl syntax'}='perlsyn'
15  }
16
17  select $page ( sort keys %desc2page ) {  # display descriptions
18      system "man $desc2page{$page}";      # display requested page
19  }
```

The script begins by storing the output of man perl in $perlpage on Line 5. Then a matching operator, as the controlling condition of a while loop (Line 11), is used to find the first man-page name (using "perl\w+") and its associated description (using ".+") in $perlpage. The m modifier on the matching operator allows the pattern's leading ^ to match the beginning, and its $ the end, of any of the lines within the variable (see table 3.6 on multi-line mode).

Capturing parentheses (see table 3.8) are used in the regex (Line 11) to store what the patterns matched in the special variables $1 and $2 (referring to the first and second set of parentheses, respectively), so that in Line 14 the man-page name can be stored in the %desc2page hash, using its associated description as the key.

The next iteration of the loop will look for another match after the end of the previous one, due to the use of the matching operator's g modifier in the scalar context of while's condition.[24]

Finally, in Lines 17–19, select displays the numbered list of sorted man-page descriptions in the form "7) Perl source filters". Then it obtains the user's selection, retrieves its corresponding page name from the hash, and invokes man to display the requested page (in the case of figure 10.1, "perlfilter").

As you might imagine, this script is very popular with the students in our classes, because it lets them find the documentation they need without first memorizing lots of inscrutable man-page names (such as "perlcheat", "perltoot", and "perlguts").

> **TIP** You can use the only Shell loop that Larry left out of Perl by getting the Shell::POSIX::Select module from the CPAN.

10.8 SUMMARY

Perl provides a rich collection of looping facilities, adapted from the Bourne shell, the C shell, and the C language.

The closely-related while and until loops continue iterating until the controlling condition becomes False or True, respectively. You saw while used to incrementally compress images until a target size was reached (in compress_image, section 10.2.2) and to extract and print key/value pairs from a hash with the assistance of the each function (in show_pvars, section 10.2.3).

Perl also provides bottom-tested loops called do while and do until, which perform one iteration before first testing the condition. Although these aren't "real" loops, the savvy programmer can construct functional replacements using while and until with continue blocks to allow loop-control directives to function properly (as shown in confirmation, section 10.6.4).

The foreach loop provides the easiest method for processing a list of values, because it frees you from the burden of managing indices. You saw it used to remove files (rm_files, section 10.4.1) and to perform text substitutions for deciphering acronyms in email messages (expand_acronyms, section 10.4.4).

The relatively complex for loop should be used in cases where iteration can be controlled by a condition, and which benefit from its index-management services. An example is the raffle script (section 10.5.1), which needs to process its arguments in pairs.

---

[24] The meaning of the matching operator's g modifier is context dependent—in list context, it causes all the matches (or else the captured sub-matches, if any) to be returned at once. But in scalar context, the matches are returned one at a time.

The implicit loop provided by the n (or p) option is a great convenience in many small- to medium-sized programs, but larger or more complex ones may have special needs that make the use of explicit loops more practical.[25]

You can use the only Shell loop that Larry left out of Perl by getting the Shell::POSIX::Select module from the CPAN.[26] It provides the select loop, which prevents you from having to re-create the choose-from-a-menu code for managing interactions with a terminal user. That loop was featured in programs for browsing Perl's man pages (perlman, section 10.7.3) and monitoring users (show_user, section 10.7.2), which were simplified considerably through use of its services.

Directions for further study

This chapter provided an introduction to the select loop for Perl, which is a greatly enhanced adaptation of the Shell's select loop. For coverage of additional features that weren't described in this chapter, and for additional programming examples, see

- http://TeachMePerl.com/Select.html

The Shell allows I/O redirection requests to be attached to control structures, as shown in these examples:

```
command | while ... done
for ... done > file
```

Although Perl doesn't support an equivalent syntax, you can arrange similar effects using open and Perl's built-in select function, as explained in these online documents:[27]

- perldoc -f open
- perldoc -f select
- man perlopentut   # tutorial on "open"

---

[25] E.g., see the discussion on *variable scoping* in section 11.3.

[26] The downloading procedure is discussed in section 12.2.3.

[27] This function selects the default *filehandle* (see man perlopentut) for use in subsequent I/O operations. The select keyword is also used by Shell::POSIX::Select for the select *loop*, but the intended meaning can be discerned from the context.

C H A P T E R   1 1

Subroutines and variable scoping

11.1 Compartmentalizing code
   with subroutines 363
11.2 Common problems with
   variables 370

11.3 Controlling variable scoping 373
11.4 Variable Scoping Guidelines for
   complex programs 376
11.5 Reusing a subroutine 386
11.6 Summary 387

Thinking logically may come naturally to Vulcans like *Star Trek*'s Mr. Spock, but it's a challenge for most earthlings. That's what those millions of VCRs and microwave-ovens blinking **12:00** … 12:00 … **12:00**—since the 1980s—have been trying to tell us.

What's more, even those who excel in logical thinking can experience drastic degradations in performance when subjected to time pressures, sleep deprivation, frequent interruptions, tantalizing daydreams, or problems at home—i.e., under *normal* human working conditions. So, being only human, even the best programmers can find it challenging to design programs sensibly and to write code correctly.

Fortunately, computer languages have features that make it easier for earthlings to program well. And any JAPH worth his camel jerky—like you—should milk these features for all they're worth.

One especially valuable programming tool is the *subroutine*, which is a special structure that stores and provides access to program code. The primary benefits of subroutines to (non-Vulcan) programmers are these:

- They support a Tinkertoy programming mentality,[1]
  - which encourages the decomposition of a complex programming task into smaller and more easily-understandable pieces.
- They minimize the need to duplicate program code,
  - because subroutines provide centralized access to frequently used chunks of code.
- They make it easier to reuse code in other programs,
  - through simple cutting and pasting.

In this chapter, you'll first learn how to use subroutines to *compartmentalize*[2] your code, which paves the way for enjoying their many benefits.

Then, you'll learn about the additional coding restrictions imposed by the compiler in *strict mode* and the ways they can—and can't—help you write better programs.

We'll also discuss Perl's features for *variable scoping*, which prevent variables from "leaking" into regions where they don't belong, bumping into other variables, and messing with their values. As we'll demonstrate in sample programs, proper use of variable-scoping techniques is essential to ensuring the proper functioning of complex programs, such as those having subroutines.

During our explorations of these issues, we'll convert a script from a prior chapter to use a subroutine, and we'll study cases of accidental *variable masking* and *variable clobberation*, so you'll know how to avoid those undesirable effects.

We'll conclude the chapter by discussing our *Variable Scoping Guidelines*. These tips—which we've developed over many years in our training classes—make it easy to specify proper scopes for variables to preserve the integrity of the data they store.

11.1   COMPARTMENTALIZING CODE WITH SUBROUTINES

A *subroutine* is a chunk of code packaged in a way that allows a program to do two things with it. The program can *call* the subroutine, to execute its code, and the program can optionally obtain a *return value* from it, to get information about its results. Such information may range from a simple True/False code indicating success or failure, through a scalar value, to a list of values.

Subroutines are a valuable resource because they let you access the same code from different regions of a program without duplicating it, and also reuse that code in other programs.

---

[1] Tinkertoys were wooden ancestors to Lego toys and their modern relatives. The mentality they all tap into might be called "reductionistic thinking".

[2] The word *modularize* could be used instead, but in Perl that also means to repackage code as a *module*, which is something different (see chapter 12).

Table 11.1 summarizes the syntax for defining a subroutine, calling it, accessing its arguments (if any), and returning values from it.[3]

Table 11.1 Syntax for defining and using subroutines

Operation	Syntax[a]		Comments
Defining a sub	`sub name { code; }`		The sub declaration associates the following *name* with *code*.

Calling a sub	`name();`
	`name(ARGS);`
	
	`$Y=name();`
	`@X=name(ARGS);`
		`# call without args`
		`# call with args`
		
		`# scalar context call`
		`# list context call`
			A sub's *code* is executed by using its *name* followed by parentheses. Arguments to be passed to the sub are placed within the parentheses.
			    The *VALUE(s)* (see below) returned by *name* are automatically converted to scalar form as needed (e.g., for assigning a list to $Y, but not for assigning a list to @X; see text).

Returning values	`return VALUE(s);   # returns VALUE(s)`
	
	`print get_time(); # prints time`
	
	`sub get_time {`
	`    scalar localtime;`
	`} # returns formatted time-string`
			`return` sends *VALUE(s)* back to the point of call, after converting a list to a scalar if necessary (see above cell). If `return` has no argument, an empty list or an undefined value is returned (for list/scalar context, respectively).
			    Without `return` (see `get_time`), the value of the last expression evaluated is returned.

Sensing context	`if (wantarray) {`
	`    return @numbers; # list value`
	`}`
	`else {`
	`    return $average; # scalar value`
	`}`
			`wantarray` yields True or False according to the list or scalar context of the call, allowing you to return different values for calls in different contexts.

Accessing sub arguments	`($A, $B)=@_; print $B; # 2nd arg`
	
	`print $_[1];           # 2nd arg`
	
	`$A=shift;`
	`$B=shift;`
	`print $B;              # 2nd arg`
			sub arguments are obtained from the `@_` array by copying or shifting its values into named variables, or else by indexing, with `$_[0]` referencing the first element of `@_`, `$_[1]` the second, etc.[b]

a. *ARGS* stands for one or more values. *VALUE(s)* is typically a number or a variable.

b. The elements of `@_` act like aliases to the arguments provided by the sub's caller, allowing those arguments to be changed in the sub; the copying/shifting approach prevents such changes.

---

[3] We won't contrast Perl *subroutines* with Shell user-defined *functions*, because functions are different in many ways, and many Shell programmers aren't familiar with them anyway.

For those familiar with the way subroutines work in other languages, the most noteworthy aspects of Perl subroutines are these:

- A subroutine's name must be followed by parentheses,[4] even if no arguments are provided.
- Subroutine definitions needn't provide any information about their expected, or required, arguments.
- All arguments to all subroutines are accessed from the array called @_.

Other features of Perl's subroutine system are natural offshoots of its sensitivity to context:

- For a call in scalar context, `return` automatically converts an argument that's a list variable to its corresponding scalar value. For example, `return @AC_DC` returns the *values* of that list (e.g., "AC", "DC") for a call in list context, but it returns that array's *number of values* (2) for a call in scalar context.
- A subroutine can sense the context from which it's called[5] and tailor its return value accordingly (see "Sensing Context" in table 11.1).

You'll see all these features demonstrated in upcoming examples. But first, we'll discuss how existing code is converted to the subroutine format.

11.1.1 Defining and using subroutines

Consider the script shown in listing 11.1, which centers and prints each line of its input, using code adapted from `news_flash` in section 8.6.1.

Listing 11.1 The `center` script

```
1  #! /usr/bin/perl -wnl
2
3  use Text::Tabs; # imports "expand" function
4  BEGIN {
5      $width=80;  # or use `tput cols` to get width
6  }
7
8  # Each tab will be counted by "length" as one character,
9  #  but it may act like more!
10
11 $_=expand $_;  # rewrite line with tabs replaced by spaces
12
13 # Leading/trailing whitespace can make line look uncentered
14 s/^\s+//;       # strip leading whitespace
15 s/\s+$//;       # strip trailing whitespace
```

---

[4] Assuming the programmer places sub definitions at the *end* of the script, which is customary.

[5] Which we'll henceforth call the *caller's context*.

```
16
17   # Now calculate left-padding required for centering.
18   #    If string length is 10, (80-10)/2 = 35
19   #    If string length is 11, (80-11)/2 = 34.5
20
21   $indent=($width - length)/2;        # "length" means "length $_"
22   $indent < 0  and  $indent=0;        # avoid negative indents!
23
24   # Perl will truncate decimal portion of $indent
25   $padding=' ' x $indent;       # generate spaces for left-padding
26   print "$padding$_";           # print, with padding for centering
```

This center script provides a useful service, but what if some *other* script needs to center a string? Wouldn't it be best if the centering code were in a form that would facilitate its reuse, so it could be easily inserted into *any* Perl script?

The answer is—you guessed it—*Yes!*

Listing 11.2 shows the improved center2, with its most important differences from center marked by underlined line numbers. Note that it uses a subroutine to do its centering, and that it supports a -width=*columns* switch to let the user configure its behavior (more on that later).

On Line 10, the current input line is passed as the argument to center_line, and print displays the centered string that's returned. Note the need to use parentheses around the user-defined subroutine's argument—in contrast, they're optional when calling a built-in function.

The subroutine is defined in Line 12, using the sub declaration to associate a code block having appropriate contents with the specified name. Notice that center_line has use Text::Tabs at its top (Line 15), to load the module that provides the expand function called on Line 25. That line could alternatively be placed at the top of the script as in center, but it's best to have such use directives within the subroutines that depend on them. This ensures that any script that includes center_line will automatically import the module it requires.

Listing 11.2   The center2 script

```
1    #! /usr/bin/perl -s -wnl
2    # Usage: center2 [ -width=columns ] [ file1 file2 ... ]
3
4    our ($width);          # makes this switch optional
5
6    BEGIN {
7        $cl_width=$width;   # center_line() validates $cl_width
8    }
9
10   print center_line($_); # $cl_width needn't be passed; is global
11
```

```
12  sub center_line {
13      # returns argument centered within field of size $cl_width
14
15      use Text::Tabs;  # imports expand(); converts tabs to spaces
16
17      if ( @_ != 1  or  $_[0] eq "" ) {  # needs one argument
18          warn "$0: Usage: center_line(string)\n";
19          $newstring=undef;        # to return "undefined" value
20      }
21      else {
22          defined $cl_width  and  $cl_width > 2  or  $cl_width=80;
23
24          $string=shift;           # get sub's argument
25          $string=expand $string;  # convert tabs to spaces
26          $string =~ s/^\s+//;     # remove leading whitespace
27          $string =~ s/\s+$//;     # remove trailing whitespace
28
29          # calculate indentation
30          $indent=($cl_width - length $string )/2;
31          $padding=' ' x $indent;
32          $newstring="$padding$string";
33      }
34      return $newstring;            # return centered string, or undef
35  }
```

The subroutine needs access to two pieces of information: the string to be centered, and the column-width to be used for the centering. It accesses the string as an argument and the field width as a *global* variable.[6] (Global variables are the type we've been using in this book thus far; we'll discuss their properties and those of other kinds of variables later in this chapter).

Although the column-width specification arrives in the variable $width (Line 7), the subroutine uses a slightly different name for its corresponding variable—formed by prepending cl_ (from **c**enter_**l**ine) to width, to create $cl_width. This is done to reduce the likelihood that the subroutine's variable will clash with an identically named one used elsewhere the program. (You'll see a more robust approach for avoiding such *name clashes* in section 11.3.)

In cases where the optional -width switch is omitted by the user, the *undefined* value associated with $width is copied to $cl_width on Line 7, and it's detected and replaced with a reasonable default value on Line 22 in the subroutine.

A subroutine that requires a specific kind of argument should provide the service of reporting improper usage to its caller. Accordingly, center_line detects an incorrect argument count or an empty argument on Line 17, and issues a warning if necessary. Moreover, to ensure that any serious use of the value it returns on error will

---

[6] Although both items could be accepted as arguments—or as widely scoped variables—for educational purposes, we're demonstrating the use of both methods.

be flagged,[7] the subroutine employs the `undef` function (Line 19) to attach the *undefined* value to the variable `$newstring`. Any attempt to use that value after it's returned (by Line 34) will trigger a warning of the form "Use of uninitialized value in print", thus making the error apparent.

The line to be centered is loaded into `$string` using `shift` on Line 24, and then centered, with the final result placed in `$newstring`.

You can see echoes of `center`'s Lines 11–25 in the `else` branch of listing 11.2's subroutine, but the coding is a little different. That's because a well designed subroutine should accept most of its inputs as arguments and copy them into descriptively named variables—like `$string`—rather than assuming the needed data is already available in a global variable—as `center`'s code does with respect to `$_`.

Now that you know how to use subroutines, we'll shift our focus to the use of the compiler's special *strict mode* of operation, which can help you write better programs.

11.1.2   Understanding use strict

When you make many substantial changes to a script—such as those involved in converting `center` to `center2`—there's a good chance the new version won't work right away. If you can't fix it yourself, an accepted way to obtain expert help is to post the script to the mailing list of the local Perl Users Group (i.e., Perl Mongers affiliate; see http://pm.org) and ask its members for assistance.

However, posting a script like `center2` in its current form wouldn't have the desired effect. That's because the first response of the seasoned JAPHs subscribing to the group's mailing list would undoubtedly be:[8]

> *Modify your script to compile without errors under* use strict, *and if it still doesn't work, post that version, and **then** we'll be happy to help you!*

You see, you can make the Perl compiler enforce stricter rules than usual by placing "use strict;" near the top of your script. When running with these additional *strictures* in effect, certain loose programming practices—which probably wouldn't trip you up in tiny scripts, but may do so in larger ones—suddenly become fatal errors that prevent your script from running.

For this reason, a script that runs in *strict mode* is viewed as less likely to suffer from certain common flaws that could prevent it from working properly. That's why your fellow programmers will be reluctant to spend their valuable time playing the role of `use strict` for you; but once your script runs in that mode, they may be willing to scrutinize it and give you the kinds of valuable feedback that only fellow JAPHs can provide.

---

[7] As mentioned earlier, *non*-"serious" uses of a value, such as copying it or testing it with `defined`, don't elicit warnings.

[8] How can I be so sure what their response would be? Because I managed the mailing list for the 400+ member Seattle Perl Users Group for 6 years, that's how!

Even if you have no intention of seeking help from other people, you might as well avail yourself of the benefits of complying with the compiler's strictures, because the adjustments they necessitate might help you heal a misbehaving script on your own.

We'll talk next about what it takes to retrofit a script to run in strict mode.

Strictifying a script

With most Perl programs, you're most likely to run afoul of the strictures having to do with *variable scoping*. As a test case, let's see what messages we get when we run center2 in strict mode, and determine what it takes to squelch them.

A quick and easy way to do this—which is equivalent to (temporarily) inserting "use strict;" at the top of the script—is to run the script using the convenient perl -M'*Module_name*' syntax to load the strict module (see section 2.3):

```
$ perl -M'strict' center2 iron_chefs
Global symbol "$cl_width" requires explicit package name ... line 7
BEGIN not safe after errors--compilation aborted at center2 line 8
```

The compiler is obviously unhappy about the global symbol $cl_width, which appears on Line 7. That's because a global variable is accessible from anywhere in the program, which can lead to trouble. You can address this concern by properly *declaring* the script's user-defined variables in accordance with the Variable Scoping Guidelines, which we'll cover in section 11.4.

With a small script like center2, a few minor adjustments will usually suffice to get it to run in strict mode. Listing 11.3 shows in bold type the four lines we had to add to center2 to create its strict-*ified* version.

> **Listing 11.3 The center2.strict script**

```
1   #! /usr/bin/perl -s -wnl
2   # Usage: center2.strict [ -width=columns ] [ file1 file2 ... ]
3
4   use strict;
5
6   our ($width);           # makes this switch optional
7   my  ($cl_width);        # "private", from here to file's end
8
9   BEGIN {
10    $cl_width=$width;     # center_line() validates $cl_width
11  }
12
13  print center_line($_); # $cl_width needn't be passed
14
15  sub center_line {
16    # returns argument centered within field of size $cl_width
17
18    use Text::Tabs;    # imports expand(); converts tabs to spaces
19
```

```
20   my $newstring;      # private, from here to file's end
21   if ( @_ != 1  or  $_[0] eq "" )  {  # needs one argument
22      warn "$0: Usage: center_line(string)\n";
23      $newstring=undef;          # to return "undefined" value
24   }
25   else {
26      defined $cl_width  and $cl_width > 2  or  $cl_width=80;
27
28      my ($string, $indent, $padding);  # private, from here to }
29      $string=shift;                # get required arg
30      $string=expand $string;    # convert tabs to spaces
31      $string =~ s/^\s+//;       # remove leading whitespace
32      $string =~ s/\s+$//;       # remove trailing whitespace
33
34      # calculate indentation
35      $indent=($cl_width - length $string )/2;
36      $padding=' ' x $indent;
37      $newstring="$padding$string";
38   }
39   return $newstring;            # return centered string, or undef
40   }
```

The most significant change is that variable declarations using my have been added to restrict the scope of the user-defined variables to the relevant portions of the script, which helps to avoid several kinds of problems.

So that you'll understand how to make these adjustments to your own programs, we'll discuss later in this chapter what variable declarations do, what variable scoping is, and some recommended techniques for properly declaring and scoping your variables.

But first, we'll discuss some scoping problems that use strict can't detect, so you won't be tempted to join the hordes of Perl newbies who drastically overestimate this tool's benefits.

11.2   COMMON PROBLEMS WITH VARIABLES

Most of the variables we've used in our programs thus far have had what's loosely called *global scope*, which is the default. The special property of these variables is that they can be accessed by name from anywhere in the program.

Global variables are convenient to use and entirely appropriate for simple programs, but they are notorious for causing problems in more complex ones. Why? Because you're more likely to accidentally use a particular variable name—such as $_ or $total—a second time, for a different purpose, in program that is complex. This can cause trouble, as you'll see in the following case studies.

11.2.1   Clobbering variables: The `phone_home` script

Let's look at the `phone_home` script, whose job is to dial the home phone number of its author and user, Stieff Ozniak, while he's traveling:

```perl
#! /usr/bin/perl -wl

$home='415 123-4567';                   # store my home phone number
print 'Calling phone at: ",
        get_home_address();             # show my address
dial_phone($home);                      # dial my home phone

sub get_home_address {
    %name2address=(
        ozniak => '1234 Disk Drive, Pallid Alto, CA',
                                # I'll add other addresses later
    );
    $home=($name2address($ENV{LOGNAME})  or  'unknown');
    return $home;
}
sub dial_phone { ... }            # left to the imagination
```

Did you notice that Oz is using the same variable ($home) to hold a postal address in the main program and a home phone-number in the subroutine? In such cases, each assignment to the variable in one part of the program accidentally overwrites the earlier value of its twin. That's a bad situation, as indicated by the violent connotations of the terms *clobbering* and *clobberation* that are used to describe it.

In this case, the stored phone number will have been replaced by the address retrieved from the hash by the time the subroutine returns. In consequence, the `dial_phone` subroutine will cause Oz's modem to dial the number "1234 Disk Drive, Pallid Alto, CA", which will be a long distance call—even if it is made *from* Pallid Alto—because the 234 area code is in Ohio!

Was the problem caused by Oz neglecting to `use strict`? No! Although that was unwise, using it would not have prevented this problem anyway.[9]

> **TIP**   Perl's strict mode is not the *magic shield against JAPHly mistakes* that many new programmers like to think it is!

However, when additional measures are combined with `use strict`, a program can safely use the same variable name in the main program and a subroutine. You'll see a demonstration of this later when we discuss the `phone_home2` script (in section 11.4.6).

In the meantime, let's hope Oz will be able to think up a different variable name to use in the subroutine, which is all that's needed to avoid the clobberation his script is currently experiencing.

---

[9] Because after enabling `use strict`, declaring the first reference to $home with my wouldn't cure the clobberation problem—but that's all that would be required to let the program run (see section 11.4.6).

In addition to being careful to avoid clobbering a variable's value, which causes it to be irretrievably lost, in some cases you must avoid *masking* a variable's value, which makes it temporarily inaccessible. We'll discuss this issue next.

11.2.2 Masking variables: The `4letter_word` script

The famous rapper, Diggity Dog, has a reputation to uphold. So, he understandably wants to ensure that each of the songs on his new CD contains *at least* one four-letter word. Toward this end, he's written a script that analyzes a song file and reports its first four-letter word along with the line in which it was found. The script can also show each line before checking it, if the –verbose switch is given.

Diggity D, who has a talent for "keepin' it real" and "tellin' it like it is," calls his script `4letter_word`:

```
#! /usr/bin/perl -s -wnl
# Report first 4-letter word found in input,
#   along with the line in which it occurred

use strict;

defined $verbose  and  warn "Examining '$_'";    # $_ holds line

foreach (split) {        # split line into words, and load each into $_
    /\b\w\w\w\w\b/   and
        print "Found '$_' in: '$_'\n"   and        # DOESN'T WORK!
            last;
}
```

Diggity may be raw—but he ain't stupid, so he's not surprised that his new script correctly finds the first four-letter word in each file and then terminates, as he intended.[10] However, the output he's getting from print is not what he was expecting.

Here's a sample run of the script, which probes the pithy lyrics of his latest song:

```
$ 4letter_word –verbose FeedDaDiggity
Examining 'Don't be playin wit da Dog'
Examining 'Giv Diggity Dog da bone!'
Found 'bone' in: 'bone'
```

He's not happy with that last line, because he wanted

```
print "Found '$_' in: '$_'\n"
```

to produce this output instead:

```
Found 'bone' in: 'Giv Diggity Dog da bone'
```

---

[10] But if he were a bit cleverer, he'd look for *profane* words rather than four-letter words using the Regexp::Common module, as does Lingua::EN::Namegame's script that squelches profane lyrics for verses of The Name Game song (see http://search.cpan.org/~yumpy).

But clearly, in a case where the first reference to $_ in print's argument string yields "bone", it's unreasonable to expect the *second* reference to that same variable in that same string to yield something different—such as the contents of the current input line, as $_ generated in the warn "Examining ..." statement.

What's happening here is simply this: The scope of the implicit loop's $_ variable is the entire script, but that value is temporarily *masked* within foreach—because that loop is presently using (the same) $_ to hold the words of the current line.[11]

It's not possible for the program to have simultaneous access to the different values that $_ holds within the implicit loop and its nested foreach loop, because those loops are *timesharing* the variable—i.e., they're *taking turns* storing their different values in that same place.

But the solution is easy: Diggity needs to employ a user-defined loop variable in foreach rather than accepting the convenient—but in this case troublesome—default loop variable of $_. Here's a modified version of the foreach loop that produces the desired result, with the changes in bold:

```
foreach $word (split){ # split line into words; store each in $word
    $word =~ /\b\w\w\w\w\b/  and
        print "Found '$word' in: '$_'\n"  and
            last;
}
```

Now that $word is the loop variable for foreach, there's no obstacle to accessing the surrounding implicit loop's $_ from the foreach loop's print statement.

Note that the script's use of strict mode did nothing to prevent this particular problem of variable usage from occurring. That's because the compiler assumed that Diggity D knew what he was doing when he accepted $_ as the loop variable for the nested foreach, which wouldn't necessarily lead to trouble.

11.2.3   Tips on avoiding problems with variables

To avoid most problems in the use of variables, avoid unnecessary reuse of common names (such as $_ and $home), and employ the tools provided by the language to confine a variable's use to its intended scope. We'll cover those tools next.

11.3   CONTROLLING VARIABLE SCOPING

The *scope* of a variable is the region of the program in which its name can be used to retrieve its value. Specifying a variable's scope involves the use of the my, our, or local declaration, as shown in table 11.2.

---

[11] Specifically, the foreach loop has its own *localized* (i.e., declared with local) variation on the $_ variable, which holds a different value.

Table 11.2 The my, our, and local variable declarations

Declaration	Example	Explanation

my	`my $A;`
	`my $A=42;`
	`my ($A, $B);`
	`my ($A, $B)=@values;`
		The my declaration creates a *private* variable, whose name works only within the scope of its declaration. This is the preferred declaration for most user-defined variables in strict mode.

our	`our $A;`
	`our $A=42;`
	`our ($A, $B);`
	`our ($A, $B)=@values;`
		In strict mode, our disables fatal errors for accessing global variables within its scope that use their simple names (e.g., $A) rather than their full names ($main::A or the equivalent $::A).[a] In Minimal Perl, this declaration is used in strict mode for all switch variables and variables exported by modules.

local	`{ # new scope for modified "$,"`
	`  local $,="\t";`
	`  print @ARGV; # tab-separated`
	`} # previous "$," restored`
		local arranges for the previous value of the modified variable to be restored when execution leaves the scope of the declaration. local is most commonly used with print's formatting variables ("$," and '$"') in Minimal Perl.

a. Using our is like pushing the "hush button" on a smoke alarm, to temporarily silence it while you're carefully monitoring a smoke-generating activity.

We'll discuss the three types of declarations in turn.

11.3.1 Declaring variables with my

my creates a *private* variable, whose use by name is strictly confined to a particular scope. This is the preferred declaration for most user-defined variables, and the one that's most commonly applied to a script's global variables when it's converted to operate in strict mode.

The other declaration that may be needed is one that's less selfish with its assets, so it's rightfully called our.

11.3.2 Declaring variables with our

Because global variables can be troublemakers, the compiler prevents you in strict mode from accidentally creating them. For example, while attempting to increment the value of the private variable $num, you might—with a little finger-fumbling—accidentally request the creation of the global variable $yum:

```
my $num=41;
$yum++;
```

You won't get away with this mistake, because your program will be terminated during compilation with the following error message:

```
Global symbol "$yum" requires explicit package name at ...
Execution of scriptname aborted due to compilation errors.
```

But you can still use global variables in strict mode—as long as you make it clear that you're doing so *deliberately*, by declaring them with our.[12] However, in most cases, it's a better practice to use a widely scoped private variable instead.

In part 1, we used the our declaration on switch variables (e.g., $debug) to identify their associated command-line switches (e.g., -debug) as optional (see table 2.5). However, because all switch variables are global variables, they must be declared with our in strict mode. (This means Perl can't automatically issue a warning for a required switch that's missing in strict mode; but by now you've learned how to generate your own warnings for undefined variables (in section 8.1.1), so you no longer need this crutch.

The our declaration is also used for variables exported by Perl modules (as you'll see in section 12.1.1).

In summary, for a script to be allowed to run under use strict, each of its user-defined variables must be declared with either our or my. Although both declarations permit abuses that are analogous to silencing a pesky smoke alarm by removing its batteries,[13] they have beneficial effects when used properly.

For completeness, we'll discuss Perl's other type of variable declaration next—although it's not used to satisfy strictures.

11.3.3 Declaring variables with `local`

local is used to conveniently make (and un-make) temporary changes to built-in variables (see table 11.2). It doesn't create a new variable, but instead a new scope in which the original variable can have a different value.

local is very useful in certain contexts. As a case in point, this declaration is automatically applied to $_ when it's used as a default loop variable, which ensures that the prior value of $_ (if any) will be reinstated when the loop finishes.[14] Although this special service can be a great convenience, the local declaration is never needed in converting a script for strict-mode operation.

For the rest of this chapter, our focus will be on the use of special guidelines that help programmers write better programs.

11.3.4 Introducing the Variable Scoping Guidelines

In programs that don't use explicit variable declarations, certain declarations are still in effect—the default ones. These can lead to unpleasant surprises, but by applying our *Variable Scoping Guidelines* (*Guidelines* for short), you'll be able to defend your

---

[12] Global variables can always be accessed by their *explicit package names*; the strictures we're discussing only disallow references using their *simple* names (see row two of table 11.2).

[13] Such as declaring every variable in the script with our or my at the top of the file, which gives every variable file scope. This may delude you into thinking that use strict is helping you sidestep the pitfalls of variable usage, but in actuality you've disabled its benefits!

[14] However, as Diggity D showed with 4letter_word (see section 11.2.2), a nested loop that needs access to the loop variable of an outer loop needs to use a different name for its own loop variable.

programs against common pitfalls. These Guidelines have been extensively tested and refined to their present form using feedback from throngs of IT professionals who've attended our training classes. They're divided into two sets, which apply to programs of different complexity levels.

SIMPLE PROGRAMS: *Those that can be viewed in their entirety on your screen, and don't have subroutine definitions or nested loops.*
COMPLEX PROGRAMS: *All others.*

Guidelines for simple programs

Variable scoping in Perl is a subject that's more easily managed through the application of Guidelines than by attempting to learn all its intricacies and applying that understanding. To cite a well-known analogy from the world of Unix shell programming, it's a lot easier to fix a misbehaving command by "adding (or subtracting) another backslash to see if that fixes it", than it is to study the myriad ways in which backslashed expressions can go wrong, and try to identify which case you're dealing with—*before adding (or subtracting) another backslash to see if that fixes it!*

The most important Guideline applies to programs that can be viewed in their entirety on your screen, and that lack nested loops and subroutine definitions:

- **Relax.** Enjoy the friendliness, power, and freedom of Perl. Don't use strict, don't declare variables, and don't worry—*be happy*!

Although this advice may sound too good to be true, it really works. And you *know* that, because none of the dozens of Perl programs we discussed in the previous chapters needed to declare or create a special scope for a variable, in order to function correctly.

But life as a programmer isn't always that carefree, so we'll examine the Guidelines that apply to more complex programs next.

11.4 VARIABLE SCOPING GUIDELINES FOR COMPLEX PROGRAMS

These are the Guidelines, shown in the order in which you apply them, along with the numbers we use in referring to them:

1 Enable use strict.

2 Declare user-defined variables and define their scopes:
   a Use the my declaration on non-switch variables.
   b Use the our declaration on switch variables and variables exported by modules.
   c Don't let variables leak into subroutines.

3 Pass data to subroutines using arguments.

4 Localize temporary changes to built-in variables using local.

5 Employ user-defined loop variables.

The Guidelines apply to any program that has one or more of these properties:

- It's larger than one screenful.
- It has a nested loop.
- It has a subroutine definition.

They also apply to all files that define Perl modules (discussed in section 12.1).

We'll show how these Guidelines are applied to existing scripts, so we can refer to their specific deficiencies. However, you should ideally use the Guidelines from the outset when developing scripts that are expected to become complex, or when developing modules.

> **TIP**   Following the Variable Scoping Guidelines will help you avoid trouble in your programs.

Like Perl scripts themselves often do, we'll begin with `use strict`.

11.4.1   Enable `use strict`

Put "`use strict;`" at the top of the file, but below the shebang line if present (a module won't have one). *Congratulations!* You've probably just broken your program, until you make the modifications described in the *following* Guidelines.

But before we proceed, a word of warning is in order. It's important that you resist the temptation to cease applying the Guidelines *prematurely*, because the compiler operating in strict mode[15] may unleash your program after a variable declaration or two has been added, but well before it has a chance to function correctly.[16]

We'll discuss the proper use of variable declarations next.

11.4.2   Declare user-defined variables and define their scopes

Properly defining the scope of user-defined variables is a critical step in defending a program against programmer oversights. You do so by declaring the variable at a certain position in the file, and in a certain relationship to enclosing curly braces.

Declarations that aren't enclosed in curly braces are said to have *file scope*, which means they apply from the point of the declaration to the file's end. Other declarations are restricted to the region that ends with the next enclosing right-hand curly brace, yielding *block scope*.

In either case, you must take care to properly demarcate the variable's scope, which may require adding curly braces in some cases, or taking steps to avoid the undesirable effects of existing curly braces in others.

Some declarations may be conveniently made within existing curly-brace delimited code blocks, such as those enclosing the definition of a subroutine, an `else`

---

[15] Henceforth referred to as the *strictified compiler*.

[16] See the discussion of the `phone_home` script in section 11.2.1 for a dramatic example of this principle.

branch, or a `foreach` loop. In other cases, you can freely add new curly braces to define custom scopes for the variables you'll declare within them.

Two types of declarations are used to convert a program for strict mode: `my` and `our`. We'll discuss each in turn.

Use the `my` declaration on non-switch variables

Most user-defined variables should be declared with `my`, which marks them as *private* to their scope. One way to make such a declaration is to place `my` before the variable's name where it's first used. Another approach is to provide declarations for a group of variables at the top of the subroutine, main program, or code block in which they're used (as shown on Line 28 of listing 11.3).

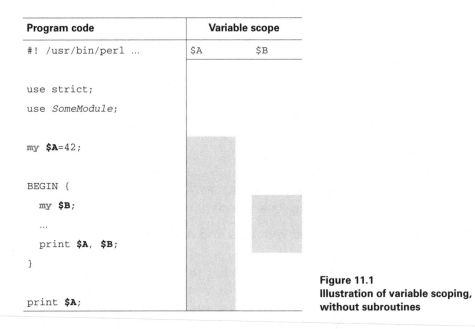

Program code	Variable scope	
`#! /usr/bin/perl ...`	`$A`	`$B`
`use strict;`		
`use SomeModule;`		
`my $A=42;`		
`BEGIN {`		
`    my $B;`		
`    ...`		
`    print $A, $B;`		
`}`		
`print $A;`		

Figure 11.1
Illustration of variable scoping, without subroutines

For example, user-defined variables that will only be accessed within the `BEGIN` block should be declared there with `my` (like `$B` in figure 11.1). However, variables used in the `BEGIN` block that will also be accessed *below* it can't be declared in `BEGIN`, because its curly braces would restrict their scope. Instead, such a variable (e.g., `$A` in figure 11.1) needs to be declared on a line *before* `BEGIN`, to include the `BEGIN` block and the following region in its scope.

Our next Guideline is a critical one that helps prevent messy situations.

Don't let variables leak into subroutines

Before delving into the details of this Guideline, we must first define a term. The *Main program* (*Main* for short) is the core portion of a program. In a script having BEGIN and END blocks, it's the code that falls between those sections. In a script lacking those blocks, Main is the collection of statements beginning after the initial use statement(s) and ending just before the first subroutine definition or the end of the file, whichever comes first.

One of the most dangerous mistakes that new Perl programmers make is to inadvertently let variables *leak* from Main into the subroutines defined below. But all it takes to plug those leaks is to routinely enclose Main in curly braces in scripts that have subroutines.[17] The beneficial effect of this simple measure is to restrict the scope of variables declared *in* Main, *to* Main.

This technique is illustrated in figure 11.2 and discussed in more detail in section 11.4.6.

Notice in the figure's right column that A's final scope is constrained by the locations of the curly braces that enclose its declaration, which exclude the subroutine.

If the script has BEGIN and/or END blocks, the same set of Main-enclosing curly braces may be extended to include either or both of those regions as needed, with the declarations being shifted to the top of the new scope.

Initial scope of $A	Final scope of $A
`#! /usr/bin/perl …`	`#! /usr/bin/perl …`
`use strict;`	`use strict;`
`use SomeModule;`	`use SomeModule;`
	`{`
`my $A=42;   # Main`	`my $A=42;   # Main`
`print $A;   # Main`	`print $A;   # Main`
	`}`
`sub C { }`	`sub C { }`

Figure 11.2
Preventing a variable from leaking into subroutines by enclosing Main in curly braces

For instance, example B of figure 11.3 allows variable V to be accessed in the BEGIN block, Main, and the END block—but not in the subroutines. In contrast, examples C

---

[17] Unfortunately, this fact has not been well documented in the Perl literature (at least, until now).

Variable scope				
A: Entire program	**B:** BEGIN, Main, and END	**C:** BEGIN and Main	**D:** Main and END	**E:** Main only
use strict;	use strict;	use strict;	use strict;	use strict;
			BEGIN { }	BEGIN { }
	{	{	{	{
decl **$V;**	*decl* **$V;**	*decl* **$V;**	*decl* **$V;**	*decl* **$V;**
BEGIN { }	BEGIN { }	BEGIN { }	Main	Main
Main	Main	Main		
		}	END { }	}
END { }	END { }	END { }	}	END { }
	}			
subs	*subs*	*subs*	*subs*	*subs*

NOTE: Variable $V, declared with my or our (***decl***), is accessible by name only within the shaded regions.

Figure 11.3 Effects of curly braces on variable scoping

and D allow access in Main and either BEGIN or END, respectively, whereas example E only allows access to the variable in Main.

Note that examples D and E differ from the others in having their BEGIN blocks above the new scope's opening curly brace, whereas C and E have their END blocks below the closing one. The guiding principle is to include only the desired program regions within the variable's scope-defining curly braces.

Example A of figure 11.3 shows a scoping arrangement that you should generally avoid, because making the variable available to all program segments makes it susceptible to name clashes and clobberations.[18] However, the use of file scope, as this is called, can be appropriate for variables that aren't storing mission-critical information.[19]

---

[18] As demonstrated with the phone_home script of section 11.2.1.

[19] File scope can also be appropriate in Perl modules, which may contain little more than variable declarations made for the benefit of their following subroutine definitions.

HEALTH WARNING!	Just as a sick person should finish his prescribed course of antibiotics even though he suddenly feels better, you should complete the application of *all* Variable Scoping Guidelines even if your script starts running after you've merely applied the first few. Otherwise, you may not eradicate all your bugs!

Next, we'll discuss the other type of declaration that might be needed to let a script run in strict mode.

Use the our declaration on switch variables and variables exported by modules

All switch variables must be declared with our in strict mode.[20] With the following command format, this allows the value ("maximum") provided with the command-line switch (-urgency) to be accessed via its corresponding switch variable ($urgency) within the script:

```
$ scan4intruders -urgency='maximum'
...
```

As with my, the positioning of an our declaration and the optional curly braces surrounding it define a variable's scope. For example, to make the variable available throughout the script, you would place the declaration below the use statements but above the BEGIN block (see example A of figure 11.3). The file scope that results is appropriate for making a $debug switch-variable available to all program segments—for example, for the benefit of widely scattered statements like this one:

```
defined $debug  and  warn "$0: Entering the XYZ phase now\n";
```

On the other hand, for switch variables that will be accessed in all program segments except subroutines (i.e., BEGIN, Main, and END), you should place a curly brace before the declarations above BEGIN and one after END, as shown in example B of the figure.

Figure 11.4 illustrates the use of variable scoping to restrict access to distinct program regions for a number of variables, showing code that more closely resembles that of a real (albeit rather ineffectual) script.

Note that neither $A nor $B can leak into sub conscious, because the outermost curly braces enclosing their declarations limit their scope to BEGIN, Main, and END. The variables $C, $D, and $E have even tighter scopes, restricting their use to BEGIN, END, and conscious, respectively.

---

[20] As discussed in section 11.3, this directive applies to both optional and required switches.

Program code	Variable scope				
	$A	$B	$C	$D	$E

```perl
#! /usr/bin/perl ...
use strict;
use SomeModule;

{ # Beginning of special scope
  our ($A);      # switch variable
  my $B;

  BEGIN {
    my $C;
    print $A, $B, $C;
  }

  print $A, $B;      # Main program

  END {
    my $D;
    conscious($A, $B, $D);
    print $A, $B, $D;
  }
} # End of special scope

sub conscious {
  my $E;
  print $E;
}
```

Figure 11.4   Illustration of variable scoping, with subroutines

It's important to keep in mind that scoping imposes limits on the use of variable *names*, not on variable *values*. For this reason, the values of $A, $B, and $D in figure 11.4 can be successfully passed as arguments to the subroutine `conscious` from the call in the END block, despite those variables being inaccessible by name from within that subroutine. In other words, although a subroutine can't access variables outside its scope, you still have the freedom to pass the value of any variable that's in scope at the location of the subroutine call to that subroutine.

Once you've applied private scopes to Main's variables, you have to take explicit steps to make their values available in subroutines, as we'll discuss next.

11.4.3   Pass data to subroutines using arguments

With the measures implemented by the preceding Guidelines in effect, user-defined variables won't be able to accidentally leak into subroutines defined at the end of a script. As a beneficial side effect, subroutines that knowingly (or unknowingly) *depended* on data leakage will suddenly start generating "Use of uninitialized value on line *X*" messages. This signifies the need to modify the calls to those subroutines to convey the data items they require as arguments.

In section 12.1, we'll discuss the application of this Guideline to the design of custom modules, which may use special features to obtain information from the programs using their subroutines. As an example, a variable could be exported from a module for initialization within the user's program, as an alternative to having the call to the module's subroutine convey the same information as an argument.

Next, we'll discuss a good way to exploit the specialized behavior of the `local` declaration.

11.4.4   Localize temporary changes to built-in variables with `local`

As stated in table 11.2, a declaration with `local` causes a variable's earlier value to be automatically restored when execution leaves the scope of the declaration.[21] To take advantage of this useful feature, enclose temporary changes to Perl built-in variables within curly braces, and declare those variables with `local`:

```
{
  local  $,="\t";
  print  @items_getting_tab_separation;
}
# $, now reverts to value it had before "\t" was assigned
print @items_not_getting_tab_separation;
```

Following this Guideline will prevent you from someday wondering, for example, why the `print` on Line 300 of your script is separating its arguments with tabs, only to discover later that an assignment to the formatting variable "`$,`" on line 15—which *should* have been temporary—is still in effect. Using `local` to ensure that such "temporary" changes get properly undone will save you a lot of unnecessary anguish, head scratching, and debugging time.

Another source of trouble is the reuse of the same variable for different purposes, as you'll see next.

11.4.5   Employ user-defined loop variables

For loops of the types shown here on the left that are nested within others—including those nested within the easily overlooked implicit loop—make the user-defined loop-variable *private* by adding the underlined text shown on the right:

---

[21] This is how `foreach` declares its default loop variable, `$_` (see section 11.2.2).

```
foreach    (  LIST  )       →   foreach my $V ( LIST  )
while      (   <>   )       →   while ( my $V=   <>    )
for ($V=0;     <>   ; $V++) →   for   ( my $V=0; <>   ; $V++)
```

Following this Guideline prevents masking of the outer loop's $_ value by that of the inner loop, which occurs in the 4letter_word script (see section 11.2.2).

Next, we'll revisit an earlier example of a program that suffers from *variable leakage* and fix it by applying the Guidelines.

11.4.6 Applying the Guidelines: the `phone_home2` script

Oz has been busy applying the Guidelines to his dysfunctional phone_home script (discussed in section 11.2.1), so let's inspect the new version, phone_home2:

```
#! /usr/bin/perl -wl

use strict;

my $home='415 123-4567';              # store my home phone number
print 'Calling phone at: ",
        get_home_address();           # show my address
dial_phone($home);                    # dial my home phone

sub get_home_address {
...
        $home=($name2address($ENV{LOGNAME})  or  'unknown');
...
```

Oz made the (highlighted) changes by following Guidelines 1 and 2a (see section 11.4). He was a little upset when the addition of use strict prevented the script from running again, but after he responded to "Global symbol "$home" requires explicit package name" by declaring $home with my, it recovered. However—despite the fact that it now complies with the compiler's strictures—*the script still doesn't work correctly!*

Here's why. After Oz declared the first occurrence of $home with my, the *other* occurrences of that variable (also underlined) were seen as falling within the (file) scope of the new declaration and therefore as references to the same variable. That left no global symbols (i.e., undeclared user-defined variables) for the strictified compiler to complain about, so the script was allowed to run.

Of course, all the references to $home still access the same variable, so the only thing that's changed is that a private variable is being clobbered by the subroutine in phone_home2, rather than the global variable of the original!

The bottom line is that the compiler has already given Oz all the help it has to offer, but it's not enough to correct the script's fatal flaw. What's the solution? Simply for Oz to apply the remaining Guidelines, to correct his mistake of considering the script's rehabilitation complete after it started running in strict mode.

This script needs its Main program enclosed in curly braces so badly that it could be the *poster child* for Guideline #2c—"Don't let variables leak into subroutines" (discussed in section 11.4.2). That adjustment would restrict the scope of the my $home declaration to Main and therefore cause the strictified compiler to require a separate declaration for the subroutine's $home—before permitting the script to run again.

The only remaining Guideline that applies to this program is the one about passing all data needed by subroutines as arguments, and the script is already doing that.

The changes that create phone_home3 from phone_home2 are shown in bold type:

```
#! /usr/bin/perl -wl

use strict;

{   # Braces cause two $home's to require separate declarations
  my $home='415 123-4567';              # store my home phone number
  print 'Calling phone at: ",            # show my address
            get_home_address();
  dial_phone($home);                     # dial my home phone
}

sub get_home_address {

...

    my $home=($name2address($ENV{LOGNAME})  or  'unknown');

...
```

The end result of the modifications is that two private variables are created, having totally independent scopes and values—despite the fact that they share the same name.

Of course, in a tiny program like this one, it's easy to spot the duplicated variable name and pick a different one to avoid variable clobberation. But in larger programs, you can't keep track of everything so easily, so it's a good practice for Main and every subroutine to declare all their locally used variables as private, in order to prevent name clashes.

> **TIP** Complying with the requirements of use strict doesn't guarantee that your program isn't doing dumb things with variables. To have greater assurance that it's correct, you need to apply the Variable Scoping Guidelines.

Tips on using Variable Scoping Guidelines

Some of the Guidelines involve coding techniques that are easier to implement from the start than to retrofit after problems become apparent. Therefore, if you know in advance that you'll be using a subroutine or nested loops in a new program (which will qualify it as "complex"), you should follow the Guidelines from the outset. Alternatively, at the time you decide to add the first one of those features to your program, you'd be wise to implement the Guidelines before doing so, to pave the way for its arrival.

Don't forget that our definition of program complexity also incorporates a size criterion, so as soon as your script requires scrolling to be read on the screen, it's time to apply the Guidelines.

Most important, don't become overly paranoid—after all, this is Perl, a relatively forgiving, easily programmed language. But an ounce of prevention is still worth several pounds of cure, so keep these Guidelines in mind.

QUESTION: *How well does* use strict *do the job of monitoring variable usage?*
ANSWER: *About as well as an automatic Bathroom Hand-Washing Monitor that won't let you leave until you've wet your hands—but can't tell if you used any soap!*

11.5   REUSING A SUBROUTINE

Once the Guidelines have been properly applied to a subroutine, you'll be able to use it in other scripts by pasting in its code and properly using its interface. For example, here's an enhanced version of the mytime2 script you saw in section 7.2.2, called mytime3. It centers its output on the screen with the help of the center_line subroutine added at its end:

```
#! /usr/bin/perl -wl
# Shows time in custom format centered on screen

(undef, $minutes, $hour)=localtime;  # we don't care about seconds
$am_pm='AM';
$hour > 12  and  $am_pm='PM'  and  $hour=$hour-12;
print center_line("The time is $hour:$minutes $am_pm.");

sub center_line {
...
    defined $cl_width  and  $cl_width > 2  or  $cl_width=80;
...
    return $newstring;
}
```

The subroutine can be given a custom column-width setting, but because the programmer wanted to accept the default of 80 characters, he didn't create the $cl_width variable. Apart from inserting the subroutine's code, the only other change he made to mytime2 was to pass the time-string to center_line, to get it centered before printing.

But what if the existing script already had a $cl_width variable—perhaps to specify cherry lozenge widths—set at 9 (mm)? Then the programmer would have had to take measures to prevent the subroutine from accidentally using 9 as the subroutine's column-width specification (e.g., by confining the clashing variable's scope to Main or renaming it $cl_meds_width).

Such name clashes are always a possibility when communicating information by widely scoped variables—which is why subroutine designers must weigh their convenience of use against the probability of future trouble, and choose to receive data by arguments in many cases.

Reusing software through cutting and pasting certainly increases productivity, but we can do better. We'll spend the next chapter exploring the more convenient and sophisticated alternative of using Perl *modules*, which let you import subroutines and variables from source code repositories.

11.6   SUMMARY

Subroutines, declared with `sub`, compartmentalize single-minded chunks of code to allow them to be conveniently executed on request. This prevents duplication of code that needs to be accessed from different program regions, and also provides a rudimentary way of sharing code between programs. (But you'll see an even better method based on modules in chapter 12.)

Perl provides three types of variable declarations. Two of them—`my` and `our`—are used to precisely define the program regions in which the names of specific variables can be used. The other declaration, `local`, causes a variable to automatically recover its former value when execution leaves a defined scope. This declaration is routinely used when a formatting variable (`$,` or `$"`) needs to be changed for a particular `print` statement, without affecting all subsequent `print` statements.

The primary function of `use strict` is to prevent a program from running until all its user-defined variables have been declared with `my` or `our`. Although this restriction is meant to encourage you to define proper scopes for all your variables, all that `use strict` actually requires is that you *make* variable declarations—not that you make them *intelligently*.[22] For this reason, `use strict` is not the magical tool for warding off scoping problems that some think it is.

However, proper use of scoping techniques—along with judicious application of our Variable Scoping Guidelines—can make your programs significantly more correct and trustworthy. The seven Guidelines for *complex* programs—ones that have subroutines or nested loops or can't fit on one screen—are discussed in section 11.4. They prescribe modifications that defend your programs against typical problems, such as variable masking and variable clobberation.

As helpful as those guidelines are, there's another one that's even more important to keep in mind—the guideline for *simple* programs, which applies to the majority of the programs featured in this book:

- **Relax.** Enjoy the friendliness, power, and freedom of Perl. Don't `use strict`, don't declare variables, and don't worry—*be happy*!

Directions for further study

The following resources provide additional information on the topics covered in this chapter.

- man perlsub   `# how subroutines work`
- man perlvar   `# how variable scoping works`

---

[22] The problem is not that `use strict` should be able to do its (very difficult) job any better, but rather that wishful thinking leads programmers to overestimate its sophistication.

CHAPTER 12

Modules and the CPAN

12.1 Creating modules 389
12.2 Managing modules 398
12.3 Using modules 403
12.4 Summary 424

Scene: A Level 3 JAPH named Alexis is describing the fallout from her latest customer demo to a sympathetic colleague.

You wouldn't believe it! Just when I had finally satisfied all of the customer's stated requirements, he insisted on having Yet Another New Feature—specifically, support for Precursive Frobination of Defragulations (PFD). So I went back to my cubicle and started coding the algorithm, when I was struck by a strange feeling of déjà vu …

Like Alexis, every programmer who sits down to write code will someday experience a creepy feeling that *she's solved this problem before.* There are at least three logical explanations for this phenomenon, leading to different actions.

One possibility is that the programmer did indeed write the code already, in which case she needs to browse through her source-code archives to locate it. If she succeeds in that quest, she should convert the code into the form of a *subroutine*[1] and give serious consideration to packaging it in a *module.*

---

[1] If it isn't in that form already; see chapter 11.

Why keep subroutines in modules? Because doing so lets you trade the cut-and-paste method of importing subroutines for the more convenient and sophisticated method based on the use function. As a result, you'll be able to import components from your own modules in the same way as you would from other modules:

```
use Text::Tabs;          # imports Perl's standard "expand" sub
use Diggity::Utilities;  # imports "4letter_word", "homeboy_george"
```

Another possibility is that Alexis never wrote the PFD code herself, but instead imported it from a module on her system. If so, her new program can import it too, also by employing use.

A third possibility is that she was mistaking some other phenomenon (perhaps induced by too many carob-iced hemp biscotti) with déjà vu, and that she never wrote, used, or even possessed the code. In the Perl world, this means her next step would be to search for a freely reusable version of PFD in the form of a module available from the *Comprehensive Perl Archive Network* (CPAN).

One of the benefits of using an existing module—and it's a *substantial* one—is that you get to use the code you need, without having the burden of writing it yourself.

In this chapter, you'll learn how to apply these techniques for managing your own code and accessing code obtained from others. Specifically, you'll learn how to create your own modules, how to use existing modules from Perl's standard distribution, and how to locate, obtain, and install modules from the CPAN.

We'll begin by showing you how to package the center_line subroutine of listing 11.3 in the form of a module. We'll end this chapter by examining practical applications built around a sampling of freely available modules—ranging from Business::UPS, for estimating shipping charges, through File::Find, for writing OS-portable programs that replace the Unix find command, to CGI (Common Gateway Interface), for generating web pages and processing web forms.

12.1 CREATING MODULES

With all of Perl's standard modules out there for you to use, plus the thousands available from the CPAN, why would you want to write your own modules? For several reasons, including these:

- To make it easier for you to reuse your own custom code
- To make it easier for you to share your custom code with others

We'll discuss how you can create your own modules next, because chances are good that you'll need to do so at some point, and this is an easy skill to acquire.

The standard way for a Perl programmer to package code for easy reuse is through an approach based on the Exporter.pm module, which is distributed with Perl. It arranges for the *importing* of a set of default components from a module—or else the ones that are explicitly requested—when the user's program runs use *Module_name* or use *Module_name* (*components*), respectively.

We'll discuss a simple method for creating such modules next.

> **TIP**   A common way to begin a new module is by editing a *template* that contains the boilerplate code for a generic module.

12.1.1   Using the Simple Module Template

Several elements are required in the definition of a Perl module, and some may be hard to remember. For this reason, a common way to begin a new module is by modifying a *template* that contains the boilerplate code for a generic module.

Listing 12.1 shows our *Simple Module Template* (*Template* for short), which works nicely for many applications.[2] We'll pay special attention to the lines with bold type, because you must modify these according to the needs of the module being defined.

Listing 12.1   The Simple Module Template

```
1  package Module_name; # puts vars and subs in module's namespace
2  use strict;
3  use Carp;              # identifies error locations from user's POV
4
5  our (@ISA, @EXPORT, @EXPORT_OK);
6
7  # List any variables or subs to be exported by module here
8  our ( module_vars, module_subs );
9
10 require Exporter; @ISA=( 'Exporter' ); # import/export services
11
12 # Classify module's exports as automatic or on-request
13 @EXPORT=qw(    module_vars, module_subs );          # automatic
14 @EXPORT_OK=qw( module_vars, module_subs );          # on-request
15
16 # The code that implements the module's functionality follows
17
18 sub lime {
19     # Contents
20 }
21
22 sub stantial {
23     # Contents
24 }
25 # And so forth ...
26
27 1;  # Indicate module's end, with True value
```

You'll learn how to use this template next.

---

[2] For a more detailed module template that handles the needs of more complex modules, see man `perlmod`.

Starting the new module

The italicized words in the Template's source code are placeholders that need to be replaced by the actual names of the items they represent. Starting at the top, *Module_name* needs to be changed to the full name of the module being created, which might be something like `Chat::Secure`, or more simply, `Center`. It's vital that the file containing the module definition be given a matching name and path, which would be `Secure.pm` in a directory called `Chat` for the first case, but `Center.pm` for the second one.

All modules should `use strict`, so that statement comes next (Line 2).

Line 3 imports the module called `Carp`, which provides the useful service of identifying the locations of errors from the point of view of the user, rather than the programmer. (The difference is demonstrated later in section 12.1.2.)

Line 5, which declares three variables that are part of the Template itself,[3] should not be modified.

The next step is to specify the module's *exports*.

Specifying exported components

Line 8 of listing 12.1 specifies all the names of the variables and/or subroutines (the *components*) that the module will export—for users to import. You allocate those components to the two categories of exports by replacing the placeholders in the `@EXPORT` and `@EXPORT_OK` initializations on Lines 13 and 14 with the desired names.

How do you decide which module-components to assign to which array? On the basis of two considerations: ease of use, and likelihood of name clashes.[4] For example, if it's inconceivable that anyone would want to use your (hypothetical) `IQ` module without importing its subroutine called `genius`—because that's all it has to offer— then by all means place that name in `@EXPORT`, to automatically export it to the module's users.

On the other hand, it's inconsiderate to export anything the user might not want, because that increases the probability of name clashes. This is especially true for components having common (and therefore clash-prone) names, such as `$output`, `$count`, and `@name` for variables, or `calculate`, `validate`, and `get_data` for subroutines.

For this reason, it might be best to provide `IQ`'s users with access to its `$statistics` variable—which shows the percentages of people falling into different IQ ranges—only *on request*, rather than automatically. That means its name should go into `@EXPORT_OK`, rather than `@EXPORT`.

Lines 13 and 14 show a special quoting syntax using the `qw` operator (see table 9.2). We haven't needed it thus far, but it has distinct advantages in contexts

---

[3] `our`, `my`, and `local` are special in that they receive the actual names of the variables provided as their arguments, rather than the contents of those variables.

[4] Discussed in section 11.2.

where variable names must be used as literal strings. Why? Because Shell-savvy programmers are understandably prone to automatically use *double quotes* in Perl statements like this one, to allow *variable substitution*:

```
@EXPORT=( "$var1", "$var2" );
```

But variable substitution needs to be *suppressed* here, not allowed, so such people need to "overcome their programming" and use single quotes instead. This allows the variable names *themselves* to be presented as the array initializers, rather than the contents of those variables:

```
@EXPORT=( '$var1', '$var2' );
```

But there's an even better solution than using single quotes. The benefit of qw( ) — which stands for "**quote words**"—is that it automatically applies single quotes to strings separated by whitespace. This provides a more easily typed and less error-prone alternative to the earlier statement (see Lines 13–14 of listing 12.1):

```
@EXPORT=qw( $var1   $var2 );
```

If you wish, you can leave either the @EXPORT or the @EXPORT_OK array empty by removing the Template's placeholders from the parentheses:

```
@EXPORT=qw( );    # no automatic exports
```

Now we need to define the module's subroutines.

Defining subroutines

Lines 18–25 of the Template are placeholders for the subroutines that implement the functionality of the module.

When you're cutting subroutines from existing scripts and pasting them into a new module, some modifications may be required. For instance, because the variables the module is exporting will already be declared with file scope on Line 8, existing subroutines need to be stripped of any redundant declarations for those variables that also appear within them. Moreover, subroutines that previously obtained information from a script's global variables will have to be modified to accept that information via arguments instead. That's because subroutines residing in the module's file won't have any other way to access, for example, the values of private variables residing in the module-using program.

Now all we have left to do is to identify the module's definition as complete.

Concluding the module with a "happy ending"

The final line of the Template (1;) may look nonsensical (see listing 12.1), but it's a vital part of the module file. It's there to satisfy the need of the use function—which loads the file—to find a success code at its end. It certainly couldn't be much easier to type!

Now that you know the procedure for defining a module, we'll use the techniques you've learned to package a subroutine from an earlier chapter in the module format.

12.1.2 Creating a module: `Center.pm`

Listing 12.2 shows the results of customizing our Template to create `Center.pm`, which provides access to the (slightly modified) `center_line` subroutine of the `center2.strict` program (see listing 11.3).

The `package Center` line at the top tells Perl to prefix all non-private user-defined variables with `Center::`, which causes the full name of the variable declared on Line 8 to be `$Center::cl_width`. The benefit of having a unique *namespace* like this for each module is that it prevents a *non-exported* variable (e.g., `$piece`, which is really `$Center::piece`) from clashing with a variable having the same simple name (`$piece`) in the user's program (where it's really `$main::piece` by default).

But typing the module's full name before every reference to its imported variables would soon become tedious. For this reason, the program's `use` directive arranges for the simple name `$cl_width` to act as an *alias* for the variable's full name in the module (`$main::cl_width → $Center::cl_width`), providing a service for a variable like the one a symbolic link provides for a Unix file.[5]

Lines 13 and 14, respectively, declare the names of the module's components that are exported automatically, and exported only on request. (Remember, from the module-user's point of view, these are the components that are *imported* automatically, or only on request.)

On Line 21, `$newstring` is declared as private from there to the end of the subroutine, so it can be accessed within the "then" (Lines 23–26) and `else` (Lines 29–40) branches of execution, as well as on Line 42 at the subroutine's end.

Next, we'll discuss the differences between `warnings` and `carpings`.

Listing 12.2 The `Center.pm` module

```
1   package Center;      # puts vars and subs in module's "namespace"
2   use strict;
3   use Carp;            # identifies error locations from user's POV
4
5   our (@ISA, @EXPORT, @EXPORT_OK);
6
7   # List any variables exported by module here
8   our ($cl_width);
9
10  require Exporter; @ISA=qw(Exporter); # import/export services
11
12  # Classify module's exports as automatic or on request
13  @EXPORT=qw(center_line);                # automatically exported
14  @EXPORT_OK=qw($cl_width);               # exported only on request
15
```

---

[5] But that could still lead to a name clash if the user program was already using a variable by the same name, which is why we recommend more distinctive names for exported variables, such as the `$cl_width` shown here, or even `$Center_width`.

```
16   sub center_line {
17     # returns argument centered within field of size $cl_width
18
19     use Text::Tabs; # imports expand(); converts tabs to spaces
20
21     my $newstring;              # private, from here to file's end
22     if ( @_ != 1  or  $_[0] eq "" )  {  # needs one argument
23       # Use warn() during development, but carp() thereafter
24   #   warn __PACKAGE__, ": Usage: center_line(line)";  # prog-POV
25       carp __PACKAGE__, ": Usage: center_line(line)";  # user-POV
26       $newstring=undef;       # arrange to return "undefined" value
27     }
28     else {
29       defined $cl_width  and  $cl_width > 2  or  $cl_width=80;
30
31       my ($string, $indent, $padding); # private, from here to }
32       $string = shift;                 # get required argument
33       $string=expand ($string);     # convert tabs to spaces
34       $string =~ s/^\s+//;          # remove leading whitespace
35       $string =~ s/\s+$//;          # remove trailing whitespace
36
37       # calculate indentation
38       $indent=($cl_width - length $string )/2;
39       $padding=' ' x $indent;
40       $newstring="$padding$string";
41     }
42     return $newstring;          # return centered string, or undef
43   }
44   1; # Obligatory "happy ending"
```

Using `carp` in production, `warn` during development

A usage message is generated if necessary from Line 24 or 25 of listing 12.2, to suit the different needs of the module's developer and the programmers who use the module. Specifically, in cases where the center subroutine is invoked without correct arguments (see Line 22), the developer wants the diagnostic message to be issued by warn, because it identifies the location *within the module* where the error originated:

Center: Usage: ... at Center.pm line 24, <> line 7. ← **warn**

But a module user who's shown a message that refers to a location in a module will probably react by emailing its author—in this case, with a request to fix the bug on Line 24!

To avoid such outcomes, a module should employ the carp function for reporting errors rather than warn, once it has been debugged and released.[6] That's because carp identifies the location in the *module user's program* from which the imported

---

6 For the same reason, a released module should also use the Carp module's croak rather than die.

subroutine was called, thereby directing the programmer's attention to the code in his own script, where the mistake usually lies:

```
Center: Usage: ... at user script line 16          ← carp
```

This problem originated on Line 16 (the last line) of the script, where a bad argument was passed to the imported center_line subroutine (see center3 in section 12.1.3).

It's prudent to identify the source of a diagnostic message in the message itself, so Perl's special __PACKAGE__ keyword is used on Lines 24–25 (of listing 12.2) to prefix the message with the module's name, Center (as shown in the earlier output from carp and warn).

As life may have already taught you, there are situations were argumentation is best avoided, as you'll see next.

Setting imported variables rather than passing arguments

As discussed in Guideline #3 (section 11.4.3), there are sometimes advantages to conveying information to subroutines through use of variables rather than arguments.

For example, some programs using Center might want to call center_line many times, to center different strings in fields of the same size. For this reason, the module allows the user's program to import and set the $cl_width variable to the desired value once and for all, rather than requiring a second argument containing that information to be passed on each call to center_line.[7]

The center3 script discussed in the next section, which covers module testing, demonstrates this technique.

12.1.3   Testing a new module

Did you notice the lack of a shebang line in the Template? That's because the code of a module is not executed from its own file, but instead from the program that imports it.

Eventually you'll write a program to use your module, but during the module's development, you should check its file for warnings (w) and syntax errors (c), as shown:

```
$ perl -wc Center.pm
Center.pm syntax OK
```

Running this command after every significant change to the module ensures that you'll hear about mistakes as soon as possible after making them. However, this is only a rudimentary form of testing, which is most sensitive to syntax errors. Accordingly, once you know that your module compiles without warnings, it's time to test it more thoroughly by writing a custom program to *use* it.

---

[7] Several standard modules, such as Text::Tabs and Text::Wrap, also use this technique.

Testing `Center` with the `center3` script

The `center3` script is a variation on `center2.strict` (see listing 11.3) that imports the `center_line` subroutine from the `Center` module, rather than including the subroutine's code in its own program file. Although it's not necessary for such a simple program, `center3` has been written for compliance with our Variable Scoping Guidelines for complex programs (see section 11.4), for educational purposes. Let's check it out:

```
#! /usr/bin/perl -s -wnl
# center3: centers input lines using a module's function

# Usage: center3 [ -width=columns ] [ file1 file2 ... ]

use strict;

our ($width);                              # switch variable

use Center  qw( center_line  $cl_width ); # import sub, scalar
BEGIN {
    $cl_width=$width;        # load value into Module's variable
}

print center_line $_;      # Note: parentheses unnecessary
```

The `use Center` line imports the desired components from the module. Although one of those—`center_line`—is automatically exported by virtue of being listed in the `@EXPORT` array, the other (`$cl_width`) is exported only on request, because it's listed in `@EXPORT_OK`. You might think that providing `$cl_width` as the lone argument to `use` would cause both components to be imported, but it won't. Here's why:

> *If you provide the names of __any__ components to `use`, you have to provide the names of __all__ the ones you want—even those that are exported automatically.*

The statement in the `BEGIN` block copies the value of the switch variable to the module's exported `$cl_width` variable. `center_line`, both checks it and uses the default of 80 columns if `$cl_width` is undefined or too small (see Line 29, listing 12.2).

The script's switch variable is called `$width` rather than `$cl_width`, both because it's easier for the user to remember, and to avoid a name-clash with the `$cl_width` that's created as an alias for the module's variable.

Notice that no declaration has to be made for `$cl_width`, both in `center3`, even though `use strict` is in effect. That's because that variable's properties were already declared in the module's file, from which it was imported.

Even if the module is written perfectly, it won't be of any use if Perl can't find it! Next, you'll learn how to tell Perl where it's located.

Specifying the module's location:
The *PERL5LIB* variable

It's time to test the program:

```
$ center3
Can't locate Center.pm ... compilation aborted
```

Perl didn't find the module, but that's to be expected. Although it maintains a list (in @INC) of system directories in which it searches for the modules named in use directives, that list doesn't include the directories in which users store their personal modules.

You can remedy that situation by adding the appropriate directory's pathname to the environment variable PERL5LIB, which augments Perl's search-list. Here's an example of appending the current directory, using the Shell's PWD variable:

```
$ export PERL5LIB=$PERL5LIB:$PWD
```

And here's how Diggity Dog could easily add his special directory, in which he keeps the custom modules he "raps out" on his own:

```
$ export PERL5LIB=$PERL5LIB:$HOME/doghouse
```

But a less creative person might be inclined to use a more prosaic directory name, like this one:

```
$ export PERL5LIB=$PERL5LIB:$HOME/mymodules
```

Either way, once PERL5LIB has been suitably adjusted and exported, Perl should be able to find your personal modules, and you'll be able to run your module-using program:

```
$ center3 marx_bros
                              Groucho
                               Harpo
                               Chico


$ center -width=11 marx_bros
  Groucho
   Harpo
   Chico
```

The module should also work when called from a Perl command, rather than a script:

```
$ grep 'French' iron_chefs | perl -M'Center' -wpl -e '$_=center $_'
                Iron Chef French      Hiroyuki Sakai
```

Although typing the export PERL5LIB command as shown earlier only affects the current Shell session, you'll probably want that variable's setting to be in effect each time you log in. To accomplish this, add that command to your Shell startup file (generally, .profile for the Korn shell and .bash_login for the Bash shell).

Now that you know how to create, test, and use your own modules, you'll see how you can identify and obtain modules written by others that might make good additions to your collection.

12.2 MANAGING MODULES

Next, we'll discuss how to determine which Perl modules you already have, and how to locate those that you don't in the CPAN. Then you'll see how to use the simplest standard method for downloading, building, testing, and installing the additional modules you need.

12.2.1 Identifying the modules that you want

CPAN modules that do a good job of providing useful services tend to get noticed. For this reason, it's wise to begin your quest for the Perl software you need by posing a question like the following to a knowledgeable colleague (or a relevant mailing list):

> *"What's the best Perl module for converting holographic gruffles to lasermorphic floobles?"*

If such a module exists, and it's one that has wide appeal (perhaps unlike the case in the example), you can expect to get some useful advice in response to that question.

But in cases where you can't discover the name of a relevant module through peer recommendations, you should use the http://search.cpan.org web site, which does a good job of reporting the modules that are associated with the keywords you specify. We'll demonstrate the use of this site next.

QUESTION: *Where do you get the modules you don't have?*
ANSWER: *From the Comprehensive Perl Archive Network—CPAN.*

Searching for a module
that calculates UPS shipping charges

Let's say you're looking for code to incorporate into your online shopping site, to calculate UPS shipping charges between warehouses and customer locations. You could begin by entering the keywords "UPS shipping charges" in the screen shown in figure 12.1 and then clicking the CPAN Search button.

The matches found by that search appear on your screen (see figure 12.2). Don't the top two listings, `Business::UPS` and `Business::Shipping::UPS_XML`, sound promising?

NOTE	Even if you don't have rootly powers, you can *still* use the CPAN shell to install modules.

Figure 12.1 Searching CPAN for "UPS shipping charges" using http://search.cpan.org

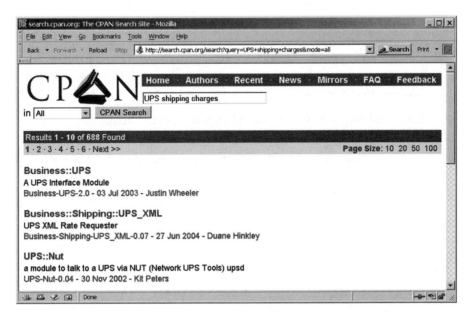

Figure 12.2 Results of searching CPAN for "UPS shipping charges" using http://search.cpan.org

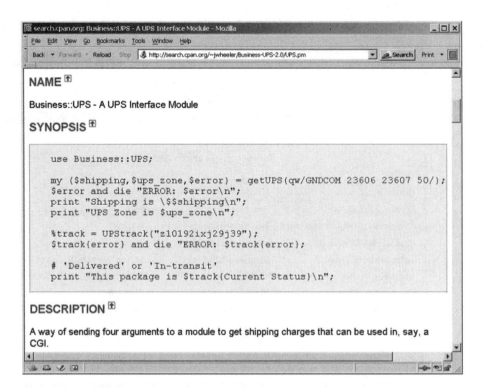

Figure 12.3   Manual page for `Business::UPS` module

Clicking `Business::UPS` displays that module's manual page (see figure 12.3).

If you could scroll down the screen shown in figure 12.3, you'd be able to read the documentation on the functions[8] called `getUPS` and `UPStrack`, which provide shipping and tracking information, respectively. The module seems to provide the desired services, so the next step is to see if you already have it.

12.2.2   Determining whether you have a certain module

Sooner or later, you'll hear about a module that sounds like it could be useful, and you'll want to try it. But how do you know whether or not you've already got it on your system?

A simple approach is to ask Perl to load the module, and see what happens:[9]

---

[8] Subroutines imported from modules are generally called *functions*, but if they're written in the object-oriented style, they're called *methods* (see section 12.3.6).

[9] The accuracy of this test depends on the suitability of your `PERL5LIB` variable's setting for your system (see section 12.1.3).

```
$ perl -M'Text::Autoformat' -e 'exit;'     # No news is good news!

$ perl -M'Business::UPS'   -e 'exit;'      # Output edited for fit
Can't locate Business/UPS.pm in @INC
(@INC contains:
/local/perl5/site_perl/5.8.7
/usr/lib/perl5/site_perl/5.8.7
...
```

It seems that you don't have Business::UPS, so now you need to get it. That's where the *CPAN access module* comes into play, which is up next.

12.2.3 Installing modules from the CPAN

The best resource in the standard Perl distribution for managing your access to the CPAN is the module aptly named—CPAN.[10]

If you have root privileges, you can run the CPAN module from that privileged account and install modules in system directories where everyone can access them. But if you only have non-rootly powers, you can still use CPAN to install modules in the directories for which you have write permission. We'll discuss the relevant configuration details next.

Configuring CPAN

You can interact with the CPAN module by starting up your Internet connection and then executing its `shell` function, using what's known as the CPAN-shell command:

```
perl -M'CPAN' -e 'shell;'
```

If you get the following response, CPAN is already configured for your system, and you're ready to go:

```
cpan shell -- CPAN exploration and modules installation
ReadLine support enabled
cpan>
```

However, if the response looks anything like this, additional preparations are needed:

```
Your configuration suggests "/root/.cpan" as your
CPAN.pm working directory. I could not create this directory due
to this error: mkdir /root/.cpan: Permission denied
```

This result indicates that the *root* user has already configured the CPAN access module, and others don't have permission to modify the existing system-wide settings.

If you are authorized to use the root account, this would be a good time to switch to it, run the CPAN-shell command again, and proceed from that more exalted footing.

---

[10] A successor with many enhancements called CPANPLUS is also available from the CPAN.

But if you can't run as root, you can still define CPAN settings for your personal use. The first steps are to create a directory and load an <u>empty assignment statement</u> into a special file:[11]

```
$ mkdir -p ~/.cpan/CPAN
$ echo '$CPAN::Config={ };' > ~/.cpan/CPAN/MyConfig.pm
```

Then, you run the CPAN-shell command again and answer a series of questions, which fill up that $CPAN::Config variable with settings appropriate for your system. For questions you don't know how to answer, either accept the [ ]-enclosed defaults or ask for help from a more experienced Perl programmer, or a system or network administrator.

It's an easy process, but there are a few questions you should be prepared for. One of them is

```
Policy on building prerequisites (follow, ask or ignore)? [ask] follow
```

Unless you want to be pestered for your approval every time a module needs to be downloaded because it's a prerequisite for another one, type "<u>follow</u>" for your answer, rather than accepting the default of "ask".

If your Internet access goes through proxy servers, you'll need to know their details to respond properly to the questions about FTP and HTTP services, which might take some research on your part.

You'll also be asked about your preferred CPAN mirror sites (*mirrors*), from which CPAN will download your modules. It pays to select reliable mirrors that can provide fast transfers to your location, so you might want to ask an informed colleague for help in choosing the best ones for your locality from the list provided.

From this point onward, different procedures need to be followed by rootly and non-rootly users, which we'll walk through next.

Installing modules as the root user

Your interest in using CPAN will be fueled by your need to install a module, whose name you probably identified through a CPAN search (as discussed earlier). If you're logged in as root, you can issue an install command as soon as you get the prompt from the CPAN-shell command. For example:

```
cpan> install Vapour::Ware
```

If the indicated module exists (this one *still* doesn't), it will automatically be downloaded, built, tested, and installed for you on the spot.

Life in the trenches of IT doesn't get much better than that! Just be careful to type the module's name properly, because colons and case variations really matter.

---

[11] Although I've never seen this procedure documented anywhere else, we've taught it in our classes for years.

Even if you're not root, you can still install CPAN modules. It just takes a bit more typing for the initial setup, as you'll see next.

Installing modules as a non-root user

After completing the initial CPAN configuration process, nonroot users need to type the following additional commands prior to installing a module:

```
cpan>  o conf makepl_arg "LIB=/your_home_dir/myperl/lib \
>             INSTALLMAN1DIR=/your_home_dir/myperl/man/man1 \
>             INSTALLMAN3DIR=/your_home_dir/myperl/man/man3"

cpan>  o conf commit
cpan>                        ⏎  install command can be issued here
```

Those o conf commands specify your HOME directory's myperl/lib (for library) subdirectory as the storage location for the modules you install, and HOME's subdirectory myperl/man as the location for storing the man pages for the installed modules.

Now you're ready to install a module, using the install *Module-name* command shown earlier, so give it a try.

But before you try to *use* any of your freshly installed modules, you'll need to update PERL5LIB appropriately (see section 12.1.3). To include the paths to your CPAN-download area and also your personal module directory, you'd use an assignment statement like this one:

```
$  PERL5LIB=$PERL5LIB:$HOME/myperl/lib:$HOME/mymodules
```

You can arrange for that variable setting to be established whenever you log in by putting it in your .profile or .bash_profile.

In the next section, we'll examine several scripts that take advantage of useful services provided by freely available modules.

12.3 USING MODULES

Now that you understand how Perl modules work, you'll benefit from seeing examples of industrial-grade modules being used to solve real problems. Well begin with a script based on Business::UPS that calculates shipping charges, and then we'll examine scripts demonstrating modules used for Internet access, menu-oriented programming, file-system maintenance, web-page creation, and processing forms submitted from web pages.

12.3.1 Business::UPS—the ups_shipping_price script

Now it's time to take our freshly installed new module out for a spin! Listing 12.3 shows a test program that I cobbled together in a few minutes after glancing at the module's manual page. It's called ups_shipping_price, and it compares the prices of two different service options for shipping a package from the origin Zip Code to the destination Zip Code in the USA.

Here's a sample run, checking on the cost options for shipping a case of CDs and autographed sweatsuits from Diggity Dog's crib in Van Nuys, CA, to a fervent female fan in Wilmington, DE:

```
$ ups_shipping_price -origin=91401 -dest=19808 -pounds=42
2DAL service to ship 42 pounds from 91401 to 19808 is $12.65
 1DM service to ship 42 pounds from 91401 to 19808 is $172.19
```

The script is fairly straightforward (see listing 12.3), apart from a few tricks that we'll discuss.

Listing 12.3   The `ups_shipping_price` script

```perl
 1  #! /usr/bin/perl -s -wl
 2
 3  use strict;                        # needed because of nested loops
 4
 5  use Business::UPS;
 6
 7  our ($origin, $dest, $pounds);  # switch variables
 8
 9  my $Usage="Usage: $0 -origin=zip -dest=zip -pounds=weight";
10
11  # Check for required switches
12  defined $origin  and  defined $dest  and  defined $pounds  or
13    warn "$Usage\n"  and  exit 1;
14
15  my $pricey='1DM';        # 1DM delivers on morning of next day
16  my $cheap='2DAL';        # 2DAL delivers on second day
17
18  foreach my $service ( $cheap, $pricey ) {
19    my ( $price, undef, $error )=
20      getUPS( $service, $origin, $dest, $pounds );
21
22    if ( $error ) {
23        warn "$0: ERROR: $error\n";
24    }
25    else {
26      my $service2=$service;
27      length $service2 < 4  and  $service2=" $service";  # align
28
29      print "$service2 service to ship $pounds pounds",
30        " from $origin to $dest is \$$price";
31    }
32  }
```

CHAPTER 12   MODULES AND THE CPAN

The variables $cheap and $pricey, which represent different shipping services, are declared on Lines 15–16, because they already need to be in scope by the time they're used in foreach's list of values on Line 18.

As you can see, getUPS takes a list of four values (Line 20) and returns a list of three values, of which $price and $error are of interest. Note the technique of assigning the list returned by getUPS directly to the my operator's list of variable names (introduced in table 11.2). This saves the programmer the burden of typing that list again in a separate assignment, after the declaration statement.

If all goes well, Lines 29–30 print the results, after the shorter "service-type" string (in $pricey) is brought into alignment with the longer one on Line 27 (by prepending a space).

Next we'll look at a script that will surely be of interest to web administrators.

12.3.2   LWP::Simple—the check_links script

In some cities, enterprising individuals wash the windshields of motorists who are waiting for traffic lights to change, and then ask for tips. Those managing their own web sites may receive attention of a similar kind from Internet entrepreneurs, who patrol the Internet for web pages having bad links, report them to the responsible web masters, and then ask for compensation.

After I got a few dozen such emails alerting me to a mistyped link on one of my web sites, I decided to start washing my own windows—I mean policing my own web-pages—more carefully. An easy way to do this is by using tools provided by the CPAN's LWP::Simple, which provides a *simple* interface to Perl's Library for Web Programming.[12]

Specifically, its lwp-request command (discussed in chapter 3) can be used to easily download web pages and extract their links, and its head function—which returns descriptive data for web pages (type, size, server, etc.)—can be used to differentiate active links from dead ones.

Before we examine the code, look at these sample runs of the script, which were conducted at different levels of verbosity for the same web site:[13]

```
$ check_links ukeworld.com
BAD: 'https://www.ukeworld.com/ppbutton2.gif', in 'ukeworld.com'

$ CL_VERBOSE=1 check_links ukeworld.com
Got 101 links for ukeworld.com
85 links are unique
BAD: 'https://www.ukeworld.com/ppbutton2.gif', in 'ukeworld.com'
```

---

[12] More precisely, it provides a *procedural* interface to the resources of LWP, which itself is based on object-oriented programming techniques (see section 12.3.6).

[13] For the lower verbosity levels, the script even spins a nifty propeller on the screen to indicate that it's working (Lines 53-54, listing 12.4). That's done by indexing into an explicit list of strings using the remainder of an integer division provided by Perl's *modulus* operator (%; see man perlop).

```
$ CL_VERBOSE=2 check_links ukeworld.com
Got 101 links for ukeworld.com
85 links are unique
Checking 'http://ukeworld.com/?D=A': OKAY
Checking 'http://ukeworld.com/?M=A': OKAY
...
BAD: 'https://www.ukeworld.com/ppbutton2.gif', in 'ukeworld.com'

$ CL_VERBOSE=3 check_links ukeworld.com   # Output edited to fit
Got 101 links for ukeworld.com
85 links are unique
Checking 'http://ukeworld.com/?D=A': OKAY
  Type: text/html      Size: N/A      Server: Apache/1.3.27 ...
Checking 'http://ukeworld.com/?M=A': OKAY
  Type: text/html      Size: N/A      Server: Apache/1.3.27 ...
...
BAD: 'https://www.ukeworld.com/ppbutton2.gif', in 'ukeworld.com'
```

Verbosity level 3 dumps out the data obtained by the head function from the web server, if any; otherwise it reports the link being tested as "BAD".

Now look at the script, which is presented in listing 12.4.

It begins by importing LWP::Simple, which exports the head function automatically. It then checks for the variable CL_VERBOSE in the environment; if it has a number in it, that number is copied to the file-scoped variable $VERBOSE, so the requested verbosity level can conveniently be determined from anywhere within the program. On Line 25, the lwp-request command obtains the list of links found within the current page, and then if tests the True/False value of the array @links to determine whether links were found. Many pages contain multiple links to other pages, so Line 32 filters the duplicates out of @links (we'll come back to this).

Listing 12.4 The check_links script

```
1   #! /usr/local/bin/perl -wl
2
3   use strict;
4   use LWP::Simple;
5
6   my $VERBOSE=0; # file scope
7   defined $ENV{CL_VERBOSE}  and  $ENV{CL_VERBOSE} =~ /^\d+$/  and
8     $VERBOSE=$ENV{CL_VERBOSE}; # if numeric value, assign
9
10  {  # MAIN program
11    foreach my $url ( @ARGV ) { check_link( $url ) };
12  }
13
14  END {
15    # If propeller was last thing written to screen,
16    # will need \n before shell's upcoming prompt to STDERR
17    print STDERR "";
18  }
```

```
19
20   sub check_link {
21     my ( $url, @links, $link, @h, $counter, $output );
22     $url=shift;
23
24     # use lwp-request command, based on LWP, to get links
25     if( @links=`lwp-request -o links '$url'` ) {
26       $VERBOSE  and
27         print "\nGot ", scalar @links, " links for $url";
28     }
29     else {
30       warn "$!\n";    # show OS error message
31     }
32     @links=uniquify ( @links );  # eliminate duplicate links
33     $VERBOSE  and  @links  and   # if link count > 0, show count
34       print scalar @links, " links are unique";
35
36     foreach $link ( @links ) {    # test each link
37       $link =~ /^(A|LINK)\s+mailto:/i  and  next; # skip mailto
38       $link =~ s/^\w+\s+//;  # strip A/IMG in "A/IMG  http://"
39       $link =~ s/\s+//g;       # eliminate any remaining WS in link
40
41       $VERBOSE > 1  and  printf "\nChecking '$link'";
42       if ( @h=head $link ) { # run LWP's head() on link
43         if ( $VERBOSE > 1 ) {
44           print   ": OKAY";
45           $VERBOSE > 2  and
46             printf "  Type: %s\tSize: %s\tServer: %s\n",
47               $h[0], ( $h[1]  or  "N/A" ), $h[4];
48         }
49         else {
50           # Show "propeller" as activity indicator;
51           # printf prints backspace, then one of - \ | /
52           # to STDERR, so stays on screen if output redirected
53           printf STDERR "\b%s",  # %s prints next arg as string
54             ('-', '\\', '|', '/')[$counter++ % 4];
55         }
56       }
57       else {        # report links for which "head" request fails
58         $output = "\nBAD: '$link', in '$url'";
59         $output =~ s|http://||g;  # save space by deleting http:
60       }
61     }
62   }
```

Then, head is called on each link in turn (Line 42). For those that yield results, a propeller is spun, or the word "OKAY" is printed, or a detailed report on the link is printed—according to the verbosity level. At levels above 2, head's output is displayed after being formatted by printf (Lines 46–47). A logical or is used to substitute "N/A" for a False value in $h[1] to provide printf's second data argument, because with some web sites, a null string gets stored in that array element.

```
63
64  sub uniquify {  # sort and "uniquify" the arguments
65    my %unique;
66    foreach ( @_ ) { $unique{$_}++; };
67    return sort keys %unique;
68  }
```

The subroutine used for unique-*ification* (Lines 64–68) uses the technique intro-duced in section 9.2.6 of registering the items of interest as keys in a hash, and then extracting the (necessarily unique) keys. The code is encapsulated in a subroutine to facilitate later reuse.

Next, we'll revisit an advanced module I wrote, which endows Perl with a new and improved control structure adapted from the Shell.

12.3.3   Shell::POSIX::Select—the menu_ls script

Apart from its many other applications demonstrated in section 10.7, the menu-oriented user interface provided by Shell::POSIX::Select can help you com-pose Unix commands, as shown in figure 12.4. The menu_ls program presents you with a series of choices for the ls command's behavior, translates them into their corresponding command options, and then runs the constructed command.

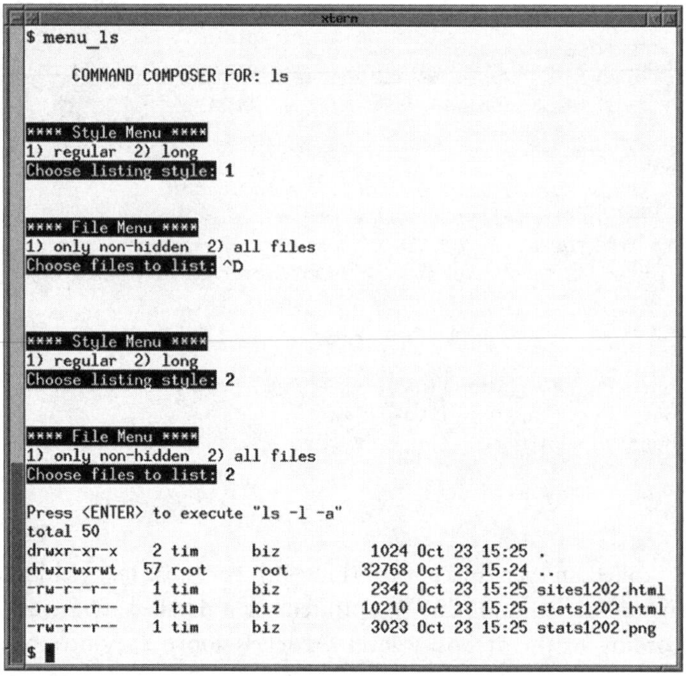

Figure 12.4   Sample run of the menu_ls script

NOTE   This implementation of `select` lets you return to previous menus to modify earlier selections.

In the session shown, the user initially selected the "regular" listing style from the Style Menu, but had second thoughts about that choice after the File Menu had already appeared. Responding to the prompt with <^D> took her back to the previous menu, where she revised her choice to "long". Then, after choosing "all files" from the File Menu, she was shown the command and given a chance to approve it before running it.

Unlike the examples of the `select` loop shown in section 10.7, this script (see listing 12.5) ignores the loop variable and focuses on the associated `$Reply` variable instead. As it does in the Shell's version of `select`, that variable contains the user's actual numerical response, which this program uses to index into the array of options (see Lines 17 and 22).

For example, a choice for the "long" listing style gets mapped into `-1` by way of the common index shared by the paired arrays `@formats` and `@fmt_opts` (see Lines 6–7). The same holds true for the choice of "all files" and the option of `-a`, which are related through the `@types` and `@type_opt` arrays. (Because the `$Reply` value reflects the numerical choices of the user from the menu, a 1 needs to be subtracted before using it as an index into the 0-based option arrays.)

In addition to `$Reply`, the `$Heading`, `$Prompt`, and `$Eof` variables are also imported on Line 2, to allow for headings and prompts to be associated with menus, and for easy detection of <^D> after a loop has been exited, respectively.[14]

Here's how that works. When the FORMAT loop is entered on Line 16, the module stores the settings of `$Heading` and `$Prompt` that are currently in effect (from Lines 14 and 15), and arranges for them to be shown when the loop is reentered, as happened in the sample session when the user exited the TYPE loop via <^D>.

Listing 12.5   The `menu_ls` script

```
1   #! /usr/bin/perl -wl
2   use Shell::POSIX::Select qw($Reply $Heading $Prompt $Eof);
3
4   # Would be more natural to associate choices with options via a
5   #  hash, but this approach better demonstrates $Reply variable
6   @formats = ( 'regular', 'long' );
7   @fmt_opt = ( '',          '-l'   );
8
9   @types   = ( 'only non-hidden', 'all files' );
10  @typ_opt = ( '',                  '-a'        );
11
12  print "\n    COMMAND COMPOSER FOR: ls\n";
13
14  $Heading="\n**** Style Menu ****";
```

---

[14] These features don't exist in Shell versions of `select`, but I've always felt they should.

```
15   $Prompt= 'Choose listing style:';
16   FORMAT: select ( @formats ) {
17       $user_format=$fmt_opt[ $Reply - 1 ];
18
19       $Heading="\n**** File Menu ****";
20       $Prompt="Choose files to list:";
21       TYPE: select ( @types ) {    # <^D> restarts FORMAT loop
22           $user_type=$typ_opt[ $Reply - 1 ];
23           last FORMAT; # leave loops once final choice obtained
24       }
25       $Eof  and  next; # handle <^D> to TYPE loop
26   }
27   $Eof  and  exit;       # handle <^D> to FORMAT loop
28
29   # Now construct user's command
30   $command="ls $user_format $user_type";
31
32   # Show command, for educational purposes
33   printf "Press <ENTER> to execute \"$command\" ";
34   # wait for input, then discard
35   defined <STDIN>  or  print "\n"  and  exit;
36
37   system $command ;        # run the command
```

The purpose of the Eof variable is to resolve uncertainties about why the loop variable is empty in the statement immediately following the loop (Line 25). The two possibilities are that the loop was never entered (e.g., due to its list being empty), or that it was exited via <^D>. Testing the $Eof variable for True detects the latter case, allowing the script to respond to the user's <^D> by reverting to the prior Style Menu (as mentioned above).

On the other hand, we don't want to hold the user hostage, so a <^D> submitted to the FORMAT loop is treated by default as a request to exit the script (Line 27), as is a <^D> response to the following "Press <ENTER>" prompt (Lines 33–35). Finally, if Line 37 is reached, the assembled command is submitted to the OS for execution by system.

Although this prototype menu_ls script handles only two of ls' many options, it nicely demonstrates your ability to write Shell-eclipsing menu-driven programs using the Shell::POSIX::Select module (see chapter 10 for additional examples).

We'll look next at a system-administration application of a module that lets Perl programs emulate aspects of the Unix find command.

12.3.4   `File::Find`—the `check_symlinks` script

A filing system is supposed to provide for reliable storage and retrieval of information. Because problems with file retrieval can have serious consequences, it's important to monitor computer file systems and take corrective action—for example, by replacing a disk drive that's going bad—as soon as problems start to appear.

One potentially vexing problem[15] on Unix systems is that of broken symbolic links—ones that formerly pointed to stored data but no longer do. To help in identifying them, the script called `check_symlinks` scans specified directories for symbolic links whose target files don't exist, and reports them in the `ls -l` style of *symlink → target*.

Here's a sample run that searches two directories on a Linux system:

```
# check_symlinks /etc /lib     # Running with root privileges

REPORTING BROKEN SYMLINKS UNDER: /etc
        /etc/X11/xdm/xdm-pid -> /var/run/xdm.pid

REPORTING BROKEN SYMLINKS UNDER: /lib
        /lib/modules/2.4.21/build -> /local/tmp/src/linux-2.4.21
        /lib/modules/2.4.19/build -> /usr/src/linux-2.4.19
        /lib/modules/2.4.19-4GB/build -> /usr/src/linux-2.4.19.SuSE

FILES BROKEN/EXAMINED: 4/6,797
TIME: 0:04 HR:MN
START: Sat Jan 28 20:35:48 2006  END: Sat Jan 28 20:39:18 2006
```

Although this run took only a few minutes, on a *disk farm* the script could run for days at a time, which is why it was designed to produce such detailed reports of its run times.

`check_symlinks` uses the `find` function from the standard `File::Find` module for its directory-searching and file-finding services, to avoid re-inventing that wheel. For each file that it finds under a specified directory, `find` calls a user-defined subroutine with `$_` set to the current file's simple name (e.g., `motd`) and the module's variable `$File::Find::name` set to its full name (e.g., `/etc/motd`). Then the subroutine is free to process that file as needed.

You can see the script in listing 12.6. As shown on Line 24, `find` needs to be supplied the *address* of the user's file-handling subroutine, which is obtained by prepending the special `\&` operator to `check_slinks`'s name.[16] Line 38 in that subroutine checks whether the current file is a symbolic link, and if so, it gets the name of its target

---

[15] I think it's *partly* a longing for the data that may never be seen again, but *mostly* a feeling of being betrayed by a trusted ally, that bothers me so about such losses. But I suppose the betrayal angle is just wishful thinking, because most broken symlinks seem to be caused by user error (e.g., rm-ing the target file).

[16] The address is needed because the user's subroutine might not be readily accessible *by name* from the `File::Find` namespace, but it can definitely be invoked *by address*.

(Line 40) using the built-in `readlink` function. If the target file doesn't exist, the full pathname of the symlink and its target are printed to report the problem (Line 48).

It's important to recognize that `check_symlinks`, like all scripts using `find`, has to work within a special constraint. Specifically, because it's `find` that calls `check_slinks`—rather than the user's script itself—`check_slinks` can't use `return` to send any information back to the script.

This leaves the programmer with two options for working with the information that's only available within `check_slinks`. He must either deal with it (e.g., print it out) once and for all in that subroutine, or else store it in a place where it will still be accessible (e.g., in a widely scoped variable) after `find` returns control to the user's program.

Listing 12.6   The `check_symlinks` script

```
1    #! /usr/bin/perl -wl
2
3    use strict;
4    use File::Find;
5
6    {  # Special scope for Main + check_slinks
7
8        my $Bad=0;      # file scope; used in sub check_slinks()
9        my $Total=0;    # ditto
10
11       my $Usage="Usage: $0 dir1 [dir2 ...]\n";
12       @ARGV  or  die "$Usage";
13
14       my $start_time=time;         # for run-time calculation at end
15
16       foreach my $startdir( @ARGV ){
17           -d $startdir  and  -r _  and  -x _   or
18              warn "$0: Bad directory argument: $startdir\n"  and
19                 next;
20
21           # find broken symlinks in or under $startdir
22
23           print "REPORTING BROKEN SYMLINKS UNDER: \E$startdir";
24           find \&check_slinks, $startdir;   # call the function
25           print "";                         # blank line
26       }
27
28       # Print final statistics, including program's run time
29       print "FILES BROKEN/EXAMINED: ",
30           commafy ($Bad), "/", commafy ($Total);
31       show_times ($start_time);
32
33       sub check_slinks {
34           my  $isbad=0;                # whether current symlink is bad
35           my  $target;                 # where current symlink points
36           my $name=$File::Find::name;      # make a shorter name
```

```
37
38          if ( -l ) { # if file (in $_) is a sym-link,
39                      #  find what it's pointing to
40              $target=readlink $_;
41              if (! defined $target  or  $target  eq  "") {
42                  warn "$0: check_slinks(): bad readlink value",
43                      " on \"$name\": $!\n";
44                  $isbad=1;
45              }
46              elsif ( ! -e $target ) {
47                  # target missing; broken link, OR NFS down!
48                  print "\t$name -> $target";
49                  $isbad=1;
50              }
51          }
52          # $Bad and $Total are still in scope
53          $isbad  and  $Bad++;        # count another bad symlink
54          $Total++;                   # count another file examined
55          return; # goes back to "find", to be called for next file
56      }
57
58  } # end of special scope for Main + check_slinks
59
60  sub commafy {            # insert commas into number strings
61      my $number=shift;
62
63      defined $number  or  die "$0: commafy(): no argument!";
64      while ($number =~ s/^(-?\d+)(\d{3})/$1,$2/) { ; }
65      return $number;
66  }
67
```

I chose to print the details of each bad symlink from within check_slinks, because I knew the script wouldn't need access to them later. However, I also needed to keep counts of the total number of files examined and those verified as bad, which would be needed later. I handled this by arranging for the scopes of $Bad and $Total to run from Lines 8/9 to Line 58—to include both Main and the check_slinks subroutine—and by incrementing those variables as needed within check_slinks. (Capitalizing the initial letters of those variable names helps me remember that they're widely-scoped.)

These measures allow the print statement to access those variables on Line 30. To enhance the readability of the printed ratio of bad files ($Bad) to all files examined ($Total), the commafy subroutine is used to insert commas at appropriate places within those numbers.

The while loop on Line 64 of commafy repeats the substitution operator—which does all the work of the loop—until it finds no more three-digit sequences to *commafy*, which is why no statements are needed in the code block.

```
68  sub show_times {
69      # argument is program's start time
70      my $stime=shift   or
71          die "$0: show_times(): bad argument";
72      my $etime=time;                  # current (ending) time
73      my $dtime=$etime - $stime;       # elapsed time
74
75      printf "\UTime:%2d:%02d HR:MN ",
76          int ( ( $dtime / 3600 ) + .5 ),
77          ( ( $dtime % 3600 ) / 60 ) + .5;
78      print "\nSTART: ", scalar localtime $stime,
79          "  END: ", scalar localtime $etime;
80  }
```

The show_times subroutine prints the program's start and end times and its run time, which involves converting some large integers returned by the built-in time function (Line 72) into formatted date strings (Lines 78–79) and calculating the elapsed hours and minutes represented by the difference of those integers (Lines 73 and 76–77).

Because the commafy and show_times subroutines are not only difficult to write but also likely to be needed again in other scripts, they're excellent candidates for inclusion with other valued tools in a programmer's personal utilities module (e. g., Diggitys::Utilities).

Now we'll take a foray into the equally timely topic of web programming, using Perl's stalwart CGI module to do all the heavy lifting.

12.3.5   CGI—the survey.cgi script

In the 1990s, Perl's strengths in the areas of text parsing, pattern matching, networking, and OS independence led to it being embraced as the language of choice for web applications. Perl became especially popular for Common Gateway Interface (CGI) programming, in which a program on a server machine receives a request from a browser, handles that request, and then sends the appropriate response to the browser for display.

For example, the user might request a graph of last week's stock prices for Acme Corp. by filling out an on-screen form and then clicking the SUBMIT button. The CGI program on the web server would then

1 Retrieve the five daily stock prices from the stock-quote server;

2 Plot those prices in a pretty graph;

3 Construct a web page that contains that graph, along with a new form for the user's next request;

4 Send the constructed page back to the browser for display.

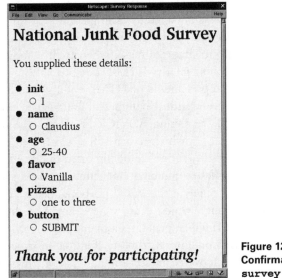

Figure 12.5
Initial screen of the `survey.cgi` script

Further details on the inner workings of the CGI protocol are beyond the scope of this book, but to give you an idea of how CGI applications can be written, we'll look at a simple example involving a web-based survey.

Figure 12.5 shows the web form that is produced by the `survey.cgi` script after it already has been filled out by the user.

When the user clicks the SUBMIT button shown in figure 12.5, a page confirming his answers to the survey questions appears next (see figure 12.6).

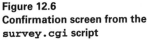

Figure 12.6
Confirmation screen from the `survey.cgi` script

Listing 12.7 shows the script that generated the previous web pages. We'll begin our examination of it with some general comments, and then we'll concentrate on how the program works.

General comments on survey.cgi

The first thing to notice about this script is that the w and l options we've routinely used throughout this book are missing from its shebang line. Although it's generally unwise to suppress warnings, doing so is proper for CGI programs running in production mode, because warnings would disrupt the functioning of the web server.

What about the missing l option, which would automatically append newlines to the output of print statements? Although it could have been used, it would have been of little benefit. That's because there are *only two* print statements in this entire (70+ line) script, but dozens of places were newlines need to be inserted (more on this later).

Another unusual feature of this script is that parentheses have been used around the argument lists of the CGI functions. This isn't required, but I find that they increase a script's readability when there are so many function having short names. (For example, Line 24 might look like a typo without its parentheses.)

Next, we'll consider some other aspects of the way functions are used in this script.

Using CGI functions in survey.cgi

A notable feature of this script is that it has almost one function call per line! (To help you spot them, the functions provided by the CGI module are shown in bold type in listing 12.7.) Although that characteristic would be highly unusual in general programming, this is quite typical of a CGI script. That's because its primary purpose is to generate the HTML code for the web pages it needs to display, and with the CGI module, each element of HTML code is obtained by calling a different function.

An advantage of this approach is that you're only responsible for calling the functions correctly (which comes easily to programmers), whereas the module has the responsibility of generating the (possible gnarly) HTML code properly.

If you're familiar with the markup elements of HTML coding, you'll be happy to learn that the CGI functions have identical names and are used in an intuitive manner. For example, the code for rendering ADVICE as a level-one heading is generated by executing h1 ('ADVICE'), which returns <h1>ADVICE</h1>.

The script requests a standard set of functions to be imported on Line 5, using the ":standard" argument (called a *tag*) to the use CGI directive. This set includes header and start_html, which generate the initial portions of the HTML code (Lines 14–15); b (bold) and i (italic), which cause style changes in the font (see Line 23); and p (paragraph, Line 24) which generates a blank line.

The use CGI::Carp statement on Line 8 imports the CGI module's counterpart to the standard Carp module (covered in section 12.1.2), which is instructed (via `fatalsToBrowser`) to show fatal errors on the browser's screen, which facilitates debugging.

The `radio_group`, `check_box`, and `popup_menu` functions (Lines 35, 41, 47) generate the HTML that displays the various groups of buttons and menu selections shown in figure 12.5.

Listing 12.7   The `survey.cgi` script

```
1   #! /usr/bin/perl
2   # survey.cgi: Demonstrates use of HTML forms with CGI
3
4   use strict;
5   use CGI qw(:standard);              # request CGI.pm components
6
7   # Carp shows errors in browser window, to facilitate debugging
8   use CGI::Carp qw(fatalsToBrowser);
9
10  # Store HTML code in variable $form; gets printed on screen, if
11  # run normally, or gets sent to browser, in CGI mode
12
13  if ( ! param() ) {      # if no parameters, we're displaying form
14      my $form=header();              # prepare HTTP header for server
15      $form.=start_html(-title=>'CGI Module Demo',
16                        -BGCOLOR=>'ivory');
17      $form.=h1('National Junk Food Survey');
18
19      # action='' means this script will handle the submitted form
20      $form.=startform(-method=>'GET', -action=>'');
21      $form.=hr() . "\n";
22
23      $form.=b('Please enter your first initial and surname:');
24      $form.=p();
25      $form.='Initial';
26      $form.=textfield(-name=>'init', -size=>1, -maxlength=>1);
27      $form.="\n";
28
29      $form.='Surname';
30      $form.=textfield(-name=>'name', -size=>12, -maxlength=>30);
31      $form.="\n" . hr() . "\n";
32
33      $form.=b('Please indicate your age group:');
34      $form.=p();
35      $form.=radio_group(-name=>'age',
36                         -Values=>['Under 25', '25-40', 'Older']);
37      $form.=hr() . "\n";
38
39      $form.=b('What are your favorite ice-cream flavors?');
40      $form.=p();
41      $form.=checkbox_group(-name=>'flavor',
42                    -Values=>['Chocolate', 'Vanilla', 'Other']);
43      $form.=hr() . "\n";
```

```
44
45        $form.=b('How many pizzas do you have monthly?');
46        $form.="\n";
47        $form.=popup_menu(-name=>'pizzas', -size=>2,
48            -Values=>['no pizzas','one to three','four or more']);
49        $form.=hr() . "\n";
50
51        $form.=submit(-name=>'button', -value=>'SUBMIT');
52        $form.="\n";
53        $form.=endform();
54        $form.=end_html();
55
56        print $form;          # send HTML document to browser now
57    }
58
59    else {    # If parameters present, we're handling submitted form
60
61        my $response=header();
62        $response.=start_html(-title=>'Survey Response',
63                              -BGCOLOR=>'snow');
64        $response.=h1('National Junk Food Survey');
65        $response.=p();
66        $response.="You supplied these details:\n";
67        $response.=Dump();
68        $response.=p();
69        $response.=h2( i('Thank you for participating!') );
70        $response.=end_html();
71        # Now send HTML string describing web page to browser
72        print $response;
73    }
```

Now it's time to talk about the script's two modes of operation.

Understanding the operational modes of `survey.cgi`

This script has two operational modes—"form display" and "form processing"—which are respectively associated with the "then" and `else` branches of the `if` construct that begins on Line 13. How does the script know which mode it's in? By checking its *parameters*, which are like command-line arguments, but delivered through other channels. The condition tested by the mode-selecting `if` is that parameters—such as the user's favorite ice-cream flavor—weren't supplied to the script.

In "form display" mode, the script displays the form and awaits its submission. When the user clicks SUBMIT after filling out the form, parameters *are* provided, causing that invocation of the script to be run in "form processing" mode. This causes the `else` branch that begins on Line 59 to be executed and the confirmation page shown in figure 12.6 to be generated.

The `Dump` function on Line 67 creates the bulleted list of name/value pairs for displaying the parameters in the confirmation page (see figure 12.6). Although the inclusion of "button" and "SUBMIT" may seem strange from the point of view of the user, these extra details can be helpful to programmers during debugging, and they can be easily removed later.

NOTE   A dual-mode CGI script knows what mode it's in by checking its *parameters*.

Next, you'll see how the script generates its web pages.

Constructing the HTML documents

The first statement in each of the "then" and `else` branches (Lines 14, 61) initializes a private variable with the header information that the HTTP server needs to find at the beginning of the document. But rather than sending output from each function to the server as it's generated, the script incrementally builds up its eventual output by appending (with `.=`) each additional piece to that same private variable—which is called `$form` in one mode and `$response` in the other.[17]

As mentioned earlier, the script inserts lots of newlines into those output variables (e.g., see Line 31). These are optional, as far as the browser and server are concerned, and included solely for the benefit of the human reader (which will be you, when we get to listing 12.8).

Next, we'll examine the script's output, which can be viewed in two forms: as raw HTML code or as a display in a browser window.

Output from `survey.cgi`

When `survey.cgi` runs in its intended environment, its HTML output is interpreted and displayed by a web browser for the user. But during the early stages of program development, its author would run this CGI-based script like a conventional Perl script and examine its output for evidence of problems. For example, the following invocation produces the HTML that displays the National Junk Food Survey form when it's sent to a web browser—but in this case, the HTML appears on the programmer's screen:

```
$ survey.cgi
...
<h1>National Junk Food Survey</h1>
...
```

The script's complete output is shown in listing 12.8, with the benefit of some light editing and manual reformatting to enhance its readability. To assist you in relating this listing to the display created by its HTML code as shown in figure 12.5, the text marked for bold presentation is shown in bold, and the window title, field labels, button labels, and menu choices are underlined.

---

[17] An alternative would be to `print` each of those pieces to the output one at a time, but it's better to keep the entire HTML document together so it can be sent to a printer, submitted to an HTML "beautifier," searched with `grep`, etc.

Listing 12.8 Output from running `survey.cgi` in form-displaying mode

```
Content-Type: text/html; charset=ISO-8859-1

<!DOCTYPE html
        PUBLIC "-//W3C//DTD XHTML 1.0 Transitional//EN"
         "http://www.w3.org/TR/xhtml1/DTD/xhtml1-transitional.dtd">
<html xmlns="http://www.w3.org/1999/xhtml" xml:lang="en-US">

  <head>
    <title>CGI Module Demo</title>
    <meta http-equiv="Content-Type" content="text/html" />
  </head>
  <body bgcolor="ivory">
    <h1>
    National Junk Food Survey
    </h1>

    <form method="get" action=""
       enctype="application/x-www-form-urlencoded">
      <hr />
      <b>
      Please enter your first initial and surname:
      </b>
      <p />
      Initial
      <input type="text" name="init"  size="1" maxlength="1" />
      Surname
      <input type="text" name="name"  size="12" maxlength="30" />
      <hr />
      <b>
      Please indicate your age group:
      </b>
      <p />
      <label>
        <input type="radio" name="age" value="
        Under 25" checked="checked" />Under 25
      </label>

      <label>
        <input type="radio" name="age" value="25-40" />25-40
      </label>

      <label>
        <input type="radio" name="age" value="Older" />Older
      </label>

      <hr />
      <b>
      What are your favorite ice-cream flavors?
      </b>
      <p />
```

```
<label>
  <input type="checkbox" name="flavor" value="Chocolate" />
  Chocolate
</label>

<label>
  <input type="checkbox" name="flavor" value="Vanilla" />
  Vanilla
</label>

<label>
  <input type="checkbox" name="flavor" value="Other" />
  Other
</label>
<hr />
<b>
How many pizzas do you have monthly?
</b>

<select name="pizzas" size="2">
  <option value="no pizzas">no pizzas</option>
  <option value="one to three">one to three</option>
  <option value="four or more">four or more</option>
</select><hr />
  <input type="submit" name="button" value="SUBMIT" />
  </form>
 </body>
</html>
```

As you've undoubtedly noticed by now, there are lots of functions with odd names to keep straight when you're using the CGI module. Never fear—help is on the way!

The CGI cheatsheets

Table 12.1 shows a summary of the CGI module's most essential functions, in approximate order of use in a program—all CGI programs use header and start_html first, and end_html last, with other CGI functions occurring between those endpoints. Likewise, table 12.2 shows the CGI module's more specialized functions used with Forms, with start_form at the beginning and end_form at the end. I'm confident that you, like the students in our classes, will benefit from having these "cheatsheets" by your side when doing CGI programming.

TIP   When you need to know the syntax of an HTML form element—such as a *scrolling list*—you'll find table 12.2 a more convenient resource than the CGI man page.

Table 12.1 Essential functions of the CGI module

Function syntax	Function output
header('*type*'**)**	HTTP header, for specified document *type*, or 'text/html' by default
start_html(-title=>'*Title*', -BGCOLOR=>'*color*'**)**	HTML header and <body> tag, along with page's title and background color
pre('*stuff*'**)**	*stuff*, with browser reformatting of it disabled
h*N* ('*Heading*'**)**	*Heading* formatted for level *N* (1 highest, 6 lowest)
comment('*text*'**)**	*text* as an HTML comment
em('*word*'**)**	*word* rendered with emphasis (usually *italics*)
b('*word*'**)**	*word* rendered in **bold**
p() hr() br()	Blank line; horizontal rule; start of a new line
ul(li('*item1*','*item2*'**))**	Unordered (*bullet*) list, with two items; same format for ordered (*numbered*) list, but use **ol()**
a({-href=>'*URL*'}, '*text*'**)**	*text* as a link to *URL*
img({-src=>'*URL*', -align=>'*position*'}**)**	Image specified by *URL* with an optional *position* specification (left, right for image itself; top, middle, bottom for image's caption text)
end_html()	HTML ending header, of </body></html>

We'll wrap up our coverage of modules with some recommendations for dealing with the "other kind" of Perl modules.

12.3.6 Tips on using Object-Oriented modules

In this book, you've learned to use Perl as a *procedural* programming language, because its similarities to the Shell and Unix cultural traditions are most apparent when it's approached from this angle. However, Perl can also be used as an *Object-Oriented* (OO) language, which may offer advantages for certain kinds of programming projects.[18] For this reason, its modules come in three flavors: procedural modules, OO modules, and modules that support both programming styles (which are rare).

How can you tell the different kinds of modules apart? It's easy, because a program that uses an OO module first calls the function new to load a variable with its output, and then it prepends that variable and an arrow (->) to the names of all of the module's subroutines that it calls. This syntax is distinctive and easy to spot in the module's documentation.

By way of illustration, let's consider some examples adapted from the documentation for the CGI module, which is one that supports both the OO and the procedural

---

[18] See *Object Oriented Perl* by Damian Conway, (Manning, 2000).

Table 12.2   Form-related functions of the CGI module

Function syntax	Function output
start_form(-method=>'*type*', -action=>'*URL*')	Start of Form, for parameter delivery *type* of POST (default) or GET. If -action is omitted, the current script processes the results.
textfield(-name=>'*Name*', -default=>'*text*', -size=>*num*, -maxlength=>*num*)	Field for text input; scrolls horizontally if -maxlength's *num* exceeds -size's *num*.
scrolling_list(-name=>'*Name*', -default=>'*starting_value*', -Values=>['*v1*', '*v2*'], -size=>*num*)	Scrolling list; same format for **popup_menu**, **radio_group**, **checkbox**, and **checkbox_group**, except -size is only for **popup_menu**. Specify NONE for no *starting_value*.
param()	All parameter names from QUERY_STRING.
param('*name*')	Value of *name*'s parameter only.
Dump()	Formatted list of QUERY_STRING parameters and values; in older CGI versions, use **CGI::dump()** instead.
submit(-name=>'*name*', -value=>'*value*')	Form SUBMIT button.
image_button(-name=>'*Name*', -src=>'*URL*', -align=>'*position*')	Image as Form SUBMIT button. X/Y coordinates of click are available as the parameters *Name.x*, *Name.y*.
reset()	Form RESET button.
end_form()	End of Form.

programming styles. The following statement calls some CGI functions in the procedural manner, with which you're already familiar:

```
print header,                       # generate the HTTP header
    start_html 'hello world',       # generate the initial HTML tags
       h1 'hello world',            # generate a level 1 heading
          end_html;                 # generate the ending HTML tags
```

Here's the same example rewritten in the OO style, with differences highlighted. Notice that after first calling new, it uses the arrow-based method calls to access the subroutines in place of the procedural approach's function calls:

```
$q=new CGI;                         # or $q=CGI::new, or $q=CGI->new
print $q->header,
    $q->start_html 'hello world',
       $q->h1 'hello world',
          $q->end_html;
```

Although these two code snippets do the same job—printing the results of calling a series subroutines from the CGI module—they're written very differently.

For your convenience, I recommend that you use procedural modules when possible, because you're better prepared by this book to understand how they work, and they'll also save you some typing. To achieve this goal, avoid modules that show only the tell-tale OO syntax ($*variable*->*sub_name*) in their documentation.

But in cases where there's an OO module that will do the job but no procedural alternative, just comply with the syntax of the examples shown in the module's documentation in writing your program.

12.4 SUMMARY

In this chapter, you learned how to increase the modularity and reusability of program code, use the CPAN, and exploit freely-available modules to enhance your productivity.

Storing code in subroutines (discussed in chapter 11) is a good first step in the right direction, but it's even better to package your subroutines in modules. Why? Because modules not only allow code to be easily imported, but they also provide an extra layer of insulation between the module's variables and those in the user's program (thanks to the package mechanism). This gives your module's variables an additional line of defense against scoping problems, which goes beyond what can be accomplished with variable declarations alone.

All it takes to create a module is to start with the Simple Module Template of listing 12.1, replace the placeholders at its top with the appropriate module-specific names, and insert the necessary subroutines at its bottom. You can then check your new module's resulting *.pm file for syntax errors and compiler warnings using the perl -wc Module_name command, prior to the more extensive testing that requires importing the module into a program. But first, you might need to adjust the PERL5LIB variable to include the name of the directory in which the module resides, to let Perl locate your module (see section 12.1.3). [19]

Thousands of extremely useful, industrial-grade modules are available from the CPAN, whose archives can be searched at the http://search.cpan.org web site. Once you've determined the name of the module you want, you can use the CPAN-access module to find it, download it (along with its prerequisites), test it, and install it— automatically! And you don't even need special "rootly" privileges to do this.

As a demonstration of code development based on CPAN modules, you saw freely available modules used to estimate shipping charges (ups_shipping_price, section 12.3.1), to check web pages for broken (hyper-)links (check_links, section 12.3.2), to help users construct appropriate invocations of Unix commands (menu_ls, section 12.3.3), and to check Unix file systems for broken symbolic links (check_symlinks, section 12.3.4).

---

[19] For additional information on creating custom modules, see *Writing Perl Modules for CPAN*, by Sam Tregar (Apress, 2002).

The mainstay of web programming with Perl is the `CGI` module, which can be used both to generate the HTML code for a fill-in form and also to parse its data after the web-surfer clicks SUBMIT (as shown in `survey.cgi`, section 12.3.5). This module can also handle cookies, file uploads, frames, cascading style sheets, and more, as you can learn from its documentation.

The CPAN is a remarkable asset to the Perl community, and the *envy of our colleagues* who program in other languages. Enjoy it!

> **TIP** Thousands of extremely useful, industrial-grade modules are available from the CPAN.

Directions for further study

The following resources provide additional information on the topics covered in this chapter:

- man perlmod   # how modules work
- man perlmodlib   # how to write your own modules
- http://search.cpan.org/faq.html   # help on CPAN searches
- man CPAN   # the CPAN-access module
- man lwp-request   # scripted interface to LWP*
- http://TeachMePerl.com/Select.html   # Perl's "select" loop
- man File::Find   # the file-finding module
- man CGI   # the CGI module
- man Business::UPS   # getUPS(), trackUPS()*
- man LWP::Simple   # lwp-request and head()*

* You'll probably need to install these modules before you can run the indicated man command successfully.

epilogue

As you've learned from this book, Perl is a great language that's just as happy to let you code quick and dirty one-liners on the fly as it is to provide the more sophisticated tools you need to write more robust applications. Most compiled languages, such as C, C++, Java, Ruby, and Python—or interpreted languages, like AWK and the Unix shells—only support programming on one end of this continuum. Perl covers the full spectrum.

This means you can whip off useful one-liners at lightning speed with the techniques learned in part 1 of this book, or carefully construct larger enterprise-grade applications like those shown in part 2—all with the same language.

What more could you ask for, than

- Perl's elegance of expression
- Its unique combination of power and succinctness
- Its portability to a wide range of operating systems
- Its ability to run the same program on a wide range of operating systems
- Its extension of the Shell-programming mindset into the 21st century
- Its wealth of freely available code from the CPAN
- Its great user community
- Its worldwide network of local Perl Mongers groups
- Its periodic international grass-roots YAPC conferences

And, we mustn't forget

- Its free price!

In closing, I hope you enjoyed learning Minimal Perl, and I wish you lots of increased productivity and enjoyment while using it.

And now, by the power invested in me by the Chief JAPH, I'm honored to say:

Welcome to Perlistan!

Just remember to boil the water before drinking it, stay away from black-market money changers, avoid the python jerky, and you'll be fine!

Perl special variables cheatsheet

`$_`
- The most recently read input record.[1]
- Used automatically by `print` and many other built-in functions.

`$"`
- The string inserted between the elements of a hash or array whose @-name appears within double quotes (e.g., "`@ARGV`").
- Set to a space by default.

`$,`
- The string inserted between the elements of a hash or array whose unquoted %-name or @-name appears in `print`'s argument list (e.g., `print @ARGV`).
- The string that replaces (unquoted) commas that appear in `print`'s argument list (e.g., `print 'NAME:', 'rygel'`).
- Empty by default.

`$0`
- The name by which the script was invoked (e.g., "`pgrep`"); for a Perl command, shows "`-e`".

---

[1] Requires use of the -n or -p option, `while (<>) { … }`, or `foreach ( … ; <>; … ) { … }`.

$$

- The process-ID number of the Shell or Perl program.

$.

- The ordinal number of the most recently read input record.[2]
- In END{ }, provides the total number of records read.[2]

$/

- A string that defines the characters (the *input record separator*) that mark the end of an input record.
- Automatically stripped by the -l option from the end of each input record read by the -n or -p option.
- By default, set to an OS-specific character sequence (represented by "\n").
- $/='-*-' means input records are terminated by -*-.
- $/="" is a special case; means input records are terminated by one or more blank lines (*paragraph mode*).
- $/=undef is a special case; means each file is one input record (*file mode*).
- The input record separator can also be set via the -0*digits* option.

$

- A string that defines the characters (the *output record separator*) that are appended after print's last argument by the -l option.
- By default, set to an OS-specific character sequence (represented by "\n").
- $\='-*-' means output records are terminated by -*-.

$?

- Contains the OS-specific exit code for the OS-command most recently run via system or command interpolation (e.g., `date`)
- On Unix systems, contains an exit code that looks to Perl like False on success and True on failure.

$!

- Contains the OS-specific exit code (when used in numeric context) or error message (in string context) for the last failed command run via system or command interpolation (e.g., system 'who').
- Shouldn't be accessed unless "$?" indicates command failure, because "$!" isn't reset by successful commands.

---

[2] Requires use of the -n or -p option, while (<>) { ... }, or foreach (... ; <>; ...) { ... }.

$a, $b

- When they appear within sort's code block or sub, these are the global variables that contain the next pair of items to be compared.

$^I

- The variable that controls in-place editing.
- Its contents define the file extension used on the backup copy of the edited file.
- Typically set through use of the -i.*ext* option.

ARGV

- The filehandle[3] of the file that most recently provided input.[4]

$ARGV

- The name of the file that most recently provided input.[4]

@ARGV

- The array that contains the program's command-line arguments.
- Contents are interpreted as filenames in programs that read input automatically.[4]

$#*array*

- The maximum index usable with @*array* (one less than the current number of elements).

@F

- The array that contains the fields of the most recently read input record (requires options -n or -p, and -a).

%ENV

- The hash that contains the program's environment variables (on Unix, keys are HOME, PATH, etc.).

---

[3] ARGV is a filehandle rather than a special variable, but it's included here with its relatives @ARGV and $ARGV for your convenience.

[4] Requires use of the -n or -p option, while (<>) { ... }, or foreach (... ; <>; ...) { ... }.

Guidelines for parenthesizing code

In this book, we've discussed several situations that require the use of parentheses around code. For easy reference, we provide here a complete summary of the cases that come up most frequently in Minimal Perl.

To demonstrate the benefit of adding your own parentheses, the parentheses you effectively get by default are shown in the comments adjoining the code samples.

You should use parentheses:

1. Around a function's arguments, to exclude following elements from that argument list:

   ```
   print sort (@F), '!';      # Default: print sort (@F, '!');
   ```

2. Around any multi-element argument list for our or chomp:

   ```
   chomp ($X, $Y);            # Default: chomp ($X), $Y;
   our   ($X, $Y);            # Default: our   ($X), $Y;
   ```

3. Anywhere the higher precedence of the logical and over or would otherwise cause your intentions to be misinterpreted:

   ```
   (X or Y) and warn;         # Default: X or (Y and warn);
   ```

4. Around assignments involving the logical and or logical or:

   ```
   $both  =(-r X and -r Y);  # Default:    ($both=-r X) and -r Y;
   $either=(-r X or  -r Y);  # Default: ($either=-r X) or  -r Y;
   ```

5 Around comma-separated list elements appearing on the right side of an assignment to a list variable:

```
@array=(X, Y);                  # Default: (@array=X), Y;
```

6 Around variables (or undefs) on the left hand side of an assignment operator, if list context is desired:

```
(undef, $Y)=@ARGV;              # Default: undef, ($Y=@ARGV);
($first_field)=@F;              # List context desired
$field_count=@F;                # List context NOT desired!
```

7 After names of user-defined subroutines—whether or not there's an associated list of arguments—unless the sub definition precedes the call in the program:

```
my_sub();                       # Call user-defined subroutine
```

glossary

argument. When used in the context of a Unix command line, this term refers to one of the "words" separated by unquoted whitespace characters that may appear after the command's name. For example, the following `ls` command has two arguments—one is an option, and the other a filename:

```
ls -l /tmp
```

The first `echo` command that follows has only one argument, because quoted strings aren't split into their constituent words by the Shell as unquoted ones are. The second command has only four arguments, because redirection requests such as "`> filename`" are removed by the Shell before arguments are allocated:

```
echo 'This is one string'          # one argument
echo  Here are four words > save    # four arguments
```

When used in the context of a Perl function or a user-defined subroutine, this term refers to the words provided after its name. For example, the following `print` function has two arguments (the comma separator isn't counted):

```
print 'Crikey!' , 'What a little beauty!' ;
```

AWK vs. awk. *AWK* refers to the language itself, and `awk` to the interpreter program that implements it. For the purposes of this book, the various flavors of AWK (such as `awk`, `nawk`, and `gawk`) are generally considered equivalent and generically referred to as AWK and `awk`. However, when it's necessary to distinguish between the flavors, their proper names are used.

AWKish. This made-up adjective expresses a resemblance to the AWK language, culture, or Pattern/Action programming model, as in "Here's an AWKish Perl program."

backslash. This is the slanted-line character that looks like it's falling backward while moving from left to right: \. *See also* **slash.**

Bell System. This term, short for Bell Telephone System, refers to the companies that were the sole providers of telephony services in the United States until the mid-1980s—including the Bell Labs, Western Electric, and various divisions of AT&T.

Camel book. Because it has a camel on its cover, this is the shorthand name used in Perl circles for the book entitled *Programming Perl*, which serves as the printed reference manual for the Perl language.

classic UNIX utility. Sometimes we need to differentiate between the versions of UNIX utilities that have historically been found on UNIX systems, and their more modern POSIX-compliant counterparts that are provided on modern Unix systems. We identify the former utilities by the word "classic," as in *classic* grep, and the latter by "POSIX," as in *POSIX* grep. We also discuss GNU versions of Unix utilities, which provide POSIX-compliant features as well as additional "GNU enhancements." For added clarity, when referring to a GNU utility that has a different name than its classic counterpart, we use it, leading to distinctions such as "classic awk" versus "gawk."

For reference purposes, we define the classic utilities as those distributed with AT&T's UNIX System V Release 0, as documented in the *UNIX System User's Manual, Release 5.0* published by Western Electric in June, 1982.[1]

Our reference point for POSIX utilities is the set provided in the directory /usr/xpg4/bin of Solaris 10.[2]

The GNU utilities we refer to are those distributed with SuSE Linux version 10, which are v2.5.1 for grep, egrep, and fgrep; v4.1.4 for sed; v3.1.4 for gawk; v4.2.3 for find; and v3.00.16(1) for bash. *See also* **UNIX, Unix, GNU, POSIX.**

clobberation. This made-up noun describes what happens to a file or variable when its former contents are destroyed by a programmer accidentally writing other data over it. *See also* **masking.**

command. We distinguish between two kinds of *commands*. A Perl command is formed by interactively typing perl and any desired arguments to the Shell. A Unix command is similar, but uses a program other than perl (echo, grep, ls, etc.):

```
$ perl -wl -e 'print "Hello world!";'   # Perl command
...
$ grep 'Waldo' hiding_places            # Unix command
...
```

See also **script, argument.**

---

[1] I taught for Western Electric's "UNIX University" at the time and made many marginal notes in my well-worn personal copy of that manual—which is still on my bookshelf!

[2] As discussed in the output of man -s 5 standards on Solaris 10, these are the X/Open Common Applications Environment Portability Guide Issue 4 extensions to the relevant POSIX standards from 1990 and 1992.

construct. A programming construct is a framework of keywords and/or symbols into which you place expressions and statements, in order to exert control over how they're executed. For example, the `if`/`else` construct tests an expression for a True/False value and then executes the branch of code for the True or False case, accordingly.

directive. This term is used to identify a built-in function whose effect is principally confined to making something happen, rather than generating data. For example, the Shell's `continue` directive starts the next iteration of a loop, and Perl's `use` directive imports components from a module. In contrast, Perl's `localtime` function returns the current date and time (data), so it isn't a directive. *See also* **function**.

<ENTER>. This represents the key that a user presses to submit a command to the Shell for execution. To avoid cluttering up displays of screen sessions, this keypress is depicted only in special cases.

explicit list. This type of list is created by parenthesizing a series of values in an appropriate context. It's typically used for initializing a list variable or copying values from a list variable into scalars:

```
@ARGV=('/etc/passwd', '/etc/host');
($one, $two)=@F;
```

As in the first example, sometimes the parentheses don't *create* a list context—they just allow comma-separated items to be treated as a list within an existing one. *See also* **undef**.

expression. An *expression* is an element of a program, or a combination of related elements, that has an associated value.

In the following example, 1 and 2 are simple expressions having the values 1 and 2, respectively (duh!). There is also a value (of 3) associated with the larger expression that associates those elements through the addition operator. Moreover, `sqrt` counts as an expression too, yielding the square root (1.732) of its argument (3).

```
sqrt 1 + 2
```

See also **statement**.

False. A False value is one considered by Perl (or the Shell, according to context) to indicate the untruthfulness of an assertion or the failure of an operation. Note that the Perl values that are considered False (or True) are opposite to those of the Shell (see section 2.4.2). *See also* **True**.

file scope. This scope, which runs from the point of declaration to the end of the file, applies to a variable declared outside any curly braces. *See also* **scope**.

function. This term refers to a subroutine that's built into the Perl language (e.g., `print`). In contrast, the Shell counterpart to a function (e.g., `echo`) is called a *command*.

See **operator** for an explanation of the purposeful lack of differentiation between the terms *function* and *operator* in this book. *See also* **subroutine, operator, command.**

GNU. *GNU* (see http://www.gnu.org) stands for *Gnu's Not UNIX* (really!) and is the brand name for the software produced by the Free Software Foundation, headed by ace programmer Richard Stallman (see http://www.gnu.org/fsf). GNU provides enhanced versions of most UNIX utilities, such as `grep`, which are distributed with UNIX-like systems including Linux, Mac OS/X, and FreeBSD. Because of their superiority, these utilities are often installed on UNIX systems as well. In this book, we sometimes need to distinguish between the different flavors of the Unix utilities using phrases such as GNU `grep`, POSIX `grep`, and the classic `grep`. *See also* **POSIX, classic UNIX utility.**

grepper, grepping. A *grepper* is a utility that extracts and displays matching records (usually *lines*) from a data source; examples are `grep` and its relatives `fgrep` and `egrep`. *Grepping* refers to the act of using a program that acts as a grepper.

identifier. An identifier is a string of characters that names a component of a Perl program, such as a variable, a subroutine, a built-in function, or a loop. A user-defined identifier can be constructed from mixtures of letters, digits, and underscores, but it can't begin with a digit, and variable names must include a variable-type symbol (`$`, `@`, or `%`) before the identifier. *See also* **variable.**

input operator. The *input operator*, often typed as `<STDIN>`, causes Perl to read input. If STDIN is omitted, the input operator is said to be *empty*, which causes Perl to read input from the program's filename argument(s) or, in their absence, from STDIN. Some people refer to the empty input operator (`<>`) as the *diamond* operator. *See also* **STDIN.**

JAPH, JAPHly. *JAPH*, which stands for "*Just Another Perl Hacker*," is a humorous title used by many Perl advocates in their email signature (`.sig`) files. JAPHly is the adjectival form of JAPH; for example, "In JAPHly parlance, `<>` is called the diamond operator."

Larry. *Larry* is Larry Wall, the revered creator of the Perl language. For more about him, see the "Essential terminology" section of "About this book."

`local` variable. This type of variable is declared with the `local` declaration. It's used in Minimal Perl to cause certain built-in variables, principally '`$,`' and '`$"`' (see appendix A), to automatically revert back to their earlier values after leaving a defined scope.

Main. *Main*, short for the Main program, refers to the central portion of a program. In a program lacking `BEGIN` and `END` blocks, it consists of the parts that would normally be positioned after the initial use statements but before the first subroutine definition (or the end-of-file, whichever comes first). In a program having those blocks, it refers to the lines between them. *See also* **scoping**.

masking. This term describes a situation in which the value of a variable associated with an outer scope is rendered temporarily unavailable due to a new local declaration of the same variable within the current scope. *See also* **clobberation**.

metacharacter. A *metacharacter* is a character that stands for something other than itself. For example, in a regular expression, the ^ character stands for the beginning of a line, rather than the ^ character itself.

my variable. This type of variable is declared with the my declaration, which makes it private to a particular scope. *See also* **our variable, private variable**.

newline. This term refers to the OS-specific character sequence that marks the end of a line, as discussed further in the "Essential terminology" section of "About this book."

operator, operand. *Operators* are symbols or keywords that request the computer to perform particular operations. The subject of the operation is the argument (or arguments) provided to the operator, called the *operand(s)*. For example, the following expressions request the addition (+) of two numeric operands and a comparison of two string operands, respectively:

```
2 + 2
$user_id eq 'root'
```

Note that the Camel book uses the term *operator* to refer to some things that we'll call functions, such as my and our. Larry, being a linguist by training, has a good reason for the terminology he's using, but the operator/function distinction is generally unimportant for our purposes. *See also* **function**.

OS. The software that controls the low-level activities of a computer is its *operating system* (UNIX, Linux, Win/XP, etc.), or *OS* for short.

our variable. This type of variable is declared with our and has scope from that point up to the nearest enclosing curly brace or, if there isn't one, to the end of the file. It's used in Minimal Perl for declaring optional switch variables, when use strict isn't in effect, or all switch variables, when use strict is in effect. *See also* **private variable**.

panel. This is a region of a table that appears below the column headings and is set off by horizontal lines. *See also* **row**.

pattern. This term refers to the sequence of literal and/or metacharacters that's used to describe character sequences that are acceptable as matches, such as \bERROR\b. In cases where multiple matches are searched for simultaneously, as in \bERROR \b|\bWARNING\b, each of the alternative parts of the regex qualifies as a separate pattern. *See also* **regex**.

Perl, `perl`. The word *Perl* refers to the language itself, whereas `perl` refers to the special interpreter program that's needed to run programs written in the Perl language.

Perlistan, Perlistani. *Perlistan* is the fabled land of the Perl-speaking JAPHs, as discussed in the "Essential terminology" section "About this book" and section 1.1 of chapter 1. *Perlistani* is the adjectival form, used mostly in referring to the residents of Perlistan.

POSIX. POSIX, the Portable Operating System Interface definition, refers to a family of standards that describe the expected behavior of UNIX-like systems, including their utility programs (such as `grep` and `awk`). We refer on occasion to the POSIX versions of certain Unix utilities, to compare their capabilities with the classic UNIX versions and Perl. Note that the GNU versions of UNIX utilities have many enhanced features enabled by default, called *GNU extensions*. You can run some of these utilities in a POSIX-compliant mode by using the `--posix` option to disable those extensions. *See also* **GNU**.

private variable. This type of variable is declared with the `my` declaration and has scope from the point of declaration up to the nearest enclosing curly brace or, if there isn't one, to the end of the file. In the case of private *loop variables*, the scope begins with the opening keyword (e.g., `foreach`) and continues through the loop's opening curly brace to its closing one. *See also* **my declaration**.

RE. This is a placeholder showing where a regex would be inserted in a Shell command or Perl code. *See also* **regex**.

regex. *Regex* is short for *regular expression*, which is the name of the pattern-matching notation used in Perl (and its UNIX forebears). This term refers to a particular sequence of literal and/or metacharacters that is used to search for matches, such as \bERROR\b. Note that a regex may consist of multiple patterns. *See also* **pattern**.

row. This is a horizontally defined region of a table that appears below the column headings, and is set off by a blank line that runs the entire width of the table. *See also* **panel**.

scope, scoping. The *scope* of a variable is the region in a program in which that variable can be accessed by name. For variables declared with `my`, e.g., the region is a consecutive series of lines consisting of statements and/or constructs. *See also* **Main, file scope, construct**.

script, scriptification, scriptified. A *script* is a Shell or Perl program stored in a file, equipped with a shebang line and execute permission. A program that has been converted from the command form to the script form is said to have been *scriptified*, through the process of *scriptification*. *See also* **command, shebang**.

shebang, shebang line. On Unix and related systems, the sequence "#!" on the first line of an executable text-file is used to identify the pathname for that script's desired interpreter, along with desired invocation options. For example, a typical Perl script might have the following first line:

```
#! /usr/bin/perl -wnl
```

Where did this peculiar name come from? In mathematical circles, the "!" character is called *bang*, so perhaps some ancient UNIX code-warrior decided to name the two-character sequence that starts a s<u>h</u>ell script the <u>*shebang*</u> and its associated line *the shebang line*.

Shell. This term, as defined in the "Essential terminology" section of "About this book," refers to the Bourne, Korn, and Bash shells of UNIX and related OSs.

slash. This is the slanted-line character that looks like it's falling forward while moving from left to right: /. It's also called the "forward slash." *See also* **backslash.**

space vs. <SPACE>. <SPACE> represents the key that generates the space character and, in some cases, the presence of that character in screen displays. In the latter case, a "ghost font" is used to make it clear that it's the presence of a space character that's being depicted, not the literal character string <SPACE> or the key that generates the space. *See also* **tab vs. <TAB>.**

standard input, standard output, standard error. These terms refer to the "standard" channels used on Unix systems for conveying input and output to programs, which have the benefit of working most conveniently with pipe and file redirections (symbolized by |, and < or >). *See also* **STDIN, STDOUT, STDERR.**

statement. A typical *statement* consists of one or more expressions followed by a semi-colon, which identifies the expression(s) as a unit that's ready for execution. The first example that follows is just an expression, whereas the second is a statement:

```
print 1 + 2
```

```
print 1 + 2 ;
```

It's important to understand that Perl will assemble a statement by gobbling up subsequent lines until it finds a semicolon, so it's a serious error to omit a required semicolon. *See also* **expression.**

STDIN, STDOUT, STDERR. These terms traditionally refer to the three standard I/O channels provided to every process on Unix systems. By extension, Perl uses them also to refer to its input, output, and error-output channels. In Minimal Perl, a line is sometimes "manually" read from the input and stored in a variable by embedding STDIN within the angle-brackets of the input operator:

```
$input=<STDIN>;
```

See also **standard input, standard output, standard error.**

strict mode, stricture, strictified. *Strict mode* is a special mode of the Perl compiler that's enabled by the use strict directive. In this mode, the program must comply with additional rules, called *strictures*—such as declaring all user-defined variables with my or our. A program that's been modified to run in strict mode is said to be *strictified*.

string. A sequence of characters used as data, such as 'Slarty Bartfast', is called a *character string*, or just a *string* for short. Quoting symbols aren't necessarily involved.

subroutine. A Perl subroutine is a named chunk of code that's executed when its name is used.

switch, switch variable. A *switch* is an argument that follows a script's name on the command line that is processed automatically by the s option. It takes the form -name, or -name=*value*. Although these might also be called "options," some could be optional whereas others might be mandatory, leading to such confusing phrases as "mandatory options" and "optional options." Using the more neutral term *switch* relieves us of such confusion. Each switch argument is associated with a corresponding switch variable, whose name is formed by replacing the switch's dash with a dollar sign; e.g., -name becomes $name.

tab vs. <TAB>. <TAB> represents the key that generates the tab character and, in some cases, the presence of that character in screen displays. In the latter case, a "ghost font" is used to make it clear that it's the presence of a tab character that's being depicted, not the literal character string <TAB> or the key that generates the tab. Here's a sample usage:

To insert a tab within the quoted string, the user presses <TAB>, yielding:

```
'Quantity:<TAB>42'
```

See also **space vs. <SPACE>.**

TMTOWTDI. This is acronym for one of Perl's official mottoes, which celebrates the flexibility Perl offers JAPHs in the coding of programs. It means *"There's More than One Way to Do It."*

True. A True value is one considered by Perl (or the Shell) to indicate the truthfulness of an assertion or the success of an operation. Note that the Perl values that are considered True (or False) are opposite to those of the Shell (see section 2.4.2). *See also* **False.**

undefined value, undef. The *undefined value* is a special value that Perl attaches to variables that have not yet been initialized. The undef function can be used to generate this value, allowing the programmer to assign it to a variable or return it from a subroutine. undef is also used in subroutine calls to request the use of a default value for its argument's position, and in explicit lists to avoid assigning a value to a variable:

```
sub42('duct', undef, 'roll') # accept default of 'tape' for 2nd arg
($size, undef, $shape)=@F;   # don't copy the array's 2nd element
```

See also **explicit list, value.**

UNIX. In the rare cases when we need to differentiate actual UNIX systems (such as Solaris) from UNIX-like systems (such as GNU/Linux), *UNIX* (always in capitals) is used to make that distinction. *See also* **Unix.**

Unix. As used in this book, *Unix* (in mixed case) refers to actual UNIX systems, such as Solaris and HP-UX, as well as their act-alikes, such as systems based on GNU/Linux. It's appropriate to lump them together, because they come equipped with a similar set of basic utility programs, and from the point of view of a Shell user or programmer, these systems feel a lot like UNIX. *See also* **UNIX.**

Unix people. These are users of Unix command-line utilities, ranging from novices who have only used `ls` and `grep`, to senior programmers who write complex scripts in the Shell language.

value. Variables are said to contain, or have, *values*, which are the data the variables store. For example, the following line stores `Klaatu` in the scalar variable `$visitor`:

```
$visitor='Klaatu';
```

Note that list variables—hashes and arrays—can store multiple values.

variable. A variable is a named location in the computer's memory where its value(s) are stored. *See also* **value, private variable, my variable, our variable, local variable.**

whitespace. Characters that don't deposit ink on paper when they're typed on a typewriter are called *whitespace characters*. These include the return, linefeed, formfeed, space, and tab characters.

YAPC. This acronym stands for "*Yet Another Perl Conference,*" which is the name for a collection of low-priced grassroots events held around the world for the benefit of those who either can't afford the expense of the more elaborately staged conferences or just prefer the company of students and geeks to corporate IT types. See http://yapc.pm.org for additional information.

how to use this index

Entries for language resources refer to Perl ones, unless otherwise indicated—e.g., "NR (AWK)" refers to an AWK resource. As an exception, entries for resources having the same name in the Shell and Perl (e.g., "exit") apply to both languages unless otherwise indicated.

Entries for *metacharacters* are found in the Symbols section and refer to resources of the regular expression notation, unless marked as FNG (for filename generation notation).

Perl's *invocation options* (such as "n" and "F") are shown with leading dashes ("−n", "−F"), but they're listed in alphabetical order as if the dashes weren't present—except options having a digit immediately after the dash, which are listed under "Numeric Options."

Variables, built-in functions, and *Unix commands* are listed under their own names.

Subroutines are listed under "subs," and significant *code snippets* are listed by their descriptions under that name.

All the *one-line Perl commands* discussed in the book are listed by description under the heading "commands (Perl)," and all scripts are listed by name under "scripts."

Perl *modules* are listed under "modules" and also under their own names (e.g., "modules: Center," and "Center module").

Featured characters are listed under their own names (e.g., Diggity Dog) as well as under the heading "featured characters."

Commands and scripts of special interest to System Administrators are cross-referenced under the heading "system administration tools."

index

Symbols

! (negation operator) 39

$ (dollar) (AWK)
  only used for field
    variables 126

$ (dollar) (Shell)
  differences from Perl in use
    with variable names 23, 25

$ (dollar) metacharacter 63
  altered meaning with /m
    modifier 69

$ (dollar), as identifying mark for
    scalar variable 23

$! (OS error-number)
    variable 341, 428
  setting to define die's exit
    value 253, 292

$\ (output record separator)
    variable 42, 127
  used for multi-character record
    separators 42
  See also output record
    separator

$" (string formatting)
    variable 43, 300–301, 435

$# (argument count) variable
    (Shell) 334

$#ARGV (maximum index) vari-
    able for @ARGV array 346

$$ (process-ID) variable 112

$& (match) variable 63, 127
  used in replacement field of
    substitution operator 95
  used to display the match
    only 64

$' (post-match) variable 127

$( ) (Shell). *See* command
    substitution

$, (print's formatting)
    variable 43, 435
  used with grep 228–229
  used with map 233

$. (record number) variable 20
  contains number of last record
    in END block 264
  used with substitution opera-
    tor for record-specific
    substitutions 97

$/ (input record separator)
    variable 42, 127, 307
  need to reset in dual input-
    mode scripts 308
  used for multicharacter record
    separators 42
  See also input record separator

$? (command error)
    variable 257, 428

$@ (eval error) variable 283–284

$^I (in-place edit) variable 429
  used in clobber-proofing edit-
    ing scripts 112

$_ (data) variable 126, 427
  as default argument for file-test
    operators 181
  introduction to 24
  may get masked in nested
    loops 373

$` (pre-match) variable 127

$0 (record) variable (AWK) 126

$0 (script name) variable
  used to show source of diag-
    nostic message 36
  used with warn and die 36

$1, etc. (field) variables
    (AWK) 126

$1, etc. (numbered)
    variables 71, 359
  used in sed-like commands 99

$1, etc. (positional parameter)
    variable (Shell) 334
  compared to $ARGV[0] in
    Perl 334
  See also positional parameters

$a (sort item) variable 429
  used in sort's coding rules 225

$ARGV (filename) variable 42,
    67, 127, 146, 191
  definition of 42

$b (sort item) variable 429
  used in sort's coding rules 225

$F[n] (field) value 126

443

$SECONDS (Shell) variable, used in clobber-proofing editing commands 112
% (modulus) operator 159, 405
%ENV (environment) hash 313–314
as inter-process communication mechanism 313
using in place of switches 315–316
&& (AWK) as similar to Perl's logical and 140
&& (Shell), as similar to Perl's logical and 35
( ) (parentheses) as metacharacters 71, 359
* (multiplication) operator 159
* (star) metacharacter 73
vs. meaning of * in FNG 237
* (star) metacharacter (FNG) 236, 259
+ (addition) operator 159
+ (plus) metacharacter 73, 109
++ (increment) operator 159, 346
- (range in character class) metacharacter (FNG) 236
- (range in character class) metacharacter 63
- (subtraction) operator 159
-- (decrement) operator 159
. (dot) metacharacter 63
becomes literal character in character class 303
. (string concatenation) operator 265–268
syntax and examples 265
tips on using 268–269
used in enhancement to most_recent_file 267
.. (range) operator, AWK-like version 152–153
used in array indexing 301
... (range) operator, sed-like version 152–153
used for logfile analysis 170

.= (string concatenation) compound assignment operator 265–267
common errors with 269
used to incrementally build HTML document 419
/ (division) operator 159
/ (slash) 438
See also slash; backslash
// (matching) operator 60
capabilities of 58
introduction to 60–62
modifiers for 68–70
when to use split instead 213
/e (eval) substitution modifier 95
for computed replacements 114–118
for function-generated replacements 116
/g (global) match modifier 69, 360
/g (global) substitution modifier 95
/i (ignore case) match modifier 69, 95, 187
/m (multi-line mode) match modifier 69, 95, 359
/s (single-line mode) match modifier 69, 95
/x (expanded format) match modifier 69, 95, 110
: (null) command (Shell) used in bottom-tested while/until loops 338–339, 352
< > (globbing) operator 234–239
< > (input) operator used in implicit loop 337
<=> (numeric comparison) operator 157
used with sort 224
<> (globbing) operator syntax and examples 235
tips on using 237–238

<ENTER> key
as needed but generally unshown in terminal sessions xxviii
definition 434
<SPACE> key, definition 438
<TAB> key, definition 439
=~ (match-binding) operator 60, 69, 96
? (question mark) metacharacter 99, 238
for stingy matching 124
for stingy matching, advantages over AWK 125
in Perl regex, for stingy matching 73
? (question mark) metacharacter (FNG) 236
@_ (sub argument) array 364
@ARGV (argument) array 42, 127
@EXPORT (default exports) module array 391
when to use vs. @EXPORT_OK 391
@EXPORT_OK (on-request exports) module array 391
when to use vs. @EXPORT 391
@F (field) array 127, 131–132, 141, 145
when to access using indexing vs. assignment to variable list 145
See also $F[n]
@INC (include) array, relation to PERL5LIB variable 397
[ ] (character class) metacharacter (FNG) 63, 236
[!] (complemented character class) metacharacter (FNG) 236
[^] (complemented character class) metacharacter 63

\ (backslash) (Shell)
as line-continuation
character xxx
differences from Perl in effects
of 31
See also backslash; slash
\ (backslash) definition 432
\ (backslash) metacharacter 63
See also backslash; slash
\& (function-address)
operator 411
\(\) backslash (backslashed
parentheses)
metacharacters 71
\{ \} (backslashed braces)
metacharacters 73
\040 (space) string escape 105
\047 (single quote) string escape
used as nested single quote in
commands 62
\1, etc. (backslashed-number)
metacharacter 71
\b (word-boundary)
metacharacter 63
\d (digit) metacharacter 67, 115
\D (non-digit) metacharacter 67
\E (end-modification) string
modifier 113, 289
cases where it can be
omitted 227
See also \U; \L
\E (end-quoting)
metacharacter 63
See also \Q
\L, \l (lowercase) string modifiers
used to achieve case
insensitivity 113, 227, 322
\Q (start-quoting)
metacharacter 63
See also \E
\S (non-whitespace)
metacharacter 67
\s (whitespace) metacharacter 67
\U, \u (uppercase) string
modifiers 113, 146, 348
See also \E

\W (non-word)
metacharacter 67, 324
\w (word) metacharacter 67
^ (caret) metacharacter 63
altered meaning with /m
modifier 69
_ (underscore)
as reference to previously tested file 219
_ _PACKAGE_ _ (package
name) keyword 395
` ` (Perl). *See* command interpolation
` ` (Shell). *See* command substitution
{ } (braces) metacharacter 73
| (vertical bar) metacharacter 71

Numeric Options

-00 (paragraph-mode) option 45
special setting of $/ as
equivalent 428
used in field processing 146
-0777 (file-mode) option 45
special setting of $/ as
equivalent 428
-0*digits* (input record separator)
option 17, 22, 428
only used for single-character
record separators 42
used to print records by
number 101
See also $/ (input record
separator) variable

A

a2p command
for translating AWK to
Perl 175
tips on using 175
address of function. *See* \& (function-address) operator
Alexis, featured character for
PFD project 388

aliases for Perl commands
perl_o, perl_io, etc. 46
amatch function
for approximate ("fuzzy")
matching 85
See also String::Approx
analyzing log files 81
Andy "yDNA" Sweger.
See Sweger, Andy "yDNA"
ARGC (argument count) variable (AWK) 126
argument generation 259
generating all readable, regular
files 259
argument pre-processing
256–259
filtering arguments 257–258
removing names of non-text
files 258
removing non-filename
arguments in BEGIN
block 256–257
sorting arguments 257
argument processing
dealing with multi-word
filenames 196–197
filtering out binary files
189–191
reporting names of non-text
files 258
using Perl to filter-out undesirable ones 188–192
argument, definition 432
ARGV (argument vector) variable (AWK) 42, 126
ARGV filehandle 42
definition of 43
arithmetic operators
comparing AWK's and
Perl's 158–159
array indexing
syntax 145
arrays 296–308
illustration of storage in
memory 297

arrays *(continued)*
   indexing techniques 300–304
   indexing with random
      numbers 304–308
   initialization methods
      299–300
   initialization using push 299
   piecemeal initialization 299
   Shell vs. Perl syntax
      comparison 298
   slices: better name would be
      "index groups" 301
   syntax for indexing 300
   syntax for slice indexing 301
   tips on using 308
ASCII 103
Ashanti, featured character for
   line-specific substitution
   command 98
associative array (AWK)
   is like a Perl hash 296
   See also hashes
automatic line-end processing.
   See -l (in-place editing)
   option
automatic looping. *See* -n (automatic input-reading) option; -p (automatic input-
   reading, with printing)
automatic printing. *See* -p (automatic input-reading, with
   printing) option
AWK
   advantages vs. Perl 130
   books on 123
   definition 432
   effects of delayed documen-
      tation on popularity
      123, 162
   features compared to
      Perl 123–130
   flavors of 123
   functions and Perl
      equivalents 161
   functions, list of 160

has a variable Perl doesn't
   have 123
history of 122–123
introduction to 121
special variables 126–128
summary of differences with
   Perl 129–130
See also awk command;
   GAWK; NAWK; POSIX
   AWK
awk
   definition 432
   GNU version, defined 433
AWK commands. *See* commands
   (AWK)
AWK scripts. *See* scripts
AWKish, definition 432

B

-B (binary) file test operator 182,
   187
-b (block) file test operator 182
B. B. King, on KISS principle in
   music 8
backslash, definition 432
   See also \ (backslash); slash
Bali, web-scraping for travel tips
   about 81
BEGIN block 338
   as place to validate a script's
      arguments 40
   equivalent coding for use when
      implicit loop not used 338
   introduction to 39
   used to validate a script's
      arguments 109
Bell Labs rookie, featured character for nexpr 163
Bell Labs veteran, featured character for nexpr xxvi, 163
Bell System 432
Benchmark module 315
Boulder, Fox, featured character
   for rock-star biodata
   system 133–138

break (loop control) directive
   (Shell) 349
   compared to Perl's last 349
Brian "Ingy" Ingerson. *See* Ingerson, Brian "Ingy"
bugs, Column of Ones 234
Business::UPS module 398–405

C

-c (character) file test
   operator 182
-c (check-syntax) option 395
C language
   approaches to Perl
      programming 13
   breeds mistrust in its
      programmers 7, 349
C language refugees
   are understandably phobic
      about uninitialized
      variables 317
C shell
   excluded from coverage xxvii
   fundamental differences from
      Shell xxiv
Camel book, definition 433
   See also glossary definition
carp function
   advantages over warn in
      modules 394–395
   is provided by Carp
      module 391
Carp module 391
   See also carp function; croak
      function
case conversions 113–114
cat command
   emulating with Perl
      command 12, 24
   emulating with Perl script 29
cd command, Perl counterpart is
   chdir 239
cell processing. *See* field processing, extracting data from
   tables

Center module 393–395
CGI module 231, 414–422
    :standard tag 416
    cheatsheet for essential
        functions 422
    cheatsheet for form-related
        functions 423
    Dump function of 418
    provides functions named after
        HTML tags 416
    tips on using 421
    See also CGI programming
CGI programming
    dual-mode programs
        418–419
    introduction to 414
    testing programs without a
        browser 419
    -w option not used 416
CGI::Carp module
    provides a CGI version of the
        carp function 416
character sets 104
chdir function, Unix counterpart
    is cd 239
check_links script 405
check_symlinks script 411, 414
chgrp command, related to Perl's
    chown 240
chmod function 240
Choi, Dora 347
chomp function 219–221
    example of need for 220, 339,
        357
    requires parentheses around
        multiple arguments 221
    syntax and examples 220
    tips on using 221
    Unix relatives 210
    used on find's output 274
    vs. using -l option 146
chown function 240
circle forehead marking. *See* fore-
    head markings of Perlistanis
classic AWK 123, 126–127, 164

classic grep 54, 91
classic sed 91, 93
classic UNIX utilities
    definition 433
clobberation of variables. *See*
    variable clobberations
clobberation, definition 433
clobbering variables. *See* variable
    clobberations
close function 68
cmp (string comparison)
    operator 157
    used with sort 224
code block
    $_ as final statement in, with
        map 234
    used with grep 228
    used with map 233
code blocks
    coding rules for sort 225
    used with sort 224
code snippets
    allowing zero tip for waiter, us-
        ing defined function 250
    emulating env command using
        %ENV hash 314
    for avoiding variable masking
        in nested loops 373
    for conditionally appending
        one of two strings to
        another 266
    for ensuring confirmation
        from interactive user 352
    for exiting script if no
        arguments 249
    for invoking command on dif-
        ferent files using for
        loop 336
    for obtaining confirmation
        from interactive user
        339–340
    for printing environment vari-
        ables in sorted order 342
    for removing non-text filena-
        mes from arguments 258

for responding to environment
    variables 315
for retrieving a phone number
    from a hash 309
for selecting a filename from
    a menu 355
for sorting arguments 257
for summing numeric
    arguments 334
for using names of all readable,
    regular files as
    arguments 259
make_money_fast, demon-
    strates repetition and
    compound-assignment
    concatenation
    operators 267
providing default argument for
    script 260
reporting names of non-text
    files 258
requiring non-zero tip for
    waiter 250
using local declaration to make
    temporary change to "$,"
    variable 383
coding conventions used in this
    book xxxi
col command 331
    doesn't take filename
        arguments 331
Colin "Shroomy" Meyer. *See*
    Meyer, Colin "Shroomy"
command interpolation 189,
    201, 269–275
    compared to command
        substitution 270
    doesn't work within
        quotes 274
    may require multi-level
        quoting 357
    returns output—not exit code,
        as Shell does 275
    tips on using 274–275
    See also command substitution

command substitution 189,
192, 269–275
alternative $(command)
syntax 269
compared to command
interpolation 270
returns exit code—not output,
as Perl does 275
used to provide validated arguments to grep 189
See also command interpolation
commands (AWK)
for printing rock-star
birthdays 130
Perl equivalents for simple
tasks 141
simple ones compared to Perl
equivalents 128
commands (Perl)
a one-line grepper 61
a one-line sed command 93
differences from scripts 11
emulating date command 214
emulating Shell's –nt file test
operator 217
fix_newsletter 104
for calculating space allowance
for each file in
collection 335
for data validation 66
for editing files 105–107
for extracting "File doesn't exist" errors from logfile 152
for extracting POD documentation from scripts 156
for filtering find's output 183
for finding JPEG-oriented
scripts 187
for generating a random
number 221–222
for line-specific
substitutions 96–97
for matching lines between
specified days 152

for numbering
paragraphs 150
for printing "Hello, world!",
down-under version 49
for printing first 80 characters
of each line 161
for printing rock-star
biodata 134
for printing rock-star
birthdays 133
for printing square roots 161
for processing multi-word
filenames 197
for record-specific
substitutions 97–98
for web-scraping
slashdot.org 86
like scan4oops script 174
like scan4oops script, Felix's
scathing review 174
make_meeting_page 102
matching a range of dates 154
of AWKish Pattern/Action
type 139
one-line 11, 14, 18
printing lines by number 100
printing records by
number 101
using field processing and
in-place editing 134
with nesting of single
quotes 62
See also -e (code) option
commands, definition 433
commas
permitted after last aggregate
initializer for list
variable 311
comments xxix
common mistakes 111
comparison operator
two forms of 158
comparison operators 157
See also cmp operator; <=>
operator

compartmentalize
as preferred term to modularize when discussing
subroutines 363
compound assignment
operators 140, 158–159,
348
construct, definition 434
Consultix xxi
context sensitivity
advantages of 206
continue (loop control) directive
(Shell) 349
compared to Perl's next 349
continue blocks 350, 353–355
give Perl loops an advantage
over Shell loops 355
control characters 104
string escapes for 56
convert command
(ImageMagick) 335
Conway, Damian xx, xxii, 347
as author of *Perl Best Practices*
book xxxii
as winner of Larry Wall
award 28
his foreword to this book xvii
See also Object Oriented Perl
book; *Perl Best Practices*
book
copy function, related to Unix
cp 240
cp command, related to Perl's
copy 240
CPAN
is the envy of non-Perl
programmers 425
link to advice on searching for
modules 425
searching to find modules 398
CPAN module 401
using the shell function 401
CPANPLUS module
relation to CPAN
module 401

creating modules
  checking for warnings and
    syntax errors 395
  defining subroutines 392
  specifying exports 391–392
  testing with a command 397
  testing with a script 396
  using "1;" as last line 392
  with the Simple Module
    Template 390–392
croak function
  provided by Carp module 394
  vs. use of die in modules 394
Crocodile Hunter 49
cut command, Perl relatives 210

D

-d (directory) file test
    operator 182
Dan Sugalski. See Sugalski, Dan
date command, Perl counterpart
    is localtime 210
debugging strategies, adding/sub-
    tracting another
    backslash 376
default loop variables, are auto-
    matically declared with
    local 373, 383
defined function 249–252
  advantages over testing values
    for True/False 249
  needed for testing values
    before using them 251
  tips on using 252
  used for identifying empty
    arguments 249
  used for validating input from
    keyboard 250–252
  used to test for <^D> from
    keyboard 251, 286
delete function
  used on array elements 298,
    307
  used on hash elements
    310–311

df command 248
diamond operator. See input op-
    erator
die function
  introduction to 35
  preferred to warn and exit, out-
    side BEGIN blocks 253
Diggity Dog
  featured character for
    4letter_word xxv, 372
  featured character for
    ups_shipping_price 404
directive, definition 434
directory management
    functions 239
do until loop. See do while/until
    loop
do while/until loop 338–340
  arranging for working loop
    control directives in bot-
    tom-tested loops 351–352
  compared to Shell
    equivalent 338
  doesn't respond to loop-
    control directives 340
  tips on using 339
Don, featured character search-
    ing for
    epistle2dippy.txt 185
Dora Choi. See Choi, Dora
double quotes
  for list to scalar
    conversion 209
  link to article on Shell vs. Perl
    differences 298
  permit command substitution
    but not command
    interpolation 274
  used to suppress secondary
    substitutions in Shell 325
double-quoted string
  used as output-template for
    print function 25
downloading the source code of
    this book's examples xxxii

Dump function
  of CGI module 418
DWIMity 191, 206

E

-e (code) option 11, 17, 45
  unused on Perl shebang
    line 30
E0 (end of range) marker 153
  used in scan4oops script 171
egrep command
  improving on with Perl
    70–72
  Perl relatives 223
egrep, GNU version,
    defined 433
elif keyword (Shell)
  Perl counterpart is elsif 261
elsif keyword
  Shell counterpart is elif 261
  See also if/else
END block 338
  equivalent coding for use when
    implicit loop not used 338
  introduction to 39
  used for calculating average of
    input data 264
  used to print final report 324
English module
  for using AWK variables in
    Perl 126
entertainment value of this
    book xxv–xxvi
env command
  emulating with help from
    %ENV 314
  relation to %ENV hash 314
eof function 307, 322
eq (string equality)
    operator 157, 340
errata page for this book xxxii
error messages
  BEGIN not safe after errors—
    compilation aborted 369

error messages *(continued)*
  Can't locate
    Some_Module.pm 397,
    401
  Can't open (some_file): No
    such file or directory 256
  Execution of some_script
    aborted due to compilation
    errors 374
  See also warning messages
eval function 283–292
  as used in preg 290
  examples and Shell vs. Perl
    comparison 283
  for handling user-supplied
    array indices 304
  need for 283
  security concerns for eval'ing
    user-submitted text 304
  why it's necessary 304
evaluation context
  effects of 207–208
  how programmer
    controls 207–208
  making use of 208–210
  understanding and
    managing 206–210
execution-trace mode
    (Shell) 282
  using to debug commands
    submitted by Perl 282
exists function 322
  used on hash elements 310
exit function 253–254
  examples and Shell vs. Perl
    comparison 253
  meanings of numerical exit
    values 253
expand function
    (Text::Tabs) 366
explicit list, definition 434
export command
  used to convey switch-like
    variables to scripts 315
  used with setting of
    PERL5LIB variable 397

Exporter module
  as basis for creating a new
    module 389
expr command
  shortcomings of 162
  See also nexpr; expr_p
expression, definition 434

F

-F (custom field separator)
    option 136–138
-f (regular) file test operator 182
False value
  of Shell, converting to Perl's
    False 275
  Shell and Perl definitions
    of 32
False, definition 434
fatalsToBrowser
  requests that error messages be
    displayed by web
    browser 417
  See also CGI::Carp
featured character
  Alexis, for PFD project 388
  Ashanti, for line-specific sub-
    stitution command 98
  Bell Labs rookie, for
    nexpr 163
  Bell Labs veteran, for
    nexpr xxvi, 163
  Diggity Dog, for
    4letter_word xxv, 372
  Diggity Dog, for
    ups_shipping_price 404
  Don, searching for misplaced
    file 185
  Felix, for scan4oops xxv,
    168–175
  Fox Boulder, for rock-star bio-
    data system 133–138
  Gabriella, for
    expand_acronyms 343
  Guillermo, for city rainfall
    comparison project
    143–148

  Ivan, for compress_image*
    scripts xxvi, 335–336, 344
  Martina, for Apache logfile
    analysis 151–154
  Murray, for scan4oops
    project 175
  Oscar, for scan4oops-like
    command 174–175
  Patrick, for city rainfall com-
    parison project xxvi,
    143–151
  PerlDude, for find2perl
    examples 200
  Ramon, for check_length 116
  Steffi, having "lingering
    thumb" 186
  TVM guy, rock-star biodata
    system 137–138
  Vitas, for city rainfall compari-
    son project 143–149
  WinDude, for find2perl
    examples 200
  Yoko, for fuzzy_match xxvi
Felix, featured character for
  scan4oops xxv, 168–175
fgrep command
  improving on with Perl 64
  Perl relatives 223
fgrep, GNU version,
    defined 433
field processing 130–138
  accessing fields with Perl
    131–132
  extracting data from
    tables 143–151
  introduction to 130–132
  printing fields with Perl
    132–133
  using undef in 131
  with AWK 90
  See also table processing
field separators
  customizing 136–138
  See also -F (custom field separa-
    tor) option

file management functions
239–241
tips on using 241
file mode, enabling by assignment to $/ 428
file test operators
$_ as default argument 181
comparing find and Perl
180–184
syntax 181
file tests
comparison of find vs.
Perl 181
Perl better than find for
permissions 183
File::Copy module 240
File::Find module 411–414
relation to find
command 180, 201
filehandles, using with close
function 68
file-management functions
tips on using 241
FILENAME (filename)
variable (AWK) 42, 126
filename generation 235
See also FNG
filename generation operator.
See < > operator
filter programs 12
basics of implementing
12–14
cascading filters, using grep/
egrep 72
using one Perl command vs.
multiple grep/egrep
commands 75
financial calculations
compound interest 165–167
compound interest2 166–167
Rule of 72 for estimating investment growth through
compounding 165
find | xargs, problems with multiword filenames 196

find command
as aid for finding misplaced
files 179
as argument pre-processor for
Perl 197–198
as emulated by
find2perl 198–200
augmenting with Perl
183–184
enhancing by adding Perl
command 179
-exec option 192
-exec's deficiences vs. xargs
alternative 193
filtering output of with
Perl 183
for finding recently modified
scripts 179
use of -follow option 274
used with xargs 192–197
find function (from
File::Find) 411
requires special handling 412
find, GNU version, defined 433
find2perl command
as OS-portable alternative to
find 198–200
supports -exec rm 200
finding files
by name matching 184–187
by pathname matching
187–188
having multi-word
names 186–187
fmt command 28, 280
emulating with Perl
command 28
improving on with
Text::Autoformat 28
See also Text::Autoformat
FNG (filename generation)
notation
corresponding metacharacters
from regex notation 238
FNR (file-specific record-number) variable (AWK) 126

footnotes, authors philosophy of
using xxv
for loop 345–349
good for index-oriented array
processing 345
for loop (Perl)
syntax of 345
for loop (Shell) 331
compared to Perl's
foreach 340
foreach loop 340–344
compared to Shell's for
loop 340
preferred to for loop for list
processing 346
preferred to while/until loop
for list processing 334
similarities to Perl's select
loop 356
used in emulating env
command 314
used with unlink to get file-specific error messages 341
forehead markings of
Perlistanis 6–7
format_mode function,
for converting permissions
strings 218
formatting variables
introduction to 43–44
See also '$"' variable; '$,'
variable
Fox Boulder, featured character
for rock-star biodata
system 133–138
Fox Boulder, featured character
for rock-star programs
alien conspiracy theories
of 137
Free Software Foundation 435
FS (input field-separator) variable (AWK) 126
function calls, compared with
method calls in CGI
example 423

functions
  data flows backwards vs. Unix
    pipelines 223
  definition 434
  for directory
    management 239
  for file 241
  for file management 239–241
  for list processing 223–234
  having multi-valued return
    codes 240–241
  in series are processed from
    right to left 208
  Shell vs. Perl functions 364
  using built-in ones 159–164
  vs. methods 400
functions of AWK, list of 160
functions of Perl, list of 160

G

-g (set-GID) file test
    operator 182
Gabriella, featured character for
    expand_acronyms 343
gawk 432
GAWK, capabilities of 125
  See also gawk command;
    AWK; NAWK; POSIX
    AWK
ge (string greater-than or equal-
    to) operator 157
getgrgid function 218
getpwuid function 218
global variables 367
  accessing by simple vs. explicit
    package names 374–375
globbing operator. *See* < >
    operator
GNU AWK 123–124
  See also GAWK
GNU find 180, 182
GNU grep 273
  capabilities 58
GNU sed 92–93, 107
  capabilities 91

GNU utilities versions used in
    this book, defined 433
GNU, definition 435
grep command
  capabilities compared to
    Perl's 58
  diversity of regex dialects
    for 55
  emulating -i option with
    Perl 70
  emulating -l option with
    Perl 67–68
  emulating -v option with
    Perl 65
  for validating data 66
  history of 53
  origin of name 54
  Perl equivalents for common
    cases 87
  Perl relatives 223
  relationship to ed
    command 54
  screen corruption resulting
    from binary matches 188,
    190
  shortcomings of 54–60
grep function 227–229
  as "gating" mechanism 227
  compared to map 232
  differences from grep
    command 227
  syntax and examples 228
  Unix relatives 223
grep, GNU version, defined 433
grepper
  capabilities compared to
    Perl's 57
  definition 435
grepping, definition 435
gt (string greater-than)
    operator 157
guidelines, for parenthesizing
    code 430–431
Guillermo, featured character for
    city rainfall comparison
    project 143–148

H

hashes 296
  advantages of printing with
    foreach over while/
    each 343
  advantages of printing with
    while/each over
    foreach 337
  aggregate initialization 311
  as basis for simple database
    systems 319–322
  automatic initialization to zero
    in numeric context 317
  illustration of storage in
    memory 309
  indexing syntax 312
  indexing techniques 312–313
  initialization methods
    311–312
  introduction to 308–311
  piecemeal initialization 311
  preferred to arrays for associat-
    ing strings with values 310
  printing techniques 314–315
  printing with foreach
    342–343
  printing with while/
    each 336–337
  slice-indexing a hash using an
    array 313
  slices used to impose ordering
    on retrieved values 312
  summary of indexing
    methods 313
  syntax and examples 310
  tips on initializing 311
  used as unique-ifiers 316–319
  used for counting word
    frequencies 323–325
  used to reduce list to unique
    elements 316
head command
  as poorly suited for printing
    specific lines 100

head function (from
LWP::Simple) 405–406
hickory ruler
as motivator for grammatical
correctness 166
HTML
generating with CGI
module 419–422
listing of output generated by
survey.cgi 420

I

-i (in-place editing) option 45
backing up original file
111–113
editing pantaloony file 106
for clobber-proofing editing
commands 112
for clobber-proofing editing
scripts 112
for mass editing of HTML
files 107
pitfalls of using .bak
extension 111
used in AWKish
commands 134
using .bak extension 109
if/else 259–265
advantages over logical and/
or 260–261
comparison of Shell and Perl
syntaxes 260
curly braces can't be
omitted 265
elsif keyword 261
mixing with and/or 261–264
nesting of 261
tips on using 264–265
IFS (internal field separators)
variable (Shell) 325, 327,
341
compared to split
function 211
Perl relatives 210

implicit loop 12
compared to equivalent explicit loop 338
how it works 337–338
LINE is label for 338
See also -n (automatic input-
reading) option; -p (automatic input-reading, with
printing)
Ingerson, Brian "Ingy" 102, 347
inode (Unix), accessing with
stat 215
in-place editing 109–113
input operator 13
definition 435
input record separator
automatic stripping of with –l
option 20
definition of 20
example of 42
how to change 22
newline as default 20
See also $/ (input record sepa-
rator) variable
input/output variables ($/, $\)
introduction to 42–43
installing modules
configuring the CPAN
module 401–402
determining which ones you
have 400
using non-root
privileges 402–403
using root privileges 401–402
invocation options
advice on ordering 44, 47
effects of 17
for automatic input processing. *See* -n (automatic input-
reading) option; -p (automatic input-reading, with
printing) option
for automatic line-end processing. *See* -l (line-end processing) option

for automatic switch handling.
See -s (switch) option
for loading modules. *See* -M
(module-loading) option
for one-line commands. *See* -e
(code) option
for warning messages. *See* -w
(warnings) option
introduction to 17–23
option clusters 17
standard option clusters 17
Ivan
featured character for
compress_image*
scripts 335–336, 344
featured character for compression of stamp
collection xxvi

J

jalebi (confection) 66
JAPH
as resident of Perlistan 5
definition 435
JAPHly
definition 435
join function 229–232
equivalent to using $" with
double quotes 210
for list to scalar
conversion 209
syntax and examples 229
tips on using 230
Unix relatives 223
used in constructing HTML
code 232
used in constructing passwd
file entry 230

K

-k (sticky) file test operator 182
keys function, retrieves all keys
from a hash 310

King, B. B., on KISS principle in music 8
ksymoops command (Linux) 171

L

-l (line-end processing) option 11, 17, 20
  doesn't affect input read from <STDIN> 339
  programs that omit it 226
  using instead of "\n" 21
-l (symlink) file test operator 182
Larry, definition. *See* Wall, Larry
last (loop control) directive 349
  compared to Shell's break 349
Laziness
  as a virtue 9
  in programming practice 12, 15
le (string less-than or equal-to) operator 157
Leaning Toothpick Syndrome 60, 92
length function 116
Library for Web Programming. *See* LWP::Simple
LINE, is label for implicit loop 338
Lingua::EN::Inflect module
  used to conditionally pluralize nouns 167
Lingua::EN::Namegame 372
list context
  effects of 207
  ways to request 207
list generators
  Shell vs. Perl techniques 325–327
  Shell's command substitution vs. Perl's command interpolation 327
  Shell's FNG vs. Perl's globbing 326

Shell's variable substitution vs. Perl's variable interpolation 327
list to scalar conversion
  method can be specified by programmer 208
  needed for matching against arrays 230
  tools for 209–210
list variables
  introduction to 295–296
  See also arrays; hashes
List::Util module 329
  for shuffling list elements 227
listfile script 217
local declaration
  arranges for the previous value of a variable to be restored later 374
  introduction to 375
  is automatically used for default loop variables 373, 375
  syntax and examples 374
  used for temporary changes to "$," and "$"" 383
  used with "$," and "$"" 44
  See also variable declarations
localtime function 214–215
  syntax and examples 214
  tips on using 215
  Unix relatives 210
logfile analysis 81, 168–175
  of Linux /var/log/messages file 168
logical operators
  introduction to and/or 37
  Perl's compared to Shell counterparts 37
longest-anything pattern 78, 109, 114, 117, 359
longest-something pattern 78
loop control directives
  Perl syntax example 351
  Perl's better than Shell's for nested loops 351

Shell syntax example 350
Shell vs. Perl comparison 349
looping
  comparison of Shell vs. Perl resources 331, 333
  introduction to 330–331
  Shell vs. Perl differences in concepts, terms, and basic syntax 332
loops
  basic types of 332
  nesting within others 350–351
  using loop control directives 349–355
ls command
  emulating in Perl using stat 217–218
  Perl relatives 210
  See also listfile script
lt (string less-than) operator 157
LWP::Simple module 405–408
lwp-request command 80–81, 405–406
  used for web-scraping 323

M

-M (module-loading) option 27, 45
  used only with commands, not scripts 41
  used to enable strict mode 369
  using to test availability of module 400
m// (matching) operator 60
  using custom delimiters with 109, 188, 213
  See also // (matching) operator
Main (program segment)
  definition of 379, 435
  See also scoping
managing modules 398–403
map function 232–234
  compared to grep 232

map function *(continued)*
  syntax and examples 233
  Unix relatives 223
  used in emulating env
    command 314
Martina, featured character for
    Apache logfile
    analysis 151–154
masking of variables. *See* variable
    masking
matching
  across lines, step-by-step
    guide 79
  against arrays 230
  against files 77
  against paragraphs 75
  disqualifying undesirable
    matches 83
  fuzzy matching with
    String::Approx 85–86
  in context, Perl's superiority to
    greppers for 75–77
  range of records 151–157
  record separators 125
metacharacter, definition 436
method calls, compared with
    function calls in CGI
    example 423
methods, vs. functions 400
Meyer, Colin "Shroomy" 347
Minimal Perl
  as a simplified subset of Perl 8
  isn't a version of Perl 8
  minimizes problems with op-
    erator precedence 252
  motivation for creating xix
  practical and eclectic nature
    of 9
  public debut xx
mkdir function 239
modularize
  means convert code to a Perl
    module 363
  vs. the term compartmentalize
    when discussing
    subroutines 363

module
  definition of 27
  meaning of double colons in
    name 28
modules
  advantages over
    subroutines 389
  and explicit package names for
    variables 393
  Benchmark 315
  Business::UPS 398–405
  Carp 391
  Center 393–395
  CGI 231, 414–422
  CGI::Carp 416
  comparison of procedural and
    Object-Oriented 422–424
  determining which ones you
    have 400
  Exporter 389
  File::Copy 240
  File::Find 201, 411–414
  introduction to 388–389
  Lingua::EN::Inflect 167
  Lingua::EN::Namegame 372
  List::Util 227, 329
  LWP::Simple 405–408
  provide aliases to their exports
    for user convenience 393
  Regexp::Common 372
  Shell::POSIX::Select 356
  Stat::IsMode 217
  String::Approx 85–86
  Term::ANSIColor 294
  Term::Cap 271
  Text::Autoformat 28, 116,
    278
  Text::Tabs 117, 366
  Text::Wrap 395
  See also using modules; creat-
    ing modules; installing
    modules; managaing mod-
    ules; Simple Module Tem-
    plate
move function, related to Unix
    mv 240

MULTICS OS 269
Murray, featured character for
    scan4oops project 175
mv command
  related to Perl's move 240
  related to Perl's rename 240
my declaration
  definition 436
  for defining a variable's
    scope 378
  introduction to 374
  is preferred declaration for
    user-defined variables 374
  syntax and examples 374
  with aggregate assignment to
    list of variables 405
  See also our declaration

N

-n (automatic input-reading)
    option 14, 17, 19
  cases where it's omitted 229
  using non-filename arguments
    with 256
  See also implicit loop
name clashes
  are more likely in larger
    programs 385
  are more likely with file-scoped
    variables 380
  as consideration in choosing
    exports from modules 391
  avoided by using package dec-
    laration in modules 393
  other techniques for
    avoiding 367, 386, 393
natural language processing, con-
    ditionally pluralizing
    nouns 166–167
  See also Lingua::EN::Inflect
nawk command 123, 432
NAWK. *See* nawk command;
    AWK; GAWK; POSIX
    AWK

ne (string inequality)
    operator 157
new AWK 123
    See also NAWK
newline xxvi
    definition 436
    See also glossary
nexpr 163
    not a complete replacement for
        expr 163
    the legend of 162–164
    See also scripts, nexpr_p
next (loop control) directive 349
    compared to Shell's
        continue 349
NF (number of fields) variable
    (AWK) 127
NR (record-number) variable
    (AWK) 126
-nt (newer-than) file test operator
    (Shell), emulating in Perl us-
    ing stat 216–217

O

-o (owned by effective ID) file
    test operator 182
-O (owned by real ID) file test
    operator 182
Object Oriented Perl book xx,
    347
Object-Oriented modules
    tips on using 422–424
Object-Oriented programming
    vs. procedural
        programming 405
octal numbers, left-padding with
    zeroes 105
OFS (output field-separator)
    variable (AWK) 126
open function 361
operand, definition 436
operating system, definition 436
operator precedence
    use of parentheses to
        override 38, 184, 252, 351

operator, definition 436
operators, vs. functions 436
ORS (output record-separator)
    variable (AWK) 42, 126
OS, definition 436
Oscar, featured character for
    scan4oops-like
        command xxv, 174
our declaration
    allows use of simple name for
        global variable 374
    for defining a variable's
        scope 381
    for marking switch variable as
        optional 35
    introduction to 374–375
    is used for all switch variables
        in strict mode 375, 381
    is used for global variables 375
    is used for variables exported
        by modules 375, 381
    omitted for mandatory
        switches 108
    requires parentheses around
        multiple arguments 33
    syntax and examples 374
    used for optional switches 117
    See also my declaration
output record separator
    automatic printing of 20
    example of 42
    newline as default 20

P

-p (automatic input-reading,
    with printing) option
    17, 19
    used with sed-like
        command 93
    using non-filename arguments
        with 256
    See also implicit loop
-p (named-pipe) file test
    operator 182
    See also implicit loop

package declaration, why it's used
    in modules 393
paragraph mode, enabling by
    assignment to $/ 428
parentheses
    guidelines for using on
        code 430–431
    mandatory for our declaration
        with multiple
            arguments 33
    optional use of 161
    required for chomp with mul-
        tiple arguments 221
    required for our declaration
        with multiple
            arguments 374
    used in explicit list 434
    used to enclose all function
        arguments 243
    used with function
        arguments 242–243
    using to control allocation of
        arguments to
            functions 242–243
    See also appendix B
Patrick, featured character for
    city rainfall comparison
        project xxvi, 143–151
pattern ranges
    matching a range of
        dates 153–154
    matching multiple
        ranges 155–157
    syntax 153
pattern, definition 436
Pattern/Action programming
    AWK vs. Perl syntax 139
    combined with field
        processing 143
    introduction to 138–142
patterns
    longest-anything 78, 109,
        114, 117
    longest-something 78
    shortest-anything 78
    shortest-something 78, 124

patterns (AWK)
  matching type 139
  relational operator type 140
Perl
  advantages over AWK 129
  as argument pre-processor for
    other commands 192
  as derived from UNIX
    utilities xvii
  as the "Swiss Army
    chainsaw" xvii
  commands hybridized with
    Unix commands 180
  common problems of
    beginners xxv
  complexity of xix, 3, 51
  cryptic programming styles
    of 14
  definition 437
  dialects of 4, 9
  efficiency advantages over
    Shell 206
  functions, list of 160
  idiomatic programming style
    of 6
  link to article on OS-portable
    programming
    techniques 199, 201, 245
  Object-Oriented program-
    ming approach 8
  redundancies of xix, 7
  sensitivity to context 243
  similarities to Yiddish 6
  source-code beautifiers xx,
    265
  summary of advantages over
    find command 201
  summary of advantages vs.
    AWK 129
  summary of facilities superior
    to Unix counterparts 206
  syntax 10
  See also perl
Perl Best Practices book xxxii
Perl commands. See commands
    (Perl)

Perl functions. See functions
Perl Mongers xxii, 368
Perl scripts. See scripts
Perl shell. See scripts, psh
perl, definition 437
  See also Perl
PERL5LIB (library search)
    variable (Shell)
  preserving setting in Shell
    startup file 397–403
  setting to help Perl find
    modules 397–403
perldoc
  advantages over man
    command 51
  -q option, for searching
    FAQ 52
PerlDude, featured character for
    find2perl examples 200
Perlistan xxvii, 3–5
  definition 437
  need for citizens to wear dialect
    markings 6
PFD, as Precursive Frobination
    of Defragulations 388
POD documentation, example of
    script containing 155
positional parameters 198
POSIX AWK 124
POSIX find 186–187
  capabilities 180, 186–187
POSIX grep, capabilities 58
POSIX sed 92
  capabilities 91
POSIX, definition 437
Primary Option Cluster
  for Input Processing 93
print function 10
  differences from AWK's
    print 134–136
  treats commas differently than
    AWK's print 134
  with arithmetic expression as
    argument 11
printf command, Perl
  relatives 223

printf function 25, 407
  % as special character with 22
  for formatted printing 218
  for printing without automatic
    newlines 21
  used for printing floating point
    numbers 324
  used for printing with fields of
    fixed widths 324
  used for prompts 21
printing, Shell's echo vs. Perl's
    print 10
private variables, are declared
    with my 374
procedural programming vs.
    object-oriented
    programming 405
processing input, a line at a time
    using Shell vs. Perl
    341–342
program segments, list of 381
Programming Perl book 433
programs, step-by-step construc-
    tion technique 47–51
push function 305, 349
  for initializing arrays 299
PWD (present working directo-
    ry) variable (Shell) 397

Q

quoting
  clever use in nexpr* scripts 164
  differences between com-
    mands and scripts 30
  differences between Shell and
    Perl 30, 341
  introduction to 30
  link to guidelines article
    (Shell) 49, 136
  nesting of single quotes using
    backslash 62
  of one-line commands 11
  Shell-friendly Perl
    techniques 136
qw (quote words) operator 391

R

-r (readable by effective ID) file test operator 182
 unnecessary to use before -T test 274
-R (readable by real ID) file test operator 182
Ramon, featured character for check_length 116
rand function 221–222
 syntax and examples 222
 Unix relatives 210
 used to select random element from array 305
RANDOM variable (Shell) Perl relatives 210
Ravi, featured character for data validation commands, and jalebi consumption 66
RE (regular expression) notation
 corresponding metacharacters from FNG notation 238
 using for matching filenames 238
recursive grepping 191–192
redirection requests (Shell)
 can be attached to constructs, unlike case in Perl 361
reference value of this book xxiv
references. See \& operator
regex, definition 437
Regexp::Common module
 using to identify profane words 372
regular expressions
 as superior to those of Unix utilities 56
 classic dialect (UNIX) 91
 comparison of dialects 57
 essential syntax 63–64
 line-spanning 77–79
 metacharacters for grouping, and match capturing/referencing 71
quantifier metacharacters 73
shortcut metacharacters 67
relational operators
 comparing AWK's and Perl's 157–158
 used to define a range of lines 97
rename function, related to Unix mv 240
report generation
 conditionally pluralizing nouns 166–167
 using system 277–280
return function 364
 returned value automatically converted for caller's context 365
reverse function
 Unix relatives 223
 used with sort 225
reverse video terminal mode. See tput command
rm command, related to Perl's unlink 240
rmdir function 239
rock-star biodata system (AWK) 133–134
rock-star biodata system (Perl) 134
RS (input record-separator) variable (AWK) 42, 126
Rule of 72
 for estimating investment growth through compounding 165

S

-s (non-empty) file test operator 182, 197
 easier to use than stat 219
-S (socket) file test operator 182
-s (switch) option 45, 278
 used heavily in preg 288
s/// (substitution) operator capabilities of 91
converting special characters with 103–105
 differences from sed 234
 introduction to computed replacements 91
 modifiers for 95
 syntax of 95
 used to insert indentation 19
 using backreferences and numbered variables with 99
 using computed replacements 114–118
 using context addresses 96
 using function-generated replacements 116
s2p command, translates sed to Perl 118
scalar (data type)
 introduction to 23
scalar context
 effects of 208
 ways to request 208
scalar function, for overriding list context 208
scalar to list conversion tools for 209–210
scope, of type file, defined 434
scoping, definition 437
script, definition 437
scriptification, definition 437
scriptified, definition 437
scripts
 4letter_word 372, 375, 383
 a scripted grepper 84
 advantages over commands 247
 award_cruises 32
 award_cruises2 32–33
 award_cruises3 38
 beatles 313
 c2f: Celsius to Fahrenheit 233
 cd_report 261, 263
 center 365
 center2 366
 center2.strict 369, 396

scripts *(continued)*
  center3 396–397
  change_file 107, 198
  check_length 116
  check_length2 117
  check_links 405–406
  check_symlinks 411–412
  compared to Shell scripts 29
  compound_interest 165
  compound_interest2 167
  compress_image 336
  compress_image2 345
  confirmation 354
  count_words 323–324
  definition 29
  double_space 40
  expand_acronyms 343
  expand_daynames 94
  extract_cell 127, 147
  extract_cell2 149
  fcookie 305
  fcookie2 306
  fields2lists, converts input
    fields into HTML bullet
    items 231
  for editing files 107–110
  fuzzy_match 85
  greperl 248, 286
  highlight_trailing_ws 272
  how nexpr* scripts work 164
  incomplete 141
  insert_contact_info 108
  insert_contact_info2 110
  intra_line_sort 226
  introduction to 29–41,
    247–248
  listfile 217
  m2k (miles to kilometers) 115
  massage_data 254
  mean_annual_precip 145
  menu_ls 409
  most_recent_file 195
  most_recent_file2 267
  mytime 212
  mytime2 215

  mytime3 386
  news_flash 277
  news_flash2 278, 281
  nexpr (Shell/AWK) 164
  nexpr_p 164, 283
  of dual input-mode
    variety 308, 320
  perl_cat 30
  perlgrep 248, 257, 286
  perlman 358–360
  phone_home 371, 377, 380
  phone_home2 384
  phone_home3 385
  preg 286–287, 291–292
  preg, as replacement for grep-
    erl, text_grep, perlgrep, and
    rgrep 286
  psh 284–286
  raffle, demonstrates nested for
    loops 347–348
  resignation_letter 251
  rgrep 192, 273–274, 286
  rm_files 341
  running Shell commands from
    Perl scripts 248
  scan4oops 170
  scan4oops2 173
  shell_types 299
  show_fields2 302–303
  show_fields2_1 155
  show_files 34
  show_pvars 337
  show_user 357–358
  survey.cgi 414, 417, 420–421
  text_grep 190, 286
  textfile_args 228
  textfiles 184, 190, 198, 228
  unique_args 316
  unique_inputs 318–319
  ups_shipping_price 404
  user_lookup 321
  See also commands (Perl)
Seattle Perl Users Group xx, xxii,
  347
  link to interview with founder
    Tim Maher xxii

  subscribers to mailing list re-
    quired "use strict" on sub-
    mitted source code 368
Seattle.pm. *See* Seattle Perl Users
  Group
sed command
  as inferior to Perl for file
    editing 110
  capabilities compared to
    Perl's 91
  differences from substitution
    operator 234
  eclipsed by AWK 90
  emulating -f option with
    Perl 94
  history of 89–91
  matching ranges of
    records 152
  -n option compared to
    Perl's -n 137
  pattern-matching capabilities
    compared to Perl's
    124–126
  performing line-specific sub-
    stitutions with 96
  Perl equivalents for common
    uses 119
  Perl relatives 223
  printing lines by number 100
  relation to ed 90
  shortcomings of 91–93
  used to insert indentation 19
  using "l" command, for special
    listing format 137
  was eclipsed by AWK 90
sed, GNU version, defined 433
select function 361
  is unrelated to Perl's select
    loop 361
select loop (Perl) 355–360,
  408–410
  author's motivation for
    developing 356
  enhancements over Shell
    version 357–358, 361, 409

select loop (Perl) *(continued)*
  facilitates development of ter-
    minal-based menu-oriented
    scripts 355
  syntax 356
  See also Shell::POSIX::Select
select loop (Shell) 331
  syntax 356
semicolon
  as terminator of
    statement 438
  customarily omitted for one-
    line code blocks 224
  not needed at end of most
    constructs 265, 333
  required at end of do while/un-
    til loop 339
  use of 19
  used in condensed if/else for-
    mat (Shell) 260
  used in condensed looping for-
    mat (Shell) 333
  vs. Shell's <ENTER> as state-
    ment terminator 10
Senator Quimby, featured character for "matching in context" commands 76
shebang line
  as used in Perl scripts 11
  definition 438
  is not used in module files 395
shebang, definition 438
Shell xxvii
  bash version, defined 433
  meaning vs. shell xxiii
  See also glossary
Shell commands, running from
  Perl scripts. *See* command
  interpolation; system
Shell functions, vs. Perl
  functions 364
Shell processing of command line
  is difficult to understand 325
Shell programmer
  as reader of this book xxiii

skills required for readers of
  part 2 xxiv
Shell prompt
  in command-with-output vs.
    code-with-output
    displays xxxi
  primary prompt xxx
  secondary prompt xxx
Shell scripts. *See* scripts
Shell::POSIX::Select
  module 356
  link to documentation 361,
    425
  provides the select loop for
    Perl 408–410
Sherpa, Yeshe xxii
shift function 254–256
  comparison of effects in
    Shell and Perl 254
  examples and Shell vs. Perl
    comparison 255
  illustration of effect on
    arguments 254
  See also unshift function
shortest-anything pattern 78
shortest-something pattern 78,
  124
Simple Module Template 390
slash, definition 438
  See also / (slash); backslash
Solaris 433
sort function 224–227
  case-insensitive sorting 227
  programmer defines sorting
    rules 225
  random sorting 226
  random sorting with
    List::Util 227
  syntax and examples 224
  Unix relatives 223
  used in printing hashes 337,
    343–344
  uses $a and $b in comparing
    list items 225

source-code filtering 358
  as used in
    Shell::POSIX::Select 356
space character, definition 438
special characters, converting
  with substitution
    operator 103–105
special variables 23
split function 211–213
  compared to cut
    command 211
  compared to IFS variable 211
  for scalar to list
    conversion 209
  syntax 211
  tips on using 213, 227, 234
  Unix relatives 210
  used to supply iteration list to
    foreach loop 372
  when to use matching operator
    instead 213
split function (AWK), Perl
  counterpart is split 210
sprintf command, Perl
  relatives 223
SPUG 347
  links to web pages 101
  needed meeting-announce-
    ment software 101
  See also Seattle Perl Users
    Group
square forehead marking.
  See forehead markings of
    Perlistanis
squared JAPHs
  are understandably uneasy
    about uninitialized
    variables 317
standard error, definition 438
standard input, definition 438
standard option clusters, introduction to 44–47
standard output, definition 438
stat function 181–182, 196,
  201, 215–219
  syntax and examples 216

stat function *(continued)*
  tips on using 218–219
  Unix relatives 210
  using to emulate ls
    command 217–218
  using to emulate Shell's -nt
    operator 216–217
Stat::lsMode module, for converting permission
  strings 217
statement, definition 438
STDERR (standard error),
  definition 438
STDIN (standard input)
  definition 438
STDIN (standard input)
  filehandle 19, 220, 228,
  250
  as default input source for
    script 289
  avoiding as default input
    source when user omits ar-
    gument to script 274
STDOUT (standard output),
  definition 438
Steffi, featured character having
  "lingering thumb" 186
strict mode 363, 439
  enabling using -M'strict'
    option 369
  See also use strict
strictified 439
stricture 439
string modifiers, for case
  conversion 113
String::Approx module
  for fuzzy matching 85–86
strings, definition 439
sub declaration 364
sub. *See* subroutines
subroutines
  basics of 363–365
  benefits of using 362
  caller's context defined 365
  defining and using 365–368

passing data through
  arguments 367, 383, 392
passing data through global
  variables 367, 395
return value can be specially
  crafted for caller's
  context 365
reusing in other
  programs 386–387
syntax and examples 364
vs. Shell functions 364
subroutines and variable scoping,
  introduction to 362–363
subs
  center_line 367, 369, 386,
    395–396
  center_line, modularized 393
  check_link (from check_links
    script) 407
  check_slinks (from
    check_symlinks script) 412
  commafy 413
  conscious 382
  dial_phone 371
  get_home_address 371,
    384–385
  show_times 414
  uniquify (from check_links
    script) 408
Sugalski, Dan 347
Sweger, Andy "yDNA" 347
switch variable, definition 439
switch, definition 439
switches, introduction to 33
system administration tools
  change_file script 107, 198
  check_links script 405
  check_symlinks 411, 414
  command emulating Shell's
    -nt file test operator 217
  command for extracting "File
    doesn't exist" errors from
    logfile 152
  command for filtering find's
    output 183

command for processing
  multi-word filenames 197
command like scan4oops
  script 174
highlight_trailing_ws
  script 272
most_recent_file script 195
most_recent_file2 script 267
preg script 287
scan4oops script 170
scan4oops2 script 173
shell_types script 299
show_fields script 302
show_user script 357–358
unique_args script 316
unique_inputs script 318
user_lookup script 321
w command 357
system function 275–283, 410
  converting Shell's True/False
    values to Perl's 276, 335
  debugging Shell commands
    submitted by Perl 281–282
  may require multi-level
    quoting 335
  requires multi-level
    quoting 276
  syntax and examples 276
  tips on using 280–283
  used in compress_image 336
  using to generate reports
    277–280

T

-T (text) file test operator 182,
  184–185
  incorporates -r (readability)
    test 274
tab character, definition 439
table processing
  using array indexing 145
  with switch-driven scripts 147
  See also field processing
tac command (Linux), Perl
  relatives 223

tail command, as poorly suited
for printing specific
lines 100
taint-checking mode 304
template processing 101–103
advantages of Perl over
sed 103
replacing placeholders 102
See also Template Toolkit
Template Toolkit 103
Term::ANSIColor module 294
Term::Cap module, compared to
tput 271
text processing
quieting spam 113–114
upper/lowercase
conversions 113–114
text substitutions, comparisons of
sed vs. Perl 93–99
Text::Autoformat module 116,
278
as replacement for fmt
command 28
Text::Tabs module 117, 366
provides expand function 366
Text::Wrap module 395
The Perl Foundation 347
time function, returns current
time as large integer
number 414
Tinker toys 363
TMTOWTDI, definition 439
TPF. *See* The Perl Foundation
tput command 271–273
compared to Term::Cap
module 271
determining terminal's dimensions using lines and cols
options 271, 277
for displaying text in reverse-
video 285
for manipulating terminal display modes 271
for underlining text on
screen 275
testing output for error 279

tr command 113, 331
doesn't take filename
arguments 331
training on Perl, minimal vs.
maximal approaches 7
Travelers tale 3–5, 14
triangle forehead marking.
See forehead markings of
Perlistanis
True value
of Shell, converting to Perl's
True 275
Shell and Perl definitions
of 32
True, definition 439
Truthiness and Falsity 32
TVM guy, featured antagonist of
Fox Boulder 137–138
typographical conventions used
in this book xxvii–xxxi

U

-u (set-UID) file test
operator 182
umask function 240
undef function
definition 439
used in assignments to explicit
lists 132
used to return undefined value
from sub 368
undefined values
definition 439
detecting and replacing 367
only serious uses trigger
warnings 368
returning from sub 368
Unix
definition 440
skills required of readers xxiv
See also UNIX
Unix people, definition 440
Unix pipelines, data flows backwards vs. Perl
functions 223

Unix utilities, POSIX versions,
defined 437
UNIX, definition 440
See also Unix
unlink function 341
is irreversible like rm 240
related to Unix rm 240
unset command 315
unshift function 255,
303–304
illustration of effects 302
used to achieve friendlier
field numbers 302
See also shift function
until loop. *See* while/until loop
use directive
loading modules with 41
used with strict 439
use strict
as quality standard 368
as used in modules 391
efficacy compared to that
of myopic lavatory
attendant 386
implements strictures,
whose violations are
fatal errors 368
is very limited as a quality-
control tool 370–371,
373, 384–385, 387
poorly conceived declarations
undermine its benefits 375
proper placement in
script 377
purpose of 368–373
See also strict mode
user interaction, obtaining
confirmation 352–353
user-defined variables 25
using modules 403–424
augmenting Perl's search path
by setting PERL5LIB 397
must import all desired components, if not using
defaults 396

using modules *(continued)*
    preserving setting of
        PERL5LIB in Shell startup
        file 397, 403
using_defined_for_keyboard_in
    put 250
using_re_notation_for_filename
    _filtering 238

V

validating data, with grep
    command 66
value, definition 440
values function, retrieves all val-
    ues from a hash 310
variable assignment, aggregate as-
    signment to list of variables
    in declaration 405
variable clobberations 371
    are more likely with file-scoped
        variables 380
    more easily avoided in small
        programs 385
    tips on avoiding 373
variable declarations, syntax and
    examples 374–384
variable interpolation
    Perl has, AWK lacks 128–129
    with print, compared to
        AWKish approach 128
variable masking 372–373
    $_ may get masked in nested
        loops 373
    tips on avoiding 373
variable scoping
    benefits of curly braces around
        Main 379
    block scope 377
    effects of curly braces 377
    employing user-defined loop
        variables 383
    example of widely-scoped
        variable 413
    file scope 377

graphical illustrations of
    378–382
introduction to 373
loop scope 383
preventing variables from leak-
    ing into subs 379
using my declaration 378
using our declaration 381
See also Variable Scoping
    Guidelines
Variable Scoping
    Guidelines 369
case study of applying:
    phone_home2 384–385
for complex programs
    376–386
for simple programs 376
introduction to 375
tips on using 385
variable declarations. *See* my
    declaration; our declaration;
    local declaration
variables
    AWK variable names usable in
        Perl 23
    cases requiring explicit
        initializations 142
    common problems 370–373
    data variable. *See* $_ (data)
        variable
    declarations for switch
        type 436
    declared with local,
        defined 435
    declared with my,
        defined 436–437
    declared with our,
        defined 436
    default initialization values 25
    drawbacks of using spaces
        around "=" in
        assignment 27
    introduction to 23
    leakage of 363, 376, 381
    list (data type), compared to
        scalar 23

masking of, defined 436
Perl compared to AWK 126
record number variable. *See* $.
    (record number) variable
scope, defined 437
See also special variables; user-
    defined variables
variables, scalar (data type)
    introduction to 23–27
Vitas, featured character for city
    rainfall comparison
    project 143–149
void context 252

W

-w (warnings) option 11, 17–18,
    395
    not used in CGI scripts 416
-w (writable by effective ID) file
    test operator 182
-W (writable by real ID) file test
    operator 182
w command 357
Wall, Larry 347
    as apparition in Fox Boulders
        dream 134
    as creator of Perl xxii, xxvi,
        6–7, 9, 14, 20, 51, 59,
        93, 118, 123, 158, 175,
        211, 436
    as discreet critic of your
        programs 18
    debugs using print statements,
        not Perl debugger 285
    on relation of Perl to Unix xvii
    pays homage to AWK 123
    See also glossary
wantarray function 364
warn function
    introduction to 35
    plus exit preferred to die, in
        BEGIN blocks 253
    vs. use of carp in
        modules 394–395

warning messages
  Applying substitution (s///) to
    @array will act on
    scalar(@array) 230
  Can't open –
    switch_var_name: No such
    file or directory 34
  Global symbol "$whatever"
    requires explicit package
    name 369, 374
  Name
    "main::switch_var_name"
    used only once, possible
    typo 35
  odd number of initializers 312
  quantifier follows nothing in
    regex 237
  readline() on unopened
    filehandle 237
  reference found where even-
    sized list expected 312
  Scalar value @some_name[0]
    better written as
    $some_name[0] 308
  use of uninitialized value in
    print 249, 368
  use of uninitialized value in
    string ne 251
  use of uninitialized value on
    line ... 383
  used only once: possible
    typo 18

useless use of a variable in void
  context 221
useless use of defined operator
  in void context 252
See also error messages
web scraping 86
while/until loop 333–338
  comparison of Shell vs. Perl
    syntax 333
  tips on using 334
  using "infinite" version in
    replacement for do while/
    until 351–352
while/until loop (Shell), emulating advanced features of in
  Perl 353–354
whitespace, definition 440
Willy, featured character for
  insert_contact_info 108
WinDude, featured character for
  find2perl examples 200
-wl (output generation)
  cluster 45
-wnl (input/output) cluster 45
-wnla (field processing)
  cluster 45, 233
-wnlaF (custom field-processing)
  cluster 45, 138, 185
word splitting (Shell) 325
-wpl (input/output with printing
  cluster), used in sed-like
  commands 97

X

-x (executable by effective ID) file
  test operator 182
-X (executable by real ID) file test
  operator 182
x (string repetition)
  operator 265–267
  syntax and examples 265
xargs command 195–198
  advantages of Perl for sorting
    applications 193–196
  advantages over find's -exec
    option 193
  not an alternative to find's
    -exec on all OSs 200
  relation to command
    substitution 189
  used with find 192–197
XPG4 433

Y

YAPC xx
  definition 440
Yet Another Perl Conference.
  See YAPC
Yoko, featured character for
  fuzzy_match xxvi, 85

Z

-z (empty) file test operator 182